Why Do You Need this New Edition?

6 good reasons why you should buy this new edition of *Gender Roles: A Sociological Perspective.*

1. *Gender Roles* has *hundreds* of new examples in tune to the latest research and today's headlines to help you understand the powerful influence of gender on society and in your personal lives. These include the impact of gender on **Election 2008 in the United States,** how gender is playing out in the global **Millennium Recession,** and the surprising gender issues unfolding on college campuses.

2. Highlighted throughout *Gender Roles,* you will learn about how media and technology are rapidly ascending as key trendsetters of gender roles in the United States and globally. New sections include MTV and music videos (the collision of gender and race); portrayals of feminism and race and gender in media and politics (Hillary Clinton, Sarah Palin, Barack Obama); gendered comedy and reality TV (*Hannah Montana* and *America's Next Top Model*), and gender and online communication (who texts and who talks more, males or females?)

3. You will understand, and yes, even appreciate, how gender roles throughout all our social institutions are explained by sociologists. By viewing cutting edge research and theory (at least three-quarters of the references in *Gender Roles* are 2005 and later) you will also see how these explanations apply to your lives—especially your campus lives—regardless of your age. Expanded topics include **sexual scripts, love and friendship, and gender parity in college.**

4. *Gender Roles* incorporates the newest trends on our family and work lives and how each influences the other. Can men and women have it all—satisfying marriages, families, and careers—regardless of gender roles? How do gender roles affect the work and family lives of gay men and lesbians? New and expanded topics include **helicopter parents, family issues and same-sex marriage, sexual orientation and the workplace, gender and jobs during recession, and the gender mysteries of the wage gap.**

5. Selected with the lives of students in mind, new tables throughout *Gender Roles* offer the most current data available. Focusing on gendered health and well-being, these include gender in relation to: cigarette and alcohol use among young adults, marriage and divorce, undergraduate major, graduate enrollment, and income according to education. You should be able to **locate yourself in charts** on: labor force participation by gender; leading occupations and lowest paying occupations for men and women; and gender, political party and voting for president.

6. Key terms and conveniently numbered summaries are in every chapter. New terms defined in the glossary include third wave feminism, queer theory, pink collar jobs, work-family spillover, and third shift. The subject index with **cross-referenced items allows you to easily maneuver** *Gender Roles*. Along with an expanded *Table of Contents*, these demonstrate the themes in *Gender Roles* and point out places to review material, such as: the intersection of gender, race, class, and sexuality; gendered global trends; men and masculinity; and paid and unpaid work. Critical thinking questions offer opportunities to demonstrate your understanding of all these gendered connections and to thoughtfully consider how they can be applied to both the college classroom and the world outside.

PEARSON

Gender Roles
A Sociological Perspective

5th Edition

Linda L. Lindsey
Maryville University of St. Louis

Prentice Hall
Boston   Columbus   Indianapolis   New York   San Francisco Upper Saddle River
Amsterdam   Cape Town   Dubai   London   Madrid   Milan   Munich   Paris   Montreal   Toronto
Delhi   Mexico City   Sao Paulo   Sydney   Hong Kong   Seoul   Singapore   Taipei   Tokyo

Dedication
In Memory of Carrie, Mike, and Emily

Editor in Chief: Dickson Musslewhite
Publisher: Karen Hanson
Assistant Editor: Mayda Bosco
Executive Marketing Manager: Kelly May
Marketing Assistant: Gina Lavagna
Senior Production Project Manager: Patrick Cash-Peterson
Project Manager: Susan Hannahs

Senior Art Director: Jayne Conte
Cover Designer: Mollica Design
Cover Art: Stephanie Dalton Cowan, GettyImages
Full-Service Project Management: Integra Software Services, Ltd, Sadagoban Balaji
Composition: Integra Software Services, Ltd
Printer/Bindery: RR Donnelley/Harrisonburg
Text Font: 10/11, New Baskerville

Credits and acknowledgments borrowed from other sources and reproduced, with permission, in this textbook appear on appropriate page within text.

Many of the designations by manufacturers and seller to distinguish their products are claimed as trademarks. Where those designations appear in this book, and the publisher was aware of a trademark claim, the designations have been printed in initial caps or all caps.

Library of Congress Cataloging-in-Publication Data
Lindsey, Linda L.
  Gender roles : a sociological perspective/Linda L. Lindsey.—5th ed.
    p. cm.
Includes bibliographical references and index.
ISBN-13: 978-0-13-244830-7 (alk. paper)
ISBN-10: 0-13-244830-0 (alk. paper)
  1. Sex role.   2. Sex role–United States.   I. Title.
HQ1075.L564 2011
305.3—dc22

2009050860

10 9 8 7 6 5 4 3 2 1

Prentice Hall
is an imprint of

www.pearsonhighered.com

ISBN-10:   0-13-244830-0
ISBN-13: 978-0-13-244830-7

Contents

v

PART II Gender Roles, Marriage,
and the Family   175

**CHAPTER 7 GENDERED LOVE,
MARRIAGE, AND EMERGING
LIFESTYLES   175**

LOVE   176

Preface

The remarkable first decade of the millennium showcased events profoundly affecting gender roles in the United States and globally. Two of the most important events that spotlighted gender-related issues were Election 2008 in the United States, and the global economic downturn of the Millennium Recession (MR). The gender content of these events and other social trends continues to be shaped by the increasingly powerful global media. Focusing on the most recent available gender research, the 5th edition of *Gender Roles* effectively captures the gender components of these trends and interprets the research according to various sociological theories. With media as backdrop, relevant interdisciplinary bridges are also highlighted. These bridges clarify gender content for students from diverse backgrounds and representing a variety of majors.

Interest in gender-related topics in all disciplines continues unabated, and sociology is no exception. Research flowing from this interest has reshaped the discipline. Accounting for the intersection of gender with powerful social categories such as race, social class, ethnicity, religion, age, and sexuality in sociological research and theory is expected. The feminist paradigm has joined with functionalism, conflict theory, and symbolic interaction to become sociology's fourth major theoretical perspective. As reflected in the MR, economic globalization is yet another reshaping trend—a process that fuels diversity yet makes people more connected to one another than at any other time in human history. Gender role change in our relationships, homes, workplaces, and schools is a fundamental feature of globalization. This edition emphasizes the junction between sociological theory and its application to gender and issues of diversity in the United States and how it is reverberating across the globe. Students will better understand the global connection and the theory–research connection with critiques throughout the text. Students will also be able to locate themselves when examining abundant material on diversity and the intersection of gender with other social categories they occupy.

The growth of gender-related scholarship brings with it more interpretations, more sophistication, and more complexity. The good news is that there is a wealth of material from which to choose. Students are introduced to the richness and complexity of scholarship on gender and the important issues emerging from this scholarship. Because only a fraction of this abundant information can be included, material was carefully chosen to adequately and accurately represent competing theoretical views on gender and how various groups are portrayed according to these views. Interdisciplinary work aids in these portrayals. Focused choices are made from research in other disciplines that impinges on the sociology of gender roles. Although selecting new material and discarding old material is difficult, it is manageable when a sociological perspective directs the process. Students will find a solid sociological foundation that links the range of information presented.

Written as a core text for courses variously titled Sociology of Gender, Sex and Gender, Gender Roles, or Gender and Society, this text may be used for those studying the sociology of the family, psychology of women, gender and globalization, and women's or men's studies. Although it is guided by a sociological perspective, those with limited or no background in sociology will find the book easy to navigate. It also offers an excellent review for upper division students who will have their sociological expertise reinforced early in the text. All students will gain the requisite knowledge to tackle more complex gender issues they will then confront. The opening chapter provides an overview of the sociological perspective, its theories, and its basic concepts. This perspective is specifically applied to Election 2008. Basic concepts from women's and men's studies are also introduced. Key terms are defined and boldfaced. Students will quickly understand that these theories and concepts can explain the sometimes contradictory research on gender issues. Theoretical discussions and applications that are both meaningfully linked with research and critiqued reinforce this understanding.

TEXT SECTIONS

Part I provides insights into the development of beliefs about females and males, and masculinity and femininity from research in biology, psychology, anthropology, language, and history. Biological and sociocultural explanations for gender development are highlighted in the wealth of new interdisciplinary material that exposes myths and critiques essentialist explanations for gender roles. These insights are linked back to sociological perspectives of the issues being discussed. This edition considerably expands the section on health and sexuality. It explores the powerful gendered connections between family and workplace impacting the well-being of men and women. The newest data on gender outcomes of globalization and the MR highlights the paid and unpaid work roles of women, especially in the developing world. Profiles of gender-related flashpoints in selected countries, and the similarities the globe's women share in their roles round out the section. Key issues related to work–family themes set up in Part I are carried throughout the text.

The sociological perspective dominates the balance of the book. *Part II* focuses on marriage and the family and provides new research, demographic portraits, and explanations regarding gender issues in love, choosing a partner, parenting, and the changing family in a multicultural context. The impact of gendered work roles on family life is highlighted. The chapter on men and masculinity accounts for the upsurge of research in men's studies. All chapters expand this research, highlighting the challenges to traditional definitions of masculinity, how men respond to these challenges, and how they respond to the changing roles of women. *Part III* views gender continuity and change in the economy, education, religion, media, politics, and law and suggests future trends related to gender roles. Women's persistent entry into the labor force is accented as a fundamental influence on gender roles in all social institutions. The last chapter brings full circle the material from the first chapter and issues discussed throughout the text with a focus on media and the gender–race intersection in Election 2008.

EXPLORING GENDER IN OUR LIVES

As with the previous editions, this edition of *Gender Roles* offers opportunities to explore a variety of gender issues affecting our personal, academic, and professional lives. You will encounter ideas that reinforce as well as challenge your thinking about females and males, about masculinity and femininity. An objective is to raise your level of consciousness about what you take for granted concerning gender. You will grapple with research, confront stereotypes, and select theories to best explain our gendered world. As clearly witnessed in the last decade, social change is relentless. It collides with attitudes and behaviors regarding gender and forces us to confront traditional ways of thinking and doing. We may eagerly pursue new directions or stubbornly resist them. In either scenario, we will make wiser decisions in our relationships and in our homes, schools, and workplaces when we better understand the myth and reality associated with gender.

Acknowledgments

The completion of the 5th edition of *Gender Roles* relied on the time and talents of many people. Editor and mentor Nancy Roberts was with me from the beginning of my long association with Prentice Hall and throughout many professional and personal transitions. She could be called on for support and encouragement. Pearson editor Mayda Bosco continued this collaboration by orchestrating a multitude of publishing requirements to make the project a success. Her advice and enthusiasm for this edition are sincerely appreciated. Project Manager Sadagoban Balaji and the staff of Integra ensured that the manuscript was clear and accurate. Kathleen Deselle did an excellent job editing references and creating an index to serve the needs of students doing term papers and of faculty and scholars who will find this text's extensive, up-to-date references useful for research. Thank you to Robert A. Saigh, Razorsharp Communications, Inc., for creating the Subject Index. I also want to thank Naomi Larsen for the meaningful test item file. I am indebted to those who have read and critiqued various chapters, including Lucille Adkins, La Roche College; Betty Buck, Asian Studies Development Program, East–West Center; Angela Constable and Jane Prather, California State University, Northridge; Debbie Gamble, Southwest Baptist University; Kathryn Keller, Montclair State University; Linda Geller-Schwartz, Florida Atlantic University; Mary Kris Mcilwaine, Pima Community College, West; and John Toth, Hendrix College.

Those who provided research assistance, data mining, and reference checking, as well as the most current material on gender, have been extremely helpful, especially Megan Hibbeler-Judy, Ken Harris, and the East–West Center in Hawaii. The administration and staff at Maryville University and Washington University provided a range of support and technical services. I wholeheartedly thank Sandy Reeder for her valuable time and effort with my many requests, and Dan Sparling for his ongoing support. I thank my mom, Ruth, for the food and the love, and my friends and colleagues for the words of encouragement when deadlines loomed and stress magnified. These include Marsha Balluff, Betty Buck, Jane Carriker, Cheryl Hazel, Bill Nagel, Phil Loughlin, and Bob Ott. St. Louis Bread Company (Panera) offered places for proofing and editing and Internet links for reviewing bibliography and media on gender roles. Most important, these are vital spots for respite and reenergizing. I am indebted to Panera staff—especially Judy, Crystal, Jane, and Melissa in Kirkwood; Leah, Rob, Ann, and Mel in Webster Groves; and Michael and Stan in Creve Coeur—for an inviting environment to all they serve. Indeed, they served me so very well, even as I occupied tables for long periods surrounded by a computer and mounds of paper. As I completed this edition, Berlinda McNeal, long-time staff member at Kirkwood Panera passed away. Her cheerfulness, warmth, and friendship are sorely missed. Finally, thanks to my BreadCo friends who cheerfully read excerpts, provided insight about gender from their own lives, and offered ongoing encouragement to finish this edition. These include Louise and Bill Blade, Ann Bleile, Dee and Leon Rouse, Nancy English, Morris Levin, Tom Loughrey, Bob Ott, Bill Reineke, Jack Wehrle, and Wendy and Michael Zilm.

Linda L. Lindsey
St. Louis, Missouri

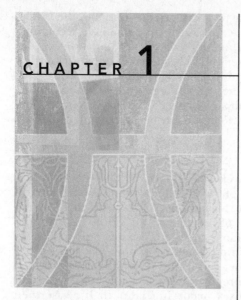

CHAPTER 1

All causes, social and natural, combine to make it unlikely that women should be collectively rebellious to the power of men. They are so far in a position different from all other subject classes, that their masters require something more from them than actual service. Men do not want solely the obedience of women, they want their sentiments.

—John Stuart Mill, *The Subjection of Women* (1869)

Events during the first decade of the millennium have profoundly affected gender roles. The study of gender emerged as one of the most important trends in the discipline of sociology in the twentieth century. The research and theory associated with studying gender issues propelled the sociology of gender from the margins to become a central feature of the discipline. To understand the powerful social effects of the *Millennium Recession* (MR) and patterns of globalization, for example, sociological analysis must account for gender. This text documents how sociologists have aided our understanding of the influence of gender in shaping our lives, our attitudes, and our behavior. This understanding is enhanced by investigating the links between sociology and other disciplines and by integrating key concepts such as race, social class, and sexuality to clarify gender relations. Sociology is interested in how human behavior is shaped by group life. Although all group life is ordered in a variety of ways, gender is a key component of the ordering. An explosion of research on gender issues now suggests that all social interactions, and the institutions in which the interactions occur, are gendered in some manner. Accounting for this gendering has reshaped the theoretical and empirical foundations of sociology. On the theoretical side, gender awareness has modified existing sociological theory and led to the creation of a new feminist paradigm. On the empirical side, gender awareness has led to innovative research strategies and opened up new topics for sociological inquiry. We open with an examination of basic concepts and theories that lay the groundwork for our sociological journey into gender roles.

BASIC SOCIOLOGICAL CONCEPTS

All societies are structured around relatively stable patterns that establish how social interaction will be carried out. One of the most important social structures that organizes social interaction is **status**—a category or position a person occupies that is a significant determinant of how she or he will be defined and treated. We acquire statuses by achievement, through our own efforts, or by ascription, being born into them or attaining them involuntarily at some other point in the life cycle. We occupy a number of statuses simultaneously, referred to as a **status set**, such as mother, daughter, attorney, patient, employee, and passenger. Compared to achieved statuses occurring later in life, ascribed statuses are those immediately impacting virtually every aspect of our lives. The most important ascribed statuses are gender, race, and social class. Since a status is simply a position within a social system, it should not be confused with rank or prestige. There are high-prestige statuses as well as low-prestige statuses. In the United States, for example, a physician occupies a status ranked higher in prestige than a secretary. All societies categorize members by status and then rank these statuses in some fashion, thereby creating a system of **social stratification**. People whose status sets are comprised of low-ranked ascribed statuses more than high-ranked achieved statuses are near the bottom of the social stratification system and vulnerable to social stigma, prejudice, and discrimination. To date, there is no known society in which the status of female is consistently ranked higher than that of male.

A **role** is the expected behavior associated with a status. Roles are performed according to social **norms**, shared rules that guide people's behavior in specific situations. Social norms determine the privileges and responsibilities a status possesses. Females and males, mothers and fathers, and daughters and sons are all statuses with different normative role requirements attached to them. The status of mother calls for expected roles involving love, nurturing, self-sacrifice, home-making, and availability. The status of father calls for expected roles of breadwinner, disciplinarian, home technology expert, and ultimate decision maker in the household. Society allows for a degree of flexibility in acting out roles, but in times of rapid social change, acceptable role limits are often in a state of flux, producing uncertainty about what appropriate role behavior should be. People may experience *anomie*—normlessness—because traditional norms have changed but new ones have yet to be developed. For example, the most important twentieth-century trend impacting gender roles in the United Sates is the massive increase of women in the labor force. Although women from all demographic categories contributed to these numbers, mothers with preschool children led the trek from unpaid home-based roles to full-time paid employment roles. In acting out the roles of mother and employee, women are expected to be available at given times to satisfy the needs of family and workplace. Because workplaces and other social institutions have not been modified in meaningful ways to account for the new statuses women occupy, their range of acceptable role behavior is severely restricted. As a result, family and workplace roles inevitably collide and compete with one another for the mother—employee's time and attention.

Key Concepts for the Sociology of Gender

As key components of social structure, statuses and roles allow us to organize our lives in consistent, predictable ways. In combination with established norms, they prescribe our behavior and ease interaction with people who occupy different social statuses, whether we know these people or not. There is an insidious side to this kind of predictable world. When normative role behavior becomes too rigidly defined, our freedom of action is often compromised. These rigid definitions are associated with the development of **stereotypes**—oversimplified conceptions that people who occupy the same status group share certain traits in common. Although stereotypes can include positive traits, they most often consist of negative ones that are then used to justify discrimination against members of a given group. The statuses of male and female are often stereotyped according to the traits they are assumed to possess by virtue of their biological makeup. Women are stereotyped as flighty and unreliable because they possess uncontrollable raging hormones that fuel unpredictable emotional outbursts. The assignment of negative stereotypes can result in **sexism**, the belief that the status of female is inferior to the status of male. Males are not immune to the negative consequences of sexism, but females are more likely to experience it because the status sets they occupy are more stigmatized than those occupied by males. Compared to males, for example, females are more likely to occupy statuses inside and outside their homes that are associated with less power, less prestige, and less pay or no pay. Beliefs about inferiority due to biology are reinforced and then used to justify discrimination directed toward females.

Sexism is perpetuated by systems of **patriarchy**, male-dominated social structures leading to the oppression of women. Patriarchy, by definition, exhibits **androcentrism**—male-centered norms operating throughout all social institutions that become the standard to which all persons adhere. Sexism is reinforced when patriarchy and androcentrism combine to perpetuate beliefs that gender roles are biologically determined and therefore unalterable. For example, throughout the developing world beliefs about a woman's biological unsuitability for other than domestic roles have restricted opportunities for education and achieving literacy. These restrictions have made men the guardians of what has been written, disseminated, and interpreted regarding gender and the placement of men and women in society. Until recently, history has been recorded from an androcentric perspective that ignored the other half of humanity (Chapter 5). This perspective has perpetuated the belief that patriarchy is an inevitable, inescapable fact of history, so struggles for gender equality are doomed to failure. Women's gain in education is associated with the power to engage in the research and scholarship offering alternatives to prevailing androcentric views. We will see that such scholarship suggests that patriarchal systems may be universal, but they are not inevitable, and that gender egalitarianism was a historical fact of life in some cultures and is a contemporary fact of life in others.

Distinguishing Sex and Gender

As gender issues have become more mainstreamed in scientific research and media reports, confusion associated with the terms *sex* and *gender* has decreased. In sociology, these terms are now fairly standardized to refer to different content areas. **Sex** refers to the biological characteristics distinguishing male and female. This definition emphasizes male and female differences in chromosomes, anatomy, hormones, reproductive systems, and other physiological components. **Gender** refers to those social, cultural, and psychological traits linked to males and females through particular social contexts. Sex makes us male or female; gender makes us masculine or feminine. Sex is an ascribed status because a person is born with it, but gender is an achieved status because it must be learned.

This relatively simple distinction masks a number of problems associated with its usage. It implies that all people can be conveniently placed into unambiguous "either–or" categories. Certainly the ascribed status of sex is less likely to be altered than the achieved status of gender. Some people believe, however, that they were born with the "wrong" body and are willing to undergo major surgery to make their gender identity consistent with their biological sex. **Sexual orientation**, the preference for sexual partners of one gender (sex) or the other, also varies. People who experience sexual pleasure with members of their own sex are likely to consider themselves masculine or feminine according to gender norms. Others are born with ambiguous sex characteristics and may be assigned one sex at birth but develop a different identity related to gender. Some cultures allow people to move freely between genders, regardless of their biological sex.

These issues will be addressed fully in Chapters 2 and 3, but are mentioned here to highlight the problems of terminology. From a sociological perspective, this text is concerned with gender and how it is learned, how it changes over time, and how it varies between and within cultures. Gender can be viewed on a continuum of characteristics demonstrated by a person regardless of the person's biological sex. Adding the concept of role to either sex or gender may increase confusion in terminology. When the sociological concept of role is combined with the biological concept of sex, there is often misunderstanding about what content areas are subsumed under the resultant *sex role* label. Usage is becoming rapidly standardized, however, and most sociologists now prefer to employ the term *gender role* rather than *sex role* in their writing. **Gender roles**, therefore, are the expected attitudes and behaviors a society associates with each sex. This definition places gender squarely in the sociocultural context.

SOCIOLOGICAL PERSPECTIVES ON GENDER ROLES

Sociologists explain gender roles according to several *theoretical perspectives*, general ways of understanding social reality that guide the research process and provide a means for interpreting the data. In essence, a **theory** is an explanation. Formal theories consist of logically interrelated propositions that explain empirical events. For instance, data indicate that compared to men, women are more likely to be segregated in lower-paying jobs offering fewer opportunities for professional growth and advancement. Data also indicate that both in the United States and cross-culturally the domestic work of women performed in or near their homes is valued less than the work of men performed outside their homes. Because the issue of gender crosses many disciplines, explanations for these facts can be offered according to the theoretical perspectives of those disciplines. Biology, psychology, and anthropology all offer explanations for gender-related attitudes and behavior. Not only do these explanations differ between disciplines, but scientists within the same discipline also frequently offer competing explanations for the same data, and sociology is no exception. The best explanations are those that account for the volume and complexities of the data. As research on gender issues accelerates and more sophisticated research tools are developed, it is becoming clearer that the best explanations are also those that are both interdisciplinary and incorporate concepts related to diversity. Sociological theory will dominate this text's discussion, but we will also account for relevant interdisciplinary work and its attention to diversity issues.

Sociological perspectives on gender also vary according to the level of analysis at which they operate. *Macrosociological* perspectives on gender roles direct attention to data collected on large-scale social phenomena, such as labor force, educational, and political trends that are differentiated according to gender roles. *Microsociological* perspectives on gender roles direct attention to data collected in small groups and the details of gender interaction occurring, for example, between couples and in families and peer groups. Microsociological perspectives overlap a great deal with the discipline of social psychology (Chapter 3). We will see that theoretical perspectives may be differentiated according to macro- and microlevel of analysis, and perspectives from each level may be more or less compatible. When theoretical perspectives can be successfully combined, they offer excellent ways to better understand gender issues from a sociological perspective.

Early sociological perspectives related to gender roles evolved from scholarship on the sociology of the family. These explanations centered on why men and women hold different roles in the family that in turn impact the roles they perform outside the family. To a large extent, this early work on the family has continued to inform current sociological thinking on gender roles. The next sections will overview the major sociological perspectives and highlight their explanations regarding the gender–family connection.

Functionalism

Functionalism, also known as "structural functionalism," is a macrosociological perspective that is based on the premise that society is made up of interdependent parts, each of which contributes to the functioning of the whole society. Functionalists seek to identify the basic elements or parts of society and determine the functions these parts play in meeting basic social needs in predictable ways. Functionalists ask how any given element of social structure contributes to overall social stability, balance, and equilibrium. They assert that in the face of disruptive social change, society can be restored to equilibrium as long as built-in mechanisms of social control operate effectively and efficiently. Social control and stability are enhanced when people share beliefs and values in common. Functionalist emphasis on this value consensus is a major ingredient in virtually all their interpretations related to social change. Values surrounding gender roles, marriage, and the family are central to functionalist assertions regarding social equilibrium.

Preindustrial Society. Functionalists suggest that in preindustrial societies social equilibrium was maintained by assigning different tasks to men and women. Given the hunting and gathering and subsistence farming activities of most preindustrial societies, role specialization according to gender was considered a functional necessity. In their assigned hunting roles, men were frequently away from home for long periods and centered their lives around the responsibility of bringing food to the family. It was functional for women—more limited by pregnancy, childbirth, and nursing—to be assigned domestic roles near the home as gatherers and subsistence farmers and as caretakers of children and households. Children were needed to help with agricultural and domestic activities. Girls would continue these activities when boys reached the age when they were allowed to hunt with the older males. Once established, this functional division of labor was reproduced in societies throughout the globe. Women may have been farmers and food gatherers in their own right, but they were dependent on men for food and for protection. Women's dependence on men in turn produced a pattern in which male activities and roles came to be more valued than female activities and roles.

Contemporary Society. Similar principles apply to families in contemporary societies. Disruption is minimized, harmony is maximized, and families benefit when spouses assume complementary, specialized, nonoverlapping roles (Parsons and Bales, 1955; Parsons, 1966). When the husband–father takes the **instrumental role**, he is expected to maintain the physical integrity of the family by providing food and shelter and linking the family to the world outside the home. When the wife–mother takes the **expressive role**, she is expected to cement relationships and provide emotional support and nurturing activities that ensure the household runs smoothly. If too much deviation from these roles occurs, or when there is too much overlap, the family system is propelled into a state of imbalance that can threaten the survival of the family unit. Advocates of functionalist assumptions argue, for instance, that gender role ambiguity regarding instrumental and expressive roles is a major factor in divorce (Hacker, 2003).

Critique. It should be apparent that functionalism's emphasis on social equilibrium contributes to its image as an inherently conservative theoretical perspective. This image is reinforced by its difficulty in accounting for a variety of existing family systems and in not keeping pace with rapid social change moving families toward more egalitarian attitudes regarding gender roles.

Often to the dismay of the scientists who developed them, scientific theories and the research on which they are based are routinely employed to support a range of ideologies. Functionalism has been used as a justification for male dominance and gender stratification. In the United States, functional analyses were popularized in the 1950s when, weary of war, the nation latched onto a traditional and idealized version of family life and attempted to establish not just a prewar, but a pre-Depression, existence. Functionalism tends to support a white middle-class family model emphasizing the economic activities of the male household head and domestic activities of his female subordinate. Women function outside the home only as a reserve labor force, such as when their labor is needed in wartime. This model does not apply to poor women and single parents who by necessity must work outside the home to maintain the household. It may not apply to African American women, who are less likely by choice to separate family and employment and who derive high levels of satisfaction from both these roles.

Research also shows that specialization of household tasks by gender in contemporary families is more dysfunctional than functional. Women relegated to family roles that they see as restrictive, for example, are unhappier in their marriages and more likely to opt out of them. Despite tension associated with multiple roles and role overlap, couples report high levels of gratification, self esteem, status security, and personally enriched lives (Chapter 8). Contemporary families simply do not fit functionalist models.

To its credit, functionalism offers a reasonably sound explanation for the origin of gender roles and demonstrates the functional utility of assigning tasks on the basis of gender in subsistence economies or in regions in which large families are functional and children are needed for agricultural work. Contemporary functionalists also acknowledge that strain occurs when there is too sharp a divide between the public and the private sphere (work and family), particularly for women. They recognize that such a divide is artificial and dysfunctional when families need to cope with the growing interdependence called for in a global economy. The "superwoman" who "does it all" in career achievement and family nurturance will be valued (Diekman and Goodfriend, 2006). Finally, neofunctionalism accounts for the multiple levels where gender relations are operative—biological, psychological, social, and cultural. A functionalist examination of their interdependence allows us to understand how female subordination and male superiority became reproduced throughout the globe.

Conflict Theory

With its assumptions about social order and social change, the macrosociological perspective of conflict theory, also referred to as social conflict theory, is in many ways a mirror image of functionalism. Unlike functionalists, who believe that social order is maintained through value consensus, conflict theorists assert that it is preserved involuntarily through the exercise of power one social class holds over another.

Marx, Engels, and Social Class. Originating from the writings of Karl Marx (1818–1883), conflict theory is based on the assumption that society is a stage on which struggles for power and dominance are acted out. The struggles are largely between social classes competing for scarce resources, such as control over the means of production (land, factories, natural resources), and for a better distribution of all resources (money, food, material goods). Capitalism thrives on a class-based system that consolidates power in the hands of a few men of the ruling class (*bourgeoisie*), who own the farms and factories that workers (*proletariat*) depend on for their survival. The interest of the dominant class is to maintain its position of power over the subordinate class by extracting as much profit as possible from their work. Only when the workers recognize their common oppression and form a *class consciousness* can they unite and amass the resources necessary to seriously challenge the inequitable system in which they find themselves (Marx and Engels, 1964; Marx, 1967). Marxian beliefs were acted out historically in the revolution that enveloped Russia, Eastern Europe, and much of Eurasia, propelling the Soviets to power for a half a century of control over these regions.

Friedrich Engels (1820–1895), Marx's collaborator, applied these assumptions to the family and, by extension, to gender roles. He suggested that the master–slave or exploiter–exploited relationships occurring in broader society between the bourgeoisie and the proletariat are translated into the household. Primitive societies were highly egalitarian because there were no surplus goods, hence no private property. People consumed what they produced. With the emergence of private property and the dawn of capitalistic institutions, Engels argued that a woman's domestic labor is "no longer counted beside the acquisition of the necessities of life by the man; the latter was everything, the former an unimportant extra." The household is an autocracy, and the supremacy of the husband is unquestioned. "The emancipation of woman will only be possible when women can take part in production on a large social scale, and domestic work no longer claims but an insignificant amount of her time" (Engels, 1942:41–43).

Contemporary Conflict Theory. Later conflict theorists refined original Marxian assertions to reflect contemporary patterns and make conflict theory more palatable to people who desire social change that moves in the direction of egalitarianism but not through the revolutionary means outlined by classical Marxism (Dahrendorf, 1959; Collins, 1975, 1979). Today conflict theory largely asserts that social structure is based on the dominance of some groups over others and that groups in society share common interests, whether its members are aware of it or not. Conflict is not simply based on class struggle and the tensions between owner and worker or employer and employee; it occurs on a much wider level and among almost all other groups. These include parents and children, husbands and wives, young and the old, sick and healthy, people of color and whites, heterosexual and gay, females and males, and any other groups that can be differentiated as minority or majority according to the level of resources they possess. The list is infinite.

Gender and the Family. Conflict theory focuses on the social placement function of the family that deposits people at birth into families who possess varying degrees of economic resources. People fortunate enough to be deposited into wealthier families will work to preserve existing inequality and the power relations in the broader society because they clearly benefit from the overall power imbalance. Social class *endogamy* (marrying within the same class) and inheritance patterns ensure that property and wealth are kept in the hands of a few powerful families. Beliefs about inequality and the power imbalance become institutionalized—they are accepted and persist over time as legitimate by both the privileged and the oppressed—so the notion that family wealth is deserved and that those born into poor families remain poor because they lack talent and a work ethic is perpetuated. The structural conditions that sustain poverty are ignored. When social placement operates through patriarchal and patrilineal systems, wealth is further concentrated in the hands of males and further promotes female subservience, neglect, and poverty. Contemporary conflict theorists agree with Engels by suggesting that when women gain economic strength by also being wage earners, their power inside the home is strengthened and can lead to more egalitarian arrangements.

The conflict perspective is evident in research demonstrating that household responsibilities have an effect on occupational location, work experience, and number of hours worked per week, all of which are linked to the gender gap in earnings (Chapter 10). Undesirable work will be performed disproportionately by those lacking resources to demand sharing the burden or purchasing substitutes. Because household labor is unpaid and associated with lack of power, the homemaker (wife) takes on virtually all domestic chores (Lindsey, 1996a; Riley and Kiger, 1999). The more powerful spouse performs the least amount of household work.

Critique. Conflict theory has been criticized for its overemphasis on the economic basis of inequality and its assumption that there is inevitable competition between family members. It tends to dismiss the consensus among wives and husbands regarding task allocation. In addition, paid employment is not the panacea envisioned by Engels in overcoming male dominance. The gendered division of household labor does not translate to significant wage reductions for employed women outside the home or reduced in-home responsibilities (Tichenor, 2005; Lincoln, 2008). In the former Soviet Union women had the highest levels of paid employment in the world, but retained more household responsibilities than comparable women in other countries, and earned two-thirds of the average male income. In post–Communist Russia, there is no change in women's domestic work, but women now earn less than half of men's average earnings (Chapter 6). Research unanimously concludes that even in those cultures where gender equity in the workplace is increasing, employed women globally take on a "second shift" of domestic work after returning home (Chapter 8).

A conspiratorial element emerges when conflict theory becomes associated with the idea that men as a group are consciously organized to keep women in subordinate positions. A number of social forces, many of them unorganized or unintended, come into play when explaining gender stratification. Functionalism's bias against social change might be matched with conflict theory's bias for social change. Compared to functionalism, however, this bias is less of a problem for conflict theory once it is stripped of some Marxian baggage. Contemporary conflict theory has made strong inroads in using social class to further clarify the gender–race–class link, suggesting that the class advantages for people of color may override the race disadvantages (Gimenez, 2001; Lareau, 2002; Misra, 2002). Most people are uncomfortable with sexism and patterns of gender stratification that harm both women and men. Women are denied opportunities to expand instrumental roles offering economic parity with men outside the home; men are denied opportunities for expanding expressive and nurturing roles inside the home. At the ideological level, sociological conflict theory has been used to support activities designed to reduce racism, economic-based disparity (classism), and sexism.

Symbolic Interaction

Symbolic interaction, also called "the interactionist perspective," is at the heart of the sociological view of social interaction at the microlevel. With attention to people's behavior in face-to-face social settings, symbolic interactionists explain social interaction as a dynamic process in which people continually modify their behavior as a result of the interaction itself. Herbert Blumer (1900–1987), who originated the term *symbolic interaction*, asserted that people do not respond directly to the world around them, but to the meaning they bring to it. Society, its institutions, and its social structure exist—that is, social reality is bestowed—only through human interaction (Blumer, 1969). Reality is what members agree to be reality.

People interact according to how they perceive a situation, how they understand the social encounter, and the meanings they bring to it. Another important step in the interaction process involves how they think other people who are part of the interaction also understand the encounter. Each person's definition of the situation influences others' definitions. To illustrate symbolic interaction's emphasis on the fluidity of behavior, I developed the concept of the **end point fallacy**, asserting that the negotiation of social reality is an ongoing process in which new definitions produce new behavior in a never-ending cycle. The end point fallacy is an excellent way to explain the inconsistencies between people's behavior as they move from setting to setting.

Social Construction of Reality. Symbolic interaction is a microlevel perspective, but it does take into account that social interaction is a process governed by norms that are largely determined by culture. Cultural norms offer general guidelines for role behavior, but symbolic interactionists assert that we have latitude in the way we act out our roles. The context of the interaction is usually a key determinant of role performance. What is appropriate role performance in one context may be inappropriate in another. Cultural norms are modified whenever social interaction occurs because people bring their own definitions about appropriate behavior to the interaction. These definitions shape the way people see and experience the world. Symbolic interactionists refer to this shaping process as the **social construction of reality**—the shaping of perception of reality by the subjective meanings brought to any experience or social interaction. Consistent with Herbert Blumer's view, every time social interaction occurs, people creatively construct their own understanding of it—whether "real" or not—and behave accordingly.

Doing Gender. Symbolic interactionists contend that concepts used to collectively categorize people—such as race, ethnicity, and gender—do not exist objectively but emerge through a socially constructed process. People called "females" or "males" are endowed with certain traits defined as feminine or masculine. Concepts such as gender, therefore, must be found in the meanings people bring to them (Denzin, 1993; Deutscher and Lindsey, 2005:5). Gender emerges not as an individual attribute but something that is "accomplished" in interaction with others. People, therefore, are **doing gender** (Fenstermaker and West, 2002). In "doing" gender, symbolic interaction takes its lead from Erving Goffman (1922–1982), who developed a **dramaturgy** approach to social interaction. Goffman maintained that the best way to understand social interaction is to consider it as an enactment in a theatrical performance. Like actors on a stage, we use strategies of impression management, providing information and cues to others that present us in a favorable light (Goffman, 1959, 1963, 1971).

Think about the heterosexual bar scene where men usually sit at the counter and operate from a script where they are expected to make the first move. If a woman is with friends, she must disengage herself if she is "selected" by the man. It is probable that the women drove separately. Data from television also illustrate these concepts. Prime time television commonly depict traditionally scripted sexual encounters according to gender and beliefs about heterosexuality that sustain power differences between men and women and between heterosexual and homosexual men (Kim et al., 2007). Although there are many cultural variations, gender-scripted rules are laid out, negotiated, and acted upon in bars and meeting places for singles and witnessed by TV viewers across the globe.

Gender roles are structured by one set of scripts designed for males and another designed for females. Although each script permits a range of behavior options, the typical result is that gender labels promote a pattern of between-sex competition, rejection, and emotional segregation. This pattern is reinforced when we routinely refer to those of the *other* sex (gender) as the *opposite* sex. Men and women label each other as opposite to who they are, then behave according to that label. The behavior serves to separate rather than connect the genders.

Doing Difference. Research on men and women in various social networks—formed at school, work, and in volunteer activities—further illustrates this process. From early childhood these groups are usually gender segregated. Gendered subcultures emerge that strengthen the perceptions of gender differences and erode the common ground on which intimate, status-equal friendships between the genders are formed (Rouse, 2002). Differences rather than similarities are much more likely to be noticed, defined, and acted on. When cross-gender social interaction occurs, such as in the workplace, it is unlikely that men and women hold statuses with similar levels of power and prestige. Once the genders are socially constructed as different, it is easier for those with more power (men) to justify inequality toward those with less power (women). Social difference is constructed into social privilege (Fenstermaker and West, 2002).

Critique. Symbolic interaction's approach to understanding gender role behavior is criticized for its overall lack of attention to macrolevel processes that often limits choice of action and prompts people to engage in gendered behavior that counters what they would prefer to do. Cultural norms may be in flux at the microlevel of social interaction, but they remain a significant structural force on behavior. In some cultures, for example, women and men are dictated by both law and custom to engage in certain occupations, enter into marriages with people they would not choose on their own, and be restricted from attending school. Larger social structures also operate at the family level to explain family dynamics. Men and women interact not only as individual family members but also according to other roles they play in society and the prestige associated with those roles. For example, a wealthy white man who holds a powerful position in a corporation does not dissolve those roles when he walks into his home. They shape his life at home, in the workplace, and in the other social institutions in which he takes part. Race, class, and gender offer a range of privileges bestowed by the broader society that also create a power base in his home. Power and privilege can result in a patriarchal family regardless of the couple's desire for a more egalitarian arrangement.

Others argue that symbolic interaction's emphasis on doing gender undermines its fluidity to recast gender norms in ways that benefit both men and women. Divorce allows for the "redoing" of gender—housework, parenting, and breadwinning roles are repudiated (Walzer, 2008). Traditional gender accountability may no longer apply in the post-divorce lives of former spouses and children.

Research on social dancing and its highly sexualized "grinding" form demonstrates the ways females challenge scripts and may be redoing gender on the dance floor. In hip-hop clubs, young women of color set the dance stage for negotiating sexual and emotional encounters (Munoz-Laboy et al., 2007). These women challenge "hypermasculine" privilege by determining the form of dance, by taking the lead, by dancing with women, and by rejecting (or accepting) sexual groping by male partners. Other data suggest that young women of all races use social dance as escapism, fantasy, and compensatory sexuality, especially when dancing with acquaintances rather than friends (Hutt, 2008).

Taking a step further, some argue that symbolic interaction's doing gender approach needs to be abandoned. If gender accountability assumes that inequality is inevitable, research on ways of "undoing gender" should be the focus of sociological analysis. (Deutsch, 2007; Risman, 2009:81). Are the young women on the dance floor "redoing" or "undoing gender"? Gendered scripts invade their dance space even as they transgress its boundaries.

> You buy into this scenario that. . . . we're all willing to pretend in this one place . . . that we're allowed to do things with each other that maybe you would think about doing off of first glance anyway. . . . it's kind of like a. . . . simulated closeness with people. (Hutt, 2008:12)

Sociological analysis of sexuality is beginning to explore the body not merely as a passive surface to be acted upon, but in its relationship to human agency (Bryant, 2007). More research is needed to determine if in the micro-worlds of post-divorce homes or in dance clubs traditional scripts can be modified enough to say that gender is "undone."

Feminist Sociological Theory

By calling attention to the powerful impact of gender in the social ordering of our relationships (microlevel analysis) and our institutions (macrolevel analysis), the feminist theoretical perspective in sociology emerged as a major model that has significantly reshaped the discipline. By the research it spawned, feminist sociological theory is not only bridging the micro–macro gap, it has also illuminated the androcentric bias in sociology and in broader society. Disagreement remains on all elements that need to be included in feminist theory, but at a minimum, the consensus is that a theory is feminist if it can be used to challenge a status quo that is disadvantageous to women (Chafetz, 1988; Smith, 2003).

The feminist perspective provides productive avenues of collaboration with sociologists who adopt other theoretical views, especially conflict theory and symbolic interaction. The feminist perspective is compatible with conflict theory in its assertions that structured social inequality is maintained by ideologies that are frequently accepted by both the privileged and the oppressed. These ideologies are challenged only when oppressed groups gain the resources necessary to do so. Unlike conflict theory's focus on social class and the economic elements necessary to challenge the prevailing system, feminists focus on women and their ability to amass resources from a variety of sources—in their individual lives (microlevel) and through social and political means (macrolevel). Feminists work through a number of avenues to increase women's **empowerment**—the ability for women to exert control over their own destinies.

Symbolic interaction and feminist theory come together in research focusing on the unequal power relations between men and women from the point of view (definition of the situation) of women who are "ruled" by men in many settings. For example, corporate women who want to be promoted need to practice impression management based on acceptable gender role behavior of their corporate setting, but at the same time they need to maintain a sense of personal integrity. The feminist perspective accounts for ways to empower these corporate women by clarifying the relationship between the label of "feminine" (symbolic interaction) and how these women are judged by peers and by themselves.

Linking Gender, Race, and Class. One of the most important contributions of the feminist perspective to sociology is its attention to the multiple oppressions faced by people whose status sets are disadvantaged due to distinctive combinations based on their gender, race, and social class. The gender–race–class linkage in analyzing social behavior originated with African American feminists in the 1960s, who recognized that an understanding of the link between these multiple oppressions is necessary to determine how women are alike and how they are different. For example, when the issue of poverty becomes "feminized," the issue is defined primarily by gender—women are at a higher risk of being poor than men. A focus on the feminization of poverty ignores the link among race, social class, and marital status that puts certain categories of women—such as single parents, women of color, and elderly women living alone—at higher risk than others. To explain poverty, racial and class oppression must be considered along with gender. When white, middle-class feminists focus on oppression of women, they may not recognize the privileges that come with their own race and class.

The attention to sociocultural diversity that originated with the gender–race–class link has reverberated throughout sociology and other disciplines, generating a great deal of interdisciplinary research. It has opened new academic programs in Women's Studies, Men's Studies, and Gender Studies and has increased dialogue between men and women. Feminist scholarship provides opportunities for men to view themselves as gendered beings and to make visible their concerns (Brod, 2003; Kimmel, 2008). With the gender–race–class link as a foundation, feminist researchers are identifying other sites of oppression that put people at risk both inside and outside their families, such as religion, sexual orientation, age, or disability.

Feminist Perspectives on the Family. Feminist scholars in the 1960s and 1970s viewed the traditional patriarchal family as a major site for the oppression of women. They asserted that when the patriarchal family is regarded as beneficial to social stability, it hampers the movement into egalitarian roles desired by both men and women. Feminist sociologists recognize that gendered family relations do not occur in a vacuum and that lives are helped or hurt by the resources outside the family that shape what is happening inside the family. In addition to gender, for example, single-parent African-American, Latino, and Native American women are disadvantaged by race when they seek employment necessary to support their families. Lesbians must deal with a system that represses same-sex relationships when they fight for custody of their children. The growing consensus of feminists in all disciplines is that women may be doubly or triply disadvantaged by their race, class, or sexuality, but they are not helpless victims. To some degree they possess **agency**—the power to adapt and sometimes to thrive in difficult situations.

Critique. With a view of gender, marriage, and the family focusing on oppression of women, the feminist perspective tends to minimize the practical benefits of marriages. This contention is that a marriage may be patriarchal, but it also includes important economic resources and social support that women in these marriages may view as more important in their daily lives than their feelings about subordination. Feminist scholars also find it difficult to reconcile research suggesting that women in traditional marriages are as satisfied with their choices as women in egalitarian marriages. Finally, emphasis on human agency may minimize situations in which women's victimization is condoned by custom and ignored by law (Chapters 6, 8, 9, and 14).

A key strength of the feminist perspective is its ability to provide bridges between sociological theories and account for social diversity in all its forms. With its challenge to the patriarchal status quo and the androcentric bias inherent in much sociological research and theory, it has created dissent that may limit its acceptance by some sociologists. On the other hand, the feminist perspective may plant the seeds for building a truly integrative theory to draw together "conceptual pieces into a web of ideas that transcend patriarchal theory building" (Ollenburger and Moore, 1992:36). Feminist theory offers a powerful new perspective in sociology. Sociology will benefit from the intellectual ferment it has already created.

FEMINISM AND ITS BRANCHES

Feminist theory and its attention to diversity offer a sound framework for organizations working to change women's inferior social position and the social, political, and economic discrimination that perpetuates it. Many of these organizations come together in networks under the umbrella of **feminism**, an inclusive worldwide movement to end sexism and sexist oppression by empowering women. Thirty years ago the women's movement faltered because it did not realistically account for how intersecting categories of oppression can divide women (Breines, 2006). Through efforts of feminist networks across the globe and under the leadership of the United Nations and the women's conferences they organized, many of these divides have been bridged (Chapter 6).

Global social change presents new and ongoing challenges for women, so a feminist agenda addressing the needs of all women is never in a finalized form. Feminists accept the goal of ending sexism by empowering women, but there is a great deal of disagreement about how that goal is to be accomplished. Because the feminist movement is inclusive, it is unlikely there will ever be full agreement on identifying problems and determining strategies to address the problems. The very inclusiveness and diversity of the movement makes unity on some issues virtually impossible. Indeed, absence of complete unity is appropriate because it fuels those worldwide debates that often result in the most creative, realistic, and innovative strategies for women's empowerment. Reflecting the difficulty of adopting one agenda, the movement has tended to partition itself into several different branches according to general philosophical differences. Women and men identify with organizations and principles that may fall under more than one branch. In addition, the branches are fluid; they continue to recreate themselves as different waves of feminism flow through society (Chapter 5). Feminist branches, therefore, are neither mutually exclusive nor exhaustive. Feminists as individuals or in the formal groups to which they belong, however, generally subscribe to the principles of one or another of the following branches.

Liberal Feminism

Liberal feminism, also called "egalitarian or mainstream feminism," is considered the most moderate branch. It is based on the simple proposition that all people are created equal and should not be denied equality of opportunity because of gender. Because both genders benefit by the elimination of sexism, men are integrated into its ranks. Liberal feminism is based on Enlightenment beliefs of rationality, education, and the natural rights that extend to all men and women. This is articulated in John Stuart Mill's (1869/2002) *The Subjection of Women*, with his statement that "what is now called the nature of women is an eminently artificial thing—the result of forced oppression in some directions, unnatural stimulation in others." Women can work together within a pluralistic system and mobilize their constituents to effect positive and productive social change. Demands will be met if mobilization is effective and pressure is efficiently wielded (Deckard, 1983:463).

Liberal feminists believe society does not have to be completely restructured to achieve empowerment for women and to incorporate women into meaningful and equitable roles. This view tends to be adopted by professional, middle-class women who place a high value on education and achievement. These women are likely to have the economic resources to better compete with men for desirable social positions and employment opportunities. Liberal feminism thus appeals to "mainstream" women who have no disagreement with the overall structure of the present social system, only that it should be nonsexist. The National Organization for Women is the formal group representing this branch, with a statement of purpose calling for an end to restrictive gender roles that serve to diminish opportunities for both women and men (Chapter 14).

Cultural Feminism. Liberal feminists may also embrace "cultural feminism" with its focus on empowering women by emphasizing the positive qualities that are associated with women's roles such as nurturing, caring, cooperation, and connectedness to others (Worell, 1996:360). The issue of how much women are alike and how much they are different is highlighted in this emphasis. Although it does not constitute a separate branch of feminism per se, the debate around the "degree of gender difference or similarity" has allowed cultural feminism to become incorporated in all the feminist branches at some level. Liberal feminists, however, are more likely to subscribe to these principles than women in other branches.

Socialist Feminism

Also referred to as "Marxist feminism," socialist feminism generally adopts the Marx–Engels model described earlier that links the inferior position of women to class-based capitalism and its alignment with the patriarchal family in capitalistic societies. Socialist feminism argues that sexism and capitalism are mutually supportive. The unpaid labor of women in the home and their paid labor in a reserve labor force simultaneously serve patriarchy capitalism. Many socialist feminists—both men and women—also believe that economic and emotional dependence go hand in hand. Fearful of the loss of economic security, a husband's power over his wife is absolute. Capitalism needs to be eliminated and socialist principles adopted to both home and workplace. Sexism and economic oppression are mutually reinforcing, so a socialist revolutionary agenda is needed to change both.

Socialist feminism appeals to working-class women and those who feel disenfranchised from the presumed economic opportunities in capitalism. It has made a great deal of headway in Latin America and has served as a powerful rallying point for women in other developing nations. It is ironic that its most vivid expression occurred in the former Soviet Union, where women continued to carry the heavy burden of unpaid household labor while also functioning in the paid labor force.

Although socialist feminism is explicitly tied to Marxist theory, there are key differences between the two. Whereas Marxist theory focuses on property and economic conditions to build an ideology, socialist feminism focuses on sexuality and gender. Men and women retain interest in their own gender group, so it is unclear if the socialism being struggled for is the same for both men and women (Hartmann, 1993). A humane socialist approach to feminism requires consensus on what the new society should be and would require men to renounce their privileges as men.

Radical Feminism

Radical feminism is said to have emerged when women who were working with men in the civil rights and anti–Vietnam War movements were not allowed to present their positions on the causes they were engaged in. These women became aware of their own oppression by the treatment they received from their male cohorts, who insulted and ridiculed them for their views. The *second wave* of feminism leading to the rebirth of the women's movement in the United States in the twentieth century may be traced to the women who found themselves derided and ignored by the people they believed to be their allies. History repeated itself. The roots of American feminism in the nineteenth century are traced to the women who were denied expression of their views by the men they worked with in the antislavery movement. The patronizing attitudes of the men of that era provided the catalyst for women to recognize gender-based oppression and then organize to challenge it (Chapter 5). A century later it happened again.

Contemporary radical feminists believe that sexism is at the core of patriarchal society and that all social institutions reflect that sexism. Whereas liberal feminists focus on the workplace and legal changes, radical feminists focus on the patriarchal family as the key site of domination and oppression (Shelton and Agger, 1993). They believe that because all social institutions are so intertwined, it is virtually impossible to attack sexism in any meaningful way. Women's oppression stems from male domination, so if men are the problem, neither capitalism, nor socialism, nor any other male-dominated system will solve the problem. Therefore, women must create separate institutions that are women centered—those that rely on women rather than men. Radical feminists would agree with cultural feminism in that the alternative path for women is to be different than men. A society will emerge where the female virtues of nurturance, sharing, and intuition will dominate in a woman-identified world.

Acknowledging the impossibility of removing sexism from all institutions, radical feminists work at local levels and in their neighborhoods to develop profit and not-for-profit institutions that are operated solely by women to serve other women, such as small businesses, day care facilities, counseling centers, and safe houses for women escaping domestic violence.

Reflecting more overall diversity than any of the other branches in its ranks, especially related to race and sexual orientation, these institutions vary considerably in structure, philosophy, and strategies to attain their goals. The blueprint for the women-identified society they envision is stamped on their activities that are much more individualized in other feminist branches. The conviction that male supremacy and oppression of women is the defining characteristic of a society is what unifies the disparate elements of radical feminism.

Multicultural and Global Feminism

The attention to diversity issues at the macrolevel is evident among feminists who organize around multicultural and global issues. This feminist branch focuses on the intersection of gender with race, class, and issues related to the colonization and exploitation of women in the developing world. Global feminism is a movement of people working for change across national boundaries. The world is interdependent and becoming more so. Global feminism contends that no woman is free until the conditions that oppress women worldwide are eliminated (Bunch, 1993:249). Multicultural feminism focuses on the specific cultural elements and historical conditions that serve to maintain women's oppression. In Latin America, for instance, military regimes have devised specific patterns of punishment and sexual enslavement for women who oppose their regimes (Bunster-Bunalto, 1993). Global feminism works to empower South Asian and Middle Eastern women who are restricted from schooling, health care, and paid employment simply because they are women.

In efforts to empower women, they do not support the idea of cultural relativism when it violates a woman's human rights, such as restricting a girl's access to education on religious grounds (Chapter 6). The women who came together for the United Nations Conferences on Women are representative of this view.

Ecofeminism

Some women are drawn into feminism by environmental activism. These women are the catalysts of ecofeminism, a newer branch of feminism. Ecofeminism connects the degradation and oppression of women with the degradation of the ecosystem. Drawing on earth-based spiritual imagery, ecofeminism suggests that the world's religions have an ethical responsilbilty to challenge a patriarchal system of corporate globalization that is deepening the impoverishment of the earth and its people (Low and Tremayne, 2001; Ruether, 2005). The planet can be healed and ecological harmony restored through political action emphasizing the principle of equality of all species (Bowerbank, 2001). With its holistic viewpoint and emphasis on interdependence in all its forms, ecofeminism is particularly compatible with global feminism.

All branches of feminism deal with the linkages of gender with other relevant social categories. Members of each branch and the groups they work with negotiate how gender is constructed according to their own needs and priorities. Different feminisms result from these constructions.

FEMINISM AND THE MEDIA

Why is feminism is considered the "f-word." Feminism is a movement to end the oppression of women. It uses women's perceptions and experiences to devise strategies for overcoming oppression. It embraces political goals that offer gender equality. We will see throughout this text that public support for feminist goals and women's empowerment is widespread. A large majority of American women agree that feminism has altered their lives for the better. Many women, however, refuse to identify themselves as feminists.

Through empowerment passivity has been replaced by open and critical debate between feminists and between those who agree or disagree with feminism. This debate is stimulating, is necessary, and fuels further empowerment. As noted earlier, inclusiveness feeds disagreement. Like the branches of feminism, feminists have different priorities and goals and they can agree to disagree. There are many feminisms and many themes of feminist thought. Feminists understand and accept the distinctions but they are presented to the public in highly distorted ways.

Portrayals of Feminsim

Media have a formidable influence in reinforcing gender role stereotypes, and the feminist stereotype is no exception. Both feminist agreement and the feminist value of disagreement are ignored or ridiculed not only in conservative media, but also throughout mainstream, cable news, and entertainment media. These portrayals also illustrate key features of **misogyny**, the contempt and disdain of women that propels their oppression. Media messages implicitly supporting misogyny propel stereotypes about feminism.

Media latch onto disagreements among feminists and present sound bytes giving the impressions that feminism has split into irreconcilable warring factions.

This negative media attention is reinforced with news format entertainment shows suggesting that women have already achieved political parity and legal parity with men, and because feminists have nothing else to fight for, they fight among themselves. Young women appear to be receptive to these messages because self-identification for feminism decreases significantly with age (Schnittker et al., 2002; Hogeland, 2007).

In addition to highlighting disagreement among feminists, media depict feminists as puritanical, man-hating, lesbain or butch, taking unfair advantage of men in the workplace, and controlling men in their homes. College students who identify themselves as "nonfeminists" believe many of these sterotypes (Blackwell et al., 2003; Houvouras and Scott, 2008). The credibility of a respected veteran female reporter was called into question by characterizing her as a "man-hating feminist" for daring to expose drug cheating in professional baseball (Burwell, 2009:B1). Prime time television series portray feminists in negative and highly stereotyped ways. Jokes deriding feminists about their appearance, sexuality and love life, and how they control their children and husbands are common. Boys who support assertive girls fear homophobic labels casting doubts about their mas-culinty (Chapter 9). Assertive girls are silenced when they are "accused" of being feminists. Young women and teens are often the targets of sexist jokes. Sexism is reinforced by the contemptuous statements about feminists routinely made by the popular and attractive characters in the shows (Chapter 13). Given the power of the media to construct gender roles, it is difficult for young women and men who may identify with feminism in principle to do so in public.

Racist comments are unacceptable in entertainment and news media. Sexist comments are acceptable. Consider the infamous response by John McCain to a female supporter (referring to Hillary Clinton) when he was asked "how do we beat the bitch?" Although momentarily taken aback by her comment, amid the laughter, he smiled and responded: "but that's an excellent question" (Kantor, 2008). Consider his probable response if his supporter had used a racist slur rather than a sexist one? The Obama campaign remained silent about sexist com-mentary or intrusion into the personal lives of opposing candidates until after the primary election.

Feminism and Election 2008

As if waiting in the wings to be re-ignited, feminist bashing made a "gut-wrenching" comeback during the 2008 election (Merkin, 2008). For the first time in U.S. history, women were very viable contenders for the highest offices: New York Senator Hillary Rodham Clinton as potential Democrat nominee for President and Alaska Governor Sarah Palin as Republican nominee for Vice President. With feminism taking center stage, a storm of gender-based commentary was unleashed during the run-up to the election. Public perception of these (and other) candi-dates was skewed via media rendering of gender and of feminism (Mandziuk, 2008; Sotirovic, 2008). Both Clinton and Palin self-identified as feminists. However, they were portrayed as very different feminists according to the media.

Hillary Rodham Clinton.   Hillary Clinton's feminist label was intermittently applauded in a few news media, suspiciously viewed throughout mainstream media, and scorned and ridiculed in right-wing media. Although Clinton ran a campaign that included, but did not focus on, women's issues, her feminism and—by extension—her personality were associated with divisiveness, "unlikability," and media-constructed views of radicalism. Feminism was further diminished when

Clinton was couched as an opportunist interested in personal ambition rather than public service and unsure of her beliefs about how far she was willing to go in support of women (Reimer, 2008; Stansell, 2008). Virtually no mainstream media source countered these stereotyped, inaccurate images of feminism associated with Clinton's campaign. Media instead spotlighted women, feminist or not, who endorsed Barack Obama's candidacy. The public heard messages that women are their own enemies, that feminism is unraveling, and that the sisterhood is split (Wiener, 2007; Valenti, 2008). Feminists who agree to disagree or those engaged in critical debate with one another were absent in media discourse. Feminism as applied to Clinton in the media represented a threat to politics as usual.

Sarah Palin. Although Sarah Palin and the social conservatives who supported her would largely disagree with a feminist political agenda (Chapter 14), she did identify herself as a feminist in the now famous interview when Katie Couric asked if Palin considered herself a feminist. Palin's response: "I do. A feminist who believes in equal rights, and I believe that women certainly today have every opportunity that a man has to succeed, and to try to do it all, anyway" (Couric, 2008). Sarah Palin's feminist label was generally applauded, regardless of the political persuasion of the media source. The McCain–Palin ticket ran a campaign that put Palin in charge of policy statements reinforcing traditional views of women that resonated with social conservatives. As applied to Palin, feminism was benignly to positively portrayed by her status as an elected official, as a mother with small children, and with a supportive husband in a marriage that did not demean his role. Feminists largely disagreed with the policy agenda (or lack of one) to meaningfully bolster women in such roles. However, they supported Palin's quest for public office, especially in her role model status for young women and for working mothers (Baird et al., 2008; Montagne, 2008). In utterly false and astonishing media messages, however, feminists were cast as *detractors* of women's "right" to have a career and a family (Young, 2008). Regardless of the feminist label, the McCain–Palin ticket embraced an antifeminist agenda. Feminism, as applied to Palin, did not represent a threat to politics as usual.

Critique. Feminism is light years advanced with two centuries of messages supporting employed mothers, equal opportunity for men and women, and equal pay for equal work. The majority of the American public accepts and approves of these feminist messages. Even while clinging to traditional views about gender roles, evangelical women now generally agree that women may have careers; some of these women may also be mothers (Riley, 2008). Are these and other socially conservative women, therefore, feminists? Symbolic interactionists argue that the authenticity of any label is only determined by self-definition and the ability of the actor to convince others to accept this definition. First Lady Michelle Obama's popularity is linked to ensuring that her children ride the wave of their White House residency as smoothly as possible. She is judged by her ability to maintain family normalcy amid the ever-present spotlight on her children, especially by conservative media (Harris-Lacewell, 2009). As she is a strong supporter of feminist goals, media attention to her "warmer side" buffers stereotypes about feminists being too strident (Stanley, 2008). Contrary to media assertions, her support by feminists will likely remain strong regardless of her willingness to engage in a pro-woman agenda outside her family roles; whereas her support by social conservatives for this type of engagement would likely erode. To maintain a broad base of support from all ranks of women she walks a narrow and difficult line.

Portrayals of Clinton and Palin for their feminist views cannot be separated from the sexism that mired both their candidacies, particularly related to their appearance and demeanor: Clinton, because she was too masculine; Palin, because she was too feminine. Journalists were suspicious of Clinton's feminist image, but she was taken seriously as a viable candidate. For Palin, media sexism was evident for failure to seriously engage her on the difficult issues related to the economic and international challenges facing the United States. Regardless of her feminist assertion, media focus on personal matters rather than on political matters served to undermine Palin's credibility as a serious candidate (Gibbons, 2008). However, the McCain–Palin ticket in turn lost credibility by claiming that the media was sexist when asking the vice presidential nominee unfair questions about her experience, and by pressing John McCain on his abysmal record of advocacy for women. The public agreed that the media focus on Palin's family life was sexist; they also believed that claims of sexism when media questioned candidates on their policies about women were hypocrisy (Quindlen, 2008).

Challenging the Backlash to Feminism

How can feminist strength and productive messages to women be projected positively when feminists dare to disagree with one another in public? Several reasons support the contention that feminism may be reframed in a more favorable light by the media. First, young women lulled into believing that sexism was in its death throes were jolted into an awareness during the campaign that feminist goals continue to be illusive. Sexism in the election served a latent function by raising consciousness that obstacles remain for women seeking success, whether in the media or in the political and business worlds (Fuller, 2008:4). Second, Hillary Clinton's vocal support for feminist goals and Sarah Palin's admission that she, too, is a feminist will be difficult to dislodge from the vernacular of media. Conservative female candidates may have difficulty recanting feminism after Palin's admission. Third, the public sees a variety of feminisms at work; at a basic level at least, feminist goals are being embraced. Antifeminist and racist attacks were unleashed in fury by right-wing extremists when Judge Sonia Sotomayor, a Latina and a Catholic, was nominated to the Supreme Court (Baker and Zeleny, 2009; Media Matters, 2009). Hillary Clinton lost her presidential bid, but she is now the third female Secretary of State. The severe backlash against feminism, ironically, is a sign that barriers may be eroding.

The theories and concepts presented in this chapter and the visions of society that they suggest are offered as tools to be used in approaching the following chapters and the array of issues related to gender roles you will be confronting. Each theoretical perspective has its own insight and explanation for any given issue. Issues are further refined when theories are used in combination with one another. As these issues are addressed, consider which perspective you believe to be the most appropriate and realistic. It is hoped that at the conclusion of this book you will have developed a perspective on gender roles that is most meaningful to you.

Summary

1. As one of the most important trends in sociology in the twentieth century, the study of gender has led to a new feminist paradigm and opened up new topics for research, especially the connection between gender, race, and social class.

2. All social interaction is gendered. Gendered social interaction is guided by status, positions people occupy, and roles, the behavior associated with a status. Sexism and discrimination result when the status and role of female and male become stereotyped.

3. *Sex* is the biological component of male and female, *gender* is the social and psychological component, and *sexual orientation* is the way people experience sexual pleasure. These terms are often confused.

4. Sociological explanations for gender roles are guided by four theoretical perspectives: functionalism focuses on how gender role contributes to social order or equilibrium; conflict theory focuses on the level of power associated with gender; symbolic interaction focuses on gender as socially constructed and how people "do" gender in everyday life; and the feminist perspective focuses on women's empowerment and draws attention to multiple oppressions due to race, class, and gender.

5. Feminism is a worldwide movement to end sexism by empowering women. Branches of feminism include liberal feminism, its most mainstream and inclusive branch focusing on working within the system to end sexism; cultural feminism, focusing on positive qualities of women's roles; socialist feminism, focusing on ending sexism by eliminating capitalism and adopting socialist principles; radical feminism, calling for women to create separate, women-centered social institutions; multicultural or global feminism, working for change across national boundaries; and ecofeminism, focusing on environmental action.

6. A severe backlash to feminism and media reinforcement of gender and feminist sterotypes occurred during the 2008 election and influenced perception of Hillary Clinton and Sarah Palin as viable candidates. Feminism can be recast in the media, so positive feminist messages are heard.

Key Terms

androcentrism 3	gender roles 4	social construction of reality 10
agency 13	instrumental role 6	social stratification 2
doing gender 10	misogyny 17	status 2
dramaturgy 10	norms 2	status set 2
empowerment 12	patriarchy 3	stereotypes 3
end point fallacy 9	role 2	theory 4
expressive role 6	sex 4	
feminism 14	sexism 3	
gender 4	sexual orientation 4	

Critical Thinking Questions

1. How would a functionalist, conflict theorist, symbolic interactionist, and feminist answer the following question: Why do men hold the most powerful economic and political positions across the globe? What social policies would theorists from each of these groups offer as mechanisms to make this situation more gender equitable?

2. Considering the intersection of gender, race, and class and the distinctions between the various branches of feminism, provide realistic alternatives for ways women can "celebrate" both their diversity and their unity at the same time.

3. The backlash to feminism (the "f-word") is often media based. Which sociological theory do you think best explains this backlash? Suggest strategies consistent with the theory you select to alter this perception.

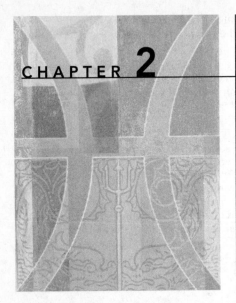

It must be stated that conceptual thought is exclusive to the masculine intellect. Her skull is also smaller than man's; and so, of course, is her brain. (Lang, 1971)

The genders are different because their brains are different. The brain is differently constructed in men and women . . . Men and women are equal only in their common membership to the same species, humankind.

—(Yassin, 2006:81)

As the quotes above from two scientists suggest, the argument used against equality between males and females is fundamentally a biological one. Despite the decades that separate these scientists and the abundant research providing alternate views, this belief stubbornly persists today. **Essentialism** is the belief that males and females are inherently different because of their biology and genes. This difference makes men and women "naturally" suited to fulfill certain roles regardless of their intellect, desires, expertise, or experiences. Like sociological functionalism, essentialism does not explicitly state that difference equates to inferiority, but the assumed quality or essence that makes men and women different is consistently drawn on to justify that conclusion. Although men are sometimes its targets, essentialism points to women's biological and reproductive makeup that refrains them from standing on equal ground with men.

The explosion of research on issues of sex and gender globally provides massive evidence refuting essentialist claims. Research does not discount the role of biology in gender development, but it clearly demonstrates that culture is a greater barrier to equality than biology. When desire and talent are combined with opportunity and encouragement, people can move into the "traditional" gender role of the other. When such movement becomes widespread, gender distinctions are blurred. Decades of research make it empirically clear that the benefits of equality for males and females alike far outweigh the disadvantages.

NATURE AND NURTURE

How much of our gendered behavior is determined by nature (heredity, biology, and genes), and how much is determined by nurture, the environment or culture in which we live and learn? Sociological explanations for gender differences are rooted in the nurture side of this question. Certainly males and females are different. Patterns of differentiation include not only physiology, but also differences related to demographics, attitudes, and behavior, especially related to sexuality. Are these differences significant enough to suggest that patriarchy is inevitable? Do the differences outweigh the similarities? What role does biology play in determining these differences? An examination of the research and theory generated by these questions—and the controversy surrounding them—will help shed light on the "it's only natural" argument. We will see that controversy and even tragedy surround how some of these questions are answered. The "only natural" argument is in fact an extension of the nature *versus* nurture debate. Because this chapter's focus is on biological issues, the categories of male and female will frequently be referred to as (the) "sexes."

Margaret Mead

Famed anthropologist Margaret Mead (1935/2001) was interested in exploring sex differences when she journeyed to New Guinea in the 1930s and lived with three different tribes. Among the gentle, peace-loving Arapesh, both men and women were nurturant and compliant, spending time gardening, hunting, and child rearing. The Arapesh gained immense satisfaction from these tasks, which were eagerly shared by both men and women. Arapesh children grew up to mirror these patterns and became cooperative and responsive parents themselves, with a willingness to subordinate themselves to the needs of those who were younger and weaker. Personality, Mead concluded, could not be distinguished by gender. What many societies would define as maternal behavior extended to both men and women. By contrast, the fierce Mundugumor barely tolerated children; they left them to their own devices early in life and taught them to be as hostile, competitive, and suspicious to others as their elders were. Both mothers and fathers showed little tenderness to their children, with harsh physical punishment being common. Children quickly learned that tribal success was measured by aggression, with violence as the acceptable, expected solution to many problems. Because both males and females demonstrated these traits, the Mundugumor, like the Arapesh, did not differentiate personality in terms of gender. Finally, the Tchumbuli demonstrated what would be considered a reversal of gender roles. This tribe consisted of practical, efficient, and unadorned women and passive, vain, and decorated men. Women's weaving, fishing, and trading activities provided the economic mainstay for the community; men remained close to the village and practiced dancing and art. Women enjoyed the company of other women. Men strived to gain the women's attention and affection, a situation women took with tolerance and humor. Contrary to her original belief that there are natural sex differences, Mead concluded that masculine and feminine are culturally, rather than biologically, determined.

Critique. Mead's work is an anthropological standard on gender differences and it is presented here in some detail. The gender roles she described almost a century ago were undoubtedly as unusual then as they are today. Yet her work still challenges the "it's only natural" argument. We know today that gender roles vary within a narrower range than suggested by Mead's research. However, "her message that gender constitutes an arena of great variability in human experience has borne out under empirical evidence" (LeVine, 1990:5). In fact, no existing theory, especially those grounded in essentialism, can explain the immense variety of meanings attached to being male and female. It is precisely this variation that has led to so much research questioning biologically based beliefs regarding femininity and masculinity. As this chapter demonstrates, we can identify biological differences and similarities between female and male, but to determine how these relate to what is considered masculine and feminine the world over is very difficult.

Evolution, Genetics, and Biology

Debates on the influence of nature and nurture on human behavior are often viewed via the lens of evolution. This Darwinian view suggests simply that sex differences (such as sexuality, cognitive ability, and parenting) and gender differences (such as toy preferences, college major, and career choice) have adaptive advantages for species survival. Genetics endow females and males with different capacities to allow this advantage to unfold productively. Other biological differences, such as prenatal androgens, reinforce genetic patterns so that girls and boys are led down different life paths.

Sociobiology. Rooted in the nature side of the debate, the field of sociobiology also addresses questions of sex differences in its examination of the biological roots of social behavior. Originally developing out of research based on insects (Wilson, 1975, 1978), sociobiologists argue that evolutionary theory can be used to draw conclusions about humans from studies of animals. The fundamental assertion of **sociobiology** is that, like other animals, humans, are structured by nature (biology) with an innate drive to ensure that their individual genes are passed on to the next generation. This is the motivating factor in all human behavior. It is as adaptive for a mother to care for her children as it is for men to be promiscuous. Each sex evolved these attributes to increase its reproductive success. Sociobiologists believe that principles of evolution pointing to species survival provide the best understanding of how gendered social behaviors developed. For example, aggressiveness not only allowed humans to successfully compete with nonanimals who shared our primeval environment but also allowed males to compete among themselves for females. The same principles explain promiscuity in men. Whereas women are highly selective in choosing mating partners, men will spread their sperm as widely as possible. For sociobiologists, other behaviors rooted in natural selection include mother–infant bonding, female dominance in child care, and male dominance in virtually all positions outside the home. As an evolutionary result of natural selection, the separate, unequal worlds of male and female emerged (Udry, 2000). Contemporary gender roles, therefore, reflect this evolutionary heritage.

Critique. Sociobiology has some success in applying evolutionary theory to animal behavior, but because it is virtually impossible to test the natural selection principles on which it is based, empirical support for evolutionary links to human behavior is weak (Nielsen, 1994). Feminist scientific critiques center on the fact that sociobiology and similar evolutionary approaches are *androcentric* perspectives, are often presented in deterministic ways, and make faulty assumptions about human behavior and disregard well-documented research about animals. Such approaches present data with overtones that may serve political agendas. Stereotypes about male dominance in all species and untested, untestable assumptions about the evolution of sex differences distort an otherwise valid approach to understanding evolution (Miller and Cosetello, 2001; Risman, 2001; Dagg, 2005). For example, it ignores the fact that the female chimp is notoriously promiscuous. Sexual selection in sociobiology emphasizes competition and aggression in male chimps, but neglects the other part of the process, in which female chimps make choices among males. Female chimps can be sexually aggressive and competitive just as male chimps can be nurturing and passive (Hrdy, 1999). It can be argued, therefore, that human females are more intelligent or more powerful in controlling human males.

Recent evidence also suggests that aggressiveness in primates is rare (probably less than one percent of all activities), with affiliated, friendly behavior, such as grooming and playing, probably a hundred times more frequent (McGinn, 2002). For humans, new research suggests that the view that humans have sex only to reproduce rather than for sexual stimulation or to experience pleasure disregards an entire range of emotions, personality traits, and sexual strategies that cannot be traced to animals (Meston and Buss, 2007). Sociobiologists may offer some productive leads for studying human social behavior, but leaping from animals to humans is tenuous at best.

Cognitive Biology. The biological basis for sex differences stems from research on prenatal hormones and brain development. Androgens help determine how our bodies, including our brains, become sexually differentiated. Higher levels of androgens predict more male-typical than female-typical behavior (Hines, 2008). Cognitive sex differences related to stronger spatial ability for males and stronger verbal ability for females, for example, may have biological roots since these differences show up very early in life before strong environmental influences kick in. These are stable differences that persist over time for individuals regardless of gender role change (Kimura, 2007). Other research suggests that infant girls come into the world with an orientation to faces and that infant boys come with an orientation to objects. In turn, the seeds are planted for them to follow different gender-based life paths. These paths usually translate to family roles for women and career roles for men (Baron-Cohen, 2007; Berenbaum and Resnick, 2007).

Other genetic approaches to sex-differentiated behavior make giant leaps by concluding that "it has been known since antiquity that gender-specific behaviors are regulated by the gonads." This research contends that female-typical responses cannot occur without a required level of estrogen and progesterone (Juntti et al., 2008). Male and female brains are so different that the sexes may be tracked over their lifespan according to brain development. For females, there are the teen girl brain, the mommy brain, and the mature female brain (Brizendine, 2006). Research on men's brains lags behind, but conclusions about nonoverlapping gender roles would be easy to predict. Return to the opening quotes in this chapter for even more blatant causal leaps.

Critique. Hormones may account for some *sex* differences in gender identity and sexual orientation, for example, but cannot account for *gender* differences in other roles such as nurturing, love, and crime behavior (Hines, 2004). There are no reliable biological data to suggest that women's underrepresentation in some sciences and men's underrepresentation in the caring professions are due to differences in biologically based cognitive abilities. Sex difference data are usually presented according to average group differences and tell us nothing about an individual's aptitude. Most research does not provide the size of the effects, only that correlations may be weak or robust, or statistically significant or not. It is difficult to pick up a newspaper today without someone claiming that males and females are different because "one millimeter of male brain tissue seems to function significantly different than the comparable function of tissue in female brains." In turn, gender stereotypes are reinforced and people lose sight of the fact that "women and men are, in most ways, more similar than different" (Crowley, 2006).

Environmental factors will determine how a person's aptitude is translated to the real world. When a girl believes that math skills are learned, she does as well as a boy on a difficult math test than if she believes that math is a gift. The effect of testosterone or estrogen on "manly" or feminine behavior must seriously account for the key role the social environment plays in understanding behavior–hormones relationships (Booth et al., 2006). Simply put, biological sex is *not* gender destiny (Dweck, 2007; Halpern, 2007). In reviewing the research on the biology of gender, developmental biologist Anne Fausto-Sterling (1992) concludes that what are considered to be the results of biology are more likely the results of culture.

The Hormone Puzzle

The chromosomal basis of sex difference is clearer. Of the two types of sex chromosomes, X and Y, both sexes have at least one X chromosome. Females possess two X chromosomes whereas males have one X and one Y chromosome. It is the lack or presence of the Y chromosome that determines if a baby will be male or female. That the X chromosome has a larger genetic background than the Y chromosome is advantageous to females with their XX chromosomes. The extra X chromosome is associated with a superior immune system and lower female mortality at all stages of the life cycle. All our other chromosomes are similar in form, differing only in our individual hereditary identities.

It is when hormones are added to the sex difference equation that the boundaries between biology and culture become more blurred. There is a subtle but significant interaction between sex hormones and psychosocial factors in gendered behavior. *Hormones* are internal secretions produced by the endocrine glands that are carried by the blood throughout the body, which affect target cells in other organs. Both males and females possess the same hormones, but they differ in amounts. For example, the dominant female hormone, estrogen, is produced in larger quantities by the ovaries, but in smaller quantities by the testes. The dominant hormone in males, testosterone, is produced in larger quantities by the testes and smaller quantities by the ovaries. The endocrine differences between males and females are not absolute but differ along a continuum of variation, with most males being significantly different than most females.

We know that sex hormones have two key functions that must be considered together. First, they shape the development of the brain and sex organs; and second, they determine how these organs will be activated. Because hormones provide an organization function for the body, their effects will be different for the sexes. For example, during fetal development, when certain tissues are highly sensitive to hormones, the secretion of testosterone both masculinizes and defeminizes key cellular structures throughout the brain and reproductive organs. The fetus first starts to develop female organs but later masculinizes itself if it possesses a Y chromosome, under the influence of testosterone. A male may be viewed as a female transformed by testosterone—the female body form is the "default" form (Mealey, 2000:14). The processes of masculinization and the development of sex differences are continuous, and influence each other by hormones, individual experiences, and social expectations.

Aggression. The debate on the influence of hormones on gender behavior is further complicated when studying sex differences in aggression. In most species, including primates, males are more aggressive than females. Higher aggression in human males is evident at about age two (Connor, 2002; Baillargeon et al., 2007). Some animal studies link testosterone to increase in aggression, and in humans, weak correlations are found between testosterone level and violence (Book et al., 2001; Browne, 2002). Girls and boys are about equal in learned aggressiveness. But because it is less socially acceptable for girls to show aggression, they are more likely to suppress their anger or carry it out verbally. They also use more *relational* aggression, purposely harming others, usually other girls, through manipulating peers, family members, and friends. Girls cause harm when a relationship suffers. Boys and young men are more likely to show aggression, but they carry it out in physical ways. They confront adversaries, usually other males, with fistfights, bullying, and shouting matches using sexually degrading language coupled with pushing and shoving (Crick et al., 2009; Salmivalli and Peets, 2009). When accounting for aggression according to key demographic features (age, race, ethnicity), key features of context (workplace, home, school), and key features of risk (abuse, developmental disability, sexual orientation), research does *not* suggest that males show predictable, higher levels of aggressiveness. Statistical significance is weak or absent for studies that do suggest some correlation (Putallaz and Bierman, 2004; Chapple and Johnson, 2007; Kuppens et al., 2008).

Although animal studies, mostly done on rodents, do show a clear, possibly causal, connection between androgens (male hormones) and male aggression, a wealth of research on humans simply cannot support the same claim (Björkqvist, 1994; Sato et al., 2008). Not only is it impossible to design ethical studies that can make the empirical causal leap from animals to people, but well-designed studies on the most intelligent social animals, especially primates, cannot make the leap either (Pavelka, 1998; De Waal and Tyack, 2003; Beauchamp et al., 2008). Perhaps the most damaging argument against the aggression–hormone link is, as noted earlier, gender differences in aggression depend on the type of aggression and the situation in which it occurs (Björkqvist and Niemelä, 1992). The cultural features of the context are powerful forces in determinants of aggression. There are different standards regarding the appropriateness of aggressive behavior, and they are learned early in life. As adults, men may feel pressured to act aggressively when publicly challenged. Hormones shift constantly as people move in and out of various social situations. Testosterone increases aggression but aggression increases testosterone. Levels of testosterone increase in winners and decrease in losers in competitions (Dodge et al., 2006; Pound et al., 2009).

Sex differences in aggression are evident, but are not very large. Testosterone is one of many components that influence behavior, including aggression, sexuality, and expression of emotions. It is clear that culture and context of aggression are as important as is any biological predisposition of the aggressor.

Motherhood. Animal studies of primates focusing on hormones released during pregnancy that allegedly fuel mother–infant bonding have been used to suggest the existence of a *maternal instinct* in human females. This research asserts that the female hormones of estrogen, progesterone, and prolactin biologically propel women toward motherhood. Furthermore, because they are elicited in larger amounts during pregnancy and after labor, women are driven to protect, bond, and nurture their infants from the moment of birth. Women's desire for babies will always trump any desire men may have to be fathers (De Marneffe, 2004; Hines, 2004). Fathering is learned but mothering is propelled by evolutionary forces. Infertile women who believe motherhood is based on a maternal instinct may view their inability to have children as inadequacy and failure (Ulrich and Weatherall, 2000).

Mothers bond, protect, and nurture their infants, but these behaviors cannot be based solely on unlearned responses. The notion of a maternal instinct is not supported by available research. A century ago sociologist Leta Hollingworth (1916, reprinted 2000) discounted the maternal instinct belief and suggested that "social devices" are the impelling reasons for women to bear and rear children. Socialization of females maximizes attachment to the young, whereas for males it is minimized. Some women suffer from postpartum depression and may even reject the child. Infanticide, voluntary abortion, and neglect by mothers, especially of their daughters, are all too common globally. The number of voluntarily childless women also continues to increase (Chapter 8). A woman's nurturing behavior will be heightened when she is in immediate contact with her newborn, but parental love emerges within the first week of the birth through repeated exposure to the infant (Maccoby, 2000). The fact that the large majority of women eagerly respond to their infants and readily take on the caretaking role is due to many factors.

The birth experience of course creates a mother–child bond that is different than a father–child bond, but this does not mean that hormones will make one parent better or more nurturing than the other. When new fathers take part in birthing, measures of infant–father bonding are as high as infant–mother bonding. If gender-typing is low, infant care can be a rewarding joint effort by parents. Consider Mead's study of the gentle Arapesh, where both sexes enjoyed child care. The intense interest fathers have for their newborns and their capacity for nurturance are not based on hormones.

Due in a large part to simplistic media accounts of the genetic basis of sex differences in human behavior, beliefs about a motherhood instinct persist, reinforce stereotypes, and justify social inequality and male dominance. The following comments suggest this scenario (Cole et al., 2007:211).

> Well I certainly think that there is the mothering instinct . . . is an instinct. I think it's a strong, very strong biological force. . . . We're almost captive to our genetics, so to speak. (Female respondent)

> In the days before there was civilizations. . . . The guys had to go out and kill the animals . . . and the women were the nurturers, and they took care of the kids . . . and that's basically the way it still is. (Male respondent)

The influence of hormones on gendered behavior is puzzling, and some research is equivocal. There is consensus among biologists and social and behavioral scientists, however, that sex differences in behavior involve a complex mosaic of nature and nurture. Biological inheritance and social experience cannot be independent of one another.

GENDERED SEXUALITY

Until fairly recently beliefs about males and females in regard to human sexuality were shrouded in myth and superstition. Research on gendered sexuality has helped dispel many of these myths, but, as we shall see, many others still persist.

Sigmund Freud: Anatomy Is Destiny

The impact of Sigmund Freud (1856–1939) on medicine and science is profound. There was no systematic psychology as a discipline before Freud. He was the first to tie a specific theory of psychosexual development to a therapeutic intervention, psychoanalysis, which he founded. Although a century of research on the foundations of Freud's work has produced questions, inconsistencies, and disagreement, he remains a powerful force on the intellectual climate in many disciplines.

The fact that a boy possesses a penis and a girl does not is the dominant factor in Freud's theory of psychosexual development. Of his five stages of psychosexual development (oral, anal, phallic, latency, and genital), the one that has received the most attention is the phallic stage as it relates to gender socialization. At ages 3–5, children recognize the anatomical difference between the sexes. They focus gratification on the genitals (the clitoris for the girl and the penis for the boy), and masturbation and sexual curiosity increase for both. Freud argued that girls come to believe that the penis, unlike the barely noticeable clitoris, is a symbol of power denied to them. The result is "penis envy," which culminates in a girl's wish that she could be a boy (Freud, 1962). She views her mother as inferior because she, too, does not have a penis. The girl's *libido*, or sexual energy, is transferred to the father, who becomes the love-object. Later writers called this experience the *Electra complex*. The resolution occurs when the girl's wish for a penis is replaced by the wish for a child. A male child is even more desirable because he brings the longed-for penis with him. In this way, the female child eventually learns to identify with her mother. Clitoral stimulation is abandoned for vaginal penetration, which is proclaimed as a sign of adult maturity for women.

A boy also experiences conflict during the phallic stage, when his libido is focused on his mother, and his father is the rival for his mother's affections. Freud called this experience the *Oedipus complex*. When a boy discovers that a girl does not have a penis, he develops "castration anxiety"—the fear he will be deprived of the prized organ. The psychic turmoil a boy experiences during this stage leads to the development of a strong superego. For Freud, conscience and morality, the very hallmarks of civilization, are produced with strong superegos. Freud believed that girls have weaker superegos because the resolution of the Electra complex occurs with envy rather than fear. Because they experience less psychic conflict than boys, personality development is tarnished. This explains why women are more envious, jealous, narcissistic, and passive than men. A boy eventually overcomes the underlying fear, identifies with his father, reduces incestuous desires for his mother, and is later ushered into psychosexual maturity. Indeed, anatomy is destiny for Freud.

Critique. Asserting that women cannot be fully mature unless they experience orgasm through vaginal intercourse, Freud's beliefs about the biological inadequacy of females ignore the clitoris serving a purely sexual and pleasureful function. Physiologically orgasms are the same, regardless of how they are reached. The sexism in Freudian theory is obvious, even though its unfortunate effects concerning the idea of female inferiority exceeded the intentions of Freud himself (Millett, 1995:61). Some critics argue that his sweeping generalizations were fueled by a personal longing for greatness (Bregar, 2000). His ideas were no doubt conditioned by the Victorian society in which he lived—one that embraced strict gender differentiation based on traditional roles for men and women in a patriarchal world. Freud was severely criticized for his ideas about infantile sexuality and the psychosexual stages of development but gained quiet acceptance for his comments on the biologically inferior design of females.

Feminism and Freud. Can feminists also be Freudians? Blatant sexism notwithstanding, the answer is "yes." Feminist scholars and therapists reject sexism but still find useful core elements of his theory and therapeutic techniques. It would be counterproductive, for example, to reject psychoanalysis when it is successful for women patients. Psychoanalytic feminism has emerged to analyze the construction of gender and its effects on women, including women's subordination (Mitchell, 2000). Freud provides a basis for "seeing domination as a problem not so much of human nature as of human relationships—the interaction between psyche and social life" (Benjamin, 1988:5). Feminist reinterpretation of psychoanalytic theory allows the problem of domination to be viewed from this unique perspective.

Another important writer representing psychoanalytic feminism is Nancy Chodorow (1978, 2001), who integrates useful aspects of psychoanalytic and socio-logical theory. She posits that because in most cultures women do the child care, mothers produce daughters who then desire to mother. Mothering thus reproduces itself. They produce sons, who devalue women for these very roles. Penis envy occurs because women, even young girls, recognize the power of males, so it is natural to desire this kind of power. There is nothing inherently biologically superior about this. It is the ability of the girl to maintain identification with her mother that achieves the desirable traits of empathy and connectedness. In this sense, there is a positive resolution of the Oedipus complex, which Freud overlooked, ignored, or rejected from his male-biased view.

Disagreements between psychoanalytic feminists and between feminism and Freudian theory have not been resolved. Feminists are searching for a theoretical and therapeutic model to replace the traditional, Freudian-based, androcentric approach (Rose, 2005). This model would encompass feminist therapy appropriate for both male and female clients. With the required reinterpretation and empirical justification, it is likely that neo-Freudian scholars will use Freud's insights for the benefit, rather than the degradation, of women.

Ambiguous Sex, Ambiguous Gender

Research on infants born with sexual anomalies helps to clarify the biological basis of sex differences. From a sociological viewpoint, it allows a rare opportunity to study the link between physiology and behavior and to understand the important distinction between biological sex and gender. Formerly referred to as **hermaph-rodites**, today the term **intersexed** describes the approximate 1–3 percent of infants born with both male and female sex organs or who have ambiguous genitals (such as a clitoris that looks like a penis). They violate the principle of **sexual dimorphism**, the separation of the sexes into two distinct, nonoverlapping categories. Assigned one sex at birth, the child's genetic sex is often discovered later.

The point of time that the child discovers his or her genetic sex makes a crucial difference in psychological adjustment and helps to determine if *sex reassignment surgery* (SRS) is an option. In SRS, genitals are surgically altered so that a person changes from one biological sex to the other. Sex reassignment has a greater likelihood of success if it occurs before age three because this is the time *gender identity* is learned—an awareness that there are two sexes who behave differently, with the child beginning to develop the first sense of self (Chapter 3). Once gender identity becomes stabilized, attempting to change it would be emotionally traumatic.

The decision by parents to alter the sexual organs or genitalia of their intersexed child either to fit the appearance of one sex or the other or to correspond to the child's male or female genetic code is very controversial. The child has no choice in the decision, and the surgery is usually irreversible. Current advice is to assign a sex at birth, provide appropriate information and counseling about the intersex condition as the child is growing up, and then have the mature person decide on what action to take, if any, for surgery. Any irreversible surgery must wait until children are old enough to know and say which gender they feel closer to. Timing of the surgery in conjunction with hormonal therapy is an important ingredient for the development of gender identity (Spriggs and Savulescu, 2006; Harper, 2007).

Transsexuals. Unlike intersexed people, **transsexuals** are genetic males or females who psychologically believe they are members of the other sex. They feel "trapped" in the wrong bodies and may undergo SRS to "correct" the problem. Only then can their gender identity and their biological sex be consistent. Transsexuals are not homosexuals. They are newly minted males or females who desire sexual intimacy with the other gender. Their ideal lover would be a heterosexual man or woman. The reality, however, is that most heterosexuals would not choose transsexuals as lovers. *Transvestites*, mostly males who are sexually aroused when they dress in women's clothing, are not transsexual. With biological sex and gender identity now consistent, transsexuals ease into their new gender role with more confidence.

Early research in the United States (1970s) on the success of SRS showed overall negative results: some transsexuals believed they made a mistake and others reported no better adjustment after SRS. Recent research, however, suggests neutral to uniformly positive outcomes. Better surgical techniques and therapeutic techniques coupled with more knowledge of transsexualism and increased tolerance in society, later research reports much more positive outcomes. Male-to-female transsexuals report few complications with SRS and that it had greatly improved their quality of life. Few express regret after the surgery. The data on female-to-male SRS is less abundant but the conclusions of satisfaction still hold (Lawrence, 2003, 2006; Spehr, 2007; Udeze et al., 2008).

Does Nature Rule? A Sex Reassignment Tragedy

Unraveling the biological and cultural ambiguities surrounding sex and gender is exceedingly difficult. This is clearly demonstrated in the infamous case of SRS performed in 1968 in Canada to one of a pair of identical male twins, Bruce and Brian. During a circumcision at eight months to correct a minor urination problem Baby Bruce's penis was burned off. Physicians concluded that constructing an artificial penis was possible but not promising. The twins' parents learned that Dr. John Money, one of the world's experts on gender identity, spoke of encouraging results with sex reassignment surgery for hermaphrodites. According to Money, gender identity was solely shaped by parents and environment. Although Bruce was *not* a hermaphrodite (intersexed) and was born with normal genitals, Dr. Money agreed to take on David's case and work with the family so he could be "taught to want to be a girl." At 22 months, Bruce underwent surgery to remove the remaining penile tissue. Bruce was transformed to Brenda. According to Dr. Money, by age five, the twins demonstrated almost stereotypical gender roles. Given girls' toys and highly feminine clothing, Brenda was being prepared for a domestic life. Brother Brian was introduced to the world outside the home, with preferences for masculine toys (soldiers and trucks) and occupations (firefighter and police officer) (Money and Ehrhardt, 1972; Money and Tucker, 1975). Brenda's case appeared to be successful. Or was it?

Directly countering Money's positive assessment was a follow-up of Brenda at age 13, when she was seen by a new set of psychiatrists. They reported a far more difficult transformation. She rebelled almost from the start, tearing off dresses, preferring boy toys, and fighting with her brother and peers. There was nothing feminine about Brenda. Her gait was a masculine gait; she was teased by other children; she believed that boys have a better life, and that it is easier to be a boy than a girl (Diamond, 1982; Diamond and Sigmundson, 1997). In therapy sessions she was sullen, angry, and unresponsive. The mere suggestion of vaginal surgery for the next step in her transformation induced explosive panic.

When did Brenda learn that she was born Bruce? At age 10, in an embarrassed fumbled attempt, her father told her that she needed surgery because a doctor "made a mistake down there." Subconsciously she probably knew she was a boy, but at age 14 she was finally told the truth. Expressing immense relief, she vowed to change back to a boy and took the name David (Bruce was "too geeky"). At age 18, at a relative's wedding, he made his public debut as a boy and married in 1990. David had a penis and testicles constructed, requiring 18 hospital visits (Colapinto, 2000).

In the media frenzy that followed David's "coming out" as a boy, the public heard only that gender identity is a natural, inborn process. Nurture's role is given little credit in the process. Three decades after the Bruce-Brenda-David transformations, John Money still makes a strong case for the social constructionist argument (Money, 1995).

Critique. Although this case may support the nature side (gender identity is inborn), there are numerous reasonable counterarguments for the nurture side (gender identity is learned). First, Brenda's estrogen therapy began at age 12, but it is doubtful that the effects of her biological sex were altered early enough to make her look—and certainly to make her feel—more like a girl than a boy. Brian was also confused and embarrassed by Brenda's tomboy behavior. Children like Brenda who do not physically or behaviorally conform to expectations are the most vulnerable to rejection and ridicule by peers. Second, in the fear she would revert to masculine preferences, unlike most girls today, Brenda was being raised rigidly to conform to stereotyped feminine gender roles. She was being prepared for a domestic life, but if her transformation had been successful, she could never have fulfilled the "ultimate" role of biological motherhood. Third, Brenda was keenly aware that boys had more prestige and a "better life" than girls. Her extraordinary opportunity to revert to the male sex may have been further prompted by these beliefs.

Finally, and most important, as we will see in Chapter 3, by age two children are marked with indelible gender stamps. Bruce became a girl nearly two years after everyone, including twin brother Brian, treated her like a boy. Bruce's life as a toddler boy was written with masculine scripts; these scripts were abruptly changed to highly stereotyped, feminine scripts. Bruce's gender identity was *already* unfolding. How did friends and family react to Brenda's transformation after knowing her as Bruce for almost two years? The family even moved at one point to get away from "ghosts and doubters" (Colapinto, 2000).

Certainly this case does not support John Money's assertion that newborns are a blank slate on which gender identity will be written. Not only did Money ignore the role of biology and genetics (Bruce was born with normal "sex apparatus") in attempting to transform Bruce into Brenda, he ignored his own suppositions about how gender is socially constructed. Social constructionists are aware of the power of the end-point fallacy—new definitions create new behaviors in an ongoing cycle. Earlier definitions and behaviors are never completely lost, regardless of how they are transformed. Bruce was expected to unlearn earlier definitions and behaviors at the core of his emerging gender identity.

John Money's rigid interpretation of David Reimer's case can be described as *cultural* essentialism. Just as biological essentialists claim sex differences due to nature, cultural essentialists claim gender differences due to nurture. Whether from biology or culture, essentialist views are unproductive because they are deterministic. They cannot adequately deal with the blurring of sex and gender in socialization. Media accounts continue to blur this distinction; most reporting on the Reimer case is in the context of intersexed infants. The media never questioned the ability of a host of players to carry out a giant pretense. Everybody may have been playing a game of science fiction, but the game of social reality was largely ignored.

Despite these criticisms, however, a social constructionist argument is still valid. Symbolic interaction emphasizes social constructionist views on gender learning but neither rejects nor ignores the powerful role of biological sex in socialization (Chapters 1 and 3). Unlike John Money's version, the sociological view of social constructionism is *not* essentialist.

The final irony is that John Money sends a Freudian-based biological message about David Reimer. Sounding like a biological essentialist, David is defined solely by his penis. At the loss of his penis, he loses both his maleness (biological sex) and his masculinity (gender). The only recourse, therefore, is castration and SRS. Rigid definitions of what males are "supposed" to be (Chapter 9) spelled doom for David Reimer.

Consider how all these threads weave together in the tragic conclusion of David Reimer's story. Treated for schizophrenia, twin brother Brian committed suicide with an overdose of antidepressant drugs in 2002. Grieving the loss of his brother and a life unraveling by depression, debt, and separation from his wife, two years later David Reimer took his own life by a gunshot to his head.

Sexual Orientation

Once familiar mainly to scientists, terms describing sexual preferences are now routinely used by the public and media. Depending on how they are used and who uses them, some of these terms are contentious. As a result, discourse about homosexuality is being reshaped though new labels, often offered by the people they refer to. In reclaiming a term once associated with ridicule and derision, **queer theory** emerged in the 1990s to examine how sexuality and sexual identity in all their forms—from sexual orientation to sexual behavior—are socially constructed. In critical reviews on gay and lesbian sexuality, for instance, queer theory alerts us to an understanding that sexuality is fluid. By transcending taken-for-granted beliefs about sexual boundaries, theorists of queer studies examine how sexual identity—whether considered deviant or not—is built up over time, emerging from the multiple contexts of our lives (Davidson, 2006; Diamond, 2008). Other terms used here reflect current sociological usage, but it is likely that they, too, will be altered as this reshaping discourse proceeds.

Sexual orientation, defined earlier as preference for sexual partners of one gender or the other, is divided into the categories of heterosexual and homosexual in most Western cultures. Like gender identity, sexual orientation is not automatically granted by biological sex. *Heterosexual* is the category of people who have sexual preference for and erotic attraction to those of the other gender. *Homosexual* is the category of people who have sexual preference for and erotic attraction to those of their own gender. Homosexual males are also referred to as *gay* men and homosexual females as *lesbians*. Although the term *gay* is often used in the media to include both gay men and lesbians, researchers use it to designate men. *Bisexual* is the category of people whose sexual orientations may shift and who are sexually responsive to either gender. Humans share the same anatomy and have the same capacity for sexual pleasure, but there is a great deal of variation in how and with whom people experience sexual pleasure. According to symbolic interactionists, sexual orientation is largely a social construction built during social interaction. Like heterosexuals, both men and women who see themselves as homosexual maintain a gender identity consistent with their biological sex. They are socialized into prevailing gender roles except for their sexual orientation (Chapter 9).

This socialization helps explain why homosexuals prefer for sexual partners those men or women who fit the standards of masculinity or femininity defined by the culture. However, because it is accompanied by gender roles that are defined as masculine or feminine, gender identity is much more susceptible to change over time than is sexual orientation. In the middle of the nineteenth century a masculine gender role was associated with employment that included elementary school teaching and clerical work. Today these same jobs are associated with a feminine gender role.

Sexual orientation, like other forms of human sexuality, is extremely varied. Research shows that the conceptual distinction between gender identity and sexual orientation is a blurry one. For example, **transgender** describes people who do not conform to culturally defined traditional gender roles associated with their sex. Transgendered people may or may not identify themselves as homosexual and may or may not choose to "pass" for the other sex in appearance (Roen, 2002). The ancient Greeks, for instance, accepted both homosexuality and heterosexuality as "natural" relationships, with few moral overtones. A man's preference for males or females was seen as a matter of taste and desire; the enjoyment of one over the other did not categorize men according to a gender preference for sexual interaction. A man who pursued males did not see himself as any different from one who pursued females. It was common for a man to change his sexual preference to women after spending his youth loving boys (Foucault, 1990; Murray, 2000). For the Greeks, gender identity existed, but sexual orientation did not. Many of these Greek males may be described as transgendered people who moved between gender roles in ways that suited their sexual preferences and lifestyles at the time.

Scientists need terms to classify groups of people by certain characteristics, but the terms they devise may be subject to criticism. To classify the wide range of attitudes and behaviors related to sexual orientation, **GLBT** is an inclusive term for gay, lesbian, bisexual, and transgendered people. The term is gaining acceptance in scientific literature and in popular culture.

Global Focus: Challenging Definitions of Sex and Gender

Transgendered people who perform specific social functions are found throughout the world today. Some people go through life with "mixed" gender identities. The *xanith* of the Arab state of Oman are biological males. They work as homosexual prostitutes and skilled domestic servants. Described as a "third" gender, they have male names but distinctive dress and hairstyles, unlike that of either men or women. Xanith are not men because they can interact with women and are not women because they are not restricted by *purdah*, the system of veiling and secluding women (cited in Lips, 2001:161). Transgender may describe the *mahus* of Tahiti. Mahus are usually young boys who adopt female gender roles early in life and find jobs usually performed by women. Mahu status is viewed as naturally evolving from childhood roles. They have sexual relations with those of their own sex but not with other mahus. Their preferred sexual partners, however, are those from the other gender. Mahu sexuality, therefore, is "same-sex but opposite(sic)-gender" (Elliston, 1999:238). Though Tahitians may poke fun at mahus, they are accepted members in society (Stanley, 2000).

India. In India, men known as *hijras* dress up in women's clothing and are called on to bless newborn infants. In order to become a hijra and perform this important cultural role, most of these men by choice are emasculated—their testicles are removed. Hijras are not homosexual. They think of themselves more as females and thus prefer heterosexual men as sexual partners. They generally live and dress as females, often in a separate subculture. In the rural areas of India where hijras practice their trade, sexual orientation and gender identity do not appear to be concerns. Hijras are ambivalent figures in India. They are teased and mocked but also valued and esteemed. The hijras have a gender role that legitimizes their function as ritual performers. As the context shifts, so does their identity. However, their gender role is at the core of their identity and affirms their positive, collective self-image (Nanda, 1997; Reddy, 2006).

Indonesia. On the Indonesia island of Sulawesi five gender identities among the Muslim ethnic Bugis are recognized. In addition to men and women, there are *calalai* (females performing male roles and dressing like men), *calabai* (males performing female roles and dressing like women, and *bissu* (transgendered people who possess spirits and can bestow blessings). Despite official Islamic discourse, these people—and the roles they perform—are "generally tolerated and even accepted" in Bugi society. There is no word for gender in indigenous Bugi language. For the Bugis, gender is made up of various understandings about sexuality, biology, and subjectivity. These understandings are necessary to understand all of Bugi life and culture (Davies, 2007).

Native Americans. For over two centuries among Native Americans, the role of *berdache* existed, a title conferred on those who did not exhibit conventional gender roles. These berdache womanly men and manly women still exist in some tribes. In tribal mythology, berdache may act as mediators between men and women and between the physical and the spiritual worlds. Native Americans refer to those who act out cross-gender roles as having "two spirits."

The hijra, xanith, mahus, berdache, and three of the five "genders" of the Bugis, are roles associated with approval and sometimes honor, rather than disdain and immorality. Like intersexed people, these transgendered people also violate the principle of sexual dimorphism and attest to the powerful impact of culture on both gender identity and sexual orientation.

Sexual Scripts

Sociologists emphasize how sexuality is based on prescribed roles that are acted out like other socially bestowed roles. **Sexual scripts** are shared beliefs concerning what society defines as acceptable sexual thoughts, feelings, and behaviors for each gender. Gender roles are connected with different sexual scripts—one considered more appropriate for males, and the other considered more appropriate for females (Wiederman, 2005). Sexual scripts continue to be based on beliefs that for men sex is for orgasm and physical pleasure, and for women sex is for love and the pleasure that comes from intimacy. Men, more than women, believe in biological essentialism, which in itself can be considered a sexual script (Smiler and Gelman, 2008). Although people may desire more latitude—such as more emotional intimacy for men and more sexual pleasure for women—they often feel constrained by the traditional scripting of their sexuality. When both men and women accept such scripts and carry their expectations into the bedroom, gendered sexuality is being socially constructed. Beliefs about gendered sexuality contribute to sexual dysfunction and sexual violence toward women and gay men. Such beliefs also hold disadvantages for both men and women by inhibiting their sexual pleasure (Dworkin and O'Sullivan, 2007). Gendered scripting clearly illustrates that biology alone cannot explain human sexuality. Sexual scripts may provide the routes to sexuality, but over time new paths offering new directions for sexuality can be built. It is unlikely that gendered sexuality will ever be eliminated. It is likely, however, that as gender roles become more egalitarian, the sexual lives of both men and women will be enhanced.

Patterns of Sexual Attitudes and Behavior

Beliefs about human sexuality have been shrouded in myth and superstition. Major assaults on these myths and on the biological determinism in sexuality were led by the pioneering work of Alfred Kinsey and his associates (1948, 1953). Just as Freud shocked science with his assertions on sexuality, Kinsey did the same on revealing his data on sexual behavior. He reported sexual activities far different from the supposed norms.

Gender and Orgasm. The original Kinsey data revealed that 92 percent of males and 58 percent of females masturbated (use of sexual self-stimulation) to achieve orgasm. Males begin to masturbate during early adolescence. Females begin to masturbate later than men, often in their twenties and thirties. These patterns have not changed significantly since Kinsey's original research (Hunt, 1974; Laumann and Mahay, 2002).

During intercourse men are more likely to have an orgasm than women. Kinsey found that over one-third of married women never had an orgasm prior to marriage and that one-third of married women never had an orgasm. Later data show that almost 90 percent of all women experience orgasm, whether married or not, and virtually all married women (98 percent) do reach orgasm, although not with every sexual intercourse. Husbands generally would like more frequent intercourse than their wives, especially early in the marriage. Later in their married life this trend may reverse; married women report more positive perception of their sexual behavior, and men report a more positive perception of their marital life.

However, for both men and women, marital satisfaction and sexual satisfaction are highly correlated. And the more frequent the sex, the higher the level of sexual satisfaction (Trudel, 2002; McNulty and Fisher, 2008). If sex keeps people happy in their marriages, low sexual satisfaction is also a good predictor of divorce.

Premarital/Nonmarital Sex. Kinsey's (1953) data reported that one-fourth of unmarried women born before 1900 had experienced coitus (sexual intercourse). He found that one-third of young women reported premarital sex by age 25. Premarital sex for men was 77 percent. Today the differences between men and women in premarital sex have all but disappeared. Men may have sex earlier than women, but by the time they graduate from college virtually all men and women are sexually experienced (Kamen, 2000; Lance, 2007). Females do have fewer sex partners than men, but they plan for their first intercourse. About half of all teenagers aged 15–19 have had sexual intercourse at least once. However, people are surprised to learn that sexual activity among teens has significantly declined (Amba and Sonenstein, 2002). What is perhaps more surprising is that the number of teenage boys reporting sexual intercourse has dramatically decreased—white, African American, and Latino alike. For girls, the rate of sexual activity has remained relatively stable. The only change to this pattern is for African-American girls, who reduced their sexual activity to levels comparable to white and Latino girls (Risman and Schwartz, 2002:18).

The overall rate of sexual risk-taking among teens has also appeared to decline. Norms about gendered sexuality explain the new pattern. Although girls have increased their sexual behavior, they define it within the bonds of a romantic relationship. A decade ago a boy was likely to have his first sexual intercourse with a pickup or casual date; today they are likely to say it was with a girlfriend. Girls whose first intercourse occurred before age 16 are more likely to report that it was coercive. When factoring in race, Asian Americans—both male and female—have their first sexual experience at an older age than white, African American and Latino (Regan et al., 2004). The premarital norm of sexual intercourse holds for teens who took abstinence pledges and who promised to remain virgin until marriage. They are just as likely to have premarital sex as teens who did not take these pledges. An ironic twist to this trend is that when the pledgers do have sex it is riskier sex—they are less likely to use condoms or other forms of birth control (Stein, 2008).

Because most people have sexual experiences with people whom they are unlikely to marry, the term *premarital* sex is inaccurate. A more accurate term to refer to these experiences is *nonmarital* sex.

Extramarital Relationships. Once called "adultery" but now commonly called "affairs," this type of nonmarital sex takes on many forms. Extramarital relationships involve different degrees of openness and include married as well as single people. They may or may not include sexual involvement. The emotional involvement with a partner other than one's spouse can be more threatening to the marriage than sexual involvement (Chapter 7). Despite the fact that most people claim to disapprove of affairs in any form, Kinsey's data indicated that 50 percent of males and 26 percent of females engaged in extramarital sex by age 40. Both genders act on their desire to have affairs, but men express a greater willingness. Estimates are that about 25–35 percent of men and 15–25 percent of women have had an extramarital affair (Atkins and Jacobson, 2001; NORC, 2008). It is clear that although most people disapprove of affairs, a significant number engage in them.

There are problems with these data. Although later research validated Kinsey's data, the high percentage of affairs he reported was suspect. It is also clear that when respondents report their knowledge of affairs others are having, the numbers increase. In addition, the fact that divorce is less stigmatized is associated with openness to extramarital relationships. Thus it is probable that reported figures for extramarital relationships are lower than the actual numbers.

The Double Standard. The **double standard** refers to the idea that men are allowed to express themselves sexually and women are not. Because the levels of nonmarital sexual behavior for males and females are now similar, does a double standard still exist? The answer is "no" when considering sexual behavior, but "yes" when considering sexual attitudes. Sexual behavior has changed dramatically. It was long assumed that, compared to men, women had weaker sex drives, were more difficult to arouse sexually, and became aroused less frequently. These assumptions have all been proven false. It is the clitoris, not the vagina, as Freud insisted, that is responsible for the multiple orgasms experienced by women. Prompted by feminist social scientists and a rejection of evolutionary views that sex for women is prompted by reproduction rather than pleasure, new models about female sexuality from women's own voices are emerging (Lloyd, 2005; Bergner, 2009). In stark contrast to Freudian views, they offer an understanding that sexuality for women is pleasureful, fulfilling, and desired.

Gender differences in sexual attitudes do persist. More women than men express the belief that emotional closeness is a prerequisite for sexual intercourse. Men report sexual pleasure and conquest as the main motives. They prefer more partners over a shorter period of time than women. When considering oral sex, masturbation, pornography, body shame, and nonmarital intercourse, women are more "sex negative" than men. Race, religion, and ethnicity do not override gender in these trends (Maher et al., 2007; Sanchez and Kiefer, 2007; Fugere et al., 2008; Griffiths et al., 2008). Men, but not women, believe that oral sex is not sex, that cyber-sex is not cheating, and that women cannot fake orgasms (Knox et al., 2008). Men daydream about sex when showering; women contemplate housework (Johnson, 2005)! Women continue to adopt a more "person-centered" approach to sex; men adopt a more "body-centered" approach. Males are less likely to feel guilty about their sexual activities than females. On the other hand, sexual dominance for men comes at a price. Men believe that women are the "symbolic keepers of masculine sexual standards" and that they (men) are judged by virility and sexual prowess. Women and men both believe that her orgasm is a sign of his success as a lover. Reflecting on a sexual encounter when he was 18, a 47-year-old man reported the following:

> She basically had to show me how to do it, and it took a few times before every-thing worked. I was a total retard. I felt great making out with her, but I didn't want to go to the intercourse part. I didn't want to wind up a failure. (Mundy, 2006:173, 183)

Pleasurable sexual activities are gendered—conditioned by sexual scripts defined as acceptable for men or women. Even with heightened public consciousness regarding the double standard, sexual behavior may have changed, but attitudes about sexual scripts remain intact.

The disappearance of a sexual double standard may not be desirable. The absence of significant gender differences in frequency of nonmarital sexual activities, number of partners, or degree of emotional involvement with partners could trigger a lifetime of more sex with more people, but also more people who are less known to their partners. Given the risks to both genders related to health and sexually transmitted diseases, sexual violence, and unplanned pregnancy, the disappearance of a sexual double standard may be hazardous to one's health and to society.

Sexuality in Later Life. Cultural barriers and gender norms also apply to sexuality in later life. For the elderly, an already difficult situation is made worse by a combination of age and gender-related stereotypes. As with gender, there is a sexual double standard regarding age and sexuality. Because it is associated with youth and virility, sexuality among the aged has been ignored or demeaned. They are perceived to be sexless. If elderly males show sexual interest, they are viewed suspiciously. Women are expected to retreat to a sexless existence after the completion of childbearing and mothering. Yet women experience more comfort and less anxiety about sex as they age. Beginning in late midlife, and contrary to sexual scripts, "bodily" sexual practices increase sexual satisfaction for women; relational intimacy increases sexual satisfaction for men (Carpenter et al., 2009). At this life stage women increase their desire for intercourse and sexual intimacy. On the other hand, widows significantly outnumber widowers, so options for sexual activity decline for women, despite the fact that sexual desire remains strong.

Research by two other pioneers of sexuality, William Masters and Virginia Johnson (1966, 1970), shows that when advancing age and physiological changes influence sexual ability for men, performance anxiety increases. A man's wife may believe his "failure" is a rejection of her. Men are socialized early in life to believe that they will be judged by their sexual potency. As suggested earlier, when a couple accept such beliefs, a cycle of less sex, less interest in sex, and increased emotional distance is perpetuated. The irony is that it is easier to cope with these incorrect beliefs if society assumes the elderly are not supposed to be sexually active anyway.

Men and women of all age groups are far less sexually different from one another than once thought. They differ more in how they negotiate sexual activities and in the kinds of sexual relationships they seek (Malesta, 2007). As pointed out by Masters and Johnson 40 years ago, cultural barriers such as traditional gender roles inhibit sexual pleasure. The social construction of women as passive sexual beings and men as sexual conquerors can be reconstructed to make them partners in a mutually pleasurable experience.

GENDER AND HEALTH

The interplay of biology and culture is necessary to understand patterns of health and well-being related to sex and gender. Various measurement techniques have been developed to determine these patterns. The simplest measure, the **mortality rate**, is expressed as a percentage of the total number of deaths over the population size (X 1000) in a given time period, usually a year. Calculating a **morbidity rate**, the amount of disease or illness in a population, is more difficult. Although it may have well-defined symptoms, illness itself is in part subjective. Many people do not recognize their own sickness, may recognize it but refuse to alter their behavior by taking off work or seeing a physician, or prefer to treat themselves. These patterns are particularly true for calculating levels of mental illness. As a result, morbidity rates are often based on treatment, and data accuracy may be compromised.

Even with these cautions in mind, however, a clear and consistent inverse pattern emerges in comparing gender differences in mortality and morbidity. Women have higher morbidity rates but live longer than men; men have lower morbidity rates but do not live as long as women.

Till Death Do Us Part: Gender and Mortality

In the United States females can expect to outlive males on an average of five years. Women and men die from the same three causes—cancer, heart disease, and stroke—but there are significant gender differences in their mortality rate (Table 2.1). Mortality rates for all leading causes of death are higher for males. Death rates for most of these causes are over 1.5 times than those for females. Only in deaths due to Alzheimer's do females have a disadvantage. Men have been gaining on women in narrowing the mortality rate, but the age-adjusted rate for men is still about 40 percent greater than that for women. When race is added to the life expectancy rate (LER) profile, white males are gaining, and they reached parity with African-American females in 2000. This parity, however, was short-lived. The gap reappeared within two years and is again widening (Figure 2.1). For all races and ethnic groups where figures are available women maintain a strong LER advantage and projected to do well into this century (Table 2.2). When factoring in social class, which has a profound health effect, females still have a more favorable life expectancy rate than comparable males. Males have higher mortality rates at every stage of life. The first year of life is the most vulnerable time for both sexes, but infant mortality rates are higher for males. By the 1990s mortality data showed all three nondisease causes of death (accidents, suicides, and homicides) in the top-15 list. For suicide, although women experience more depression than men and attempt suicide about four times more frequently, men commit suicide about four times more than women. Men choose more lethal means and are more likely to succeed. Males succumb earlier to virtually all causes of mortality, with nondisease causes showing the greatest male–female differences.

Global Patterns. The female advantage in LER holds globally as well. The graying world is a female world. The **feminization of aging** describes the global pattern of women outliving men and the steady increase of women in the ranks of the

Table 2.1 Leading Causes of Death and Male-to-Female Death Rate.

Cause of Death	Male to Female Death Rate
All Causes	1.4
1. Heart Disease	1.5
2. Cancers	1.4
3. Cerebrovascular Diseases (Stroke)	1.0
4. Respiratory Disease	1.3
5. Accidents	2.2
6. Diabetes	1.3
7. Alzheimer's Disease	0.7
8. Influenza and Pneumonia	1.3
9. Kidney Disease	1.4
10. Septicemia (Blood Poisoning)	1.2
11. Suicide	4.1
12. Chronic Liver Disease and Cirrhosis	2.1
13. Hypertension	1.0
14. Parkinson's Disease	2.2
15. Homicide	3.8

Source: Centers for Disease Control and National Center for Health Statistics. "Deaths: Preliminary Data for 2005." Selected 2005 Findings: Adapted from Table B. www.cdc.gov/nchs/products/pubs/pubd/hestats/prelimdeaths05

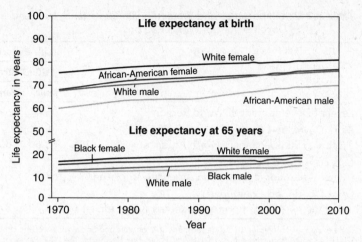

Figure 2.1 Life Expectancy at Birth in the United States by
Gender and African-American/White Race.

Sources: Centers for Disease Control and National Center for Health Statistics. *Health: United States, 2008.* Adapted from Figure 14: Data from the National Projections Program and Vital Statistics Program HYPERLINK "http://www.cdc.gov/nchs/hus" www.cdc.gov/nchs/hus

elderly. Over 50 percent of the current elderly population globally is female, and of the oldest old, 80 years and older, over 60 percent are female, a pattern projected to increase (Table 2.3). The highest overall life expectancy is in Japan, where men can expect to live to age 77 and women to age 85. In less than a decade, many countries will have only five men to every 10 women over the age of 80. In the developed world the gender gap in mortality is declining slightly as men are gaining in life expectancy. But for both the developed and the developing world, the gap favoring women

Table 2.2 Projected Life Expectancy at Birth by Gender and Race/Ethnicity, 2010–2050.

Gender, Race/Ethnicity	2010	2020	2030	2040	2050
MALE	75.7	77.1	78.4	79.6	80.9
White	76.5	77.7	78.9	80.0	81.2
African American	70.2	72.6	74.9	77.1	79.1
American Indian/Alaska Native	76.6	77.8	79.0	80.1	81.2
Asian	76.3	77.5	78.7	79.8	81.0
Native Hawaiian/Pacific Islander	76.8	77.8	79.0	80.1	81.2
Latino	78.4	79.3	80.2	81.0	81.8
FEMALE	80.8	81.9	83.1	84.2	85.3
White	81.3	82.4	83.4	84.5	85.5
African American	77.2	79.2	81.0	82.7	84.3
American Indian/Alaska Native	81.5	82.5	83.6	84.5	85.5
Asian	81.1	82.2	83.2	84.2	85.3
Native Hawaiian/Pacific Islander	81.6	82.6	83.5	84.5	85.5
Latino	83.7	84.4	85.0	85.6	86.3

Source: Population Division, United States Census Bureau, U.S. Popultaion Projections. August 14, 2008. Adapted from: http://www.census.gov/population/www/projections/files/nation/summary/np2008-t10.xls

Table 2.3 Life Expectancy and Projected Life Expectancy by Gender and Level of Development of World Regions.

	Life Expectancy at Birth (Year)			
	2005–2010		2045–2050	
	Male	Female	Male	Female
Level of Development of World Region	65.4	69.8	73.3	77.9
More Developed Regions (Australia, Europe, Japan, North America)	73.6	80.5	79.9	85.6
Less Developed Regions (Africa, Asia/Middle East, Latin America/Caribbean)	63.9	67.4	72.2	76.5
Least Developed Countries (30 of the 40 World's Poorest Countries Are in Africa)	54.7	57.2	66.7	70.4

Source: Population division of the department of Economic and Social Affairs of the United Nations Secretariat (2009). Adapted from, Table III.2, p.10. *World Population Prospects: The 2008 Revision. Highlights,* New York: United Nations.

widens again at the oldest age. Poverty combines with son preference, sex-selective abortion, and neglect and abandonment of female infants and girls in many parts of the world. The average global **sex ratio at birth (SRB)**—the number of boys born for every 100 girls—is 105 and favors males slightly. In rural areas of China and India alone between 117 and 140 boys are born for every 100 girls (French, 2007; Kogure, 2007). If a newborn is a girl, the couple tries again and again for a boy, continually increasing SRB until the desired number of sons are born (Westley and Choe, 2007). Unless gender inequality is tackled, Vietnam and Nepal will likely mirror these skewed sex ratios (UNFPA, 2007). Frequent pregnancy and lack of safe and legal abortion take another toll. Maternal mortality figures are hard to track but it is estimated that there are between 500,000 and 700,000 annual maternal deaths worldwide; 99 percent of these occur in developing countries, and most of these are preventable (Women Deliver, 2007; UNFPA, 2008). Given this reality, the female advantage in mortality is astounding.

In Sickness and in Health: Gender and Morbidity

Data from many sources consistently report that women have higher morbidity rates than men. Women's advantage in mortality may be offset by their disadvantage in morbidity in part because living longer reflects increased chronic illness and disability.

Men and Morbidity. Males are prone to certain physical and mental illnesses and injury categories in which women tend to be exempt. Overall, men have lower acute conditions but higher prevalence of chronic conditions that are life-threatening and associated with long-term disability, such as heart disease, emphysema, and atherosclerosis. Males have the highest rates of cancer at the youngest and oldest ages and are almost twice as likely to die from it as females. They are also afflicted with a range of genetic disorders much less common in females, such as myopia, hemophilia, juvenile glaucoma, and progressive deafness (Riska, 2006; National Center for Health Statistics, 2009). For mental illness, gender differences do not vary by rate, but they do vary by type. Men are more likely to suffer from personality disorders (antisocial behavior or narcissism) than women (Black, 2007; Blanco and Lopez, 2007). As a buffer against mental and physical illness for both men and women, it is better to be married. For men, it is much better to be married. Single men have the highest mortality and morbidity rates for both physical and mental disorders. Never married, divorced, and single men have higher rates of mental illness when compared to all marital categories of women (Simon, 2002; Strohschein et al., 2005; Olivardia, 2007). Since men are even less likely to seek help for emotional distress compared to their already low rates of help seeking for physical illness, rates of depression may be higher than reported (Mahalik and Rochlen, 2006; Magovcevic and Addis, 2008).

Gender roles also put more men in occupations that can be hazardous to their health, such as police and fire protection, the military, mining, and construction. Sports-related injuries are also much higher for men than women and are associated with chronic illnesses and disabilities. Males in all age groups are more likely than comparable age females to engage in a range of behaviors that increase their risk of disease, injury, and death. Regardless of the stereotype, as judged by accident and injury rate, women are better drivers than men.

Women and Morbidity. Morbidity appears to gradually emerge in females, especially noticeable in preadolescence, where girls begin to report higher levels of asthma, migraine headaches, and psychological and eating disorders than boys, a pattern that occurs in the United States and other developed countries (Wade et al., 2002; Sweeting and West, 2003). Small gender differences in self-esteem–favoring males show up during late adolescence and continue through the life course. As adults, women report more physical and mental disorders and use health services more than men. Anger, frustration, and depression are intensified when doctors face multiple, unexplained symptoms in their female patients. When a physician cannot find anything physically wrong, women—especially older women—are often dismissed as complainers; mental health issues remain unexplored for many female patients (Morris, 2001; Badgio and Worden, 2007; Levine and Weissman, 2007).

Females of all ages report more daily and transient illnesses such as colds and headaches and a higher prevalence of nonfatal chronic conditions such as arthritis, anemia, and sinusitis. Most all autoimmune disorders, such as juvenile diabetes and multiple sclerosis, are skewed toward women. Employed women and women who are identified as androgynous or less traditional in gender role orientation have better physical and psychological health. Like men, type of work is correlated to health. Professional women frequently describe their jobs as stressful, but lower-level workers are more likely to report stress-related illnesses, such as insomnia and headaches. Regardless of employment, income, age, and marital status, however, women are more likely to suffer from depression and anxiety compared to men (Worell and Goodheart, 2006; Woo and Keatinge, 2008; Zunker, 2008).

Premenstrual Syndrome. In many cultures menstruation is viewed as a disease of women and continues to be associated with pity, suspicion, scorn, and fear. Menstruating women may be isolated and undergo ritual purification at the conclusion of their periods. Medicine views this normal physiological process as a pathology and as a condition that dismisses a woman's physical pain as inconsequential or fabricated. The myths associated with it have not been dispelled, even in the health care and scientific community.

Research *on premenstrual syndrome* (*PMS*) challenges these myths. There are many faces of PMS that are variously defined by health professionals, researchers, and women themselves. Overall, PMS is widely viewed as a blanket term for a variety of physical and psychological symptoms occurring between two days and two weeks before a menstrual period. Physical symptoms include water retention, breast tenderness, and cramping, and psychological symptoms include heightened tension, anxiety, irritability, and depression. As many as 75 percent of women in their twenties and thirties experience some premenstrual *symptoms*, but only 2–10 percent experience severe to disabling symptoms, which may be defined as premenstrual *syndrome*— a serious psychiatric disorder (Mayo Clinic, 2002; Tavris, 2007). A diagnosis of PMS is vastly different from the normal bodily changes associated with menstruation.

Correlational research indirectly links PMS to fluctuations in hormones, like estrogen, that are seen to influence anxiety, depression, and other behavioral changes. Research shows that hormone concentrations change prior to a woman's period, but they do so in the same manner for all women, regardless of a woman's symptoms. Women are more anxious or irritable because of the physical symptoms, not because of the hormones. Hormones cause the reduction of the mood-altering chemical serotonin, in turn increasing anxiety or depression. PMS, therefore, is not directly caused by hormones but by their effect on the brain. Nutritional connections between hormones and serotonin also impact symptoms (Bernard, 2003). It is not only difficult to sort out the causal path for explaining PMS related to hormonal fluctuations, but to date it is virtually impossible to separate the physical symptoms from the cultural expectations associated with menstruation. Researchers who adopt both biological and cultural explanations will be more successful.

The whole notion of PMS is equivocal, but the acceptance of the term by some health-care professionals has aided those women who experience great physical and psychological difficulty with their periods. Prior to "legitimizing" PMS, countless women were turned away from a male-dominated health-care system with vague, paternalistic assurances that it was all in their heads. On the other hand, as a term, PMS is so commonly misused in the media (a staple of comedy shows, for example) that it is now equated with all menstruation. It is a convenient but erroneous explanation and justification for the behavior of women. If women "have" PMS, it reinforces the myth that up to two weeks a month most adult women have impaired judgment. Women may be put in a double bind if they attribute changes in their behavior to PMS.

Menopause and Hormone Replacement Therapy. Misinformation and cultural stereotypes surround *menopause*, when menstruation permanently ceases. Up to several years before menopause, referred to as *perimenopause*, women may experience irregular menstrual cycles and often report symptoms of irritability, depression, headaches and hot flashes. Like PMS, most symptoms are not disabling. The severe distress accompanying menopause is experienced by only about 10 percent of women. Research does not support that the physical symptoms of menopause cause serious depression in women. When combining the physical and psychological factors, menopause for most women is probably easier than was puberty. Indeed, many women look forward to the time when menstruation ends.

Medicine, however, still largely subscribes to the maternal instinct idea and views menopause as psychologically crippling because reproduction is sealed off at this life stage. The reproductive cycle cannot be reversed but women can escape the fate of menopause. Despite it being written decades ago, many gynecologists conform to beliefs advocated by Robert Wilson (1966) in his influential book *Feminine Forever* that menopause is a "disease of estrogen deficiency" treatable by *hormone replacement therapy (HRT)*. He views menopausal women as unstable "castrates," creating untold misery in the form of alcoholism, drug addiction, and broken homes because of their estrogen starvation (cited in Fausto-Sterling, 1993:336).

Until recently HRT was the taken-for-granted "remedy" for menopause prescribed by gynecologists and accepted by women taking the most commonly prescribed estrogen-progestin HRT. Benefits were thought to include decreased chance of coronary heart disease (CHD), curbing bone loss (osteoporosis), slowing memory loss and cognitive decline; risks included increased breast cancer and blood clots. The largest study ever conducted using a sample of 16,000 women followed up for over five years confirmed that the estrogen-progestin HRT significantly increased the risks of invasive breast cancer, stroke, and blood clots. Perhaps more stunning, however, it showed that HRT raised, not lowered, CHD risk in healthy postmenopausal women. Women had an 81 percent increased risk of CHD in the first year after starting estrogen-progestin HRT (Manson et al., 2003). Another unexpected finding was that HRT increased the risk of women developing dementia (AARP, 2003; Shumaker, 2003). Earlier research using female rats on the role of estrogen in cognitive functioning was inconsistent, but HRT was widely regarded as the remedy to stem memory loss, "counteract the effects of aging and delay the onset of Alzheimer's disease" (Carpenter, 2001; Znamensky et al., 2003). The benefits that HRT did confirm were fewer fractures and colorectal cancers (Cauley et al., 2003). Because the harm was considered greater than the benefit, women were advised to immediately contact their physicians to determine future HRT. This potential harm to research subjects and the need to get the information disseminated quickly was so imperative that the study was ended three years early (Women's Health Initiative, 2003).

Updated research has again altered the HRT picture. When accounting for age, perimenopausal women who start HRT may have a *lower* risk of heart disease than women who start it later. Another surprising finding is that a daily dose of estrogen may help control metastatic breast cancer in some patients by shrinking tumors as well as relieving pain (Bernhard, 2008; Ericson, 2009). These findings are intriguing, tentative, and puzzling and cannot be generalized to most women at midlife. As of this writing, HRT is advised largely for women with severe menopausal symptoms.

From a symbolic interactionist view, even with known risks, the massive prescriptions of HRT played on the fears of aging women in a society that worships youth. It also reinforced cultural views of menopause as a disease that produces psychologically unstable women. The cultural refusal to accept the realities of aging coupled with the gender stereotypes of women who are revered if they are young and fertile has compromised the health of millions of women. As reported by a 56-year-old female pediatrician who is dealing with her own menopausal symptoms,

> There's an arrogance in thinking we can go on indefinitely taking hormones that our bodies aren't supposed to take anymore. (Cowley and Springen, 2002:41)

Consider this attitude in light of research that the majority of women, if given the choice, would like to *never* have a period. New birth control pills with synthetic hormones can suppress a woman's period for months (Mishori, 2007). It is likely that advances in hormone therapy can make them cease permanently. The long-term effects of these powerful hormonal-based birth control pills are unknown for younger women who opt out of menstruation for a lengthy amount of time. Regardless of whether they are pre- or postmenopausal, women's cycles of life are defined as disease-producing processes that must be medicalized, medicated, and controlled.

If science is doing its job, it will report findings that may contradict previous findings. It is also clear from the HRT story that science is not immune from gender bias. Feminist health professionals call for a view of menopause as a normal developmental process and for providing women of all ages with accurate information to make educated choices concerning risks, benefits, and treatment (Jensen, 2004).

Eating Disorders. There are other serious health effects in the quest for youth and beauty. As the Duchess of Windsor reportedly said over a half century ago, "You can never be too rich or too thin." Such beliefs translate to eating disorders, especially *anorexia nervosa*, a disease of self-induced severe weight loss, primarily in young women. A variant is *bulimia*, which alternates binge eating and purging. The incidence rates of these "fear of fat" diseases have steadily increased since the 1950s, affecting over seven million women today. They will affect 1–2 percent of late adolescent girls and adult women, of which 6–10 percent will die. During puberty, when a girl begins to worry about attractiveness, there is an average weight gain of 20–25 pounds. In terms of race and ethnicity, African-American and Latino women have higher rates of obesity than Asian or white women. African-American and Asian women, however, are more satisfied with their body weight, and Latino women are less satisfied than white women. Regardless of satisfaction levels, increases in eating disorders with onset in adolescence are reported for females in all these groups (Chao et al., 2008; Esch and Zullig, 2008; Gravener et al., 2008). Self-esteem is fragile during adolescence for both boys and girls of all races, and weight issues contribute to their insecurity.

Males are not immune to weight obsession with their concerns focusing on body shape and muscularity. The objectification of the male body in the media form is a key factor in the rapid increase of eating disorders and abuse of anabolic steroids and supplements for all age categories of males. Over one million males suffer from eating disorders, up 50 percent from just a decade ago, with the largest increase reported for adolescents. Whereas adolescent girls diet for thinness, boys diet to obtain a muscular body image, often to gain weight. Like women, men's psychological well-being is associated with body image norms related to masculinity.

Nonetheless, men often find it easier to turn to drugs than to turn to people to deal with self-esteem issues related to body image (Tager et al., 2006; Baharke, 2007; Ousley et al., 2008). Only half of both men and women with eating disorders report being cured, a prognosis that has worsened over the last decade. Half of females with eating disorders who die commit suicide. Since men are less likely to seek help for both physical and emotional illnesses, the prognosis is even worse (Goldberg and Elliot, 2007; ANAD, 2009; Brausch and Gutierrez, 2009).

Cultural beliefs are significant influences in the development of eating disorders. Anorexia can be described as a *culture bound syndrome* because it was first associated with norms unique to American society. The power of the Western media has extended these norms to other societies. In Fiji, for example, "big was beautiful" for girls. Television came to Fiji in 1995, and within three years a teen's risk for eating disorders doubled and there was a fivefold increase of vomiting for weight loss (Goodman, 1999). A global increase in eating disorders is also linked to increased cigarette smoking by girls who are concerned about weight gain (Lindsey, 1997; Saules et al., 2008). Female models and movie stars have gotten progressively thinner throughout this century. At size 14, today Marilyn Monroe would not easily find a job in motion pictures. Whereas male celebrities have gotten more muscular, female beauty contestants average 20 percent lower than ideal weight.

Chronic dieting and excessive physical exercise are reinforced by other health messages publicizing the obesity epidemic in the United States. The messages are confusing and may seem contradictory—Americans are obsessed with thinness at the same time as an obesity epidemic has emerged. The health and diet industries bolster these messages. From a conflict theory perspective, this has resulted in a form of *medicalization*, a process that legitimizes medical control over parts of a person's life. Combined with cosmetic surgery and unhealthy body weight norms, the social pressure for thinness is supported by a billion-dollar advertising and medical industry. This industry sustains a culturally accepted belief that women's bodies—and increasingly men's bodies—are unacceptable as they are.

HIV/AIDS. A decade ago, acquired immuno deficiency syndrome (AIDS) focused on the high mortality rate of men with the disease. In the United States in 1992 it was the leading cause of death of men between the ages of 25 and 44, with the highest percentage among men having sex with men (MSM). For all categories of men and women today, AIDS mortality has significantly decreased. Even with decreased mortality rates, African-American women are still 10 times likely to die of AIDS than are white women (Centers for Disease Control, 2009). For both white men and men of color living with HIV, the primary transmission is MSM; for African-American women, the primary transmission is through high-risk heterosexual contact. Injection drug use follows as the second most likely transmission category (Centers for Disease Control, 2008a, 2009).

In the United States and the developed world, HIV infection rates have stabilized or are declining since the 1990s. AIDS mortality is re-focused to HIV morbidity. New cases of HIV are declining. The sharpest declines are for white males. One-third of new diagnoses are among women, and for all racial categories, the largest increase is among African-American women. Over two-third of females living with HIV/AIDS are African American (Figure 2.2).

When poverty and region are added to the equation, new infections are declining at a slower rate in inner city neighborhoods among poor African-American and Latino populations. Poor men and women living in the South account for a significant proportion of new cases. The largest increases are occurring among women in both these categories. Taking all these factors together, poor, heterosexual, minority women are at greatest risk for HIV/AIDS in the United States (Kaiser Family Foundation, 2008).

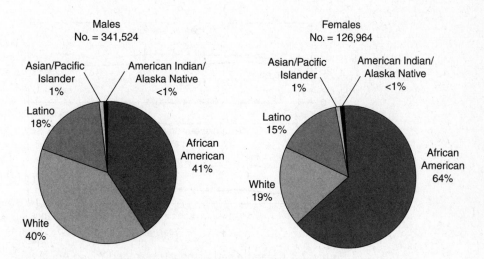

Figure 2.2 Race/Ethnicity of Adults and Adolescents Living with HIV/AIDS.

Source: Centers for Disease Control. "HIV/AIDS among African American," *CDC HIV/AIDS Fact Sheet:* August 2008. www.cdc.gov/hiv

With carefully monitored drug regimens and lifestyle changes, the AIDS death sentence has been commuted to a life sentence for HIV-infected people (Centers for Disease Control, 2008b). Although people in the developing world with an HIV diagnosis are living longer, the diagnosis remains a death sentence. The rapid spread of AIDS worldwide and the patterns that have been produced by this spread have transformed AIDS into a women's disease. Women worldwide are becoming infected with HIV at faster rates than men, with the number of annual cases for women now equaling or exceeding those of men; more than half of HIV-infected women live in sub-Saharan Africa and most of them are infected through heterosexual contact with a spouse or partner. The death rate is so alarming that the two century increase in life expectancy worldwide is predicted to drop in 51 countries (Kaiser Family Foundation, 2009). Lower LER of HIV/AIDS has already been reported in sub-Saharan African regions of Kenya, Rwanda, Mali, Chad, and Niger. Because women are infected at higher rates than men, HIV may be the biggest threat to their LER advantage.

Drug Use. For both sexes the use of alcohol and other drugs, including caffeine and nicotine, is culturally acceptable. Gender differences in morbidity rates relative to these usages are still evident (Figure 2.3). More men than women use alcohol throughout their lives, and alcoholism is significantly higher among men. However, women metabolize alcohol differently and suffer more from its acute and chronic effects. For women, impaired driving is quicker, and alcohol-induced liver disease and brain damage occur over a shorter period of time after consuming less alcohol (National Institute on Alcohol Abuse and Alcoholism, 2008). Fetal alcohol syndrome is linked to congenital heart defects, mental retardation, and low birth weight of infants. Alcohol is a major factor in rape and spouse abuse, with homicide an all-too-frequent outcome.

In coping with stress, men are more likely to turn to alcohol; women are more likely to turn to prescribed drugs. Prevalence rates for over-the-counter and prescribed

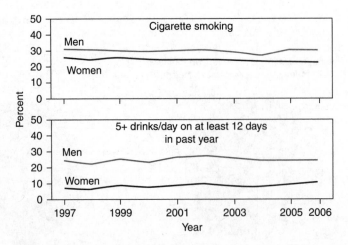

Figure 2.3 Cigarette and Alcohol Use among Young Adults (18–29 Years).

Source: Centers for Disease Control and National Center for Health Statistics. Health, United States, 2008. Adapted from Figure 31: Data from the National Health Interview Survey

drugs are double for women. Compared to men, women are almost twice as likely to receive a narcotic or antianxiety drug for a psychological problem, and are twice as likely to abuse or become addicted to them (National Institute on Drug Abuse, 2008).

If women increasingly adopt the risky health-adverse behaviors of men, the gender gap in morbidity may decrease. For example, although adult men in all age groups continue to smoke and consume alcohol at significantly higher rates, gender differences are rapidly decreasing among adolescents (National Center for Health Statistics, 2009). If these trends continue, the gender gap in mortality for lung cancer, heart disease, and cirrhosis of the liver may also narrow. To date, however, even with the movement of young women into behaviors detrimental to their health, mortality rates for these causes remain virtually unchanged.

Explaining Gendered Health Trends

Reasons for sex differences in mortality and morbidity are both biological and sociocultural. As noted earlier, females possess an additional X chromosome and protective sex hormones that are associated with a superior immune system. Since women bear and nurse children, biology offers the equipment allowing them to survive in the worst conditions, whether in childbirth or in cold, famine, or other conditions of deprivation. Women may have higher morbidity rates, but they are likely to recover from the same sicknesses that kill or disable men.

Added to this biological advantage is a gender role benefit. There are significant gender differences favoring women in their overall knowledge related to both physical and mental health, specifically related to information on sexuality and reproduction (Beier and Ackerman, 2003). Young girls are taught to be sensitive to their bodies, to be aware of changes in bodily states and physical processes, and to openly express their concerns to friends and their health-care providers. For cancer therapies, women are more likely to take advantage of new directions for preventive health care and self-care and be diagnosed in earlier, more treatable stages. This translates to lowered mortality rates for breast and ovarian cancer. Role flexibility allows women to be less constrained in seeking help for illness and psychological distress. They maintain a larger social support network and have higher degrees of connectedness than men, allowing them to call on others for help or support in stressful times. Men have higher degrees of separation and are less likely to seek out others for emotional reasons. In the United States and other parts of the developed world, widowers are more vulnerable to depression and suicide in part because their wives maintained the social networks that buffer psychological distress. When men are socialized into the belief that seeking help is a sign of masculine weakness, they may not get treatment for life-threatening diseases in time (Chapter 9). For women, however, these very patterns contribute to higher treatment rates and bolster the claim that women are sicker, weaker, and less emotionally strong than men.

THE WOMEN'S HEALTH MOVEMENT

Emerging as an organized, powerful force by the 1970s, the women's health movement confronted mainstream modern medicine by challenging androcentric practices not in the best interest of much of the population it is supposed to serve (Morgen, 2002). The movement asserts that women must be empowered to take an active role in all phases of their health and health care. Blatantly sexist attitudes regarding the sexual inferiority of women still run rampant in this system. For example, in both the pre-Kinsey and the post-Masters and Johnson eras, medical textbooks for gynecologists continue to highlight Freud's anatomy as destiny model (Scully and Bart, 2003).

Challenging Gender Bias in Research

The potential harm of an androcentric medical system to the health and well-being of women is demonstrated in many ways. Women had been virtually absent as participants in clinical trials involving drugs, uses of medical technology, and health-care options on which much contemporary health care is based. Androcentric medicine insists that biological differences between men and women have major, inescapable health consequences, but then routinely conducts research using only male subjects. Male is the medical norm. A large, now infamous, federally funded study examining the effects of diet on breast cancer used only men as sample subjects. Men are diagnosed with about one percent of all breast cancers and certainly their lack of attention to symptoms women would respond much quickly to is itself a gender-related issue (Bio-Medicine, 2008). However, the breast cancer study with only male subjects added to the growing evidence that medical research is often flawed by gender bias. Research on heart disease is another notable example where the exclusion of women in clinical trials is ominous. The key study on the effect of low doses of aspirin and the risk of heart attack used over 35,000 subjects, all of them men. The reduced heart attack risk was so spectacular that the public was made aware of results even before findings were published (Steering Committee of the Physician's Health Study Research Group, 1989). Results could not be generalized to women because hormonal differences between men and women were not studied. In addition, excluding women ignored the fact that heart disease is the number one killer for both men and women. Women receive less aggressive cardiac care, are more likely to die in the hospital, and have greater risk of death from a second heart attack in the year following the first heart attack than men (Radford et al., 2001; Rainer et al., 2002).

Progress in Women's and Men's Health

In addressing these and other health-related issues, many nongovernmental organizations (NGOs) have emerged to publicize and influence health policy. More women are entering the health-care field as physicians, especially as gynecologists, hospital administrators, clinical psychologists, and other mental health therapists. Nurses are assuming more responsibility in decision-making processes. The concept of a health-care team tied to beliefs about preventive health care and holistic health has helped in this regard. Clinical trials with female subjects representing a diversity of racial and ethnic groups will soon be normative in health research. The interplay of race and class must also be accounted for to make findings applicable to a diverse population of women.

The empowerment of women as both patients and health-care practitioners is also beneficial to men. Encouraged by successes of the health movement for women, a men's health movement has emerged. This movement is helping to train health-care practitioners in understanding how masculine gender roles are hazardous to men's physical and mental health. Although less visible than the women's health movement, toxic masculinity's influence on injury and death related to extreme sports, unnecessary occupational risks, impulsive sexual and alcohol-related behavior, and suicide is gaining public attention. Most important, young men today are more likely to be aware of symptoms and to seek help for them than those of only a generation ago (Mahalik et al., 2007; Mullen et al., 2007; Addis, 2008). There are encouraging signs that men are also seeking preventive services. Mortality rates for prostate cancer, for example, have been positively influenced through early detection. The men's health movement may be responsible for small but noticeable reductions on a range of other male mortality-related measures.

NATURE AND NURTURE REVISITED: THE POLITICS OF BIOLOGY

Biologically, women are definitely not the weaker sex. Drawing from data on human sexuality, developmental biology, animal behavior, and ethnography, anthropologist Ashley Montagu (1999) makes the case that women are more valuable than men because they maintain the species during a child's crucial development stages. From a sociobiological standpoint, Montagu used the idea of adaptive strategies, asserting that women are superior, too, because they are more necessary than men. He literally turned around interpretations of women as passive beings who are sexually and biologically inferior.

The Female Advantage in Evolution

Assertions about survival of the fittest favor women. Sociobiologists need to account for the newest data showing that human evolution probably benefited more from cooperation and the plant-gathering activities favoring women than competition and the hunting activities favoring men. DNA evidence now suggests that a "make love not war" scenario was probably the most productive, adaptive strategy of the earliest waves of human migration out of Africa. Conventional Darwinian wisdom about competition and the desire to pass on selfish genes does not conform with newer models suggesting that humans are naturally predisposed to altruism and cooperation. Attempts by humans to dominate other humans through violence, distrust, and cruelty were uncommon in early humans because they were maladaptive (Cloninger, 2004).

The primate studies sociobiologists are so fond of indicate that the dominant belief that animals compete with one another to gain resources and increase reproduction is a narrow and unsophisticated view of evolutionary theory (Cussins, 2000; Strum and Fedigan, 2000). Even the long-held belief about baboons, the "most extreme male-dominated chest-thumping society in the primate world," is being questioned. The highly affiliated baboons, who went unstudied for decades, now show males spending time with females as lovers not fighters and that females make deliberate choices about when to consort with males (Hart and Sussman, 2009; Higham et al., 2009). As primatologist Robert Sapolsky contends, female choice is built around male–female affiliation rather than the outcome of male–male aggression (Sapolsky, 2002; David, 2003). When viewed through the lens of gender, new interpretations of the biology–animal–human link emerge.

Reframing the Debate

Let us return to our original question of the roles of nature and nurture, of heredity and environment, of biology and society. Most scientists and media accounts frame the debate as one *versus* the other, such as the "nature *versus* nurture debate." All the evidence points to the impact of both in explaining sex differences. Deterministic theories that either dismiss or fail to account for biology and society are doomed as useful explanatory models in science. The problem, according to Sandra Bem (1996:11), is that there is too much of a focus on biological difference and not enough on the "institutionalized androcentrism" that transforms male–female differences into female disadvantage. Using pop-Darwinism accounts, media take hold of the sex difference theme, and soon people believe that men have math and promiscuity genes and women have caring and victimization genes that predestine their gender roles. Pop-Darwinism becomes a convenient moral guide to justify assertions about male sexuality and female passivity (McCaughey, 2008).

Genes are claiming more and more of social and individual life when scientific theories are used to serve prevailing ideologies regarding gender. Biological arguments are consistently drawn on to justify gender inequality and the continued oppression of women. Although evidence clearly suggests that the female sex is the stronger sex biologically, we have seen that differences between the sexes (genders), both perceived and real, have been used to subordinate women. Natural superiority, if it does exist, should not be used to condone social inequality, whether it occurs for women or men. Biologically based arguments that exclude culture, nurture, and environment may be ideologically embraced but are not empirically sound (Lippa, 2005). To understand data on health and sexuality, interdisciplinary work is encouraged and requires *both* sociocultural and biological knowledge. While not abandoning promising evolutionary based arguments, psychologists, anthropologists, and biologists are working together to better understand how nature and nurture weave together to produce sex differences and similarities. Chapter 3 shows that socialization has a massive, profound influence on the differences that do exist. Sociologists favor explanations for gender development and gender roles rooted in nurture and sociocultural factors. These sociological explanations account for a range of variables and imply that women and men have the potential to achieve virtually in any direction they desire. Nonetheless, a great deal of rapidly emerging data in many disciplines suggest that the nature *versus* nurture view must be replaced by the more empirically sound and productive nature *and* nurture view.

Summary

1. Arguments against gender equality are based on biology. Evolutionary approaches from animals and insects favored by sociobiology are often the bases. Massive evidence, including the work by Margaret Mead, refutes these arguments.

2. Sex hormones shape the development of the brain and sex organs and determine how these organs will be activated. Hormones play important roles in behavior but do not cause male aggression. The belief that there is a hormonally based motherhood instinct is not supported.

3. Sigmund Freud's theory of psychosexual development asserts that because boys have a penis and girls do not, females ultimately wish they were boys. Penis envy in females is resolved by the wish for motherhood. Freud was a sexist in his belief that anatomy was destiny. Psychoanalytic feminism rejects Freud's sexism but uses his theory to explain women's subordination not as part of human nature but of human relationships.

4. Infants born with ambiguous sex traits, referred to as hermaphrodites or intersexed, may undergo sex reassignment surgery. The infamous case of the sex reassignment of a male twin due to a circumcision accident illustrates that success with surgery largely depends on the age, the culture in which it occurs, and if the person freely chose it as an option.

5. Global research on sexual orientation and transgender indicates that they are extremely varied. Cultural beliefs about sex and gender determine how they are translated into patterns of behavior.

6. Sociologists emphasize the importance of sexual scripts in prescribing roles related to sexuality. This scripting clearly illustrates that biology alone cannot explain human sexuality and that sexuality is much less spontaneous than we think.

7. The double standard in sexual behavior and attitudes is declining, but gendered patterns still exist: Males have earlier, more frequent intercourse both before and after marriage, emphasize sexual pleasure as a motive for intercourse, and have more nonmarital and extramarital relationships than females. Traditional beliefs about gender roles inhibit sexual pleasure for both women and men.

8. Both in the United States and globally, females have higher morbidity (sickness) rates but live longer than men; men have lower morbidity rates but do not live as long as women.

9. Gender differences in disease and disability are clearly related to gender roles, especially in terms of occupations, drug use, eating disorders, and HIV/AIDS. Gender beliefs, and not medical evidence, related to premenstrual syndrome and hormone replacement therapy serve to harm women's physical and emotional health. Gender beliefs harm men when they do not seek help for physical or psychological problems.

10. The women's health movement has challenged androcentric medicine by calling attention to the lack of females in health-related clinical trials, by empowering women as patients, and encouraging them to become practitioners, practices that benefit men as well.

12. Both biology and culture (nature and nurture) are ingredients in explaining sex differences. Media attention to biological differences disregards how androcentrism and ideology transform these differences into female disadvantage. Women are biologically the stronger sex, but biology is used to justify gender inequality and oppression of women. Nature *verus* nurture should be replaced with a nature *and* nurture view.

Key Terms

double standard 38	GLBT 34	sexual dimorphism 30
essentialism 22	morbidity rate 39	sexual scripts 36
feminization of aging 40	mortality rate 39	sociobiology 24
hermaphrodites 30	queer theory 33	transgender 34
intersexed 30	sex ratio at birth (SRB) 42	transsexuals 31

Critical Thinking Questions

1. Based on your understanding of the research on the biological and cultural ingredients of gender, provide an empirical rationale countering the claim that gender roles are destined to be unequal.

2. Why is Freud's theory of psychosexual model considered sexist and **used** in reinforcing gender stereotypes? How has psychoanalytic feminism reconciled these issues to the benefit rather than the detriment of women?

3. Using research examples, demonstrate how patterns of mortality and morbidity are highly gendered and the consequences of this fact. How can a combination of conflict theory and symbolic interaction explain these patterns?

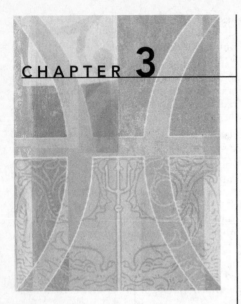

CHAPTER 3

Girls play at being pretty, but boys play cars.

Boys don't clean house and girls don't get dirty.

Boys stay outside as long as they want, but girls can't.

Boys don't play hopscotch. Girls don't play rough or get sweaty.

Girls are cute and harmless and don't get as muddy as boys.

—Comments from seven- and eight-year-olds when asked "How are boys and girls different?" (cited in Freedman, 2001:142)

As early as second grade, children have strong ideas about what boys and girls are supposed to do and be. They embrace and even celebrate smaller gender differences, in turn obscuring larger gender similarities. From the moment a girl infant is wrapped in a pink blanket and a boy infant in a blue one, gender role development begins. The colors of pink and blue are among the first indicators used in American society to distinguish female from male. As these infants grow, other cultural artifacts will ensure that this distinction remains intact. Girls will be given dolls to diaper and tiny stoves on which to cook pretend meals. Boys will construct buildings with miniature tools and wage war with toy guns and tanks. In the teen and young adult years, although both may spend their money on CDs, girls buy cosmetics and clothes, and boys buy sports equipment and technical gadgets. The incredible power of gender socialization is largely responsible for such behavior. Pink and blue begin this lifelong process.

GENDER SOCIALIZATION AND CULTURAL DIVERSITY

Socialization is the lifelong process by which, through social interaction, we learn our culture, develop our sense of self, and become functioning members of society. This simple definition does not do justice to the profound impact of socialization. Each generation transmits essential cultural elements to the next generation through socialization. **Primary socialization**, the focus of the research and theory overviewed in this chapter, begins in the family and allows the child to acquire necessary skills to fit into society, especially language learning and acceptable behavior to function effectively in a variety of social situations. **Continuing socialization** provides the basis for the varied roles an individual will fill throughout life.

Not only does socialization shape our personalities and allow us to develop our human potential, but it molds our beliefs and behaviors about all social groups and the individuals making up those groups. **Gender socialization** is the process by which individuals learn the cultural behavior of femininity or masculinity that is associated with the biological sex of female or male. The forces of social change have collided with gender socialization on a massive scale. To explain gender socialization in contemporary society, it is necessary to understand cultural diversity in all its forms.

Culture and Socialization

As a society's total way of life, **culture** endows us with social heritage and provides guidelines for appropriate behavior. Cultures are organized through **social institutions** that ensure the basic needs of society are met in established, predictable ways. Although it is the social institution of the family that sets the standards for the emergence of gender roles in children, the family itself is shaped by overall cultural values regarding gender. Parent–child interactions occur in a cultural context in which females have lower power and prestige than males. Beginning in infancy, parents socialize sons to express emotions differently than daughters in ways that support gender differences in power. Institutions overlap in their socialization functions so that one will support and carry on the work of another. For example, the institution of the family is fundamentally responsible for a child's primary socialization, but the work continues with the institution of education when the child enters preschool or kindergarten. Other institutions include the economy, religion, government, and an evolving leisure and recreational institution with a media focus. Like cultures throughout the world, the social institutions in American culture are differentiated according to expectations and norms that form the basis of gender roles. These roles show up in the jobs men and women perform, leisure activities, dress, possessions, language, demeanor, reading material, college major, and even how much they engage in sex and the degree of sexual pleasure they derive. The list is virtually endless.

Culture also provides measures of **social control** to ensure that people more or less conform to a vast array of social norms, including those related to gender. Social control mechanisms that guarantee gender role compliance are often informal but very powerful, such as ridicule, exclusion from peers, and loss of support from family or colleagues. Both boys and girls ridicule boys who play with dolls or toys designed for girls and shun girls who play too aggressively. Adults who challenge workplace norms in which gender role scripts are changing—such as when men choose occupations as child-care workers and women choose occupations as plumbers—also remain vulnerable until new norms are in place.

When socialization processes encourage the perpetuation of stereotyped portrayals of the genders, social control is particularly effective. Stereotypical thinking becomes insidious when individuals are harmed because they are defined in terms of assumed, negative characteristics assigned to their group. If we stereotype women as passive, an individual woman may be passed over for a job in which leadership qualities are required. Her own individual ability in terms of job leadership may not even be considered due to the stereotype assigned to her entire gender. A man may be denied custody of his child on the basis of stereotypes that view men as inherently less capable of raising children than women. Stereotypical thinking about gender is so pervasive that even the law is impacted.

It might appear that the power of socialization creates little robots molded by our culture who uncritically submit to mandated gender roles. However, to argue that the automatons of one generation produce their own carbon copies in the next ignores two important facts. First, socialization is an uneven process taking place on many fronts. We are socialized by parents, siblings, peers, teachers, media, and all other social institutions. We know of achievement-oriented women who are admired for their leadership and men for their effectiveness in caring for young children.

Second, we live in diverse, heterogeneous societies made up of numerous **subcultures** that share characteristics in common with the culture in which they exist, but are also distinguished from the broader culture in important ways, such as in gender patterns. In addition to gender, subcultures are differentiated according to factors such as race, ethnicity, social class, age, sexual orientation, or common interest. Age-based subcultures are especially important because they emerge at points in the life course that are strongly defined according to gender role norms. For example, age peers in elementary school determine criteria for prestige, which in turn impacts self-esteem, achievement motivation, and academic success. A boy defined as effeminate or a girl defined as a bully has much to lose in this regard. At the other end of the age spectrum, the elderly, too, are not immune to such rankings. Age and gender stereotypes combine against divorced or widowed elderly who would like to begin dating. They risk social disapproval through cultural stereotypes that devalue or view sexual activity for the elderly suspiciously. Elderly widows may be regarded as asexual and elderly widowers as "dirty old men."

Gender Socialization: The Impact of Social Class and Race

Gender combines with social class and race as key determinants in how gender roles are enacted. There is a strong correlation between social class and parental values that impact gender. Overall, middle-class parents emphasize autonomy and working-class parents emphasize conformity in socialization. These values translate into gender role flexibility more in middle-class families than in working-class and low-income families. Boys and girls from middle-class homes are offered less stereotypical gender role choices in behavioral expectations and career development and hold more egalitarian attitudes. Gender role flexibility and autonomy training for both daughters and sons are enhanced in middle-class families with career-oriented mothers. In such families, however, women express higher levels of support for such flexibility and autonomy than men do. Research is less clear on the specific variable that accounts for this pattern. Boys from middle-class homes are more achievement oriented than girls. College students describe white middle-class women in more stereotypical ways than they do for African-American women. Families of all races who move upward in social mobility are more likely to embrace traditional gender roles (Xiao, 2000; Bumpus et al., 2001; Davis and Pearce, 2007). It may be that race, mother's employment, and social mobility are more important than social class in determining gender attitudes. Because social class itself is multidimensional and determined by these very factors, it is difficult to sort out the direction of causation.

In viewing race as a separate variable the gender role socialization portrait is further complicated. Overall, available research suggests that in general children from Asian-American and Latino homes are more likely to be socialized into less flexible, traditional beliefs about gender than African-American and white children. For Asian-American children, gender roles emphasize female subordination to all males and older females in a patriarchal family structure. Within three generations of immigration, however, unquestioned female subordination weakens considerably. This is especially true among Chinese, Korean, and Japanese families and is linked to upward mobility of the family and a college education for their children. As Asian-American children become more Americanized, both boys and girls begin to exhibit less traditional gender roles (Farley and Alba, 2002; Lien et al., 2004).

Latino Families. Data from Latino subcultures (Puerto Rican, Cuban-American, and Mexican-American) report that females act out gender roles that are more deferential and subordinate than those found in other racial and ethnic groups. There is a great deal of diversity within Latino subcultures in the United States but they share a heritage related to Catholicism that has a powerful impact on gender roles. Religious socialization fosters women's subservience to men and teaches girls to value motherhood above all other roles. Women are expected to be chaste before marriage and dependent after marriage (Raffaelli and Ontai, 2001, 2004). Latino children also receive socialization messages promoting *familism*, a strong value emphasizing the family and its collective needs over personal and individual needs. Familism helps buffer hypermasculinity (machismo) in boys and serves as a source of prestige for girls, who help with the care and nurturing of the young and the old early in life (Chapter 8). The impact of socialization on familism is supported by data showing that for recreational activities Latino fathers are more involved with their children than either African-American or white fathers (Yeung et al., 2001; Loukas et al., 2005).

African-American Families. Compared to other racial and ethnic groups, research on gender socialization in African-American families is more extensive as well as more contradictory. On the one hand, research shows that compared to children of other races, African-American children are socialized into views of gender that are less rigid and less stereotyped. African-American girls from homes with nontraditional gender roles have high achievement motivation and self-esteem. Compared to white males, African-American males—both older children and adults—participate more in housework and child care. Views of what is considered masculine and feminine are often blurred in African-American homes (Theran, 2004; Buckley and Carter, 2005).

On the other hand, evidence suggests that African-American women encourage independence and self-reliance in their daughters but at the same time encourage them to accept other parts of a female role that are highly traditional. Mothers are less likely to grant freedom to explore expanded roles. Daughters report that their mothers are overly protective and mothers report that their daughters' behavior needs to be closely monitored, especially in relation to sexuality (Townshend, 2008). African-American women are also likely to adopt patriarchal beliefs regarding marriage and family through messages heard in African-American churches. Both mothers and fathers prepare their daughters more for racial bias than for gender bias (Cole and Guy-Shetfall, 2003; Shearer, 2008). The net effect of these socialization practices is a reinforcement of traditional gender roles.

African-American views about gender are also mediated by setting, such as family and school, and the race/social class intersection in the setting. In father-present lower-income homes, for example, sons hold more rigid beliefs about masculinity. In father-absent lower-income homes, socialization fosters daughters to adopt more masculine roles and sons to adopt less masculine roles (Mandara et al., 2005). Young African-American girls attending predominantly white middle-income schools are less assertive than those attending predominantly African-American lower-income schools (Scott, 2000). African-American boys and girls attending predominantly African-American summer camps construct gender more rigidly than those attending interracial camps (Moore, 2000).

To sort out findings that appear to be contradictory for African Americans, a host of variables need to be accounted for. The socialization work of African-American parents is strongly influenced by social inequalities in American society that work against beliefs about gender equity (Hill, 2005). African-American children who are already facing a difficult road because of racial discrimination may find it easier to adopt rather than challenge traditional gender roles if it means one less barrier must be overcome. Historical patterns of gender role configurations in African-American subcultures also help understand the contradictions. High regard for the independence and initiative of African-American women is normative in these subcultures. In this sense, the "traditional" gender role of women is one of strength and resilience rather than weakness and resignation (Chapter 8). Mothers teach daughters not only to resist oppression but also to accommodate African-American institutions, such as the Church, that may be more in line with patriarchy existing in the broader culture (Pittman, 2005). Most important, African-American children tend to adopt less polarized views of gender. Males and females are not "opposites" with completely different expectations. Both men and women are encouraged to be nurturing and assertive. Research clearly suggests that the concepts of masculinity and femininity are simply not theoretically useful if they continue to be polarized. The research is inconsistent only when race, class, and gender are separated and when white, middle-class standards of masculinity and femininity are applied to all of the African-American experience.

The concepts and research reviewed here are important for understanding the three major theories of gender socialization—social learning, cognitive development, and gender schema theories—and the newest variety, social cognitive theory.

THEORIES OF GENDER SOCIALIZATION

All theories of gender socialization focus on primary socialization and how children learn **gender identity**, when they become aware that the two sexes (male and female) behave differently and that different gender roles (masculine and feminine) are proper. Like socialization overall, gender socialization is mediated through a number of important elements, such as biology, personality, social interaction context, and the social institutions. Different theories give different weight to each element. Freudian psychologists and sociobiologists contend that unconscious motivation and biologically driven evolutionary demands are powerful socialization forces (Chapter 2). Sociologists, social psychologists, and many personality psychologists emphasize social interaction taking precedence over biology as the key socialization force. This focus on the context of social interaction has allowed for significant interdisciplinary work between psychology and sociology in building theories of gender socialization.

Social Learning Theory

Unlike Freud's psychoanalytic approach, which focuses on internal conflict in socialization, social learning theory focuses on observable behavior. For social learning theorists, socialization is based on rewards (reinforcing appropriate behavior) and punishments (extinguishing inappropriate behavior). They are concerned with the ways children model the behaviors they view in others, such as cooperation and sharing or selfishness and aggression. Imitation and modeling appear to be spontaneous in children, but through reinforcement, patterns of behavior develop that eventually become habitual.

As with other behaviors, gender roles are learned directly, through reprimands and rewards, and indirectly, through observation and imitation (Bandura and Walters, 1963; Mischel, 1966). The logic is simple. In gender socialization, different expectations lead to differential reinforcement from parents, peers, and teachers for doing either "boy" or "girl" things. Boys may be praised by peers for excelling in male sports such as football but derided for excelling in female games such as jump rope. Girls may be praised by peers for embroidering table linen but derided for preferring to play with toy soldiers rather than baby dolls. Gender identity is developed when children associate the label of boy or girl with the rewards that come with the appropriate behavior and then act out gender roles according to that perception. Parents and teachers model gender roles during the critical primary socialization years and children imitate accordingly. This results in continued reinforcement of the valued gender identity. Social learning theory thus assumes that "knowledge about gender roles either precedes or is acquired at the same time as gender identity" (Intons-Peterson, 1988:40).

Gender Socialization for Boys. According to social learning theory, boys and girls are not parallel in the acquisition of gender role knowledge during the primary socialization years. Early research on gender socialization conducted by David Lynn (1969) accounts for his assertion that boys encounter more difficulty on the socialization path than girls. Lynn asserted that because fathers are not as available as mothers during early childhood, boys have limited opportunities to model the same-gender parent. And when the father is home, the contact is qualitatively different from contact with the mother in terms of intimacy. Since male role models are generally scarce in early childhood, boys struggle to put together a definition of masculinity based on incomplete information. They are often told what they should not do rather than what they should do. "Don't be a sissy" and the classic "big boys don't cry" are examples. Girls have an easier time because of continuous contact with the mother and the relative ease of using her as a model.

Lynn further contended that it is the lack of exposure to males at an early age that leads boys to view masculinity in a stereotyped manner. For males, masculine gender roles are more inflexible than those offered to females. It is this gender role inflexibility that is a critical factor in making male socialization difficult and may explain why males express more insecurity about their gender identity. The consequences of this narrow view of masculinity are many. Male peer groups encourage the belief that aggression and toughness are virtues. Males exhibit hostility toward both females and homosexuals, and cross-gender behavior in boys ("sissies") is viewed more negatively than when it occurs in girls ("tomboys"). Women are more accepting of children who cross gender lines in their behavior (Chapter 8). Men's fear of ridicule propels them to exaggerated antihomosexual and sexist remarks to ensure that others do not get "the wrong idea" concerning their masculinity (Kimmel, 2009).

Although research does not confirm that modeling per se is responsible for gender role acquisition, it does indicate that gender-appropriate behavior is strongly associated with social approval. Although laden with uncertainty and inflexibility, boys express adamant preference for the masculine role. A boy learns that his role is the more desirable one and brings with it more self-esteem.

Gender Socialization for Girls. Other social learning theorists state that it is a mistake to conclude that the socialization path for girls is easy simply because mothers are more available to girls as models during early childhood. Even young children are bombarded by messages suggesting that higher worth, prestige, advantages, and rewards are accorded to males compared to females. Boys can readily embrace the gender roles flowing from these messages. Girls, in contrast, are offered subordinate, less prestigious roles that encourage deference and dependence and must model behavior that may be less socially valued. Research on teen movies shows that girls are often portrayed in negative, gender stereoypical ways—as socially aggressive, bullying, selfish, and disloyal to female friends (Behm-Morawitz and Mastro, 2008). If modeling and reinforcement are compelling enticements to behavior, as social learning theory suggests, a girl would understandably become quite anxious about being encouraged to perform roles or model behavior held in lower esteem. For socialization overall, girls have the advantage of gender role flexibility, but boys have the advantage of a higher prestige gender role.

Social learning theory provides the foundation for a great deal of research on socialization, especially when it is combined with a symbolic interaction perspective. In emphasizing the importance symbolic interactionists attach to role taking, this approach suggests that when children take on a variety of roles, including those related to gender, opportunities are available for behavior to be rewarded, punished, and imitated. Roles are also carefully defined to determine the relative influence of some people compared to others. Data on adolescents planning for the future, for example, show that they not only model parents and peers but also judge the level of influence of both in determining their plans. This research shows that they use both processes, but the judgment of the level of influence (symbolic interaction theory) is more important than the modeling (social learning theory) (Starrels and Holm, 2000). Congruent with gender socialization, same-gender parents and peers would be defined as more influential than other-gender parents and peers.

Critique. Children are not the passive recipients of rewards and punishments that social learning theorists envision. Because children routinely choose gender-inconsistent behavior, the reinforcement and modeling processes are far more complex. First, children may not model same-gender parents, teachers, or peers or may choose other-gender models outside the family who offer alternatives to gender role behavior that enhance self-esteem. A girl may be rewarded for a masculine activity, such as excelling in sports, but she keeps a tight hold on other aspects of her feminine role. Second, social learning theory minimizes the importance of social change, a significant factor in gender socialization. Families are much more diverse than the stereotyped "at-home mother and outside-home father" that are used to explain the rocky socialization paths for girls and boys. Divorce, blended families, single parenting, and an increasing number of nonresident parents who are mothers instead of fathers have created a wide range of models for gender socialization (Chapter 8). Third, other statuses also vie for the attention of both child and parent during primary socialization. Birth order and age of child may be as important as gender in determining how parents behave toward their children. Finally, children experience subcultural family influences in which siblings and adults take on a range of nontraditional roles, such as in single-parent families. And regardless of the different paths offered to them, both girls and boys learn to prefer their own gender and strongly endorse the roles associated with it.

Cognitive Development Theory

Cognitive development explanations for gender socialization contrast sharply with social learning theory. Jean Piaget's (1896–1980) interest in how children gradually develop intelligence, thinking, and reasoning laid the foundation for cognitive development theory. His work is consistent with symbolic interaction theory regarding his ideas that cognitive abilities are developed in stages through ongoing social interaction. Simply stated, the mind matures through interaction with the environment. Behavior depends on how a person perceives a social situation at each cognitive stage (Piaget, 1950, 1954). Cognitive theory stresses a child's active role in structuring and interpreting the world.

Building on Piaget's work, Lawrence Kohlberg (1966) claimed that children learn their gender roles according to their level of cognitive development; in essence, their degree of comprehension of the world. One of the first ways a child comprehends the world is by organizing reality through her or his **self**, the unique sense of identity that distinguishes each individual from all other individuals, and a highly valued part of the child's existence. Anything associated with the self becomes highly valued as well. By age three, children begin to self-identify by gender and accurately apply gender-related labels to themselves and often to others. By age six *gender constancy* is in place. Gender is permanent: A girl knows she is a girl and will remain one. Only then, Kohlberg asserts, is gender identity said to be developed. Gender identity becomes a central part of self, invested with strong emotional attachment. Studies on gender concepts of children aged three to five offer support for the cognitive development approach to using gender identity to organize and label gender-related behavior. These labels form the basis for gender stereotypes and expectations about gender-related behavior (Martin et al., 2004). Thus cognitive development theory offers a good explanation for the development of gender-typing during primary socialization: When children finally figure out what gender means in their lives, they embrace that understanding in ways that create and then reinforce gender stereotypes.

Once gender identity is developed, much behavior is organized around it. Children seek models that are labeled as "girl" or "boy" and "female" or "male" and, in turn, identification with the same-sex parent can occur. Although children base much of their behavior on reinforcement, cognitive theorists see a different sequence in gender socialization than do social learning theorists. This sequence is "I am a boy, therefore I want to do boy things, therefore the opportunity to do boy things (and to gain approval for doing them) is rewarding" (Kohlberg, 1966:89). Reinforcements are important, but the child chooses behavior and roles according to the sense of self. Individual differences in gender roles are accounted for by the different experiences of children. Children may subsequently repeat these experiences based on reinforcement, so there is some consistency with social learning theory. There is wide support for the cognitive development approach to gender role socialization. Children are gender detectives. Research consistently finds that children's choices, interests, and activities—such as play, toys, and friendships—are based on their beliefs about gender compatibility (Martin and Ruble, 2004:67). Children value their own gender more and believe theirs is superior to the other. Early in life children develop the ability to classify characteristics by gender and choose behavior according to that classification (Miller et al., 2006).

Critique. Like social learning, cognitive development theory cannot account for all of gender role socialization. The cognitive development model has also been criticized because a key assertion is that children will actively choose gender-typed behaivor only after they understand gender constancy. Gender constancy appears at age six, but gender-typed preferences in play and toy selection are already in place by age two or three. Cognitive development theory assumes that these preferences are based on gender identity. For the model to fit neatly with the stages outlined in cognitive development, gender identity must come before understanding gender constancy. To date research has been unable to confirm this sequence. In countering this criticism, cognitive theorists suggest that all that is needed for gender identity is simple, rudimentary knowledge about gender. *Gender stability*, where the child views the same gender role behavior over and over in a variety of contexts, will suffice even if the child cannot fully comprehend gender constancy. Simple knowledge about gender stability allows children to begin to accurately label who is a girl and who is a boy. Critics still argue, however, that the acquisition of knowledge about gender stability is not as simple as cognitive development theorists describe. For children to determine patterns of gender stability, they must experience social interaction in a relatively large number of contexts. It is unlikely that this interaction will be either uniform or consistent in terms of gender. Understanding the supposedly simple idea of gender stability may be as complicated for children as understanding gender constancy (Renk et al., 2006; Stockard, 2007).

Gender Schema Theory

Gender schema theory is an important subset of cognitive development theory. **Schemas** are cognitive structures used to understand the world, interpret perception, and process new information. Sandra Bem, one of the most prominent gender schema theorists, contends that once the child learns cultural definitions of gender, these schemas become the core around which all other information is organized (Bem, 1981, 1983, 1987). Consistent with cognitive development theory, before a schema is created to process gender-related information, children must be at the cognitive level to accurately identify gender. Infants as young as nine months can distinguish between male and female, but it is between ages two and three that this identification becomes associated with giant leaps in gender knowledge. Schemas tell children what they can and cannot do according to their gender. Schemas affect their behavior and influence their self-esteem. A child's sense of self is linked to how closely his or her behavior matches accepted gender schemas. When a girl learns that prescriptions for femininity in her culture include being polite and being kind, these behaviors are incorporated into her emerging gender schema, and she adjusts her behavior accordingly.

Gender schemas of parents impact how they behave toward their children and, in turn, how this influences their development. Significant, positive correlations between parent and child gender schemas are consistently reported. Parents with traditional gender schemas are more likely to have children with gender-typed cognitions than parents with nontraditional schemas (Leaper and Friedman, 2007). By 18 months children can associate cultural symbols with gender—pictures of fire hats and hammers are associated with males, and pictures of dolls and teddy bears with females (Eichstedt et al., 2002). As adults, gender-based processing directs people to use language according to gender role orientation (Crowley, 2001). These studies support Sandra Bem's contention that the way parents behave toward children and the way symbols are classified are directed by a gender schematic network of cultural associations that we learn to accept. In cultures that rigidly adhere to beliefs about gender differences, gender schemas are likely to be even more complex.

Other support for the influence of gender schemas comes from research indicating that people have a selective memory bias for information congruent with gender. Children and adults can recall personal experiences, activities, people, media, and reading material more accurately and vividly when the information is presented in gender stereotypical ways (Martin et al., 2002; Ruble et al., 2006). Schemas are guided by gender to fill in gaps when other information is ambiguous. In the absence of relevant information about the strengths of a political candidate, for example, people default to gender of the candidate to process the information (Chang and Hitchon, 2004). We also revert to gender schema to sort out information that is gender-inconsistent. Gender stereotype–congruent tasks are completed more quickly. Boys can manipulate a Transformer™ faster than girls; girls can dress a doll quicker than boys (Knight et al., 2004). Children presented with pictures of girls and boys engaged in nontraditional roles, such as a girl sawing wood or a boy sewing, will recall the picture in a gender-consistent way—the boy is sawing and the girl is sewing. Beginning in early childhood we tend to exaggerate or invent male–female differences even if none exist (Martin and Ruble, 2004:68).

Cultural Lenses. The cultural impact on gender acquisition can be refined further using a gender schema model. Referred to as *cultural lenses,* every culture contains assumptions about behavior that are contained throughout its social institutions and within the personalities of individuals (Bem, 1993). Sociologists assert that these lenses consist of a society's values, beliefs, and norms. She suggests that in American culture, three gender lenses are most prominent: gender polarization (shared beliefs that females and males are different and opposite beings), biological essentialism (biology produces natural, inevitable gender roles), and androcentrism (males are superior to females). Despite massive research evidence against gender polarization and biological essentialism, the beliefs persist, and in turn are used to justify androcentrism. These beliefs become another set of gender schemas in which to organize behavior. Children accept them without recognizing that alternatives are possible. As adults they cannot envision their society—or any other for that matter—organized according to a different set of gender schemas. Gender schema theory helps explain why a person's world becomes so differentiated by gender over the life course.

The notion of cultural lenses provides a good interdisciplinary link to macrolevel sociology. Functionalists are interested in identifying core cultural and subcultural gender lenses that influence social order and social change. Monitoring these gender cultural lenses over time can offer insight into the functional and dysfunctional consequences of gender roles for society as a whole. In cultures that rigidly adhere to beliefs about gender differences, gender schemas are likely to be even more complex. The influence of gender schemas may help explain why it is so difficult to dislodge gender stereotypical thinking once it is placed during childhood.

Gender schema theory may be the best alternative in explaining not only how people develop gender identities but also how gender stereotypes can be modified. Boys who view reading as a feminine activity can be introduced to boy-friendly books to encourage reading development and enhanced literacy (Sokal et al., 2005). Research on computer use and information technology (IT) suggests that there is a gendered digital divide, but when people are made aware of the influence of gender on their thinking about computers, gender schematic thinking may be reprocessed to be more aschematic. Two generations of children have grown up with computers as integral to their daily lives, but the centrality of computers to adolescent girls is less important than it is for adolescent boys. Coursework on computers and video game imagery are designed according to gender schemas of boys, in turn contributing to the underrepresentation of women in IT careers. However, when girls who identify with more traditional gender roles are introduced to website development with gender-friendly aspects, such as those designed around gender schematic themes of inclusion, social connectedness, and flexibility, interest in computers is heightened. Research also demonstrates that IT women have different gender schema than women in the general public and IT men have different gender schema than men in the general public (Agosto, 2004; Cooper, 2006; Lemons and Parzinger, 2007). When taken-for-granted notions about gender are examined, coursework can be modified to account for gender schemas in a productive manner.

Critique. As a cognitive model gender schema theory is subject to the same set of criticisms noted earlier, but two other also need to be considered. First, it has difficulty explaining gender schemas of those who consider themselves transgendered. Are transgendered people who identify only a few traits associated with their own sex "gender aschematic"? Gender schema theory rests largely on the assertion that virtually everyone is gender schematic.

Secondly, gender schema theory has difficulty explaining inconsistent developmental aspects of gender-related perceptions and behaviors. Gender schema theorists would predict that because early childhood is so rigid and inflexible in gender stereotyping the path is set for gender intensification to continue to increase. Adolescents, especially girls, however, are more flexible and less stereotyped in many of their gender-related activities and choices (Ruble et al., 2006). Environmental cues shift as contexts change. These appear to be powerful influences on role preferences even if they are inconsistent with gender schemas (Signorella and Frieze, 2008). Other schemas—such as those based on age, ethnicity, and religion— may compete, crosscut, or intersect with gender schemas as guides to behavior (Campbell et al., 2004). Gender stereotypes may be in place by adulthood, but ample evidence suggests that they tend to weaken over time (Campbell et al., 2004; Cherney, 2005).

Social Cognitive Theory

Notice that the criticisms of the theories of gender socialization reviewed here fall short in accounting for inconsistent messages children receive about gender from a variety of ever-changing sources. As a newer model, social cognitive theory taps into the strong points of all three theories to understand the degree to which children actively choose their gender roles (a key element in cognitive development and gender schema theories) and how much imitation and reinforcement are needed for gender roles to be learned (a key element in social learning theory) (Kunkel et al., 2006). As articulated by Albert Bandura, a prominent name associated with social learning theory, a social cognitive approach to gender socialization highlights the rapid expansion of knowledge from observations, the self-regulation of behavior once knowledge is gained, and the self-reflection that evaluates the selected behavior (Bussey and Bandura, 1999; Bandura and Bussey, 2004).

Social cognitive theory has been used to explain the connection between gender and the selection of sports role models. As predicted by social learning theory, girls and boys overwhelmingly nominate role models of their own gender. However, when girls choose role models from among sports figures, they often pick males rather than females. Social cognitive theory explains these choices according to the image of sports as a male domain and the level of influence wielded by men in the domain (Adriaanse and Crosswhite, 2008). Not only are girls more likely than boys to be outsiders, but sports from an outsider perspective makes their gender stereotypes stronger. Level of inference is also accounted for when children evaluate their parents on the importance of sports for health behavior (Shakib and Dunbar, 2004). Adolescents receive subtle messages about gender and sports from fathers and mothers and evaluate how their parents act out these messages. Do both parents actively participate in sports for the benefit of physical exercise? Do fathers participate more or less than mothers? Social cognitive theory might argue that gender stereotypes about sports communicated in families during primary socialization make fathers more influential role models than mothers for boys but mothers are more influential role models than fathers for girls. In this way social cognitive theory accounts for apparent contradictions in selection of gender role models for children.

When combined with a symbolic interaction perspective, social cognitive theory provides a good foundation for interdisciplinary approaches to gender role socialization. In emphasizing the importance symbolic interactionists attach to role taking, social cognitive theory may suggest that when children take on a variety of roles, including those related to gender, opportunities are available for behavior to be rewarded, punished, and imitated. Roles are also carefully evaluated to determine the relative influence of some people as models compared to others. Data on adolescents planning for the future, for example, show that they not only model parents and peers but also judge the level of influence of both in determining their plans. This research shows that they use both processes, but the judgment of the level of influence (symbolic interaction and social cognitive theory) is more important than the modeling (social learning theory) (Starrels and Holm, 2000). Congruent with gender socialization, same-gender parents and peers would be defined as more influential than other-gender parents and peers.

Critique. Of all the theories of gender socialization, social cognitive theory appears to offer the best integrative model to explain contradictory research results on gender related to the influence of a child's choice of role models. However, social cognitive theory has yet to provide answers to two important questions about primary socialization: First, when does "active self-socialization" occur, before or after the selection of role models? Second, which is more important in the process, the child's active choices or the availability of the role model itself? In other words, can a child internalize and act out beliefs about gender if there are no role models already in place?

Social cognitive theory does resonate with sociology's assertion that various subsystems, or agents, operate interdependently in the process of gender socialization. Social cognitive theory is a psychological view of social interaction that focuses on the individual and how social interaction shapes his or her feelings, thoughts and behaviors. Nevertheless, for social cognitive theory to be a good bridge between the disciplines, it needs to more fully incorporate a sociological view of social interaction, and account for ongoing social interaction in social situations according to how individuals change because of the interaction. How are gender stereotypes of adolescent boys altered when they interact with star school athletes who also enjoy activities such as cooking and child care?

Social cognitive theory offers very productive leads for explanations of gender role socialization, but it is not a fully integrative model. Such a model must incorporate key elements of social learning, cognitive development, and gender schema theories and also integrate the psychological and sociological approaches. Understandably, this tall order has yet to be filled.

AGENTS OF SOCIALIZATION

Agents of socialization are the people, groups, and social institutions that provide the critical information needed for children to become fully functioning members of society. Functionalists point out that if these agents do not carry out their socialization tasks properly, social integration may be compromised. Conflict theorists point out that these agents offer varying degrees of power, allowing socialization advantages to some groups and disadvantages to others. These agents do not exist independently of one another and are often inconsistent in the gendered messages they send. Later chapters will be devoted to each agent, but the focus here will be on those agents that are the most influential in determining gender roles during primary socialization.

The Family

The family is by far the most significant agent of socialization. Although social change has increased family diversity and created more opportunities for children to be influenced by other social institutions, the family continues to play the pivotal role in primary socialization. The family is responsible for shaping a child's personality, emerging identity, and self-esteem. Children gain their first values and attitudes from the family, including powerful messages about gender. Learned first in the family and then reinforced by other social institutions, gender is fundamental to the shaping of all social life. Gender messages dominate and are among the best predictors of a range of later attitudes and behaviors.

Do You Want a Boy or a Girl? The first thing expectant parents say in response to this question is, "We want a healthy baby." Then they state a gender preference. Preference for one gender over the other is strong. Most couples agree on their preference for male over female children, especially for a first or only child, a finding from studies over time conducted in the United States and one that holds true for most of the world. Males are stronger in these preferences than females (Baunach, 2001; Kemkes, 2006). There are important exceptions, however, to the son-preference finding when surveying individuals rather than couples. Reviews of recent data from the United States and some European countries, including gender-equitable Scandinavia, find that college women, first-time pregnant women, and middle-class young adults state a daughter preference or no preference more often than a son preference (Andersson et al., 2006; Dahl et al., 2006; Strow and Brasfield, 2006).

The key issue in understanding parental gender preferences is parity. The ideal for couples in the United States and much of the developed world is to have two children, one boy and one girl. It is well documented that couples with two children of the same gender are more likely to try for a third child than those with one son and one daughter (Andersson et al., 2007; Kippen et al., 2007). Parity is also related to sex selection technology (SST), which increases the chances of having a child of the preferred gender. Data on attitudes toward use of SST for a firstborn child show a preference for a firstborn son. When considering the gender balance issue, couples who use SST are more likely to try for a boy if they have two girls compared to couples who try for a girl if they have two boys. Such choices have a major impact on these families since the number of children is significantly higher in families with firstborn girls (Swetkis et al., 2002; Dahl and Moretti, 2008). And, as we will see, the decreasing son preference in the developed world does not predict its decline globally.

Gender Socialization in Early Childhood. Gender-typing of infants by parents begins on the day of the child's birth. Gender of the child is one of the strongest predictors of how parents will behave toward their children, a finding that is reported globally and one that crosses racial and ethnic lines in the United States (Parke, 2002; Sidanius and Pena, 2003). Both parents are likely to describe infant sons as strong, tough, and alert and infant daughters as delicate, gentle, and awkward, regardless of the weight or length of their infants. Fathers are more stereotyped in their assessments than mothers. Socialization by parents encourages gender-appropriate norms allowing separation, independence, and more risk taking for boys, and connection, interdependence, and more cautious behaviors for girls. While Dick is allowed to cross the street, use scissors, or go to a friend's house by himself, Jane must wait until she is older.

Gendered Childhood: Clothes, Toys, and Play. On leaving the hospital with their newborn, proud parents deposit their infant in a household ready to accommodate either a boy or a girl. The baby is also welcomed into the home by greeting cards from friends and family that display consistent gender-stereotyped messages. Indeed, gender-neutral cards for any age are largely nonexistent. Pink- and pastel-colored cards for darling, sweet, and adorable girls and cards in primary colors for strong, handsome, and active boys are standard. The first artifacts acquired by the infant are toys and clothes. In anticipating the arrival of the newborn, friends and relatives choose gifts that are neutral to avoid embarrassing themselves or the expectant parents by colors or toys that suggest the "wrong" gender. They breathe a sigh of relief when they know the gender of the child in advance so these selections are much easier. Teddy bears and clothing in colors other than pink or blue are safe bets.

Most parents know the sex of their baby before birth and decorate the child's room accordingly. If parents choose not to know the sex of the baby in advance, decorations for either gender will be chosen. But within weeks of the baby's arrival, the infant's room is easily recognizable as belonging to a girl or a boy. Until recently toys for toddlers were likely to be gender-neutral, but that pattern has changed dramatically in less than a decade. Manufacturers offer gender lines for almost all their toys, even if the toys have the same function. Girls and boys play with the same building blocks but in different colors; girls' are pink and purple and boys' are in darker primary colors. Infant girls cuddle pink—clad teddy bears and dolls and infant boys cuddle blue-clad teddy bears and dolls. When you inspect toy ads note that these dolls are virtually indistinguishable in all the features except for the color of their clothing. By age two children begin to reject toys designed for the other gender and select those designed for their own gender. By preschool, children have a firm commitment to own-gender toys and tend to reject other-gender toys and the children playing with other-gender toys, especially if a boy is playing with a girl's toy.

Color-coded and gender-typed clothing of infants and children are widespread and taken for granted. Pink and yellow on girls are sharply contrasted by blue and red on boys. Although jeans for school and casual wear are now more common than dresses, girls' clothing is likely to be in pastels with embroidered hearts and flowers. Since pants for girls often do not have pockets, a purse becomes a necessity. Both boys and girls wear T-shirts and sweatshirts. Boys wear those that have superhero and athletic motifs, and girls wear those depicting female television characters or nature scenes. Pictures of outstanding male athletes are typically represented in nonathletic clothing for boys and sometimes for girls, but it is unusual to find female athletes depicted on clothing for girls. Halloween costumes provide a good example of gender-typing in clothing. Gender-neutral costumes are rare at Halloween, with hero costumes highly favored for both boys and girls. Girl heroes are clustered around beauty queens and princesses, and boy heroes are clustered around warrior themes of masculinity, especially villains and symbols of death. Animal costumes are favored for younger children, but these, too, are gender-typed. The pink dragon is female and the blue teddy bear is male (Nelson, 2000). Gender-oriented clothing and accessories provide the initial labels to ensure that children are responded to according to gendered norms. If her gender is not readily identifiable by her clothing, an infant girl of three months may have a bow attached to her bald head in case onlookers mistakenly think she is a boy.

Dolls. A clothing–toy link carries a formidable force for socialization, especially true for girls who buy "fashions" for their dolls. Dolls for girls, especially Barbies™, and "action figures for boys" (advertisers will never call them dolls) are standard gifts to children from parents. Not only are messages about beauty, clothing, and weight sent to girls via Barbie™, but girls also learn about options and preferences in life. An older version of the doll "Teen Talk Barbie™" said, "You look great!" and "Want to go shopping? Okay, meet me at the mall." Barbie™ has held a variety of jobs, including flight attendant, ballerina, fashion model, teacher, and aerobics instructor. At the height of the women's movement in the 1970s she graduated from medical school as a surgeon and joined the army in the 1980s. She broke up with Ken™ after 43 years together but they recently reunited. Celebrating her fiftieth birthday in 2009, she has earned over $1.2 billion dollars (Towner, 2009). Barbie™ remains a powerful socialization icon for girls throughout the world.

A generation ago the male counterpart of Barbie™ was G.I. Joe.™ Although today G.I. Joe™ is sold mainly to nostalgic adult men, it was the prototype for subsequent action figures. The action figures currently sold to boys have larger body frames and are more muscular than the original figures. Girls equate beauty with Barbie™. Boys equate handsomeness and ruggedness with heroic action figures. Messages about masculine and feminine embodiment ideals are sent to both boys and girls through these toys. Combined with an entertainment-based youth culture, gendered toys are another link to lower self-esteem and the origins of eating disorders in children (Powers, 2001; Grogan and Richards, 2002; Thomas, 2003).

Toys and Gender Scripts. Toys for girls encourage domesticity, interpersonal closeness, and a social orientation. Boys receive more categories of toys, their toys are more complex and expensive, and they foster self-reliance and problem solving. Toys for boys are much more likely to be designed for leisure (race cars and trains); toys for girls are more likely to be designed for housework (ironing, cooking, sewing, cleaning) and beauty (hairstyling, cosmetics, glamorous clothing for dolls). As they get older, Dick and Jane acquire toys that encourage more imagination, pretense, and role taking. Pretend play is developed earlier in girls, but by second grade, boys surpass girls in imaginative play. Girls script their play and stage their activities more realistically, largely having to do with caretaking dolls and playing house. The major exception to this pattern is the formidable "princess" scenario that girls are increasingly embracing, often to the chagrin of their nontraditional parents

Source: © Baby Blues Partnership. Reprinted with permission of King Features Syndicate.

(Orenstein, 2006). Boys script their play around fantasies related to superheroes, dragons and dinosaurs, wars in space, and aliens. The toys associated with the scripts are rated as competitive, violent, exciting, and dangerous (Blakemore and Centers, 2005). Girls do have one advantage over boys in their toy selections: they are allowed to cross over and play with toys originally designed for boys (Green et al., 2004). Playing with masculine toys in childhood is associated with sports participation and early development of manipulative and mechanical skills. Since boys are not allowed to cross over and play with toys designed for girls, if boys are restricted in their play it is due to lack of encouragement in scripting activities suggestive of domestic roles, such as caring for children (no dolls allowed) and housework.

Both parents and children express clear preferences for gender-typed toys. These preferences reinforce the persistent gender-related messages that are sent to children through the toys. On your next outing to a toy store, note how shelves are categorized according to gender and how pictures on the boxes suggest how boys and girls should use the toys. Little Jane uses her tea set to give parties for her dolls in her room, whereas same-age Dick is experimenting with sports or racing trucks outside in the mud. Siblings and peers ensure that the children will play with toys or stage games in gender-specific ways. The gender-related messages, in turn, show up in differences between girls and boys in cognitive and social development in childhood as well as differences in gender roles as adults. Despite massive social change impacting the genders, gender-typed preferences in toys not only persist but appear to be growing.

Gendered Parenting Practices. As social learning theorists suggest, through the toys and clothes children receive during early childhood, parents send powerful messages about what is or is not gender appropriate. In turn, children come to expect that their mothers will respond to them differently than their fathers. Parenting practices thus vary not only according to the gender of the child but also according to the gender of the parent (Pomerantz et al., 2004; Friedman et al., 2007). By preadolescence, children expect responses from their parents according to traditional instrumental-expressive gender role stereotypes. Children as young as three years believe not only that their parents will approve of them more when they play with gender-typed toys but that fathers will disapprove more if boys play with girls' toys. Children expect mothers to soothe over hurt feelings more than fathers. They expect to have more time with their fathers for recreational activities. Household chores are usually divided according to gender, but mothers are more likely than fathers to encourage both their sons and daughters to take on chores that would usually be assigned to the other gender. These patterns of gender intensification increase as children get older (Leaper, 2002; Galambos, 2004; Freeman, 2007). Fathers may be more traditional than mothers in their stereotypes, but both parents have strong convictions about which gender is better suited to which activities. Parents perceive the competencies of their children in such areas as math, English, and sports in regard to their child's gender, even if these influences are independent of any real differences in the children's competencies (McHale et al., 2003; Marmion and Lundberg-Love, 2004; NSTA, 2007). Children may recognize the inequity in their parents' actions, but largely accept the behavior as appropriate to their parents' gender roles. This acceptance of stereotypes is consistent with cognitive development theory by suggesting that the development of gender role identity is linked to children's perception of adult behavior.

Gender of parent does not predict the level of responsiveness—both parents respond swiftly and appropriately to the demands of their children—but it does predict the type of response. There are clear differences between men and women in gender role expectations concerning child rearing. Children of all ages are seen more frequently with women than men. Girls do housework with mothers, and boys do yard work with fathers. Mothers talk to their children, are emotionally expressive, and stay closer to them more than fathers, regardless of the child's gender. Both mothers and fathers expect more risky behavior from their sons and believe that there is little they can do to prevent it. Mothers give daughters more guidance in safety issues and express disappointment for misbehavior that causes injury; they get angry at sons. Fathers are much more involved with their sons, a pattern that increases as their sons get older. They focus acitvities with their sons on instrumental learning—how to repair things and how to earn and manage money—and engage in more rough-and-tumble play with sons than daughters (Gleason and Ely, 2002; Mellen, 2002; Morrongiello and Hogg, 2004).

Today's parents are much more likely to support beliefs about gender equity and feminist values than their parents. A growing new generation of feminist parents are socializing the next generation of feminist children. Parents who are forerunners of change, however, face some difficult obstacles. This ideological shift toward equity is more strongly supported by mothers than by fathers. Fathers have less support for gender equity when they have sons only, but more support when they have daughters only. Feminist fathers may lag behind feminist mothers because the fathers tap into the gender differences that were part of their own socialization experiences (Risman and Myers, 2006; Blakemore and Hill, 2008). According to symbolic interactionists, beliefs about equity cannot fully erase these early family influences. In addition, children from egalitarian households—whether their parents are defined as feminist or not—are continually exposed to patriarchal families outside their homes, especially in the media. Until egalitarian behavior becomes normative throughout all social institutions, a cultural lag persists (McCorry, 2006; Friedman et al., 2007). On the other hand, we have seen that socialization is a powerful force serving both gender role continuity and gender role change. As beliefs about gender equity become more widespread, the next generation of parents should socialize their children in less traditional ways than they were socialized.

Peers and Preferences

Children transfer gender role patterns established in the family when they begin to form friendships with their peers. With family gender role models as a foundation, peer influence on children's gender socialization is even more powerful. Parents initiate the first peer relationships for their children, with these often developing into later friendships chosen by the children themselves. Two- and three-year-olds delight in playing with their same-age companions, and parents are not compelled to separate them by gender at this early age. As school age approaches, however, this situation is altered dramatically.

Activities, games, and play are strongly related to gender roles and become important aspects of socialization. These are easily seen when a brother and sister play together. When Jane pressures Dick into playing house, she is the mommy and he is the daddy. Or she can convince him to be the student while she is the teacher and relishes the prospect of scolding him for his disruptive classroom behavior. On the other hand, if brother Dick coerces Jane into a game of catch, he bemoans her awkwardness and ridicules her lack of skill. What would social learning theory say about the likelihood of Jane becoming an expert in catch? Games such as these are usually short-lived, dissolve into conflict, and are dependent on the availability of same-gender peers with whom siblings would rather play.

Games. Peer play activities socialize children in important ways. The games of boys are more complex, competitive, and rule-governed and allow for more positions to be played and a larger number of participants than games played by girls. Girls play ordered games, like hopscotch or jump rope, in groups of two or three, which take up less space, minimize competitiveness, and tend to enhance cooperation. Playgrounds shape the spaces of children, and boys are offered more space and earlier access to space for their games than girls. Small boys learn that intentional body contact through rough and tumble also gains teacher attention (Kelle, 2000; Kim, 2008). Both boys and girls play kickball, but boys play it at younger ages than girls and graduate to more competitive, physically demanding sports much sooner than girls. There are significant consequences of gender differences in games. When girls are weaned from sports and physical activities in early childhood they lose strength, are less interested in exercising, stay indoors, and watch television more than boys (Cherney and London, 2006). By adolescence they show some loss in bone density and are at increased risk for obesity, which can have severe health consequences later in life. An important early study of these effects bitterly concluded that girls' games "teach meaningless mumbo-jumbo—vague generalities or pregame mutual agreements about 'what we'll play'—while falsely implying that these blurry self-guides are typical of real world rules" (Harragan, 1977:49–50).

Later research does lend support to the notion that girls lose out in early skill development related to competition. Girls may also take longer to develop the ability to take on the roles of several people at once—referred to as the *generalized other* by symbolic interactionists—which is valuable in understanding group dynamics by anticipating how others will react in a given group situation. Complex games such as team sports require this ability. Yet this learning process may have negative effects for both girls and boys. The games of young boys do provide earlier guidelines that are helpful for success later in life, such as the importance of striving for individual excellence through competition as emphasized in American culture. However, boys may be at a disadvantage because it takes them longer to learn values such as cooperation and intimacy, which are also essential for interpersonal and economic success.

Cognitive development and social learning theory highlight the importance of peers in fueling gender segregation during early childhood. Peer group influence increases throughout the school years, exerting a powerful effect on children. When children interact, positive reinforcement for the behavior of same-gender peers occurs more frequently than with other-gender peers. Boys are mocked by other boys for displaying fear or for crying when they are picked on and applauded when they are aggressive. Boys are more tenacious in their gender role behavior and exhibit strong masculine stereotyped preferences through preadolescence. But boys must walk a fine line between displaying too much or not enough aggression openly since it is the very behavior that is likely to get them expelled from school (Smyth, 2007).

Children prefer to interact with other children who have the same style of play as their own. In preschool gender segregation is enforced by peers but high-activity girls originally interact more in games with boys. Over time gender resegregation occurs, but low-activity girls and and high-activity girls interact in separate groups. (Hoffmann and Powlishta, 2001; Pellegrini et al., 2007). Boys interact in larger groups and have more extensive but less communal peer relationships; girls interact in smaller groups and have more intensive and more communal peer relationships. Research consistently shows that early intimacy with peers carries over to higher levels of self-disclosure and trust between women, especially best-friend pairs (Fagot and Leve, 1998; Maccoby, 1998, 2000). The trust and openness that enhance same-gender relationships could inhibit later cross-gender friendships. Since gender boundaries are strictly monitored and enforced by peers in childhood, the worlds of male and female are further divided. Because they learn different styles of interaction, when boys and girls meet as teenagers they may do so as strangers.

In interpreting the results of research on peer enforcement of gender segregation and how behavior changes for one gender in the presence of another, keep in mind that the context of the peer interaction must be considered. In some contexts, for example, boys support other boys who are more communal and helpful. Like girls, boys do have high levels of approval for expressions of happiness and offer sympathy and acceptance for children who have physical or learning disabilities (Ferguson et al., 2000; Hepler, 2000; Sorber, 2001).

School

Family life paves the way for education, the next major agent of continuing socialization. The intimacy and spontaneity of the family and early childhood peer groups are replaced by a school setting environment in which children are evaluated impersonally with rewards based on academic success. School will play a critical role in the lives of both parents and students for the next 12–20 years. We will view the gender impact of the educational institution fully in Chapter 11. The intent here is to briefly consider its role in primary socialization. Regardless of the mission to evaluate children impersonally—by what they do rather than who they are—schools are not immune to gender role stereotyping and often serve to foster it.

Teachers who honestly believe they are treating boys and girls similarly are unaware of how they inadvertently perpetuate sexist notions. When Jane is ignored or not reprimanded for disruptive behavior, is encouraged in her verbal but not mathematical abilities, or is given textbooks showing women and girls in a narrow range of roles—or not showing them at all—gender stereotyping is encouraged, and Jane's self-esteem and achievement motivation decrease (Skelton, 2006; Brown, 2008). Dick discovers that his rowdiness will gain attention from his female elementary school teacher, that he can aspire to any occupation except nurse or secretary, and that he is rewarded for his athletic skills at recess. Unlike Jane, who may be grudgingly be admired when engaged in "tomboy" behavior, Dick is loath to even investigate school-related activities typical for girls, lest he be called a "sissy." A decade of research on students of all grade levels conducted by Myra and David Sadker (1994) brings this point home. Their study asked, What would it be like to become a member of the "opposite sex"? Both boys and girls preferred their own gender, but girls found the prospect intriguing and interesting and were willing to try it out for a while. As girls wrote, "I will be able to be almost anything I want" or "I will make more money now that I am a boy." Boys, on the other hand, found it appalling, disgusting, and humiliating. Comments from two sixth-grade boys suggest the intensity of these feelings: "My teachers would treat me like a little hairy pig-headed girl"; and at the extreme: "If I were turned into a girl today I would kill myself" (Sadker and Sadker, 1994:83).

Functionalists emphasize the responsibility of the schools to socialize children to eventually take on positions necessary to maintain society. Schools provide experiences that offer technical competence as well as the learning of values and norms appropriate to the culture. American culture places a high regard on the values of competition, initiative, independence, and individualism, and schools are expected to advocate these values. We have already seen how these values are associated more with masculinity than femininity. Also, from a functionalist viewpoint, schools are critical ways of bringing a diverse society together through the acceptance of a common value system.

Unfortunately, many schools unwittingly socialize children into acquiring one set of values to the exclusion of the other. Stereotypical thinking assumes that in filling breadwinning roles, boys will need to be taught the value of competitiveness; in filling domestic roles, girls will need to be taught the value of nurturance. Though both are positive values and both are needed to function effectively, they are limited to, or truly accepted by, only one gender. As schools begin the task of fostering gender-fair behavior in the curriculum and in school culture, differential gender role socialization harmful to both girls and boys can be altered (Chick et al., 2002; Sadker and Zittleman, 2007).

Television

Television aimed at young children is a commanding source of gender socialization. This observation is empirically justified, considering that a child may spend up to one-third of the day watching TV. Heavy television viewing is strongly associated with traditional and stereotyped gender views. Children are especially vulnerable in believing that television images represent truth and reality. Television is by far the most influential of the media. Television establishes standards of behavior, provides role models, and communicates expectations about all of social life. Children are increasingly using messages from television to learn about gender and sexuality—a pattern found for both genders and for children of all races in the United States (Cantor et al., 2001; Opplinger, 2007). When television images are reinforced by the other mass media, like movies, magazines, and popular songs, the impact on socialization is profound (Chapter 13).

Television Teaches. Strongly supportive of social learning theory, children as young as two years of age copy what they see on TV, with imitation increasing through the elementary school years. Television encourages modeling. Children identify with same-gender characters. Boys identify with physically strong characters, especially athletes and superheroes. Girls identify with beautiful models, girls who are popular and attractive in school, and plain girls who are transformed into lovely and rich princesses (O'Reilly, 2001; Scharrer, 2001).

Television is gender stereotyped. Gender role portrayals in shows that are deemed acceptable for children are highly stereotyped, especially female roles. Data from two popular shows for preschool children, *Barney & Friends* and *Teletubbies*, show some changes in more flexible gender role portrayals for boys, but that traditional gender roles are reinforced for girls (Powell and Abels, 2002). Even *Sesame Street*, arguably the most popular children's show for preschool children of all time, highly underrepresents female characters—human or Muppet™—and portrays males more than females as dominant and in roles of authority. In cartoons for preadolescents, male characters outnumber female characters ten to one. Females are portrayed more in family roles and are more physically attractive and sexualized than male characters. Cartoons influence girls in their beliefs about female roles. Cartoons are usually either all male or have one or two females, often in helping or little sister relationships. Many of you may recall from your childhood the lone Smurfette™ among all the other male Smurfs™. When girls are portrayed with boys in dangerous situations, boys determine the story line and the code of values for the group. Girls are defined in relation to the boys. Television influences self-image. On Saturday morning TV boys are more significant persons than girls, if only by the sheer number of male characters compared to female. This is bolstered by television's consistent and stubborn portrayal of female characters existing primarily as add-ons to males (Leaper et al., 2002; Nathanson et al., 2002).

Children's television is supported by commercials aimed at products for children, mainly toys, fast food, and sugared cereal. In the early days of television, advertising for children's items was targeted to adults. Today children are more likely than adults to actually watch the commercials. Marketing to the "child consumer" is a key tactic of the toy industry with age- and gender-linked ads designed to entice a specific niche of children (Pike and Jennings, 2005; Desmond and Carveth, 2007). Advertisers prompt children to believe doing without these toys or other products is an unfortunate hardship. Commercials are blatant in creating desires for toys encouraging domesticity and passivity in girls and high activity in boys; girls play cooperatively and boys play competitively and aggressively. Not only do these patterns show no sign of decreasing, but gender stereotypes are intensifying.

The entertainment industry has melded toys into television and the child consumer it increasingly caters to is getting younger. Toy manufacturers such as Fisher Price and producers of children's programs such as Disney have joined in creating a "baby market" targeting the 0–3 age niche. This industry defines babies as "early learners" and markets products such as Baby Einstein as "educational" and "developmental" (Hughes, 2005). As symbolic interactionists tell us, when these definitions are accepted, the product is approved as more than merely a toy. The fact that these toys are packaged and sold as "gender appropriate" is ignored.

Regardless of how gender stereotyped toys are, television succeeds in pressuring parents to buy "learning tools" that are also fun for their children. Those who resist pressure to buy products or find that the products children want are unavailable are made to feel guilty, by advertisers and children alike. Remember the frantic search for limited supplies of Cabbage Patch™ dolls, Power Rangers™, and Tickle Me Elmo™ by parents who feared a disappointed child during holidays or on his or her birthday? Picture, too, the angry exchanges we have witnessed between parent and child in front of the toy, candy, or cereal displays. Parents searching for nonstereotyped toy alternatives may feel demoralized when the offer of a tea set to their son or a truck to their daughter is met with resistance. Tantalized by television, the child's desire is within reach. The desire is likely to be gender role–oriented. The parent stands in between. Who is likely to give up the fight first?

SOCIALIZATION FOR GENDER EQUITY

Socialization is neither consistent nor uniform. It occurs via diverse agents at the cultural and subcultural levels. Yet identifiable gender role patterns still emerge, and children are taught to behave in feminine or masculine ways. But major contradictions also arise in this process. Girls climb trees, excel in mathematics, and aspire to be surgeons and professors. These same girls are concerned about physical attractiveness, financial success, finding the right husband, and raising a family. Boys enjoy cooking, babysitting, and cry when they are hurt or sad. These same boys are concerned about physical attractiveness, financial success, finding the right wife, and raising a family.

Androgyny

The socialization theories and research overviewed in this chapter strongly support the notion that views of masculinity and femininity need to shift in the direction of gender role flexibility. Regardless of how the various theories explain gender socialization, it is quite clear that they all agree that masculine and feminine traits are changeable. Ideally, then, socialization toward gender flexibility paves the way to increased gender equity. The concept of **androgyny** refers to the integration of traits considered to be feminine with those considered to be masculine. Large numbers of people can be identified as androgynous on widely used scales to measure the concept. Both men and women can score high or low on either set of traits or have a combination of them. People not only accept their biological sex (being male or female) and have a strong sense of gender identity, but also acknowledge the benefits of gender role flexibility. Gendered behavior does not disappear, but we adapt it according to the various situations and contexts confronting us and at the same time act on our own talents and desires. Parents who are identified as androgynous are less stereotyped about masculinity and femininity and offer a wider range of behavioral and attitudinal possibilities to their children. Many of these are the forerunner parents to the feminist kids mentioned earlier.

Critique

Although androgyny is an encouraging concept, it has moved more out of favor as applied to socialization for several reasons. It suggests that people can be defined according to a range of gendered behaviors and then classified accordingly. This in itself is stereotypical thinking. Media-inspired popular conceptions stereotype the "androgynous man" as feminine and often portray him as weak or ineffectual. When a woman exhibits masculine traits she is less likely to be portrayed negatively. Since it is viewed as redundant, she is rarely referred to as the "androgynous woman." Androgyny for many people is associated more with femininity than masculinity; thus it lacks the envisioned positive integration of gender traits. It may be masculine-affirmative for women but it is not feminine-affirmative for men. According to Sandra Bem, a pioneer in measuring androgyny, even if we define what is masculine and feminine according to our culture and subcultures, we need to stop projecting gender onto situations "irrelevant to genitalia" (Bem, 1985:222).

In order for parents and teachers to enthusiastically embrace a socialization model for gender equity, they must believe that feminine traits in boys are as valuable and prestigious as masculine traits in girls. Because of lurking stereotypes and the higher cultural value given to masculinity, an androgyny model for socialization has been less successful but a "gender-neutral" model has yet to be developed. Androgyny does recognize, however, that socialization into two nonoverlapping gender roles is not a productive way of meeting the demands of a rapidly changing society. Nor do such roles offer the best options for fulfilling a person's human potential. Agents of socialization must be altered to meet these demands. Consider this pronouncement when we view the role of language (Chapter 4), another powerful agent of socialization.

GLOBAL FOCUS: SON PREFERENCE IN ASIA

Level of economic development is strongly associated with preference for sons. In regions where economic development is higher, such as in North America and Northern Europe, son preference appears to be weakening. In less developed regions, particularly throughout Asia, favoritism for sons is bolstered by the poverty of the couple, women's subordinate status, the low economic value given to the work women perform, religious beliefs, inheritance norms, and naming customs.

China

In China, where son preference is centuries old, a family name may be "lost" if there is no son to carry it on. Confucian practices related to ancestor worship, which trace the family name only through male lines, combine with marriage customs requiring newly married rural women to move into the household of their husbands and inheritance laws keeping women economically dependent on their new families. Low-income Chinese women living in mountain villages express even stronger son preference than urban women who earn cash income, because they need their sons to provide for them in old age. Women are outsiders and remain so even after marriage, and women without sons may be abandoned by their in-laws if they are unable to carry out household or farm work. A daughter not only loses her name at marriage but is viewed as a temporary commodity (Li and Lavely, 2003; Ball, 2008). The Chinese proverb "Raising a daughter is like weeding another man's garden" attests to the strength of preference for sons.

East and South Asia

Son preference is pervasive globally, but it is strongest throughout East and South Asia, in developed countries such as Taiwan, Hong Kong, and South Korea, and in developing countries such as India, Pakistan, Bangladesh, and Vietnam. It persists in rural and urban areas and among all religious faiths (Yu and Su, 2006). A major shift favoring males in the average *sex ratio at birth (SRB)* is growing through-out Asia. The worst SRB imbalances occur in poor, rural areas in China, India, and Bangladesh. SRB in India and Bangladesh has worsened over the last century but in China it has worsened over the last three decades, traced to the introduction of the one-child policy in 1979. Consequences of this inflation for girls are profound. These include underreporting of female births, female infanticide, neglect of female infants and girls resulting in their premature death, and the use of ultrasound technology leading to sex-selective abortions of female fetuses (see Chapters 2 and 6).

In India and Bangladesh, female infanticide and neglect are associated with the economic survival of the family, which is dependent on the number of sons and the control of the number of daughters, who are regarded as financial liabilities. As in China, a rural woman generally moves to her husband's household at marriage. She is expected to bring money and goods in the form of dowry to help offset the expenses associated with her upkeep. When dowries are considered too paltry by the groom's family the bride may be tortured and poisoned by her husband or in-laws or she may commit suicide (Vindhya, 2000; Johnson and Johnson, 2001). After a long dormant period, dowry abuse is increasing in India. In many cases the women are doused in kerosene and set on fire, in what is supposed to look like a cooking accident (Narasimhan, 2000; Diamond-Smith et al., 2008).

Gendered Effects

In addition to the blatant human rights violations the artificially inflated SRB has huge economic and social implications. Because women continue to have babies until they have a son, larger families consist mainly of girls and have higher poverty rates than smaller families, which consist mainly of boys. Although larger families are more likely to be in poverty overall, it is deepened when girls face lower pay than boys when they seek employment outside the home. This economic issue collides with social repercussions of a serious bride shortage in China, India, and Korea. "Bachelor villages" are growing at alarming rates, particularly in China and India. These are populated by young, jobless unmarried men and few unmarried young women. China is estimated to have 50 million unhappy, unmarried men and the number is growing. This "surplus" restive population is being closely monitored by government authorities concerned about their potential for social and political unrest (Coonan, 2008).

It may appear that because women are viewed as objects—a commodity of exchange—the principle of scarcity would make them more valuable from a market perspective. The scarcity principle of supply and demand, which would put a premium on women, is not borne out by research. In Asian cultures where the SRB is highest and gender equity the lowest, the scarcity of women is associated with selling and kidnapping of young girls and women, keeping unmarried girls cloistered in their homes, and violence and domestic abuse by husbands and fathers. Fewer girls are available to care for the daily needs of infirm mothers and grandmothers, who usually outlive fathers and grandfathers. Because boys will soon shoulder more than the traditional financial responsibilities for their elders, elder abuse by sons is likely to increase as well.

Despite overall improvements in health care, education, and paid work for Asian women and outlawing fetal sex screening in China and South Asia, son preference persists and has dire consequences for the well-being of females. Socialization practices regarding son preference in much of developing Asia are strong and growing. Since these practices are in place for over half of the world's population, efforts at economic development and poverty reduction are severely compromised.

Summary

1. Socialization is the process by which we learn culture and become functioning social members. Gender socialization tells us what is expected cultural behavior related to masculinity and femininity.

2. Gender role socialization in children is patterned by important cultural factors, especially race and social class. Middle-class parents are more flexible than working-class parents. Children from Latino and Asian-American homes are generally socialized into less flexible gender roles than African-American and white children.

3. Four major theories of gender socialization explain how children learn gender identity, an awareness of two sexes, and the behavior associated with them. Social learning theory focuses on the rewards and punishments for acting out appropriate gender roles; cognitive development theory asserts that gender identity allows children to organize their behavior. Once they learn gender identity, they choose their behavior accordingly; gender schema theory, a subset of cognitive development theory, asserts that of all cognitive structures, or schemas, a child learns, gender is the core one around which information is organized. Social cognitive theory, the newest model, offers ways to integrate the other three theories by accounting for behavior in terms of imitation and observation, self-regulation and self-relfection.

4. Socialization, including gender socialization, occurs through specific agents—people, groups, social institutions—that provide children the information they need to function in society. These agents are interdependent and often send inconsistent messages. The family, the most important agent, provides the child's first values and attitudes about gender.

5. Expectant parents in the United States usually state a son preference for a first or only child. College women and first-time pregnant women in the United States and Europe, however, are more likely to state a daughter preference or no preference.

6. Gender of the child is a strong predictor of how parents behave toward their children and in the selection of the toys and clothes they give to them. Boys are allowed more independence, separation, and risk taking, and the toys they receive encourage these behaviors. Toys for girls encourage domesticity and social orientation. Girls have the advantage of playing with toys for boys, but boys cannot cross over and play with toys for girls.

7. The gender of a parent predicts gender role expectations in child rearing. Although today both mothers and fathers support beliefs about gender equity, the shift to these beliefs is much swifter for mothers.

8. Peer play activities are highly gendered. Boys play more complex, competitive games in larger groups. The play of girls fosters cooperation, intimacy, and social skills. Peer groups monitor and enforce gender segregation.

9. Teachers are often unaware that they treat boy and girl children differently, such as encouraging more cooperation in girls and more competitiveness in boys. Gender socialization in schools often inhibits learning both these necessary skills.

10. Television teaches children about gender in highly stereotyped ways. In cartoons, male characters outnumber female ten to one. In popular and acclaimed shows males outnumber females and are in more dominant, important, and active roles. Commercials aimed at children reinforce these gender stereotypes, especially showing girls in domestic settings and boys in aggressive settings.

11. Androgyny in socialization suggests that people can integrate femininity and masculinity in their personalities. People can be classified according to gendered behavior, but socialization into nonoverlapping roles based on that behavior is harmful.

12. Son preference has artificially inflated the sex ratio at birth throughout Asia. In China and East and South Asia son preference is associated with abortion of female fetuses and female infanticide, neglect, and abandonment.

Key Terms

agents of socialization 66	gender identity 58	social control 55
androgyny 75	gender socialization 55	social institutions 55
continuing socialization 55	primary socialization 55	socialization 55
culture 55	schemas 62	subcultures 56
	self 61	

Critical Thinking Questions

1. With reference to research on parental expectations for behavior, gender segregation, and peer play activities, explain patterns of gender socialization in early childhood from the perspectives of social learning and cognitive development. Which explanation better accounts for the research?

2. Through specific research examples, demonstrate how gender schema theory can help "bridge the gap" between sociological and psychological approaches to gender role socialization.

3. Based on your understanding of the theory and research on gender socialization, what suggestions would you offer to parents and teachers who want to socialize children into more androgynous and flexible gender roles? Demonstrate how your suggestions counter the negative gendered impact of agents of socialization.

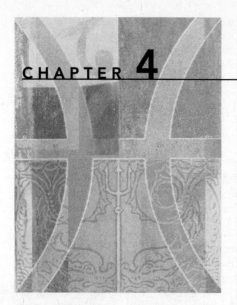

Man: An individual human; especially an adult male human

Woman: An adult female person

—*Merriam-Webster Dictionary*, 2009

GENDERED LANGUAGE AND SOCIALIZATION

Language wields a powerful but taken-for-granted force in socialization. Primary socialization literally bombards children with mountains of information and learning they must absorb. This process includes learning both the verbal and the nonverbal rules and complexities of their language. Language reflects culture and is shaped by it; therefore, it is fundamental to our understanding of gender. Language tells us about how the culture defines and categorizes the genders. In learning language children are taught that the genders are valued differently. However, since language socialization is a lifelong activity, we continually modify it in response to social change. As we shall see, it is the taken-for-granted part of language socialization that makes language such a powerful element in determining gender role continuity and change. For speakers of English, unless stated otherwise, everyone begins as a male. Decades of research on American English suggest that all people are male until proven female.

THE GENERIC MYTH

The English language continuously focuses attention on gender. The best example of this attention is when the word *man* is used to exclude woman and then used generically to include her. This is demonstrated when we speak of culture as *man-made* or the evolution of *mankind.* Other examples may be less clear, such as referring to a voter as the typical "man on the street" or finding "the right man for the job." Are women included as voters or workers? More often the word is used to distinguish man from woman, such as in the phrases "it's a man's world" and "this is man's work." The word is definitely ambiguous and may be subject to interpretation even within the context. Although it is unclear where women belong, it does imply that they are "part" of man. Sometimes no interpretation is necessary. At a wedding ceremony when a couple is pronounced *man* and *wife,* she becomes identified as his. Not only is generic language ambiguous, it is discriminatory.

It is awkward to change language to make it more precise. If *man* is supposed to refer to *woman,* then *he* is also supposed to mean *she.* Because English does not have a neutral singular pronoun, *he* is seen as the generic norm, with *she* as the exception. A doctor is he and a nurse is she. Most neutral designations are also "he" words. A consumer, employee, patient, or parent is *he,* despite the fact that women represent over half of these categories. Now we see that language is ambiguous, discriminatory, *and* inaccurate. The generic use of *he* is presumed to include all the *shes* it linguistically encompasses. It is quite apparent from research, however, that this is not the case.

People develop masculine imagery for neutral words, a pattern firmly in place by preadolescence. The pattern cuts across race, ethnicity, and social class, but males in all these categories adopt the pattern more than females. Generics are supposed to be neutral, but children and adults report primarily male, sex-specific imagery when hearing generic terms (Flaherty, 2001; Lambdin et al., 2003; Gygax et al., 2008). People visualize male and interpret the reference as male rather than male and female. When an encyclopedia states that "man is the highest form of life on earth" and that "his superior intelligence has enabled man to achieve things impossible for other animals," the response of a young boy is likely to be "wow!" while the response of a girl to the same information is "'who?,' does that mean me, too?" (Miller and Swift, 1993:73–74). A child's emerging gender identity is intimately connected to the way words are perceived (Speer, 2005). The belief that the word *man* is a clear, concise, and universal reference to mean person persists, but the mass of evidence is squarely against this view.

Inclusive Language

To encourage inclusiveness and avoid sexism, several suggestions are offered in dealing with the generics issue. Many writers use he/she, she/he, or s/he, or they explicitly note that both males and females are being discussed, using forms you will find throughout this book. Of these options, "they" is the most accepted. However,

To be fair

when the "he and she" or "she and he" alternative is used, people overestimate the rate of female pronouns—regardless of which pronoun comes first—and say the language is biased in favor of women (Madson and Hessling, 2001). Another suggestion is to offer inclusive replacements for outmoded terms. For instance, some colleges use "first-year student" to replace the archaic and noninclusive use of the word *freshman*. These examples offer the least cumbersome and most accurate solutions to the generic problem, but they are also the least accepted. People tend to oppose what they perceive as invented language—an issue we will return to later.

Titles and Occupations

Linguistic sexism abounds in the usage of titles and occupations. We write "Dear Sir" or "Dear Mr. Jones" even if we are unsure of the gender of the addressee, especially if it is a business letter. After all, business*men* are considered to be the likely occupants of these positions. The same can be said for chair*men*, fore*men*, congress*men*, news*men*, and garbage*men*. Physicians, attorneys, and astronauts are men. Nurses, schoolteachers, and secretaries are women. If either gender deviates occupationally and enters the other's field, we add linguistic markers (male nurse) to designate this surprising fact. The media, too, are grappling with these issues and remain extraordinarily inconsistent in use of generics, as a quick read of your Sunday paper will verify. Women are referred to as chairmen or chairwomen for charitable events or are referred to as "he" when they are business executives and grouped with men who are also executives. The nonsexist designations would be "chair" of the event or "they" to refer to all the executives.

Children confront this usage issue in their reading material. They may assign meaning to words quite differently than what the adult assumes the child understands. Consider a child's shock on discovering that a cat burglar is not a cat at all. Children also use linguistic markers in referring to females in traditionally male roles or males in traditionally female roles. What emerges is the idea of a female scientist, lady spaceman, or male secretary. Since reading is slower when gender and role names are perceived as mismatched, children may need these markers when they find a mismatch between what they see and what they perceive to be true (Sturt, 2003; Irmen, 2007). The stereotyped gender role thus remains unscathed.

When women enter predominantly male occupations, little attention is given to how they are named. A woman may become an engineer and be referred to as a female engineer, lest people mistakenly think most engineers are women. The male occupation becomes linguistically protected from invasion by females. However, when males begin to enter predominantly female occupations in greater numbers, a language shift occurs rather quickly. Although women are the majority of elementary teachers and nurses, men are rapidly entering the fields, making the use of *she* as a label a subject of controversy. It is now considered improper to refer to teachers and nurses as *she* when more than a token number of men enter the occupations. The same can be said for referring to stewardesses as flight attendants and waitresses as servers. Women will soon comprise the majority of clergy, pharmacists, attorneys, and physicians but the generic *he* is likely to be retained for a longer period of time when referring to them as a group. Another linguistic marker involves adding appendages or suffixes to words to show where women belong occupationally. A poet becomes a poetess, an usher becomes an usherette, and an actor becomes an actress. Women are defined as the exceptions to the male-as-norm rule. The linguistic markers are not necessary for men who already own the occupations.

Titles of address for women also reinforce the idea that women are part of men. The title "Mr." conveys the fact that the person addressed is probably an adult male. But for women, marital status is additionally conveyed in forms of address. When a woman fills out a form where she must check either "Miss" or "Mrs." she is conveying personal information not required of men. These titles define women according to their relationship with a man. This distinction historically served the purposes of providing information regarding a woman's availability, and pressure was on the single woman to think about marriage. To counter this titular sexism, "Ms." was offered as an alternative to both married and unmarried women who believe that their marital status is private information they chose to convey or not.

Yet language change does not come easily. When first introduced, "Ms." was ridiculed and maligned in the media as a radical, feminist invention used by women trying to cover up the shame of a divorce or not being married. Editors bemoaned its style while ignoring its precision. These objections have largely disappeared. Although married women and homemakers prefer "Mrs.," single women and professional women prefer "Ms." As a form of address, Miss is moving into linguistic oblivion for adult women; it is reserved today for younger girls. In written Business English "Ms." is used almost 10 times more than "Mrs." and "Miss" (Lawton et al., 2003; Fuertes-Olivera, 2007). Today "Ms." is a normative, standard form of address with a high level of acceptance (Wiser, 2007).

What's in a Name?

A simple one-word answer to this question is "identity." Whereas a name symbolically links us to our past and provides us a sense of self-definition, in many cultures girls are socialized early in life to expect the loss of their surnames upon marriage. A woman may also lose her complete name and be called someone different. Jane Smith becomes Mrs. Richard Jones. The new name and title alter the earlier identity legally, socially, and even psychologically. Mrs. Jones is now linguistically encompassed by her husband. Today the legal requirements for a woman to abandon her name at marriage have all but disappeared, but the belief that a woman should take her husband's surname is strong for both men and women. The change in status from single person to wife or husband carries with it other linguistic conventions. Newspaper articles often identify women of accomplishment according to their husbands' names, such as Mrs. Richard Jones, rather than Jane Jones. In dictionaries of famous people, women are typically listed with male names, even if the males did not contribute to the reasons the women are in the dictionary at all. How many of us are aware that Mrs. George Palmer Putnam is Amelia Earhart and that Mrs. Arthur B. Nicholls is Charlotte Brontë (Nilsen, 1993)?

The surname change at marriage has grave implications for women whose accomplishments are recorded under their birth ("maiden") names. These women can literally lose the professional recognition that impact their income, tenure, notoriety, and career choices. Contemporary strategies women use to offset such liabilities include retaining their birth name for professional purposes or hyphenating their birth and married surnames. Such strategies are likely to increase because research shows that college students have positive perceptions of both men and women who choose to hyphenate their names. Compared to other married women, those with hyphenated names are perceived to be friendly, well educated, and intellectually curious. Men with hyphenated names are perceived to be accommodating, nurturing, and more committed to their marriages (Forbes et al., 2002). Women students are more positive about hyphenation than men students, but the generally positive perceptions of both bode well for future shifts to more equitable gender roles.

Another linguistic dimension involves the ordering and placement of names and titles. Husband and wife, Mr. and Mrs., and Dr. and Mrs. give prominence to men. If she is a doctor and he is not, Dr. and Mr. would not be used, and if they are both doctors, Dr. and Dr. would not be a form of address. Men own the province of placement so their names and titles come first. An exception to this ordering rule is bride and groom. Considering that her wedding is treated as the most important event in the life of a woman, this is understandable. *Her* wedding day, the *bridal* party, *brides*maids, *bridal* path, and mother and father of the *bride* indicate the secondary status of the *bride*groom in the whole affair. His status is resurrected, however, by phrases such as "giving the bride away," indicating his new ownership of her.

Children's Names. As with occupations, children's names are chosen to ensure that people readily distinguish boys from girls. As you would expect, boys' names are ripe for the picking as girl's names but not the reverse. Popular boys' names for girls include Madison, Morgan, Taylor, Cameron, Dylan, and Bradley. It is also permissible to append a name normally given to a boy to refer to a girl, such as Paul to Paula, Christopher to Christie, and Gene to Jean or Jeanette. Female names are easier to identify because the last letters are usually a, e, or i (Barry and Harper, 2000). A boy's name will often be used to designate girls, especially in shortened form. Pat, Lee, Dale, Chris, and Kelly are examples. But when boys' names are co-opted by girls, such as Shirley, Jody, Marion (John Wayne's given name), Ashley, and Beverley, they quickly lose their appeal for boys. As expressed by a concerned writer for a devastated boy whose name has been co-opted by girls,

> In schoolyards . . . permanent damage is already inflicted on budding male psyches of defenseless . . . Taylors and Jodys. . . . It's not like little guys have names to spare. Even before the young ladies hijacked Bradley and Glenn, there were fewer boys' names than girls. . . . Girls names were more like fanciful baubles for the decorative sex. (Goldman, 2000:22)

The obvious sexism in such comments bear out the taken-for-granted assumption that the superiority of boys over girls must be preserved. The equity option is ignored.

Linguistic Derogation

English can be very unsympathetic to women. Women are typically referred to in derogatory and debased terms that are highly sexualized. There are several hundred such sexually related terms for women and only a handful for men. A few of the examples for females include *broad, chick, doll, bitch, whore, babe, wench, fox, vixen, tramp,* and *slut.* When men want to insult other men, they often use these same terms. Sexually derogatory terms are used almost exclusively by men and frequently in the context of sexually related jokes. Men who use and hear sexist jokes find them more amusing and less offensive than women, but both men and women judge the object of the jokes or the person who is sexually degraded as foolish, less intelligent, and less moral (Greenwood and Isbell, 2002; Sunderland, 2006). And consider the sexual connotations of *mistress* and *madam* and the male counterparts of *master* and *lord.* The word *girl* suggests both child and prostitute. It would be insulting for grown men to be called "boys," but grown women are routinely referred to as "girls." College students take for granted the "guys–girls" distinction so that males do not have to be referred to as boys. Linguistic practice regularly implies that males are complete beings who take on adult qualities, and females are childlike and incapable but at the same time seductive and sexual. Females linguistically retain these statuses throughout their lives.

Over time English words for women acquire debased or obscene references. Words such as *lady, dame, madam,* and *mistress* originally were neutral or positive designations for women (Henley, 1989:60). The masculine counterparts of lord, baronet, sir, and master escaped pejoration. Another example is the word pair *spinster/bachelor.* Which word would you select to fill in the blank: "One attractive eligible _____ is always invited to their parties."? When a man chooses to remain unmarried he is a "confirmed" bachelor. A woman may be an "old maid." Positive terms for an adult, unmarried female are unavailable, or, if available (i.e., bachelorette), are not commonly used. If women occupy a secondary position in society, stereotyped language continues to reinforce this placement.

Language frequently trivializes women. The phrases *women's work, women's place,* and *wine, women, and song* suggest this. When the word *lady* is substituted for woman in other contexts, implicit ridicule occurs. The nonseriousness of the "lady" designation is demonstrated by substituting it for "women" in the following: National Organization for Women and League of Women Voters and *The Subjection of Women* by John S. Mill *and Vindication of the Rights of Women* by Mary Wollstonecraft (Bosmajian, 1995:390). If the terms *man* and *woman* imply maturity, the term *lady* minimizes any woman's adulthood. A wife or child may be referred to as "the little lady" of the house. When the term woman is used in this context, an adjective often accompanies it, serving to bolster the childlike reference. Thus we have "the little woman." The male equivalent term is nonexistent. Until our linguistic consciousness is raised and such references are abandoned, women internalize a language that is belittling to them.

GENDERED LANGUAGE USAGE

We are socialized into the language of our culture and subcultures. Women and men occupy overlapping subcultures but ones that also have distinctive differences. Although overlap is much more apparent than even a decade ago, it is well documented that subcultures continue to be differentiated according to gendered language.

Registers

Sociolinguists use the term **register** to indicate a variety of language defined according to its use in social situations. Registers are gendered in that males and females who share the same formal language, such as English, also exhibit distinctive styles of communication, including vocabulary, grammar, sentence structure, and nonverbal communication. They are socialized into overall linguistic systems that are culturally shared but also into speech communities that are subculturally separate.

Female Register. Research identifies important aspects of female register that also highlight issues related to gender equity (LaFrance and Harris, 2004; Holmes and Meyerhoff, 2005; Stockwell, 2007).

1. Women use more qualifiers than men. These words usually hedge or soften evaluative statements: A friend is defined as "sort of" or "kind of" shy rather than simply "shy" to soften the statement. Another qualifier is when the sentence already begins with words that make it doubtful. "This may be wrong, but . . . " is an example.
2. Women may end a sentence with a tag question. When tags are used, a question follows a statement: "I enjoyed the concert, didn't you?" or "It's a beautiful

day, isn't it?" Less assertive than declaratory statements, tag questions appear as if she were asking the other person's permission to express her opinion or feelings. Use of qualifiers and tag questions may suggest that women are uncertain, tentative, or equivocal in what they are saying. They may be used as defenses against potential criticism. Consider the impact of the following statements that use both qualifiers and tag questions in the same sentences:

I guess this is correct, don't you?
This sort of makes sense. Does it to you?
I kind of liked the movie. What do you think?

3. Women use more intensifiers than men. Many of these words are employed as modifiers—adjectives and adverbs—that make up many word lists used by females: "This is a divine party," "Such a darling room," or "I think croissants are absolutely heavenly" serve as examples. Men do use intensifiers, but a pattern exclusive to women is literally to intensify the intensifier by heavily emphasizing and elongating the word. In describing a fine dining experience, for example, both men and women may say "It was so wonderful," but women will draw out and accent the adverb to become "It was so-o-o-o wonderful." An emotional overtone is added to a simple declarative sentence.

4. In those areas where women carry out their most important roles, vocabulary is more complex and descriptive than men's. Women express a greater range of words for colors, textures, food, and cooking. They are able to describe complex interpersonal relationships and emotional characteristics of themselves and others using a greater variety of words and communication styles that are adapted to the setting, a pattern found cross-culturally. Both parents talk to daughters more than sons but mothers' conversations are more interpretive for their daughters and more instructional for their sons (Fivush et al., 2000; Clearfield and Nelson, 2006).

5. Female register includes forms of speaking that are more polite and indirect. By keeping the conversation open, asking for further direction, and not imposing one's views on another, polite requests rather than forced obedience result. Women will make polite requests to others, including children ("Please answer the phone" or "Will you please answer the phone?"). Men are more likely to use imperatives ("Answer the phone.").

Both men and women share the same view of what is considered polite speech—by what is said and who says it.

Male Register. For both men and women, specialized vocabularies and communicative styles emerge from specialized roles and gendered expectations. Male register, like female register, has important implications for gender equity.

1. Men use a wider range of words related to mechanics, finance, technology, sports, and sex. They choose words related to objects, properties of objects, and to topics that are impersonal. Sexually related words are used much more frequently by men. Males in all age groups direct derogatory sexual slang to females ("bitch," "cunt") and gay men ("fag," "prick"). When males use homophoic language it is rarely challenged, especially by other males who are also present (Athanases and Comar, 2008; Newman et al., 2008).

2. Although the use of profanity in public by both genders is now normative, profanity, especially sexual profanity, remains the province of men. Men and boys do not mask profanity, use it more frequently, use it in more settings, and, compared

to women, are not judged harshly—and may be judged more positively—when using it (O'Neil, 2002; Coates, 2007).

3. Because men are more likely than women to be in authoritative roles, features of male register include being direct, succinct, instrumental, and personal. The personal feature may appear contradictory, given a man's tendency to emotionally distance himself from others. In the male register context, however, personal usage denotes language that is more informal and less precise. Men in leadership positions can be relaxed, friendly, and therefore more personal with subordinates of either gender. They can also be more direct and less polite.

4. Men talk more than women. Contrary to the stereotype of the bored man listening to the talkative woman, in mixed-gender conversations in a variety of contexts, research clearly indicates that men do the bulk of the talking. In classroom interaction at all educational levels, male students talk more and for longer periods than female students and are listened to more by teachers, a pattern found in the United States, England, and Canada (Julé, 2004; Swann, 2005). Men talk more than women opponents in arguments, political debate, business negotiations, workplace meetings, and trials. Where time is limited men are offered extra time to speak and exceed formal and informal time limits more often than women. However, the perception that women are more talkative than men persists. When men outspeak women by margins of two to three times longer, the men feel they did not have a fair share of conversation (Kosberg and Rancer, 1999; Tannen, 2001a; Sidnell, 2005). In turn, the stereotype that women, like children, should be seen but not heard is reinforced.

5. Because men dominate women in amount of talking, it is not surprising that communication domination of women by men carries over to what is talked about, how topics are switched, and the frequency of interruption. In conversing with women, men use interruption to indicate boredom and impatience and pave the way to a topic change. In conversing with men or with other women, when women interrupt conversations, they do so mainly to indicate interest in what is being talked about, to respond, and to show support. Gender role expectations regarding a man's right to dominate and structure a conversation are taken for granted by both men and women (Okamoto and Smith-Lovin, 2001; Litosseliti, 2006; Andersen, 2008).

The Language of Friendship

Gendered registers are important contributors to conversational strategies in building friendships between the genders and within single-gender groups.

It is common to see several women in a restaurant engaged in lengthy conversation long after they have eaten, young girls intently and quietly conversing in their rooms, or teenage girls talking on the phone, in text-messaging, or online for hours. When comparing talk within same-gender groups, women talk more frequently and for longer periods of time, enjoy the conversation more, converse on a wider variety of topics, and consider coming together to "just talk," a preferable social activity.

Gossip. All these talk-related activities may suggest that a great deal of gossiping is going on. The term *gossip* is used almost exclusively to indicate a specific kind of talk engaged in by females—talk that is often viewed as negative and pointless. To the contrary, research clearly shows that in all age groups, friendships are cemented between females when experiences are shared and dissected and personal information is revealed (Mandelbaum, 2003; McDonald et al., 2007). In gossip begins friendship. Gossip allows girls and women to talk to one another in their common roles, share secrets, and support the needs of each other as well as themselves. These high affiliation strategies serve to strengthen their friendships.

Conversation strategies of males are frequently defined as low-affiliation ones: using commands, threats, withdrawal, and evasiveness to get demands met. Adolescent boys, for example, are less concerned with the needs of who they are talking to than getting their own needs met, a pattern that carries through to adulthood (Strough and Berg, 2000; Leaper and Ayres, 2007). Popular girls will modify their behavior to account for the needs of an unpopular girl. When paired with popular boys, unpopular boys often use appeasement tactics, such as smiling or offering small toys as gifts (Murphy and Faulkner, 2000). When men want to encourage or cement friendships with a few other selected males, they play golf or tennis, go to football games, fish and hunt together, or play poker. These activities tend to discourage lengthy conversations but encourage time together and open up possibilities to discuss more serious matters. Whereas women use open, free-flowing conversations in bonding and appreciate self-disclosure, men often feel uncomfortable in this regard. Safe topics like sports and politics deter men from revealing details of their personal lives to one another.

Do women gossip more than men? It depends on how gossip is defined. If it is defined as talking about others then men and women do not differ. If it is defined as talking about others or oneself by revealing *personal* information, then women may gossip more than men. Men gossip about others and reveal personal information about the people they gossip about. But when men talk about themselves, they do so cautiously and minimize the amount of personal information revealed. There are no significant gender differences in derogatory tones of gossip. Although men gossip more about acquaintances and celebrities and women gossip more about close friends and family, gossip topics are converging. Both genders gossip about dating, sex, celebrities, colleagues, and personal appearance (Coates, 2003; McAndrew et al., 2007; McAndrew, 2008). As topics converge, it is likely that male self-disclosure will increase in their gossip with other males.

Except for the greater reluctance of men to self-disclose, any gender differences in gossip depend on which aspect of gossip is being investigated. If men "talk" and women "gossip" but are conversing on similar topics in the same manner, what separates the two is simply the gender stereotype associated with gossip. Gossip defines women but not men.

In mixed-gender relationships with romance as a goal, conversational strategies differ over time. At the beginning of a male–female relationship, men talk more than women, but once the relationship "takes hold," communication decreases. Women would like to talk more, men would like to talk less. As she attempts to draw him out, he appears to wordlessly resist, frequently using silence as a mechanism of control (Tannen, 2001b). Women fear that lack of communication indicates a failing relationship or that he has lost interest in her. Married women are more likely to identify communication as a marital problem than married men do (Chapter 7).

NONVERBAL COMMUNICATION

The language we verbalize expresses only one part of ourselves. Communication also occurs nonverbally, often conveying messages in a more forceful manner than if spoken. In addition to bodily movement, posture, and general demeanor, **nonverbal communication** includes eye contact, use of personal space, and touching. We will see that women are better at communicating nonverbally and appear to be more accurate in decoding nonverbal messages, but men may have an advantage in communication online.

Facial Expressions and Eye Contact

In decoding nonverbal cues, females rely more on facial information and exhibit a greater variety of facial expressions than men do. The accurate decoding of emotions is associated with better social adjustment of children, with girls doing better than boys, a pattern found in many cultures (Hess et al., 2000; Leppänen and Hietanen, 2001). Females of all ages can accurately identify an emotion more often than comparable males and have less difficulty distinguishing one emotion from another (Hall et al., 2006; Beek and Dubas, 2008). Although the context may explain why males and females display certain facial expressions, the nonverbal expression of smiling is clearly gender differentiated.

Smiling. Photographs taken throughout the twentieth century show steady increases of both genders smiling, but women are still more likely to smile and smile more fully than men (LaFrance and Hecht, 2000; Krumhuber et al., 2007). At all age levels, females smile more than males, a pattern that peaks in adolescence and remains relatively constant through adulthood. As a test of this, take a look at your high school yearbook. Smiling increases for females in situations where gender-appropriate behavior is more conspicuous (being in a wedding party) or more ambiguous (entering a mixed-gender classroom for the first time). In candid and posed photographs, females not only smile more, but are more rigid in posture, seeming to show a higher level of formality than males (Hall et al., 2001; LaFrance et al., 2003). Gender roles for females appear to offer less latitude for ease in situations where they feel that they are "on display." In these cases smiling is likely to be staged and less spontaneous.

Anger. Boys are taught to resist displaying emotion and to mask it in facial expressions. Girls are allowed to display their emotions more openly. The notable exceptions to this pattern are fear and sadness and anger. Parents allow girls to display fear and sadness but not anger, and they allow boys to display anger but not fear and sadness (Plant et al., 2000; Garside and Klimes-Dougan, 2002). What happens, therefore, when girls get angry and boys get sad and fearful? For girls, anger may be masked by crying, an acceptable outcome for young children in some settings. In contexts such as the workplace, when a woman's anger results in tears, she is judged as weak. If she does not confront the aggressor, she can be exploited. If she counters the anger with a verbal barrage, she is too aggressive. Compared to men, however, women have a greater repertoire of acceptable anger-coping styles and anger diffusion strategies (Linden et al., 2003; Guerrero et al., 2006).

For boys, anger is often expressed during sports, physical fights, or barrages of profanity, which may be acceptable for both younger and older children in some settings. For adult men, overt aggression in the workplace is certainly discouraged, but occasional outbursts of anger are often overlooked. There are few instances where males of any age can express fear and sadness by crying. The "big boys don't cry" reprimand is frequently used by parents and teachers. Peer disapproval for male crying is another effective mechanism of social control. For adult men, the expression of fear and sadness by crying in a workplace setting can amount to career suicide.

Compared to research on gender differences in anger and fear, people are usually surprised by data showing that women engage in more eye contact than men. The stereotype is of a woman who modestly averts her eyes from the gaze of an adoring man. In both same-gender and other-gender conversational pairs, females of all ages look at the other person more and retain longer eye contact, a pattern found in children as young as one year old. Men have more visual dominance than women—a pattern of looking at others when speaking but looking away from them when listening (Leeb and Rejskind, 2004; Hall, 2006a). Direct eye contact increases perception of power, whether it comes from a man or woman (Aguinis and Henle, 2001). When men look at one another "eye to eye," it is often in an angry confrontational manner. In countering verbal and nonverbal behaviors that may put women at a disadvantage in certain settings, women may capitalize on their ability to retain eye contact without expressing anger to gain prestige and power.

Touch and Personal Space

Because touch can suggest a range of motives—such as affection, dominance, aggression, or sexual interest—the context of the touching is extremely important. Men touch women more than women touch men, and women are touched more often than men overall. Subordinates are touched by superiors, such as a hand on the shoulder or pat on the back. But when female flight attendants and bartenders are pinched and poked or when a man nudges and fondles a status equal in the office, sexual overtones cannot be dismissed. The increase in sexual harassment cases calls attention to the fact that women feel threatened by them, especially if the "toucher" is a boss or superior. With the glaring exception of spontaneous displays related to sports, men seldom touch one another. It is even more rare if touching is associated with emotions such as fear, nervousness, timidity, or sadness.

Space Invasion. Men are more protective of their personal space and guard against territorial invasions by others. In his pioneering work on personal space, anthropologist Edward Hall (1966) found that in American culture there is a sense of personal distance, reserved for friends and acquaintances, that extends from about one and a half to four feet, whereas intimate distance, for intimate personal contacts, extends to eighteen inches. Men invade the personal space of women more than the reverse, and this invasion is more tolerated by women. The space privilege of males is taken for granted. The next time you are on an airplane or at a movie, note the gender differences in access to the armrests. In walking or standing, women yield their space more readily than men, especially if the person who is approaching is a man. Men retreat when women come as close to them as they do to women and feel provoked if other men come as close to them as they do to women (Payne, 2001). Even in their own homes, women's personal space is more limited. An office or study primarily used by the husband may be off limits to the rest of the family. Wives and mothers rarely "own" such space.

The Female Advantage

The ability to accurately understand nonverbal language for the sender and the recipient in a variety of settings can be of enormous benefit. In the workplace, female managers who accurately perceive emotional expression of their employees and then use this information to support them receive higher satisfaction ratings. Male managers who are more accurate in decoding emotional expression of their employees receive higher employee rating if they use the information to be more persuasive (Byron, 2007:721). Female supportiveness and male persuasiveness may suggest gender stereotypes, but the accuracy of decoding nonverbal cues that works to the advantage of women is the key element in employee satisfaction. In schools and in dating and romantic contexts, research clearly shows that men often misperceive women's friendliness as sexual intent, regardless of the extent of the couple's relationship (Kelly et al., 2005; Humphreys, 2007; Farris et al., 2008). A women who recognizes the misperception via accurate nonverbal decoding can adjust her behavior accordingly, offering a more satisfying, safer dating relationship as well as a better work environment. In any relationship, couples can be taught about the power of verbal and nonverbal cues to enhance their communication, even for topics that are difficult to emotionally confront (Parr et al., 2008).

In health-care settings, patients attended by physicians and nurses who adopt nonverbal behaviors that are supportive, affiliative, and empathic show better medical and psychological outcomes (Mast, 2007). Holistic health care relies heavily on accurate reading of the nonverbal behavior of patients that works to the advantage of female medical personnel and all patients. In recognizing this benefit, coursework for health professionals incorporate material on effective communication strategies, including understanding patients' nonverbal cues. Since women are socialized early in gaining nonverbal expertise, it is understandable why they receive higher grades in these courses than men do.

GENDER AND ONLINE COMMUNICATION

The explosion of Internet and other computer-based communication offers insights into how language is adapting to new formats. Whether this communication occurs via written form, such as email or text-messaging, through speech that allows people to see one another on a computer screen, or through virtual worlds, gendered interaction is occurring. Online communication and other rapidly developing forms of computer-based communication are hybrids of verbal and nonverbal—overlapping what is seen and what is unseen. The frequency of e-communication appears to be converging for men and women, but how messages are sent and received mirrors gendered communication in other contexts. Gender is a critical marker in how e-communication is carried out.

Men Online

E-communication is a boon for men. Internet communication has increased the overall communication of males in all age groups. Men are less likely than women to keep in contact with friends and family by phone or postage, but they are increasingly turning to e-mail and text-messaging for these purposes. Men's relationships can be enhanced with more frequent communication, even if its computer-based form is less personal—or perhaps *because* it is less personal.

In online written communication men prefer to use style and content that are impersonal. They use authoritative language and are more formal in messages to both friends and colleagues, regardless of the gender of the recipient. We can inspect our own work and school emails, for example, to demonstrate these patterns. In emails related to answering questions, discussing issues, or planning meetings, men send fewer emails to resolve the issue. Their emails tend to be terse and to end abruptly. Compared to women's emails, sentences are shorter and more direct ("Meet in the cafeteria at 12:30."). In online discussion groups men are less supportive and tend to respond more negatively to interactions (Guiller and Durndell, 2007). In online situations that are more ambiguous because of the lack of visual cues, men are likely to rely on formalized, prescribed language styles.

Virtual environments with visuals paint a different online picture for males. Men apparently feel more comfortable in virtual worlds where they can manipulate the environment and stage events. In an experiment using a mechanical device to mimic a handshake, for example, men liked people who mimicked their handshakes more than females did. For men, virtual interpersonal touch may be a gratifying form of social interaction (Bailenson and Yee, 2007). Gendered space and interpersonal distance (IPD) in the virtual world mirror the nonverbal norms in the physical world. Research on nonverbal patterns in "Second Life," a virtual community allowing for control and manipulation of avatars, demonstrates clear gender patterns. For both male and female avatars the closer the IPD the less likely avatars look directly at one another. However, male-to-male avatars interacting indoors with less IPD are least likely to look at one another (mutual gaze) than any other combination of gender and location (outdoor/indoor) (Yee et al., 2007). In both virtual and physical worlds males avert their gaze when their interpersonal space is invaded, especially when it is invaded by other males. Males as avatars or as "real" people express their discomfort by widening interpersonal distance as soon as they can. Males may be less accurate in nonverbal communication than females but when visual cues are present and when they have a measure of control over their space, interaction with other avatars in a virtual world appears to offer "relationship" satisfaction.

Women Online

We saw that women decode information and read nonverbal cues more accurately than men do. Nevertheless, when the nonverbal environment extends to the virtual environment, women's advantage appears to diminish. Men create the games, the rules, and the language used in most all virtual worlds. Virtual entertainment is based on masculine gender preferences. Women are much less likely to be socialized into the technological expertise that enhances their enjoyment of online entertainment.

E-communication for women mirrors their verbal communication. As expected, therefore, emails and text messages used by girls and women are frequent, longer, supportive, and affiliative. Women use more intensifiers, tentative language choices, and polite requests, and respond more positively to interactions ("Let's meet in the back of the cafeteria for lunch, OK?"). Women reference emotions and personal connections more than men, regardless of the gender of the recipient. In both style and content they are more relational and expressive (Colley et al., 2004; Palomares, 2008). Young women represent a slight majority of MySpace users (Chapter 7). In online discussion groups women post more messages and have significantly higher participation rates than men (Caspi et al., 2008). Since men dominate face-to-face classroom discussion, women may feel more at ease in the online environment. Overall, women are more likely than men to write the way they speak—both in the choice of words and in the manner the words are conveyed.

E-communication, however, lacks important nonverbal cues women rely on to enhance the satisfaction they receive from online interaction. Women's lack of comfort with the technology and the enormous amount of effort needed to compensate for the nonverbal void in text-based language may explain the decrease in the number of female participants in virtual learning environments

(Stokar von Neuforn, 2007:209). These factors may also explain why females use computer technology more for education and instruction and less for entertainment and diversion. There is a definite gender gap in perception of communication in the virtual world.

GLOBAL FOCUS: THE LANGUAGE OF JAPANESE WOMEN

The language of Japanese women has been recognized as a separate social dialect for a thousand years. Its origins can be traced as far back as the eighth century. One of the most important novels in all of Japanese literature, *The Tale of Genji*, was written in 1016 by a woman, Lady Murasaki, in women's language (Shirane, 2008). Although Japanese women's language today is an expression of language used in women's quarters for centuries, with young women at the forefront, it is being reconfigured in response to rapid social change in Japan.

Style and Syntax

Japanese women's speech is highly formal and polite, much more so than the polite gendered varieties of other languages such as English. Japanese women's speech exceeds the politeness norms in a language system that is already one of the "politest" in the world. Japanese women, for example, rarely use profanity. Politeness is also expressed by their use of honorific and humiliative speech much more frequently than men's use of these forms. Women use far fewer interrogatives, assertions, and requests, and construct them differently from men when they are used. These patterns are demonstrated in the media, in the workplace, at school, and even at home (Ohara, 2000; Ohara and Saft, 2003). In conversations, women speak of different things than men and say things differently when they converse about the same topic.

In addition to style of communication, Japanese female register has distinctive formal linguistic patterns in vocabulary, topic, grammar (syntax), and phonology (sound and intonation). Unlike English, there are grammatical forms in Japanese used exclusively by women and numerous forms for which men and women use entirely different terms. Rules of grammar governing how words are combined to form sentences may also differ according to the gender of the speaker. For example, the words for "box lunch," "chopsticks," and "book" differ depending on if they are spoken by a female or male. Special terms of self-reference and address through different sets of first- and second-person pronouns distinguish speakers by gender. Female speakers may avoid second-person pronouns ("you") entirely (Ohara, 2001; Endo and Smith, 2004).

Gender differences are most evident in Japanese gender-related syntax focusing on the end of the sentence. Choice of verb endings is particularly constrained by the gender of the speaker. Women are obliged to select endings that have the effect of rendering their sentences ambiguous, indirect, indecisive, and less assertive. With gender distinctions built directly into the syntax, women's speech is not derived from female applications to (supposedly) gender-neutral grammar as it is in English.

When styles of discourse are combined with the formal linguistic features of Japanese women's language, the image of a Japanese woman that emerges is one who lacks self-confidence and is timid, overly polite, formal, and tentative in her speech. The consequences of these speech forms are linked to social powerlessness putting women at a disadvantage when they venture into nontraditional roles outside the home. Japanese women who are in positions of authority may experience linguistic conflict when they use less feminine forms of even the polite speech used by men (Takano, 2005).

Consider the case of a mid-level manager in a Japanese corporation. As a manager, she cannot display linguistic traits indicative of women that give the impression she is indecisive or indirect in her talk. At the same time, however, she cannot be as authoritative as her male counterparts. She must not be too informal with employees she supervises or with other managers, the majority of whom are male. If she effeminizes (or masculinizes) her speech too much, she may be perceived as a threat to established business and social norms, which she has already violated by becoming a manager in the first place. Men must maneuver their language to account for the politeness of Japanese language as well, but they have much more linguistic flexibility. Japanese language has a much greater impact on the way Japanese women carry out their lives (Ohara, 2004; Takemaru, 2005).

Manga

Despite these patterns, language change follows social change and Japanese women are adopting linguistic strategies to deal with linguistic conflict. Fueled by media, globalization, and social diversity, women from a variety of social class and subcultures are using various formats to gradually defeminize traditional language. Research on *manga*, the hugely popular Japanese comics consumed by Japanese from all backgrounds, supports this trend. Manga is niched to serve all varieties of readers. *Shojo manga* targets elementary through high school girls, and *ladies manga* targets women in their forties and older who are in more traditional roles, especially home-based mothers whose lives revolve around family, children's schooling, and accommodating in-laws (Ito, 2002).

As expected, shojo manga pushes linguistic limits with discourse that is much less traditionally feminine than found in ladies manga. Shojo's characters use language defined as moderately feminine, moderately masculine, or neutral. When angry they may use strongly masculine forms. Ladies manga reflects stronger feminine forms but this, too, demonstrates that "unconventional" feminine speech linguistic changes are creeping. Gendered formal linguistics can be readily identified in written Japanese and manga for all audiences shows less feminization. As suggested below, what is written about, however, is still likely to mesh with traditional roles stereotyped by gender and age (Ueno, 2006:22–23):

LADIES MANGA
An irritated mother–in-law talking to her son: You just heard it, didn't you? Isn't it awful? Your wife yelled at her husband's very important mother.
An irritated mother talking to her daughter: Things like your childhood dreams often change, so for now, just study hard. Understand?

SHOJO MANGA
Daughter speaking to her friend about her father: He is just
a stubborn old man. I wonder why mom married someone like that.

Manga reinforces other communication styles that are rapidly emerging in subcultures of young women throughout Japan. Online virtual communities have "re-appropriated" women's language in enactments of "gothic/Lolita" displays of fashion and appearance. Referred to as "costume play" or *kosupure*, young women create subcultures that are linguistically and role distinctive, but definitely nontraditional (Gagne, 2008). The virtual worlds transfer to the physical world as young women congregate on safe Tokyo street corners in their online "outrageous" costumes and speak a language only they understand. On Monday morning they return to high school wearing their traditional, conservative uniforms almost indistinguishable from those worn by their mothers and grandmothers.

Research is needed to determine the degree to which women's language will be enacted as the youthful occupants of the gothic/Lolita subcultures and the readers of shojo manga get older. We will see in Chapter 6 that gender roles associated with marriage and the family in Japan remain quite traditional.

EXPLAINING GENDERED LANGUAGE PATTERNS

Explanations for the gendered language patterns revealed in this chapter can be grouped according to what sociolinguists describe as dual-culture, dominance, and social constructionist models. Each of these models is also generally compatible with one of the three guiding perspectives in sociology and as such is associated with corresponding strengths and criticisms.

The Dual-Culture Model

The **dual-culture model** argues that the interactional styles of males and females are separate but equal. Also referred to as the difference or separate world's approach, the dual-culture model emphasizes that because childhood socialization puts boys and girls into separate subcultures, they develop different communication styles. If miscommunication occurs, it is due to lack of cultural (subcultural) understanding rather than male power or deceit (Burleson and Kunkel, 2006). Girls learn language to negotiate relationships and establish connections, and boys learn it to maintain independence and enhance status. The dual-culture model avoids women-blaming or female deficit in language.

In important ways, the dual-culture model is compatible with functionalism. Functionalists maintain that language serves to bind people to their culture and that social equilibrium is helped when one language, including its nonverbal elements, is used and accepted by everyone. Functionalists suggest, therefore, that any gender differences in language are useful for maintaining this equilibrium and minimizing confusion in communication. The research on children's use of linguistic markers when there is a mismatch between stereotyped perception and reality suggests argument. Research on problems people have in comprehending when a pronoun does not match the gender stereotype shows that confusion is created (Kennison and Trofe, 2003). From this perspective, it is better to avoid the confusion than to change the pronoun. It also implies that when people communicate in ways that reinforce traditional gender roles, there is less possibility for disrupting social patterns.

Critique. There is support for the separate tenet, but not the equal tenet, of the dual-culture model. The model overlooks the cultural context of conversation and does not consider that along with gender, people bring with them other statuses that offer varied degrees of power that influence communication. Both micro- and macrolevel sources of behavior must be accounted for. The multiple statuses of race, class, and gender held by all people highlight this criticism. Stereotyped beliefs about style of speech are stronger for race than gender. When race and gender are connected, white males and African-American females are much more likely to hold their conversational grounds when challenged than white females (Lindsey, 1975; Smith-Lovin and Brody, 1989; Popp et al., 2003).

Research on housing suggests that rental agents have the opportunity to discriminate against people of color because they can determine race from a phone conversation (Massey and Lundy, 2001). A white woman compared to a man or woman of color has an advantage in this regard. However, social class may also be inferred from speech patterns. A poor woman of color may be more disadvantaged in her housing choices than men of any race. Whether the language differences stem from any combination of gender, race, and social class, they are not value-neutral and can lead to inequity. Separate is not equal.

The Dominance Model

Robin Lakoff's (1975, 2005) groundbreaking work was influential in the **dominance model**, arguing that gendered language is a reflection of women's subordinate status. Nancy Henley (1977, 2002) extended this hypothesis to nonverbal behaviors, including facial expressions, body movements, gaze, and interruptions. Compatible with conflict theory, the dominance model explains gendered language use according to the power differences between men and women. The structure and vocabulary of English, such as the accepted uses of male generics, have been fashioned by men, and they retain the power to name and to leave unnamed. Data on interruptions provide another example. Interruption is an attempt to dominate and control a conversation by asserting one's right to speak at the expense of another. The dominance model views men's interruption of women as the right of a superior to interrupt a subordinate. Female subordination is reinforced through their use of hedges, tag questions, and conversational cooperativeness. Gender differences are explained by socialization of girls into less powerful feminine roles that teach them to be demure, attractive, and aiming to please. Girls and women adopt language patterns that keep them from acting as independent or nonsubordinate agents.

Critique. Contrary to the dominance model, research suggests that differences in status do not explain gender differences in nonverbal behavior and that the gender differences persist even when men and women occupy the same status. For example, females still smile more than males and talk less than males, even when they have equal statuses (Hall, 2006b).

For verbal behavior, the dominance model's emphasis on the superiority associated with male speech and the inferiority associated with female speech implies that women are victims of culturally determined speech patterns that they may not be aware of or cannot control. Feminist reinterpretations of the dominance model suggest that women gain power by using gendered communication patterns to their advantage (Burgoon and Dunbar, 2006). For example, a greater amount of direct eye contact may be interpreted as assertive, with strength rather than meekness being communicated. Status equals look directly at one another. Status unequals do not. Women who want career advancement can adjust their eye contact so that they appear not quite as watchful, but still deferential, to their superior. A female executive in the boardroom adjusts her nonverbals—such as amount of eye contact—to the situation according to the image she wants to project. She is practicing *impression management* to highlight her (superior) executive status and de-emphasize her (subordinate) gender status. If men dominate women in verbal arguments women's visual behavior during the argument may be more dominant.

If the language of cooperation is more beneficial than the language of competition in certain contexts, then women's communication skills honed in developing friendships may offer an advantage. It is sexist to conclude that women's speech is weak just because a woman is doing the talking. If female register is associated with powerlessness, it occurs in a society that appears to value consensus less than competition, and connection less than independence.

Finally, social change in the direction of gender equity in other institutions is making its way into language. Since female and male communication patterns are demonstrating more and more similarity, the dominance-power explanation is losing research support (Aries, 2006; Kalbfleisch and Herold, 2006). Overall, this may bode well for the decrease of linguistic sexism.

The Social Constructionist Model

The ascending explanation for gendered language is the social constructionist approach. By highlighting how language as a symbol shapes our perception of reality, how reality is redefined by altering language, and how interpersonal communication is negotiated, the social constructionist model is embedded in a symbolic interaction view. There is much evidence to indicate that the use of masculine generics, for example, makes it difficult to actually "image" women mentally. The use of male generics gives more prominence and visibility to men. During the crucial primary socialization years when language learning occurs, children internalize views that contribute to the marginalization of women.

The key feature of the social constructionist model is its focus on the context or setting of the conversation and on the use of impression management in interpreting gendered language. It is clear that both women and men organize their talk via gendered norms but alter it to their advantage as they move between conversational settings (Eckert and McConnell-Ginet, 2003; Reid et al., 2003). Gender differences in conversational topics are largely determined by opportunities to express the interests of the speaker regardless of the power the speaker brings to the setting. For example, women may reframe negotiations to adhere to the expectation of politeness associated with female register, but they still get what they want out of the negotiations (Small et al., 2007). Research suggests that for moderated online courses, the constructionist model offers more support than either the dual-culture or the dominance models. Men and women use very nuanced gendered language that is manipulated according to the specific features of the online context (Hayslett, 2008). As we move into more multicultural contexts of speaking, social constructionists alert us to be attuned to not only gender, but also the backgrounds and cultural characteristics of all speakers. It is the flexibility and choice offered by various contexts of conversation that distinguish social construction from other models (McElhinny, 2005).

Critique. The very strength of the social constructionist model's reliance on the context of conversations and the impression management practiced in specific contexts makes it difficult to generalize explanations for gendered language to other settings. Generalization is a necessary ingredient for science. Research is lacking on the features of various communication contexts to predict how speakers will adjust their linguistic strategies as they move between contexts. In addition, contrary to social costructionistist claims, the harmful effects of gender stereotypes are not overcome with individual attempts at impression management through altering language. Gendered social structures are ushered into all communication contexts. To effectively attack such stereotypes, social institutions at both the micro- and macrolevels must be part of the effort.

THE IMPACT OF LINGUISTIC SEXISM

We have seen that language subtly, and not so subtly, transmits sexist notions that are harmful to both men and women. Language influences our perceptions of what is proper, accepted, and expected. When we hear the words *man* and *he*, we conjure up male images. When *she* is associated with nurses and homemakers, men are linguistically excluded. Alternative images remain unexpressed because they remain unimagined. Language supports a powerful "nonconscious ideology" (Bem and Bem, 1970).

Cognition and Self-Esteem

Research plainly shows that ambiguous interpretations of masculine generics not only bias cognitions but differentially affect the self-esteem of people who read, hear, and use them. Those who use sexist language in written form are also likely to use it in oral form. During primary socialization, boys internalize masculine generics that they apply to their expanding environment. Their own sense of well-being is linked to that environment. When girls begin to expand their environments, they have no such set of referents. They must adopt symbols that are different and separate from the symbols used to identify people in general.

Language learning also produces a double bind for women who are socialized into believing they must speak politely and refrain from "man talk." Women's language is associated with maintaining femininity. Whether it is an acceptable assessment or not, female register may serve to deprecate, ignore, and stereotype women. In turn women can internalize beliefs that they are lesser persons. Research on sexist remarks and jokes made by men suggests that women respect women when they confront the person who made the remark, but that men do not like being confronted. The typical responses to women who express their dislike of being the targets of profanity and degrading sexual humor are "Can't you take a joke?" and "Don't take it personally." With the negative repercussions that come with confrontation, women may believe silence is justified. Language learning for girls may be the counterpart for the difficulty boys may experience in gaining a sense of identity from incomplete information they are offered during primary socialization (Chapter 3). In either case, the socialization road is not easy.

Toward Language Change

The evidence that sexist language creeps into our perceptions and does damage to both men and women is strong. Yet despite this evidence, people who would fervently work on other gender issues, such as equal pay or violence toward women, are mystified or even angry at calls to change language to make it more inclusive. Similar to the type of ridicule that came about when "Ms." was introduced, media reports tell us that *he* is now a loaded word and that no one

> dares to show insensitivity to gender-neutral terminology in public, with people preferring to offend against rules of grammar rather than against women's sensibilities. Women should not be insulted but should remember that gender may be unrelated to sex in language. (*Economist*, 2001:20)

In this condemnation, rules of grammar are more important than how they are used against people, and women are denied any emotional response by being told how they are supposed to feel about the issue. Those who advocate for gender-inclusive language are often labeled "politically correct" in the media. The label sarcastically implies that people are required to change terminology on frivolous, inconsequential, and unreasonable grounds.

Formal Change. Attempts to introduce language change are also resisted when changes are viewed as artificially imposed rather than naturally evolving. Examples from linguistic history counter this argument. The use of *he* as the required pronoun for referring to a single human being of indeterminate sex came into usage during the eighteenth century in England and the United States (Curzan, 2003). Formerly, *they* or *he* or *she* were considered proper choices. The use of *they* as a plural word to identify a single entity was disdained by several powerful educators and self-styled language reformers, who were able to establish *he* as the rightful substitute. In 1850 the British Parliament passed a law declaring that "in all acts, words importing the masculine gender shall be deemed and taken to include females" (Miller, 1994:268). In both instances language change occurred by fiat, not through "natural" evolution. Although the earlier usage may not have been as grammatically sound, it was certainly more accurate. It also created a great deal of interpretive problems. Today we have a term that is presumed to be both generic (*he* = *he* and *she*) and nongeneric (*he* = *he*). The quick acceptance of the generic rested on cultural definitions that gave males more worth than females. In order to make language gender-neutral today, it is necessary to challenge the taken-for-granted belief that males are regarded more highly than females. Such challenges are met with resistance.

Gradual Change. On the positive side, there is gradual but steady progress in efforts to make language more inclusive and gender equitable. Recognition of the harm of sexist language is widespread. At the macrolevel, people are more supportive for incorporating inclusive language in government, schools, and media. Female teachers are leading the way as agents of change, selecting reading material with inclusive language, offering students ways to avoid the gender-exclusive generic "he" in their writing (Pauwels and Winter, 2006). Organizations, professions, and academic disciplines are adopting inclusive language standards in their style guides, publications, and websites (Amare, 2007).

At the microlevel, although gender differences cut across context on many linguistic behaviors, girls and boys are more alike than different. Differences that do exist, especially in nonverbal communication, are differences in degree—not in kind (Dindia, 2006). Gender differences in conversational topics persist but are getting smaller over time. The language of consensus and cooperation is moving into the workplace; its benefit for both employee satisfaction and company profit is increasingly recognized. Men are displaying more self-disclosing nonverbal behaviors, such as hugging another man as a greeting rather than using the mechanical handshake of the past. Some media portrayals of men support this contention. Watch a night of Jay Leno, Conan O'Brien, or David Letterman as confirmation. Such behaviors are approved by both men and women and improve the rating of the show and the likability of male television hosts.

News media have powerful influences on public perception. Broadcasters now routinely report on the "men and women" soldiers or "service members" serving the United States. Ironically this neutral designation explicitly calls attention to gender and marks the fact that both men and women are in harm's way. Written and broadcast media are also much less likely than even a decade ago to use the generic "he" to refer to politicians, journalists, scientists, and world leaders. There are simply too many exceptions to expect audiences to overlook glaring noninclusive language. And for the trekkies still in abundance, the following is offered:

> . . . to boldly go where no *man* has gone before.
>
> —Capt. James T. Kirk, *Star Trek*

> . . . to boldly go where no *one* has gone before.
>
> —Capt. Jean-Luc Picard, *Star Trek, The Next Generation*

> . . . I don't like being called "sir" . . . I prefer "Captain."
>
> —Capt. Kathryn Janeway, *Star Trek, Voyager*

Summary

1. Research shows that the generic use of words such as *man* and *he* is ambiguous, discriminatory, and inaccurate. Inclusive replacements are suggested to counter this usage.

2. Linguistic sexism in titles and occupations abounds. Children often use linguistic gender markers, such as lady spaceman, when they see a mismatch between what they see and what they perceive to be true.

3. Customs about names are highly gendered. On marriage women are expected to take their husbands' last names. Children's names ensure that boys and girls are distinguished. It is common for girls to take or append boys' names but not the reverse.

4. There are several hundred English words that refer to women in derogatory or debased and obscene ways. Over time words for women that were originally neutral acquire debased references.

5. People use language according to gendered registers. Females use a register with more qualifiers, tag questions, intensifiers, and politeness. Males use a register with more profanity, directness, and imperatives. Males outtalk females and interrupt females more than females interrupt males. These patterns are largely taken for granted by both men and women.

6. Conversational strategies for females are high affiliation ones used for intimacy, rapport, and cementing friendship. Conversational strategies for males are low affiliation ones used to get demands met. If romance is a factor in mixed-gender conversations, men initially outtalk women, but later talk less and use silence as a control mechanism.

7. In nonverbal communication females rely on facial information and decode emotions much better than males. Females smile more and are allowed to display sadness and fear but not anger. Males can display anger more, but not sadness and fear. Men touch women more than women touch men, and women are touched more than men overall. Men invade the personal space of women more than the reverse. Men are provoked when other men come as close to them as they do to women.

8. Online communication mirrors nonverbal behavior. Men write online using authoritative language. In virtual environments men are more comfortable when they manipulate avatars and stage events. E-communication is more frequent, longer, and supportive for females compared to use by males. Females have an online communication advantage but are less likely than males to use computer technology for entertainment.

9. The language of Japanese women is a separate social dialect that differs by vocabulary, topics, grammar, and phonology. Women are often defined as being timid and lacking self-confidence. Led by young women, linguistic strategies through formats like manga are being adapted to counter these images.

10. The dual-culture model of language is compatible with functionalism and asserts that the language styles of males and females are separate but equal. The dominance model is compatible with conflict theory and asserts that gendered language reflects women's subordinate status. The social constructionist model focusing on the context of conversation appears to offer the strongest explanation. Although it is compatible with symbolic interaction, it has difficulty generalizing results of gendered language use from one context to another.

11. Language transmits sexist notions but people often resist changing language to counter sexism. With media influence, progress is being made, however, to make language more gender equitable.

Key Terms

dominance model 95

dual-culture model 94

nonverbal
communication 87

register 84

Critical Thinking Questions

1. With reference to the gender patterns of generics, titles, naming, derogation, and registers, demonstrate how language is a potent agent of gender role socialization. Which sociological theory do you think best accounts for these patterns? Justify your choice.

2. Explain how both gendered verbal and nonverbal language cement relationships between women but inhibit close relationships between men. How can gender socialization provide more opportunities for crossing the linguistic boundaries important for bringing men and women together?

3. How can sociological and linguistic perspectives (dominance, dual-culture, social constructionist) combine to explain gendered verbal and nonverbal language?

CHAPTER 5

WESTERN HISTORY AND THE CONSTRUCTION OF GENDER ROLES

Men have had every advantage of us telling their own story. Education has been theirs in so much higher a degree; the pen has been in their hands.

—Jane Austen, *Persuasion*, 1818

Echoing Jane Austen's sentiments, in 1801 an anonymous author wrote in the *Female Advocate*, an American publication: "Why ought the one half of mankind, to vault and lord it over the other?" Reflecting an egalitarian model far ahead of its time, these writers identified a critical need to explore the other half of humankind. Distinguished historian Gerda Lerner extends this message to contemporary scholars. She suggests that the recognition that women had been denied their own history "came to many of us as a staggering flash of insight, which altered our consciousness irretrievably" (Lerner, 1996:8). This insight reverberated throughout the academy, and as a result, the field of women's history rapidly expanded.

101

It is impossible to understand the present without reference to the past. Historians say that they search for a "usable past," for a record that will clarify and give meaning to the present (Carlson, 1990:81). In order to explain the differential status of women and men in contemporary society, it is necessary to examine the impact of powerful historical forces constructing gendered attitudes. Scholarly work is scrutinizing the past with the goal of uncovering the hidden elements of a woman's history. As we shall see, such a history is vastly different from centuries of discourse that highlighted the proper roles of women in society.

These discourses date back to the earliest writings of the Greek philosophers and center on debates about women's place, women's souls, and women's suitability for domestic functions. Writings of this type were used, and often continue to be used, to justify a patriarchal status quo. What is clear is that the centuries of debate on "women's themes" do not constitute a women's history. As pioneer women's historian Mary Ritter Beard asserts, in the 2,500 years history has been written, most male writers overlooked the histories of females. In historical writing, the whole of human experience has been dominated by the political, economic, and military exploits of an elite, powerful group of men. Through the historical glimpses in this chapter, we will find that throughout history women have assumed a multitude of critical domestic and extradomestic roles, many of which were previously ignored or relegated to inconsequential historical footnotes.

PLACING WOMEN IN HISTORY

The revitalized women's movement of the 1960s provided the catalyst for the independent field of women's history to emerge. Although there is general agreement as to what is *not* women's history, scholars do not agree on what the approach, content, and boundaries of the field should or must include. There is broad consensus, however, that because women and men experience the world around them in qualitatively different ways, the starting point must be on those very experiences. Women's history asks why women have a profoundly different historical experience than men.

Because women have basically been left out of historical writing, the first attempts at reclaiming their historical place centered on combing the chronicles for appropriate figures to demonstrate that female notables of similar authority and ability to males existed. If there was Peter the Great, there was also Katherine the Great. Referred to as **compensatory history**, this approach chronicles the lives of exceptional, even deviant, women and does not provide much information about the impact of women's activities to society in general. Another track is **contribution history**, documenting women's contributions to specific social movements. Their activities, however, are judged not only by their effects on the movement but also by standards defined by men. Lerner suggests that we can certainly take pride in the achievements of notable women, but these kinds of histories do not describe the experience of the masses of women who still remain invisible to the historical record.

If females are peripheral in history, then some groups of females are even more peripheral. Both compensatory and contribution history parallel historical standards that, until recently, also ignored society's *nonelites*—the men and women of classes and races defined as marginal to society. An inclusive approach to the past must account for their lives and cultures. A balanced history makes visible women and other marginalized groups and, in turn, affirms their identity.

The Gender, Race, and Class Link in History

Despite the fact that the relation of gender to power is the foundation of women's history, African-American and Latino women historians are reluctant to use a gender-based male/female dichotomy that falsely homogenizes women. The critical intersection of gender, race, and class must be in the historical foreground. Women's history is again being reconceptualized to understand the power relations between men and women and between the races and classes of women. Related to this is the concern that when the historical experiences of women of color become chronicled, they may be acknowledged according to race, yet within another dichotomy—people of color versus white. Other elements such as sexual orientation or ethnicity, however, are still missing. A multicultural framework also should be adopted because it explores simultaneously the interplay of many races and cultures and provides what may be the only way to organize a truly inclusive history of women (Ruiz, 2008). As women's history becomes both more sophisticated and mainstreamed, feminist scholars must account for all these dimensions.

Historical Themes about Women

It is impossible to provide a full historical reckoning of women's history in this chapter. The intent here is to overview key historical periods important in influencing attitudes and subsequent behavior concerning gender. The focus is Western society and the paths that lead to the gender roles of American women and men. As mentioned in the first chapter, history illustrates the impact of *misogyny*, the disdain and contempt of women, that propels their oppression. This reflects the first of two important themes of women's history to be overviewed. The first is the theme of patriarchy, and it relates to the power of men over women and the subjection and victimization of women. This theme is central to all feminist scholarship on women, regardless of discipline.

Countering the women-as-victim approach, the second theme explores the resistance of women to patriarchy, focusing on stories of courage, survival, and achievement. This alternative view indicates that although women's history is still unfolding, it has issued a formidable challenge to traditional thinking on gender roles. Feminist historical scholarship has challenged gendered dichotomies, related not only to race and class, but also to nature versus nurture, work versus family, and private versus public spheres of men and women (Bock, 2003). Similar to feminist scholarship in sociology, this theme reflects interdisciplinary elements in the field of *social history*. This field employs theories and methods of sociology to understand the linkage between social and historical patterns. I suggest an additional dichotomy— unicultural versus multicultural. This dichotomy reflects the second theme and considers how gender–race–class links to other cultural components, such as region and religion. Culture is used in the broadest sense to highlight diversity and to provide for more inclusiveness in women's historical record. Many of these cultural components will be explored from a global perspective in Chapter 6.

This approach has several objectives. First, the roots of patriarchy will be discovered in a format that is manageable. Second, misconceptions about the roles of women and attitudes toward these roles will become evident. These misconceptions are often at the root of current debates about gender and social change. Third, it is a history of "most women," a massive group whose contributions to their societies and whose response to the multiple oppressions they faced have been overlooked historically. This is the perspective of social history, in that it addresses social change by connecting larger social structures with everyday life and experiences (Elliott, 1994:45). Finally, this overview has a consciousness-raising objective. A discovery of an alternative historical account allows us to become aware of our culturally determined prejudices and stereotypes. *Her* story allows for a balance to the historical record.

CLASSICAL SOCIETIES

The foundation of Western culture is most often traced to the Greek and Roman societies of classical antiquity. Western civilization is rooted in the literature, art, philosophy, politics, and religion of a time that extends from the Bronze Age (3000–1200 B.C.E.) through the reign of Justinian (565 C.E.). The period between 800 B.C.E. and 600 C.E. witnessed spectacular achievements for humanity. With the achievements came ideological convictions that persist in modified form today. The dark side of classical societies was laced with war, slavery, deadly competitions, and a brutal existence for much of the population. Inhabiting another portion of this cordoned-off world was democracy, literacy, grace, and beauty. These opposites serve as a framework from which to view the role of women. Like the societies themselves, the evidence concerning women's roles is also contradictory. This contradictory evidence must be viewed in light of the fact that no authentic historical voice of classical woman survived into the Renaissance (Spongberg, 2002). What we know about women and gender relationships in these societies is almost entirely from sources written by men.

The Glory That Was Greece

The Greek view of women varies according to the time and place involved. Greek literature is replete with references to the matriarchal society of Amazons. Though shrouded in mystery, Greek mythology saw the Amazons as female warriors, capable with a bow, who had little need of men except as sexual partners. Greek heroes were sent to the distant land on the border of the barbarian world to test their strength against the Amazons. Because the Amazons invariably lost and eventually were raped by, or married to, the heroes sent to defeat them, some feminist historians suggest these myths are used to reinforce beliefs about the inevitability of patriarchy. Too much evidence exists, however, to dismiss the stories outright (Geary, 2006). We know that throughout Asia Minor and the Mediterranean during this period there are innumerable references to physically strong women who were leaders and soldiers. The admiration for the skills of these warrior women is used to support the belief that ancient Greek women were held in higher esteem than women of later times.

Partnership. Archaeological material from the Neolithic to the Early Bronze Age period immediately predating the birth of Greek civilization provides substantial evidence of matrilineal inheritance, female creator images, the sexual freedom of women, the goddess as supreme deity, and the power of priestesses and queens (Joyce, 2008; Mina, 2008). Some contend that these ancient societies show neither matriarchy nor patriarchy as the norm. In this view, the inference that if women have high status, then men must inevitably have low status does not necessarily follow. A generally egalitarian or partnership society is also possible.

The egalitarian zenith was reached in the goddess-worshipping culture of Minoan Crete. It is defined by cultural historians as a high civilization because of its art, social complexity, peaceful prosperity, and degree of technological sophistication. The social structure of Minoan Crete conformed to a partnership model, with a key part of that partnership being a free and equal sexual relationship between men and women (Eisler, 1995b). At the birth of civilization women enjoyed more freedom, including sexual freedom, and less restraint on their modesty. Interaction and unity rather than separation and isolation may describe the gender norms of the time (Stikker, 2002; Knoblauch, 2007). The mythology of such cultures points to the absence of warfare, private property, class structure, violence, and rape. Referred to as the Golden Age, the mythology bolsters the view of a society where stratification based on gender was largely unknown. Evidence from the Amazonian myths through to Minoan Crete does not necessarily suggest that matriarchy existed, but it does suggest plausible alternatives to patriarchy. Claims about women's power in prehistory remain contentious (Eller, 2000). Some claim that that patriarchy is inevitable today because it was inevitable throughout history. Regardless of historical accuracy, however, images of women in powerful, respected roles and of men and women working together as partners prove empowering to all women.

Over time, a *matrilineal* system tracing descent from the female line was replaced by a patrilineal system. Goddesses who dominated the ancient world and then lost their central position as gods were added to religious imagery (Chapter 12). The mother of the later gods may have been an earlier goddess (Munn, 2006). Maternal religion declined as patriarchal theology was grafted onto it. Patriarchy eventually prevailed. Patriarchy did not completely dislodge the revered goddess from later Greek mythology. Religion was the realm where the women of ancient Greece maintained a degree of power and prestige.

Oppression. The Amazon legends and goddess images perpetuated the belief that Greece revered women. Except for religion, however, the Greek world saw women as inferior in political, social, and legal realms. Plato called for girls to be educated in the same manner as boys with equal opportunities open to them to become rulers, believing that a superior woman is better than an inferior man. In the *Republic* he stated, "There is not one of those pursuits by which the city is ordered which belongs to women as women, or to men as men; but natural aptitudes are equally distributed in both kinds of creatures." Alongside his supposed enlightened image of women, however, is Plato's disdain and antipathy of women. In championing the democratic state, Plato was a pragmatist as well as a misogynist. He believed an inferior class of uneducated women might work against the principles of democracy, so he appeared to champion the emancipation of women. Women may "naturally participate in all occupations," Plato continues, "but in all women are weaker than men." Women were excluded from his academy and no woman speaks in his dialogues. Indeed, women's sexual nature could distract men from reason and pursuit of knowledge so men and women must exist in separate worlds. In the end Plato's emancipated women were likely to be illiterate, isolated, and oppressed.

It is Aristotle who is more representative of the Greek view of women. In *Politics*, Aristotle explicitly stated that a husband should rule over his wife and children. If slaves are naturally meant to be ruled by free men, then women are naturally meant to be ruled by men. Otherwise, the natural order would be violated:

> Man is full in movement, creative in politics, business and culture. Woman, on the other hand, is passive. She stays at home, as is her nature. She is matter, waiting to be formed by the active male principle.

Because the active elements of nature are on a higher level than the passive, they are more divine. This may be why Aristotle believed women's souls were impotent and in need of supervision.

Athens. The women of Athens can be described as chattels. At one point in Greek history, even a wife's childbearing responsibilities could be taken over by concubines, further lowering a wife's already subordinate status. Divorce was rare but possible. As a group, women were classified as minors, along with children and slaves. Aristotle speaks of a propertyless man who could not afford slaves but who could use his wife or children in their place. Husbands and male kin literally held the power of life and death over women. Some upper-class women enjoyed privileges associated with wealth and were left to their own devices while their husbands were away at war or serving the state. Considering the plight of most women of the time, these women achieved a measure of independence in their households only because of the absence of their husbands for lengthy periods. But Athenian repression of women was so strong that wealth could not compensate for the disadvantages of gender. From a conflict perspective, the class position of a citizen woman belonging to the highest class was determined by her gender, "by the fact that she belonged to the class of women" (De St. Croix, 1993:148). Her male relatives could be property owners, but she was devoid of property rights. As a woman, therefore, her class position was greatly inferior. In Marxian terms, women were an exploited class, regardless of the socioeconomic class to which they belonged.

Athenian society did not tolerate women in public places except at funerals and all-female festivals, so for the most part they remained secluded in their homes. Mourning was ritualized, and women could not express their grief in public or at the funerals they were allowed to attend (Loraux, 1998). Athenian households were segregated as well. Women had special quarters that were designed to restrict freedom of movement and to keep close supervision over their sexual activities. Supervision was so strong that evidence suggests Athens established a formal police force to monitor and protect the chastity of women (Keuls, 1993).

The few successful women in this world of men were of two groups. One group consisted of those women who practiced political intrigue behind the scenes to help elevate their sons or husbands to positions of power. The second group were the *hetairai*, high-level courtesans whose wit, charm, and talent men admired. When pederasty was in vogue, men sought boys or other young men for their sexual and intellectual pleasure. It was common for a man to change his sexual preference to women after spending his youth loving boys. By the fourth century B.C.E. Athenian men "rediscovered" women, but not their wives, because they had no desire to become family men. The uneducated wives could not compete with the social skills and cultural knowledge exhibited by either the hetairai, thoroughly trained for their work since they were girls, or the sexually experienced, educated males they frolicked with earlier in life (Murray, 2000). Throughout much of history, courtesans had a better life than wives.

Sparta. The subordinate position of Athenian women extended to most of the Greek world. When comparing Athens to Sparta, some differences can be ascertained. Sparta practiced male infanticide when newborns were deemed unfit enough to become warriors. Whether girls were killed is unclear. Regardless, it cannot be said that male infanticide indicated a higher regard for females in

Sparta. It is significant only to the extent that Spartan society was organized around the ever-present threat of war and strongly influenced the roles of Spartan women. If Athenian men were separated from their wives by war, the situation was magnified in Sparta. Spartan men were either at war or preparing for it. Army life effectively separated husband and wife until he reached the age of 30. These years of separation, marked by infrequent visits by their husbands, allowed wives to develop their own talents and capabilities that would have been impossible in Athens.

While the men were away, the women enjoyed a certain amount of freedom. Although the woman's responsibility was to bear male children who would become warriors, girls were also to be physically fit. Gymnastic training to promote both fitness and beauty was encouraged. Compared to women in Athens, young unmarried Spartan women enjoyed a higher degree of freedom. Euripides, an Athenian, commented on this scandalous state of affairs:

> The daughters of Sparta are never at home! They mingle with the young men in wrestling matches, their clothes cast off, their hips all naked. It's shameful! (Cited in Miles, 1989:31)

In addition to physical activities, citizen women were expected to manage the household and all the associated properties. Women retained control of their dowries and were able to inherit property. In comparison to Athens, the free women of Sparta had more privileges, if only because they were left alone much of the time. But in the context of the period as a whole, the vast majority of women existed in a legal and social world that viewed them in terms of their fathers, brothers, and husbands. Subordination and suppression of women was the rule.

The Grandeur That Was Rome

The founding of Rome by Romulus, traditionally dated at 753 B.C.E., led to an empire that lasted until overrun by invading Germanic tribes in the fifth century C.E. The Roman Empire evolved and adapted to the political, social, and cultural forces of the times and in turn influenced these very forces. Changes in gender roles mirrored the fortunes and woes of the empire. The prerogatives of women in later Rome contrasted sharply with the rights of women in the early days of the republic. It is true that women remained subservient to men and cannot be portrayed separately from the men who dominated and controlled them. But compared to the Greeks, Roman women achieved an astonishing amount of freedom.

Male Authority. Early Rome granted the eldest man in a family, the **pater familias**, absolute power over all family members, male and female alike. His authority could extend to death sentences for errant family members and selling his children into slavery to recoup the economic losses of a family. Daughters remained under the authority of a pater familias throughout their lives, but sons could be emancipated after his death. Even after marriage, the father or uncle or brother still had the status of pater familias for women, which meant the husbands could exercise only a limited amount of control over wives.

The absolute authority of the pater familias may have helped women in the long run. The right of guardianship brought with it a great deal of responsibility. A daughter's dowry, training, and education had to be considered early in life. If she married into a family with uncertain financial assets, the possibility existed that she and her new family could become a continued economic liability. The pater familias exercised extreme caution in ensuring the appropriate match for the women under his guardianship. This system allowed for total power of the pater familias, but it also caused a great burden for that very power to be maintained. By the first century C.E., legislation was passed that allowed a freewoman to be emancipated from a male guardian if she bore three children. The roles of childbearer and mother were primary, but they allowed for a measure of independence later in life. Like Sparta, Rome was always involved in warfare, and a declining birth rate was alarming. The abandonment of the pater familias rule functioned to decrease the economic burden women caused for the family. Emancipation in exchange for babies was an additional latent function.

Female Power. Like other women throughout history, Roman women could amass some power without the authority granted to men via law. Compared to the Greeks, Romans recognized a wider role for women. In the civic realm Romans acknowledged women's productive role in the origins of the state and offered select women citizenship. Religious life still retained vestiges of goddess worship, and women shared in the supervision of the religious cult of the household. The comparative power women held in the religious life of the empire is reflected in goddess cults and the revered *Vestal Virgins*. These mortal women symbolized Rome's economic and moral well-being. Though vestal virgins were open only to a select few, these women took on roles of great public importance. Roman women in general, however, knew that their lives would be carried out as wives and mothers. Nonetheless, wives also carried out the business of the family while their husbands were on military duty. These roles gradually extended so that it became common for women to buy and sell property as well as inherit it and participate in the broader economic life of the society (Wildfang, 2006; Green, 2007; Takacs, 2008).

Their expertise was both praised and criticized, especially as women amassed fortunes in their own names. The necessity for economic decision making led to a much less secluded lifestyle. The Greeks would have been astounded to see women in public roles and seated with men at dinner parties. Although most women remained illiterate, including upper-class women who had the most independence, women had greater opportunities for learning and were taught to cultivate music, art, and dancing. These women challenged a system where they were chained to their husbands or fathers. Roman women were eventually granted the right to divorce.

Freedom is relative. Roman society allowed a few women of higher social standing privileges unheard of in Greek society. Religion was the one area where women exercised much control, but with few exceptions, religious dominance did not expand into other realms. The abhorrent misogynistic texts of the poet Juvenal are more representative of beliefs about women (McLeod, 1991). Agreeing with Aristotle and Plato, these texts warn men that women are dangerous and distracting. Women may have been important in the establishment of the Roman state, but women's evil is also represented as a cause for the decline of the Roman Empire. The emancipated woman was a rarity even in Roman times. That a sexual double standard existed is unquestionable. Women may have been more visible, but they were definitely not autonomous. Rome was a brutal, slave-based society in which a dominator model of male control over women and the control of "superior" men over "inferior men" regulated all existence at all levels, whether personal, familial, national, or international (Eisler, 1995b:123). When compared to almost any free males in Rome, the most assertive, independent, and visible women were still in bondage to men.

THE MIDDLE AGES

When the Roman emperor Constantine reigned (306 and 337 C.E.), the empire was already in the throes of disintegration. Constantine's decision to wed the empire to Christianity was politically astute because Christianity seemed to offer an integrative force in a period when the empire's decline was accelerating. Constantine's foresight on the impact of Christianity was remarkable. He did not envision, however, that the collapse of Rome itself would be instrumental in allowing Christianity to gain a firm grip on Europe that lasted throughout the Middle Ages. The Renaissance and feudalism combined did not radically diminish this powerful hold. Christianity profoundly influenced the role of women. Compared to the preclassical era, women's status in the classical era markedly deteriorated. This already bleak situation was considerably worsened when Christianity dominated Europe during the Middle Ages.

Christianity

To its credit, the Church, in the form of a few monasteries and abbeys, became the repository of Greek and Roman knowledge that surely would have been lost during the sacking, looting, and general chaos following the disintegration of the Roman Empire. The decline of a literate population left reading, writing, and education as a whole in the hands of the Church. The power of literacy and the lack of literate critics permitted the Church to become the irreproachable source of knowledge and interpretation in all realms. The Church's view of life was seen as absolute.

If certain sentiments of the early Church had persisted, Christianity might not have taken on such misogynous overtones. Extending from Jewish tradition, the belief in the spiritual equality of the genders offered new visions of and to women. The ministry of Jesus included women in prominent roles, demonstrating spiritual equality in the steadfastly patriarchal society of the time (Chapter 12). Also, the Church recognized that women provided valuable charitable, evangelistic, and teaching services that were advantages to the fledgling institution. Some positions of leadership in the Church hierarchy were open to women and served as models for women who might choose a religious life. The convent also served as a useful occupation for some women, particularly of the upper classes, who were unsuited for marriage. It provided a place of education for selected girls and a sacred space for women to worship together without interference. Talented nuns were also poets, composers, and artists. Whereas the convent may have offered opportunities for women, the measure of independence that they achieved in becoming nuns was viewed with suspicion. Education for nuns eroded, and with more restrictions put on women's ownership of land, it was difficult to found new convents. Distrust of the independent woman in Catholic Europe served to strip nuns of their autonomy, and in Protestant Europe women were left without an acceptable alternative to marriage (Bardsley, 2007; Tibbetts, 2008).

Misogyny eventually dominated as the Church came to rely heavily on the writings of those who adopted traditional, restrictive views of women. Women were excluded from the few covenant communities teaching reading and writing. Biblical interpretations consistent with a cultural belief of the inferiority of women and placing the blame squarely on Eve for the fall of humanity became the unquestioned norm. As a fifteenth-century minister told his flock when Eve conversed with Satan,

> Eve . . . told him what God had said to her and her husband about eating the apple; . . . the fiend understood her feebleness and her unstableness, and found a way to bring her to confusion. (Cited in Bardsley, 2007:173)

Christianity also altered attitudes about marriage and divorce. Unlike in classical society, marriage could not be dissolved. Because divorce was unobtainable, women may have benefited if only for the fact that they could not be easily abandoned for whatever transgressions, real or imagined, their husbands attributed to them. Whereas childlessness was grounds for marital dissolution throughout history, even this was no longer an acceptable cause. However undesirable the marriage, the marriage was inviolable in the eyes of the Church.

Witch Hunts. With the medieval Church as a backdrop, misogyny during the late Middle Ages created an outgrowth for one of the most brutal periods of history concerning women—the time of the witch hunts. The woman who deviated from gendered norms generated the greatest distrust. If she remained unmarried, was married but childless, was regarded as sexually provocative, or was too independent or too powerful, she could be denounced as a witch (Briggs, 2002). Women who were not economically dependent on men—husbands, fathers, or brothers—may have been higher in social class, but like their sisters in classical societies, their gender class dominated all other statuses. Money and power condemned rather than protected them from the witch hunts. The power of the Church was directly related to the poverty of the people. Women who survived economically in their paid roles as healer, midwife, and counselor were particular targets of the witch hunts. Such women were admired for their expertise and sought out by the communities in which they practiced their professions. They were transformed into witches who symbolized evil and the wrath of God.

Female power was on trial but so was the fear of female sexuality, reinforced by Christian theology's view that sexual passion in women is irrational and potentially chaotic (Reineke, 1995). The majority of the victims of the European witch hunts were women. It displayed an eruption of misogyny that remains unparalleled in Western history. Accused of sexual impurity and in order to appease God's anger, thousands of women were burned as witches. Although confession as a witch meant death at the stake, the horrible tortures used to extract confessions were impossible to endure. It was common for women to publicly confess to such absurdities as eating the hearts of unbaptized babies and, the most used condemning confession, having intercourse with the devil (Stephens, 2002). God and the devil are enemies, and the methods of the devil worked well on weak women with evil temperaments, so burning the witch upheld righteousness and morality and claimed a victory over Satan (Kramer and Sprenger, 2000). It cannot be denied that the medieval Church's attitudes about women played a prominent role in sanctioning the witch craze.

Feudalism

The feudal system was adapted to the ongoing threat of war. Serfs and their families were protected by lords, who in turn expected their serfs to fight when called upon. All serfs owed their lives to the lord of the manor, and the wives of serfs owed their lives to their husbands. The lack of respect for serfs in general and their wives in particular is indicated by a custom that allowed the lord to test the virginity of the serf's new bride on their wedding night.

Women of noble standing fared somewhat better in that they were valued for their role in extending the power of the family lineage through arranged marriages, though here, too, the lord of the manor had to grant permission for any marriage. An unmarried noblewoman was a property worth guarding, her virginity a marketable commodity, assuring the legitimacy of a male heir. Her marriage united two houses, perpetuated a lineage, and expanded the economic fortunes of both families.

At marriage the bride would be given in exchange for a dowry of money or jewelry, and in some places, the custom required her to kneel in front of her husband-to-be to symbolize his power over her. As her husband was controlled by the lord of the estate, she was to be controlled by her lord and husband. Whether serf or noble, feudal wives had much in common.

The Renaissance

The last 300 years of medieval Europe, which included the Renaissance and Reformation, were years of ferment and change that inevitably extended into women's realms. It can be said that the Renaissance had generally positive effects on women of all social standing (Thomson, 2005). Educated aristocratic women became patrons of literature and art, many of them as authors in their own right. Notably the women who emerged as scientists, writers, and artists were literate women largely of noble blood. As such, they were accorded some prestige for their accomplishments. But other forces were at work that kept traditional images of women from being seriously challenged.

Martin Luther and the Reformation. With the Reformation came the startling notion that the Church hierarchy may actually exclude people from worship. Preaching a theology of liberation from the Church he indicted as too restrictive, Martin Luther advocated opening Christianity to everyone on the basis of faith alone. Critical of Aquinas's view that a woman was imperfect, in essence a botched male, Luther argued that those who accused her of this are in themselves monsters and should recognize that she, too, is a creature made by God. Many women embraced Luther's justification by faith principle, but some paid a heavy price as a result. For example, Ann Boleyn was beheaded in England in her effort to introduce Protestantism; Jane Grey and Anne Askew, who dared to criticize the Catholic mass, were tortured and executed (Zahl, 2001). The degree to which the first women embraced Protestantism for personal, political, or social justice convictions is unclear. The Reformation did appear to offer an opportunity to present different interpretations of Christianity highlighting men and women's spiritual equality that would elevate the position of women.

This was not to be the case. Luther himself presents a paradox. Women may not be "botched males," but he still believed they were inferior to men. Though woman is a "beautiful handiwork of God," she does "not equal the dignity and glory of the male" (quoted in Maclean, 1980:10). Theological statements of the time abound with themes of superior man and inferior woman. Women bear the greater burden for original sin because of Eve's seduction by Satan. God's natural order assigns women functions related to procreation, wifely duties, and companionship to men. Upsetting the natural order, such as a woman's adultery, justified her being stoned to death, but the sentence did not extend to an unfaithful husband (Karant-Nunn and Wiesner-Hanks, 2003; Peters, 2003). As the Reformation reverberated throughout the Western world, no dramatic changes relative to the Christian image of women occurred.

The Renaissance generated the rebirth of art, literature, and music in a world that was rapidly being transformed by commerce, communication, and the growth of cities. As a force in people's lives, Christianity now competed with education. Literacy expanded to more men and some women, opening up intellectual life that had been closed to most except clergy and nobility. Women made some economic headway by working in shops or producing products in the home for sale or trade. As money replaced barter systems and manufacturing increased, a new class of citizens emerged who were not dependent on either agriculture or a feudal lord for protection.

Critique. Like other periods in history, the Renaissance presents contradictory evidence about women. The question of whether women had a Renaissance depends on the answer to other questions: Which women? Where were they located? What was their social class? Historians have scoured the hundred years (1580–1680) of this Golden Age for records of female notables, and hundreds have been discovered or rediscovered (Spongberg, 2002; Wiesner-Hanks, 2008). These records provide abundant testimonies to the intellect, talent, and stature of women poets, artists, artisans, and musicians.

Although they provide an image of the past that is affirming to women, they remain, as always, a witness to extraordinary rather than ordinary women of the day. Social history provides a more inclusive view, and from this several plausible conclusions can be drawn. The Renaissance witnessed women in more diverse roles. Many women, particularly lower-class women, migrated to the expanding cities and were employed as servants, barmaids, fishmongers, textile workers, and peat carriers, to name a few. More educated women established themselves as actresses and midwives. Although a woman was protected from financial destitution by marriage, a surplus of women in some European cities such as Amsterdam may have made marriage unattainable, but less disastrous, if she was employed. Prostitution also burgeoned during this period. Compared to wives and unmarried women (spinsters), widows in England enjoyed the most freedom because they could inherit property and were free to continue their husbands' businesses (Prior, 1994). But misogyny continued to govern Europe. Women who ventured outside prescribed gender roles found themselves in precarious positions, both socially and economically.

THE AMERICAN EXPERIENCE

Women's history and American social history are fundamentally intertwined, a productive association for the growth of both areas. Because social history focuses on previously neglected groups, such as minorities and the working classes, women are brought in as part of that cohort. Until recently, the interest in women was largely confined to issues related to the attainment of legal rights, such as the suffrage movement. Only in the last few decades has women's history in the United States come into its own. This new women's history issues three challenges: to reexamine gendered social relations, to reconstruct historical generalizations, and to reconfigure historical narrative (De Hart and Kerber, 2003). Similar to the new sociological paradigm based on feminist theory, these challenges from women's history are laying the foundation for a paradigm shift in history.

The First American Women

As a prelude to this paradigm shift, women's history is bringing to the surface a range of taken-for-granted assumptions about women in America. The first

American women were Native American women, but this fact has been historically ignored until recently. In those instances when it was not ignored, stereotyped and inaccurate portrayals based on European, Christian, patriarchal beliefs prevailed.

Prior to colonization, in the fifteenth and sixteenth centuries, at least 2,000 Native American languages existed. Given such tribal diversity, it is certainly difficult to generalize about the status of Native American women as a group. The archaeological and historical record, the latter based mainly on diaries, letters, and some ethnographic descriptions from the period, does allow some reliable conclusions, especially for coastal and Midwestern tribes, such as the Seneca of western New York, the Algonquins distributed along the Atlantic coast, and a number of Iroquoian tribes scattered throughout the territories east of the Mississippi River.

Accounts of American Indian women during this period can be interpreted in many ways, and much of this is dependent on their particular tribe. Missionary and European views of women on the Eastern shores during the 1600s saw them as beasts of burden, slaves, and "poor creatures who endure all the misfortunes of life" (Riley, 2007). This led to the stereotypical and derisive "squaw" image that was perpetuated by zealous missionaries, who generally saw Native Americans as primitive savages (Fischer, 2005). This image contrasts sharply with the historical record.

Gender Role Balance. Ancient tribal systems can be described by balance, and functional separation of gender roles. Men and women represented two halves of the same environment (Kowtko, 2006). Gender segregation was the norm, but it provided women a great deal of autonomy. The success of the system depended on balanced and harmonious functioning of the whole. The work of both men and women was viewed as functionally necessary to survival, so even if a leadership hierarchy existed related to leadership, one group would not be valued or, more importantly, devalued in comparison to the other. In sociology this would be recognized as the ideal functionalist model, void of judgments that define inferiority or superiority based on the tasks performed. Many tribal units were matrilineal and matrilocal, a man living in the home belonging to his wife's family. Women were farmers and retained control over their agricultural products, feeding hungry settlers with their surpluses and influencing warfare and trade with the settlers through the power to distribute economic resources.

Tribal Leadership. They were also tribal leaders, many who represented gynocratic systems based on egalitarianism, reciprocity, and complementarity. Venerated for their wisdom, women were sought as advisers and as arbitrators in tribal disputes (Fur, 2002; Macleitch, 2007). As early as 1600 the constitution of the Iroquois Confederation guaranteed women the sole right to regulate war. The Iroquoian gynocracy was referred to as a "petticoat government" by John Adair. Among Virginia Indians, women often held the highest authority in their tribes and were recognized as such by white colonists. The English, fresh from the reign of Elizabeth I (1558–1603), "knew a queen when they saw one" (Lebsock, 1990). Another significant source of authority and prestige for Native American women was through their roles as religious leaders and healers. When roles of shaman and war leader coincided women held very powerful positions. Spiritual roles were so important that in some tribes the gods were women (Daly, 1994). In North American creation myths, women are the mediators between the supernatural and the earthly worlds. Men and women sought spiritual understanding through individual quests for vision. Again, the worlds of men and women were rigidly separated. Fasting and seclusion were part of a woman's spiritual quest. Menstruating women were believed to be so powerful that they could drain the spiritual power men required for hunting. Women would withdraw to menstrual huts outside of the villages during this time. Is this interpreted as taboo and banishment? Women probably welcomed the respite and saw it as an opportunity for meditation, spiritual growth, and the enjoyment of the company of other women (Evans, 2000). The balanced and cooperative functionalist system represented by these practices would serve to enhance gender solidarity.

Colonization and Christianity. Colonization and Christianity were the most disruptive forces of ancient tribal patterns and, by extension, the status of women. The Iroquois Confederacy provided an image to the Europeans of a self-ruling inclusive democracy. But female participation in a democracy that was economically based on matrilineal–matrilocal clans mystified them. With increased European contact, women were gradually stripped of tribal political power and economic assets, becoming more defined, hence confined, by their domestic roles. They began to look more and more like their subordinated European sisters. Christianity further eroded their powerful religious roles. The impact of Christianity on Native American women continues to be debated among historians. There is evidence from the writings of Father Le Jeune in 1633 about the tribes living on the St. Lawrence River that women were the major obstacles to tribal conversion. They resisted being baptized and allowing their children to be educated at mission schools run by Catholic Jesuits. The women were accused of being independent and not obeying their husbands, and under Jesuit influence, the men believed that the women were the cause of their misfortunes and kept the demons among them (Devens, 1996:25). Women were acutely aware that conversion to Christianity brought severe role restrictions.

On the other hand, New England and Puritan missionaries, specifically the Quakers, had greater success in converting women. If change was gradual and the Indians could retain key cultural elements, the belief was they would willingly accept the Christian message. This Christian Gospel did not obliterate native culture but "offered membership in God's tribe" and attracted women by "honoring their traditional tasks and rewarding their special abilities" (Rhonda, 1996). Their culture could remain simultaneously Christian and Indian. Although historians disagree on the extent of Native American women's resistance to Christianity and colonization, most scholars accept that these women had a high standing in precontact societies (Smith, 2006; Stone, 2006; Riley, 2007).

The Colonial Era

The first white settlers in America were searching for religious freedom that had been denied expression in the Old World. The Puritans sought to practice a brand of Christianity without bureaucratic or doctrinal traditions they viewed as hampering devotion to God. In challenging the old order, however, the Puritans retained traditional beliefs about women.

Gendered Puritan Life. Christian assumptions about male superiority carried easily into the New World. Males were subordinate to God as females were subordinate to males. Puritan settlements such as the Massachusetts Bay Colony extracted a high degree of religious conformity considered necessary to the well-being and survival of the community. The Puritan community existed on the basis of obedience to the civil and moral law of the Old Testament as defined by the clergy. Social harmony and order were praised. As a sociological functionalist would support, deviation from a clergy-sanctioned order was a threat to the social fabric. Nonetheless, Puritanism placed spiritual power in the individual. Cultivating women's spiritual autonomy and religious development was encouraged, but only within the confines of a rigid patriarchal family structure. In 1637 Anne Hutchinson was banished from Massachusetts Bay for criticizing the minister's sermons, for holding separate meetings for men and women who were of similar mind, and as documents from her trial indicate, for not fulfilling her ordained womanly role.

Along with the threat of banishment, the convenient accusation of witchcraft kept potentially ambitious women in tow. An epidemic of witchcraft persecutions ravaged the Puritan colonies, fueled by images of independent and disobedient women who defied authority. The infamous Salem witch trials of 1690–1693 occurred when a few adolescent girls and young women accused hundreds of older women of bewitching them. Invariably the older women were viewed as aggressive and threatening, out of character with the submissive women who knew their proper place in the Puritan community. With the community's strict hierarchy at stake, it was not difficult to condemn people who swerved from their expected roles. Family relationships of many accused witches were marked by conflict. Women were brought to court for witchcraft for "railing" at their husbands or "speaking harsh things" against them (Demos, 1996:59). There was also a powerful economic rationale to witchcraft. Many women condemned as witches had no male heirs and could potentially inherit larger portions of their fathers' or husbands' estates. These women were "aberrations in a society designed to keep property in the hands of men" (Karlsen, 2004). An inheritance could produce more economically independent women. Being burned as a witch was a convenient way to rid the colony of its aberrations, foil challenges to gender norms, and maintain the desired social order.

Because religion extended to all areas of life and only men could be citizens, women were denied any public expression. When married, colonial women entered a legal status known as civil death. Based on English Common Law the marital union meant that she could not vote, own property, sue or be sued, administer estates, sign contracts, or keep her children in the event of divorce. She had some control over property she brought to the marriage and could inherit property at the death of her husband, but she could not sell it. Marriage was sacrosanct, but divorce was possible, mostly in cases of adultery or desertion. Family arrangements and limited divorce options ensured family harmony and prevented destitute women to become the community's responsibility. Puritan society was rigidly divided into public and domestic spheres. Though women had essential tasks in the domestic area, Puritan men still controlled both spheres.

The other side of the picture required Puritan men to not only provide for the economic and physical needs of the family, but also love their wives. The revolutionary idea that love and marriage must be connected was historically unprecedented; until this time marriage was simply seen as an economic necessity (Chapter 7). If the couple happened to love one another, so much the better. The ideal family was patriarchal, and marriage, although based on love, fit into a family power structure that required a wife's obedience to her husband.

Puritan women were also valued because they were scarce. Most settlers were male, and because many colonies were obliterated by disease or starvation, the colonists knew that it was vital to repopulate or see their religious visions doomed. Though wives were valuable, when it came to starvation, patriarchy prevailed, as the following excerpt from a Jamestown, Virginia, historical record documents.

> And one amongst the rest did kill his wife, powdered (salted) her, and had eaten part of her before it was known, for which he was executed, as he well deserved. Now whether she was better roasted, boiled, or carbonadoed (grilled), I know not, but of such a dish as powdered wife I never heard of. (quoted in Frey and Morton, 1986:40)

Women were important for their economic productivity within the family. Family survival, hence community survival, was tied to the efforts of both men and women. But vegetable gardening, weaving, canning, and candle and soap making contributed to the family's economic fortunes, and these tasks were largely confined to women. Subsistence living was the rule, but surplus products could be bartered or sold. The family was the basic social unit for the colonists, and women were integral to its well-being.

A Golden Age for Colonial Women? Historians are at odds about the prestige of women during this period. Because there were far fewer immigrant women than men, and women were considered valuable, this leads some to suggest that the colonial period was a golden age for women. Although the colonists came to the New World with patriarchy strongly in place, adapting to the harshness of the environment required the modification of many beliefs. Strict adherence to gender roles was impossible for survival. Women had to be economically productive and had to have expanded roles. Outside the home women engaged in merchant, trade, and craft functions. English Common Law intruded into the colonies, but it was often circumvented.

If a golden age existed, it had clearly declined by the late eighteenth century. The family lost its centrality as the economic unit in society, to be replaced by a wider marketplace dominated by men. Women's work was once again confined to activities that were not income producing. Colonial women became more dependent on their families for how their lives were defined. The American economy did not allow many opportunities for women to be wage earners. Resistance increased for women who out of necessity, more than desire, sought work outside their homes. The crucial element, however, is that Puritan ideology was based on the unquestioned assumption of female inferiority and subordination. The colonial environment was a modified version of Old World notions about women. The thesis that between the seventeenth and the nineteenth centuries a status decline occurred for women from a golden age (in the colonial period) is still contested (Lewis, 2002; Hoff, 2003; Norton, 2003). Although there may not have been a golden age, political participation and education enhanced women's autonomy during the Revolutionary era. These changes kindled public discourse on women's roles that served as a catalyst for later gender role change.

The Victorians: True Womanhood

The struggle for survival gradually diminished as Americans prospered on farms and in shops. As judged by economic contributions to the family, a middle-class woman's productive role lessened, and her life solely revolved around housekeeping and child rearing. By the nineteenth century her world had changed considerably. Victorian examples of womanhood made their way into magazines and novels directed toward women. Despite an undercurrent of liberal feminism that was fermenting during this period, periodicals targeted to middle-class women presented them with a cult of domestic femininity. Magazines popularized the new feminine ideal as **True Womanhood**, associated with the cardinal virtues of piety, purity, submissiveness, and domesticity. The Victorian middle-class home was to be a bastion of morality, and women were glorified in the pulpit and in print as the high priestess of the home (Plante, 1997:35). These were the standards on which society would judge them and on which they would judge themselves.

Tied completely to her family, the middle-class woman found herself with time on her hands, a luxury not shared by her colonial sisters. Idleness was the reality but it was transformed into gentility that many families strived for. Gentility ushered in attitudes putting women on pedestals. Women were to be protected from the harshness of the world outside the home. Victorian femininity was equated with sexual, social, and political repression. The doctrine of separate spheres for the activities of women and men became firmly entrenched in the American consciousness.

The strength of the True Womanhood cult was generally effective in silencing many voices of feminism that were being heard in Europe and America during the Victorian era. From pulpits throughout America, women were told that their home is the route to happiness and to resist voices calling them to other spheres. Supposedly, a woman did have a choice to define her rights and roles either inside or outside the home, as attested to by the Rev. Mr. Stearns:

> Yours is to determine whether the beautiful order of society . . . shall continue as it has been (or whether) society shall break up and become a chaos of disjointed and unsightly elements. (Welter, 1996:122)

The Victorian era conjures up images of rigidity and repression that cannot be denied, but explorations into women's history are providing alternative views. Karen Lystra (1989) demonstrates that middle-class Victorian America exhibited marked sexual expression and erotic intensity through the private correspondence of lovers. Her analysis of this intimate correspondence from the perspective of Victorian social conventions is sociologically a symbolic interaction approach. Romantic love and sexual expression flourished at a time when public prudery was the norm. Though hidden, this intimate reality is also culturally significant. "The system of ideas and behavior commonly referred to as romantic love provided one significant means of integrating private and public worlds" (Lystra, 1989:6). Because one's true self was disclosed in this correspondence, it can be argued that women gained a sense of mastery not allowed in other parts of their lives.

Other historical research confirms that women exercised active control in adapting conditions of their domestic, sexual, and intellectual lives to meet their personal needs and to work toward the social justice causes they embraced (Thompson, 1999; Passet, 2003). Although the patriarchal family remained firmly entrenched and basic gender inequities intruded into domestic life, Victorian women were able to achieve a modicum of autonomy. Gender role segregation enabled gender solidarity, which was nurtured by the emotional segregation of men and women. This allowed for the existence of a female world in which a supportive, intimate network of female friendships and intimacy flourished and could serve to empower women. Contemporary functionalism suggests that a focus on the rigidity associated with the Victorian era and the True Woman model overlooks the latent functions these very patterns provided for women.

Frontier Life

Idleness was impossible on the frontier. Victorian America extolled the gentility and supposed frailness of middle-class women. Frontier society was disdainful of these very traits. As with the colonial era, women were needed for any settlement to be successful and were valued for their work both inside and outside the home (Montrie, 2008). During the early frontier expansion, women were scarce, yet colonial society never seriously questioned the notion of woman's inferiority; hence, her relative status remains unclear. Through the hardship and deprivation of frontier life combined with less adherence to religious proscriptions concerning gender, it is evident that the pioneer woman achieved a degree of freedom and respect unlike previous periods of America's brief history.

The frontier experience began with the grueling trip West, which often took six months to complete. Faced with the deprivation of the trail, surviving the trip meant that the normal gender division of labor was suspended, with both women and older children filling expanded roles. Rather than viewing the situation as an opportunity for male–female equality, diaries from these women suggest that they saw themselves as invaders of a male domain. Although few women who emigrated West on the Oregon or Overland Trails came from the northeastern middle classes where the cult of True Womanhood reached its zenith, they were not immune to it either. In the journey West, women and men maintained separate worlds of existence as much as possible. Women created a specific female culture based on their roles of mother, healer, and nurse. Compared to men, however, trail life precluded sustained interaction and deep attachments to other women (Faragher, 1996:207). Whereas men used the trip to fulfill dreams of "camaraderie, action and achievement," many women found the experience lonely and isolating.

Life on the trail and later settlement in the West threw their domestic roles in a state of disarray, but women appeared reluctant to redefine their boundaries to create anything but a temporary alteration of affairs. Although women often shared work and had overlapping functions with their fathers and husbands, gender remained the key variable in determining their duties and interests and kept them focused on their domestic lives.

It is not safe to conclude, however, that frontier women were passive. They exhibited a spirit of nonconformity, adventure, and extraordinary adaptation. Frontier settlements saw the necessity of woman's labor not being confined to the home. The Homestead Act of 1862 propelled women to own and establish farms independently of fathers or husbands or to maintain their farms as widows (Lindgren, 1996). Child rearing was often left to siblings as wives worked in the fields. Subsistence farming required that as many goods as possible be produced and consumed within the home. Women took the major responsibility in this area. Isolated farms, prairie loneliness, and the daily harshness of frontier living generated the understanding that men and women, wives and husbands, depended on one another for physical and emotional survival. Both prior to and after the Civil War, African-American men and women also trekked West, carving out new lives on frontier farms they purchased. In their struggle to eke out new lives on remote farms dotting the Western landscape, African-American women and white women shared much in common. These experiences served to elevate the status of women.

Popular images of women as saints in sunbonnets, Madonnas of the prairies, and pioneer mothers abounded during the era of westward expansion as well as accounts of the deprivation, ardor, and premature aging associated with frontier life. Diaries and letters of pioneer women demonstrate that Victorian domesticity and compliance existed side by side with new roles ultimately challenging this compliance.

Accounts of women who emigrated to the Kansas frontier during the latter part of the nineteenth century provide testimony to these critical roles. In her diary a daughter recalls the birth of her brother on a day when her father was away. Her mother was alone with two babies, no neighbors, and no doctor, when the stork arrived.

> So my brave mother got the baby clothes together on a chair by the bed, water and scissors . . . drew a bucket of fresh water from a sixty-foot well; made some bread-and-butter sandwiches; set out some milk for the babies. . . . So at about noon the stork left a fine baby boy . . . and when my father came in he found a very uncomfortable but brave and thankful mother, thankful that he had returned home with the precious wood, and that she and the baby were alright. (cited in Stratton, 1981:87)

Such accounts are characteristic rather than exceptional. They speak of women who, with their families, endured prairie fires, locusts, droughts, disease, and the ever-present loneliness. Most did not return to their homes in the East, but accepted their new life with stoicism and a hope for making their farms an economic success. Through hundreds of excerpts from diaries, letters, and oral histories, writers provide a picture of matter-of-fact women who adapted to and thrived in their frontier existence.

The intent is not to idealize the brutal existence pioneer women confronted. It is to suggest that adversity was important in bringing men and women together more equitably on the frontier, even if the participants themselves did not acknowledge the altered gender roles.

Industrialization

It appears incongruous, but as the cult of domesticity ascended, the first mass movement of white women into industrial employment was also occurring. From the founding of the United States, women have always participated in paid labor and were not completely circumscribed by their domestic roles. When teachers or shopkeepers or planters or traders were needed and men were unavailable, women were encouraged to fill these roles. Industrial expansion during the nineteenth century required an entirely new class of workers. Faced with a shortage of males who continued to farm, industrialists convinced women that, although they were too weak for agriculture, work in the mills could suit their temperaments, was good for them, and was good for the nation. For the less marriageable, factory work saved them from pauperism. The Civil War and its aftermath accelerated the need for women in industry. Thousands of women and many children answered the call.

Race and Class. By the latter part of the century, the shift from an agricultural to an urban industrialized economy rapidly accelerated. The family was no longer a critical unit of production and work was to be performed for wages at other locations outside home and farm. By the turn of the century, agriculture required less than 10 percent of America's labor power, with 20 percent of all women in the United States over the age 16 employed outside the home (Balanoff, 1990:611). These women were young, single, or the wives and daughters of working-class families, whose income was necessary to keep the family out of poverty. Married women worked only out of dire necessity, often driven into the labor market by widowhood. Middle-class married woman were expected to devote time and talent to the emotional well-being of the family. Labor-saving products and appliances were introduced to the home. By 1900, housework and child care were no longer a full-time occupation, leading to more leisure, boredom, and restlessness for women who were, however, discouraged from seeking paid employment outside the home. There were two important results. First, many middle-class women became involved in social reform work, including the growing feminist movement. Second, the already existing schism between working-class and middle-class women widened. As we shall see, to date this schism has not been completely mended.

Working-class women were confronted with different issues. Industrial growth increasingly demanded cheap labor and looked to poorer women and immigrants to take on this load. The rapidly urbanizing Eastern states accommodated the flood of immigrants who settled in areas close to the factories, mines, and mills in which they worked. Immigrant women were overrepresented as unskilled laborers in jobs that cut them off from wider society and African-American women continued to toil on farms and as domestics because factory labor remained closed to them in the North. In the South, an oversupply of African-American female labor made their position worse. In the West, Asian women worked in small family-owned businesses. In this era, gender was disregarded as a qualification for factory work; race was not.

The working conditions faced were appalling, even by the standards of the day. Unsanitary conditions, no rest breaks, rules against sitting down, 54-hour, 6-day work-weeks, and grueling, rote tasks were characteristic. In combination with an unsafe environment in which machines had no safety guards and buildings were poorly ventilated and lacked fire escapes, it is understandable why job-related injuries and deaths skyrocketed. In 1911, the Triangle Shirtwaist Company in New York caught fire, killing 146 workers, many of them women. Doors were kept locked so that workers could be inspected for theft of company merchandise, and available fire escapes needed repair, buckling under the pressure of those fleeing the fire. The owners of the factory, accused of locking the doors, were tried on manslaughter charges but acquitted. Civil suits brought by relatives of 23 victims ended with payments of $75 to each family (Getzinger, 2009). The garment industry was notorious in its treatment of lower-level workers. A system of subcontracting finishing work to people, primarily immigrant women, became common. Women would work in what came to be called "sweat-shops," in basements and workrooms of low-rent tenement apartments, thereby saving the company much in the way of production costs (Banner, 2005). What made an already dismal situation worse was that it was necessary for workers to purchase their own equipment, which would then require years of arduous labor to pay off.

When men and women were employed in the same factories, women held less prestigious jobs and were paid less. Men resisted being employed with women in the same job. Gender segregation by type of activity led to a stratification system that justified the lower wages paid to women. Because both women and their employers viewed employment as temporary, gender segregation of jobs perpetuated low wages and kept women from training programs, and job benefits. The nineteenth-century roots of gender-typing in jobs carries over to contemporary debates about comparable worth (Chapters 10 and 14).

The Union Movement. The Triangle fire also ignited massive protest over the scandalous conditions under which people worked, generated much sympathy nationally, and created a ripe atmosphere for unions to flourish (Von Drehle, 2003). The major growth period occurred from the 1870s through World War I. Union activist Mary Harris ("Mother") Jones reported on the horrendous plight of women and children in industry:

> condemned to slave daily in the washroom (of breweries) in wet shoes, and wet clothes . . . in the vile smell of sour beer, lifting cases . . . weighing from 100 to 150 pounds.

In 1881 the **Knights of Labor** was opened to women and African Americans calling for equal pay for equal work. In 1885, 2,500 women members of the Knights of Labor endured a six-month strike marked by violence in Yonkers, New York, at a mill where they worked as carpet weavers. The *International Ladies' Garment Workers Union* (ILGWU) gained recognition in many shops as a result of a strike that lasted through the winter of 1909, involving 20,000 mostly female shirtwaist workers (Wolensky et al., 2002). With the support of the Women's Trade Union League and public outrage from the Triangle fire, legislation was passed requiring more stringent safety and inspection codes for factories.

Compared to the union movement involving men, women's attempts to unionize were not nearly as successful. Union efforts were not supported by a broad spectrum of people, including the police and courts. Many unions still refused to admit women, and even with an official policy urging equal pay to women, the most powerful union, the American Federation of Labor (AFL), was unwilling to exert the pressure necessary for its affiliates to conform to the rule. The AFL was also becoming a union of skilled craftsworkers made up exclusively of men, and there was fear that the success of the union would be diluted if it took on the numerous women still in the ranks of the unskilled. Originally welcoming women as members, a period of economic recession saw members of the Knights of Labor competing with one another for scarce jobs. In 1895, only five percent of all union members were female, and by 1900 only three percent of all women who worked in factories were unionized. The ILGWU had become the third largest affiliate of the AFL by 1913, and it did capitalize on the power that was being wielded by the AFL itself. But because men and women were segregated by job, the unions representing women had less success. Unionization was obstructed by men's fears of job competition and the tenacious belief that women's place was in the home. By 1900, women represented half the membership of unions in five industries (women's clothing, gloves, hats, shirtwaist and laundry, and tobacco), and they earned about half of what men earned; African-American women earned half of what was earned by white women.

The characteristics of the female labor force also made unionization efforts difficult. Work for women was unstable, temporary, and subject to economic ups and downs. In jobs performed by both genders, men were given preference in slack periods and women were laid off. Young women worked until marriage, which was the preferred exit out of the factories and into a middle-class lifestyle. Although they did provide opportunities for women to develop leadership skills and agendas representing their own interests, unions of women workers tended to be small, more isolated, and financially weak. Overall, unions were most helpful to women when they were allowed to join with men.

Women advanced more in the labor force during periods of growth as well as in periods of war. During the Civil War women served as nurses, clerks, and copyists and produced uniforms and munitions. World War I also saw an expansion of job opportunities both in Britain and in the United States. Government campaigns to rally support for war, its supply needs, and women's labor force participation have been seen throughout American history. World War I was also the first war where women in America and Europe were actively recruited for military service. After the war British women who had worked in engineering (on buses, railways, and trams), in the services, and in government offices were dismissed and expected to return home. Those who persisted on jobs were often labeled as "hussies" or as women who stole men's jobs (Beddoe, 1989:3). Such statements were echoed in the United States. Public support for the war effort made the transition to the labor force easier for women who, if they had a choice, had not considered working outside the home. In most instances women were summarily dismissed after the men returned.

Women who ventured outside the home were caught in conflicting roles, but it is apparent that both industrialization and war were the catalysts for creating the "new woman" of the 1920s. Lamenting the demise of the True Woman, people both hailed and damned her new counterpart as she strove for equality with men. She "entered the 1920s with high expectations, ready for challenge and for choice" (Brown, 1987:30–31,47). The flapper era saw a loosening of sexual and social restraint. Searching for independence from parents and excitement from one another, working women migrated to cities, seeking each other out in the crowded boarding houses in which they lived. These furnished rooms created new peer-oriented subcultures where women charted sexual terrain that other women later followed (Meyerowitz, 1990:150). While retaining a separate political sphere from men, many of these new women worked for social and legal change. Prosperity, hope, and the formation of an identity that included volunteer and paid work led many of these women to pursue feminist causes.

The Depression. In less than a decade, much of this hope was dashed. The rule that scarce jobs should go to men first continued through the Depression. Job segregation and the belief that there was women's work and men's work ironically protected the jobs of women employed as waitresses, domestics, or clerks. Rather than accepting the loss of prestige that would be associated with doing a "woman's" job, some men abandoned their families because they were no longer breadwinners. In those instances in which a job was not defined completely in gender terms, such as teacher, it was rare to see a woman either obtain it or keep it if a man could be employed instead.

In general, industrialization saw women make steady headway in the world of paid employment. Older attitudes about women's functions in the family continued to compete with the needs of an expanding economy. But the precedent for women working outside the home gained strength and was nurtured by gradual public acceptance for newer roles. Once the industrial era established this trend, World War II provided the most important catalyst for expanding employment options.

World War II

Throughout history, war is latently functional for social change that otherwise might not have occurred or would have occurred at a much slower pace. War suspends notions of what is considered typical or conventional and throws people into novel situations, which in turn sensitize them to an awareness of potential never dreamed possible. In addition to the impacts documented here, for example, World War II gave women the only opportunity in U.S. history to play professional baseball (Corey, 2003). Novel situations occur both on and off the actual battlefield.

As this chapter documents, by choice and necessity women have consistently taken on expanded roles in wartime. Considering, too, that the history of the world has been marked by frequent and prolonged periods of war, the roles women assumed during wartime were essential for social stability. Usually these newer roles have been short-lived, with the prewar social order swiftly reestablished when the men returned home. Although this was indeed the case with World War II, it is also true that this particular war profoundly influenced American women in unprecedented ways. The liberating effects of the war effort not only endured but also had powerful consequences for the next generation of women. The impact was seen most in the areas of employment and family.

Demand for Women's Labor. When America officially entered the war in 1941 there was quick recognition that victory depended on the total commitment of the nation. One task of the Office of War Information (OWI) was to monitor public opinion to determine the degree of commitment and willingness to sacrifice for the war. Accustomed to men taking the lead in both politics and war, women were less enthusiastic about the war and less receptive to military themes and staged events about the war than were men. Within a few months of Pearl Harbor, when patriotism was at its height, a concerted national policy to fully mobilize the civilian population in the war effort was initiated. Much of this policy was focused on women.

The powerful War Production Board (WPC) and War Manpower Commission (WMC) were set up to convert to a wartime economy, coordinate labor for the various sectors of the economy, and allocate workers for both war and civilian production. The booming wartime economy rapidly ended the Depression. It became apparent that the war machine required uninterrupted production schedules and an increased labor supply. Women were essential in filling the roles in the war production industry as the men were called into military service. An efficient propaganda program was put into effect that prompted women to respond to the employment needs of a nation at war.

The battle abroad could be won if women acknowledged and acted on their patriotic duty to be employed on the home front. After the Depression years, many women eagerly sought the higher pay and better working conditions offered in the war industry. When jobs became available, women were first hired in traditionally female positions, as clerks or semiskilled laborers in factories producing uniforms or foodstuffs. Women were rebuffed from the defense plants that offered higher pay.

Defense industry employers were at first reluctant to hire women, even if it meant paying men overtime or creating shortages in production. If continued, these policies would have had disastrous consequences for the war effort. As labor shortages reached crisis proportions job training and opportunities for women in almost all phases of defense work soared. Within six months after Pearl Harbor, employers hired women in a variety of semiskilled, professional, and managerial jobs. OWI was responsible for selling the war to women and created images of defense work as exciting, glamorous, and economically rewarding. Campaigns appealed to patriotism and guilt for slacking off when the war effort needed women. "Rosie the Riveter," popularized through a wartime song, became the new home-front heroine. She represented the millions of women who worked at munitions plants, foundries, and quarries as lumberjacks, shipbuilders, and plumbers. OWI was successful in recruiting women for the civilian labor force as well as for the armed services. Women's corps of all branches of the military were formed during World War II, and by January 1944, over 100,000 women joined. The employment of women reached its wartime peak in July 1944, when 19 million women were employed, an increase of over five million from 1941.

Women's Diversity in the Labor Force. Once the gender barrier eroded, women's opportunities in the war industry flourished, with less concern about age, marital status, and race. However, preferences were still given to women who were white, single, and younger. The war allowed African-American women access to employment in defense plants, which significantly decreased their reliance on agricultural and domestic labor. Employment prospects for both African-American men and women were increased by defense contracts, which contained clauses prohibiting racial discrimination. Nonetheless, some companies refused to hire African-American women throughout the war. Labor shortages did increase their numbers, but they were hired for the lowest-level jobs and, unless they were protected by a union, were paid less than either white women or African-American men. The mixed feelings of this situation—patriotism and pride along with disenchantment—are poignantly expressed by an African-American woman who worked in a defense plant.

> I'm not fooling myself about this war. Victory won't mean victory for Democracy—yet. But that will come later . . . maybe a hundred years later. But doing my share today, I'm keeping a place for some brown woman tomorrow. (Johnson, 1943/1996)

As the war continued and the demand for defense workers grew, the demographic balance of the female labor force shifted considerably; both older and married women were recruited. Some industries reported an even division between single and married workers. Near the end of the war married women outnumbered single women in the labor force.

What about the Children? The new encouragement for married women to enter the labor force challenged a society that firmly believed that a mother's place was at home with her children (Langley and Fox, 1998). By the close of the war, 32 percent of women who worked in the major defense centers had children under the age of 14. Day-care centers, foster home programs, and other variations of child care were developed throughout the country. By tying defense production to provisions for child care, day-care services increased dramatically. The Federal Works Agency administered a program that, at its height, enrolled 130,000 children in over 3,000 centers.

Rather than viewing child care as a menace to children and an indictment for mothers, such options were praised. Mothers with young children could enter the workforce where they were sorely needed, assured that their children would be well looked after. Overall, day-care centers were not that abundant and were used by relatively few employed mothers, with most relying on friends and relatives for child care. Some women remained suspicious of organized day care and preferred to remain unemployed rather than believe the media campaigns. Regardless of whether women took advantage of child-care options or not, when they were needed in the war industry, innovative strategies were developed for day care and traditional beliefs about mothering were suspended. An effective government propaganda program allowed the nation to view day care, at least for a time, as the virtuous, acceptable choice. Mothers were working in defense plants in unprecedented numbers, but their children were not regarded as being socially, physically, or psychologically at risk as a result.

The view that women could and should shoulder more of the responsibility for the war effort was widely accepted. But a paradox remained. Men on the battle-fields were seen as protecting the cherished values of home and family, and yet these very values could be threatened by altered roles of women on the home front. To get around this problem, another propaganda campaign was launched. Women were told they were in it only "for the duration," would return home to domestic duties after the war, and gladly give up their jobs to the returning men. Although joblessness for men was to be alleviated, female unemployment, of course, was never an issue. Devotion to country meant temporarily employment for women, but the home is where women would and should want to be. To a great extent, this belief was accepted by both men and women after the war.

Peacetime. The ideal for which the war was fought—nation and family—remained unshaken. Romantic visions of wives and mothers in resumed, postwar lives abounded during the war, alongside the images of capable women working in defense plants. Hovering in the wings during the war years, the cult of the home made a triumphant comeback to entice even the most reluctant women out of the labor force. For some women who remained in the labor force, a return to prewar job segregation caused mobilization and protest. But with no fully articulated class consciousness or feminist movement to bolster them, they had no real basis for a sustained challenge to the system (Milkman, 2003).

The conversion to a peacetime economy was accelerated with soaring marriage and birth rates. Labor-saving devices and technological innovations were introduced that revolutionized housekeeping but, ironically, did not decrease women's domestic responsibilities. Whereas wartime media appealed to a woman's efficiency in the home to keep her productive in the defense plants, propaganda after the war appealed to her homemaking roles. She was also held to a higher standard of excellence for these roles. Wives were made responsible for the psychological adjustment of husbands in their return to civilian life. Her needs were to be subordinated to his. Women were cautioned to be sensitive, responsive, and above all feminine because this was what civilian life meant for men.

It is clear that new roles for women created during the war existed alongside traditional beliefs concerning their primary domestic duties. Some historians suggest that World War II represented a watershed for gender role change; others argue that continuity and persistence of gender roles was the reality (Kaledin, 1984; Banner, 2005; Meyerowitz, 2005). The women themselves were divided in their postwar plans. Although many enjoyed the work, they saw it as temporary and only for the duration of the war. Many women who gained a sense of independence from their wartime jobs were bitter when postwar cutbacks forced them out of the labor force. Single women, war widows, and those who had to support themselves anyway had no choice but to continue to work. The loss of pay and respect during the postwar years weighed heavily on many women.

The Postwar Era to the Millennium

Despite the emergence of the "back to the home" ideology, the postwar era represents the massive reentrance of women into the labor force over the next half century. Due to its huge gendered effects, this labor force trend (through to the Millennium Recession) is the foundation for much material in this text. Debates continue about the level of impact, but it is impossible to ignore the liberating effects of World War II on women. The war itself contributed to broad social changes in American society. The seeds of social change were planted during the war and took root in an atmosphere of economic growth. Recovery from the Depression, narrowing the gender wage gap, and urban expansion profoundly affected both women and men. Home and family remained integral to women's aspirations, but a doctrine of the spheres that separated women from any other outside existence was doomed after the war. The roots of the sociocultural trends of the 1950 and 1960s can be traced to the war years. World War II was a key catalyst in the emergence of the global economy that profoundly and irrevocably altered gender roles in all social institutions. In later chapters we will see that the global economy at the millennium is linked to both advantages and disadvantages for women and their families worldwide.

Attitudes do not change as quickly as behavior. Efforts that sought to restrict the nondomestic roles and activities of women in the postwar years relied on beliefs about biological determinism that were difficult to reject. Throughout history we have seen scores of women who have successfully broadened narrow role definitions. But World War II provided models for gender role change on such a grand scale that women's accomplishments could not be conveniently relegated to a forgotten footnote in history. Assumptions about essentialism and separate spheres continue to bolster gendered norms and restrict opportunities for both women and men. Attitudes will inevitably erode in the face of massive evidence that contradicts these assumptions. The progress made by women during the war, coupled with rapid postwar social and economic changes, provided the framework for the reemergence of the women's movement in the United States.

THE WOMEN'S MOVEMENT

> In the new code of laws . . . I desire you would remember the ladies and be more generous and favorable to them than your ancestors. (Abigail Adams, March 31, 1776)

In writing to her husband John when he was attending the Second Continental Congress, Abigail Adams cautioned him that if the ladies were ignored and denied the rights for which the Revolutionary War was being fought, they would eventually create a revolution of their own. Women should not be bound by laws that they had no hand in creating. To John Adams she also wrote as follows:

> That your sex is naturally tyrannical is a truth so thoroughly established as to admit of no dispute; but such of you as wish to be happy, willingly give up the harsh title of master for the more tender and endearing one of friend. Then put it out of the power of the vicious and the lawless to use us with cruelty and indignity and impunity . . . so whilst you are proclaiming peace and good will to men, emancipation for all nations, you insist on retaining an absolute power over wives. But you must remember that arbitrary power is like most other things which are hard, very liable to be broken.

John Adams, later to become the nation's second president, dismissed these warnings while helping to draft humanistic documents that proclaimed that all men are created equal. As he wrote to Abigail, "As to your extraordinary Code of Laws, I cannot but laugh. . . . We know better than to repeal our masculine system." For the *Founding Fathers*, the business at hand was to build the infrastructure for an enduring democracy. That this democracy denied basic rights to females, as well as to blacks, was overlooked by most. The challenges that did emerge, even from such influential women as Abigail Adams, did not provide the momentum for organized protest. Although Abigail Adams accurately predicted that women would ferment another revolution, it took another half century before it happened in America.

Two other events helped fuel the rise of feminism and the beginnings of a women's movement in the United States. The French Revolution's ideals of liberty and equality inspired the *Declaration of the Rights of Man* in 1789. A reply by Olympe de Gouges came two years later with the *Declaration of the Rights of Woman*, where she declared that "woman is born free and her rights are the same as those of man" and that "the law be an expression of the general will" and "all citizens, men and women alike" should participate formulating such law (Bock, 2002). For the first time, humanistic standards were explicitly applied to both genders. More importantly, the democratic fervor was sweeping France and influencing other parts of Europe and England, creating an atmosphere that at least considered these radical writings. Had such a work appeared first in America, it would have been rejected, dismissed, and buried.

Second, in 1792, English writer and activist Mary Wollstonecraft (1759–1797) wrote what was to become the bible of the feminist movement, *A Vindication of the Rights of Woman*. In this remarkable work, Wollstonecraft argued that ideals of equality should be applied to both genders, and that it is only in bodily strength that a man has a natural superiority over a woman. As she writes,

> Not only the virtue but the knowledge of the two sexes should be the same in nature, if not in degree, and that women, considered not only as moral, but rational creatures, ought to endeavor to acquire human virtues (or perfections) by the same means as men, instead of being educated like a fanciful kind of half being.

She maintained that women must strengthen their minds, become friends to their husbands, and not be dependent on them. When women are kept ignorant and passive, not only do their children suffer but also society as a whole will be weakened. In advocating full partnership with men, Wollstonecraft explicitly called for a "revolution in female manners" to make women part of the human species by reforming themselves and then the world:

> Let women share the rights and she will emulate the virtues of man; for she must grow more perfect when emancipated . . . . (Excerpts from Wollstonecraft, 1792/1970)

The Early Movement: 1830–1890

The Industrial Revolution radically reorganized the process of production. By the 1830s, employed women worked in factories for low wages under dismal conditions. Manufacturing altered home production of items such as soap, bread, candles, and clothing, and middle-class women lost much economic power. Whereas factory women used unions as vehicles for organized protest, middle-class women believed that higher education and political rights could best serve their aims. These women had different class-based ambitions and used divergent strategies to meet their needs. Unique to American history, they organized into their respective groups, but as women meeting the needs of women.

The dire economic condition of women stimulated working-class and middle-class women to first organize. This humanistic catalyst for the early women's movement also provided middle-class women an outlet to work for a social cause. It was only during the latter suffrage movement that women from both classes joined together for a common goal. Before suffrage, the rallying issue for women was slavery. When Wollstonecraft was calling for the emancipation of women, women were already playing a critical role in the abolitionist movement.

It soon became apparent to the women who worked in the antislavery movement that they were not on the same political level as their male counterparts. Women abolitionists were often not allowed to make public speeches, and with the formation of the American Anti-Slavery Society in 1833, they were denied the right to sign its *Declaration of Purposes*. When the World Anti-Slavery Convention met in London in 1840, women members of the American delegation, including Lucretia Mott and Elizabeth Cady Stanton, had to sit in the galleries and could not participate in any of the proceedings. They became painfully conscious of the fact that slavery had to do with gender as well as race.

The Seneca Falls Convention. Women abolitionists began to speak more openly about women's rights. As progressive as the abolitionist movement was, the inherent sexism of the day served to divide and alienate its members. Men feared that abolitionist goals would weaken by attention to women's rights. While continuing their work for antislavery, women were now more vocal about legislative reforms related to family rights, divorce, women's property, and temperance issues. Recognizing that the inferior status of women needed to be urgently addressed, in 1848 the **Seneca Falls Convention** was held in upstate New York, an event hailed as the birth of the women's movement in the United States.

The Seneca Falls Convention approved a *Declaration of Sentiments* modeled after the Declaration of Independence, which listed the forms of discrimination women had to endure and which they vowed to eliminate. Excerpts from the Declaration clearly demonstrate the continuities of past and present concerns of women.

1. We hold these truths to be self-evident: that all men and women are created equal; that they are endowed by their Creator with certain inalienable rights; that among these are life, liberty and the pursuit of happiness.
2. The history of mankind is a history of repeated injuries and usurpations on the part of man toward woman, having in direct object the establishment of an absolute tyranny over her.
3. He has compelled her to submit to laws, in the formation of which she has no voice.
4. He has made her, if married, in the eye of the law, civilly dead.
5. He has monopolized nearly all the profitable employments, and from those she is permitted to follow, she receives but a scanty remuneration. He closes against her all the avenues to wealth and distinction that he considers most honorable to himself. As a teacher of theology, medicine or law, she is not known.

6. He has endeavored, in every way he could, to destroy her confidence in her own powers, to lessen her self-respect, and to make her willing to lead a dependent and abject life.

This list of discriminatory practices against women as well as 11 of the 12 resolutions aimed at ending such practices was accepted by the convention. It was agreed that women had to submit to laws they did not help create, but there was no unanimous agreement about whether they should seek the vote. History honors Seneca Falls as originating the suffrage movement, but the suffrage resolution was passed only by a small majority. Although the early women's movement has become synonymous with suffrage, this was the very issue that initially split its supporters. Perhaps difficult to understand by today's standards, many women believed that equality was possible without the vote.

In the following years conventions for women's rights were held throughout the North and West. Since abolition was part of its platform, the movement never spread to the South before the Civil War. During the war, activities on the behalf of women *per se* were dormant, but they emerged in earnest soon after. Despite the lack of a national agenda and disagreements on strategy, the movement grew under the leadership of a few women who had the strength and time to work for its causes. Several outstanding women with unique talents are credited for this growth: Lucy Stone, the movement's most gifted orator; Elizabeth Cady Stanton, philosopher and program writer; and Susan B. Anthony, the organizing genius (Clift, 2003; Million, 2003). They spoke on social, economic, and legal issues affecting women and pressed for reforms in education, wages, organized labor, child welfare, and inheritance.

As the movement grew, so did its opponents. First as abolitionists, then as feminists, and always as women, many people despised and ridiculed the movement. Suffrage women were accused of being unnatural, masculine, and female sexual inverts who would doom America to sociobiological disaster (Behling, 2001). By the standards of the day, militant methods fueled opposition. Ever-present verbal abuse and threats of mob violence at rallies caused some supporters to downgrade the importance of the vote. The ranks of the movement were divided and by the end of the Civil War, it was split into two factions.

Division and Unity. Although both factions agreed that getting the vote was necessary, they split on ideology and strategy. In 1869 two organizations were formed. Susan B. Anthony and Elizabeth Cady Stanton founded the National Woman Suffrage Association (NWSA). NWSA did not admit men, was considered militant in tactics, focused on controversial issues such as husband–wife relations, and wanted the vote to achieve other rights for women. Enfranchisement, then, was seen as a means to a greater end.

The second organization, the American Woman Suffrage Association (AWSA), led by Lucy Stone and Julia Howe, was more moderate, attracting many middle- and upper-class women. To make the suffrage question more mainstream, the AWSA refrained from addressing issues thought to be controversial, such as marriage and religion. AWSA focused its work on state-by-state ways to achieve the vote. In 1869 Wyoming was the first state to grant the vote to women, but did so for pragmatic rather than strictly democratic reasons. Women were scarce in the territory, and the right to vote was thought to encourage more migrants. Wyoming was almost not granted statehood because Southern congressmen argued that the states did not have the right to grant suffrage. Because the legislature was elected with women's votes, supporters for statehood asserted that Wyoming "will remain out of the Union for a hundred years rather than come in without the women." By a small margin Wyoming was admitted to the Union in 1890.

AWSA strategies succeeded in gaining many advocates, with suffrage gaining the respectability it needed to attract a broader base of support. In the meantime, NWSA increasingly turned its attention to suffrage and campaigned for political and legal rights. In 1890, the two groups merged to form the **National American Woman Suffrage Association (NAWSA)**. A key consequence of the merger and its gain in "respectability" was that the organization generally distanced itself from the plights of black women, immigrant women, and working-class women. African-American women worked diligently in the suffrage movement but were aware that a double standard existed for black and white women suffragists. Black suffragists called on their white sisters in the movement to "put aside their prejudices and allow black women, burdened by both sexism and racism, to gain political equality" (Terborg-Penn, 1991:133). Their words were largely unheeded. The exclusion of these potential allies at the turn of the century impacted the movement for the next half century. It took another half century before the schism appreciably narrowed.

The Nineteenth Amendment

The next 30 years saw renewed energies for passage of a suffrage amendment, though NAWSA actually accomplished very little. Strategies deemed as too radical were disavowed, militant members were expelled, conservatism set in, and a crisis in leadership occurred. Some of the expelled faction joined a group founded by militant suffragist Alice Paul in 1913. Embracing the tactics of the more militant English suffrage movement, Paul headed the Congressional Union, later known as the Woman's Party. To bring the constitutional amendment to America's public consciousness, the Woman's Party staged mass demonstrations. In the meantime, as new president of NAWSA, Carrie Chapman Catt began a rigorous suffrage campaign in 1915. NAWSA distributed leaflets, lobbied, and addressed influential organizations. Woman's Party members held rallies, went on hunger strikes, and used unorthodox, definitely unfeminine means to spotlight suffrage. Although tactics varied, the common goal was passage of a suffrage amendment that had been introduced and defeated in every session of Congress since 1878.

By the end of World War I, giving the vote to women had widespread support. In 1919 the Nineteenth Amendment was passed by margins of 304 to 90 in the House and 56 to 25 in the Senate. The struggle could not be over until two-thirds of the states ratified it. On August 26, 1920, by only two votes, the amendment was ratified in Tennessee, making the Nineteenth Amendment part of the U.S. Constitution.

The Contemporary Movement

Once the right to vote was gained, feminism literally died in the United States for the next 40 years. The end of the arduous campaign resulting in ratification of the Nineteenth Amendment found some feminists insisting that broader social reforms, rather than narrower feminist goals, were now necessary, because they believed political equality had been achieved. Others, including Alice Paul, called for passage of the Equal Rights Amendment (ERA), which would prohibit all forms of discrimination against women. The ERA was first introduced in Congress in 1923, but even by this time the unity of support for a specific cause had been dissolved.

Coupled with the Depression and a conservative national mood, most activism for women's issues was abandoned.

Second Wave Feminism. It was not until after World War II that the women's movement emerged again on a national scale. Referred to as **second wave feminism**, this phase of the movement (1960–1980s) sought to raise the consciousness of women about sexist oppression in the power structure of society and about using political means to eradicate it. Under the banner "the personal is the political," second wave feminists focused on ways to counter sexism in popular culture and other social institutions.

Three major events provided catalysts for this reawakening of feminism. First, President John Kennedy established the Commission on the Status of Women in 1961. The Commission issued a report documenting the inferior position of women in the United States and set up a citizen's advisory council and state commissions to address problems identified in the report. Second, in 1963 Betty Friedan published her landmark work, *The Feminine Mystique.* Friedan argued that women's only road to fulfillment is as wife and mother. Referring to it as "the problem with no name," women had no identity apart from their families. Despite restrictive roles and a society that condoned and applauded such restrictions, women were beginning to voice their unhappiness. "It is no longer possible to ignore that voice, to dismiss the desperation of so many American women" (Friedan, 1963:21). The second-class status of women, which was pointed to in the Kennedy report, was bolstered by Friedan's assertions and research.

National Organization for Women. The third event heralding the return of feminism was the founding of the **National Organization for Women (NOW)** in 1966, with Betty Friedan serving as its first president. These three events are interdependent. Many of the women first met when they worked on state commissions set up after the Kennedy report. They were also unhappy with the progress being made on their recommendations and felt that a separate effort to deal with issues related to women was important. The creation of NOW can be viewed as an indirect result of the Commission on the Status of Women.

NOW was formed during the turbulent 1960s, an era of heightened political activism and social consciousness. The drive to organize women occurred during a time when African Americans, Native Americans, Latinos, poor people, students, and anti-Vietnam War activists were also competing for public attention through mass demonstrations for their respective causes. In comparison to many of the organizations spawned as a result of these causes, including other women's groups, NOW was, and is, more moderate in its approach. NOW's ability to survive as a viable organization is in part tied to its mainstream emphasis.

White, college-educated, middle-class women were attracted to NOW and became the base for its original growth. However, NOW adopted a top-down structure that tended to limit diversity. NOW remains hierarchically organized with a national body and formal constitution, but with local chapters more autonomous growth and diversity are aided. In the decades since its founding, NOW's membership has expanded considerably, bringing in more nonprofessional and younger women and women of color. This is vital to the ultimate success of feminism in America. A feminist consciousness among African-American women, for example, can only be nurtured through a framework that addresses the ideology of racism in America (Higginbotham, 2003). In 1967 the first NOW national conference adopted a Bill of Rights that included support for an Equal Rights Amendment to the Constitution, women's right to work at all types of jobs, maternity leave rights, and the right of women to control their reproductive lives. As suggested by these goals, NOW has a broad agenda of areas affecting women, but it focuses on political tactics to achieve goals.

Offshoot Groups. The second branch of the feminist reawakening consisted of women representing a wider range of backgrounds who came together in loose coalitions to work on common interests. This branch attracted younger women and women who were involved with other social movements of the time, especially the civil rights movement. During the 1960 and 1970s these women founded many groups, but they tended to match NOW's tactics using mass-based demonstrations, mailings, and media attention for political ends. These included the National Welfare Rights Organization focusing on public assistance to poor women and their families and the National Women's Political Caucus (NWPC), which promotes women as candidates for public office.

Other groups, more radical in orientation, shunned the formal structure of organizations like NOW and believed that its focus on institutional reforms inhibited individual expression. Unlike NOW, some groups excluded men from their ranks, others worked solely for reproductive rights, and many came together under the broad banner of sisterhood, simply for consciousness raising and dialogue. Known for "street theater" and vocal, disruptive demonstrations, groups such as the New York Radical Feminists and Redstockings also used consciousness-raising, but with specific attention to the ongoing power men have over women in all phases of their lives, including sexual and interpersonal relationships. Although less viable in the long run these groups are good examples of some of the many divergent paths of feminism and the women's movement (Chapter 1).

Third Wave Feminism. The extraordinary legal and political successes extending women's rights in the postwar era suggest that the women movement accomplished many of its goals. In the 1990s, however, backlash to feminist initiatives began in earnest and stalled political progress. The mass-based demonstrations of all the postwar social movements were no longer part of the public consciousness. Unlike second wave feminists, young women were introduced to feminism in college coursework (positively) or through media depictions (negatively). Young women embracing feminist causes in the 1990s were less likely to identify with a concept such as sisterhood, with its assumptions of homogeneity of women, and were cautious about identifying openly as feminists. **Third wave feminism** suggests that there is no universal feminism and women define for themselves what it is and what it can become. Despite the lack of a common definition of feminism, third-wavers tend to focus on the intersection of gender with race, class, and sexuality, in both scholarship and activism.

Critique. Despite the historical chronicle of second and third wave feminism according to post–World War II decades, the lines may be divided by generation and by tactics, but there is a great deal of overlap in their areas of interest and their goals. They all acknowledge the importance of the Equal Rights Amendment to the Constitution, for example, but may disagree on where to place it on an activist priority list (Chapter 14). It is more productive, perhaps, that

> . . . thinking about feminist waves as *movement* highlights the variations within generational groups as well as continuities between them. (Aikau et al., 2007) (Italics mine)

The emergence of third wave feminism with younger women filling its ranks is an energizing force for the movement and the array of agenda items still to be tackled. As it has been for over two centuries, the diversity of its members and the inclusive nature of the movement will be forces for both divisiveness and unity. The next chapter demonstrates that the diversity of women worldwide is more conducive than detrimental for a strong global women's/feminist movement.

Summary

1. Women's history emerged to uncover the hidden elements of the other half of humankind, which had been ignored by male historians writing about the exploits of a few powerful, elite men. The first compensatory and contribution histories focused on exceptional women. Today women's history accounts for the race, class, and gender links. Historical themes include misogyny and women and victims but also the resistance women have used against patriarchy.

2. Predating Greek civilization, Minoan Crete may have been a partnership society with a matrilineal system, Amazon legends, Goddess worship, and high gender egalitarianism.

3. Illustrated by the writings of Plato and Aristotle, Greek society relegated women to inferior legal and social status. Described as chattels, in Athens the vast majority of women were segregated and restricted. A few high-level courtesans and wealthy women exercised some privileges. Women in Sparta were expected to be physically fit and manage households when the men were at war.

4. Roman women had more freedom. Vestiges of goddess worship remained, and women had important religious roles. Selected women could become citizens, some amassed fortunes in their own names. But even the most independent and wealthy women were in bondage to men.

5. During the Middle Ages Christianity enveloped Europe, and the misogyny of the Church carried over to the lives of women. The most notable misogyny occurred with witch burning. The Renaissance and Reformation offered some women opportunities for education and more diverse roles overall. But Luther's image of women generally coincided with earlier views, and misogyny continued to govern Europe.

6. The first American women were Native American women from gynocratic tribal systems based on gender reciprocity and balance, often holding important leadership roles. With colonization and Christianity, women's high standing was largely lost.

7. Colonial white women in the Puritan era lived under Christian views imported from Europe. Some scholars argue that because women were scarce and had vital economically productive roles in the household, they enjoyed a measure of prestige and that this era was a golden age for women.

8. The Victorian era saw the rise of True Womanhood—telling women to be pious, pure, and submissive. Despite these messages middle-class women controlled their lives to meet personal needs and engage in social activities.

9. Frontier women were valued for their work in and outside their homes. They lived adverse lives, but adapted and often thrived on their frontier farms.

10. Industrialization opened up employment to women from all walks of life. The appalling working conditions and the Triangle fire that killed 146 workers, mostly women, helped trigger the union movement. The Knights of Labor was opened for women and African Americans. Women's attempts to unionize were not as successful as men's. Gains in pay and employment for women were lost with the Depression.

11. World War II opened up employment for women. The demand for female labor led to higher paying defense jobs and acceptance of married women and women of all races

and classes in the workplace. The cult of the home emerged after the war. But World War II altered gender roles, and the next half century saw increased opportunities for women.

12. Several yardsticks mark the Women's Movement and rise of feminism: The publication of *The Vindication of the Rights of Women* in 1792; the denial of women to sign the *Declaration of Purposes* of the Anti-Slavery Society in 1833 or speak at the World Anti-Slavery Convention in 1840; the Women's Rights Convention in Seneca Falls, New York, in 1848; the passage of the Nineteenth Amendment in 1920; second wave feminism was reawakened by the Commission on the Status of Women by President Kennedy in 1961; the publication of the *Feminist Mystique* by Betty Friedan in 1963; and the formation of the National Organization for Women in 1966. Third wave feminists are more diverse, interested in the links between race, class, gender, and sexuality and offer no one definition of feminism. All groups agree that the Equal Rights Amendment should be passed.

Key Terms

compensatory history 102

contribution history 102

Knights of Labor 121

National American Woman Suffrage Association 130

National Organization for Women 131

pater familias 107

second wave feminism 131

Seneca Falls Convention 128

third wave feminism 132

True Womanhood 117

Critical Thinking Questions

1. With the intersection of race, class, and gender as a framework, demonstrate through specific historical examples how the theme of misogyny and women as victims exists alongside themes related to women's resistance to subjugation and women in esteemed and powerful roles.

2. Considering the historical record, demonstrate how periods of gain and loss for women tend to offset one another. Overall, what historical events provided the opportunities to sustain gain in gender equality?

3. Based on your knowledge of gender and history, and with specific references to feminism in the United States, what suggestions would you offer to contemporary feminists who are working for the passage of the Equal Rights Amendment?

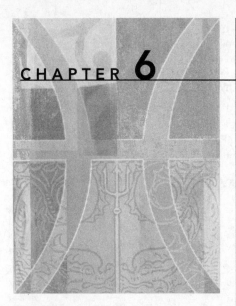

CHAPTER **6**

Development, if not engendered,
is endangered.

—United Nations Development Program

GLOBAL PERSPECTIVES ON GENDER

135

ISRAEL

Religion, Family, and Employment
Jewish Feminism

THE MUSLIM WORLD

Islamization: Iran and Afghanistan
The Arab Middle East
North Africa: Female Genital Mutilation
To Veil or Not to Veil

SCANDINAVIA

Norway
Sweden
The Equality Future

Social change is a central concern of sociology. The discipline emerged as a way to understand and explain the paths to modernity that transformed the world. With the backdrop of the Millennium Recession (MR), this chapter explores the profound gender impact of global social change for women in general and in selected societies. The focus will be on the two commanding change-related processes—globalization and development.

It is not redundant to say that the globe is globalized. It is also safe to say that no one is immune to the effects of a globalized world on their personal and social lives. The world is globalized because all societies have paths to borrow, learn, cooperate, and compete with one another. How they fare on these paths is largely dependent on the powerful forces of "globalization." It is a term defined in many, many ways by different players interested in how these forces affect their constituencies. Adopting the United Nations model, **globalization** is defined as the removal of barriers to increase the flow of capital between and within nations. Implicit in this definition is that globalization is synonymous with capitalism; *economic* globalization is redundant. Globalization is a highly gendered process; it plays out differently in the lives of males and females. It is clear that globalization connects us in a single social and economic space, but it does not unite us.

Unlike definitions of globalization, there is more consensus that **development**, focuses on programs designed to upgrade the standard of living of the world's poor in ways that allow them to sustain themselves. This chapter focuses on gender issues in **developing nations**, also referred to as the *developing world*, the United Nations designation for those less-developed countries with poverty-level incomes per capita. Most of these nations are in Africa, Asia, Latin America, and the Caribbean, and also include the small island nations of the South Pacific. As we will discover, the processes of globalization and development go hand in hand, and are not benign in their effects.

The gender issues selected for review are flashpoints identified by activists, scholars, researchers, and feminists across the globe that serve as culturally defined gender markers on a given nation or region. Even with such a limited focus, the task is formidable. Science demands generalizations but countless exceptions exist. The sociological objective, therefore, is to identify gendered patterns of life and living and to illustrate what women share in common as a result of these patterns. Of all the globe's institutions, the United Nations, through its focus on the gendered consequences of globalization and development, has allowed for many of these issues to be assessed. Unless otherwise noted, statistics and trends mentioned in the chapter are taken from the following sources: UNDP, 2009; UNFPA, 2009; World Bank, 2009.

THE UNITED NATIONS CONFERENCES ON WOMEN

In its Charter of 1945, the United Nations (UN) announced its commitment to the equality of women and men. The year 1975 was declared International Women's Year; the next decade was designated the *UN Decade for Women*. Official conferences to work on a global agenda of women's issues were held in Mexico City in 1975, Copenhagen in 1980, Nairobi in 1985, and Beijing in 1995. Under the banner of "equality, development and peace," each conference assessed the progress of commitments made by various nations on behalf of women.

Alongside each official UN conference ran a parallel one, a forum consisting of hundreds of **nongovernmental organizations (NGOs)**—privately funded nonprofit groups concerned with relief and development and advocacy for the poor—that brought together women from all over the world and all walks of life. NGOs are largely grassroots organizations, representing a wide diversity of opinions and agendas. Because inclusiveness both enhances and fuels dissent, the conferences were marked by divisive cultural issues. The gendered issues related to politics, religion, ethnicity, and economics created the most friction. Efforts by conservative groups to discredit and interrupt the proceedings also occurred. Women attending the NGO Forum in Copenhagen saw the conference becoming more and more politicized. The split between women in the developing and developed world appeared to widen, deterring dialogue about what they shared in common. They left the forum, however, with a better understanding of diverse perspectives and priorities. Five years later in Nairobi, dissention was much less evident; dialogue opened and consensus was reached on key issues. A central change from Copenhagen was acknowledgment that political issues and women's issues cannot be separated. Whether called "a women's movement" or "a feminist movement," when women come together to work on common issues, it is fundamentally a *political* movement.

These gains in political astuteness were clearly evident a decade later. In 1995 the international women's movement took center stage when Beijing, China, hosted the largest UN conference in history. With 50,000 in attendance, Beijing was historic not only in terms of numbers, but also because a woman's agenda moved from the sidelines to the center of global debate.

The Legacy of Beijing: A Personal Perspective

As with the past conferences, in covering the largest gathering of women in history, international media again focused on controversy and conflict rather than the atmosphere of unity and support that emerged during the conference. The Beijing gathering and the parallel NGO Forum in nearby Huairou represent landmark developments in global understanding and cooperation among women of the world.

As addressed in a number of sessions at the conference, women exemplify a glaring blind spot for the media. News outlets in many countries, including the United States, too often approach women's issues with stereotypes, misconceptions, and bias. When addressing a public believed to relish controversy, the seeds for reinforcing these stereotypes continue to be sewn. I believe, however, the truly remarkable events in Beijing helped alter this trend.

Even while attending the conference, many of us were acutely aware that the international media dwelled on issues generating the most controversy, especially by religious fundamentalists who staged frequent demonstrations. The Iranian delegation of fully veiled women and their male "escorts," for example, provided the media much camera time. Their efforts were met by what I would describe as "bemused toleration." The international media toddled behind with cameras and microphones and reported on the nightly news that religious fundamentalism was tearing the conference apart.

This could not have been further from the truth. Although religious fundamentalism was certainly one of many controversial topics, the NGO Forum was remarkable in its ability to gather women of all faiths to engage in dialogue over matters that affected their daily lives—including reproduction, caring for children, domestic violence, and health and well-being—all of which have religious overtones. Workshops brought together women from diverse religious and spiritual heritages. Politics, religion, and cultural traditions were met head on, for example, between Palestinian and Israeli women living under the constant specter of war or between Muslim and other women who disagreed about veiling or female genital mutilation (discussed later). Whether practices were accepted or rejected became less important than how they were discussed. Toleration and understanding emerged in an atmosphere where opinions were voiced and everyone could agree to disagree. What became clear, however, is that the die was cast against religious fundamentalism when it restricts women's human rights. Religious fundamentalism was recast so that it became liberating, used as a weapon against sexism and for empowerment (Lindsey, 1995).

What is the legacy of Beijing? I speak from the perspective of attending the gatherings in Copenhagen and Nairobi as well as Beijing. The previous conferences were more divisive, but also smaller, less inclusive, and with fewer women in the organizing bodies or as official delegates. Although the Beijing conference was racked with negative international media attention, Chinese obstructionism, logistical nightmares, and inadequate facilities, the ability and perseverance of the women who attended and worked to get the Platform of Action adopted were nothing short of spectacular. As Hillary Rodham Clinton stated in her address to the Forum, "NGOs are where the action is." With thousands of NGOs as watchdogs, governments continue to be monitored for pledges made to women and their families through the ratified UN document. This document addressed 12 critical areas of concern, including education, health, and employment, outlining action steps to implement objectives. The number one issue was women's poverty. Actions for this issue included developing gender-sensitive economic policies, placing economic value on women's unpaid work, and offering increased education and training programs for poor women.

After the following overview of gender issues from a global perspective, it should be clear how Beijing served as a watershed for the women's movement worldwide. Despite the inevitable backlash any global movement for social transformation must endure, the women's/feminist movement has successfully sent its message across the globe. This message is that women will no longer be ignored, that women's rights are human rights, and that nations will be held accountable for their progress, or lack thereof, in ending gender inequality. Numerous follow-up conferences, seminars, and workshops held since Beijing by NGOs monitor progress and ensure accountability. The gathering of women in Beijing attests to the recognition that women's empowerment is beneficial to everyone. Despite media misconceptions and a long and rocky path ahead, emerging global sisterhood is a sociopolitical reality to be reckoned with.

WOMEN, GLOBALIZATION, AND DEVELOPMENT

The United Nations Development Program spearheads major efforts to reduce the gender gap in human capability—areas such as literacy, access to health care, job training, and family planning. Much of this effort is directed at the eight *Milliniuum Development Goals (MDGs)*, to be achieved by 2015, that target the major development challenges in the world. Goal 3 is to promote gender equality and empower women. Women in the developing world are the most restricted in important areas of human capability. The good news is that since 1985 the gap in education and health has been cut in half. The bad news is that the global economic crisis has stalled MDG implementation and patterns of gender inequality have intensified. These patterns include the following:

1. Seventy percent of the 1.4 billion people worldwide in abject poverty (living on less than one dollar a day) are women and girls.
2. Over two-thirds of the illiterate adults worldwide are women.
3. If the unpaid work women perform—such as subsistence farming and domestic labor—was counted in economic terms, the world's gross domestic product would triple. Eighty percent of Africa's food is grown and processed by women.
4. Women's employment rate is plummeting; at the same time the number of women who are household heads skyrockets.
5. After years of decline, since 2002 the refugee population has steadily increased half of the world's 32 million refugees are women; women and their dependent children represent three-fourths of the refugee population (UNHCR, 2008).
6. In virtually every Sub-Saharan African nation, women constitute over half of all cases of HIV/AIDS.
7. Ninety percent of all countries have organizations that promote the advancement of women, but women make up about 10 percent of the world's legislative seats.

The underlying cause of the inequality of women is that their roles are primarily domestic (mother, wife, homemaker, subsistence farmer), and although these are vital to the well-being of their families and to society, they are undervalued and unpaid. Most of the world's women work in the **informal sector**, the economic activities of people who work as subsistence farmers, landless agricultural laborers, street vendors, or day workers. Much informal sector work is undocumented because services and goods rather than cash income is often the exchange basis. Globalization capitalizes on the informal sector work of women and reinforces existing gender inequality.

The Impact of Globalization on Women

The role and status of women in development has emerged as a major global social issue. Beginning with Ester Boserup's (1970) pioneering study on women in development, the argument that development has adverse effects on women—often leading to further impoverishment, marginalization, and exploitation—is well documented (Lindsey, 1996b; Jaquette and Summerfield, 2006; Tiessen, 2007). The path to negative development outcomes for women is a deceptively simple one. In societies characterized by powerful patriarchal institutions, men and women rarely share equally the limited resources available to families, a situation that deteriorates with globalization.

Rural Families. The hardest hit are rural women whose work outside the home consists of subsistence farming. Even though they were not landowners, Latin American and African women for several centuries managed farms and retained control over their produce. Colonialism, agricultural development projects, and technology-based cash crop farming virtually eliminated traditional economic resources available to women through farming. Subsistence farming is vital to the livelihood of a family but it is considered domestic work with no cash exchanged and no surplus for profit in the marketplace (Waring, 1988). Development programs typically use standard international economic definitions, which exclude the majority of work women perform, such as child care, domestic labor, and subsistence farming.

Development policies have also ignored gender implications of other work activities. At the family level, *the trickle-down model* is supposed to operate. Policies are designed to upgrade the economic standards of families by concentrating on the assumed male head of household, who is the breadwinner, with his dependent wife in the homemaker role. Development programs assume that the whole family benefits by improving the employment of men. This assumption is based on an urban, middle-class model that does not acknowledge the productive roles of women, especially rural women. Women's work, therefore, remains undercounted, undervalued, and underpaid (Staudt, 1998).

Men often migrate to cities in search of paid work, leaving women with loss of help in remaining subsistence activities. Employment options available to rural women usually consist of low-paid domestic work or commercial farm labor. Some women are recruited for work in the transnational corporations' (TNCs) assembling and light-manufacturing plants dotting the urban fringes in less-developed countries. TNCs favor teens and young women for their willingness to work for low wages in substandard conditions. Others migrate internationally, joining the massive ranks of maids and nannies employed in the households of the world's wealthy. Development planners failed to account for the various ways that women and their families are impacted by the global economy and the supposed economic benefits that come with it (Cagatay, 2001).

On the positive side, the correlation between globalization, development, and women's impoverishment is no longer ignored. Propelled by the international women's movement, strong women-oriented NGOs and the Beijing Platform of Action, the gendered impact of development is being addressed. Development projects funded through the UN and World Bank, for example, must prepare a gender analysis at the planning stages to determine how the project differentially affects women and men.

A Model of Women and Development

A sociologically informed model of women and development can offer planners useful leads to explain, understand, and design appropriate development projects. The following elements should be included in the model (Lindsey, 1995, 2004, 2006; Deutscher and Lindsey, 2005).

1. It must be informed by sociological theory and account for the global stratification system that keeps the developing world economically dependent on richer nations. Capitalism and colonialism intertwine to determine the economic structures that ultimately shape the subordination of women.
2. It must account for the market-driven economic globalization that, paradoxically, may serve to both empower and disempower women.
3. Sociological theory for development planning must be translated into practice. Fieldwork and policy inform one another and contribute to new ways of using social science concepts for real-world applications. As envisioned by sociology's founders, a "sociology of usefulness" is encouraged.
4. Economic definitions of productivity need to account for women's unpaid work in their homes, as farmers, and in the informal sector (see Eisler, 2007).
5. It needs to be interdisciplinary and capitalize on the rich conceptual and empirical work of the social sciences. Sociologists, economists, and anthropologists need to talk to one another, to practitioners who work in development, and most important, to the women and the community affected by development decisions.
6. A feminist perspective emphasizing women's empowerment should inform the model. This perspective fits well with conflict theory because it challenges a patriarchal status quo (Chapter 1). Women's empowerment enhances quality of life for women, their families, and their communities.

Development projects that neglect gender analysis and ignore broader definitions of production are both unrealistic and unsuccessful. Gender disparities are now being recognized as injustices and obstructions to development.

RUSSIA

The collapse of the Soviet Union ushered in beliefs that democracy would envelop the world. Former Soviet Premier Mikhail Gorbachev's policies of *glasnost* ("openness") combined with *perestroika* ("restructuring") were to be the keys to transform the Soviet Union into a democratic nation with a free-market economy. Gorbachev's vision of a democratized, capitalistic Soviet Union was not to be. The USSR rapidly crumbled into independent nation states, most which embraced capitalism but not democracy. Russia, the largest and most economically and politically influential of the former Soviet republics, continues on a rocky path in a transitional economy. Russia's economy rebounded from a 1998 financial crisis then sank again in the global MR. The number of Russians who are better-off in the transitions is not balanced by the number whose quality of life deteriorated during the same period. Even before MR, the restructured economy deepened poverty and unemployment and slashed or eliminated subsidies for health and welfare (Khasbulatova and Egorova, 2002). Russia is in important ways similar to many developing world nations in quality-of-life indicators, particularly with regard to gender.

Russian women have been further marginalized or pushed into poverty by the combined effects of globalization and the transition to a free-market economy (Dawson, 2002; Glass and Marquart-Pyatt, 2008). The impact of these processes reverberated throughout most of the other post-Soviet republics. In Azerbaijan, for example, educational and health-care subsidies were drastically cut and public sector jobs, which disproportionately employed women, were eliminated. Loss of paid work propelled women into poverty, and simultaneously, loss of subsidies for child care and elder care increased their caregiving responsibilities. In a decade, Azerbaijan dropped from 71 to 90 in the UN Development Index (Najafizadeh, 2003). Although women's advocacy organizations filled some of the gaps left by the ravages of transition, the Millennium Recession may offset these benefits.

The Soviet Legacy

The Soviet constitution stated, "Women and men have equal rights." In 1917, Lenin's regime mandated upgrading women's position by abolishing all forms of discrimination that women endured in tsarist Russia. Women were granted full equality in educational and employment opportunities, family and property rights, and competition for administrative offices. Women secured almost half the positions as deputies in state legislatures and were well represented in the trade unions. Political positions with the most influence, however, were essentially devoid of women. The rhetoric of equality masked the continued oppression of women in the former Soviet Union.

Employment

The Soviet Union had a larger percentage of women in the labor force than any other industrial society during its rapid expansion. In no country in the world did women constitute such a significant part of the labor force in so short a time. In today's Russia, the large majority of women are employed. With MR, however, the already pervasive gender stereotypes about women workers run rampant and males are the preferred employees. Employers view women workers as less profitable. Working mothers benefit from even the limited subsidies for child and health care offered by employers. A woman's load as mother, wife, and worker decrease time available for training to upgrade her skills; in turn she is viewed as a "second-rate" employee (Rimashevskaia, 2008). Russian women have high levels of professional credentials in law, medicine, and engineering as well as in the skilled trades. Like American women, however, they are overrepresented in low-paying and menial jobs, are underrepresented in managerial jobs, and hold lower ranks as managers and less prestigious specialties as professionals (Harden, 2001; Riska, 2001).

Despite the official doctrine of equal pay for equal work, and regardless of qualifications, gender discrimination in hiring and promotion and in wages is taken for granted. Under the communists, the average female worker earned two-thirds of the average male income; women now earn less than half of what men average. The wage gap decreased briefly after the 1998 financial crisis, stagnated after 2002, and is increasing again during MR (Brainerd, 2000; Kazakova, 2007). The pay gap is larger for professional women who are in feminized jobs, such as teaching, nursing, and social work—occupations considered an extension of women's "natural" aptitude for caregiving (Iarskaia and Iarskaia-Smirnova, 2002). Already entrenched in unskilled jobs, in feminized professional jobs, and within a gender-based system of job segregation, women's economic losses are expected to increase.

Gender inequity persists in unemployment as well. Globalization moved workers out of industry into a newly created service sector. For-profit companies rapidly emerged in all industries and government oversight of these companies virtually disappeared. The decline of government bureaucracy and subsidies exert a heavy toll on women and their families. Female unemployment is at an all-time high at the same time that unemployment benefits are slashed. Men and women adapt differently to the stark realities of the new labor markets in Russia. Women report lower levels of control during transition but appear to adapt better than men. Rural women benefit when gardens are transformed into profitable small businesses. NGOs are more likely to support the causes of women rather than men during transition (Ashwin, 2005; Barrett and Buckley, 2009; Sweet, 2009).

The Collision of Family and Employment. The glaring disparity between men and women in the labor force is explained by a unique combination of ideological and cultural factors. Referred to as a *double burden* rather than a second shift in a Russian context, powerful family barriers hinder women's career advancement. Compared to men in almost every other developed nation, and most nations undergoing economic transition, Russian men take on the least amount of domestic duties when their wives, sisters, and mothers are also in the paid labor force. On average, husbands have 30 hours more free time per week than wives. Both rural and urban women report a slight decrease in work hours outside the home but a sharp increase in work hours inside the home (Karakhanova, 2003). Women are torn by how to deal with *peregruzhenost* (overburdening). Heightened by the chaos generated by the collapse of the state-controlled economy, traditional views of family roles, coupled with a chronic labor shortage in rural areas, serve to maintain this situation.

The Russian government is alarmed about a falling birth rate and the increased preference for smaller families. Nonetheless, the economy depends on the cheaper labor of women who can be hired part-time or as temporary workers. Professional women are being pushed out of the labor force but manual workers are still in demand. The economy could not withstand a mass exodus of women from the ranks of paid labor, but private enterprises are not offering benefits such as day care and pregnancy leave to entice women to stay in the workforce. Another confounding factor is that although Russian couples do not want large families, available and affordable birth control options are limited. Abortion is costly but abortion rates are very high. Official figures show that for every one birth there are two abortions in Russia. This ratio does not capture the number of illegal abortions, estimated to be as high as eight abortions for every birth (Bodrova, 2002). Russia's pronatalist call has fallen on deaf ears largely because the government is unwilling to subsidize birth control options and employment benefits for new parents.

Marriage and Family

Despite the fact that women take on virtually all domestic responsibilities, the prospect of marriage and children, albeit a small family, is a strong priority, especially among rural women. Women are more preoccupied with romance and appear to accept the far from egalitarian arrangement that will emerge after marriage. Russian women are more family oriented than men and place a higher value on child rearing. Family, children, and social order continue to be the highest values for women, with the importance of paid work declining significantly as a value

(Goodwin and Emelyanova, 1995; Karakhanova, 2003). They may be agricultural workers, professionals, or clerks, but their main concern is to be married and raise a family.

Russia is promoting the image of women as homemakers. Women in the workplace are caricatured as masculine and blamed for social problems such as divorce, teen pregnancy, drug abuse, and juvenile delinquency (Dement'eva, 2001; Boyko, 2002). Although employed women are needed for national productivity and as income earners for their families, there is still no reprieve from social disapproval. Officials openly portray women as taking good jobs away from deserving men. Talk shows and newspapers describe how workplace and family suffer when women work outside the home. Women lament the lost masculinity of contemporary men and men reproach women for their lack of femininity (Lipovskaya, 1994; Clements et al., 2002).

Support or Backlash to Feminism?

In the transition period Russian women face a number of difficult issues. The restructured economy intensified sexual inequality, but glasnost at least opened discussion on the plight of women, particularly rural women. NGOs and universities began publicizing the benefits of a women's movement and women's rights. Glasnost rekindled a hidden but viable feminist spirit that the Soviet Union had driven underground. On the other hand, the revival of feminism appears to be weak. Feminists are portrayed in popular culture as threatening to Russian values and leading to a war with men. Men's loss of income and jobs is offset by media increasingly portraying Russian women as aggressive, vengeful, and dominant (Kay, 2006; Voronina, 2009). The feminist movement in Russia suffers from a lack of younger women filling leadership positions, the failure of Russian-bred NGOs to become organizationally viable and financially sustainable, and minimal political representation for women's issues. Feminism has a "shadow existence" in contemporary Russia—with few footholds in univerisities or in the country as a whole (Zdravomyslova, 2002; Kukulin, 2008). It appears easier to mobilize activists and advocates for Russian women outside Russia than inside Russia (Sperling et al., 2001). Civil activism for Russians is a relatively new idea. Both men and women are suspicious of feminists who, for example, applaud full-time employment for women but who neglect to address their double-burden work (Sperling, 1999; Conze, 2001). Because the Soviets imposed gender egalitarianism—whether it was to be objectively viable or not—by decree from the central government, feminism in Russia has been unable to shed the image that it is not so different from communist ideology.

As disheartening as it sounds to Western feminists, many Russian women would agree with the words of a woman who, although very poor, has the luxury of being a stay-at-home wife. "Women will never win in the fight within the establishment for power. Why should I try when I can achieve so much more at home?" (Tavernise, 2003:4). Contrary to Marxian assertions, the life of toil inside the home for no pay is eagerly embraced by women who toil for low pay outside the home. Glasnost paved the way to openly debate critical problems faced by women. The government, however, is disinterested in the debate; neither have women mobilized enough to challenge the government to do so. The ironic twist to democratic trends in Russia, in the short term at least, is the erosion of women's rights.

CHINA

Even before the revolution elevating Mao Tse Tung as head of the new People's Republic of China (PRC), the Chinese Communist Party (CCP) recognized that women were valuable allies in building socialism. For the peasant revolution to maintain momentum during the construction of a new regime, it was believed that women's issues must be given priority. Because women were inextricably bound to an ancient, oppressive, and seemingly immutable family structure, women's rights in the home were given highest priority. Priorities, however, were (and are) mediated with more immediate goals in mind, specifically economic growth. For the CCP, as long as women's rights and economic development conveniently coincide, they remain a government priority.

Similar to the ideology of the former Soviet Union, China's goal to increase women's employment is linked to the argument that if women gain economically, they will also gain in the family. Whereas Karl Marx articulated the structure of classical social conflict theory, it was Friedrich Engels who applied this approach to the family (Chapter 1). Engels argued that the family is the basic source of women's oppression. The patriarchal family is a microcosm of a larger, oppressive capitalistic society. By this reasoning, therefore, once women expand their roles outside the family to become economically productive in the new socialist system, servility to men will cease. Popularized as the "liberation through labor" ideal, the improvement of the economic status of women continues as the foundation for achieving gender equality. Family reform would inevitably follow.

Reform and the Chinese Family

The record of Chinese family reform since the revolution is mixed. The traditional Chinese family was based on Confucian principles, which gave complete authority to males. The family was patriarchal, patrilineal, and patrilocal. In Confucian classic writings, females are seen as naturally inferior, unintelligent, jealous, indiscreet, narrow-minded, and seductive to innocent males (Chapter 12). Given these views, it is not surprising that women's lives were severely restricted and that laws would reflect these values. A woman's marriage was arranged; she could not normally inherit property, would move into her husband's household at marriage, and had to survive under the unquestioned authority of her husband, his father, and his grandfather, as well as other assorted male relatives. A female hierarchy also existed. Her mother-in-law exercised strict control, and she could beat or sell her daughter-in-law for disobedience or for running away. The bride occupied the lowest rung in the domestic hierarchy of the traditional Chinese family.

Footbinding. Running at all was impossible for those women who endured the technique of footbinding, which could reduce a foot to as small as three inches. Dating to the early part of the twelfth century, this crippling procedure was more extreme for women from the upper classes who did not have to work in manual labor or in the fields. Besides becoming a status symbol and a prerequisite for marriage among the upper classes, footbinding ensured that women remained passive and under the control of men. Indeed, for the family and hence Confucian-based society to function smoothly, the subordination of women was required, and practices such as footbinding helped ensure this.

Marriage. The Marriage Law of 1950 abolished many practices that had oppressed women in the traditional Chinese family. The fundamental principle on which the new law was based was free-choice marriage. It was expected that this would lay the foundation for releasing women from their abysmal existence in feudal marriage and alter the ancient belief that men are superior to women. Not only did both genders gain equal rights to divorce, but marriages had to be monogamous; bigamy and other forms of plural marriage, as well as concubinage, were abolished. Also eliminated were child betrothal, bride prices, and any restrictions placed on the remarriage of widows.

Again with women's rights in mind, in 1980 a sweeping new law was passed to update the older law. The 1980 law specified that husband and wife hold equal legal statuses in the home and both have the freedom to engage in paid work, to study, and to participate in social activities. Neither party is allowed to restrain or interfere with the other. It is clear that the 1980 law bolstered the rights of women—especially urban women—in their homes. In rural areas, however, the law was met with less enthusiasm. Enforcement was minimal and progress stalled. In the next two decades China witnessed alarming increases in domestic violence, child abandonment, a quadrupled divorce rate, and large increases in poverty rates of divorced women. After years of legislative debate, amendments to the 1980 law were passed in 2001 that are largely efforts to protect women's rights in their families. Adultery and cohabitation were outlawed, and property division in divorce was extended to include all property gained in a marriage, including salary, profits, and inheritance. Bigamy and forced marriage were already illegal, but ancient concubinage practices continue. Like the older law, however, the new law resists enforcement.

Laws abolishing blatant abuses of the feudal Chinese family have been beneficial to women. But these successes must be tempered with the cultural realities of an ancient patriarchal society as well as official policies that have undermined gender equality. For example, although three-fourths of marriages are "free-choice" marriages, it is still difficult to provide the conditions for young people to meet and develop relationships. Cultural restrictions on girls' activities combined with lack of privacy make reliance on arranged meetings and matchmakers acceptable alternatives. It is not easy to determine the extent to which these alternatives are freely chosen, regardless of the marriage laws. Founded on egalitarian principles, the law envisions "mutual responsibility and faithfulness in marriage," but these ideals are far from reality. Husbands' resistance to egalitarian pressures may translate into lower marital quality for wives (Pimentel, 2006). It is also difficult to enforce the provision for wealthier men who have second wives and jeopardize the families of all their unions. Kin customs pervade, and parents of potential partners still wield much authority in arranging marriages. A patrilocal extended family structure in rural areas continues to put new brides at a disadvantage and reinforces the preference for sons. Parents know that daughters are only temporary commodities. Ancient Chinese proverbs such as "Raising a daughter is like weeding another man's field" continue to be quoted and attest to the strength of the preference for sons.

The One-Child Policy

As noted in Chapter 3, the extent of ancient traditions that put a premium on sons and serves to devalue daughters has taken a more ominous turn. From its founding, PRC policy focused on upgrading the status of women. It simultaneously introduced a stringent campaign to reduce population growth. These two goals have disastrously collided with one another. In 1979, the central government initiated the **one-child policy**, which, as the name implies, allows only one child per couple, with severe penalties for violation. Whereas China had other programs to curb its rate of population growth, the one-child policy is unique in that enforcement is stricter, more uniform, and with more severe consequences for noncompliance. Massive public campaigns make prospective parents aware of the incentives or penalties related to the policy.

Couples receive one-child certificates entitling them and their child to an annual cash subsidy. For subsequent children, an "excess child levy" is imposed as compensation for the extra burden placed on the state in educating and feeding additional children. Rewards for the single child must be returned with the birth of the second. If an employed woman with a one-child certificate gets pregnant again, she is encouraged to have an abortion. If she refuses she loses her bonus, will be left out of the next wage increase, and will suffer scorn by her coworkers. Powerful beliefs about male sexuality and power persist. Male sterilization is dismissed as an option. The policy largely applies to China's 90 percent Han population; minorities such as Muslim Uighers and Tibetans are allowed more than one child or are exempt from the policy. In a culture priding itself on families who care for and respect the elderly, the one-child policy is also on a collision course with the rapidly increasing elderly population. Between 2006 and 2050, the elderly population is projected to increase from 8 to 24 percent, with few children available to support them (Kaneda, 2006; Liu, 2008). By 2035 over 70 percent of all families in Beijing and Shanghai will be one-child families (Rong, 2005). Acknowledging the emerging care crisis, if an only child marries an only child, the couple is allowed to have two children.

There are other exceptions to the formal policy. It is more relaxed in rural areas for farm families who produce their own food in private plots for subsistence and profit, and "excess" children can be pressed into agricultural labor. Birth rates are declining in rural areas, too, but peasant communities know that enforcement of the law is weaker. Farm couples with one or two female children are more successful in getting approval to try for a son. Penalties for excess children for poorer urban couples are much more detrimental in their overall effect. Richer couples in urban areas like Shanghai and the exploding cities in Guangdong Province are more successful in skirting the policy. Wealthy couples have high-quality housing and can provide private schools to several children. Since they do not rely on government subsidies, they are confident that they will be quietly ignored by local authorities.

Son Preference. Regardless of location, the one-child policy reinforces the preference for sons. Strong vestiges of ancestor worship exist throughout China. Ancestors are powerful and could bless or curse a family, so offerings and prayers must be bestowed frequently. A woman gains ancestral status only through her husband and sons. Without male descendants she could have no afterlife. Chinese women who trace their family trees back three thousand years do not find any women on them. Dismal indeed were the prospects of a wife who conceived no male children or who remained unmarried or a childless widow.

With one child as the option, that child had better be a male. Female infanticide has been practiced in China for centuries, but it diminished considerably after the Chinese revolution in 1949. Directly linked to the one-child policy, illegal practices such as female infanticide, sex-selective abortion, and the neglect and abandonment of girls have dramatically increased. Maternal deaths for unapproved pregnancies also increase (Hesketh et al., 2005; Jackson et al., 2006). Coupled with large numbers of international adoptions of unwanted girls, these practices translate to China's lopsided sex ratio at birth, estimated between 112 and 135 depending on region. Each birth cohort of women is smaller than the previous one (Chapter 2). Since women marry men who are a few years older, the one-child policy favoring sons makes fewer brides available to grooms (Potts, 2006).

Critique. When enacted in 1979 the one-child program was the most unpopular policy in contemporary China. It was announced as a short-term measure that would lead couples to voluntarily reduce size of their families. Despite the huge and negative demographic, financial, and cultural effects of gender imbalance and the lack of uniform enforcement, China has reaffirmed intentions to continue the policy and to crack down on couples who violate it (Feng, 2005; Yardley, 2008). Rich people and celebrities, for example, will pay stiff fines and will be publicly named. Penalties for children born overseas will not be overlooked when the couple returns to China.

Much has changed since 1979. Research suggests that 75 percent supports the policy and believes it was (and is) necessary for China's continued economic growth (Li and Zhang, 2007). Chinese couples increasingly say they desire only one child, many believing that future generations of women will be better-off when the one child is a girl. Among college-educated, urban couples not only is son preference decreasing, but females who want one child are now more likely to express a daughter preference (Greenhalgh, 2001; Merli and Smith, 2002; Ding and Hesketh, 2006).

The latent functions of a one-child policy include reducing the significance of patrilineal heritage and encouraging women to make nontraditional career choices. In the long run, the one-child policy may improve the status of women and make daughters more valued overall. On the other hand, debate about the one-child policy inside China focuses on the economic benefits and concerns about the care crisis. Sexist overtones and dire consequences of the policy for girls are dismissed. The large portion of China's population residing in poverty-stricken rural and fringe urban areas maintain strong cultural beliefs about the value of a boy over a girl. The well-being of girls is compromised in human capability relative to their education, health, and economic outlook. International discourse on the one-child policy revolves around China's economic and demographic "challenges" rather than as a human rights violation.

To Get Rich Is Glorious

Under the banner of Chinese-style capitalism, the slogan "To get rich is glorious" is eagerly embraced throughout China. Market-driven globalization fueled the massive entry of women into paid labor, one of the most consequential socioeconomic transformations in late-twentieth-century China (Cartier, 2001). In rural China, where women are valued for their domestic work, female employment rates are historically lower. With relaxed restrictions on migration, however, opportunities for off-farm income continue to accelerate. Women's employment soared, many finding jobs near their villages and others migrating to the mushrooming global factories in China's Special Economic Zones (SEZs). As hosts to foreign investment firms, SEZs are a major engine driving capitalism in China—where the profit motive thrives unfettered. Others migrate as couples, the more educated among them bypassing factories for higher paying service and technical jobs (Xu, 2000; Fan and Li, 2002). The migration of millions of Chinese between village and city constitutes the largest internal migration of any nation in history.

The Gender Paradox of Globalization and Development

State policy and economic reform appear to be mutually supportive, fostering both gender equality and women's economic integrity. Support for this contention is strong. Women's new activities in both rural and urban areas significantly increase household income. Rural poverty among women is eroding. Women carry on farm work when husbands and children migrate, but household decision-making power increases (Matthews and Nee, 2000; De Brauw et al., 2002). Women welcome market-driven reforms that offer flexibility for their on-farm work and opportunities for off-farm employment. Women report more independence and freedom from patriarchal and parental control over their lives. For urban working couples, women have more freedom to choose jobs according to their educational and professional priorities (Zhou and Moen, 2001). The prediction that globalization fuels gender inequity and increases women's disadvantage is not necessarily borne out by research in both rural and urban areas (Rozelle et al., 2002:21).

On the other hand, it also appears that China is not that different from the "classic" pattern documenting the downside of globalization and development for women. Globalization widens gender disparities in state sectors that employ more women, and they are the first to be laid off. In areas where family-based rather than communal-based agriculture is now normative, farming shifts to older, less-educated women who experience sharp increases in domestic responsibilities (Wang, 2000; Lee, 2002). Current and future earnings are compromised when family members migrate because not only must additional help be hired, but girls often drop out of school to work on the farm. Urban women are employed in gender-segregated jobs and are paid less than men. For employed rural women, the gender disparity in income is even greater. The government is officially committed to women's equality, but legal means to enforce it in the workplace are weak or absent (Lindsey, 2007).

China's globalization paradox for women has several key dimensions. First, women's employment has skyrocketed at the same time as massive increases in unemployment for both men and women occurred. Second, there are major gains in household income, especially in rural households, but women gain less than men. In female-headed households there is an overall net loss. Third, essentialist beliefs about the proper place of women are reemerging. If job and family are incompatible for women, any problem of unemployment will be "solved" when women return to hearth and home. At the same time, women hear other messages that they are needed in the labor force (Lindsey, 2006, 2007).

China is not a democracy, but its enviable position as the world's largest market allows it to navigate its development course with more freedom from international regulation than its developing world neighbors. To date, MR downturn bringing other nations to their knees appears to be less severe in China. More data are needed to resolve the paradox. It remains uncertain if women in China will be culturally permitted to share in the "to get rich is glorious" ideal.

INDIA

India is confronting challenges that threaten its economic and political stability. Now with over one billion people, it is second only to China as the world's most populous nation. Considering the staggering problems related to population growth, land and food shortage, unemployment, and growing disparity between poverty and wealth, India looks to all segments of its very heterogeneous society for solutions. Opportunities for women are a major factor in solutions, but planners have barely acknowledged this reality.

The Religious–Political Heritage

India is similar to Western nations in that its history and religious heritage reflect inconsistencies regarding the role of women. Goddess images, important female religious occupations, and critical economic roles for women in the pre-Vedic and Vedic eras (2500–300 B.C.E) demonstrate a modicum of prestige for large numbers of women. Coupled with technological changes that excluded women, the ascendance of Hinduism gradually eroded this prestige and sent more women into a chattel-like existence. Indian women share a religious legacy with Western women. Their freedom and status are severely compromised when religion gains an institutional foothold (Chapter 12).

By the beginning of the first century, India decentralized the authority of the various Indian states. High-caste Brahmin scholars were powerful enough to interpret the ancient *Smitris* (laws). The *Laws of Manu* now enveloped India and demonstrated how much the position of women had deteriorated. Manu made a woman completely dependent on a man (husband, father, or son). Manu forbade widow remarriage and reduced a widow's status to such a lowly extreme that the ritual of burning widows (satis) steadily took hold (Chapter 12). The Laws of Manu demonstrated "the polarized male perception of the female" but were also used to legitimize gender inequality as well as protect the interests of the ruling Brahmin class (Mitter, 1991:87).

The Social Reform Movement

Shaping the roots of a reform movement, new ideas concerning the status of women emerged by the nineteenth century. Glaring examples of the inhumane treatment of women were attacked, including child marriage, lack of property rights, purdah (seclusion of women), and the dismal condition of widows. Reformists were most successful when accounting for religious proscriptions embedded in these customs. They argued that, regardless of caste or religion, such customs were responsible for the condition of women. Education and literacy, however, would make women better wives and mothers. Although many women were helped by these strategies, reformists accepted the belief that a woman's life was restricted to her family life. Today the majority of rural and lower-caste women remain untouched by the reforms. Divorced, widowed, and single women are in peril when they have no source of male support but cannot be employed for pay outside their homes. Cultural beliefs about women and marriage and the patriarchal organization of the Indian joint (extended) family impose huge economic hardships on women.

The Gandhis and Nehru. Serious questioning of women's roles came with Mahatma Gandhi, who believed that women were not only essential to India's quest for independence, but also that social justice demanded their equality. Given the nationalist sentiment and the charisma of Gandhi, women of all castes and regions flocked to the independence movement, assuming leadership roles and participating in all manners of political dissent (Desai, 2001; Sarkar, 2001). Jawaharlal Nehru shared Gandhi's vision. As India's first prime minister, and against much opposition, Nehru pushed through legislation giving women the right to inherit, divorce, and vote. As with the reforms a century before, however, the effect was minimal for most women. A strong women's movement in India worked for gender equality 30 years before independence. But its effectiveness was curtailed by agendas set by British colonialists and Indian nationalists who supported women only when their interests happened to coincide. Patriarchal bias held on in the post-independence era, and not only were the contributions of women forgotten, but women became victims in further conflicts (Anjum, 2000). The overall effect was, and to a large extent continues to be, that the vast majority of Indian women have not seen the effects of a women's movement on their daily lives.

The Nehru factor in Indian politics continued to be played out after independence. Nehru's daughter, Indira Gandhi, succeeded to the post of prime minister in 1966 largely because she was a member of the Nehru dynasty and because her party believed they could control her. Her skill and strength proved them wrong. She was politically astute, using her gender as an asset rather than a liability. She identified herself as a member of the oppressed but also appealed to those looking for a mother–goddess figure, so imbued in the Hindu tradition (cited in D'Souza and Natarajan, 1986:373). Until her assassination in 1984 by her bodyguards, Indira Gandhi ruled with an authoritarian hand for 15 years.

The Gender Gap in Human Development

Mahatma Gandhi's vision to elevate the position of women in India is far from realized. About 50 percent of females are literate compared to about 75 percent of males; about 20 percent more boys continue to secondary school level. Education translates into paid employment. When compared to the masses of unskilled female laborers in India, most of whom work in agriculture, professional women comprise only a tiny minority. Although there has been an expansion of female employment in general, this has not offset the decrease in the employment of unskilled women. The most important statistic related to gender and paid work is that virtually all Indian women are engaged at some level in informal sector work. The United Nations' Human Development Index (HDI) is a composite measure of a nation's achievement in three categories related to health, education, and employment. India's rank of 128 out of 177 countries is directly linked to the fact that women and girls represent the largest proportion of the population living in absolute poverty.

Health. Regarding health and reproduction, and despite development efforts, mortality rates have increased and life expectancy rates have decreased in some regions. Similar to China, the sex ratio at birth in India favors males, a pattern that is increasing. Son preference contributes to higher mortality rates for females than males, with female infants less likely to receive the necessities for survival in poverty-ridden households. The neglect of girls is also linked to a strong, continuing dowry tradition in India. In highly stratified societies such as India, dowries, like other properties, are a means of social mobility where men use rights over women to compete for social status. Males and females are closer to parity in nutrition and healthy life expectancy, but the harmful consequences of dowry and son preference for females continue (Chapter 2).

Despite knowledge about family planning and desire to have fewer children, frequent and excessive childbearing severely compromises the health of women. In addition to strong cultural beliefs about a husband's right to have frequent and unprotected sex on demand, many women remain unaware of methods enabling them to space births; less than 10 percent use any spacing method. The most widely used method of contraception is female sterilization; one-fourth of married women are unaware of male sterilization as a method of contraception. The inability to space births is correlated with both maternal mortality and infant mortality. When a mother dies in childbirth, it is also likely that her infant will die soon thereafter.

The increased mortality rate for females in India is also linked to the explosion of HIV. Ten percent of the world's HIV-positive population is in India, and women are infected at faster rates than men (Heine, 2003). HIV in India is not restricted to high-risk groups such as sex workers or drug users. The virus is on the rise in rural areas and among all castes. Many women have not heard of the disease and others report never seeing a condom. These are the women who are infected by their husbands but cannot refrain from sex with them. Can poor women insist their husbands to wear condoms? "Yes, in an ideal world, but in India most women are forced to treat their husbands like God" (Sify, 2003). Sex workers also have limited choices regarding their sexual partners. Knowledge about the disease does not reduce fatalism. "What can we do?" asks one young woman. "We have to earn a living. The choice is dying of AIDS or dying of starvation" (Roy, 1994).

Feminism in an Indian Context

The disheartening Human Development Index does not go unnoticed by officials at all levels of government. A revitalized feminist movement led by strong NGOs is promoting governmental attention in efforts to put beneficial principles of development into practice. The central government has taken steps to combat the negative impact of a restructured economy on poor women and those who toil in the informal sector. Violence against women, especially dowry-murder, is also a priority. The Indian women's movement has increased public awareness to domestic violence, calling attention to the power differences between men and women that serve to disempower women in their families. They also act as watchguards to ensure that laws are passed and enforced rather than passed and ignored (Rudd, 2001; Singh, 2007; Vindhya, 2007). A five-year plan that specifically addresses the issues of excessive female mortality and low literacy rates of women was recently adopted. Programs designed to combine traditional and modern medicine in a way that is acceptable to the rural population are underway. For example, efforts to combat AIDS through education and awareness that account for traditional beliefs and cultural practices will be more successful.

Through their efforts on social and welfare measures, women's organizations are increasingly being drawn into the political process. In the world's largest democracy, political parties are recognizing the importance of the women's vote. Training is a component of this process as well. Outreach programs for poor, marginalized producer women are enhancing their empowerment and self-reliance. Family-owned microenterprises in India are more productive when women have joint decision making with men. At the community level, they are starting to participate and influence decisions in local self-governing bodies and for the first time are exerting their voting rights at all levels.

As successful as these efforts may be, the feminist movement in India is constrained by many issues faced by feminism worldwide. The movement has not been successful in expanding diversity to attract rural women or to effectively mentor poor women as grassroots leaders. NGOs that make up the movement continue to be led by women from elite castes. Landmark scholarship about women and by women addresses many of these concerns, but applying it to the lives of women outside the academy is difficult (Purkayastha et al., 2009). Whereas the activists working for independence in the early twentieth century were able to create a sense of sisterhood that transcended caste and cultural boundaries, the contemporary movement has been unable to replay that achievement. New strategies to address everyday experiences of women (microlevel analysis) and to account for globalization (macrolevel analysis) are necessary for feminism to achieve the inclusive, gender-equitable social order envisioned by Mahatma Gandhi (Subramaniam, 2006; Gangoli, 2007).

JAPAN

When comparing gender role patterns in Japan to other developed nations, we quickly confront a series of contradictions. During World War II, Japanese and American women had much in common—both were responsible for the functioning of the "home front," yet both were denied leadership positions in the government and industries that relied on their services.

The Occupation

After Japan's surrender in 1945, Occupation forces were determined to establish policies supporting the emergence of a democracy compatible with Japanese cultural values. Japan's remarkable advances in economic growth, health, higher education, and overall prosperity attest to the spectacular success of the experiment in guided social change introduced during the Occupation. Major shifts in attitudes about overall social equality, especially involving women and men also occurred. It can be argued that the single largest beneficiary of this experiment was the Japanese woman.

Occupation policy was in part dictated by the provisions of the Potsdam Declaration of July 26, 1945, mandating that democratic tendencies among the Japanese people be strengthened and that freedom of speech, religion, and respect for fundamental human rights be ensured. With the enactment of the *Showa Constitution* on May 3, 1947, five articles provide for rights of women. Included are equality under the law with no discrimination because of race, creed, sex, social status, or family origin; universal adult suffrage; equal education based on ability (women could be admitted to national universities); granting women the right to run for public office; and marriage based on mutual consent. Japanese women in 1947 in essence had greater rights than American women because Article 24 of their new constitution had an unprecedented equal rights clause for women. The clause was inserted after much debate but has withstood a half century of criticisms (Brooke, 2005). In contrast, the Equal Rights Amendment to the United States Constitution has yet to be passed.

Gender Equity and Public Policy

Legal assurances of equality had their greatest impact on Japanese employment practices beginning with the Occupation. Laws were enacted guaranteeing women protection from long work hours, and pregnancy and menstrual leave; they emphasized that a new Japan required the strong support of women as the producers and socializers of the next generation (White, 1991). It is obvious today that such laws serve to inhibit women's advancement and stereotype women as less physically capable than men. Yet it took 30 years before the disparity was acknowledged. The Equal Employment Opportunity Law (EEOL), passed in 1986, calls for equal pay and other improvements in hiring and working conditions. Unfortunately, without viable enforcement provisions, many employers simply do not adhere to the law. Others believe the failure of the law is due to the principle of Japanese *gradualism*, which companies use to block unpopular initiatives by invoking cultural norms emphasizing social order over the potential for disorder by policy enactment (Knapp, 1999). Gradualism can take so long that, without continued advocacy, a policy will never be enacted. Some changes have occurred in terms of overt discrimination and public consciousness of and support for activism relating to women in the labor force have increased. However, the law remains weak and can neither prevent gender-based personnel policies nor tackle the monumental problems of indirect discrimination (Gelb, 2000; Lindsey, 2010).

Gender Equity Plan. A more recent governmental approach to gender issues is the creation of the Gender Equality Bureau, a Cabinet level council created in 1994 and upgraded by an act of the Japanese Diet in 1997. Envisioned as a policy to take a stand on women's issues well into the twenty-first century and with new receptiveness to feminist input, this council produced a *Basic Plan for Gender Equality* in 1999. Like EEOL, however, the Plan's enactment is seriously hampered by competing views about traditional values related to women's place in society and by lack of funds to oversee the reforms needed (Osawa, 2000). The Bureau is directed by virtually all male high-level officials who seek input from the few women holding political office in Japan, by NGOs, and through UN initiatives on gender equity. Men thus hold virtually all the decision-making power about gender equity in Japan.

Support for elements of the Plan is evident. Issues related to human rights and violence against women, gender equality training for teachers, and on the global level, funding programs aiding women in the developing world have met with fairly high levels of public enthusiasm (Gender Equality Bureau, 2003). On the other hand, key provisions of the Plan related to gender equality at home, at work, and in the community reveal large and persistent attitude gaps between women and men, between the married and the unmarried, and between homemakers and employed women. Men talk about the economic burden of marriage, and women talk about the difficulty of harmonizing home and family life. Employed women and homemakers report being overburdened with household responsibilities and caregiving to elderly parents-in-law; almost 100 percent of caregivers in Japan are women (Ogawa et al., 2003). Highly educated women serve tea or are secretaries to male superiors with less education or training. Cultural values about the proper roles of men and women in Japan remain largely intact. Japan is facing a huge labor shortage, but rather than violating a cultural norm of providing equal opportunities for women, the government is willing to violate another taboo—encouraging large-scale immigration by foreign men to fill Japan's labor shortage (French, 2001).

Despite decades of litigation, gender discrimination in recruitment, employment, and pay remains untouched and lack of opportunities for women outside their homes persists. Women have equal rights but, in addition to discrimination, negative attitudes about ambitious, rebellious women who do not conform to social norms are rampant (White, 2001:152). Annual campaigns such as "Gender Equality Week" are designed to raise awareness of gender issues, but awareness of equality is not matched by behavior to reduce it.

Work and Family: A Nondilemma

The cultural belief that women in the labor force are temporary commodities until marriage is so taken for granted that the issue of a work–family collision may be viewed as a "nondilemma." Japanese couples certainly discuss the issue and may express regrets over how it is played out in their lives. Married women know that their roles as wife and mother will limit employment opportunities, but the issue is almost always resolved in favor of home over workplace. As woman often point out, a "guillotine falls on their careers on their wedding day" (Off-Centre, 2001).

Like other women globally, employed women in Japan are constrained by restrictive, stereotyped gender roles. Though women represent half the workforce, they are concentrated in lower-level jobs with poorer working conditions and insecure long-term prospects. Occupational gender segregation is powerful in Japan; very few employees cross over to the jobs of the other gender. Feminized jobs command little respect and much less pay than even the few comparable jobs held by men. Japan has the largest wage gap of all developed countries, hovering between 60 and 66 percent for several decades. The slight converge is explained by number of years on the job as full-time workers (A. Kawaguchi, 2009; D. Kawaguchi, 2009; Shuto, 2009). The gender education gap has virtually disappeared, but women are excluded from management positions in most Japanese firms. Firms define women as part of a peripheral, impermanent labor force, easy to hire or fire. Women increase company profits not because of their job performance but because of lower wages and few, if any, fringe benefits, such as the potential for lifetime employment which is reserved for selected male employees (Hori, 2009; Kodama, et al., 2009).

Japanese women enter the labor force largely as re-entry employees after children are reared. They are likely to be middle-aged women who are concentrated in part-time or temporary employment and who take lower-level jobs not commensurate with their education. They face discrimination due to a combination of gender, age, and family status factors (Weathers, 2001; Sano, 2009). Many of these women would like to be in full-time, permanent positions but face systemic cultural barriers locking them into a secondary labor market (Broadbent, 2002; Yu, 2002). The large number of re-entry women bolsters the belief that women should not be hired or trained for permanent positions because they will inevitably leave their jobs when they get married (less likely today) or when they become mothers (highly likely today). This pattern continues unabated for women and the gendered division of labor remains universal and unchallenged.

Marriage and the Family

It is said that Japanese women walk with their feet pointing to the inside, toward *uchi* (home). The pulls toward home and any perceived incompatibility between home and family life are so powerful that the uchi-pointing path is seen as the only realistic one for the vast majority of Japanese women. Girls are socialized into traditional gender role values early in life. High school continues to drive their preparation to become full-time homemakers even as they tackle the courses preparing them for the difficult university entrance exams. Girls are ambivalent about the gendered paths laid out before them and are aware of the stereotyped messages they receive, but, like women throughout Japan, they know they will be full-time homemakers for a portion of their lives (Shikakura and Hougham, 2000; Nishimura, 2001).

In comparison to other industrialized nations, Japan is also unusual in that women's labor force activity and fertility both declined in the twentieth century.

The common global pattern is that a lower fertility rate, especially for highly educated women, is associated with higher labor force participation. At 1.22 in 2008, Japan has the lowest fertility rate in the world. This trend reflects the notion that educated women can offer their one or two children the highest-quality home environment.

Given powerful cultural beliefs that a woman's life goal is to have children, this trend is not surprising. Motherhood remains the essence of a woman's social and personal identity. A women's role is ranked as mother first and wife second. Employment is not even considered in the ranking hierarchy. This expectation is so strong that it is virtually impossible for employed women with preschoolers to escape social judgment if anything is amiss at home when she is at work (Kashiwagi and Hasuka, 2000). A mother is solely responsible for her child's well-being. Those few professional women who remain in their jobs may compensate by employing "substitute housewives" or relying on their mothers who live with or near them. Such an arrangement provides no assurance that they will be viewed more seriously as employees, nor does it eradicate role overload. Nonetheless, it allows some measure of occupational success for women who refuse to give up domestic roles of mother and wife.

Demography and Family Change.　Demographic shifts are impacting marriage and the family in Japan. Besides the world's lowest fertility rate, Japan has the happy distinction of having the world's highest life expectancy rate. By 2030 Japan will have the largest percent of the oldest old (those 85 and older) in the world. Women are marrying later and waiting longer to have children, preferring instead to embark on university education offering them more options for employment (Retherford et al., 2001; Raymo, 2003).

Japanese Men.　Delayed marriages for women, who marry at younger ages than men, result in a huge number of bachelors. In Tokyo alone over 40 percent of men in their early thirties are bachelors who live with their parents. Young people with university degrees who are employed full-time and live with their parents often into their thirties are derisively referred to as "parasite singles" or "spongers" in the media. Despite the fact that men are not expected to possess domestic skills necessary to survive on their own, male parasite singles are more disparaged than females. They may lament a bride shortage, but they are in no hurry to prove to a potential spouse that they will participate in housework or child care. The vast majority of husbands do not engage in domestic work in meaningful ways. A generation ago most husbands filled the ranks of "salarymen"—company men with lifetime employment in one firm who are expected to spend 10–14 hours a day on and off the job with their colleagues. These traditional salarymen are fast disappearing, replaced by men eager to live a fuller life outside the confines of conventional jobs and conventional marriages. Whether this generation of men will live out their married lives with more equality and task sharing in their homes remains to be seen (Tsuya et al., 2005).

Japanese Women.　Another contradiction relates to the role of women in the Japanese family. After the war, laws removed the language related to the incompetency of women. Parental consent was abolished for marriage beyond a certain age, divorce by mutual agreement was possible, and in a divorce property would be divided between husband and wife. Such laws appeared to bolster a wife's lowly status in the family. Herein lies the paradox. On the one hand, Japanese women are depicted as powerless, destined to domestic drudgery; buffeted by the demands of her husband, her child's school, and her in-laws; and expected to be humble and submissive. However, these stand in opposition to a strong tradition of decision making in the family; Japanese housewives are viewed as being in full control of domestic life, with virtually unlimited autonomy.

To shed light on this paradox, it is likely that most women fall between a submissiveness–assertiveness continuum; there is gradual, steady movement toward the assertiveness pole. Women are highly specialized in the domestic sphere. They also have lower levels of self-esteem, power, honor, privilege, and authority relative to men. Women as a group are defined by the principles of domesticity, seclusion, and inferiority, although individual women can be placed at some point along the continuum for each element (Lebra, 2007). Inferiority outside the home is balanced by the power inside the home. The long-held view of the submissive Japanese woman is challenged by research showing that women are active agents in constructing their identities in positive ways in their family, and are influential players in its decision making (Liddle and Nakajima, 2000).

Motherhood. Being a Japanese woman is synonymous with motherhood. Mothers are revered, almost idealized, by their children and the mother–child bond is viewed as a sacred dyad (Notter, 2002). With such strong mother–child attachments and concern that the mother–child role may be compromised, children in Japan are reared for more dependence and less autonomy than American children, a socialization factor contributing to the parasite single syndrome noted earlier. From a functionalist view, the more dependent the child, the more indispensable the mother. Husbands, too, assume a childlike dependence on their wives. Patriarchy exists outside the home, but a husband who does household work deprives his wife of domestic matriarchy. Nowhere is domestic matriarchy more evident than in how household expenses are divided. Although it is expected that the husband is the provider, the wife maintains control over the financial management of the household. Paradoxically, his authority is demonstrated when he hands over his paycheck to her. In this sense, patriarchy and matriarchy are reciprocal. Earning the money is his responsibility. Managing the money is hers.

A Japanese Woman's Profile

Given all these contradictions, how can contemporary Japanese women be portrayed? Two general portraits emerge. The first is of a woman who values family life and will sacrifice for it, who is unwilling to divorce even in an unsatisfactory marriage, who believes she is discriminated against by both society and the family, but who is proud of her role as decision maker in her family, especially in financial matters. She is more egalitarian and more individualistic in her role values than were women in the 1970s but does not openly identify with feminism (Yamaguchi, 2000; Ezawa, 2003). She probably worked outside the home until her first child was born and then returned to the labor force when the oldest child entered high school. She sees herself as a professional homemaker and enjoys the status of being a "good wife and wise mother." This is the portrait of Mariko, a 44-year-old, middle-class Tokyo suburban woman with three children, two part-time jobs, and a disengaged husband.

It was a Japanese life, a woman's life, no worse and no better than so many others, a life spent largely in reaction to children, to a husband, to sick parents. . . .

> Mariko knew how hard it was . . . to do the few things she wanted to do, to feel a sense of accomplishment. . . . Her children were getting older and would soon be gone, just in time, it seemed, for her to turn around and be a parent to her parents. (Bumiller, 1995:289)

The second portrait reflects the desires of young Japanese women to be much more independent than their mothers. They do want marriage, but will be very selective in choice of husband. After centuries of arranged marriages in Japan, by the 1970s love matches were normative. Both young men and women want to marry for love, but romance is difficult to find. After graduation they enter a highly gender-segregated labor force comprised of full-time married men and part-time married women. Women want to delay marriage so eligible brides for men are in short supply. These highly educated women are financially independent but employed in jobs at lower levels than suggested by their credentials. Some believe they are not feminine enough for Japanese men; others do not want to marry men who only want housewives. Dilemmas related to work and marriage are suggested in the comments below. The first woman seems to display envy and bitterness for married friends; the second is very assertive about who she believes is an "eligible man" (Nemoto, 2008:230, 232).

> Some married friends say they envy my lifestyle, traveling frequently and going out all the time. But they don't mean it. They are saying that they are . . . better than me because . . . they have house, children, and husband. They think I am the loser.

> I am not interested in men at the workplace. They are not the best of the best. They are kind of left over.

Women are vital for Japan's global economic prominence, in achieving a high standard of living, and in amassing the globe's best overall health record. With the help of media images of modernity, legal reform paved the way for challenges to the ancient patriarchal model in Japan. These reforms prompted limited, but increased support for gender equity in the home and workplace and more involvement from husbands in child rearing (Bassani, 2003; Sato, 2003). Linking in-country women's groups with women-centered NGOs outside Japan under a common banner also fuels feminist activism. The movement is being energized by international conferences on how Japanese women deal with multiple discriminations based on gender ethnicity and race (Chapman et al., 2008). Compared to the women's movements in other countries, however, mass-based feminism in Japan is still embryonic.

Feminists in Japan are less vocal, preferring to orchestrate activism in a manner meshing with Japanese cultural norms of gradual social change. The "gradualness" strategy may be successfully playing out. Strong patriarchal gender norms about family and workplace are eroding. Young women assess the opportunity costs of marriage, especially early marriage, and motherhood versus singlehood. Women now expect expanded roles and greater autonomy for those roles. Rising expectations provide the basis for reforms aimed at equalizing the positions of women and men. Support for these reforms bode well for addressing the crises in employment, in population growth, and in child and elder care.

LATIN AMERICA

Latin America exhibits a great deal of diversity in terms of ecology, politics, and culture, but common features can be identified, including a rigid class structure, the prevalence of Catholicism, and a colonial heritage from Spain and Portugal that help to define the region. Latin American women also demonstrate both diversity and common features that unite and divide them. Although there has been a marked improvement in the overall situation of Latin American women, a gender gap in all human development indicators persists.

The Gender Divide

As discussed in Chapter 8, the socialization of men and women in Latino cultures hinges on the concepts of *machismo* and *marianismo*, which are viewed as mutually exclusive beliefs separating the genders. Because machismo emphasizes virility, sexual prowess, and the ideological and physical control of women, it is associated with legitimating violence against women as well as compromised physical and mental health among men. Its long-term ideological effect reproduces male privilege throughout all social institutions. Machismo allows for male dominance in the household and is invoked to restrict socioeconomic, sexual, and other lifestyle choices of women. Reinforced by teachings of the Roman Catholic Church, marianismo is associated with glorification and spiritual verification of motherhood, a stoic acceptance of one's earthly lot, and the endurance of an unhappy marriage. Unlike men, the moral superiority of women maintains that hardship is suffered in silence. It has evolved as a nearly universal model of behavior for Latin American women.

These rigid images are more likely to be embraced by *mestizos,* people of mixed Indian and Spanish descent. Before the Spanish conquest there was apparently more egalitarianism and role complementarity between men and women. The conquistadors brought views of women stemming from Old World religious and feudal attitudes that allowed marianismo and machismo to become entrenched in the New World. Over time women's behavior was not merely a response to machismo but also a survival strategy due to their economic dependence on men.

On the other hand, cracks in the gender divide are evident. Women who achieve higher levels of education and work in well-paying jobs are less likely to embrace marianismo ideology, trends identified in Brazil, Costa Rica, and Chile. Research on men in Nicaragua finds them coming together to form groups such as the Association of Men Against Violence which challenge machismo ideology. In "unlearning" machismo, they improve the well-being of both themselves and all the women in their lives and "reclaim the human dimension of their beings." Indeed, in postrevolutionary Nicaragua the unlearning of machismo is truly revolutionary (Welsh, 2001:190).

Family Planning. Discourses on issues surrounding family planning and reproduction provide other indications of a potential machismo–marianismo crack. NGO initiatives resulting from the UN conference in Beijing include persuading governments to review family planning and birth control issues. Both politically and culturally, Latin America remains solidly linked to the Catholic Church. In Chile, for example, the close relationship between the State and the Catholic Church has greatly impacted women's lives and thwarted widespread efforts at family planning (Willmott, 2002). In contrast, Peru has collided with the Vatican in policies to disseminate birth control material and to ensure that women have counseling to achieve their desires with respect to birth spacing. Although women and their families will certainly benefit from this, it is also in response to the doubling of Peru's population since 1960, about half of whom live in extreme poverty, and a fertility rate of 6.2 among women with little or no education. Despite Church stubbornness, Peru's family planning policies have been generally successful. In 1990 the fertility rate was 4.1; by 2008 it dropped to 2.4. Women's appointments to top-level cabinet posts in Peru provides more clout to implement state-supported family planning efforts.

Nicaragua has followed suit with government policy stating that reproductive health, sex education, and services in family planning are available to women. While continuing to condemn abortion to prevent pregnancy and for population control, Nicaragua recognizes a woman's right to decide when and how frequently she will have children. These positions are advocated despite Church policy banning any form of birth control other than the rhythm method. Political influence for Latin American women occurs mostly within informal settings and in regard to accepted cultural norms that do not seriously challenge gender roles. Feminist NGOs are altering this pattern. Even in more conservative Chile, feminist discourse on human rights related to reproductive and sexual rights is being heard and is unleashing the potential for policy changes on issues of birth control (Willmott, 2002).

Latin American Women, Globalization, and Development

Research also confirms the link between the erosion of women's position and globalization-based development strategies that harm rather than help women. *Structural adjustment programs* (SAPs), designed to increase foreign investment, eliminated some jobs in the private sector but many more in the public sector, which employ more women. Women shoulder the brunt of negative SAP effects. In Mexico and Costa Rica, for example, SAPs increased levels of female unemployment, malnutrition, poor health, and illiteracy. Women's empowerment was severely compromised—impoverishment and disempowerment go hand in hand (Anastaskos, 2002).

As in other developing nations, globalization also removes subsistence farming from women's income-producing activities. When men migrate to cities for work, women and children are often abandoned on farms. Thus in addition to religion and the survival of feudal attitudes, economic factors loom large in explaining the inferior position of women in Latin American cultures.

Except for certain regions, most notably in Brazil and Argentina, Latin America remains underdeveloped after almost 500 years of European colonization, after the establishment of independent republics in the nineteenth century, and after the elimination of dictatorships in the twentieth century. Underdevelopment can be explained by *dependency theory*, which looks at the unequal relationships between Latin America and world markets and between women and men. Unequal opportunities due to fluctuations in world markets negatively influence the region, but the effects on women are disastrous. Not only are women and children the most vulnerable when the subsistence economy erodes, but in response to debt burdens, governments cut welfare budgets first. State policy and agricultural reform are not gender neutral and indeed serve to diminish the status of rural women.

Feminist Agendas

Latin American women are not passive observers of these economic events and continue to engage in collective action to ensure their survival. In contrast to women's movements in other parts of the developing world, the Latin American movement has been much more successful in consensus building and developing a feminist agenda embraced by women from a wide variety of backgrounds (Friedman, 2002; Vargas, 2002). Large numbers of peasant women, for example, are grassroots leaders, core organizers, and mentors for the next generation of leaders from their villages. In coalition with international NGOs, Latino feminists actively participated in those struggles leading to the establishment of democratic regimes throughout Central and South America (Luciak, 2001). This organizational legacy provided strength in numbers and the political shrewdness to challenge economic and social policies detrimental to women. Feminist voices are heard when states prioritize reforms and when questions about gender-based discrimination are addressed. Unlike women in India, who are hindered in gender equity by peasant reform movements, such tactics by Latin American women allow them to become more politically astute and to develop both class and gender consciousness.

The Class–Gender Link. The plight of the majority of Latin American women who are in poverty contrast sharply with that of upper- and upper-middle-class women who are employed in professional occupations or who are part of the elite leisure class. Career women are supported by their husbands, parents, and other institutionalized devices that allow them to combine professional and family roles. The irony is that professional success is to a large extent dependent on the hiring of domestic help. Domestics provide services that help to blunt the impact of a career on the family. Domestic servants in Latin America—many of whom migrate from other countries to these jobs—represent the majority of female wage earners. There is disagreement about whether working as a servant provides a channel for upward mobility or whether it reinforces a rigid stratification system based on class (Pappas-Deluca, 1999; Radcliffe, 1999).

Feminist scholars and political activists in Latin America have yet to resolve the issue of whether class or gender is the overarching issue that serves to perpetuate the low status of women. Over two decades ago consensus emerged among Latin American feminists that both categories are valid. Women's liberation reinforces class struggle. In sociological terms, this supports a strong conflict theory orientation. It also fits the socialist/Marxist branch of feminism asserting that patriarchy influences women to uphold a system that perpetuates their inferior position. Only when class and gender barriers are simultaneously assaulted can equality for all people be realized.

ISRAEL

Issues of gender equality have been salient in Israel since its new beginning as an independent nation. We are aware of impressive experiments partly challenging traditional forms of gender stratification, such as in the military and in the kibbutz (discussed below). The rise of Golda Meier to the highest political position in the fledgling state is another often-cited instance in how far women can progress. Legislatively, women in Israel have achieved what women in the United States continue to fight for, such as paid maternity leave and equal opportunities with men in education and employment. What is the success of these experiments?

Despite egalitarian gender role ideology, feminists contend that gender equality in Israel is illusory. The system that informally serves to limit the choices of women remains intact. The military, for example, is displayed as the height of gender egalitarianism because Jewish Israeli women have been conscripted since the State was founded. The Israeli Defense Force (IDE), however, is probably the most gendered of all social institutions in Israel. Women are exempt if they marry, get pregnant, or declare that they are religiously observant. They are excluded from many military jobs offering promotion and higher pay. IDE jobs are strongly gender segregated. The majority of women soldiers are secretaries, clerks, or health personnel (Frankfort-Nachmias, 2001:135). Similar to other countries, the Israel's military is a rite of passage for males into adulthood and identity. Individual women may transgress gender boundaries in the military, but ultimately they, too, "learn to identify with the patriarchal order of the army and the state" (Sasson-Levy, 2003:440).

Gendered military policy shapes public discourse about gender in other social institutions. The thrust of Israeli public policy reinforces traditional gender roles. This thrust is related to three key institutions: religion, family, and government. All of these are intertwined and all are concerned about national security.

Religion, Family, and Employment

Israeli society is organized around the principle of the family as the dominant institution and the family as the cradle of Jewish heritage. As such, the Jewish family is tied to ancient religious traditions, which are unquestionably patriarchal in nature. The family is what defines the woman's role. Israel is neither a religious nor a secular state, but rabbinical courts have jurisdiction over matters of marriage and divorce, and their interpretations tend to favor Judaism's most traditional branch—that of Orthodox Judaism (Graetz, 2003b). Women in all branches, however, are expected to be in charge of domestic functions and prepare their households for religious observances. These roles in turn free men to study, to teach, to be breadwinners, and to be more fully engaged in the religious life of the community. A woman may contribute to her community's social and economic life, and she may see the division of household tasks as unfair, but religious ideology takes precedence over gender ideology in most Jewish Israeli families (Blumen, 2002).

Kibbutzim. Dating from a century ago, the **kibbutz** is an Israeli agricultural collective in which children are raised together in a gender egalitarian arrangement allowing parents to be full participants in the economic life of the community. Initially designed as a radical departure from the patriarchal family and traditional gender division of labor in the family, the kibbutz is an effort at eliminating distinctions between the work of men and the work of women.

It is the child-centered approach to cooperative living that distinguishes the kibbutz from other communes worldwide, such as nineteenth-century Shakers in the United States and contemporary communes in Denmark (Brumm, 2008). Until about 1970, kibbutzim (plural form) were characterized by collectivization that minimized gender role differences and maximized instrumental and expressive role sharing. In the spirit of communal socialization, between one and two months after birth, infants were moved to a children's house, where they spent the next 12 years of their lives living with their peers. The Sabbath was reserved for children and their parents to be together, but teachers and nurses were responsible for the daily socialization of children.

Parents were still critical to their children's development; children identified with parents, deriving security, love, and affection from them. Ideally, such an arrangement frees parents from child-care responsibilities, allowing them to work for the betterment of the community as a whole. Based on the principle of gender equality, it was assumed that the roles performed by women and men are basically the same.

These principles, however, have not been sustained. Raising children communally increases women's dissatisfaction with kibbutz life and distances men from their children. Some men report the same feelings of dissatisfaction. Research shows, for example, that men's satisfaction with fatherhood increases significantly when children sleep at home rather than with their peers (Lev-Wiesel, 2000). The "child-centered" approach is being gradually replaced by the "family-centered" approach—"nuclear like" in structure—with children raised by their parents and living at home. Regardless of this change, however, women are still more likely to leave the kibbutz than men. Second- and third-generation kibbutzim children are abandoning the kibbutz in favor of urban-living and nuclear families. The loss of agricultural profit fuels outmigration of young people and further undermines the strong egalitarian ideology of the traditional kibbutz (Gavron, 2000). In addition, once financial stability and numbers sufficient for kibbutz survival were assured, gender stratification and segregated jobs accelerated. Today women function almost exclusively as child-care workers, nurses, teachers, and kitchen workers.

Kibbutzim members are equipping themselves with the social and economic tools to bolster community survival. The change in kibbutzim from relationships based on cooperation, community, and equality are also traced to globalization and market relationships. As in other countries, the market approach to life has a negative impact on women in Israel (Palgi, 2003). Overall, however, the legacy of equalitarianism in the kibbutz has not vanished and will be evident in emerging kibbutzim forms.

Education. The gender gap in Israeli education has disappeared. Higher education for both genders is encouraged and normative. Education and religion intertwine, however, to influence beliefs about marriage and the family for Israel's youth. Religious schools inculcate a religious-based conception of womanhood that is shaped by both divine law and the male world (Rapoport et al., 1995). Education is also a powerful factor in moderating the views of Jewish women when women have the authority to interpret scripture. Women have increased their numbers in seminaries and are ordained as rabbis in all branches of Judaism except Orthodox (Chapter 12).

The Workplace. Israel represents the global pattern related to gender and paid work. Women venturing into the workplace face gender gaps in earning, higher rates of unemployment and underemployment, and occupational gender segregation regardless of their job level. They also face the effects of globalization. They lose more public sector jobs, and in existing private sector jobs they are paid less. When conflict arises between family and job, employment is abandoned (Kulik, 2000; Yaish and Kraus, 2003). Despite the Equal Opportunity Law passed by the Knesset in 1988 prohibiting discrimination in advertising, training, promotion, and severance pay, and later provisions prohibiting sexual harassment and unequal fringe benefits, these patterns persist. Laws are ineffective if enforcement is lax and if women do not challenge the discrimination they routinely experience (Kraus, 2002). Most important is that women continue to be viewed—and often view themselves—as wives and mothers first and, much further down on the scale, as secondary breadwinners.

Jewish Feminism

Public policy has not significantly helped with the burdens women must face in carrying out their roles and the contradictions they face within these roles. To counter ancient traditions hampering gender equity, policy makers must translate the needs of women into effective and culturally acceptable legislation.

The feminist movement in Israel is clearly the front-runner to do this translation, but lack of unity among Jewish women is hampering goals. Feminism was imported to Israel from the West in the 1970s, and like in the West, its agenda was shaped by the leadership of educated professional women. For two decades the movement remained dominated by Ashkenazi women—largely white, European-oriented, and solidly middle class (Freedman, 2003). Feminist conferences in the 1990s were marked by dissent from Jewish women of color and working-class women representing women from Mizrahi, Palestinian, Bedouin, Asian, and Ethiopian backgrounds. Mizrahi women—whose heritage is traced to Arab North Africa, the Middle East, and East Asia—led the rallying cry that signaled hidden, deep divisions within Jewish feminism (Motzafi-Haller, 2000, 2001). They asserted that feminism as constructed by Ashkenazim could not speak for the diversity of women in Israel. They accused feminism of ignoring poor and marginalized Jewish and non-Jewish women. This accusation led to the formation of a separate branch of feminism that remains ideologically and strategically separate from mainstream feminist organizations (Dahan-Kalev, 2003:108).

Feminists in Israel have been less successful than their Western sisters in dealing with the contentious, fundamental connections between race, class, ethnicity, and gender that hinder efforts for feminist progress. The peace process, however, represents a new era for Israeli feminism that is poised to better deal with some of these divisive issues. Not only are there more women than men in the peace movement, but Jewish and non-Jewish women representing a diversity of ethnic groups are in key leadership roles. In orchestrating dialogue between Palestinian and Israeli women, these women are raising awareness about issues women face in common, such as living under the constant threat of terrorism, domestic violence, and sexual oppression (Svirsky, 2003; Plonski, 2005; Hunter, 2006). By embracing issues of social justice and new ways of dealing with peace and security, the movement can hopefully mend diversity fences and regain the political prominence necessary to be an important player for policies that help all women (Herzog, 2008).

THE MUSLIM WORLD

The Muslim world represents a range of contradictions to Westerners. On the one hand, oil-rich Muslim nations have taken development efforts seriously, creating better living standards and enhanced educational and job opportunities for their citizens. On the other hand, in Islamic nations, development occurs within unique cultural frameworks that Westerners view with curiosity and suspicion. Existing suspicion heightened with the 9/11 terrorist attacks in 2001. Nowhere do these conflicting images emerge more forcefully than when viewing women in Islamic cultures.

Given the stereotypes surrounding Islam, many are surprised to discover that Islam first developed both as a new religion and as a social reform movement aimed at changing the lowly status of women (Chapter 12). Reforms are possible, however, only in the context of a culture's willingness to undergo change and endure stressful transitions. This has simply not been the case in Arab, South Asian, and African cultures dominated by Islam. Regardless of the position of women in the pre-Islamic world, the Qur'an continues to be drawn on as a moral rationale for restricting women. A resurgence of religious fundamentalism has bolstered Qur'anic interpretations endorsing the inferior status of women. Islamic legal reform does have many advocates, and they can provide evidence from the Qur'an for upgrading rather than degrading the position of women. But reform has barely kept up with fundamentalist resurgence.

Islamization: Iran and Afghanistan

This resurgence is fueled by **countermodernization**, or antimodernization—a social movement that either resists modernization or promotes ways to neutralize its effects. Throughout much of the Muslim world, countermodernization takes the form of **Islamization**, a religious fundamentalist movement seeking a return to an idealized version of Islam as a remedy against corrupt Western values. With Islamization, religion and state are inseparable, and all laws governing public and private life have a religious basis. Islamization is replayed in South Asia (Pakistan and Bangladesh), in the Middle East (Saudi Arabia and Iraq), and North Africa (Egypt and Sudan).

Until the Taliban takeover of Afghanistan in 1996, its most virulent expression worldwide was the Iranian revolution that propelled Khomeini to power after the overthrow of the Shah of Iran in 1979. As elsewhere in the Muslim world, in both Afghanistan and Iran, Islamic authorities ("mullahs") have long played an influential role in all aspects of social life. Countermodernization is selective in its ideas and technologies used to convey the ideas; Iran and Afghanistan are the extreme versions of this movement, but powerful elements can be found in most Arab cultures as well as in other Islamic societies, such as Pakistan, Bangladesh, and Sudan (Lindsey, 1984, 1988; Hashmi, 2000). The resurgence of countermodernization and Islamic fundamentalism was masterminded for political power and relied on the subordinate status of women to attain its goals (Shehadeh, 2007). Despite Islamization couched as a benefit to women, they are its likely victims.

Islamization in Afghanistan, for example, targets women as key vehicles to restore Islamic identity when they return to exclusive domestic roles. Islam is invoked to deny reproductive choice, educational opportunity, and paid employment. With "gender apartheid" taking effect, Islamization under the Taliban banned women from employment and schools for girls and hospitals serving women were closed, lest women come into contact with men to whom they are not related. Women were executed for adultery and prostitution, often defined as simply being seen with a nonkin male. Beheading, amputation, shooting, and public beating occurred for religious infractions such as clothing not sufficiently covering a woman's entire body, for illegally teaching girls to read and write, and for going out in public alone—even if completely veiled (Lindsey, 2002a). The Taliban decreed out of existence even the minimal rights women and girls gained as Afghanistan began the process of economic development during the Soviet era.

After a respite from its brutality, women are again targets of the Taliban resurgence in Afghanistan and Pakistan. The resurgence is responsible for burning down schools for girls, threatening and beating their teachers, bombing women's micro-businesses, and assassination of women activists and development workers (Boone, 2009; Filkins, 2009). In Taliban-controlled areas of Afghanistan, the search for a formula to protect traditions under Islamic law while dealing with inevitable social change was resolved in favor of an extreme form of countermodernization.

The Shah and Khomeini. Islamization in Persian Iran was (and is) not as extreme in its treatment of women. Women receive medical care in facilities designed for them and girls are in gender-segregated schools. However, women in Iran remain under the strict control of their fathers or husbands, are restricted from a variety of paid employment, and must answer to Islamic authorities for violations of dress and traditional gender roles, most related to marriage, family, and motherhood. Iran provides the best example of how countermodernization can serve to restrict women. What is startling about the overthrow of the Shah of Iran in 1979 and the establishment of the Islamic regime under the Ayatollah Khomeini is that women were a force in propelling the Ayatollah to power. As exploitation under the Shah grew, women became more politically active and took to the streets in mass anti-Shah demonstrations. At a time when the veil was becoming a remnant of the past, women embraced it as a symbol of solidarity against the Shah. The images of veiled women protesting in mass demonstrations shocked many. Veiling seemed to contradict the progressive view of women that was supposedly a hallmark of the Shah's regime.

The veil served several purposes. It prevented the easy identification of the protesters that could make them targets of the secret police, and it was a symbolic gesture halting the modernization and Westernization of Iran. When that identity is linked to women, by restoring the veil as the Islamic marker, broader social identity is also restored (El Guindi, 1999). Many women saw the veil as a symbol of solidarity, to be discarded or worn at will after the fall of the Shah. These women believed that they would be rewarded for their sacrifices and militancy. The new religious leaders would expand rights for women, including educational and employment options and more self-determination in their domestic roles.

Khomeini's position during the anti-Shah movement increased women's support for him. He opposed the idea of women-as-objects and saw a woman as a man's equal: "She and he are free to choose their lives and their occupations." He stated that the "Shah's regime has destroyed the freedom of women as well as men" (cited in Sanasarian, 1982:117). The new Islamic republic would not oppress women, according to Khomeini. Less than a month after the ousting of the Shah, illusions of equality were shattered. Legislation was enacted to alter gender relations so they would not resemble anything like those existing in the West. The tragic paradox for the women of the Iranian revolution is that they were harmed by their support (Moallem, 2005). Gender segregation in all parts of public life intensified (Kazemzadeh, 2002). The minimum legal age for girls to marry was lowered from 18 to 13 and then to 9. An extreme example of loss of freedom was physical brutality and loss of life. Women were executed for adultery and prostitution and beaten for improper dress. No longer was the veil a symbol of militant solidarity. In the eyes of many Iranian women, it became a symbol of oppression.

With Khomeini's blueprint, the next regime systematically undermined the freedom of women. Religious righteousness originally compelled both men and women to work in overthrowing the Shah. Once this succeeded, women were literally pushed out of public life and into the home. It is likely that many women would have embraced domestic roles anyway, but the new regimes severely circumscribed all other options (Mir-Hosseini, 2001).

Toward Reform. Attempts at reform, however, have not been silenced. Islamization continues, but it is taking a different course. Globalization thwarts excessive countermodernization. Despite efforts to maintain the fervor of earlier Islamization, under Iranian President Ahmadinejad, it takes a back seat to the broader anti-Western and anti-American strategies. How this plays out for women remains to be seen. One scenario suggests that issues related to globalization and nuclear capability are in the foreground; Islamization, especially with women as targets, are in the background. Women remain at the forefront of political protest. Despite blackouts, camera videos showed (literally) tens of thousands of Iranian women protesting the re-election of Ahmadinejad, accusing the government of election fraud. Many women protested without traditional veils. Some of these women rallied around Zahra Rahnavard, wife of opposition leader Mir Moussavi and outspoken critic of the regime. Similar to the movement against the Shah 30 years ago, with cries of "God is great," she galvanizes young women to vote and evokes Islamic principles and the strong women in Mohammed's family to support her stance. She vocally supports veiling, "arguing that it liberates women," and herself wears a modest chador (head-covering). On the other hand, although she states that it should be a choice for women to wear it or not, she had an important role in forming the female police units harassing women and enforcing their "Islamic behavior." (Addley, 2009; Kazerounian, 2009).

Women retain the right to run for public office in Iran. Despite diminished authority, they have not been ousted from their offices under the regime. Women also use Iranian traditions and Islamic principles and law to speak out for women's rights. Prominent women such as Shirin Ebadi may be put under house arrest, but they are somewhat protected by their notoriety. Women comprise over half of university students in Iran and their potential political clout is acknowledged. Religious intellectuals are debating, albeit reluctantly, how the "woman question" can be addressed in Iranian Islamic law (Moghadam, 2002; Moallem, 2005). Although acceptable economic reasons, rather than unacceptable feminist reasons, are cited for these changes, it is clear that women on the whole can benefit. Feminists in Iran are divided by degree of support for Islamic principles and how their highly praised roles as wives and mothers can be used to their benefit (Povey, 2001; Barlow, 2008). These divisions do not bode well for seeking reform with a unified voice. But the fact that feminism is even minimally viable in Iran signals potential reopening of dialogue between women and, hopefully, between women and the state (Ezazi, 2009).

Given the ongoing instability in Iran, however, it is difficult to predict which of these scenarios may play out. For example, will ousting an unpopular president, even one whose policies are orchestrated by more powerful clerics, serve to re-ignite Islamization in Iran? Women helped topple the Shah 30 years ago and their rights were severely curtailed. Some of the same messages to women appear to be used today. It remains to be seen if the call for the end of discrimination against women using Islamic principles will succeed.

In Afghanistan, reform addressing women's issues has stalled. Despite the resounding global call to focus on rebuilding Afghanistan's crumbling infrastructure, funding for the war is almost 90 percent of the allocation; development efforts get the leftovers. Efforts in Afghanistan and Pakistan focused on building infrastructure and ensuring education for both girls and boys are beginning to pay off. Despite the rhetoric that Afghan women are "saved" by military strategies, education, employment, and safety for families, rather than more troops, are needed to defeat terrorist ideology (Evans, 2009).

NGOs continue to bolster infrastructure in Afghanistan that includes keeping schools for girls open and safe, and offering reproductive health services for women. They are at the vanguard ensuring that violations of women's human rights are in the public forefront (Maley, 2008). In the last edition of this book and elsewhere I argued that the extreme version of Islamic countermodernization as represented by the Taliban—condemned by Muslims throughout the world—would have eventually dislodged them from power (Lindsey, 2002b). Although theTaliban are now associated more with terrorism than with Islam in the eyes of the world, I doubt if my argument holds today.

The Arab Middle East

Iran and Afghanistan are at one end of a continuum regarding Muslim women. Other Muslim nations present their own traditions, beliefs, and interpretations about gender in Islam. Some feminist scholars contend that there are no effective models for women's liberation that can appeal to Muslim women. They are either too Western or too pre-Islamic (Fernea, 1998). Others say that Islamic societies are based on such rigid definitions of family that tampering with these definitions brings fear of social chaos. Strongly functionalist in orientation, traditional male dominant–female subservient relationships existing in Islamic nations are accepted (Mernissi, 1987:174).

On the other hand, Islam regards women as powerful and potentially aggressive—images that are empowering to women. In their quest for modernization, women are not only embracing but also testing traditional norms. In Saudi Arabia women run investment firms, manage shops, and are employed in hospitals. Corporations are still gender segregated, but opportunities for women's employment in reshaped business roles are increasing. By stretching the limits of male-dominated Saudi society, women endure public criticism, but believe that productive change is inevitable. In Egypt middle-class professional women have overcome social pressures and religious taboos for success outside the home. Influences on them are both modern—Western capitalism and socialist egalitarian ideology—and traditional—the images of formidable females such as Queen Nefertiti and the Prophet Muhammad's strong-willed wife. The latter images bolster interpretations by feminist Islamic scholars that challenge fundamentalist views denying social justice to women. These scholars are increasing interfaith dialogue and are bringing human rights issues related to women in all religions to the forefront (Safi, 2003; Mayer, 2008).

In Arab cultures as diverse as Jordan, Saudi Arabia, Kuwait, and Palestine, women's gains are apparent in health, literacy, and political reform. Even with the severe separatist policies against women in Saudi Arabia and on Pakistan's borders, and the less severe in Iran, media cannot be completely restricted. The irony of the wars in Afghanistan and Iraq is that Muslims see women as competent, successful, and esteemed in a variety of roles—as soldiers, journalists, diplomats, politicians, and aid workers. The shortage of women peacekeepers is being addressed by the United Nations. Women are being trained for these roles to serve in Muslim nations throughout the world. Throughout history, war is latently functional for altering perceptions of women.

North Africa: Female Genital Mutilation

Islam is not uniform across Muslim societies, so women's roles in those societies cannot be approached simply by a rendering of religious texts. However, these societies are linked by certain cultural practices regarding women. Although the veil may be a symbol of oppression from a feminist viewpoint, other customs suggest an even more frightening reality. It is the practice of female genital mutilation that has stirred global debate.

Female Genital Mutilation. Also referred to as *female genital cutting,* **female genital mutilation (FGM)** refers to a variety of genital operations designed to reduce or eliminate a girl's sexual pleasure and ensure her virginity. If she is a virgin she is marriageable. If not, she can be condemned, living as an outcast. Sometimes she is murdered. FGM is practiced throughout North Africa, in parts of the Middle East, and in some Sub-Saharan regions. The total number of living females who have undergone FGM ranges from 80 to 100 million, including children as young as age four. It is practiced by the wealthy and the poor and in rural and urban areas. Although most girls who undergo the procedure are Muslim, it is also practiced by Coptic Christians and those who adhere to tribal religions (UNICEF, 2008). FGM's past is untraceable. It predates Islam, although some Islamic cultures justify it today on religious grounds.

Referred to incorrectly as female circumcision, FGM is not at all equivalent to the far less radical procedure of male circumcision. FGM ranges from a partial clitoridectomy to full removal of the clitoris, a woman's most erotically sensitive organ. In its more extreme form, practiced in Egypt, Somalia, Sudan, and some parts of Ethiopia, FGM removes the clitoris and then the vagina is sewn almost completely shut, leaving an opening just large enough to release urine and menstrual blood. The effects of these mutilations range from psychological trauma to hemorrhage, blood poisoning, painful intercourse, lack of sexual pleasure, and death from infections or complications during childbirth. The vagina is cut open again on the woman's wedding night, an experience reflected by the following lines in a poem by a Somalian woman:

And if I speak of my wedding night; I had expected caresses. Sweet kisses. Hugging and love. No. Never! Awaiting me was pain. Suffering and sadness.

I lay in my wedding bed, groaning like a wounded animal, a victim of feminine pain.

At dawn ridicule awaited me. My mother announced: Yes, she is a virgin. (Muse, 2000)

As brutal as it is, the practice continues. With the elimination of sexual pleasure, virginity is likely to be ensured before marriage and chastity after marriage. It forms a core cultural identity of many traditional people. Girls who refuse or "deny" the procedure bring shame to their families. Women who were forced to undergo the painful procedure and midwives who know the health consequences are often its strongest advocates. A Muslim and the fourth of 11 children, a Mali woman reports the consequences when she opposed her parents and relatives in refusing to be "excised":

I was beaten and tortured. I was ostracized by the whole village. . . . No women had ever refused. . . . All my grandmothers had been excised. . . . There are many women who have no support, there are many who have died, there is so much pain—all of which I can bear witness to.

Only by fleeing to France with the help of friends and filing for refugee status did she resist the procedure. She could never return to her village or to her family. She was accused of heaping more shame on her people by disclosing excism traditions to Europeans (Cited in Merry, 2009:137–138). Resistance comes with grave costs.

Three UN Conferences on Women have taken up the FGM issue. In 1980 African delegates argued that FGM was essential to guarantee a girl's marriage. Delegates from Western cultures, appalled by FGM, were accused of interfering with hallowed cultural traditions. Five years later the issue was discussed with much less confrontation. A decade later, under the broad mantle of "violence against women," cultural boundaries were transcended and consensus was reached that FGM was a human rights violation (Boyle, 2008:273). Egypt, Nigeria, and Ghana have banned the practice. The United States may grant asylum to a girl returning to a country practicing FGM. Previously women feared that daughters could not be married without being "circumcised." When entire villages do not allow their girls to undergo the procedure, men must look for marriage partners elsewhere or marry uncircumcised women. Women's empowerment now suggests the latter.

It is unfair to regard FGM as the defining characteristic of an entire region, but it calls attention to the issue of cultural change through women's empowerment. The controversy also illustrates symbolic interaction's "definition of the situation" in two ways. First is the relabeling of "female circumcision" to "female genital mutilation" or "female genital cutting." The former label suggests something mild or benign. The latter labels clearly do not. Second, the movement against FGM has been redefined as a defense of human rights rather than as cultural interference (Ibhawoh, 2000). The new definition of the situation is fast becoming the reality. In the last decade all major international bodies and most governments in nations where it is practiced have committed to its suppression. Cultural beliefs regarding women remain strong, however, and despite laws to the contrary, the practice continues.

To Veil or Not to Veil

Thirty years of debate have allowed for a broad consensus on the elimination of FGM. This section ends with another contentious issue—one debated for over two centuries in various contexts—that remains far from settled. The issue of veiling (hijab) that is praticed in purdah-system gender-segregated societies has produced two strands of feminist thought on the topic: one strand condemns it as oppressive and the other reframes it as liberating and a sign of resistance. A middle view suggests that veiling is neither liberating nor oppressive. Power relations emerging from veiling must be considered in light of the context in which it occurs (Shirazi, 2003). Critics of veiling are accused of denying the integrity of Islamic culture and the agency of Muslim women (Mojab, 1998). Given these debates, Western feminists tend to shy away from either indicting or celebrating veiling because of charges of cultural interference and that they misunderstand or disregard the link between gender, religion, ethnicity, and politics (Lindsey, 2002a).

SCANDINAVIA

When compared to gender equity in the developing world, the Scandinavian countries and Western Europe stand in sharp contrast. By every measure of overall human development and assessment of equality between men and women, Scandinavian nations are consistently ranked the highest. In the global gender gap index, five of the seven nations with the best gender equity scores are in Scandinavia: Norway, Finland, Sweden, Iceland, and Denmark. The four pillars to assess gender equity are economic participation and opportunity, educational attainment, political empowerment, and health and survival (World Economic Forum, 2008). Scandinavian women hold between 35 and 45 percent of national legislative seats and about half at the municipal level. Perhaps more than women in any other region in the world, Scandinavian women's well-being is enhanced by the benefits of gender parity.

Gender equality goals in Scandinavia are in general pursued through generous child-care policies supporting women in the workplace and shared parenting. Spearheaded by women's organizations throughout the Nordic countries, these goals have widespread support. More than any other place in the world, there is stronger convergence between state and civil society in the Nordic countries (Bergman, 2009:320). Norway and Sweden in particular provide the global standard for gender egalitarian models.

Norway

At 41, Grö Harlem Brundtland ascended to prime minister of Norway, holding the seat for 16 years. Under her leadership Norwegian society became synonymous with social democracy elevating gender, health, and environmental issues to the highest levels. In the last two decades, although not elected, women candidates for prime minister outnumbered men. This demonstrates the clear association between political power and gender equality. Women have clout when they are represented by other women in the legislative bodies of their nations.

Norway represents sociological understanding that gender floods our lives in countless ways. Decisions that on the surface appear to be gender neutral have a different impact on women than on men. Norway's goal is to mainstream the gender perspective into all public activities. This does not mean that attention is exclusively directed toward women. The goal is equality and the gender perspective promotes it. The Norwegian government's long-term objective is that the gender perspective is an automatic one influencing all important decisions, whether in politics, in employment, or in education. To understand how gender influences social institutions and everyday life, all public servants acquire knowledge of the gender perspective (Kristiansen and Sandnes, 2006).

Norway does not attempt to eliminate gender roles. Women and men have different priorities and organize their lives accordingly, such as by job preferences, consumer patterns, and leisure activities. Such differences, however, should not be grounds for unequal access to social benefits and economic resources. The gender perspective ensures that the different behaviors and aspirations of women and men will be equally favored in the organization and governing of Norway. For example, parental leave for new fathers has been in existence for three decades. A high priority on the political agenda is to make it easier for parents with young children to combine family with work responsibilities outside the home. This is the key issue affecting American men and women and their families (Chapters 7 and 8).

Sweden

Like Norway, Sweden's trend toward gender equality advances through public policy, fueled by the gradual increase in the number of women in elective office. But Sweden is unique in that egalitarian principles emphasize gender role change in males. Sweden has gone farther than any other government in stipulating that economic support and daily care and nurturing of children is the equal responsibility of both parents. Like most of the globe, women do more housework and child care than men and are employed more in occupations that are care oriented for children and adults, such as preschool teachers and companions for the elderly. Swedes believe, however, that men have great stakes in gender equality. They want to set examples for children to become gender-equitable partners and to reject gender stereotypes harmful to the partnerships.

The Equality Future

Compared to most of the world, particularly the developing world, gender equity programs in Norway and Sweden are highly advanced. The costs for these programs are high and therefore contentious. The level of support and cost for the social and welfare benefits Norway and Sweden provide to their citizens are extraordinary from an American perspective. Although these benefits have translated into overall well-being and an enhanced quality of life, it is unclear if this path will continue in the same manner (Bergqvist and Nyberg, 2002). Globalization in Scandinavia translates into an upsurge of migrant workers, many of them poor, many of them women, and most of them bringing traditions that counter gender equality (Daugstad and Sandes, 2008; Vuori, 2009). Like health care, gender equity initiatives will be scrutinized carefully to determine their cost-effectiveness. It is doubtful that either nation will retreat from efforts aimed at reducing gender disparity, but in the Millennium Recession, funds for these efforts are reduced. Norway and Sweden, however, still stand as powerful role models for gender equality.

Summary

1. Globalization and development affect men and women in profoundly different ways. Bringing together policy makers, government leaders, and NGOs, the UN convened four major conferences to assess this impact. The 1995 UN Conference on Women was a watershed for the women's movement and for women's rights worldwide.

2. Globalization serves to hurt women when they are denied access to technology, subsistence farms are sold, men abandon families to seek work elsewhere, women's unpaid labor in their homes, on farms, and in the informal sector is uncounted.

3. A model of women and development needs to account for sociological theory and global stratification, the impact of market-driven economic development, a theory–practice feedback loop, interdisciplinary work, accounting for unpaid work, and a feminist perspective emphasizing women's empowerment.

4. Russian women have lost economic and political power with the collapse of the Soviet Union. In its transitional economy women have lost jobs, their pay has declined, and they have sharply increased work hours in their homes. The importance of paid work has declined, and the importance of family and social order has increased for women. Feminism and women's rights have eroded.

5. The PRC ushered in reform for women. Footbinding, concubinage, and child betrothal were abolished, free-choice marriage was instituted, and women had equal rights to divorce. Cultural barriers undermine these reforms. The one-child

policy reinforced ancient son preference and has dire consequences for girls. In the long run the policy may make daughters more valued. Research on Chinese women under market-driven development shows a paradox—women report both gains and losses in their homes and in their workplaces.

6. Women's progress in India is eroded by strict interpretations of Hinduism. In the twentieth century social reform gave women rights to inherit, vote, and divorce. The gender gap in human development related to education, literacy, and employment in India is huge. Female neglect and HIV/AIDS are rising due to son preference and a woman's lack of control over sexual intercourse. India has a strong feminist movement, but it is constrained by lack of diversity, disagreement on a common agenda, and difficulty of attracting poor and rural women to its ranks.

7. Gender roles in Japan are highly paradoxical. Japanese women benefited from postwar social reforms, including equal pay, improvement in hiring and working conditions, and access to higher education. Reform is hampered by Japanese gradualism, traditional views of women, women's abandonment of career at marriage, and motherhood as the essence of a woman's social and personal identity. Women have high levels of power and decision making in their households.

8. Machismo–marianismo ideology in Latin America serves as a powerful gender divide. The level of power of the Catholic Church explains the mixed success of family planning, sex education, and reproductive health throughout Latino cultures. Globalization and the shift from subsistence to commercial farming have hurt women. A strong and inclusive, politically astute Latin American feminist movement is being heard by government leaders. Debate continues on whether class or gender is the key factor in women's low status.

9. Israeli women have achieved equal rights and opportunities by law, but other polices related to religion, family, and government reinforce traditional gender roles. In most families religious ideology takes precedence over gender ideology. The egalitarian ideology of the kibbutz is also eroding. Jewish feminism is strong but divided between middle-class women and women of color and working-class women. This division has hindered feminist progress for all groups.

10. In most of the Muslim world the Qur'an is interpreted by men and used as the moral rationale to restrict women. Fundamentalist resurgence through Islamization has fueled countermodernization movements, with Iran under Khomeini and Afghanistan under the Taliban as the most extreme examples. Reform related to education, jobs, and elected offices was evident in Iran but has stalled under Ahmadinejad. In Afghanistan, after a respite, Taliban resurgence is harming women, including closing schools for girls, assassinating women leaders, and bombing women's businesses. In Arab cultures, even with extreme separatist policies, women are seeing gains in health, literacy, and political reform.

11. FGM (also called female genital cutting) is practiced largely in North and Sub-Saharan Africa. With the belief that a girl cannot be married unless she undergoes FGM, the brutal practice continues despite laws to the contrary. By defining it as a human rights violation, international efforts to combat it are more successful.

12. The issue of veiling remains contentious among Muslim women and among feminist scholars. Some see veiling as oppressive, whereas others see it as liberating and a sign of resistance and the integrity of Islamic culture.

13. Scandinavia has the highest global human development rank and the highest gender equality. In Norway the gender perspective is central to all government decisions. In Sweden gender equity is advanced by concentrating on changing men's roles. Social and welfare benefits serving gender equity initiatives may suffer if costs rise too quickly.

Key Terms

countermodernization 165

developing nations 136

development 136

female genital mutilation (FGM) 169

globalization 136

informal sector 139

Islamization 165

kibbutz 162

Nongovernmental organizations (NGOs) 137

one-child policy 146

Critical Thinking Questions

1. Discuss the factors that erode the status of women during the process of development. Demonstrate how these factors can be accounted for in a model of women in development that is useful for policy makers working to make development a success.

2. Identify the key cultural, political, and religious barriers that impede women's progress in Russia, China, Japan, India, Israel, and Latin America. Of these six nations/regions, select the two you believe will be most successful in overcoming these barriers and provide the rationale for this selection.

3. Considering the profound consequences of Islamization and controversial practices such as FGM and veiling customs for women in the Muslim world, what advice would you give to NGOs and feminists both inside and outside Muslim nations working to elevate the status of women? Make sure you account for the role of religion in this advice.

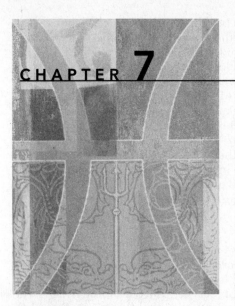

The story of Cinderella promotes love and marriage as an escape from a world of drudgery and lack of fulfillment into one of enchantment and "living happily ever after." Indeed, the term *Cinderella story* has now come to symbolize the lives of those few beautiiul women who have gone from rags to riches when the right prince comes along. The 1949 Disney version of *Cinderella* is still alive and well. By the 1990s, instead of a cartoon prince we had Richard Gere carrying Debra Winger and Julia Roberts away from their preprincess existences as factory worker *in An Officer and a Gentleman* and as prostitute in *Pretty Woman*. The millennium Cinderella is

Annette Bening, the highly educated (and beautiful) career woman who is swept off her feet by Michael Douglas, portraying the most powerful man in the world, in *The American President*. Movies about teenage Cinderallas have exploded in the last decade. Through complicated and bizarre plot lines, ordinary high school girls are transformed into beautiful princesses and whisked away from their mundane existences by handsome teenage princes who will later become kings (Chapter 13). These movies suggest "modern" themes related to sexuality, alternative lifestyles, and women's roles outside the home. At the same time, however, they highlight "traditional" themes about the power of love to overcome all obstacles and propel females into marriages that will fulfill all their dreams. The finale of the hugely popular *Sex and the City* television series and movie found all female lead characters in happily ever after relationships or marriages. This chapter examines the myth and reality associated with such media images.

LOVE

Americans are so accustomed to viewing love and marriage as inseparable that it is rather startling to realize they have been paired only since the nineteenth century in the United States (Chapter 5). Romantic love as an ideal existed in Europe and throughout Asia centuries ago, but it was not regarded as a basis for marriage. The poets and philosophers who sang the praises of courtly love during the European feudal era elevated love to something unattainable in marriage. The ladies of the court would bestow gifts, blessings, and an occasional kiss on suitors who would do battle or endure hardships for such prizes. Love was feared for the sexual passion it might produce, so was discouraged. Courtly love games were reserved for the aristocracy and excluded the vast majority of the population who did not have the luxury of playing at romance. Personal fulfillment and compatibility of the couple were irrelevant.

Linking Love and Marriage

Marriage, on the other hand, was the mundane but necessary alternative to the enchantment of feudal romance. Although the aristocracy glorified romantic ideals, their marriage decisions were based on rational rather than romantic goals. Marriage was an economic obligation that affected power, property, and privilege. From a functionalist perspective, without the assurance of marriage which produced legitimate heirs, the entire stratification system might be threatened. This held true for the king was well as for the peasants. Passionate love could not serve as a realistic option for choosing a mate.

The Puritan era in the United States ushered in the revolutionary idea that love and marriage should be tied together. This was a radical departure from early church teachings, which warned men that even looking on their wives with lust made them sinners. In the new ideal, if love was not the reason for marriage, it was expected to flourish later. Parental control over approval of marriage partners remained the norm, but the belief that love should play a part in the process became etched into the fledgling American consciousness. Today the belief that love should be a strong factor in choosing a marriage partner is fast becoming a global norm. Initially, however, it was a phenomenon uniquely associated with the United States.

Dramatic social change also eroded the separation of love and marriage. A political climate receptive to egalitarian attitudes was bolstered by the leveling effects of the Industrial Revolution, serving to decrease class stratification and the segregation of the genders. Consistent with a conflict perspective, as women moved into the world of paid employment, their economic power increased. Social change combined with economic assets enhanced choices for both genders, but particularly for women. By the 1890s couples were receptive to the idea of **companionate marriages**—those based on romantic love—with an emphasis on balancing individual needs with family needs. Less traditional beliefs about gender were also bolstered in companionate marriages. Responsibilities that had formerly been under the control of one or the other spouse began to be shared.

Love as a basis for marriage is strengthened in societies where gender equality is fostered and women and men can express sexuality in a more open manner. Women's improved economic position, opportunities for youth to interact without being under the constant surveillance of parents, and increased time for leisure allowed romantic love to blossom. By the beginning of the twentieth century love, marriage, and the belief that a spouse should be freely chosen had become inseparable.

Friends and Lovers

"Love is three-quarters dream and one-quarter reality—but problems rise when you fall in love with the dream and not the reality." (cited in Fulghum, 1997:19)

Defining Love. Because love is such a complex emotion and so difficult to define to everyone's satisfaction, it is easy to understand why it is ladened with folklore, superstition, and myth. Love is extolled for its virtue and damned for its jealousy. *Euphoria, joy, depression, restlessness, anger,* and *fear* are all words used to describe love.

The love for a friend, sibling, parent, or child is certainly different from the feelings accompanying romantic love and the strong passion it stimulates. Nonetheless, distinguishing between the varieties of love is exceedingly complicated. The distinction between romantic love and other varieties of love includes *eros,* or the physical, sexual component of love; *agape,* its spiritual and altruistic component; and *philos,* the love of deep and enduring friendships (Lindberg, 2008). Although romantic love ideals are supposed to include all these components, agape and philos indicate other kinds of love relationships, such as the love between friends or siblings, and parents and children. What is interesting is that the sexual dimension of eros is the key component distinguishing romantic love from friendship, but is also its most selfish aspect. The need for sexual gratification may counter the altruism idealized in beliefs about romance. As we shall see, this is an important element in female and male views of love.

Distinguishing Love and Friendship. Like with lovers, the profile for good friends and best friends includes acceptance, trust, respect, open communication, mutual assistance, and understanding. Friends, like lovers, are the champions of one another and advocate their friendship by loyalty and sanctions against those who speak or act harshly against them (Baxter et al., 2001; Canary and Dainton, 2003). If these good friends, best friends, or other friends become lovers, the sexual passion dimension is added to the profile.

Same-Gender Friends. When asked who are their nonromantic best or close friends, both men and women usually identify someone of their own gender.

Same-gender friends know each other longer, spend more time with each other, and are more committed to the friendship. Early socialization emphasizes patterns of gender segregation that carry through to adulthood (Chapter 3).

Compared to males, females report higher levels of intimacy, spontaneity, and openness with their same-gender friends, a pattern that crosscuts race and age (Granger, 2002; Johnson, 2004). Males are more competitive and less open with their same-gender friends and are more likely than women to identify someone of the other gender as among their best or close friends. This is also consistent with gender role socialization patterns that promote instrumental and goal-oriented friendships for males and expressive and emotion-centered friendships for females (Johnson et al., 2007). From a symbolic interaction perspective, same-gender friendships are enhanced and stabilized when each party accepts the role definitions attached to gender.

Friendships for both men and women are important for emotional and social well-being, but women appear to capitalize on them more than men. Females of all ages who maintain friendships with other women report being less lonely and depressed, but paradoxically, they also report romantic liaisons with males as simultaneously euphoric and depressive (Joyner and Udry, 2000; Knickmeyer et al., 2002). Women's friendships with other women are at risk if they believe their friends are sexually active or are their romantic rivals. Women are more threatened by the physical attractiveness of rivals; men are more threatened by the status-related characteristics of rivals (Bleske and Shackelford, 2001; Buunk and Dijkstra, 2004). From a feminist perspective, beliefs about male power in love and mate selection encroach in friendships between women.

Other-Gender Friends. Same-gender friends may be more stable and emotionally supportive because the passion dimension lurks behind other-gender friendships. Even on social networking sites like *MySpace*, females tend to be more interested in friendships with men but men are more interested in dating. This may explain why females keep their profiles private (Thelwall, 2008). Other-gender close friends are endangered if liking turns into loving. Men perceive that sex with their women friends is beneficial to the friendship, whereas women perceive it as more detrimental, beliefs that distort the friendship balance. Men are much more likely to endorse and act on the sexual liaisons of "friends with benefits" (Afifi and Fulkner, 2000; Monsour, 2002; Puentes et al., 2008). Media images showing other-gender friendships doomed by romance reinforce these patterns. In the classic movie *When Harry Met Sally*, Billy Crystal (Harry), believes that it is impossible for men and women to be "just friends." Sally disagrees. Harry is right: he marries Sally at the end of the movie. In the reverse but rarer direction, *Seinfeld's* Elaine and Jerry move from a romantic to a platonic relationship. It is difficult to return to being friends after having been lovers, particularly if one partner is in another romantic relationship.

Consider, too, the friendship–love–friendship–love scenarios in the television series *Friends*. If the name of the series is supposed to imply that other-gender roommates and neighbors can maintain ongoing platonic and intimate relationships, it certainly was difficult for this group of "friends." In *Will & Grace*, it is Will's homosexuality that allows them to remain best friends. Close other-gender friendships can weather the gender storms. However, in addition to the loving–liking difficulty, these storms also include gender beliefs working against egalitarianism that create the path for not only the demise of the friendship, but also difficulties in sustaining other romatic relationships (Underwood and Rosen, 2009). The potential for rewarding and enduring other-gender friendships is limited by formidable gender barriers.

Gendered Love and Love Myths

It is clear that our ideas about love depend on whom we are considering as the object or target of our affection, whether a spouse, sex partner, sibling, child, best friend, or parent. Friendship and romantic love are distinguished by more than passionate sexual desire. Compared to friends and family members, lovers have heightened enjoyment for each other's company, are preoccupied with thoughts about the lover, are fascinated by all that the lover says or does, and want to frequently communicate with their lover. According to Robert Sternberg (2008), love is a triangle formed by three interlocking elements: intimacy, passion, and commitment. Through open communication, intimacy brings with it emotional warmth and bonding. Physiological arousal and sexual desire are part of the passion component, where feelings of romance take precedence. Commitment involves the choice to continue and maintain the love relationship. All relationships undergo change and transformation, so each vertex of the triangle will not be equal, but if there is too much mismatch between the components, the prediction is that the relationship will fail. Research confirms that males and females differ in levels of satisfaction and skill for each of the three elements of the triangle. Mismatches are associated with loss of passion, unrequited and obsessive love, and depression (Regan, 2000; Engel et al., 2002; Mikulincer and Goodman, 2006). Because gender role socialization makes it difficult to maintain equal balance in the vertexes, the joy and awe associated with romantic love may be compromised.

Regardless of its definition, romantic love is idealized in the United States. Americans are bombarded with romantic stimuli throughout their lives which serve to reinforce these idealizations. The most complicated of emotions has produced a range of myths that demonstrate how we romanticize love. To the extent that these myths carry over into beliefs and behaviors related to gender roles, marriage, and the family, romanticization can have dire consequences.

1. **Love Conquers All**. The "all" that is supposedly conquered in this myth involves the inevitable problems and obstacles of daily living. By idealizing the love-object, problems are even more difficult to solve. Total agreement with another person's views on life and love is impossible. Romantic love is certainly paradoxical. Idealization requires remoteness to be maintained (keeping the lover on a pedestal), but intimacy evaporates remoteness (the pedestal collapses). One's partner cannot fulfill all needs and make all problems disappear.

2. **Love Is Blind**. This myth asserts that true love dissolves social boundaries and anyone can become the romantic love-object. The belief that "it doesn't matter, as long as I love her/him" fuels this myth. As we will see, mate selection and the love that it allegedly encompasses is not a random process but one that is highly structured. We are socialized to fall in love at specified life stages and with specified categories of people. No longer exclusive to Western cultures, the faith in romance is quite high. But love is conditioned by a number of social and demographic variables that exert a tremendous influence on us.

3. **Love at First Sight**. Because falling in love is a rational process, it counters the belief that people fall in love at first sight. Physical attractiveness certainly

provides the initial impression. Until verbal interaction occurs, information comes indirectly from the person's overall appearance. The "love at first sight" myth is bolstered by what psychologists refer to as the *halo effect*—people who are attractive are assumed to possess more desirable qualities than those who are less attractive. Beauty and good looks are associated with other positive characteristics, such as morality, competence, warmth, and sensitivity. Initial attraction based on appearance is more important in chance encounters such as on airplanes or at one-time events.

The love at first sight myth works against women because they are judged more strictly on level of attractiveness, especially related to body weight. Men are more likely to believe in the myth than women (Montgomery, 2005). Love requires ongoing, sustained interaction, and attractiveness issues tend to fade in the long run. As a prerequisite to love, interpersonal attraction is enhanced by the *mere exposure effect*—being frequently exposed to a person increases liking for that person. Familiarity does not breed contempt; it breeds liking. This explains why college dormitories are major marriage markets where love can flourish. It also explains why the adage "Absence makes the heart grow fonder" is incorrect. Its opposite, "Out of sight, out of mind," is the empirical reality.

4. **One and Only Love Forever**. The belief that there is a "one and only" person in the world eligible to marry is pervasive, even among people who are divorced or who have ended long-term relationships. Clearly the cycle of love–breakup–love–breakup refutes this belief. Like love at first sight, men appear to accept the belief more than women.

5. **Women Are the Romantic Sex (Gender)**. Women are thought to be the starry-eyed romantics who fall in love quickly. This belief is associated with stereotypes about women's emotionality that consume them when they fall in love. Research shatters this myth. Men express a higher level of romantic love than women and fall in love earlier and harder than women. Men also score higher on romantic idealization of love. Men, including gay men, are more idealistic and romantic and women are more cautious and pragmatic in attitudes about love and romance (Cobb et al., 2003; Missildine et al., 2005; Schmitt, 2006).

However, when women do decide to fall in love, they exceed men in levels of emotion and euphoria. Women are defined as the experts who will work harder and sacrifice more to maintain the relationship and keep the romance alive. In Robert Sternberg's (2008) theory of love, women attach greater importance to the commitment vertex of the triangle. For women, the rational behavior eventually leads to the romantic idealism characterizing love in America. It is at the passionate first stage of love where men are more romantic.

6. **No Sex Without Love**. Both men and women express the attitude that love is a prerequisite for sex, but their behavior certainly suggests otherwise. The vast majority of people engage in nonmarital sex, and many enjoy sex solely for its physical pleasure (Chapter 2). Research does show that the most satisfying sexual experiences are with spouses and committed partners because attributes of love, such as caring and commitment, characterize the relationship. However, "permissiveness without affection," known today as "hookup culture" or "friends with benefits," is fast becoming a sexual standard. Today's causal sex culture is different than the singles bar scene only few decades ago when sex wasn't the inevitable result.

Now they go in groups but drive separately. If somebody hooks up, they can all get home. . . . For men and women, once they hook up, sex is going to happen. It's not a sexual revolution, it's sexual evolution. (Scott, 2007)

Women are less likely to agree with the standard and are judged more strictly when they engage in any nonmarital sex, whether with a lover or an acquaintance. Women are now less likely to endorse beliefs about sacrifice and submissiveness in a sexual relationship. But they are also more likely to engage in nonmarital sex when they hear love messages, even if these are not marriage messages (Kamen, 2003; Mongeau et al., 2006). The double standard continues.

7. **The Opposite of Love Is Hate**. Since love is so difficult to define, the final myth is perhaps easier to understand. If there *is* an opposite to love, it is not hate, but indifference.

Gender and Styles of Romance. The openness and sharing that most agree are important components of love, serve to separate women and men in the later stages of love and marriage. Gender role socialization commands that masculinity be associated with lack of vulnerability. One becomes vulnerable through self-disclosure; therefore, to love fully is to self-disclose fully. Men have higher levels of openness, communication, and self-disclosure than women at the beginning of a relationship. They use more direct, open, and active strategies to initiate a romantic relationship (Clark et al., 1999; Trost and Alberts, 2006). As the relationship continues, even into marriage, men tend to retreat in communication and responsiveness, but women expect more of both. Women become resentful and irritated when men appear unwilling to express thoughts and feelings (Chapter 4). Men in all racial categories are less likely than women to regard emotional satisfaction and communication as important ingredients in preserving a marriage or maintaining a relationship (Sprecher and Toro-Morn, 2002; Canary and Wahba, 2006). For heterosexual married couples, cohabitants, and dating partners, it is the man's behavior that sets the direction for the level of intimacy in the relationship that in turn predicts the level of satisfaction and adjustment to the relationship for both partners.

Men in Love. Explanations for this change of behavior center on a man's discomfort in opening himself to the emotions and intimacy demanded in ongoing romantic or other close relationships. Men may be blamed for their lack of emotional expression and self-disclosure that women have honed throughout their lives. Because romantic love is so identified with the expressive dimension and self-disclosure in which women are supposedly more skilled, we tend to disregard the instrumental dimension and physical aspects that men prefer. Rather than talking, men demonstrate love when they "do" masculine things for a wife or lover, such as repairing the car or cleaning out the gutters.

Men also put more emphasis on the eros/sexual component that is the distinctive marker of romantic love. Men are more likely to believe that portrayals of sex on television are accurate and represent reality; women believe the same about portrayals of love on television (Diamond, 2004; Punyanunt-Carter, 2006). Because love is so idealized for its agape/altruistic quality, even its key sexual marker is played down. Men, in turn, are viewed as "incompetent" at loving. A male deficit model defining women as "relationship experts" has led to an incomplete and overly feminized perspective of love (Cancian, 2003).

Critique. It is clear that males and females are socialized into different attitudes and behaviors regarding romantic love and that the idealism associated with romantic love serves to weaken women's endorsement for its sexual component. But the claim that men do not have the skill for the effective communication necessary to satisfy both partners in the relationship is not justified. Because gender scripts call for men to be the initiators of a romantic relationship, they demonstrate these skills at the beginning of a relationship when they need to entice women into dating. Women give high marks to men who talk about goals, reveal otherwise private beliefs and attitudes, and disclose personal weaknesses to their potential partner. If men have good communication at one point, this skill does not suddenly disappear later. According to symbolic interaction and conflict theory, men have the skill to communicate, but the will to do so may be constrained by gender scripts suggesting that they can retain power in a relationship by determining what is left unsaid rather than said.

Androgynous Love. Regardless of which gender is more skilled at communicating, for relationships to become more loving, the rejection of polarized gender views of love is necessary. *Androgynous* love may integrate masculine (instrumental) and feminine (expressive) styles. If love and loving are gender typed, androgyny should help overcome the imposed limitations. Research does reveal that highly masculine or highly feminine gender roles—both of which suggest gender inequality—are not conducive to expressing love and also negatively affect intimacy (Rodman et al., 2001).

Traditional gender roles jeopardize love and loving and the marriages on which they are founded. A woman's relationship script calls for a more passive role eventually allowing her to exchange sex for commitment. A man's relationship script calls for an active role allowing for sexual conquest. Women's enjoyment of sex and their agency in sexual relations are compromised by these scripts. Both scripts are in the throes of change, and some research indicates that women's and men's conceptions of love and sexuality are converging (Cramer et al., 2003; Kamen, 2003). The courtship game, however, continues to function according to gender role stereotypes. Moving toward an androgynous love ideal may overcome some gender barriers. Loving relationships that endure the harsh reality of shattered love myths may result.

MATE SELECTION

Americans fueled the global trend that links romantic love with selecting a marriage partner. Even in the developing world where the selection of a spouse is often in the hands of marriage brokers, parents, or other relatives, elements of "love" are increasingly factored in as conditions for sealing the arrangement. Regardless of whether it is in America or India or Brazil, however, the idealism of love is modified. Before any marriage commitment, a prospective mate is dissected and evaluated on cultural qualifications important for a marriage. Like the love that propels a couple toward marriage, gender differences abound in the process of mate selection. Unless otherwise noted, statistics for this section are from the U.S. Census Bureau (2009).

The Marriage Gradient

Sociological research documents the influence of **homogamy**, becoming attracted to and marrying someone similar to yourself. If romantic love was the sole basis for mate selection, coupling would occur by chance; instead, homogamy results in **assortive mating**, coupling based on similarity. Assortive mating assumes that people who are culturally similar to one another have more opportunities to meet those similar to themselves than more dissimilar to themselves (Kalmijn and Flap, 2001). College, for example, is a powerful marriage market where people meet, date, fall in love, and marry. Mating requires meeting. Parents send children to certain colleges with the expectation that an excellent education also allows them to meet potential partners from similar backgrounds. The view of college as a marriage market may edge out career priorities for some women, especially with media accounts lamenting that suitable partners for women are lacking when they outnumber men on campus (Berlin, 2006). To test predictions about homogamy, count the number of seniors you know who are engaged.

Demographic characteristics such as age, race, social class, and religion are among the first elements that demonstrate this structure and are of enormous importance in mate selection (Jepsen and Jepsen, 2002; Pallone, 2003). Though considered *nonaffective* in nature—that is, not tied to the emotional expressiveness and highly charged passion of love—these variables predict partner selection and marital stability more than the prized notion of romantic love. It is these nonaffective elements that help to determine with whom we will fall in love. Romantic love is tempered by a market approach to mate selection. This results in a process that appears to be radically different from the ideology surrounding it.

Whereas homogamy is the marriage mate selection norm, it is filtered by the **marriage gradient**, in which women tend to marry men of higher socioeconomic status (SES), the conventional practice used by women for upward mobility. Although this practice is weaker today, data still clearly support that "marrying up" is the path many women choose to bolster economic security. The marriage gradient is functional for women who prefer well-educated men who have the earning capacity necessary to support a family. Women place greater value than men on the instrumental qualities of a prospective mate and assess men on their suitability as good providers. Decades of research attest that this continues to be true, even for college-educated women who express high levels of egalitarianism, expect high-paying jobs, and want to combine career and marriage. Women do want to provide for their families but are uncertain about "how much providing to do" (Melton and Lindsey, 1987; Loscocco and Spitze, 2007; Bjerk, 2009).

In addition to any SES differences between men and women at marriage, the marriage gradient also predicts a degree of dissimilarity between marriage partners related to age, race, and attractiveness, all of which demonstrate the highly gendered mate selection process.

Age. The key variable influencing mate selection is age. Most people marry others within a few years of their own ages. If there is an age difference, the man is usually older than the woman. Traditional gender expectations dictated that men must gain the education and job skills necessary to support a family, thus keeping them out of marriage longer than women, who are socialized primarily for domestic roles. Since the 1950s there has been a gradual increase in the marriage age for both genders. With women now representing over half of all college students and half of the labor force, traditional gender roles are being altered significantly. The median age at first marriage is now higher for women than at any time since 1890 and is approaching that of men (Table 7.1). In later marriages or remarriages, age differences are likely to be greater, but usually favoring the same younger woman–older man pattern.

Table 7.1 Median Age at First Marriage by Gender, Selected Years

Year	Men	Women
1890	26.1	22.0
1910	25.1	21.6
1920	24.6	21.2
1930	24.3	21.3
1940	24.3	21.5
1950	22.8	20.3
1960	22.8	20.3
1970	23.2	20.8
1980	24.7	22.0
1990	26.1	23.9
1995	26.9	24.5
1998	26.7	25.0
2000	26.8	25.1
2005	27.0	25.5
2007	27.7	26.0
2008	27.4	25.6

Source: U.S. Census Bureau, Annual Demographic Supplement to the March 2002 Current Population Survey, Current Population Reports, Series P20–547; *Current population Reports, 2008; American Family and Living Arrangements, 2008.*

However, a new minitrend indicates that younger man–older woman marriage is becoming more acceptable, most common among the elderly. Generally, elderly widows are at a disadvantage for a homogamous remarriage because men marry younger women at all life stages and women outlive men by over seven years. New role models for women, success in economic spheres, divorce and remarriage, the marriage squeeze (discussed later), and less constraints from family and society will likely accelerate the pattern for all but the youngest women.

Race. Of all demographic variables, homogamy is strongest for race. Between 1970 and 2000, interracial marriages tripled. In Hawaii, over half of all marriages are interracial. Because the U.S. Census now allows an option of multiple racial responses, it is certain that the numbers of interracial marriages will surge. Marking off more than one racial category provides a more accurate picture of diversity in the United States but also a more complex one, especially when determining interracial marriages. Interracial marriages are estimated between 4 and 7 percent of all marriages. Of these, about one-fourth are African-American–white marriages, with about 70 percent of these consisting of a white wife and an African-American husband.

The other three-fourths of interracial marriages are between whites and nonblacks, the most typical pattern being Native American or Asian women of Japanese, Filipino, or Korean descent marrying white men. For Asians, gender role beliefs help explain these patterns, but in a paradoxical way. More acculturated Asian-American women seek marriage to men who are more egalitarian and hold less traditional views of women. White men seek Asian-American women for the opposite reason. They may desire a stereotyped Asian female—"good at housekeeping, service oriented, willing to stay at home, and sexy" (Kitano and Daniels, 1995:188). Although both may get what they want initially, patterns of acculturation toward egalitarian gender roles predict more marital satisfaction among Asian-American women than among white men.

Race and SES. When comparing race and class in these marriages, the data support homogamy in SES. This suggests that class is more important than race in these marriages. Interracial marriages among those with similar SES preserve social class boundaries. Although interracial couples have higher rates of divorce, like other couples, higher levels of education and SES appear to buffer racial barriers and bolster marriage (Fu, 2007, 2008; Bratter and King, 2008). Barack Obama, America's first biracial President, is the son of a white mother and a black father who was African rather than African American. His parents met when they were attending college in Hawaii.

Attractiveness. The importance both men and women attach to physical attractiveness in selecting a serious dating or marriage partner has increased dramatically in the last two decades. Media obsession with celebrities walking the "red carpet"—by how they look and what they wear—and the fairy tale weddings they have help explain why this is now a global trend (Ingraham, 2008). Both genders today report communication skills important in choosing a partner, and men are now like women in that they add a woman's economic prospects to their marriage partner shopping list. Men, however, continue to place a higher value on good looks, weight, and facial attractiveness than women. Women are well aware of the value men place of attractiveness. Women with lower body esteem also express less confidence in their relationships (Ambwani and Strauss, 2007; Lippa, 2007). For a quick confirmation of gender beliefs about attractiveness, pick up any newspaper devoted to ads for dating partners. Men's are more likely to mention that they are looking for "beautiful and slender" women or those who have proper "weight in proportion to height." Women are more likely to say they are looking for a long-term relationship with a man who is affluent and dependable as well as kind and caring (Fetto, 2000). Male preoccupation with physical attractiveness cuts across race, social class, and sexual orientation. Because men value it more than women and it is the first trait they notice when checking out possible dating partners, physical attractiveness is an important factor in explaining why men fall in love sooner than women.

The Marriage Squeeze

Age at marriage is also affected by the proportion of women and men who are available. When there is an unbalanced ratio of marriage-age women to marriage-age men, a **marriage squeeze** exists, in which one gender has a more limited pool of potential marriage partners. Most people marry in their mid-twenties, and men marry women who are a few years younger than themselves. After World War II the birthrate increased considerably (the "baby boom" era). There were more women born in 1950 than men born in 1940. By the 1980s there was a shortage of marriageable men. Because of the steep decline in birthrates in the 1960s and 1970s, men in their mid-twenties faced a shortage of women.

If younger men are tangled in a current marriage squeeze, the same is true for women at midlife. The trends of women marrying men two to three years older than themselves combined with higher male mortality rates and economic independence for women help explain this. Although the proportion of single women at the prime marrying age is steadily increasing, widows make up a large portion of the single-women-living-alone category.

Women are caught in a paradox that both restricts and expands their choices for marriage. They are restricted in the number of acceptable partners precisely because of their own successes outside the home. The marriage squeeze has little to do with women's willingness to marry men who are dissimilar to them. Strong cultural meanings of marriage and forces of attraction propelling people into marriage are more important factors. Women, like men, want to eventually marry. But women today are less likely to marry simply for financial security. This flexibility narrows the range of partners when these women are seriously thinking about marriage. Many may opt to remain single because they do not want to settle or settle down with the single men who are "left." The marriage gradient results in two categories of those who may be squeezed out of the marriage market: highly educated, economically successful women and poorly educated, lower-SES men.

African-American Women. When considering demographic trends related to race, age, and education, the marriage squeeze is acute for African-American women as a subgroup. We saw in Chapter 2 that for both race and sex, life expectancy rates are lowest for African-American males. It is estimated that there are eight African-American men for every ten African-American women. These women are also more likely to be college educated; for every ten college-educated African-American women, there are two comparably educated men. African-American women outnumber employed African-American men in every age category by two to one. African-American–white marriages are infrequent, but when they occur, we saw that the pattern is of African-American men marrying white women. African-American men who marry women of other races are also likely to be highly educated. Highly educated African-American women are less likely to racially intermarry (as are highly educated white men).

These patterns significantly restrict the field of eligible partners for African-American women. As a result, in comparison with white women, African-American women are more likely to marry men who are older, are of a lower educational level, and have been previously married. If African-American women select mates of their own race who are otherwise significantly different than themselves, this lack of homogamy, as it is for all races, predicts less marital stability and happiness.

The marriage squeeze may be responsible for the hard choices men and women of all races must make in today's marriage market. Demographic trends help us better understand these choices, but they do not tell us why some people are more acceptable partners for marriage than others. Eligibility in the marriage market is determined by strong gender, race, and age norms regarding what is "appropriate" to marry—norms that direct us toward some people and away from others. The marriage squeeze itself is a by-product of these influences. As these norms are altered, the marriage squeeze also fluctuates. In this sense, a symbolic interaction views the marriage squeeze not as an objectively determined demographic process, but as a socially constructed one.

Sociological Perspectives on Mate Selection

Theoretical perspectives in sociology offer competing explanations for the marriage gradient and a social class marriage gap that may result. According to the functionalist perspective, traditional gender socialization—expressive roles for women and instrumental roles for men—contribute to social stability. An attractive woman may have more of an advantage in "marrying up," but she, her family, and society as a whole will benefit. According to conflict theory, men do not need to be as attractive because they possess greater economic power and prestige in society than women. Once economic power is achieved outside the home, men will use it to maintain dominance within the home. In extending conflict theory, the feminist perspective suggests that when excluded from power, women become objects of exchange. The marriage gradient in mate selection serves to reduce women to objects based on appearance while disregarding their other statuses, such as personal accomplishments and occupational success. Symbolic interactionists assert that the marriage gradient may produce a self-fulfilling prophecy—women may come to view themselves the way they are viewed by men—merely as objects of exchange based on varying degrees of beauty.

GENDER ROLES IN MARRIAGE AND THE FAMILY

Social change related to love and marriage is enormous. Marriage and the families that become "legitimate" by it are both idealized and frightening for couples on the way to the altar. Images of loving couples with contented children coexist with those of abandonment, divorce, and domestic violence. The enchantment of romance has a bleak shelf life. Regardless of perception or reality, and although their numbers are smaller, the vast majority of people will marry. Shifts in gender roles have altered our views of "traditional" marriage and families and prompted the emergence of a variety of lifestyles for those seeking alternatives to these traditional views. These shifts are also largely responsible for significant demographic changes in marriage trends.

The Marriage Gap

Led by young adults who have higher rates of cohabitation and lower rates of marriage, since 1950 the United States has experienced a steady *marriage gap*. For the last half century, the marriage rate shows a consistent decline (Table 7.2). The lower

Table 7.2 Marriage and Divorce Rate, 1960–2008, Selected Years

	Rate per 1000 population	
Year	Marriage Rate	Divorce Rate
1960	8.5	2.2
1970	10.6	3.5
1980	10.6	5.2
1990	9.8	4.7
1995	8.9	4.4
2000	8.3	4.1
2003	7.7	3.8
2005	7.5	3.6
2008*	7.0	3.4

*Provisional.

Source: Table 77, *Statistical Abstract of the United States, 2009*. U.S. Census Bureau; Table A3, *National Vital Statistics Report*. Volume 57(15). U.S. Department of Health and Human Services, Centers for Disease Control and Prevention.

Table 7.3 Marital Status in the United States by Gender, 2007

All Adults	Percent	Men	Women
Married	56.0	58.1	54.1
Unmarried	41.7	40.0	43.3
Widowed	6.2	2.5	9.8
Divorced	10.3	8.9	11.5
Never Married	25.2	28.6	22.0
Separated	2.2	1.8	2.6

Note: Adults = 18 years and older.

Source: Adapted from DePaulo and Trimberger, 2008:17.

divorce rate may be associated with the decline in marriages and an increased acceptance of cohabitation (Chapter 8). Fueled by the share of women who are not married, or who stay married, the gap is widening. More people—especially more women—who are also in committed relationships are choosing to remain single. Even with a lowered divorce rate, divorced women have lower remarriage rates than divorced men (Chapter 8). Women who delay marriage or remarriage may choose not to marry at all. In addition, life expectancy is increasing, and since women outlive men, widows may find themselves without partners several decades after their husbands die. For the first time in American history more women are living without a spouse than with one (Roberts, 2007). It is unlikely, therefore, that American women can expect to live out most of their adult lives in marriage (Table 7.3).

The marriage gap is also an economic gap. Poor people are less likely to get married (and stay married) than the nonpoor. The gender–social class connection as a factor in the marriage gap is an important one. Although both men and women who are poor are more likely to be squeezed out of marriage, poor women with children are even less likely to marry (Wax, 2005). This demographic trend has spawned a geat deal of media attention we will discuss later.

Regardless of a marriage gap and the decreased time spent with spouses, marriage is still the preferred choice for couples regardless of race and SES. Marriage is also the preferred route for long-term commitment for gay and lesbian couples. Marriage is emotionally and economically beneficial to both men and women. Gender roles are critical mediators of the benefits.

Theoretical Perspectives on Marriage and the Family

Sociologists find it easier to describe what families *do* than what they *are*. In many regions of the developing world, large families are functional for subsistence agriculture and to produce goods for family use or for sale or exchange when surpluses are available. As long as it can feed itself, a larger family unit of production provides an economic advantage. Because women are responsible for feeding the family, subsistence farming is considered to be a domestic role and is assigned to women in many parts of the world. In the developed world, the family has been transformed from a unit of *production* to one of *consumption*. Extended families— consisting of parents, dependent children, and other relatives, usually of at least three generations living in the same household—are typical in rural areas throughout the developing world. In urban areas, larger families are at an economic disadvantage because families consume but do not produce goods. Thus **nuclear families**, consisting of wife, husband, and their dependent children who live apart from other relatives in their own residence, are more typical globally in urban areas.

Because the conventional definition is too limited to encompass the structural diversity of households in the United States, especially those without marriage partners, a more inclusive definition is needed. The U.S. Census Bureau now uses the term *family* to describe a group of two or more persons related by blood, marriage, or adoption who reside together. A *subfamily* consists of a married couple and their children or one parent with one or more never married children under 18 living in a household. The term *subfamily*, then, combines the "traditional" nuclear family with other family forms. Notice that all varieties of families are not the same as households. A **household** is a person or group of people who occupy a housing unit. There are family households, nonfamily households, and households made up of both family and nonfamily members. All these definitions emphasize family structure, but tell us nothing about how the family is organized according to functions.

Families have been profoundly altered by industrialization and urbanization, the two key processes propelling modernization. In this sense, gender role change in families is a by-product of modernization. Family change over the last century was fueled by women entering the labor force, but women entering the labor force was fueled by the forces of modernization. The contemporary reality is that the "traditional" nuclear family is but one of many variations of family structure and household structure (Table 7.4). When adding family function to the variations, households with homemaker wives, breadwinning husbands, and their at-home children under age 18 represent only 10–12 percent of all married-couple households. These distinctions may appear to be academic, but how marriage and family are defined provokes a great deal of controversy and influences the lives of many people when definitions are translated into public policy. We will see that the controversy surrounds gender role change related to family function.

Table 7.4 Households and Family Groups, 2008

	Total	White	African American	Asian	Latino (any race)
Percent	100.0	100.0	100.0	100.0	100.0
Married couples	73.1	77.3	44.5	80.1	64.4
With children under 18	31.3	32.4	20.2	40.7	40.3
Without children under 18	41.8	44.9	24.3	39.4	24.1
Unmarried parent couple	1.9	1.8	2.2	0.9	3.9
Mother only with children under 18	11.9	9.2	30.7	6.2	16.6
Father only with children under 18	2.2	2.2	2.7	1.4	2.1
Householder and other relative(s)	10.9	9.4	19.9	11.4	13.0
Grandparent householder with grandchildren under 18	1.4	1.0	4.0	0.6	1.4
Householder with adult children	5.8	5.2	10.7	3.6	5.5
Householder with young adult child age 18–24	2.3	1.8	5.1	1.3	2.4
Householder with parent	2.5	2.1	3.9	5.0	4.1

Source: *American's Families and Living Arrangements: 2008.* Adapted from Table FG10. *Current Population Survey*, March. U.S. Census Bureau www.census.gov/population/www/socdemo/hh-fam.html

All theoretical perspectives in sociology recognize that families are pivotal in carrying out functions for family members and society as a whole. There is also general agreement that the functions can be carried out within a variety of marital and nonmarital family structures found across the globe. However, sociologists disagree about the benefits and liabilities to the family and society that are associated with gender role change.

Functionalism. Functionalists argue that marriage and eventual parenting are good for society and the individual couple. Marriage and the family provide social benefits, including regulation of sexual behavior, socialization of the children, economic cooperation, safety and protection, and an environment in which love and commitment can be freely expressed. Married couples benefit from ongoing companionship and ego support that combat depression and bolster emotional well-being. Families provide *social capital* to members. This includes a family's resources, such as level of education, income, housing, and material goods, and emphasizes the social placement function of families in the larger social stratification system.

The functionalist perspective highlights these family tasks as vital for social stability. If the institution of the family is ineffective in carrying out requisite social "duties," and other institutions have not picked up the slack, social equilibrium will be compromised. From the functionalist perspective, the socialization of children into nonoverlapping and accepted social roles—instrumental for boys and expressive for girls—is central to social stability. Gender role change and ambiguity of roles are disruptive to family harmony. If one partner takes on the roles typically prescribed for the other, marital dissent and family disruption result. If too many families are disrupted by such change, broader social harmony is threatened. Functionalists favor a nuclear family model that functions with a wage-earning husband, who has final power over household decisions, and a dependent wife and children. This model becomes the ideal to which all families should adhere.

Critique. The problem with the functionalist view is that change is inevitable, so what is considered to be traditional changes over time. Although the traditional model is believed to be the historical and contemporary U.S. norm, it emerged only a century ago and was associated with white, middle- and upper-class families. Throughout the nineteenth century, poor women, especially immigrants and their children, worked in "sweatshops" or at home doing piecework. Nostalgia is expressed for a family form that was never the American norm and is far from the norm today (Coontz, 1997, 2000). Functionalist snapshots of families taken at different times in history show that the model for the "traditional" family varies over time. The multigenerational family living in the same household was believed to be the U.S. norm in the early twentieth century. This belief was perpetuated by television shows such as *The Waltons*, which depicted a three-generation farm family surviving the Depression by hard work, faith, and devotion to family. A "new" traditional family emerged in the 1950s and has served as the ideal ever since. Television gave us *Leave It to Beaver* (The Cleavers—Ward, June, Wally, and the Beaver) and *Father Knows Best*. These extremely popular shows portrayed a patriarchal family model with a breadwinning husband, a bread-baking homemaker mother, and their at-home children. At the millennium the Cleavers have disappeared, and alternative families and households are emerging on television. These may become the "traditional" families of the future.

Conflict Theory. Conflict theory focuses on the social placement function of the family in preserving existing inequality and power relations in the broader society. Social capital provided by wealthier families is maximized through marriages that ensure its safekeeping within their own social class. According to conflict theory, when social placement operates through patriarchal and patrilineal systems, wealth is further concentrated in the hands of males, which promotes female subservience, neglect, and poverty. When applied to the household, conflict theory argues that married couples and other family members possess differing amounts of resources and will defend their individual interests and resources to maximize their power base in the home. A husband's power base is maximized by the economic leverage that comes with his earnings. When women gain economic strength by being a wage earner, conflict theorists assert that her power inside the home is also strengthened. More egalitarian household arrangements result.

Critique. With its focus on control of economic resources in the family and the jealous guarding of family property both between and within families, conflict theory has been criticized for disregarding the cooperation and agreement that are also part of family life. Family members are highly altruistic, and kin and nonkin networks offer major sources of support to families in a variety of ways—even when their own well-being is compromised. A paycheck for women does not guarantee egalitarian roles in their homes.

Feminist Perspective. Feminist scholars in the 1960s and 1970s viewed the traditional patriarchal family as a major site for the oppression of women. Feminists expressed concern that when the patriarchal family is viewed as beneficial to social stability, it hampers the movement into egalitarian roles desired by both men and women. They also argued that the idealized view of the family did not account for the varied experiences of women whose daily lives were lived out in multiple family forms. Since the 1980s the feminist perspective broadened considerably to include not just gender, but race, class, and sexuality as other avenues of oppression to women in the family. Feminists recognize that gendered family relations do not occur in a vacuum and that lives are helped or hurt by the resources outside the family that shape what is happening inside the family (Wells and Zinn, 2004). Along with gender, for example, single-parent African-American, Latino, and Native American women are disadvantaged by race when they seek employment necessary to support their families. Lesbians must deal with a system that represses same-sex relationships when they fight for custody of their children. However, feminists suggest that women may be doubly or triply disadvantaged by their race, class, or sexuality, but they are not helpless victims—they possess *agency*, the power to adapt and even thrive in difficult situations.

Critique. With a view of marriage and the family focusing on oppression of women, feminists tend to minimize the practical benefits of marriage, including economic resources and social support (Sweeney, 2002). Feminist scholars also find it difficult to reconcile research suggesting that women in traditional marriages are as satisfied with their choices as women in egalitarian marriages. Finally, when feminists accept all forms of family diversity and highlight and emphasize a woman's informal power and human agency, they may disregard situations such as domestic abuse, where both law and custom sustain women's victimization (Umberson et al., 1998).

Symbolic Interaction. Symbolic interactionists suggest that there are many subjective meanings attached to what a family is "supposed" to be and what its members are "supposed" to do. In our daily lives, however, we adapt these beliefs to fit our own definitions and accommodate our own needs. As we saw from the census classifications, the definition of a family is not written in stone. It shifts with the broader social changes going on outside the family itself. These shifts show up in how people are labeled. The offspring of unmarried women are less likely to be referred as "illegitimate," for example. Symbolic interactionists also focus on how couples take on family roles that become traditionally gendered, even when they desire egalitarian marriages. The definitions of what a man and women are supposed to do in the home are powerful and are reinforced every time we carry out our family roles. However, because family members can negotiate these definitions, over time the roles may change to what a couple desire rather than what they currently have.

Research on marital satisfaction also demonstrates the importance of perception of marriage and family roles. The majority of married couples say they are happy in their marriages, but males express higher levels of happiness than females (Stets and Hammons, 2002; NORC, 2008). A key factor in marital satisfaction is the extent to which a couple agrees on expectations regarding traditional gender roles. Marital quality decreases when a couple holds divergent views, such as how spending decisions should be made or how children should be disciplined. When wives adopt less traditional gender role attitudes (I'll decide how to spend my own income; women need time away from their families), the couple's perceived marital quality goes down. When husbands adopt less traditional attitudes (I'll do the ironing; a woman should be President) it goes up. Marriages with the lowest evaluation of marital satisfaction are those with a traditional husband and a nontraditional wife. Regardless of how traditional or nontraditional they may be, marital satisfaction is highest when gender role attitudes and behavior are congruent (Guilbert et al., 2000; Amato et al., 2003). Symbolic interactionists suggest that when a couple brings ideals related to gender roles into their marriages they will continually negotiate them to maximize marital satisfaction for both partners.

Critique. Symbolic interaction's microlevel perspective tends to minimize the importance of larger social structures in explaining family dynamics. Men and women interact not only as individual family members but also according to other roles they play in society and the prestige associated with those roles. For example, a wealthy white man who holds a powerful position in a corporation does not dissolve those roles when he walks into his home. They shape his life at home, in the workplace, and in other social institutions in which he takes part. Race, class, and gender offer a range of privileges bestowed by the broader society that also allows for a power base to be established in his home. Power and privilege foster a patriarchal family regardless of the couple's desire for a more egalitarian arrangement.

Gender and the Family Values Debate

Sociological perspectives on gender roles in marriage and the family are embedded in the highly politicized "family values" debate that fluctuates according to media focus and election year. One side of the debate centers on the argument that new family forms and alternative lifestyles are breaking down the family and creating social havoc—children are neglected, illegitimacy rates soar, marriage is scorned, and divorce is rampant. Propelled by poor women with children who remain umarried, the marriage gap itself is the fundamental reason behind America's growing income inequality (Hymowitz, 2006). The underlying message is that a return to the traditional family will solve these social woes. Led by the New Right linkage of conservative politicians and fundamentalist Christian churches, "family restorationists" often use sociological data to support their claims (Chapter 14). In the idealization of the traditional, patriarchal nuclear family, they suggest that males are disempowered in companionate marriages that emphasize equality and balancing individual needs with family needs. Such marriages and families, they believe, undermine traditional values of self-sacrifice and family commitment. The welfare state steps in to take over what should be family responsibilities (Popenoe, 2003; Morgan, 2008). Gender role change led by women who sought roles outside their home usurped men from their positions of dominance. When men return to their position as the unchallenged head of the family, families and society will benefit.

Arguments in defending the idealized model advocated by family restorationists are pervasive. At the extreme is Phyllis Schlafly (2003), who maintains that feminists are responsible for social havoc because they encourage women to challenge patriarchy. She argues that feminism and women who work outside the home take jobs from males, create male wimps, promote sex outside of marriage, sabotage family stability, and undermine motherhood. Family restorationists believe that conflicts are resolved when women accept the houshold responsibilities they abandoned when the workplace demanded more of their attention than their families.

Critique. The major shortcomings in the family restorationist model center on several key points. First, the model ignores the reality of social change, especially related to gender roles. There are all kinds of "new" traditional families depending on the time frame used. How a family is defined has changed and will continue to change over time. The demand of the restorationists is for an ideal family that has never been normative. The view that women's employment is the culprit in the so-called family decline is not borne out in research. Divorce was increasing even before women's widespread entrance into the labor force. Women with children who may be married or not or or who are third-shift caretakers do not have the full-time homemaker option. If they receive public assistance, they are required to be employed or in training for employment. Women may celebrate feminist progress in the workplace but their paychecks are needed to support their families, whether they are married or not.

Second, although the class divide in marriage is a demographic fact, it is not the fundamental cause of social inequality; neither is marriage the panacea for fighting poverty. Poverty begets poverty for women from the most disadvataged neighborhoods—whether they or married or not or whether they are single parents or not (Coontz, 2005, 2008). A great deal of evidence suggests that economic downturn reverberates throughout all social institutions and has a huge impact on both family structure and family function, not the other way around (Brand and Cohen, 2007). The unmarried poor were not responsible for the widening income inequality in the first decade of the millennium and poor people marrying will certainly not stem the tide of the income inequality caused by one of the worst economic declines in U.S. history.

Third, the link between family change and child well-being is both far more complex and more positive than the uniform negative effects family restorationists emphasize. Surveys of parents for over four decades suggest that mothers today spend at least as much time—and perhaps even more—"interacting with their children as mothers did decades ago." To the benefit of children, and despite the increased time mothers devote to the workplace, the amount of time for recreation has not decreased. Although housework is given less time, women are more efficient in juggling home and workplace demands (Bianchi et al., 2006).

Finally, American couples increasingly desire egalitarian gender role in their marriages, in direct opposition to the patriarchal family model advocated by restorationists (Amato et al., 2007). Egalitarian marriages and other nontraditional family structures offer lifestyles condemned by family restorationists but, as we will see, these can enhance a marriage and bolster rather than hurt a child's well-being.

Ongoing legal and political challenges in extending the rights of the married to the nonmarried and to kin and nonkin partnerships will keep the issue of "what is a family"—and the gender roles in these families—in the public spotlight.

Housewives

The image of the housewife is bombarded with contradictions. The term *housewife* is used here instead of *homemaker* to specifically indicate the females rather than the male who carry out the role. On the one hand, the traditional housewife role is associated with fulfillment of the American dream for women. It is seen as the height of a woman's aspirations, a deliberate choice that gives her the maximum amount of pride and satisfaction. In overseeing her home, she can be expressive, creative, and autonomous. Research suggests that many women view housework as complex and intellectually challenging. They may believe that their roles as housewives and mothers are less valued than the workplace roles of men and women, but their roles offer paths to build self-confidence, skills, and a sense of well-being. These beliefs are important given data that women in all household patterns do more housework than men, but that the gender gap is widest for married women (Caplan and Schooler, 2006; Davis et al., 2007).

Housewife Status. When housewives suggest that their position is a devalued one, they focus on the intense time demands that are essential for the job but are taken for granted by their husbands, family, and society. A woman must continually be on call to the needs of her family while her own needs are put on hold or ignored (Dempsey, 2001; Phipps et al., 2001). The more she sacrifices for her family the more she becomes securely bound to it and the more she is blamed for family-related problems. For example, children in full-time homemaker families are perceived by their fathers as less disciplined and able to manipulate their mothers more than children in homes where mothers are employed (Baker et al., 2003). In addition, a housewife's time demands have not decreased, despite the wonders of microwaves and coffeemakers and the conveniences of dry cleaners and fast food. When her domestic roles include all that is related to child care, there are enormous increases in time demands. Baking brownies for an elementary school party is part of the housework and cooking time, but added to this is the time spent getting to and attending the party itself. At the societal level, a conflict perspective explains the most important reason for the devaluation of the housewife role: It is not a paid role. Women receive no remuneration for the vital services they provide (Chapter 10).

The full-time homemaker is caught in a struggle to positively affirm her role at a time when women are completing college and entering professional careers at record rates, and are marrying later and delaying childbirth. She takes pride in her domestic work and derives a measure of satisfaction from this work. Her well-being is conditioned by how her role is socially defined in and outside of her family and how she perceives the fairness of her duties. Those whose spouse and children support their household work express more satisfaction with housewifery. Homemakers who have support from family, friends, and organizations important in their lives, such as a church or volunteer group, counteract the boredom and loneliness they may experience and are also higher in marital satisfaction (Jalilvand, 2000; Grote et al., 2002; Mirowsky and Ross, 2003).

A related issue is how patriarchy functions to undermine all women, whether they are homemakers or work for pay. The homemaker role may be devalued, but it is the very role women are expected to enthusiastically embrace. A woman who works outside the home is held accountable for anything that may be construed as going awry in her family due to her workplace commitments. From a feminist view, patriarchy inserts a wedge of suspicion and accusation between full-time homemakers and women who work outside the home. Rather than considering the gendered factors that encourage dependency for the homemaker and guilt for women who work for pay, feminists are viewed as the causes of the devalued position of housewife. The broader patriarchal economic and marital arrangements that encourage the devaluation are ignored.

The housewife role is obviously an ambiguous one. The label of "housewife" is gradually being replaced by the inclusive label of **homemaker**—the person responsible for the "the making of a home." From a symbolic interaction perspective, the change of label plants the seeds for revised definitions affirming the importance of home-based roles for women and men.

The Issue of Housework

As we see throughout this text, there is a research boom on the impact of women's paid labor force activities on all social institutions. At the household level, a great deal of this research focuses on the impact of wives' employment on the division of household labor. For American couples, who does what housework and how much each family member does is one of the most contentious issues families must resolve. The manner in which the housework issue is resolved has an enormous impact on family lifestyle, gender socialization of the children, and marital satisfaction of the couple.

Global Trends. The gender gap in housework is a global phenomenon. Throughout the world, regardless of whether women are full-time housewives or employed outside the home, they shoulder the primary responsibility for housework. Cross-national comparisons show that in countries with higher levels of gender-egalitarian attitudes men take more responsibility for domestic labor, including cleaning, cooking, shopping, and child care. In industrialized countries, Swedish men and Hungarian women do the most housework and Japanese men and Russian women do the least. The United Nations and the World Bank report that in both the developed and the developing world, women's literacy, business ownership, technological training, and paid employment increase the likelihood that men spend more time and women spend less time on domestic responsibilities (UNDP, 2009; World Bank, 2009). Tracking since 1965 shows that American men have increased their share of housework by about one-third, and women have decreased their share by over 10 percent (ISR, 2002). A key point to understand, however, is that the increase in the proportion of his tasks is not offset by the decrease in hers. It is exceedingly difficult for a woman who works 40 hours a week outside the home to add another 40 or 50 inside. This gives no respite from work, whether it is paid or unpaid. For households in the United States as well as globally, the nonessential tasks wives leave uncompleted are not likely to be completed by husbands and children.

Dual Earners. Research on dual-earner couples in the United States usually starts with the logical assumption that a married woman's labor force activity translates into more equitable domestic role sharing with her spouse. Studies conducted since the 1960s indicate that husbands feel obligated to take on a substantially larger share of the housework when their wives are also working outside the home. When these attitudes are matched with actual behavior, however, this largely has not happened. Both homemakers and employed wives spend as much as 50 percent more time on household chores than their husbands. For dual-earner couples of all races, a half century of research finds that a husband's contribution to domestic work has increased gradually over time but remains small in proportion to that of his wife (Blood and Wolfe, 1960; Press and Townsley, 1998; Pinto, 2006; Cunningham, 2007). Like dual-earner couples worldwide, the decline in her household labor is largely accounted for by her increased time in paid work, and demographic factors such as advancing in education, marrying later, having fewer children, and having them later.

The expanded household tasks that husbands are doing favor traditionally masculine chores. Lawn care, house repairs, plumbing and electrical work, and automobile maintenance are the household tasks that husbands assume. Tasks for men are usually related to time-limited or seasonal projects, such as arranging for car repairs or mowing the lawn and shoveling snow. When child care is involved, fathers are increasing their recreational time with children more than in the past. Nonetheless, wives take on a significantly greater share of a family's total share of housework (Kroska, 2004). Women do the traditional feminine chores (laundry, cleaning, ironing, child maintenance) as well as housework that is becoming more gender neutral (cooking, grocery shopping, child care, pet care). These are the ongoing, taken-for-granted daily tasks that consume huge amounts of time and energy for employed wives. Children share some chores but these, too, reproduce the gendered division of household labor. Boys take out the garbage and girls do the dishes. Daughters, however, are more likely to take on tasks that sons perform than the reverse. Gendered household tasks are reduced if dual-earner families have only sons or only daughters.

Multicultural Variations. Household task sharing in dual-earner families is also mediated by race, ethnicity, social class, and religion. Middle-class wives may be able to afford paid help, but they maintain the responsibility for organizing child care, investigating day-care options, and hiring and monitoring nannies or other domestic helpers. These ongoing activities may not significantly decrease their total hours of domestic labor. Mothers of all social classes have more difficulty balancing work and family roles, but professional couples have higher incomes and therefore more control over how these roles can be balanced. Adding race and ethnicity to the picture, compared to white men, African-American, Mexican-American, and Puerto Rican men in dual-earner families take on a greater share of housework and child-care tasks; Asian-American men take on the least amount. Dual-earning couples who express high degrees of religiosity assign more household and child-care tasks to wives. For African-American couples, higher religiosity is associated with less likelihood of divorce. This holds true for white wives but not for white husbands (Ellison and Bartkowski, 2002; Brown et al., 2008). These tasks take up a greater amount of her in-home labor time if she is employed in a nonprofessional job.

For dual-earning couples of all races, because men's increased share of domestic responsibilities are taken up by recreational time with children and male chores, women perceive the household division of labor as unjust. Wives are less concerned about the total time they spend in housework compared to their husbands than about the type of tasks that are accomplished. They point out that men do not equitably share the mundane, routine home and child maintenance tasks that neither partner prefers to do (Baxter, 2000). Women clearly are aware that when a man "helps out" his wife in the home on traditionally masculine tasks, it is not an indication of true task sharing. Women employed full-time for pay walk into their homes after work and begin what sociologists now refer to as a **second shift** of unpaid work (Hochschild, 2003). This second shift leads into a **third shift** of caregiving for employed women who simultaneously care for their children and frail parents, grandparents, or other friends and relatives (Chapter 10).

A cultural lag between liberal attitudes about fairer task sharing in housework and how the housework is actually accomplished indicates persistent gender inequity. According to men, wives have such high standards for housework that whatever they do is not good enough. The perception of unfairness that women harbor about household task sharing decreases marital happiness and increases the likelihood that they will end the marriage (Frisco and Williams, 2003). There are many reasons for husbands to get more involved in housework. They have happier marriages, better physical health, less anxiety and depression, and even better sex lives than men who don't (Shelton, 2000; Ogletree et al., 2006; Coltrane and Adams, 2008). "Chore wars" remain the thorn in the side of dual-earner couples and compromise egalitarianism for both men and women (Thornton and Lasswell, 1997).

Extramarital Relationships

Sexual betrayal shatters the commitment that is fundemental to marriage. Americans express high levels of intolerance for sexual infidelity in any relationship that is expected to be monogamous, whether the couple is married or not. These levels of intolerance significantly increase when the infidelity occurs between married partners. However, people frequently engage in the infidelity they denounce (NORC, 2008). Betrayal of commitment can be emotional as well as sexual. Half of married men and 40 percent of married women engage in sexual or emotional extramarital relationhips; two-thirds of young adults in commited, dating relationships engage in sexual infidelity (Orzeck and Lung, 2005). Even these large numbers are suspect because single women and men are involved with married women and men, but figures often only give the married estimates. These relationships may still be referred to as "affairs," but labels of "cheating" and "sexual betrayal" are now commonly used.

Arrangements are extremely varied, involve different degrees of openness, and include married as well as single people. Many extramarital relationships are more open, with the spouse and other friends aware of the relationship. In this sense, the label of "affair" is erroneous with its implication of secrecy. A sexual component may or may not be part of it, although the potential is certainly there.

Job mobility and career-related travel for both men and women, more time away from home, more permissive sexual values, and greater sexual opportunities are linked to the higher likelihood of sexual infidelity among all categories of couples, married, cohabiting, and those in long-term commited relationships. These trends take place in a culture that continues to idealize romantic love. Americans who are more likely to be prompted into an affair are those who orginally believe that a spouse can satisfy all sexual and emotional needs.

Gender Differences. As would be expected, men and women differ as to their desires and expectations for pursuing extramarital relationships. Although men and women may eventually act on their desire to have an affair, men express a greater willingness to pursue a "spousal alternative." Women view monogamy more as relationship enhancing; men view monogramy more as a sacrifice. Women emphasize love and fidelity in their commited relationships; men emphasize commitment but not fidelity (Gonzalez and Koestner, 2006; Schmookler and Bursik, 2007). Both African-American and white men report more distress and less forgiveness when their partners are sexual cheaters; women in these same categoies report more distress and less forgiveness when their partners are emotional cheaters (Abraham et al., 2003; Phillips, 2006). In these examples, there is less of a gap between what men say and actually do compared to what women say and actually do.

Sexual excitement is a stronger rationale for men to pursue such relationships than it is for women. Married women report that their affairs are less for sexual fulfillment and more for emotional support and companionship. Men report the reverse (Atkins et al., 2001). The frequent reasons men give for having sex outside marriage is the sexual rejection by their wives and the boring nature of repeated sex with the same person. It is not clear which comes first. Men who examine why they are bored with their wives, and who talk to friends or counselors about their situations, emerge over time with a healthier sense of well-being than those who continue a pattern of interim affairs (Duncombe et al., 2004). More data are needed to determine if this signals a trend in which nonmarital sexuality is so normative that what it "means" to be married or in a long-term relationship is now largely focused on emotional commitment rather than sexual commitment for both men and women.

Single Women. Affairs between single women and married men demonstrate a gendered double standard. Although they are primarily secret relationships that appear to protect both parties, the woman's reputation is more threatened by exposure of the affair, with fewer penalties accruing for her married counterpart. A single man is also more likely to be absolved of an affair compared to his married counterpart. Female adulterers are treated more harshly than male adulterers, both socially and legally (Batten, 1992:90). We have the "other woman," but where is the "other man"?

Single professional women may opt for relationships with married men. Many of these women have no desire to marry their extramarital partner or any-one else. Rather than the other women and mistresses of the past, these "second" women have a different agenda. They want to finish their education and build their careers. Others want to recover from divorce and explore their sexuality (Richardson, 1986:24). However, if she does desire to eventually marry, her relationship with the married man will effectively keep her out of the marriage market. By having her needs met by him, she does not avail herself of opportunities to meet other men. This is especially true for younger single women with low-paying, uninteresting jobs who enjoy the material benefits a successful married man can bring to the relationship. The feeling of power that may have prompted the relationship can also lead to powerlessness for women who get caught up in a relationship in which each partner is there to gratify the internal longings of the other (Tuch, 2000). These women end up staying in a relationship that decreases rather than increases their autonomy and independence.

If the relationship is discovered, there are huge costs to the single woman and the wife, who both bear the larger burden of the infidelity. Certainly the marriage will be threatened. The unaware wife also can experience stages of grief that are akin to the loss of a loved one through death (Boekhout et al., 2000).

It is likely that there will be more second women in the future, some who are satisfied in their relationships but others who invest too much and end up with a great deal of pain that is not easily, if ever, overcome. Despite the adventure, sexual freedom, and independence from the entanglements of an exclusive relationship, feminists suggest that affairs lead to distrust between women as well as reinforce beliefs about male power and privilege. In the long run, women may have more to lose than to gain by extramarital relationships.

Global Focus: The Second Wives of Hong Kong Men

Every Friday evening the first-class compartments in trains between Hong Kong and Mainland China are filled to capacity with Hong Kong men toting well-appointed suitcases filled with exotic food, luxury household products, and designer clothing. These men will spend the weekend with their "second wives" across the border in Shenzhen. Sometimes referred to as "China's Tijuana," Shenzhen was decreed a Special Economic Zone in 1980, where capitalism is allowed to thrive unfettered. The result, according to one journalist, is that Shenzhen is a city of "laissez-faire business and institutionalized lust" (Perry, 2001). Thousands of women from impoverished rural areas migrate to Shenzhen in search of love and money. Hong Kong men flock to Shenzhen for the same two reasons (So, 2001). They find young, attractive, and eager Mainland women willing for the chance to become the second wife of a rich man. For the most part the second wives are in stable relationships and are provided apartments, gifts, and generous monthly allowances to support themselves and the children that they often have with their "husbands" from Hong Kong.

Why does a man want a second wife? From his perspective she is affordable and available. She gives "needed" psychological and sexual release when he is away from home. And because a new family is established and provided for by the liaison, he justifies the union as legitimate. Peer pressure also plays a role. The "good boys" (*houdzai*) are teased by other men and told that the first wife (*silai*) is getting old, dull, dumb, and losing her feminine qualities. Why does a woman agree to be a second wife? From her perspective, a second wife is far superior to being a sex worker or having a passionate but brief extramarital affair. Even if she is "less than" a wife, she is "more than" a mistress. More important, compared to her impoverished life before she migrated to Shenzhen, he offers her higher status, stable income, and upward mobility. Her children could become Hong Kong citizens. When he dies she may inherit half his wealth, with the other half going to his legal wife across the border. From the mass media's perspective, men are seldom blamed for their cross-border lives. *Funglau*—sexual potency and activity—is at work, and men succumb to seduction by Mainland women. It is the first wife who is at fault—she needs to be retrained to serve her husband better (Daswani, 1999; Perry, 2001).

Bigamy is illegal, but the concubine heritage is centuries old. Like the generations of concubines before her, a second wife is not legally married but retains a normative social role. Given the large number of philandering men from Hong Kong who have second wives and families in Mainland China, the new marriage law imposes stricter regulations regarding the rights of the women and children from these unions. Although first wives have some legal recourse, it is costly and embarrassing to track down the "second" families, prove bigamy, and sue their husbands.

To date the new marriage law has not met with much success—either legally or culturally—in cracking down on Hong Kong's philandering husbands (Lindsey and Beach, 2004:201). Poor women throughout China migrate in search of a better life. If it means becoming a second wife, their children may escape a life of poverty. Although it is clear that the marriages and families of Hong Kong's first wives are jeopardized, the second family counterparts across the border may be in peril if her husband "succumbs to seduction" again. The law has been unable to deal with cultural beliefs that implicitly condone the behavior of these men.

GENDER ROLES IN EMERGING MARRIAGES AND LIFESTYLES

Rapid social change has significantly altered coupling in all its forms. How gender roles are enacted in these arrangements is a key feature in explaining why some couples stay committed to one another and why others do not.

Egalitarian Marriage

The alternative to the traditional family is one in which the marriage, and hence the family, is egalitarian in both structure and function. There has been a steady trend endorsing gender equality in families for the last 50 years (NORC, 2008). In an **egalitarian marriage**, partners share decision making and assign family roles based on talent and choice, rather than on traditional beliefs about gender. She may enjoy lawn care, he may enjoy cooking, and together they do gardening chores they both enjoy. The undesirable chores, such as cleaning or laundry, are equitably distributed. It is the sharing of the domestic chores that creates the most difficulty for the egalitarian couple, because they, too, have been socialized into a world of traditional marriage and family patterns in which gender roles continue to intrude.

Scandinavia. The Scandinavian countries, specifically Norway and Sweden, consistently rank the highest in all measures of human development, including gender role egalitarianism and public policies designed to translate it to the family (Chapter 6). Parental leave for new fathers and programs to bolster women's economic status outside the home and men's child-rearing functions in the home have enhanced egalitarian marriages. As in the United States, Scandinavian men adopt more egalitarian attitudes about the division of labor in child rearing than they actually practice, but public policy will continue to support the objective of gender equity. In Scandinavia and the United States, egalitarian attitudes about career and child rearing are increasing, but for marriages to be truly egalitarian husbands need to participate fully in housework.

Instead of ranking husband over wife, egalitarian marriage presumes a partnership pattern, one that is strongly associated with paid employment for wives and an effective work–family balance for the couple. When wives contribute financially to the family, their decision-making powers are enhanced and traditional assumptions about feminine duties in the household are challenged. Perceived imbalance in decision making lowers marital satisfaction for both husband and wife and bolsters the patriarchal nature of marriage (Zimmerman et al., 2003; Amato, 2007). Egalitarian marriage fosters better communication and sharing and builds on a strong, empathic friendship between spouses. Because the couple does not accept gender role beliefs about a husband's dominance and a wife's acceptance of it, discussion is open and disagreement is expected. Disagreement is not a sign of marital weakness—the couple "agrees to disagree." Conflict may be a by-product but it is an expected and beneficial cost of the open communication encouraged in egalitarian marriages (Schwartz, 2002).

Equity Benefits. Children also benefit from egalitarianism because parents share the joy and burden of child rearing more equitably, and the needs of the couple are balanced with the needs of their children. The two sets of needs cannot be separated. This balance is very important to women who are happy in their egalitarian marriages but who must deal with the ongoing concern that their "mothering" is compromised. The egalitarian family helps women openly talk about both the rewards and the turmoil of motherhood that are hidden behind embedded beliefs about motherhood. As suggested by Susan Maushart's (1999:3) research, egalitarianism "unmasks" motherhood. She states that the mask of motherhood is revealed in cultural values glorifying the ideal of motherhood, but takes for granted the work of motherhood, and in debates about child care that pass judgments on "what's best for the child," as if the child's needs were separable from those of the mother, father, and siblings.

Despite the household task overload women face, the trend toward egalitarian marriages is unlikely to slow down. Men are marrying later and living independently for a longer period of time. These are the men who are more egalitarian in their beliefs, including that men should share housework. Even highly traditional marriages and families show more companionate qualities than those of a generation ago. They, too, cannot remain isolated from social change. We have seen that marital satisfaction, gender equity, and communication are enhanced when men and women are partners, when women engage in satisfying employment, and when men get involved in housework. One of the strongest predictors of marital satisfaction for both husbands and wives is decision-making equality in the famiy (Bartley et al., 2005; Amato et al., 2007; Pitt and Borland, 2008). As society becomes more gender equitable, marriages will become more egalitarian.

Commuter Marriage

The dual-location couple is not new. Men and women who serve in the armed forces, for example, have homes maintained by their spouses thousands of miles away and see them during leaves determined by the military. Economic recession, company mergers and buyouts, and job loss requiring relocation also foster dual-location arrangements of a couple. Almost all of the home-maintainers, however, are women. What is new is a dual-career couple evolving into a dual-location couple for reasons of the wife's, rather than the husband's, career. Historically, the common pattern is for the woman, literally, to follow her man from city to city as he advances up the career ladder. Her own career, if she has one, is expected to be secondary to his. Today many couples who are firmly committed to their marriages also have wives who are unwilling to abdicate their careers if a move is required. To maintain both marital and career commitments, marriages with commuter wives are growing in number. These marriages generally consist of highly educated, well-paid spouses who are managers, executives, and in professional careers, who see one another on weekends or less frequently, and who may continue these arrangements for several years. These patterns apply to white and African-American couples, although in the latter, wives are more likely to be in professional careers than husbands (Jackson et al., 2000; Tessina, 2008).

Commuter marriages help overcome the unhappiness and stress that wives express when they put their careers on hold earlier in the marriage. Earlier career subordination on the part of the wife leads to unhappiness and stress that the eventual commuter marriage helps overcome. Research suggests that despite the inconveniences, constant travel, and missing their family, commuter wives willingly make their treks because of immense career satisfaction that they find healthy for themselves and their marriages. Couples report quality time when they are together, communicate better, and enjoy the independence (Coolidge, 1997). As a commuter–marriage wife, who is a university professor, states,

> This is the best job I've ever had. I love it! I'm so grateful to my family for the chance to do this. What a great way to continue my career. (Harris et al., 2002)

Critique. The career advantages of a commuter marriage may be offset by disadvantages related to the considerable stress of living in two locations with little overall time together. Self-sufficiency and independence are enhanced, but loss of emotional support and dissatisfaction with the couple's marriage and family life increase. Strains are also associated with increased costs for maintaining two residences that may not be balanced by two incomes (Seifert, 2000). Couples in commuter marriages have less stress if they have been married longer before the dual-location arrangement began. Older couples, those whose children are already launched and those where one spouse is already established and successful in his/her career, also appear to fare better in a commuter marriage (Rhodes, 2002).

It may be difficult to resolve the logistical and emotional strains of a commuter marriage. But the marriage itself is unlikely to be sustained if the career ascendancy on the part of a husband leads to the career subordination of his wife. The guilt and regret commuter couples feel when they are not together are often due to the fact that they accept two standards that are not easy to reconcile: the standard that career success applies to both husband and wife and the standard that family success applies to wife but not husband. Both standards are based on traditional gender role beliefs that invade even this highly nontraditional form of marriage.

Cohabitation

Until relatively recently, *cohabitation*—an unmarried couple living together— was cause for condemnation. As increasing numbers of people choose cohabitation as their preferred lifestyle, whether they intend to marry later or not, this is no longer the case. Social support for cohabiting couples does vary, however. Peers and friends are more accepting than parents and relatives. Although parents may not openly express discomfort with the arrangement, they breathe a sigh of relief if their cohabiting child decides to marry. Increased support for cohabitation may account for the dramatic increase of cohabitants and the decrease in the marriage rate.

The number of cohabiting couples has soared from about half a million in 1970 to almost 6 million couples today, including almost 800,000 same-sex partners, representing close to 4 percent of all households in the United States (U.S. Census Bureau, 2009). These households are highly varied and include college students, who report it as preparation for marriage; persons over age 65, who cohabit for financial and emotional security; and couples with children present, this last group representing close to half of cohabitant households. The U.S. Census Bureau admits that these are probably conservative numbers because people may be reluctant to report themselves as "cohabiting" and may call themselves "roommates." In addition, these figures probably undercount gay and lesbian couples. They may refer to cohabiters as *POSSLQs*—"People of the Opposite Sex (sic) Sharing Living Quarters." Over half of people in their twenties and thirties have cohabited, and half of all couples married since 1985 have lived together at some point before marriage. Cohabitation is now so normative that it is an accepted stage between marriage and dating. However, as a stage, it is very unlikely that it will replace marriage as the preferred lifestyle.

Gender Differences. Although it would be reasonable to think that cohabitants are more egalitarian than married couples, the striking gender differences in cohabiting couples challenge this logic. Unlike married couples, cohabiting couples are less homogamous. Women tend to be younger, have higher levels of education, and earn more money than their partners. Males also express less commitment to the relationship and to later marriage than females. Women tend to view the relationship as temporary and leading to marriage. Men tend to view it as temporary but not leading to marriage. If children are involved, marriage is the more likely outcome but having children does not protect the couple form later divorce (Rhoades et al., 2006; Sassler et al., 2006; Thornton et al., 2007).

Issues of housework and money also signal the gender divide between cohabitants. Cohabiting women spend less time on housework than married women. But married and cohabiting women do more housework than married and cohabiting males, and like married women in traditional households, cohabiting women tend to accept the responsibility (Ciabattari, 2002). Compared to women in cohabiting households, women in egalitarian marriages would consider the larger housework burden as unfair. In household finances, money is rarely pooled, which has the advantage of financial independence, but the couple gives precedence to the man's career over the woman's. Gender norms about housework and finances persist in cohabitant households.

Contrary to popular belief, cohabitation is not a good screening device for a later successful marriage. Research concludes that cohabitants who marry have higher rates of depressive symptoms, lower marital satisfaction, adjustment, and commitment to marriage than noncohabitants and, perhaps more significant, have divorce rates that are equal to or higher than noncohabitants (Kline et al., 2004; Brown et al., 2005; Stanley et al., 2006). Both male and female cohabitants who break up are likely to cohabit again, setting up a cycle in which one failed relationship may predispose them to another one. Living together lessens total commitment—the door to leave is always open.

Considering these findings, it is somewhat surprising to witness the increasing population of cohabitants. Perhaps they are drawn to the idealism that is inherent in an arrangement that, on the surface at least, offers more benefits than liabilities. But the benefits appear to erode as cohabiting time increases. Playing house and keeping house are fundamentally different.

Singlehood

Historically, failure to marry was linked to perceptions about personal or social deficiencies. For women the stigma was, "She was never asked," and for men, "He's probably gay." Bolstered by the women's movement and gay rights activism, these stigmas are fast disappearing. It is also difficult to maintain such negative perceptions considering that unmarried adults in the United States represent over 40 percent of the population (see Table 7.3). Nonfamily households have grown rapidly since 1960, and that increase is largely due to the growth of one-person households. Almost one-third of all nonfamily households are now one-person. Women living alone represent almost two-thirds of these households and include widowed, divorced, and single people. In 1900 only one in ten adults was unmarried; today it is one in four. The large majority of both men and women eventually marry, but the percent of never-married people, especially women, continues to increase.

Many young people no longer view marriage as necessarily better than remaining single. The number of single people reporting that they are "very happy" has increased steadily for almost three decades (NORC, 2008). High school seniors and college students in particular say that although they plan to marry, it is not in their near future. Finishing college and getting a good job are more important, so for now they favor a lifestyle free of long-term commitments (Plotnick, 2007).

Gender Differences. Highly educated, financially independent women are likely candidates for choosing singlehood. For every age category, the higher a woman's income, the lower the rate of marriage. These women express a sense of control in their lives that is offered by remaining single. The availability of eligible partners and the marriage squeeze do not account for this trend. Market conditions offering either mate surpluses or deficits will not propel women to marry men who do not offer what they can achieve without being married (Lichter and Landale, 1995).

Men are also choosing singlehood at increasing rates. For men, singlehood frees them from financial burdens they associate with a demanding instrumental role (Edwards, 2000; DePaulo, 2006). There are no significant gender or race differences in terms of what is liked or disliked about being single. Professional African-American women report that they are very aware of the advantages and disadvantages of singlehood, but describe their lives as satisfying and meaningful (Fuller, 2001). Men and women of all races enjoy its mobility, freedom, and social options. However, they must deal with loneliness, the uncertainties of dating, and the pressure to marry from family and friends. Despite many new options available for parenthood, women who want to be biological mothers may feel acute distress due to their single status. Being single in a "couples" world brings added pressures, and many singles, particularly men, report higher levels of emotional distress than married people (Phillips, 1999; Cole, 2000; Lewis, 2001).

Gender Stereotypes. As the ones traditionally responsible for the marriage proposal, men are thought to seek out attractive, desirable women and leave unattractive, undesirable women in the unasked category. She is the lonely spinster; he is the carefree bachelor who must be wary of single women interested in matrimony. The image of a man snagged into marriage by a woman in hot pursuit has been a popular one. The media perpetrate images of women doomed to singlehood and childlessness by a marriage squeeze that leaves them desperate as their biological motherhood clocks are ticking away, a perception we will explore in the next chapter. In women's magazines and popular media, the few upbeat articles about singlehood are overshadowed by multiple negative ones such as anguished interview with (people like) hapless *Desperate Housewives* star Teri Hatcher, a tragic figure not for the sexual abuse she suffered as a child but for her perpetual single status (Mapes, 2007: xiii).

These are simply untrue stereotypes. Women singles express high levels of self-confidence and happiness in choosing singlehood. The mental health benefits of marriage for men are higher than other marital categories but marriage does not free them from pervious states of depression (French and Williams, 2007). Men who are comfortable in their choice are bolstered by married friends and a supportive family. Men and women singles are often more more involved with their families and extended kin network than their married siblings. This involvement includes caretaking roles for children and elderly relatives. They retain the autonomy they desire but share in the joys and responsibilities of family life (Sarkisian and Gerstel, 2008).

As the current generation of never-married people age, it is likely that many will remain unmarried and many women will forego childbearing whether they cohabit or not. Contemporary singlehood represents opportunities for happiness for a significant subset of the population who may reject marriage and any permanent and/or exclusive sexual relationship.

Summary

1. Love and marriage were linked during the Puritan era. Love includes components of sex (eros), altruism (agape), friendship (philos), and allegiance (nomos). Sexual passion distinguishes love and friendship.

2. Best friends are usually of one's own gender. Other-gender friends are endangered if liking turns to loving and if gender role beliefs intrude. Love is also seen as a triangle of intimacy, passion, and commitment.

3. Romantic love is idealized and produces many myths. These include "love conquers all, live is blind; love at first sight; women are the romantic gender; sex should not occur without love; and the opposite of live is hate."

4. Men are more open and communicative at the beginning of a relationship and show love by doing things for their lover. The male deficit model of love ignores men's skill at communication and self-disclosure early in a relationship. Androgynous love can integrate masculine and feminine qualities.

5. Mate selection is highly structured and based on homogamy. People choose partners based on age, SES, race, and attractiveness. African-American women are caught in marriage squeeze when the marriageable men of their own race are less educated and less economically successful.

6. Functionalists regard traditional expressive and instrumental gender roles as socially beneficial in mate selection. Conflict theorists say men do not have to be attractive but only economically successful. Feminists say women have less power and are objects of exchange in a marriage market. Symbolic integrationists say women may accept the view of themselves as objects of exchange.

7. Gender role change in families is a product of modernization. Functionalism regards marriage as aiding social stability, which gender role change can disrupt. The functionalist ideal family form of employed husband with his dependent wife and children is recent in history and pertains to white, middle-class families.

Conflict theory asserts when wealth is concentrated in the hands of males at the household level, it leads to women's subservience. She can gain power by becoming a wage earner. Feminists contend that race, class, and sexuality are also avenues of oppression to women in their families. Symbolic interactionists emphasize how people take on traditional gender roles despite beliefs about egalitarianism.

8. In the family values debate, family restorationists believe that society will be better-off when women stay home and men are unchallenged heads of the family. Their model ignores that families have changed over time, many women must be employed for their families to survive, children are not harmed when their mothers work, and couples increasingly desire egalitarian gender roles.

9. Housewives may express satisfaction in their roles but feel devalued. Patriarchy undermines bridges between homemakers and employed women. Whether employed full-time or not, married women across the globe do the majority of the housework.

10. Extramarital relationships are increasing. Married women say affairs are less for sex and more for emotional support; married men report the reverse. Single women and unaware wives have more liabilities if the affair is discovered.

11. Wealthy Hong Kong men often have "second wives" in Mainland China. New marriage laws to counter this trend have been largely ineffective.

12. Household chores and imbalance in decision making create the most difficulty for egalitarian couples. Egalitarian marriages are desired and are correlated with paid employment for wives, better communication, and task sharing.

13. Commuter (dual-location)-married couples are committed to their marriages and to both their careers. Couples must reconcile gender standards related to career and family success.

14. The number of cohabiting couples continues to increase. Males are less committed to the relationship than females. Couples who have cohabited have equal or higher divorce rates than noncohabitants.

15. The number of people remaining single is increasing. Highly educated, financially secure women are more likely to choose singlehood and report high self-confidence and happiness. Women who want to be biological mothers express distress at being single.

Key Terms

assortive mating 183	homogamy 182	nuclear families 189
companionate marriages 177	household 189	second shift 197
egalitarian marriage 200	marriage gradient 183	third shift 197
homemaker 195	marriage squeeze 185	

Critical Thinking Questions

1. Using research evidence, argue for or against the following statement: We are socialized to fall in love with only certain people, therefore the notion of romantic love is a myth.

2. Construct an ideal family form and marital relationship from the perspectives of functionalism and conflict theory. Account for how marital success and happiness are determined in this idealized construction.

3. What are the gender factors working against the contentment of full-time homemakers, equalitarian marriages, commuter marriages, and cohabiting couples? How can these factors be modified to make these household forms more successful?

CHAPTER **8**

Desire for a feminine destiny—husband, home and children—and the enchantment of love are not always easy to reconcile with the will to succeed.

—Simone DeBeauvoir,
The Second Sex (1953)

GENDER AND FAMILY RELATIONS

The majority of people globally will eventually become parents. Like those from many other cultures, Americans are propelled into parenthood by the gendered processes of love, cohabitation, and marriage that prime the couple for their new roles as mothers and fathers. Parenthood is structured by gender beliefs and produces powerful gender outcomes. These gender beliefs are so completely embedded in family practices that the differences and inequalities they produce are largely taken for granted. As we saw in previous chapters, challenges to taken-for-granted definitions about the family provoke highly contentious debates. These debates have profound consequences when one or another definition is used to determine public policy on a variety of family-related issues, including divorce, child custody, and benefits for single parents, cohabitating couples, and partners and children in gay and lesbian families. Political rhetoric usually highlights beliefs that when the traditional family structure is changed to accommodate change outside the family, such as women's massive entry into paid employment, disastrous social consequences follow. Other views celebrate family diversity, flexibility, and the creation of new roles for all family members in response to social change. Gender-based parental roles are called into question as alternative definitions of the family emerge. We will see in this chapter that narrow views of gender severely restrict opportunities for exploration and growth for both children and their parents. (Unless otherwise noted, statistics in this chapter are taken from U.S. Census Bureau, 2009).

THE PARENTHOOD TRANSITION

The transition from couple dyad to family triad is a momentous one. The first child brings numerous changes that affect the marriage and alter the lifestyle of the couple. New parents report that enormous joy is tempered with increased marital tension. To say that parenthood is filled with uncertainty is an understatement. Parenting is based on skills that need to be learned but cannot be effectively accomplished, if at all, until after the child is born. Socialization for parenthood is based on one's own family experiences, involvement with others' children, formal classes, folklore, and reading - child-care and parenting manuals. Whatever the degree of preparation, new parents discover that the anticipation of what it means to be a parent is far different from the reality. Gender is a key factor in accounting for this anticipation gap. Parenthood brings different experiences and produces different results for mothers compared to fathers.

Early sociological work on the transition to parenthood focused on parenthood as *crisis*. In this model, first-time parents encounter anxiety, uncertainty, loss of confidence—even shock—during the first days and weeks of parenting. The strains of parenthood can be overwhelming, and the demands alter the quality as well as quantity of time spent on the marital relationship. More time and energy are spent on children-related issues than on marriage-related ones. When couples nurture their children but not their marriage the risk for divorce is heightened. Traditional gender roles can also drive a wedge between the new parents. When women do virtually all of the infant care and take on the added housework demands, men tend to retreat to workplace roles, neglect the emotion work in the newly created family, and find themselves distanced from both wife and newborn (Erickson, 2005; Bell et al., 2007). The crisis of parenthood is eased when gender roles are more flexible and couples make a determined effort to enhance closeness.

Parenthood as crisis has been modified with the emerging view that parenthood is a normal developmental stage. The disorganization and seeming chaos when the newborn enters the household gradually give way to new routines and family norms. The major shifts in lifestyle associated with tension and undesirable role change are more than offset by the joy and gratification the child brings to the new parents (Feeney, 2001).

Obviously, parenthood will alter marital roles and create new family roles. Whether the parenthood transition is seen as a crisis, a stage in normal development, or something in between depends on how a family responds to meet the parenting challenge. This response will be largely dependent on beliefs regarding gender roles. The labels "husband" and "wife" suggest different realities; the same can be said for motherhood and fatherhood.

Motherhood

The belief that a woman's ultimate fulfillment will be as a mother is a powerful socialization message girls hear very early in life. The **motherhood mandate** issues a command to females of all ages instructing them that motherhood demands selfless devotion to children and a subordination of one's own life to the needs of children and family. Although many other activities that she feels personally worthwhile are halted, the mandate assumes that a woman willingly submits herself first to her child-rearing responsibilities. The power of this mandate instills guilt in women with small children who work outside the home, regardless of whether they are employed because they "want to be" (employment is personally rewarding) or they "have to be" (they need the money).

The Motherhood Mandate. American culture idealizes motherhood, but the actual support new mothers receive varies considerably. If women are socialized into believing that being a good mother comes easily, they are severely jolted by parenting responsibilities. The tension and strain experienced by first-time mothers can be perceived as personal failure, in turn lessening their motivation to seek help. The notion of a maternal instinct is not empirically supported (Chapter 2), but the view that all females want to become mothers and that a mother's role "comes naturally" stubbornly persists. Ideal mothers are expected to enjoy the work of mothering and caring for home and family, regardless of how demanding or tedious the work is. Exclusive devotion to mothering is good for her children and promotes husband happiness and marital contentment (Hoffnung, 1995; Ridgeway and Correll, 2004).

Given the huge social changes accompanying the large-scale entry of women into paid employment, it would be expected that mothers have more latitude navigating their motherhood roles. A new version of the mandate has surfaced, but it may exert even more of a toll on mothers. This "new momism" is media-driven and pressures mothers to conform to impossible standards of perfection. In marketing the cultural ideals of motherhood, media images, self-help books, and toy manufacturers put enormous strain on women's performance as mothers. In sympathizing with the demands mothers face, "skill building toys" are offered as compromises for children's less time with their moms (Pugh, 2005). Women are expected to seek out the latest information offering guidance in fulfilling their roles as mothers. In parenting magazines, despite the use of the supposedly neutral word "parent" in their titles—mothers are the target audience (Zimmerman, 2004). These images of moms appear to "celebrate" work and family at the same time—achieve at work but self-sacrifice at home. The end result, however, is a paradox rather than a celebration, as suggested by Susan Douglas and Meredith Michaels (2009:244):

Now here's the beauty of this contorting contraction. . . . Both working mothers and stay-at home mothers get to be failures . . . intensive mothering has lower status . . . (stay-at-home mothers are boring), but occupies a higher moral ground (working mothers are neglectful).

The new momism further divides women who work outside the home and those who don't into opposing camps. Room mothers and cookie bakers make way for soccer moms and vanpool drivers. It is a no-win situation for mothers. She is blamed for too little or too much time with her children. Although she delights in her child's development, her own development stalls and her sense of self can be diminished.

Functionalism. In emphasizing that the motherhood mandate is essential for social equilibrium, functionalists would support these qualities. Mothers are both the biological reproducers and the social reproducers. As the primary socializers of children, they provide the necessary ingredients for maintenance, productivity, and continuity of society. If socialization does not instill girls with the motherhood mandate, and the "aura" associated with it, society may be compromised. Functionalism assumes that the traditional division of labor of nonoverlapping gender roles within a patriarchal family is the most efficient and least contentious arrangement. It is a mother's fault if something "goes wrong" with the children. She takes the responsibility, the blame, and ultimately the guilt (Garey and Arendell, 2001).

Functionalists point to the responsibilities associated with motherhood. But rights accrue as well. The motherhood mandate is in tandem with the motherhood mystique, which is a glorification of the role. Child rearing brings joy and pride for a child's accomplishments, for which mothers take a great deal of credit. It is apparent, nonetheless, that mothers are more likely to share the credit for what goes right, but assume the burden of blame for what goes wrong.

There is no argument that the family is the critical institution for socialization. Contemporary functionalists recognize that there are social benefits when women, including those with school-age children, work outside the home. They assert that family maintenance today hinges on the incomes of employed mothers. Women, like men, need to be encouraged to pursue the work that offers the highest income. Functionalists agree that equality in the workplace is beneficial to families and to society. However, with the ever-present motherhood mandate lurking, women are always on family alert. Parents and children accept the mandate and take for granted any arrangements permitting men less in-home responsibility. Functionalists have difficulty transferring beliefs about gender equity outside the home to gender inequality inside the home. In other words, how are women supposed to be equal and different at the same time?

Often overlooked is the fact that the motherhood mandate is relatively recent in the United States. Until the mid-nineteenth century a frontier economy based on subsistence farming required women to carry a multitude of productive roles. In her role set, a woman's child-rearing function was less important for family survival than her farm and household-related money-raising activities (Chapter 5). It is only since the beginning of the twentieth century that the notion of having children for purely psychological reasons became firmly ingrained in the American consciousness.

Conflict Theory. Conflict theorists focus on the motherhood mandate as contributing to the social powerlessness experienced by women in their household and roles outside the home. Because a woman's earnings from paid employment alter the power relations within the family, men will evoke the motherhood mandate to ensure that women concentrate their energies on domestic roles. Careers and personal growth are impeded when family responsibilities intrude in the workplace. The choices wives make regarding child rearing weaken their bargaining power at home and on the job and reinforce economic dependence on their husbands. In the workplace this translates into lower salaries and sagging careers (Chapter 10). At home it translates into shouldering the bulk of child-care tasks (Guendouzi, 2006). From a conflict perspective, not until as many men as women truly want to stay home with the children can women hope to achieve real economic parity.

Challenging the Motherhood Mandate. An acceptance of the motherhood mandate/new momism precludes much individual growth for women. By this definition, motherhood is the key worthwhile role that overrides all others. The obvious problems and contradictions emanating from the mystique are conveniently overlooked. Can women feel good about themselves as mothers if they also seek other roles?

One answer lies in the demographics of motherhood which have changed significantly since the 1950s. As women achieved career and educational goals, marriage and motherhood were delayed. The median age at first marriage for both women and men has risen steadily (Chapter 7). The decline of the fertility rate since World War II is linked to higher levels of education, rising wages, and the opportunity costs of child rearing for women. This explains why so many women in their 30s and 40s are now having children for the first time. It also supports the idea, however, that mother-hood remains a fundamental goal. Most women are unwilling to give up biological parenthood but opt for smaller families than in their parents' generation. Because career-oriented women are also unwilling to give up either motherhood or profes-sional roles, they are adapting their beliefs about family and parenting accordingly.

Young women assume that motherhood, as the mandate suggests, gives them their most meaningful sense of personal fulfillment. But unlike their mothers and grandmothers, they are also challenging the idea that motherhood is the necessary ingredient for making them "complete." Motherhood is a role most seek, but it must be complemented with other personally fulfilling roles. For both men and women, the acceptance of childlessness has gradually increased since the 1970s, but contrary to the motherhood mandate, women are more likely than men to hold positive attitudes toward childlessness (Koropeckyj-Cox and Pendell, 2007). This is especially true for younger professional women, who already demonstrate higher rates of childlessness than older professional women. These women may be either less confident or more realistic in their ability to successfully carry out roles associated with motherhood and still have a satisfying career. If this is indeed the case, it may indicate a further weakening of the motherhood mandate.

Feminism. The acceptance of feminist values by a larger proportion of women also affects notions about motherhood. Women who hold traditional gender role orientations desire larger families when compared to less traditional women. Traditional women are also likely to express higher levels of religiosity and have lower levels of education. College women who subjectively identify with feminism are less interested in motherhood or intend to delay marriage and motherhood until after they are established in their careers. Regardless of media hype, however, feminism and motherhood are not incompatible. Feminists who intend to become mothers or those who already have children are realistic about the gendered pitfalls of mothering but also believe that motherhood offers opportunities for assertiveness, learning and mastering new skills, and ensuring that feminist principles are passed to the next generation of sons and daughters (Baker, 2000; O'Reilly, 2000; Howitz, 2001). The old view of motherhood is unacceptable because paid work has become so important to the identities of mothers. They recognize that simply staying home all day with preschoolers does not automatically qualify one as a good mother.

The idea of a motherhood mandate is shifting to viewing motherhood in much more flexible ways to fit the lifestyles of contemporary women and couples. This shift accounts for the well-being of children and the marital satisfaction of parents. The qualities we associate with motherhood can be more widely shared by both men and women in a variety of family contexts. This variety is very important since many women are choosing motherhood but not marriage. It is expected that like other gender roles, qualities associated with motherhood will continue to change as we experience more diversity in our families and workplaces.

Fatherhood

Cast into primary breadwinning roles, American fathers are viewed as more peripheral in nurturing and child care compared to mothers. This is a far different picture than the colonial fathers who were expected to provide for not only the economic needs of their children, but also for their moral and spiritual development. In this sense, colonial fathers were nurturers as much as mothers. Public policy and legislation regarding custody of children, child support, definitions of desertion, and child neglect reinforce the emphasis on the father's role as the economic provider for the family. Increases in divorce and cohabitation have undermined father–child relationships, and nonresident fathers are increasingly absent from their children's lives. To get women off welfare, public policy focuses on finding unwed, divorced, and married fathers who deserted their families. A father is targeted in order for him to meet his financial obligation to the family; his emotional involvement with his children is largely ignored.

The fact that fathers do take their breadwinning role very seriously does not diminish the interests or love they have for their families. Like women, men also see raising a family as a major life goal. Fathers today spend more time with their children and report greater overall family satisfaction. Strong evidence also suggests that quality family relations and supportive social connections are associated with better psychological health and well-being for fathers (Hall, 2005; Auerbach and Silverstein, 2006). Compared to nonfathers, contemporary dads exhibit two models of fatherhood: the "good-provider model," encouraging them to work more hours, and the "involved-father model," encouraging them to work less hours. The "forces pulling women out of the home are stronger than the forces pulling men into it" (Gerson, 2009:327). The models may seem contradictory, but they suggest that men regard the fatherhood role as a very significant one.

New Fathers. As first-time parents, men adapt more easily to the rigors of fatherhood than women do to motherhood, and husbands can predict with more success than their wives what kind of parents they are likely to be. In the transition to parenthood, personal goals of husbands do not change substantially, and husbands are less ambivalent about parenting responsibilities (Salmela-Aro et al., 2000; Simpson et al., 2003). Fathers see themselves as less competent than mothers in dealing with daily child care. They internalize strong beliefs about their paternal responsibility, but largely surrender actual responsibility for child care to their wives. A father's level of engagement, accessibility, and responsibility are a fraction of the mother's. A father's time is spent more on recreational activities with their children than with their ongoing physical upkeep. The existing gender gap in housework increases with the birth of the first child and widens with more children. Women's housework and child maintenance tasks increase significantly; men's show "extraordinary stability" (Craig, 2006; Baxter et al., 2008).

Children's Development. Because the prime directive for fathers is to provide for the economic support of their families, in comparison to mothers, the father's effect on the development of their children is often overlooked. Chapter 3 demonstrated that parental influence on childhood socialization is vitally important. Mothers accept the major responsibility in socialization of their children, but fathers send important early messages, especially regarding gender roles. These messages are powerful because fathers have reduced contact and quality of interaction with their children. Compared to mothers, fathers expect their adolescent sons to conform to gender roles much more than their adolescent daughters. Fathers are more likely to take into account gender when dividing chores and privileges, when showing affection, and when disciplining their children. Fathers are likely to use harsher discipline on sons, believing it enhances a son's masculinity. Increased parent–child conflict during adolescence is typical, but conflict is heightened for fathers compared to mothers and for sons compared to daughters. These gender preferences decrease the attachment adolescent sons have with their fathers (Kurtz, 2002; Tucker et al., 2003). Fathers who are less traditional and stereotyped in their gender role beliefs have sons who match their fathers' beliefs.

Traditional fatherhood may bring less of the profound personal and marital changes that mothers experience, but fathers can and do form strong bonds with their young children and are successfully taking on child-care tasks and nurturing roles more than fathers in the past. When fathers change, daughters—and especially sons—will follow. Egalitarian parenting clearly benefits children and enhances marital satisfaction.

A Fatherhood Mandate. Continued gender role stereotyping severely limits options for fathers to explore new roles. Conflict theory and the feminist perspective argue that the motherhood mandate is a barrier to gender equity. But the opposite is true for a fatherhood mandate. Young men have not adopted a fatherhood mandate allowing them to move in the direction of androgynous, flexible gender roles. Functionalists would also support a fatherhood mandate that moves beyond the provider role so fathers can effectively meet the challenges of social change and the new family processes that emerge as a result. After the terrorist attacks on September 11 in New York City, for example, children sought protection, safety, and security from both parents, but particularly from fathers (Warren, 2001). Those fathers who listened to their children and responded to them with warmth and compassion began to carve out a tentative fatherhood mandate combining instrumental and expressive roles. The involved-father model appears to be gaining in prominence and, as discussed on Chapter 9, it may signal a crack in a masculine ethic that deters men from more meaningful parent–child relationships.

Voluntary Childlessness

The motherhood mandate may be weakening, but couples who choose not to have children must still contend with a prochild social message. Childless marriages are steadily increasing and more women of childbearing age will not have children.

It is unlikely, however, that this signals a revolution against a childbearing, pronatalist ideology, or that cultural definitions equating women with (sexual) reproduction will be altered any time soon. Media are replete with stories of women who "successfully" challenge their biological clocks and have children before it is too late. A billion-dollar fertility and adoption industry has mushroomed to meet this challenge. The belief that couples should have children is so strong that those who choose not to do so, especially the women, continue to be denigrated, often regarded as incomplete and selfish (Meyers, 2002; Bulcroft and Teachman, 2004).

Critique. Married couples who are voluntarily child-free can be viewed with a combination of pity, scorn, and suspicion. Married women who do not mother children are thought to live a childless existence. These are stereotyped views that are fundamentally different from empirical reality. Voluntarily childless couples express similar levels of marital happiness as couples with children. Voluntarily childless married women express higher levels of well-being than married mothers. Women who are childless do not lead childless lives. They choose not be mothers, but children are central to their lives and provide them with a sense of generativity that compares favorably to biological mothers (Joseph, 2001; Letherby, 2002). They take on a variety of meaningful child-related responsibilities through their networks of kin, friends, voluntary organizations, and employment.

Although couples continue to view parenthood as desirable, the increased number of voluntarily childless couples implies that, along with the weakening of the motherhood mandate, there is also less pressure to conform to traditional family norms regarding parenthood. Support for those couples who choose to remain childless is growing.

PARENTS AS DUAL EARNERS

Again, it is the entry of women into paid employent that significantly altered the structure and function of families in the United States. Paid employment benefits women socially and psychologically, especially when they work in positions that they find challenging, rewarding, and personally meaningful. Their marriages and sense of well-being appear to be enhanced, and shared decision making increases marital satisfaction for both wife and husband (Han and Moen, 2001; O'Keefe, 2002; Kendall, 2007). As suggested in Chapter 7, dual-earning couples are more likely to have egalitarian marriages than those with a wife as full-time homemaker. The cost for women involves maintaining responsibilities at home and for the children when husbands do not share household and child-care chores on anywhere near an equal basis. Multiple roles of employed women also include other caregiving demands, such as caring for frail parents, which may compromise the benefits of employment and life satisfaction (Chapter 10). In general, however, the evidence from dual-earner families shows that women are enriched by their labor force activities.

The dual-earner family is now the normative family. There are more dual-earning nuclear families with children present than one-earner nuclear families with children present (Chapter 7). The largest overall increase is in families with preschoolers. Because women are traditionally responsible for child care, particularly in the preschool years, all eyes turn to them when questions arise as to how children are affected when both parents work outside the home. It is the wives rather than their husbands who reap society's disapproval if children suffer when both parents are in the labor force. How accurate is the "suffering children" theme?

Children of Employed Women

If parents are happy and the family is enhanced by a dual-earning family structure, this should logically carry over to the children. Not so, states writer Kate O'Beirne (2006;23–24), who maintains that

> . . . . we know what is true about the bond between mother and child. Women fall madly in love with babies in a way that devoted fathers don't . . . Women would have to be snookered to leave their young children in the care of someone else.

This view asserts that a positive, sustained relationship with a caregiver is essential to healthy, emotional childhood development but a mother must be that caregiver. A person caring for a child out of love will do it better than one doing it for pay.

If parents, especially mothers, are not filled with remorse and guilt by these views, it increases with messages that care options must not include "paid strangers." These strangers are the female day-care workers who will teach babies and young children "values, fears, beliefs and behaviors" (Robertson, 2003:48). Of course, the only option is mother care, because even "devoted fathers do not fall madly in love with their babies like mothers do." These messages ignore or dismiss any "damages" to children of parents who do not have the option of working for pay. They also tell fathers that they do not (and cannot) love their children as much as mothers.

The Child-Care Issue. The contention from such writers is that a generation *denied* love when they were children will create havoc on them as adults and do untold damage to the social structure, an argument echoed by the family restorationists mentioned in the previous chapter. Parents are abandoning their children to day care so they can selfishly pursue their own careers, which in later years will harm the next generation of their children. What is the evidence to warrant this conclusion?

One major source of information is often overlooked in debates on this issue. When women were desperately needed during World War II to work in defense plants, they were recruited by the thousands in propaganda campaigns designed to alleviate anxiety and guilt about leaving their children with others (Chapter 5). Creative approaches to day care became the norm of the day. Because women were needed, day-care centers multiplied quickly and many had no other care options for their children. Any potential negative, long-term consequences on these children were ignored. After the war traditional attitudes prevailed and women were expected to return home and be full-time housewives and mothers. They were not guilty of being neglectful mothers during the war, but if they chose to continue to work outside the home afterward, the guilt returned. The script that employed mothers are "bad" mothers returned with a vengeance.

Over a half century after World War II, there is near consensus by developmental psychologists that surrogate child care is not the major risk factor in the lives of children of dual-earner couples (Burchinal et al., 2000; Colwell et al., 2001). The key problem is poor quality care. Fortunately for married, white-collar and professional women, many employers provide benefit packages offering high-quality care options. The same cannot be said for many low-income, dual-earning couples and single-parent women who rely more on informal, less costly, and less desirable options of lower quality. On the other hand, an enriched group child-care experience can stimulate the moral development and prosocial behavior of infants and preschoolers. Poor children or those from troubled families may have resources in their child-care centers that are absent in their homes. Low-income mothers who gain entrance into good-quality subsidized child care are able to maintain steady employment and spend half as much income on child care (Brooks, 2002a; Honig, 2002). Probably the greatest challenge to these families is the availability of affordable, safe, accessible child care (Hawkins and Whiteman, 2004). Their satisfaction with child care carries over to the well-being of their children.

Children's Time with Parents. There are no significant differences in the home environment or development of children in two parent households with employed mothers than those whose mothers who are not employed. Children with employed mothers gain their strongest sense of well-being and attachment from parents (Harsch, 2006). "Paid strangers" who are caring and compassionate may supplement primary socialization but they will not substitute for it. Dual earners build in "quality" parent–child time in homes where mothers are employed and both parents spend more time on homework and reading with their children than in homes where a mother is not employed (Zick et al., 2001; Roxburgh, 2006). Working mothers with a college education spend significantly more time with children than women who do *not* work outside the home. They also spend more time with children than working fathers (Guryan et al., 2008). The amount of time working parents spend with their children or communicate with their children continues to increase. Early in life children do express that they would like their mothers to be at home more and are concerned about the confusion, rush, and scheduling headaches that are the inevitable effects of job, school, and recreational demands. Nonetheless, children's appreciation for their employed mothers' accomplishments grows over time (Hoffman, 2000; Dorfman, 2001; Moen, 2003). As children get older they report more advantages than disadvantages of arrangements that allow their mothers to work for pay (Heaven and McCluskey-Fawcett, 2001). Fueled by media stereotypes and guilt messages received from a variety of sources, parents still agonize over decisions to use surrogate care in order for a mother to return to paid employment.

Adolescents. The adverse effect of maternal employment would be expected to show up during adolescence, because this is often a stress-filled time for families. Again, research does not warrant this conclusion. Adolescents from dual-career families, especially daughters, appreciate the jobs their mothers have, often want to follow in their professional footsteps, and not surprisingly, have less traditional gender role attitudes than children from single-earner homes (Hoffman and Youngblade, 1999; Kinelski et al., 2002). Adolescents and adults reflecting on the effect of their mother's paid employment when they were children viewed their family lifestyle positively and reported high degrees of parental closeness, supportiveness, and interest in their personal problems (Gambone et al., 2002).

Summary. Decades of research on the effects of the dual-earner family on children do not support the "suffering child" or "abandoned child" theme. Employed mothers do not neglect their children nor are the children jeopardized by maternal employment. The benefits of growing up in a dual-earning family are bolstered by longitudinal research on children of all races who were followed over a 14-year period that compared them according to whether their mothers worked outside the home or not. The results show that on measurements of self-esteem, academic achievement, language development, and behavior problems in both family types, children are not harmed in their development. This study is important because the results applied to mothers who worked outside the home when their children were babies and preschoolers (Harvey, 1999). To the relief of egalitarian and dual-earner couples, results such as these continue to be confirmed. Motherhood and working for pay do not harm children—to the contrary, they are likely to improve children's social and intellectual development (Jacobson, 2004; Gottfried, 2005; Bianchi et al., 2006). When children are provided with high-quality out-of-home options, employed mothers enrich the human capital of their families.

Helicopter Parents

The irony of the child-care debate is that the majority of current college students were in some form of child care outside the home, attended preschool, and had employed mothers. These students represent the cohort termed the *millennial generation*, born between 1980 and 2000, who grew up with Internet, cell phones, and text-messaging. Often referred to as *helicopter parents*, their mothers and fathers continue to hover over their children in college as they did throughout their precollegiate years. Compared to the baby boomers and "Generation X," millennials from middle-class homes see their dual-earning parents more frequently, communicate with them more often, and count on parents to intervene when problems arise in school and sometimes even in the workplace. Contrary to media messages on the lack of involvement in their children's lives, dual-earning helicopter parents are overprotective and over-involved. Although parents are often accused of meddling, college students report that they expect parents to run interference for them and prefer they do it more rather than less (Shellenbarger, 2006; Graves, 2007; Hoover and Supiano, 2008). From the students' view, over-involved parents produce happier students (Marklein, 2008).

Hovering Moms. Do mothers or fathers do more hovering? Most information on gender of parent and gender differences in type of hovering is still anecdotal. However, these reports suggest, as we would predict, that mothers hover more overall. They are concerned with their children's lifestyle on campus, from food, clothing, and health, to roommates, relationships, and grades. Fathers hover on issues related to choice of major and career, and on college costs. One survey of parents reported that three-fourths communicated with their college-student-young adults two to three times a week; and one-third did so on a daily basis (Rainey, 2006). It is likely that mothers use cell phones and fathers use emails as the preferred way to stay in touch with their children. One mother reports that she supplemented her two to three daily conversations with her daughter with *Facebook* (Flanigan, 2008). Mothers have contacted companies to speak to managers about why their sons were not hired and to speak to deans and professors about why their children received a lower-than-expected grade (Tresaugue, 2006; Rose, 2007).

These anecdotal reports support early research showing that mothers are indeed more likely than fathers to be the hoverers and that mothers of sons do most of the hovering (Jayson, 2007; Shellenbarger, 2007). Mothers are vulnerable to the charge of "supermom" for their overzealous hovering (Robb, 2008). Supermom in the helicopter parent context is more of a criticism than an approval of her behavior. Considering the motherhood mandate, over-involved parents, especially over-involved mothers, who base their self-worth on the accomplishments of their children rather than their own accomplishments express more sadness and have less self-esteem.

Intrusive mothering in the name of school success often results in fostering uncertainty in their children. Children themselves believe they are incompetent students, and mothers inadvertently promote failure when their children are low achievers (Pomerantz and Eaton, 2001; Shellenbarger, 2005; Marsh, 2007). Given these trends, concern is expressed that overprotected children who are less than autonomous as adults will be unable to withstand the demands of life in the global economy once mom and dad are out of the picture. Believing that "mom will fix it," psychologists fear that when childhood is too "sanitized," young adults cannot be confident enough to make their own decisions (Marano, 2004; Newbart, 2005). We saw in Chapter 2 that the empty-nest syndrome is largely a myth, but more research is needed to determine if it is emerging for helicopter mothers.

For mothers who do and do not work outside the home, the meddling helicopter mom image sends yet another mixed message about the level of involvement they are expected to assume in their children's lives. They can be blamed for too much involvement (smothering their children) or not enough involvement (abandoning their children). The new momism keeps a tight reign over all mothers.

FAMILIES IN MULTICULTURAL PERSPECTIVE

The multicultural heritage of the United States is reflected in its families. Because this heritage is linked to race and ethnicity, minority families are impacted by the same disadvantages that affect them outside their homes. To account for gender patterns in these families, the multiple risks and experiences from their unique cultural histories must also be considered. Keep in mind, however, that white and European-American families also vary in social class, cultural history, and other variables that impact gender roles in their families. Although not profiled in this section, they should not be viewed as the default, normative family in the United States.

African-American Families

Contrary to stereotypes, there are two parents present in over half of African-American families, and over half of the fathers in these families work full-time. Data from the turn of the century (1910) reveal that African-American households were less likely to be nuclear and more likely to be headed by women, a pattern that persists today. The half of the African-American households without two parents present are those headed by single parents and 90 percent of these are single-parent women. Compared to European Americans, African-American family life cycles are marked by less formal marriages, parenthood earlier in marriage, later, less likelihood of remarriage, and a higher divorce rate (U.S. Census Bureau, 2009). Over three-fourths of African-American children are likely to live part of their life in a female-headed household, often with a female grandparent. The households are likely to consist of both kin and nonkin. The key factors in the development of these patterns are the legacy of slavery and economic oppression rooted in discrimination that led to the underemployment of African-American men. These factors have a profound impact on gender roles in contemporary African-American families.

Compared to all other racial groups, African-American females have had a much longer legacy of paid employment essential to the stability and survival of their families. This legacy fueled the variety of family and household structures African-American families exhibit. Paid employment is central to African-American women's mothering and to their family experience. It is the most important reason for the greater degree of role sharing by wives and husbands and has strengthened these families in several fundamental ways. First, families demonstrate a strong willingness to absorb others into kin structures by creating a network of **fictive kin**, where friends "become" family. African Americans tend to define the boundaries of their families with more flexibility than in families of other races, so distant kin become primary kin, and close friends and neighbors become fictive kin. Women fill the fictive kin ranks. Women-centered networks of "bloodmothers" and "other-mothers" who share mothering responsibilities bring an array of exchange and support that benefits all household members. In turn, children are offered a diversity of parenting models that are seen as enriching children with a more multifaceted form of nurturing (Collins, 2009). Employed mothers who are the family's breadwinners often turn to these networks for child-care needs.

Second, compared to white couples, for working-class and middle-class married couples, family structures are likely to be more egalitarian. These families have dual-earning husband and wife in stable employment. Egalitarian arrangements are bolstered by middle-class African-American women who work outside the home by choice rather than economic necessity and who do not view their roles as wife–mother and wage earner as mutually exclusive (Higginbotham, 2000; Hines and Boyd-Franklin, 2005). Research by sociologist Burt Landry (2000) suggests that these women were practicing an egalitarian lifestyle decades before white couples. Third, African-American husbands appear to be more willing than white husbands to take more responsibility for child rearing and adapt themselves and the household to the needs of their employed wives (Hofferth, 2003). This last pattern is interesting because African-American working-class and lower-class men tend to hold traditional ideas about gender roles. The intersection of race and social class helps account for this pattern.

The Myth of Black Matriarchy. The paid work of African-American women has been a necessary and constructive adaptation to the reality of economic and social inequality in the United States. Yet this very strength has been viewed as a weakness in these families. An early influential report purporting to explain the poverty of African-American families by Daniel Moynihan (1965) intimated that a "black matriarchy" exists in which decision making and other family powers and responsibilities rest with women rather than men. By this way of thinking African-American men are emasculated, stripped of authority, and driven from the family under an aura of self-defeat. The family is left with fewer defenses against poverty, delinquency, and illegitimacy.

The Moynihan report reminds us of the connection between sexism and racism. The report was attacked largely because black men were usurped of their rightful place as family head. To untangle the pathology surrounding the black family, the father must be returned as the dominant person in the household. Assertive and independent women can wreak havoc on both the family and the race. Black women apparently do not suffer the same humiliation as black men and "neither feel nor need what other human beings do either emotionally or materially" (Smith, 1995:157). The demographic reality of African-American households, and the household structures that accommodate the legacy of economic oppression, challenges the notion of black matriarchy. However, this has done untold damage by creating and reinforcing stereotypes of superhuman women and weak and absent men, who are then blamed for the circumstances in which they find themselves. Many African-American men may have internalized its assumptions, which in turn creates tension between the genders.

Multiple Risks of Race, Class, and Gender. Despite stellar educational, health, and professional gains and ongoing career success, African-American women have the lowest earnings of both genders and all races, an earning pattern that may be getting worse (Newsome and DoDoo, 2006; Kaba, 2008). African-American women must carry the double burden of their minority group status. Few would argue that these women are exploited by virtue of both race and gender. If she is a single parent, the prospects of decent wages to maintain her family above the poverty level are severely reduced. This is intensified by the kind of jobs they typically have. Although women of all races earn less than men overall, the likelihood of poverty is significantly higher for women in occupations dominated by African-American women and lower in occupations dominated by white women. This is despite a strong commitment to employment and socialization messages to girls emphasizing self-reliance, independence, and resourcefulness (Collins, 2004).

While African-American women are worse-off economically and face the double-minority burden, African-American men must contend with a double bind of their own. African-American men, like other men in the United States, are socialized into instrumental family roles that tie masculinity with being a good provider and father. This standard for masculinity is accepted by African-American men, but opportunities for carrying it out are restricted. In seeking masculinity standards that are available and acceptable in poor neighborhoods, African-American teens often turn their attention away from school and home to life on the streets. Coping mechanisms include "compulsive masculinity" that is often violent in and outside the home (Chapter 9).

The African-American community is not immune to other stereotypes concerning black male–black female relationships. African-American men often perceive that black women have more opportunity and are held responsible for the status of black men. Tension may be heightened because African-American women now have higher levels of education than black men and are outpacing men in gaining professional occupations. The marriage squeeze and the marriage gap are more acute for African-American women searching for same-race men of comparable age and educational levels. Increased joblessness, underemployment, incarceration, and higher death rates from violent crime, disease, and poor health care deplete the pool of marriage-able black males in absolute numbers and render those who are available as less desirable to marry (Chapters 2 and 7). Interviews of African-American women who live with violence and poverty in their daily lives expressed what they looked for in a man: "To a one, they all indicated that they wanted a man who was employed and had not been in jail" (Hattery and Smith, 2007:54–55).

Stereotyping increases during periods of economic uncertainty. The high unemployment rates of black men may counter the legacy of role flexibility and egalitarianism evident in many African-American families. It is the economic position of men that will significantly determine the course of many African-American families and how gender roles will be enacted.

Latino Families

For the first time in U.S. history, there are now slightly more people who identify themselves as Latino or Hispanic (15 percent) than who identify themselves as black or African American (14 percent), making them the largest minority in the nation. Most significant, by 2050 the African-American population is projected to increase by 1 percent and the Latino population is projected to double; one in three U.S. residents would be Latino (Bernstein and Edwards, 2008). Latinos are very diverse and the enactment of gender roles is a major indicator of that diversity. There are significant cultural and historical differences between Latinos, especially economic well-being and number of generations in the United States, that are important determinants of gender roles in their families. The three largest subgroups are Mexican Americans, Puerto Ricans, and Cuban Americans. Although all three groups suffer the economic burdens of minority status, poverty is most acute for Puerto Ricans and least acute for Cuban Americans.

Although Mexican Americans hover near the poverty line as a group, there are wide variations in overall economic status. Latinos share a heritage of Spanish colonialism and, through this, a solid connection to the Catholic Church. Several fundamental values related to gender and the family link these diverse groups. First, family relations are characterized by respect and honor. Second is the notion of **familism**, a strong cultural value emphasizing the family and its collective needs over personal and individual needs and any other groups to which a family member belongs. Familism creates strong bonds between nuclear and extended family members in terms of support, loyalty, and solidarity. Familism is associated with emotional protection and guidance for Latino youth and a buffer against negative influences outside the home (Azmitia et al., 2009; German et al., 2009). These bonds ensure that family members will remain intimately connected to one another throughout their lives.

Third, and the most important element related to gender roles and the family, is that familism is strongly gendered. There is an adherence to patriarchal gender roles in a well-defined system of mutually exclusive beliefs that separate men and women; these roles are found throughout all social classes in Latino cultures. Derived from the Spanish word *macho* ("male"), the man's role is associated with **machismo**, seen to include virility, sexual prowess, and the physical and ideological control of women. The woman's role is associated with **marianismo** (from the Virgin Mary's name, Maria), seen to include the beliefs of spiritual and moral superiority of women over men, the glorification of motherhood, and the acceptance of a difficult marriage. Women are expected to have an infinite capacity for sacrifice in their role as mothers and to be submissive to the demands of the men in their family. These attitudes are associated with compromised emotional health for women (Stevens, 2000; Bedolla et al., 2006; Steidel, 2006).

The beliefs that support marianismo remain strong, but changes are evident in what were once entrenched patriarchal gender roles in the family. Higher education for both males and females in Latino subcultures is associated with more gender role flexibility in the home and a loosening of stereotyped beliefs about humble women and aggressive men. Older Latino males are more likely to resist these changes than younger Latino females. Latina adolescents and young women entering new careers armed with college degrees are in the forefront of these changes (Denner and Guzman, 2006). It is clear that education, SES, and degree of acculturation affect how these values are translated into the home.

Puerto Rican Families. By far, research on gender and the family in Latino subcultures centers on the link between employment and home for women and their families. Puerto Ricans have the lowest income of any Latino group, and it is the critical gender–family link that explains this fact. Half of all Puerto Rican households are headed by women, and only half of Puerto Rican women are high school graduates. Women have been employed in low-paying jobs, such as light manufacturing, and these are quickly disappearing. Coupled with global economic recession, companies are moving operations to Asia, where even lower-paid female workers are hired. Families are often divided, with children being raised by grandparents in Puerto Rico and husbands migrating back and forth between the island and New York in search of employment. Marriages are fragile, but marianismo and the stigma of divorce keep many couples legally married but separated. About half of all heterosexual couples form *consensual unions*, different from cohabitation, that are recognized as informal marriage (Manning and Landale, 1996). Births to unmarried Puerto Rican women have soared over the last four decades, today comprising over 60 percent of all their births in the United States. Women who are recent migrants, especially those who are spouses in middle- and working-class couples, strive to maintain a continuity of family life. These families are more nuclear in structure and are at the forefront of the trend toward fewer consensual unions and more legal marriages.

Better-educated women are more likely to value both career and family roles and this is reflected in their parenting practices (Safa, 2003; Guilamo-Ramos et al., 2007). However, girls are often caught between two cultures that mirror one set of values more than the other. Echoing the marianismo–machismo duality, for example, Judith Ortiz Cofer (1995:204–205) writes of her experiences growing up in a Puerto Rican community in New Jersey.

> As a girl I was kept under strict surveillance, since virtue and modesty were, by cultural equation, the same as family honor. . . . But it was a conflicting message girls got, since Puerto Rican mothers also encouraged their daughters to look and act like women. . . . The extended family and church structure could provide a young woman with a circle of safety; if a man "wronged" a girl, everyone would close in to save her family honor.

She asserts that her education gave her stronger footing to survive this kind of duality in mainstream culture and saved her from the harsher forms of racial and ethnic prejudice. Familism may buffer girls from the "harshness" of the outside world, but it does not adequately prepare them for the role conflict they will inevitably face when they enter it as wives, mothers, and employed workers.

Mexican-American Families. Mexican-American (Chicana) women also confront gender roles tied to ideology surrounding marianismo–machismo and familism, factors that keep divorce rates low. The nuclear family is embedded in a network of kin who maintain intergenerational ties by passing on cultural traditions, fostering ethnic pride, and serving as social and economic support (Rinderle and Montoya, 2008). Early research interpreted machismo as a male defense against racial discrimination and poverty. The belittling daily world faced by Mexican-American laborers is reproduced in the home, so men are bolstered when women are "kept in their place." Notice how the concepts of machismo and black matriarchy can be used to justify the same conclusion and then used to perpetuate gender inequality.

Subordination of women to men in families is evident, but recent research is challenging the model of the all-dominant and controlling male. Families are not as patriarchal as had been assumed, and there is a trend toward gender equity. Couples do report that the spheres of men and women are still separated, but that they share child rearing and household tasks. Joint decision making is more apparent, especially when women are employed outside the home. Gender roles are less traditional because extended family ties are also weakening. There is a trade-off: families may receive less child-care support from older kin, but children are less likely to hear messages about female subordination. When family cohesion is threatened by pressures outside the home, such as job loss, a health crisis, or neighborhood deterioration, families rally around traditional cultural values. However, these values are being adapted to fit family needs, even if they counter traditional beliefs about gender. Women may need to enter the world of work and men may need to be family caretakers. Children see more open communication between their parents and less of a retreat into defined roles (Crockett et al., 2007; Behnke et al., 2008; Robles, 2008; Sanchez, 2008). In these cases, family stress functions to bolster family cohesion as well as encourage productive gender role change.

Compared to their immigrant parents, traditional patterns have been altered significantly for children born in the United States. Poverty significantly decreases by the second generation of immigration, college education for both men and women is increasing, and families are moving upward in SES. On the negative side, Chicana women are largely employed in occupations segregated by gender and offering little job mobility—both functioning to keep income levels low. Teen pregnancy rates are on the decline, but more Mexican-American women are entering the "single parent" ranks. With weakening familism, child care and financial support are less available. The risks of class, race, ethnicity, and gender will determine if the economic prosperity of second-generation Mexican Americans can be sustained (Mendoza, 2005; Callister and Birkhead, 2008; Coltrane et al., 2008).

Cuban-American Families. Cuban Americans enjoy the highest standard of living of all Latino groups. Immigrants in the 1960s were highly educated, many drawn from Cuba's professional ranks. Even though women were not likely to be in the labor force, education for middle- and upper-class women was encouraged and helped bolster the prestige of the family. The double standard of sexual morality lives on in the Cuban-American subculture. Parents want their daughters not only to be educated but also to remain virginal, uncorrupted, and sequestered. Later immigrants were poorer, families more fragile and prone to breakup, and women in the workplace more common, a trend that continues today. However, Cuban-American families are demographically more similar to European Americans. Compared with other Latino subgroups, these families have fewer children, are economically stronger, and are more likely to be headed by a married couple. Married couples with higher levels of education are less traditional and are slowly moving toward more gender-equitable family roles. Unlike European Americans, Cuban-American families are more likely to be extended and children are expected to live with their parents until they get married. The elderly in these families offer child-care services and in turn expect to be taken care of as they become feeble. The increased number of Cuban-American women in the work force is associated with child care by elderly kin (Skaine, 2004). More egalitarian family and work roles are in line with the future expectations of Cuban-American girls. As they become more acculturated, younger women are less likely to accept restrictions based on gender.

Asian-American Families. The Asian-American and Pacific Islander population is the fastest growing of all racial minorities, with projections that by 2050 they will represent just fewer than 10 percent of the population, double from 2008. Their numbers increase by immigration rather than reflecting increases in the resident population. Asian Americans—primarily Chinese, Japanese, and Filipino—have the highest number of married couples and the lowest divorce rate of all other racial minorities at a number similar to whites. Compared to other racial minorities in the United States, there is also a widerspread in income and poverty level. Cambodians and Pacific Islanders have the highest poverty rates and Japanese and Indians have the lowest. Chinese are in between, but on the higher rather than the lower side of income levels. Gender is the one factor that shows least diversity related to income: regardless of subculture and education, Asian-American women have lower incomes than Asian-American men.

On the other hand, even more so than in Latino families, Asian Americans exhibit striking cultural diversity. In religion, for example, Koreans are predominantly Protestant Christian, Filipinos are Catholic, Japanese are Shinto and Buddhist, Pakistanis are Muslim, and Indians are Hindu. Religion has a powerful influence on beliefs about gender that are carried into the family (Chapter 12).

Asian-American families share several other patterns that have important gender implications. Gender roles from the originating Asian cultures demonstrate collectivistic kinship traditions in which personal needs are sacrificed for family needs. Extended families are normative, and children are socialized to be obedient in the family and loyal to parents and elders. Conformity to cultural and family traditions are expected in children but much more for girls than boys. Obedience is played out by marriages that are commonly orchestrated by kin rather than left solely to the devices of children. These family traditions emphasize female subordination to all males and older females in a patriarchal family structure (Ternikar, 2004; Espiritu, 2008; Ahluwalia and Suzuki, 2009; Hall, 2009; Park et al., 2009). The comments of the baby boomer daughter of Chinese immigrants is a good representation of these traditions.

> Despite my deference to traditional Chinese behavior, the day finally came when I had to disobey my father. I had received several offers of full scholarships to attend college. . . . When the time came for him to sign the college registration forms, he refused. "The proper place for an umarried daughter is at home with her parents," he insisted. He wanted to keep me out of trouble until I found a husband to do the overseeing. (Zia, 2009:44–45)

Education is the key for Asian-American women from all cultures to challenge such subordination. Today Asian-American women lead women of all racial minorities in obtaining college degrees and are close to par with white women. But shattering the barriers also takes an emotional toll by disappointing one's family and in the constant juggling of different cultural expectations (Dyke and Johnson, 2003).

The extent to which these patterns occur is linked to length of residence in the United States. Recent arrivals are strongly connected to their ethnic community, for example, which provides social support and jobs in family businesses. Chinese and Koreans in particular appear to benefit from community ties—they have high levels of education for both females and males and enjoy relatively fast upward mobility. Although still quite low, the divorce rate and the number of female-headed households are steadily increasing among all Asian-American groups. When children become more "Americanized," intergenerational conflict increases, with males more likely to challenge restrictions imposed by parents

(Chen, 2009; Kim, 2009). Among Chinese Americans, for instance, children will gladly provide economic help for their parents but resist their parent's advice on personal matters such as who they choose as friends or dates. Traditional expectations for marriage are eroding, and emerging norms are now emphasizing choice of partners based on romantic love. Whereas arranged marriages have not disappeared among Chinese Americans, formal arrangements have been replaced by "strong suggestions" from parents and elders, which children are at least expected to investigate (Luo, 2008). And as expected, boys are less likely than girls to take their parents' suggestions for investigating a possible marriage partner.

Native American Families

Native Americans comprise less than 1 percent of the U.S. population and include those reporting American-Indian and Alaskan (Eskimo and Aleut) origin. Native Americans are rapidly being assimilated into majority culture, and intermarriage rates have soared. At the same time, resurgent cultural pride has fueled tribal diversity and contributed to a rise in the number of people claiming Native American origin. Nonetheless, Native Americans share some key patterns related to gender roles in family life.

About one-third of Native American households are female headed; most of these are in poverty. The remaining two-thirds are made up primarily of married couples. These households are at risk for social problems related to their poverty status, such as unemployment, dropping out of high school, illiteracy, and alcoholism. Historic governmental policy is fundamentally responsible for the current economic plight of Native American populations (U.S. Commission on Human Rights, 2000).

Colonialism, which was accompanied by Christianity, altered ancient tribal patterns drastically, particularly those related to gender roles in the family. Women's power and prestige varied by tribe, but historical evidence indicates that women lost status with colonialization. Many tribal units were *matrilineal*, the family name being traced through the mother's line, and *matrilocal*, a couple moving into the bride's home at marriage. Although gender segregation was the norm, complementarity, balance, and gynocratic (female-centered) egalitarianism also existed both in the home and outside it. Women held important political, religious, and other extradomestic roles. With increased European contact, women were gradually stripped of these roles (Chapter 5). In order to assimilate native people, the U.S. government first sought to obliterate ancient traditions—a policy that become known as "cultural genocide" (Churchill, 2007). Altered family patterns were its first expression, and an egalitarian family structure changed to a patriarchal one.

Cultural genocide did not succeed. Although ancient tribal customs were altered, they were not eradicated, and they continue to reinforce family strength and stability. Women retain spiritual, economic, and leadership roles offering prestige and power in their families and communities (Cheshire, 2001; Coles, 2006). For those who live off the reservation, these roles contribute to more equally shared household and parenting responsibilities (Hossain, 2001). Unlike other racial, ethnic, and religious groups, a return to cultural traditions among Native Americans may signal more, rather than less, egalitarianism.

DIVORCE

An enduring marriage is not necessarily a successful one. Because Americans say romantic love is the primary reason for marriage, "falling out of love" is a reason for divorce. The two variables in combination that most consistently predict divorce—as well as breaking up after cohabitation—are age and social class. Teenage marriages and cohabitors of lower SES are the most likely to dissolve, probably within five years. For teenage couples who start out with less education, fewer economic resources, and less emotional maturity, the idealization of love quickly fades when confronted with the stark reality of married life. Whether married or not, teenage males lose the idealization quicker than teenage females (Forste, 2003; Sawhill, 2006). Though subject to historical anomalies like the Depression and World War II, the divorce rate steadily increased throughout the last century, peaking in the 1980s, but decreasing continuously, although modestly, since. The marriage rate is also declining (see Table 7.2).

It is easier to calculate marriage rates than divorce rates. Depending on which standard for calculating divorce rates is used, the future of marriage in the United States as well as for its individual couples appears rather bleak. When comparing the number of divorces to the number of new marriages, it is fair to say that half will end in divorce. The problem with this comparison is that it does not account for how long a couple was married, so it may inflate the failure rate of new marriages. It is more revealing to look at annual divorces per 1,000 married women (half of married couples), which is at about 20. This indicates a less discouraging four-in-ten marriage failure rate. By all measures, however, the divorce rate is rising throughout the world, but the United States remains near the top (Figure 8.1).

Gender and Adjustment in Divorce

Divorce has profound social, psychological, and economic effects on the divorcing couple and their families. Research shows that divorce is strongly gendered—in how it is carried out and in its differential impact on women and men.

Gender Role Beliefs and Emotional Well-Being. Although it is difficult to separate economic from noneconomic factors, women tend to adjust better to divorce than men. However, both men and women who are nontraditional in their

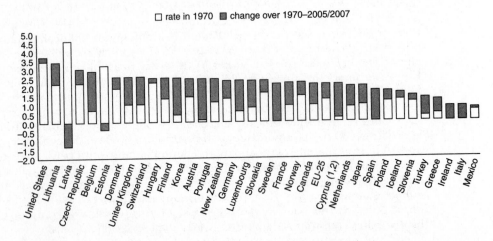

Figure 8.1 Increase in Divorce Rates from 1970 to 2007 in OECD* Countries

*Organisation for Economic Co-operation and Development

Source: OECD Social Policy Division, Directorate of Employment, Labour and Social Affairs. OECD Family Database www.oecd.org/els/social/family/database

gender role orientation adjust better than those who are traditional. Androgynous men and assertive, independent women are better at reconciling themselves to divorce than men and women who hold more conventional gender role beliefs. Women of all races who have higher levels of self-esteem and independence opt out of unsatisfactory marriages at a faster rate and adjust better to their post-divorce lives. Nontraditional gender role beliefs, however, are less protective for divorced women with young children (Zimmer, 2001; Williams and Dunne-Bryant, 2006; Baum, 2007). The powerful emotional toll of motherhood ideology works against a woman's well-being. Men who adjust better to divorce are likely to be connected to a new partner and quickly reestablish their preferred gender role pattern, whether it is a traditional one or not. Ex-spouses appear to adjust better when they attribute the cause of the divorce to the relationship itself rather than to themselves or each other (Oygard and Hardeng, 2001; Amato and Previti, 2003). In this sense, they leave the marriage with a more intact sense of self that serves as bolsters as they face a postmarried future.

Age. Younger people are better at rebuilding their lives after a divorce, and the spouse who first sought the divorce adjusts to it more readily. Women are more likely to initiate a divorce than men, and younger women do so at higher rates than both older men and older women. Women under age 40 report that divorces lead to a wider range of growth options and enhance their well-being over the long run. Older women suffer greater psychological trauma in divorce and may be more likely to stay in an unhappy marriage until a new partner is on the horizon (Sweeney, 2002; Pedrovska and Carr, 2008).

Employment. Although most women are employed, and may have the financial latitude to end unhappy marriages, their income contributes more to marital happiness than marital dissatisfaction. A husband today is not only less likely to feel threatened by a wife who matches or outearn him, but he may celebrate the mismatch. Some estimates suggest that almost half of married dual-earner couples have wives with higher incomes. For dual-earner couples, it is housework rather than income that fuels marital problems (Rogers and DeBoer, 2001; Menninger, 2006). The most dissatisfied couples are those in which wives want joint decision making and household task sharing by husbands whereas husbands prefer a more traditional, patriarchal style of family functioning—a pattern that holds for couples of all races (Saginak and Saginak, 2005; Ono and Raymo, 2006). Shifts in gender role ideology help explain why today's women are now more likely than their mothers and grandmothers to initiate divorce.

The Impact of Gendered Law in Divorce

Divorce is no longer a legally difficult process. The legal ease of ending a marriage is linked to the *no-fault divorce*, which allows one spouse to divorce the other without placing blame on either. Divorce is readily available to those who want it, such as women in abusive marriages, older men hoping to remarry younger women, and young couples who married quickly and confronted marital conflict just as quickly. "Irreconcilable differences" has become the generic, default category used by divorcing couples (Watkins, 2006). No-fault divorces now represent the large majority of all divorces in the United States.

Custody. Mothers gain custody of children about 70 percent of the time, usually without further legal action by fathers. Father custody and other joint arrangements constitute about one-third of child custody decisions. Although all states have gender-neutral child custody laws, custody is still likely to be granted to the mother, the preferred pattern for mothers and fathers (Stamps, 2002). Most often fathers give in to the mother's demand for full custody without further legal action. Women must now take on an array of roles they previously shared. Even if she is working outside the home, the divorce increases financial obligations, child care, and household responsibilities. Conflicts at work involving children can intensify and create a greater sense of insecurity. For those divorced mothers who recognize that they simply do not have the financial capability to adequately provide for their children, the decision may be to give up custody. The belief that children—especially young children—should stay with their mothers is pervasive. Unlike a noncustodial father, a mother who voluntarily gives up custody is stigmatized; often she is viewed as abandoning her children. She may relinquish custody out of love, knowing that her ex-husband is financially in a better position to offer them what she cannot. Reinforced by social stigma, contact with her children may also be reduced, and guilt can continue for years (Rhoades, 2002; Kielty, 2008).

Fathers are now more likely to gain full custody in contested divorces. Custody revisionists have begun to challenge the maternal preference argument, citing the best-interest-of-the-child standard (BICS) (Krauss and Sales, 2000; Goel, 2008). Fathers can be favored over mothers because they are financially better-off. The courts rarely award alimony and even less so to women capable of earning a living, so divorce requires women to give up any thought about staying a homemaker, if that was her predivorce existence. Earning a living can jeopardize her chances of gaining custody, especially if she has young children. Not only does the father make more money, but if he remarries, he has the possibility of another full-time caretaker. Although uncontrollable economic factors are the key reasons that most mothers lose custody battles, they are cast into the stigmatized role of unfit parents. The case for fathers' rights in custody decisions is often more of a case against mothers, with claims that men are the victims in a family law system that priviliges women (Adams, 2006). Gender-neutral standards are supposedly in effect to ensure parity in divorce and child custody decisions, but gender stereotyping of parents works against this in both principle and practice.

Joint Custody. To deal with problems associated with child custody, *joint-custody* arrangements—where parents share decisions related to their children, including how much time children will spend in the home of each parent—have skyrocketed. Joint custody is now the most prevalent court-ordered divorce arrangement. Co-parenting occurs in a variety of contexts, from simply sharing day-to-day decisions about children with their ex-spouses, to actually moving children, and sometimes parents, to different homes on a rotating basis. There are vigorous debates on the effects of such arrangements on children. Joint-custody fathers are more involved in their children's lives, have increased contact with them, and actively participate in shared decision making regarding their children. Complicated scheduling is a downside, but less strain is reported than if one carries the full burden of parental responsibilities (Bauserman, 2002; Melli and Brown, 2008; Peters and Ehrenberg, 2008). A huge issue is the degree of parental cooperation. If channels of communication remain open and children are not used as pawns, a joint-custody arrangement may be a constructive option. If parental cooperation fails, joint custody serves to increase conflict between parents. The quality of the coparenting relationship is the key factor in how a child adjusts to divorce. Gendered beliefs about who is a "good" or "better" parent intrude, however, and often thwart adjustment for parents as well as their children (Bokker, 2006; Goel, 2008).

Joint-custody fathers have a better record at maintaining contact with their children and supporting them financially. But as equitable as the arrangements may seem on paper, women are less able to take on the greater economic burden that is clearly associated with joint custody.

Divorce and Poverty. Although women appear to fare better than men in the psychological trauma of divorce, the economic consequences are often disastrous for women in the United States as well as globally. Research shows that in the first year of the breakup, one in five women enter into poverty compared to one in thirteen men and women are at higher risk than men for chronic poverty (Gadalla, 2008). Adding parenthood to gender, compared to divorced fathers, divorced mothers have a disproportionate share of the economic burden of the divorce. Approximately 40 percent of divorced mothers enter poverty (Yamokoski and Keister, 2006; Aranat and Michaels, 2008). For both African-American and white women, divorce increases a woman's financial burdens in two important ways. First, child support payments do not match expenses of maintaining the family; and second, women must work outside the home, often in low-salary jobs, a situation compounded by both race and gender discrimination (Molina, 2000; Arnstein et al., 2007; Steiner, 2007). Older women, housewives, and those reentering the labor force after a long absence are in an extremely precarious position. They are at a distinct disadvantage in the job market at the exact time when they need an adequate income to support the family.

Dividing Assets. No-fault divorce makes a bad economic situation worse for women when courts mandate an equal division of assets, such as the family home and savings. Coupled with no-fault divorce, joint custody puts women at great financial risk. Joint custody may be agreed on during a divorce mediation process in which parents meet with an impartial third party to reach mutually acceptable agreements. However, mediators may usher in beliefs about gender-neutral standards that are anything but neutral as far as finances are concerned (Comerford, 2006). Most women do not have the economic resources to coparent on an equal basis with their ex-husbands.

Misconceptions abound about women who are "set up" for a life of leisure by their wealthy ex-husbands. Actually, court-ordered alimony—"maintenance"—is awarded to only a small percentage of women and in amounts so low that they barely match welfare or Social Security. Laws in many states are not kind to the few women who do receive alimony. In Florida a judge is allowed to reduce alimony if a former spouse enters into a "new supportive relationship." If money is received from a boyfriend, for example, a divorced woman's alimony can be reduced, regardless of if she has custody of children or if she is living with her boyfriend (Caputo, 2008). If the relationship ends, alimony is unlikely to be reinstated, as much for the legal cost as for the lack of sympathy she will receive from the system. Divorced and cohabitating women of all races who end long-term relationships are often cast into dire economic circumstances (Avellar and Smock, 2005).

Child Support. The issue of what is awarded is related to the issue of what can be collected. Fewer than half of all custodial mothers are awarded child support; half of these mothers actually receive it from nonresidential fathers and only 25 percent receive the full amount. The amount of unpaid child support is staggering. Over 11 million families are owed support, forcing 10 million children into welfare. In half of divorced families, by two years after the divorce there is no contact with the nonresidential parent, usually the father (Magnuson and Gibson-Davis, 2007). The deep emotional loss fathers experience at divorce may help explain the financial distancing from their children.

The severe economic consequences of divorce are played out among women of all races. Although young minority men are not well-off economically, their postdivorce financial situation tends to be better than that of their ex-wives. A man's standard of living tends to show a moderate decrease in the immediate aftermath of a divorce but improves considerably over time. Although declines in postdivorce income are less for women than in years past, data still show only decreases, and losses much greater than men's postdivorce income (McManus and DiPrete, 2001; Bedard and Deschenes, 2005; Daniels et al., 2006). A loss of half the family income is typical. Divorce is a principal reason for the high poverty rate of single-parent women and their dependent children. In addition to the population of never-married women with dependent children, divorce contributes to the **feminization of poverty**—a global trend showing an increase in the percentage of women in the poverty population. Women at highest risk of poverty are single-parent women of color. The feminization and the *juvenilization* of poverty go hand in hand (Bianchi, 1999).

To help get divorced women off public assistance, states are more vigilant in enforcing child custody orders. To recoup the cost of collecting the money from fathers, however, many states keep the money rather than passing it on to ex-wives and children. The benefits of getting men to live up to their financial obligations, however, are greater when programs encourage men to maintain active contact with their children and are nurtured in their identities as fathers (Nepomnyaschy, 2007; Garasky et al., 2007). In addition, the men who have been slipping out of their children's lives can be brought back, especially poor men of color. Welfare programs that work on issues to reconnect poor, absent fathers to their children may be more successful than programs that criminalize fathers when they do not or cannot pay (Curran and Abrams, 2000; Bialik, 2008). Changes in divorce law may also help with a women's postdivorce income loss. States could retain the no-fault option while recognizing that men and women enter divorce with very different levels of economic vulnerability.

Remarriage. The United States has a decreasing marriage rate, and is near the top of the globe's divorce rate, but it also has the world's highest remarriage rate. Almost three-fourths of divorced people remarry, and about one-half of all marriages are remarriages. The marriage–divorce–remarriage pattern is referred to as **serial monogamy**. Combined with a rising rate of cohabitation, remarriages are the primary reasons for the formation of a **blended family**, in which children from parents' prior relationships are brought together in a new family. This now normative form of kinship represents over half of children in the United States today; half of families with children are blended families.

About 75 percent of divorced men and 66 percent of divorced women remarry. The large majority of men remarry within five years of their divorce. Most divorced men with children are free from sole custody and economically better-off than their ex-wives, allowing for greater latitude in the remarriage market. Men have an age advantage as well. There is more acceptance of the older man–younger woman pattern than the reverse. A 10 year age difference favoring men is common in remarriages. Women who are poorly educated are most likely to remarry. Their remarriage chances decrease if they have dependent children because they represent a financial liability for men. Financially independent women are attractive to men for remarriage, but these women have less to gain in a remarriage, especially if they do not want to raise children. When adding race to the remarriage picture, African-American women are the least likely to remarry and white women the most likely. Latino women fall in between (Bramlett and Mosher, 2001; Goldscheider and Kaufman, 2006).

These different remarriage rates are best explained by the influence of race, class, and gender in combination. Among women of all races, marriage and remarriage offer opportunities for economic stability. They seek married partners with work stability—they can get employed and stay employed. But low-income African-American single mothers attach more importance to respectability and control in their lives. Low-income white single mothers mention trust and domestic violence as more important. The meaning of marriage differs for these women. Many believe that marriage will make their lives more difficult and hence choose to remain single (Edin, 2005). It is difficult to determine, therefore, if remarriage for these women offers more costs or more benefits.

SINGLE-PARENT FAMILIES

In 1950 fewer than 7 percent of all families were headed by single parents; today that number is about 30 percent. Over 40 percent of all families with children under age 18 are single-parent families (Table 8.1). Over half of children in poverty live with single parents, and single-parent mothers outnumber single-parent fathers four to one. Almost half of African-American children live in families headed by women, often with a female grandparent. The staggering statistic today is that almost two-thirds of U.S. children will live part of their life in a single-parent household or in other households with adults who are not their parents before age 18.

Because the media focus most on the never-married rates of single-parent mothers, people often forget that single parents include divorced parents and an escalating subset of highly educated women who choose motherhood but not marriage. These are college-educated—often postgraduate—degree-holding, financially secure women who adopt children—usually girls—or may choose birth through artificial insemination. These risk-aversive women often wait until after 30 for their first child

Table 8.1 Single-Parent Families with Own Children under 18, Selected Years

Year Married	Couple Families	Mother-Only Family	Father-Only Family
2008	25173	8374	2162
2005	25919	8270	2021
2000	25248	7571	1786
1995	25241	7615	1440
1990	24537	6599	1153
1980	24961	5445	616
1970	25541	2971	345
1960	23358	2099	232
1950	18824	1272	229

Note: Numbers in thousands

Source: Adapted from Table FM-1. *Current Population Survey,* March and Annual Social and Economic Supplements, 2008 and earlier. U.S. Census Bureau. www.census.gov/Press-Release/www/releases/archives/families_households

(Schmidt, 2008). With careers on track, financial security for their families is better ensured. They are single mothers with adopted children who spend time with each other and whose children grow up in the company of children much like themselves. Their households and families can be described as extended, platonic, female centered, and middle class. They have the resources and networks for support but rely on one another for help in a pinch. Mothers do not rule out dating, but rather than searching for a husband or male life partner, many prefer to give their children another sibling rather than a father. These women suggest that they are "one another's primary asset." As one mother explains,

> If I had a great job opportunity somewhere else, I wouldn't move now. . . . If I went somewhere else I'd have to reform what we have here, and I don't know if I could. . . . The next 8 to 10 years is my time for child-rearing. I'd like to keep that protected. (Bazelon, 2009:33)

Although the number of such financially secure unmarried mothers is growing, their percentage in the ranks of single-parent mothers is still quite small. It is the ever-present issue of money that separates them from the majority of their single-mother counterparts.

Despite the drop in marriage rate, increased cohabitation, and the increased number of single parents, the nonmarital birth rate has actually *fallen*. However, the decreased birth rate of unmarried women does not offset the even steeper decline of births for married women (Mather et al., 2006). The net result is that unmarried women have a larger share of overall births and this share of women are at high risk for poverty. Over half of the children in poverty live with single parents, and single-parent mothers outnumber single-parent fathers four to one. Almost half of African-American children live in families headed by women, often with a female grandparent. Even with the increased number of fathers gaining sole custody in contested divorce, the number of never-married poor women with children continues to escalate. About half of all single parents are divorced; the other half have never been married. The divorced half of single-parent mothers appear to fare better than their never-married counterparts—they probably finished high school, live in their own homes, and have higher incomes. If children from divorced homes are living with their fathers the median family income is over one-third higher than if they live with their mothers. Overall, median family income is almost four times less in single-parent families compared to husband–wife families. Poverty rates for all single-parent families are expected to creep even higher as economic recession deepens.

Mothers and the Single-Parent Household

In mother- or grandmother-headed single-parent families, economic vulnerability is a way of life. Not only are female-headed families the fastest-growing type of family in the United States, but the odds that it is in poverty approach one in two (Figure 8.2). Over half of all poor children in the United States live in families headed by women, and median income is an astonishing four times lower than in husband–wife families (Sawhill, 2006). Poverty rates increase significantly for single-parent women who are also racial minorities.

Many factors contribute to this situation. We know that child support, alimony, and joint custody are not the financial salvation for these women. Neither are welfare payments in a restrictive system, which can contribute to, rather than deter, the cycle of poverty (Press et al., 2005). Because women are more likely than men to be in menial

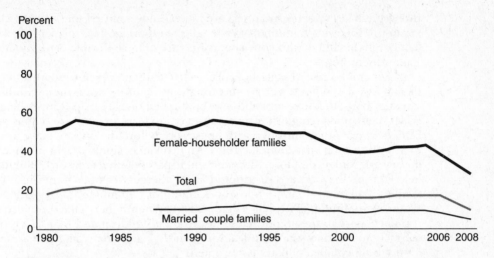

Figure 8.2 Children Ages 0–17 Living in Poverty by Family Structure, 1980 to 2008

Source: Adapted from Figure 4, *America's Children in Brief: Key National Indicators of Well-Being, 2008,* Federal Interagency Forum on Child and Family Statistics. Office of Management and Budget. http://childstats.gov/americaschildren and Table 3, *Current Population Survey,* 2007 and 2008. U.S. Census Bureau

or low-paying jobs, if employed at all, their income is far from adequate to meet the needs of the family. The financial burdens of the single-parent family headed by a woman who is divorced, never married, or was cohabiting fuel the feminization of poverty. The distinctive character of a woman's poverty is that she has the economic responsibility for children.

Financial uncertainty heightens the physical and emotional demands on single-parent women. Compared with married couples, they rely more on children for housework, have fewer social supports, and raise children who are also more likely to become single parents. Single mothers report higher rates of depression and lower levels of self-esteem than married mothers, especially if they were teenage mothers and did not graduate from high school (Sarlo, 2000; Heard, 2007). In African-American households, daughters raised by single-parent mothers have lower levels of educational achievement than those raised in single-father households (Alderman-Swain and Battle, 2000). Money is the key factor in these patterns. Women who are more financially secure adjust better to single parenting, feel better about their family and their jobs, and have better child-care options. Their children tend to have better educational outcomes and fewer behavioral problems. Single women perched on the poverty line, however, experience chronic life strain, which impacts their physical, social, and psychological well-being.

Fathers and the Single-Parent Household

As single parents, men face a situation far different from that of women. Nearly 15 percent of all single-parent households are headed by a man, and about 4 percent of children live with their fathers only. These numbers are expected to increase as more fathers gain custody of their children. Custodial fathers have fewer problems of adjustment to single parenthood than custodial mothers (Hilton and Kopera-Frye, 2004). Fathers are usually better educated, occupy higher-level occupations, and continue their careers after becoming single parents. Remember, too, that financial strength is a key reason why fathers are increasingly awarded sole custody when they request it. Like single mothers, single fathers report problems balancing work and family. Single fathers who cope successfully have more flexible work situations and support networks.

For child care and household tasks, single fathers appear to adapt well, perceive themselves as competent, are meaningfully involved with their children, and shoulder household responsibilities without much outside help (Linnenberg, 2007). When they become single fathers, many set out to learn new tasks and domestic skills. Fathers who are more involved with housework before the divorce make a smoother transition to their new domestic roles. After divorce, single-parent mothers do less housework; fathers do more. Although single-parent fathers rely on their children to help with housework, it is distributed along the gender lines found in two-parent families. Daughters do more housework, and more "feminine" housework than sons (Pasley and Minton, 2001; Raley et al., 2006). When fathers take on the role as the "primary" parent, they report close ties to their children and high levels of family satisfaction. But they still must deal with gender role stereotyping that assumes they cannot be as competent parents as women.

GENDER PATTERNS IN GAY AND LESBIAN FAMILIES

As society's most conservative institution, the family is highly resistant to change. Political debate concerning definitions of the family is also linked to antigay campaigns focusing on homosexuality as the enemy of the patriarchal family and the American way of life. Gay and lesbian families do exhibit characteristics in opposition to the structure and behavior patterns of the patriarchal family. As we will see, this seems more to the credit of these families than to their detriment.

Same-Sex Marriage

In 1995 Utah became the first state to expressly prohibit same-sex marriages. In 1996 Hawaii became the first state to legalize same-sex marriage but reversed the ruling two years later. In 2004 a San Francisco judge began issuing marriage licenses to same-sex couples. Massachusetts judges followed. A firestorm of controversy ensued as other states grappled with how to deal with the large influx of same-sex couples demanding marriage licenses. California legalized same-sex marriage in the summer of 2008, but five months later voters approved Proposition 8, which again banned it. Maine also overturned same-sex marriage by referendum. Although these are setbacks, supporters are gathering signatures to put the issue on the ballot in these and other states. It is likely that support for same-sex marriage will continue. As of this writing, Iowa, Massachusetts, Connecticut, New Hampshire, and Vermont have legalized same-sex marriage.

The other states represent a mixed bag of unions granting rights similar to marriage, unions granting limited and specified rights, recognition of foreign same-sex marriages, and statutes or outright constitutional bans on same-sex marriages and same-sex unions. To thwart these same-sex couples a "marriage amendment" to the Constitution, defining a marriage only as a union between a man and a woman, is making some headway in Congress. As a way of sidestepping the definition of a marriage, many states allow same-sex couples to enter **civil unions**. Although statutes may refer to marriage as a union between a man and a woman, civil union is a new legal classification entitling same-sex couples to the rights and responsibilities available to married partners, such as inheriting a partner's estate and filing joint tax returns. If these states uphold same-sex marriages, reciprocity with other states is the key issue.

International. Since Canada also legally recognizes same-sex marriage the reciprocity issue concerning Canadian-American same-sex marriages adds more confusion. The European Union (EU) is confronting the same issue. By the 1990s same-sex marriages were legal in Denmark, Norway, and Sweden, but only in Norway, and later in Belgium and Spain, do same-sex couples enjoy the *complete* range of marriage benefits heterosexual married couples receive. In 2001 the Netherlands approved a bill to legally recognize same-sex marriages and same-sex adoptions. It was the first country in the world with *full* marriage rights for gay and lesbian couples. Like in the United States, reciprocity is expected between EU countries but to date most countries have not complied. The fallout from any legal recognition of same-sex unions is far from over.

The highly contentious politics around same-sex marriage involves definitions of marriage that revolve around images of traditional, patriarchal families. Although the courts often uphold these definitions, they are being challenged in the workplace, in the unions, and in the schools in support of couples choosing more nontraditional family structures and lifestyles related to sexual orientation, nonpatriarchal parenting, gender roles, or cohabitation (Mackinnon, 2003; Harding, 2007). A productive twist to the same-sex marriage issue is that people who identify themselves as transgendered and transsexual will be able to skirt issues related to "what sex they claim to be or what sex they became" (Chapter 2) in order to obtain marriage license.

Children, Egalitarianism, and Gender Roles

The U.S. Census reported in 2000 almost 600,000 LGBT families, divided almost equally between gay male and lesbian families. These numbers are expected to increase to about a million such families by the 2010 census. Gay men and lesbians who form families and stepfamilies tend to incorporate a network of kin and nonkin relationships including friends, lovers, former lovers, coparents, children, and adopted children. These families are organized by ideologies of love, social support, flexibility, and rational choice (Joos, 2003; Johnson and O'Connor, 2005; Ryan, 2007). Notice how this structure is similar to the fictive kin and familism evident in African-American and Latino families.

Same-sex families with children are highly child focused. The most important conclusion about the adjustment and psychological development of children and adolescents raised by same-sex couples compared to other-sex couples is that "research fails to reveal any important differences." The quality of the relationship between parents is more important for children than the sexual orientation of the parents (Patterson, 2006; Tasker and Patterson, 2007; Shiller, 2007). Perhaps out of concern for any stigma attached to homosexuality, gay and lesbian parents closely monitor their children in all facets of their development, including emotional health, peer influences, and school progress. When problems arise, they are likely to seek the support and counseling services that are now more available from therapists specializing in lesbian and gay psychology, many of whom adopt a feminist perspective in their therapeutic approaches (Negy and McKinney, 2006).

An early literature review of homosexual couple families showed more equality in their household arrangements than those of heterosexual couples (Maccoby and Jacklin, 1974). The conclusion of more egalitarianism was confirmed in the first comprehensive study that compared homosexual and heterosexual couples

(Blumstein and Schwartz, 1983) as well as in research that followed. These studies generally discount the stereotypical image of a gay relationship with one dominant and one submissive partner. The egalitarian pattern tends to occur for both lesbians and gay men, although lesbians are more successful in maintaining it over the long term.

Domestic Task Sharing. Although household work is divided by talent and interest, research does suggest that, like heterosexual couples, gay men and lesbian couples show one partner taking more domestic responsibilities than the other and that domestic work is hidden and devalued (Carrington, 1999; Hagewen, 2002). In addition, the monogamy that gay men value is harder to achieve. Mirroring gender role norms in the wider society, gay men also value sexual prowess and, like heterosexual men, fall prey to its power as a defining mark of masculinity. On the other hand, young gay men are leading the pack to the altar. With a marriage license as the monogamy standard, these young men are "a lot more like married heterosexual couples than they are like older gay couples" (Denizet-Lewis, 2008:34). And like heterosexual women, lesbians view sexual prowess as less important than emotional commitment, particularly in the beginning stages of a relationship. Lesbian couples frequently adopt a peer-friendship bond that later culminates into a sexual one as physical closeness grows and the relationship progresses (Glazer and Drescher, 2001; Connolly and Sicola, 2006).

Gay and lesbian families live under a microscope in the way they conduct their lives as couples, but particularly as parents. They pose a threat to traditional gender roles by their egalitarian beliefs. In housework and in child rearing they act out these beliefs more than heterosexual couples. But they must live their lives as couples and parents under a microscope that defines them according to "heteronormative" expectations (Shattuck, 2005; Berkowitz, 2007).

The debate about levels of egalitarianism in same-sex couples has implications for the same-sex marriage issue overall. If same-sex couples are more egalitarian, would legally recognized marriage make them less so? Overall, marriages are more likely to be patriarchal rather than egalitarian, so legally married same-sex couples may succumb to patriarchal family lifestyles. Symbolic interactionists suggest that, in turn, egalitarianism may be compromised.

Lesbian Mothers

Whether as a civil union or as a marriage, legal acceptance does not mean social acceptance. We have already seen that in divorce mothers usually gain custody of children. With lesbians, however, this is less likely. Some women hide their lesbian identity to win custody and then live in fear of being exposed by their husbands and having the courts reverse the decision. Others who are granted custody after bitter court battles may endure continual harassment from their ex-husbands or their own relatives. Some mothers fear their children will be traumatized by a publicized custody fight and voluntarily accede to their husbands' demands (Duran-Aydintug and Causey, 2001; Sherman, 2005). Lesbians may be less stigmatized than gay men when they raise children with their partners. But their "mainstream" motherhood identity exists alongside their stigmatized lesbian identity, and they walk a fine line between the two. They must negotiate these two identities in a society that takes for granted heterosexist notions about ideal mothers raising perfect children (Hequembourg and Farrell, 2001; Henehan et al., 2007; Massey, 2007).

Gay Fathers

Just as lesbian mothers can lose the opportunity of raising their children, gay fathers are even more likely to be denied custody. About one-third of gay men have been married at least once, and many of these men are natural fathers. The coming-out process can trigger a domino series of events that reverberate through the family, including separation, divorce, child custody disputes, loss of support from family and friends, and loss of job. Children may feel alienated from their fathers and may cast blame on their mothers. Gay fathers can find that visiting their children is so discouraged that they may be reluctant to subject themselves and their children to the turmoil that visits may bring. If their children remain unaware of their fathers' gay identity, the gay fathers lead compartmentalized existences that compromise their emotional well-being. Like lesbian mothers, they fear that their gay identity will be exposed and their children traumatized. When courts endorse beliefs about "family values" gay fathers are viewed as "bad parents" and custody is less likely to be granted (Warwick and Aggleton, 2002; Vescio and Biernat, 2003; St. John, 2006).

On the other hand, research also shows that most children of gay men do reconcile with their fathers and reinstate contact. Being gay may not be compatible with traditional marriage and the family, but it is compatible with fathering (Better, 2005; Berkowitz and Marsiglio, 2007; Brinamen and Mitchell, 2008). Gay men without biological children express strong desire to parent with a life partner through either adoption or surrogacy (Friedman, 2007; Galvin, 2008). For families with publicly gay fathers who do have custody of their children, research shows positive histories. Problems in rearing children certainly exist, but once men productively resolve their gay identity issues, gay fathers are comparable to single heterosexual fathers who have custody of their children. The research conclusion is that the adult children of gay men—who were raised by gay men—do not differ in terms of life satisfaction, self-esteem, sexual attitudes, or sense of well-being (Hicks, 2005; Johnson and O'Connor, 2005; Macatee, 2007).

Future Families

Alternative families consisting of gay men and heterosexual women are also evolving. Some gay men maintain liaisons with heterosexual women with whom they may have children. Women who desire children without the confines of marriage may choose to have a child with a gay man with whom she may or may not be emotionally attached, who provides financial support and help with parenting. There is no legal obligation, they do not live together, and the child is "hers." In this way, desires on both sides are met. Success with such arrangements varies considerably, but it is likely that more couples will choose this new family form to fit distinctive life goals in a rapidly changing society. This form adds another diversity piece to nontraditional family and household arrangements.

Overall, a growing number of gay men and lesbians have gained custody, have brought their biological children into an "openly" lesbigay home, have adopted children, and live in permanent households with their homosexual partners and their children. Positive research outcomes on children raised in lesbigay homes are bolstering claims for adoption and custody. Gay adoptions are legally banned only in Florida. States have a variety of confusing statutes that may or may not allow for gay fostering under specific circumstances. The courts tend to view gay adoptions, however, as private, contractual matters (O'Neill, 2009). Gay and lesbian families tend to be child centered, egalitarian, financially well-off, and with parents who have levels of psychological health comparable to heterosexual parents (Malley and McCann, 2002; Henehan et al., 2007). These families face hostility and suspicion with society's stereotypes about homosexuality, idealized notions about families, and the manner gender roles should be enacted in their families. Even with legal recognition, rights may still be denied. Legal interpretations continue to work against gays and lesbians by defining them as unfit to raise children. It is likely, however, that family law will be swayed in support of homosexual couples as more children with good development outcomes are raised by gay and lesbian couples, and as same-sex marriages or civil unions become more normative.

Summary

1. The transition to parenthood is seen as both a crisis and a normal development stage. The motherhood mandate makes parenthood more stressful for women. The motherhood mandate is supported by functionalism for its socialization benefit to children; conflict theory challenges this view because it ignores individual growth for mothers; feminists are redefining motherhood to fit the new lifestyles of women who desire career and children.

2. Fatherhood is tied to the good-provider role but the involved-father role is gaining in importance for men. Fathers are taking on more child-care and nurturing tasks than in the past. An emerging fatherhood mandate would combine instrumental and expressive roles.

3. Voluntarily child-free married couples express similar levels of marital satisfaction as couples with children.

4. Dual-earning families are now the norm. Children of employed women are not harmed by their employment and neither are children who are in high-quality day care. When mothers work for pay, social and intellectual development of children is often improved.

5. Underemployment of men and employment of women in African-American families is typical. Working-class and middle-class couples are likely to be in dual-earner, egalitarian family roles. African-American husbands adapt themselves to their employed wives more than white husbands. Multiple oppressions of race and gender keep earnings low for African-American women. African-American men who cannot affirm their masculinity with provider roles may do so with "cool pose."

6. Gender roles in Latino families are tied to economic well-being, number of generations in the United States, and which subgroup they represent. Half of Puerto Rican families are headed by women who hold low-paying jobs. Machismo ideology serves to subordinate Mexican-American women. Compared to other Latino families, Cuban Americans have fewer children, are economically better-off, and are headed by a married couple with a college-educated wife. For all Latino subgroups, trends toward gender equity are growing.

7. Asian-American families are also diverse and share gender patterns from their originating Asian cultures. Overall, women are subordinate to all males and older females in a patriarchal family structure. Traditional expectations for arranged marriages are eroding.

8. One-third of Native American households are headed by women and likely to be in poverty. The U.S. practice of cultural genocide altered but did not erase tribal customs related to family strength and stability and women's leadership roles. A return to cultural traditions signals more, not less, gender egalitarianism.

9. Women tend to adjust better to divorce than men, especially those who are nontraditional in their gender roles, those who are younger, and those who have the financial latitude to end an unhappy marriage. Mothers usually gain custody in a divorce, but

joint custody is becoming more common. Many women are propelled into poverty after a divorce. Remarriage rates for both men and women are high, but men have an age and income advantage for remarriage.

10. Single-parent families headed by women are likely to be in poverty. Mothers report high levels of depression and low self-esteem. Single-parent families headed by men are likely to be finically secure, have flexible work and support networks.

11. Same-sex marriage is legal in a number of states. Gay and lesbian families are child focused and show high levels of egalitarianism. Lesbian mothers walk a line between mainstream motherhood and stigmatized lesbian identity. Gay fathers who resolve gay identity issues are comparable to single heterosexual fathers who have custody.

Key Terms

blended family 230	feminization of poverty 230	marianismo 221
civil unions 234	fictive kin 219	motherhood mandate 209
familism 221	machismo 221	serial monogamy 230

Critical Thinking Questions

1. Demonstrate how gender ideology permeates beliefs about motherhood and fatherhood in the United States and creates a paradox for parents. Document the benefits and/or liabilities of this ideology for couples and their children. As a result of this evaluation, what conclusions do you draw about the relationship between gender beliefs and parenthood and the likelihood of a productive resolution of this paradox?

2. Compare African-American, Latino, and Asian-American families in terms of gender socialization of children and the influence of the multiple oppressions of race, gender, and social class. Based on this comparison, determine the prospects for movement toward more gender equity in these families.

3. Identify the similarities and differences between homosexual and gay and lesbian couples in terms of their family arrangements, gender roles, and child rearing. Demonstrate how functionalism, conflict theory, and symbolic interaction account for these patterns. How does the feminist perspective provide an overarching framework that incorporates all three theories?

CHAPTER **9**

- Boys don't cry.
- Don't get mad, get even.
- Take it like a man.
- Size matters.
- Nice guys finish last.

What it means to be a man: Selections from the "The Guy Code"

—Michael Kimmel, 2008:45

MEN AND MASCULINITY

Devoting a separate chapter to men and masculinity in a book on gender roles is not without controversy. Although comparisons between men and women—how we are alike and how we are different—are explicitly incorporated throughout this text, some may argue that men are cast into the "default" category and marginalized in a book focused on women. As we saw in the first chapter, feminists from all disciplines were the catalysts for early research on gender and the development of women's studies. An explosion of scholarship on women *and* gender followed. This scholarship made clear that books, research, law, history, and literature that did not mention women were about men. In this sense women are the default category and men the unquestioned norm. This argument is less meaningful today because of the parallel explosion of scholarship devoted to the rapidly emerging discipline of men's studies. It is difficult to sort out viewpoints about how much space should be devoted to men and how much to women. *Gender studies* may be the "legitimate" default category. It is through gender studies that men and masculinity are made visible (Hearn and Kimmel, 2006:53). As this chapter documents, therefore, men's issues are not excluded; neither are they marginalized.

Men are regarded as superior to women. Whereas women wage battles for economic, political, and social equality, men wield the power that will often determine the outcome of the fight. All roles are made up of both rights and responsibilities, but *both* men and women perceive the rights and privileges of the male role as enviable, desirable, and well worth the responsibilities associated with the role. Men have careers; women have jobs. Men are breadwinners; women are bread bakers. Men are sexual leaders; women are sexual followers. A man's home is his castle. Father knows best. Is this the true story? The male mystique is based on a rigid set of expectations that, as we shall see, few men can attain. The social and psychological consequences of striving for the impossible plus the impractical can be devastating. We shall see that the role that appears to offer so many rewards also has its deadly side. In discovering more about this role, we will realize that a men's liberation movement is not a contradiction in terms.

HISTORICAL NOTES AND MASCULINE MARKERS

Images of masculinity are often confusing and contradictory. Over a half century of media heroes show men as courageous, competent, and always in control, such as Clint Eastwood, Tom Cruise, Russell Crowe, Brad Pitt, Leonardo DiCaprio, and Matt Damon, and the enduring images of Sylvester Stallone's *Rocky* and *Rambo*. Leonardo DiCaprio's early movie successes in *Romeo and Juliet* and *Titanic* painted him as a romantic, sensitive leading man. Considered to be typecast for "chick flicks" and unfit for "more masculine" roles, he is now likely to star in movies containing extreme violence, such as *The Departed* and *Blood Diamond*. All these images exist side by side with fallible antiheroes such as Dustin Hoffman, Jack Nicholson, Robin Williams, and Tom Hanks. Women praise the sensitive man who can admit to his vulnerability yet admire the toughness of the man who refuses to bend in the face of overwhelming odds. Most men fall short when attempting to satisfy both standards. History provides some insights into how this situation arose.

Patriarchy and History

Patriarchy is tied to male dominance, a theme in Western and Eastern civilization. It is a theme that remains accepted, unquestioned, and taken for granted. From a Western civilization perspective, male role standards can be described in terms of five historical periods, ranging from the Greco-Roman era to the eighteenth century (Table 9.1). Except for the standard of "spiritual male," contemporary views of

Table 9.1 Historical Ideals for Male Roles

Ideal	Source(s)	Major Features
Epic Male	Epic sagas of Greece and Rome (800–100 B.C.)	Action, physical strength, courage, loyalty, and beginning of patriarchy.
Spiritual Male	Teachings of Jesus Christ, early church fathers, and monastic tradition (400–1000 A.D.)	Self-renunciation, restrained sexual activity, antifeminine and anithomosexual attitudes, and strong patriarchal system.
Chivalric Male	Feudalism and chivalric code of honor (twelfth-century social system)	Self-sacrifice, courage, physical strength, honor and service to the lady, and primogeniture.
Renaissance Male	Sixteenth-century social system	Rationality, intellectual endeavors, and self-exploration.
Bourgeois Male	Eighteenth-century social system	Success in business, status, and worldly manners.

Source: Doyle, 1995:27.

masculinity continue to be based on these historical models. The fundamental features of a male ideal that persist after two centuries attest to the stubborn rigidity of a definition that defies even global social change.

With patriarchy already firmly entrenched, the peculiarities of American history tightened its hold. From the Puritans to the frontier era to the Civil War and World War I, the value of individualism was propelled as the hallmark of the United States. Not only did Americanism and individualism soon become inseparable as key masculine markers, but the line between nationality and masculinity was also blurred. Virtually unlimited opportunities beckoned men into farming, politics, business, or wherever their imagination and ambition led them. The fact that men of color and women were largely excluded from these opportunities was overlooked in the quest for individual success. The image of the solitary, independent man against the world was a powerful image throughout the period of preindustrial expansion. Nothing could stand in the way of dedicated American males setting out to achieve their objectives. Initially these objectives related to material success through hard work and physical endurance, with intellectual skills coming in second. Success based on material wealth and getting ahead were, and are, integral to American validation of masculinity.

War and Soldiering. Masculinity was also validated by soldiering. Historically war is associated with the idealized rhetoric of virtue and glory, but ignores its destruction and sheer horror. There are secret attractions for war: "the delight in seeing, the delight in comradeship and the delight in destruction" (Gray, 1992:25). Functionalism views war as a way to integrate society by bringing former rivals and other disparate elements together as comrades in arms to confront a common enemy. In both World Wars military training was seen as the way to build the manhood of the nation. Women served men as nurses, clerks, or during World War II, builders of war equipment. Women were considered helpmates to the men who fought the real battles. War and the preparation for war encourage men to perform according to the highest standards of masculinity. Several forms of masculinity are interfaced in war—physical violence, heroic independence, risk taking, dominance, and competition. War becomes the supreme guideline for defining masculinity (Braudy, 2003).

The Depression. The American version of masculinity was assaulted during the Depression. The loss of jobs and daily economic uncertainty for those fortunate enough to have jobs during this time trampled the self-esteem of men accustomed to their role of breadwinner. The fact that men throughout the nation faced similar circumstances offered little assurance. Many blamed themselves for their inability to get or retain a steady job. When their wives were able to find work outside the home, their emasculation may have been complete. Male self-indictment reverberated throughout the United States. Beyond the economic wreckage of high joblessness, the psychological toll was also sadly demonstrated. Many men became estranged from their families; others coped by deserting them. Alcoholism, mental illness, and suicide increased. Contrary to the image of the American man as invincible and able to overcome any obstacle, men and women alike recognized how vulnerable they were.

Vietnam. The Depression offered insights into how impractical masculinity ideals had become, but these were largely ignored. World War II helped bring the nation out of the Depression and revitalized traditional images of masculinity. The harshness of the Depression added luster to these images. Even considering that Korea and Vietnam were not the victories Americans had learned to expect, beliefs about war as a proving ground for manhood continued. A "cult of toughness" emerged to sway public opinion in favor of escalating the war in Vietnam (Fasteau, 1974). America, like its fighting men, was tough. Politicians cultivated this image of toughness, but the battle carnage, the rising body count of young draftees, and the untenable political situation in Asia served to fuel protest against the war. The first young men who burned draft cards or sought asylum in Canada or Sweden were viewed as cowards and sissies, afraid to face the test of war. As the protesters grew in number and the war became increasingly unpopular, more potential draftees joined in the antiwar movement. Comments about bravery and cowardice were not wiped out, merely driven underground.

Kuwait, Iraq, and Afghanistan. Other opportunities to challenge what it means to be a man emerged. War, at least as embodied in Vietnam, was not the answer. Nevertheless, the cult of toughness reasserted itself in the 1980s, continuing into the millennium. The Reagan era was predicated on a show of toughness and "staying the course." The administrations of George Bush and George W. Bush continued the cult of toughness in relation to the Gulf Wars. Like Reagan, they were "men's men." Indeed, the height of popularity for George Bush came with Operation Desert Storm. George W. Bush also sought to continue this toughness and manliness legacy to bolster support for the continuing Iraq war that, like Vietnam, became increasingly unpopular. The image of the President in his commander-and-chief role sharply improved sagging approval ratings when he guided an airplane to land on a carrier. Global media coverage of the staged event spotlighted Americanized masculinity norms—courage, individualism, toughness, and especially, independence. The world may not support Iraq (or Vietnam), but the United States, like its president, will not yield. Politicians believe that this image must be maintained at all costs. George W. Bush garnered the worst approval ratings of almost any president in history, but these were due primarily to policies fueling the Millennium Recession (MR) rather than the Iraq War. Although the Obama administration has softened the tone considerably, the war in Afghanistan continues to be reported according to masculinity images that are synonymous with toughness. Behind this assumed toughness lurks aggression and vulnerability.

These wars did not alter the image of masculinity. The first Gulf War was perceived as a victory that avenged Vietnam (Pettigrew, 2007:264). The media and the President "gendered" the moral discourse of war to "reaffirm the dominant, masculine identity of America as the world's one remaining superpower" (McBride, 1995:45). Although media now routinely report on "the men and women" troops serving the nation, there is no hint that the women are any less masculine than the men.

Suicide. I suggest that after periods when assaults on traditional masculine ideals are at their heights, the old definitions reemerge with a greater tenacity and more deadly consequences. An epidemic of suicides is sweeping the soldiers, the veterans, and even the recruiters of the Iraq and Afghanistan wars (Thompson, 2009). The military is dealing with them in a decidedly masculine way. Soldiers are urged to "fight their internal insurgents" (if you expect to suffer you will) and accept the horrors of war as empowering rather than as traumatizing. Men who commit suicide are blamed for harming their families, their units, and other soldiers. Mental health counseling is translated into sessions on "warrior resilience and thriving" and soldiers are encouraged to open up about their troubles. However, soldiers are reluctant to seek counseling for fear that it will damage their careers (De Luce, 2009; Gomez, 2009). We will see later, that exposing one's mental anguish is viewed as incompatible with masculinity and soldiering. Despite the acknowledgement that mental health is an issue that urgently needs to be addressed, it is apparent that war continues to reinforce traditional images of masculinity.

Sports

Most men today do not rely on war for validating masculinity. Whether as athletic competitor or spectator, sports have unquestionably emerged to fill this need. Sports and war metaphors—"jump on the team and come in for the big win"—are used in the military to train recruits and by coaches to train athletes (Pettigrew, 2007). Like the military, sports build character and comradeship, provide heroes and role models, teach about courage, and show how to overcome adversity against all odds. Fathers are powerful socializing agents for introducing their children to sports, especially their sons. Children learn early in life to associate sports with males, with hypermasculinity, and with the spectacle of violence (Aitchison, 2006; Hickey, 2008). The intellectual aspects of masculinity have not kept up with the physical aspects where sports are concerned. Bill Gates may be one of the richest men on the globe, but he is less of a role model than is Michael Jordan. A billion-dollar industry flourishes on contests where winning can literally call for the obliteration of the athlete. Boxing, race-car driving, football, hockey, skiing, diving, and gymnastics often brutalize competitors. Sport is an area where boys learn that pain is more important than pleasure (Sabo, 2004). Bodies and emotions are injured, but they are hidden or ignored in the name of competition, efficiency, teamsmanship, and of course, winning.

Brutalized Bodies. Men are not immune to the issues of weight and body image usually considered the province of women. The enormous pressure males feel early in life to achieve athletically is linked with psychological obsession and brutalized bodies. If brutalization is the price for winning friends and carving out one's place in the male pecking order, then so be it. The quest for the muscular ideal perceived as needed for athletic success and admiration by female admiration leads to steroid abuse, eating disorders, and overexercising that injures rather than strengthens the body (Thompson and Cafri, 2007). Athletes indicate that injury is framed as a masculinizing experience and reinforces highly valued notions of masculinity. A jock image in college is associated not only with injury risk, but also with prized masculinity roles acted out by athletes (Miller, 2008). With sport as such an intense masculine marker, it offers self-esteem for some but crippling insecurity for others. Consider, for example, the case of men with physical disabilities:

> Paralytic disability constitutes emasculation . . . and the weakening and atrophy of the body threaten all the cultural values of masculinity: strength, activeness, speed, stamina, and fortitude. (Gerschick and Miller, 2004:349)

Sports Violence. Other than the military, sport is the only social institution that condones violence in achieving a goal. Deliberate fouls in basketball, high sticking in hockey, late hits in football, and the taken-for-granted intentional injuries in rugby are frequently overlooked by referees and applauded by spectators. As social learning theory suggests, if sports violence on the playing field is associated with admiration, respect, money, and media attention, sports violence off the field is likely. Much of that violence is directed toward women. College athletes in contact sports are significantly more likely to be involved in all forms of aggressive behavior, but especially sexual assaults, partner battering, rape, and date rape. Consider, for example, Mike Tyson, O. J. Simpson, and Kobe Bryant. Sports heroes have figured so prominently in violence toward women that efforts are being made in schools and through prosocial media messages to provide young athletes with messages that do not equate male strength with dominance over women. Scandals involving payoffs and kickbacks to athletes and college programs and coverage of rape trials of sports figures do not dampen the thirst for sports. Sports remain one of the most powerful markers of masculinity. The physical and mental stamina required of modern athletes allow men who are not themselves athletes to validate their own masculinity, if only in a vicarious manner.

ON MASCULINITY

Definitions of masculinity have remained remarkably consistent over time. All sociological perspectives on masculinity highlight how masculine role ideals embodied in the historical standards have been adapted to the lives of contemporary men. Although the definitions may be consistent, as a result of these adaptations, masculinity is enacted in myriad ways.

Hegemonic Masculinity

Given the consistent definitions of masculinity, it may seem paradoxical that masculinity can be viewed as fragmented and uneven and at the same time tenacious and steadfast. The notion of **hegemonic masculinity** makes this paradox more understandable. This notion asserts that a number of competing masculinities are enacted according to particular places (contexts) and particular times. The characteristics of masculinity that become the idealized norm are those acted out by the most powerful men, likely to be those who are white, middle class, and heterosexual. In this process all other masculine styles are rendered inadequate and inferior (Beynon, 2002:16). Hegemonic masculinity harms men in subordinate statuses (men of color, poor men, nonheterosexuals) because it narrows their options to chose other enactments masculinity. It also harms women because it positions masculinity in opposition to women (Gardiner, 2002). The key is to recognize who has the power in a given situation to determine what is a dominant masculinity and what is a subordinate one. Hegemonic masculinity of the white, middle-class and heterosexual variety is not only the dominant form but also, in relation to women, *is* masculinity.

Masculinity's Norms

Decades of research on hegemonic masculinity show us that there are a number of ways masculinity (manliness) can be "successfully" acted out (Brannon, 1976; Smiler, 2006; Jandt and Hundley, 2007). These different enactments can be subsumed under categories that serve as both traditional norms of masculinity and emerging ones. I adapted the categories to incorporate recent work on masculinity and to use it as a framework for approaching a variety of issues concerning masculine gender roles. Most of these informal rules have become institutionalized norms (also referred to as standards, markers, or themes) that have strengthened over the decades.

Antifeminine Norm. This powerful norm stigmatizes all stereotyped feminine characteristics and the qualities associated with them, including openness in expressing emotions related to vulnerability. It is so closely tied to every other norm of masculinity that may be viewed as the overarching norm that literally defines masculinity. Males are socialized to adamantly reject all that is considered as feminine. Women and anything perceived as feminine are less valued than men and anything perceived as masculine. Acceptance of the antifemininity norm and the traditional scripts it includes comes with huge costs.

Interpersonal Relations. Beliefs about feminine behavior disallow many men from revealing insecurities and vulnerabilities to others who could help them cope with difficult life situations. Restraints in emotional openness are associated with suicide, Type A behavior, heart disease, and stress-related conditions such as ulcers, stroke, back pain, and tension headaches. Concealing emotions also inhibits the development of the repertoire of interpersonal skills essential for successful relationships in all areas of life. Intimate friendships between males are discouraged, and intimate friendships between females are blocked by messages that tell men they will be judged negatively if they exhibit "too much" emotion or sensitivity (Chapters 2 and 3). They believe emotional expression drives others away rather than bringing them closer.

Boys of all ages learn quickly that gestures of intimacy with other males are discouraged and that expressions of femininity, verbally or nonverbally, are not tolerated. Male role models—fathers, teachers, brothers, school athletes, peers—provide the cues and the sanctions to ensure compliance on the part of the young boy. The "boy code" is monitored carefully by other boys. Anger is accepted but displays of "soft" emotion are swiftly censured (Serriere, 2008; Oransky and Fisher, 2009). As we will see, the culturally inbred antifemininity norm especially keeps teenage boys from expressing feelings toward other boys on pain of being ridiculed as "sissies" at best or "fags" at worst.

To bolster their formative masculinity, boys strictly segregate themselves from girls in school. This segregation means that intimacy with boys must be achieved in other culturally acceptable ways. Throughout childhood and into adult life, male camaraderie occurs in male-only secret clubs, fraternal organizations, the military, sports teams, or the neighborhood bar. Although men are taught that too much intimacy among males is forbidden, the human desire for informal interaction is powerful. The separate groups allow men to act out this human need in safety and according to masculinity's antifeminine norm, otherwise people would be suspicious of such close male interaction. Men rarely talk about friendship in these groups. "Instead we hear about something called male bonding, as if all possible nonsexual connection between men is rooted in some crude instinctual impulse," and even this is viewed as something either "terribly juvenile or possibly dangerous" (Letich, 1991:85). The antifemininity norm blocks the expression of the deepest feelings of affection between men. The norm also reinforces stereotypes about homosexuality and, in turn, breeds anger and antigay aggression (Parrott et al., 2008).

Men may be guaranteed sociocultural superiority over women, but at the enormous expense of remaining psychologically defensive and insecure (Chodorow, 1993:60). Males of all ages are more likely to express feelings of uncertainty and anxiety to females, but the healthiest men are those who have an array of both male and female friends with whom they feel comfortable in expressing their emotions and concerns. Overall, men's endorsement of the antifemininity norm's quest for invulnerability has the opposite effect: It makes them more vulnerable than less vulnerable.

Success Norm. This norm suggests that men are driven to succeed at all costs. Also referred to as the status norm, men need to be looked up to, and prestige is associated with the belief that money makes the man. Manliness is tied to career success and the ability to provide for a family in his breadwinner role. The positive "good provider" role is salient in this norm, but it comes with more than an economic price. Men feel compelled to emulate other men, and in doing so, families become display cases for masculine success. Because prestige is gained from their work outside rather than inside the home, competency as a parent is less important than competency in the world of paid labor. It is expected that the wives, children, colleagues, and peers of these men judge them accordingly. As the Depression so aptly demonstrated, self-esteem is assaulted with the loss of a job. We saw earlier that unemployment for men is correlated with an array of risks to emotional well-being. Men are told that ensuring the family's financial security is their top priority in life, a message that eclipses every other role.

Gendered Occupations. In the workplace men are threatened by women's competence and their entry into traditional masculine occupations, thereby kindling controversy about what constitutes a "man's" job. Blue-collar men express the most hostility, but the resistance comes from men in the professions as well. Consistent with both the antifemininity and the success norms, they may believe that their jobs will be tainted by femininity and regarded as less manly. Men who succeed in feminine jobs are frequently viewed as less competent than those who succeed in masculine jobs. An influx of women in an occupation decreases its attractiveness to men. Males who do work in predominantly female fields may be viewed as less competent by those outside the job, but they have more advantages than females in these fields (Chapter 10). From a symbolic interaction view, a labeling cycle producing a self-fulfilling prophecy occurs: The job is "feminized," men desert it, working conditions deteriorate, and pay decreases. The job is resegregated, going from almost all men to almost all women. Success at a job where women are doing essentially the same work can be demeaning for men who favor conventional gender roles. Males are bound to a concept of masculinity that assumes they will dominate women occupationally and that they will enact a strong breadwinning role, with their self-esteem tied to both. Females reinforce these beliefs by viewing men as success objects.

In the bleak economic times of the decade leading to the MR, men flocked to female jobs, as nurses, caseworkers, elementary school and preschool teachers, and even as nannies. Men report that even with lowered pay, working with children and in caregiving roles offers flexibility, satisfaction, and a belief that they are "making a difference." However, masculinity's stubborn success norm erodes these beliefs. If men feel others view them as lacking ambition or being deficient in their provider role, they may wait out the economic downturn in female jobs but jump back into higher-paying, more prestigious male jobs when conditions improve (Cullen, 2003).

Men also face confusion when they are challenged by the reality of a new economy that has transformed the traditional provider role for men. Dual-earner couples are not the exception but the norm. Although beliefs about egalitarianism in the workplace are being expressed much more than in the past by both men and women, a retrenchment favoring the conventional norm of male superiority in terms of the success norm remains. When wives work outside the home, both spouses—but particularly husbands—are reluctant to define her as on equal footing in the provider role. Conflict theory suggests that one reason married men embrace the breadwinner role is that it entitles them to privileges in the home, including less housework, more time for leisure and recreation, and more services provided to them by wife and children.

Intellectual Success. In addition to economic success, males are expected to demonstrate intellectual superiority over women. The feminist movement ushered in the idea that intellectual companionship between the genders is possible and preferable. With a few modifications, however, traditional beliefs still hold. Men now expect that their wives will be wage earners, and they express admiration for their wives' careers. But they also believe that the bulk of child-care and household responsibilities should rest with a wife and that her career should be interrupted if these responsibilities are jeopardized. Men also believe that a husband should outearn his wife and that her career success is less important than his. Men are threatened by female coworkers who are promoted over them, and husbands are threatened by wives who equal or excel them occupationally. Young men have lower self-esteem if they see their wives as "winning" over them occupationally. Despite these trends, gender-related attitudes of men are reemphasizing work roles for men and maternal roles for women. Men's attitudes are strongly influenced by the social and historical period in which they live as much as they are by personal experiences. This suggests that cultural mandates for the success image of masculinity remain entrenched.

Toughness Norm. As embodied in war and sports, the toughness norm of masculinity tells men and boys to be strong, confident, self-reliant, brave, and independent. Any male must express confidence in his ability to carry out tasks that appear insurmountable. He must do so with a sense of stoicism that shows he is in command of the situation. Leadership is reinforced by toughness. Men believe that "if I ask for help, they may think I lack self-confidence or need reassurance." Any behavior associated with anxiety or lack of self-confidence is the antithesis of traditional male role behavior embodied in the toughness norm (Bruch, 2006:287). Antifeminine elements intrude here by implying that compliance and submissiveness are the negative qualities that the tough male disdains.

The harried husband of the Dagwood Bumstead, Al Bundy, or Homer Simpson variety possesses such qualities. The opposite of the tough male is the "wimp." Men may be labeled wimps for crossing boundaries and relating to their partners, wives, and children in "sensitive" ways. Indeed, this view suggests that a "male" wimp is redundant.

Sensitivity may be the opposite of toughness, but in the strongly gendered world of oil rig crews, for example, tough guy behavior can be dysfunctional as well as dangerous. Displays of risk-taking and masculine strength interfere with safety and performance in a potentially deadly environment, especially when they try to prove themselves by toughness. When tough guy hypermasculinity is abandoned in favor of teamwork, admitting mistakes, and interdependence, improvements in performance, safety, and efficiency follow (Ely and Meyerson, 2008). As explained by symbolic interaction, by risking a blow to their image, these men adjust their sense of self to accommodate a different, but nonetheless prized, form of masculinity.

Aggression Norm. As a key marker of manliness, aggression is associated with daring, lack of compromise, and unbending will in the face of adversity. Manliness as connected to aggression has been central throughout history, and is often played out in revenge, a theme that endures today. Abundant research indicates that males who adhere to traditional masculinity norms are more aggressive in the worlds they inhabit—whether in school, in the workplace, or in their families, compared to men who adhere less to these norms. Masculinity ideology is a better predictor of aggression than is gender (Cohn and Zeichner, 2006; Richardson and Hammock, 2007). Boys learn early that turning the other cheek is less respected than fighting one's way out of a difficult situation, especially if bullied. Media reinforce these images by aiming stories at youngsters that glorify violence and revenge in the name of a good cause. The cause itself is one that is usually defined as patriotic, but often portrayed ambiguously or personally, showing that war is comprised of guts and glory on the battlefield of honor. The title of "hero" is readily bestowed on those who win by using physical force. Diplomats who quietly work behind the scenes hammering out vital peace agreements are less likely to command public admiration than frontline soldiers. President Jimmy Carter, who pursued a diplomatic solution to the Iran hostage situation, was seen as soft for his refusal to use military channels. An ill-fated rescue attempt was a way to escape this pressure.

Aggression and war are at times necessary. Functionalists emphasize that by socializing boys into masculinity with the aura of violence and aggression surrounding it, the soldier role, which they may eventually assume, will be easier to accept. In this view, the aggressive masculinity needed in wartime is latently functional. Such views are also linked to the antifemininity norm. Toughness, the repression of empathy, less remorse for "accidental" violence, and less concern for moral issues are deemed essential for winning. The human cost of war is cast aside. As a marine serving in Iraq reports,

> We had a great day. . . . We killed a lot of people . . . we dropped a few civilians . . . but what do you do? . . . (and for killing an Iraqi woman). I'm sorry . . . but the chick got in the way. (Filkins, 2003)

The problem with this view is that aggression and masculinity become inextricably linked and carry over into the nonwar existence of men. As another marine reports,

> When I go home, people will want to treat me like a hero, but I'm not. . . . If I
> have to kill the other guy, I will, but that doesn't make me a hero. I just want
> to go home to my wife and kids. (Myers, 2003)

The men in these stories openly expressed masculinized marine aggression. The hypermasculinity associated with the Iraq War and its warriors is simultaneously acknowledged and hidden (Pettigrew, 2007). Many also expressed great remorse about killing to journalists only under conditions of anonymity. They do not utter these things to other soldiers. A soldiering mentality is maladaptive in a man's daily life, but he hauls its baggage as surely as his battlefield pack.

School Violence. The deadly influence of three masculinity norms— antifemininity, toughness, and aggression—is plainly evident in two decades of school violence resulting in the death and injury of students and teachers in small cities and suburbs across the United States. Toxic masculinity is a critical factor in understanding this violence, but one that is ignored by almost all media accounts and many professional ones. Reporters, educators, parents, and scholars refer to the perpetrators as "violent youths," "isolated adolescents," "lonely teenagers," and "unhappy students" and rarely mention the fact that all the killers are boys. Many of these boys were considered good students but were also identified as passive, alienated, and ostracized or shamed by their peers—especially the schools' "popular" clique. They were called "nerds," "wimps," and "sissies" and targeted for homosexual slurs. The Columbine killers were also addicted to a diet of extremely violent video games, such as *Doom* and *Quake*, specifically designed with adolescent boys in mind. Research suggests that isolation and humiliation by peers were likely triggers for the violence. Regardless of race and social class, antisocial behavior is one result of low self-esteem and is the single best predictor of later aggression (Kerr and Nelson, 2002). All these patterns have traceable links to the way masculinity is defined and acted on by men and boys.

Sexual Prowess Norm. The theme of sexuality permeates a norm that may be referred to popularly as "macho man." In this image, men are primarily sexual beings living and having ongoing heightened interests in sexuality in all its forms. In the sexualized world they create and function in, men are judged according to their sexual ability and sexual conquest. Men who sustain injuries that compromise their beliefs about sexual prowess are prime candidates for depression, self-neglect, and suicide. Strong masculine role ideology, for example, is associated with barriers to effective rehabilitation (Schopp et al., 2007). Male sexual identity is experienced as sensation and action. Sexual harassment is a case in point. This identity is so taken for granted that men's ogling, touching, or sexual remarks or jokes are dismissed as harmless fun rather than as sexual domination or exploitation. Men are mystified or angered when they are accused of harassment because they view it as normal gendered interaction (Quinn, 2002).

This form of sexual identity is reinforced by essentialist beliefs that masculinity is biologically rather than socially constructed. An "impotent" man is cast into a stigmatized, demeaned category because the term is used to describe more than just his penis. Media depict a man's sexual performance as a way to confirm his masculinity, with success in sex linked to success in life (Lehman, 2004). Mostly used as a front, boys develop stories and routines documenting their sexual escapades and describing successful pickup ploys. As boys mature and strive to be "masculine," they soon understand that credibility and bonding are achieved with male peers through sexual talk laced with aggressive overtones and sexist joking, with girls and women as their unflattering targets (Curry, 2004). As a staple for preadolescent boys, pornography provides their initial foray into sexual images of male and female. Of the numerous masculinity and guy code lessons learned from pornography, boys often choose two as standards to chart their fledgling sexuality: "porn makes the man" and "size matters" (Jensen, 2007). When boys and men rely on sexuality to define masculinity, their vulnerability will inevitably increase. They gain a measure of respect for sexual talk and bravado of the locker room, but at the same time they understand that they can never live up to the sexualized selves they present to others. And they are well aware of the disastrous consequences if they acted on the aggression in their sexual talk. In the pursuit of the illusion of masculinity, one set of vulnerabilities is exchanged for another.

Tenderness Norm. This emerging norm is identified by men who reject a rigid cultural construction of masculinity that disallows them from displaying sensitivity or tenderness to others. Tenderness masculinity encompasses beliefs that expressions of sensitivity are beneficial to men, both personally and in their relationships with others. Referred to positively as "sensitive guys," men accepting this norm strive for more emotional openness with men and more egalitarian relationships with women.

Research suggests that because tenderness masculinity allows for less emotional restriction, it is the healthiest of the masculinity norms (Harris and Thoresen, 2005; Lawler-Row et al., 2008). Willingness to forgive, reconcile, and keep a positive outlook after the episode, for example, is associated with psychological benefits. Although "anger-out" is masculinity's accepted emotional display, it is not only the least healthy for men, it is also socially unproductive. Men and the people they display anger toward do not "forgive and forget." If forgiveness is viewed as feminine, then men also tend to reject it, a belief that cuts across race and social class. Men in supportive networks that include both genders are also more likely to forgive and to feel good about it (Hammond et al., 2006; Miller et al., 2008). The tenderness norm is emerging, but it competes with the more powerful aggression and antifeminine norms.

Whereas the sensitive guy image is one that resonates with men and women seeking equitable partnering roles, it is a masculinity image that remains subordinate to all the others. When images of tenderness masculinity make their way into the media, they are undermined by the more normative images. Think of Arnold Schwarzenegger in *True Lies* and *Kindergarten Cop* to understand how tenderness masculinity is subverted to the other types. Heterosexual men are often portrayed as exploitive sexual beings who also strive to create pleasure for their partners. The latter more "sensitive" view is not particularly progressive or egalitarian if masculinity is still associated with control. The male takes charge of sexual activity and decides the sequence, the pace, the positions, and how best to stimulate his partner. Women may want to lead or to communicate other needs. Whenever the "crisis of masculinity" becomes a media focus, it is usually because women are outperforming men in traditionally male spheres, and men are not being assertive enough to retain or regain their positions of dominance. Their lack of assertiveness is associated with being too nice, too tender, or too sensitive.

Images to Reject or Accept? Masculine images have a contradictory quality that may seem confusing to men. Men are presented with alternative images that challenge the traditional version of a male mystique. In accepting these revised images as legitimate and offering more benefit than liability, men could rally behind new definitions of masculinity. The tenderness option is one that is sought by men and women as individuals. But when men come together in groups, the older images of masculinity surface and the newer images are subverted. Both genders adhere to quite rigid views of masculinity. Men are threatened by changes in definitions of masculinity, regardless of the virtual impossibility of meeting the traditional standards. Men's roles have not kept pace with the changes in women's roles. The evidence is clear that attitudes toward masculinity have served to hamper those men seeking to free themselves from restrictive male stereotypes. The majority of men, however, are on no such quest.

On an optimistic note, new masculinities like the tenderness option—however small the breakthrough may be—emphasize the development of a deeper awareness of the mutuality of the two genders. This awareness needs to be taught to children. Stunned by escalating school violence, for example, educators are adopting socialization practices emphasizing nurturance and nonaggressive means of resolving conflict. Boys learn about positive forms of masculinity that steer them away from traditional forms that can do more harm than good (Kiselica et al., 2008). As the director of one such program reports,

> We live in a society that accepts behaviors that men can be possessive of women and use women for any purpose, even sexually . . . If we have a corps of young men who say: "that's not acceptable" men will change the norm within society. (Jewett, 2007)

By accepting attitudes that have been traditionally labeled as feminine, tenderness masculinity is necessary for the development of full human potential.

Social change has influenced the behavior of men in their masculine roles, whether it is acknowledged or not. But cultural lag remains: Attitudes have not caught up with the behavior change that is evident. As far as masculinity is concerned, the disheartening overall conclusion is that the more things change, the more they remain the same.

HOMOPHOBIA

The world is primarily based on **heterosexism**—people view relationships only in heterosexual terms, and in doing so, other sexual orientations are denigrated. Reflecting the taken-for-granted view that the world is heterosexist, at various times in history homosexuality was a sin, a disease, a crime, a mental illness, an immoral choice, an alternative lifestyle, and an unavoidable tragedy (Tin, 2008).

To be masculine means more than being nonfeminine; it means antifeminine. A taken-for-granted heterosexist view fuels **homophobia**, the fear and intolerance of homosexuals (gay men and lesbians) and homosexuality. Researchers identify homophobia as integral to heterosexual masculinity. Compulsive heterosexuality spells out to men that in order to be a man, one cannot be a homosexual. The logical extension from this definition is that homophobia in men translates into the fear of other men. Data from the United States, Britain, and Australia suggest that homophobia is learned early and reinforced through the media, peer interaction at school, and in the workplace (Clum, 2002; Keller, 2002). In the United States, the majority of teenage males express high levels of homophobia. More positive media images may temper these beliefs as they get older, but they are not likely to be erased.

The Demography of Homophobia

People with higher levels of homophobia are also likely to be heterosexual, elderly, not college educated, living in the South, and religiously, sexually, and politically conservative. They also tend to be more authoritarian and hold rigid, highly traditional views of masculinity and femininity. Homophobia is also correlated with sexism and racism (Cohler and Galatzer-Levy, 2000; Embrick et al., 2007; Szymanski et al., 2008). People who have LGBT friends and who believe that homosexuality is due to biology are less homophobic (Hegarty, 2002; Kantor, 2009). Homophobia translates into stigma, depression, and fear in the lives of gay men. Homophobia and violence against homosexuals are all too common occurrences.

The Risks of Race and Ethnicity. When the minority status of "homosexual" is added to an already disadvantaged position due to race or ethnicity, stigma for gay men increases. Those disadvantages may be higher within their own subcultures: African-American gay and bisexual men, for example, may be at higher risk for violence and HIV infection because they need to maintain a facade of heterosexuality and adhere to heterosexist masculinity norms in their homophobic subcultures. Although secrecy may protect them against violence, it does not protect them against HIV risk. Risky sexual behavior is associated with the sexual prowess masculinity norm that works against all men, but especially gay men (Lichtenstein, 2000; Constantine-Simms, 2001). Among Latinos, a similar scenario is played out and impacts both homosexual and heterosexual men and women. Throughout Latino cultures in North and South America, Latino males are expected to be dominant, tough, and fiercely competitive with other males. This exaggerated machismo masculinity is displayed more frequently in poor and working-class neighborhoods. Unprotected sex with multiple partners is proof of virility and masculinity, and therefore not homosexuality. Young Latinos are aware of the dangers, but cultural norms about manhood and homosexuality continue (Schifter and Madrigal, 2000). Although homophobia in Latino communities is very strong and male-to-male sexual liaisons are kept secret, they may be accepted as transitory until marriage because they say a sexual outlet is needed. A gay identity, however, is not acceptable (Diaz et al., 2001).

Among Asian Americans, especially in Chinese communities, gender roles and images of masculinity are extremely rigid. Gay Chinese Americans express high levels of anguish not only because they were socialized for strong family ties, but because their families trace their heritage only through male offspring. An only son who is gay dooms a family line. Though it is difficult to generalize about levels of homophobia within different racial and ethnic groups, it is clear that gay men must contend with another layer of minority status that will undoubtedly impact their lives.

Gender. Homophobia has declined significantly for most demographic categories. Today there is more support for extending the same rights related to employment and military service to all people, regardless of sexual orientation (Andryszewski, 2000). The increasing number of states allowing legal marriages for gay couples also attests to this decline (Chapter 8). Media representations of gay men are becoming mainstream and popular and are portraying positive, affirmative friendships between gay and straight men (think *Will and Grace, Queer Eye for the Straight Guy, Brokeback Mountain*). Overall, young adults can be described as somewhere between tolerant and accepting of homosexuals (NORC, 2008).

Gender differences in level of acceptance of homosexuality are the single most important contradiction to the trend. Males may be less homophobic than in the past, but they have been slower to change than other groups. For adolescent males, the gender gap in homophobia may be widening.

Masculinity and Homophobic Labels

The feminine labels that boys use in name-calling denigrate other boys precisely because the word is associated with a devalued group—females. The most popular, taken-for-granted label males use to insult other males is "girl."

When stereotypes about femininity and homosexuality collide, boys then combine two devalued groups (females and gay men) in using their denigrating labels. These labels range from "sissy," "wimp," and "pussy" to "homo," "fag," or "cocksucker." Rap icon Eminem routinely uses homophobic labels in his repertoire as a slur less against a man's sexuality, but more related to his gender. With "fag discourse" rampant in high school, the "specter of the fag" is a powerful mechanism to regulate the behavior of boys, with "gay-baiting" an accepted practice (Pascoe, 2007; Tharinger, 2008). Boys distance themselves from any behavior suggestive of these labels. They are reluctant to challenge the inconsistencies and stereotypes associated with their usage because, just by doing so, they may be threatened themselves with the label of "faggot." As adults, men continue to fear these labels and subtly use homophobia to control other men. Men who are highly homophobic are likely to enact hypermasculinity to dispel any notion that they may be viewed as feminine, hence homosexual.

Gay Men. Homophobia takes its toll on gay men who are socialized to accept the same masculinity norms as heterosexual men. Gay relationships, whether they are sexual or not, demonstrate the impact of socialization into masculinity standards and the homophobia of the standards. For example, in gay subcultures throughout the world a powerful gay machismo element is evident. Exaggerated masculinity takes the form of dress (leather, motorcycle regalia, military uniforms), rough language, and risky, sometimes violent sexual encounters. Beliefs about masculinity can propel gay men into risky behaviors related to drugs, alcohol, and sexual practices (Hamilton and Mahalik, 2009). Gay machismo presents an image of masculinity that gay men have been taught as the proper one. Sexual prowess, power, and control are its central characteristics. When gay men adopt the heterosexist masculine standard, however, their reality is distorted because they are still gay and open to the rejection and homophobia existing in the broader society.

Gay men must contend with feelings of self-worth in a society that labels them as deviant. Compulsory heterosexuality and hegemonic masculinity ideals takes a huge psychological toll on gay men and boys, whether they reveal their non-heterosexual status or not. By internalizing the negative labels of the dominant group, gay men may learn to accept the stereotyped, pejorative view of themselves. The other side of homophobia is its counterpart in gay men: diminished self-esteem and shame (Szymanski and Carr, 2008).

Gay Rights. The emergence of a strong gay rights movement has helped gay men to affirm positive identities and the right to sexual self-determination. In this manner, both individual and political agendas are being met. Patterned after the women's movement, one faction is working to escape the bonds of a sexist culture in which they recognize the common oppression and levels of discrimination they share with women. They are working to cast aside restrictive role playing that distances them from other men and to challenge masculinity norms that are harmful to the well-being of all males, whether gay or not.

On the other hand, a significant number of gay men recognize that because women and gay men are both subordinate in society, it may be better to capitalize on their advantage of being male—regardless of how it undermines women. From this "male advantage" view, a gay male executive moving up the corporate ladder can wield power over any competing female. As conflict theory suggests, males are higher in the stratification system than females. Males are socialized into accepting the masculinity norms described earlier, whether they are gay or not.

MASCULINITY AND FATHERHOOD

Can men have it all? This phrase is usually connected to women who want to combine a career with marriage and children. Femininity norms have been flexible enough to accommodate women with such aspirations. Masculinity norms have not. The success and toughness norms dictate that men take on the responsibilities of parenthood primarily through their breadwinning roles.

Like women, men envision the American Dream in terms of successful marriage, satisfying career, contented spouse, and happy children. Idealism notwithstanding, men willingly abdicate the daily household and child-care responsibilities to their wives. Masculine images of success tied to career priorities do not allow the latitude necessary for the degree of family commitment many men desire. Contrary to belief, men do not "have it all."

Images of Fatherhood

Fatherhood means more than paternity. The word *fathering* is associated with sexual and biological connotations. The word *mothering* is associated with nurturance. The biological father who takes his provider role seriously has met the necessary criterion for masculinity. This narrow outlook disregards, even belittles, those men who want to expand their parenting roles or choose to be stay at home fathers (SAHFs). Employed fathers are viewed more positively than SAHFs; employed mothers are viewed more negatively than homemakers (Brescoll and Uhlmann, 2005). In families where men are SAHFs and women are breadwinners, ceding control of parenting to men is difficult. Men are cast into a suspicious light by women, as one SAHF explains at a playground:

> . . . you will get this stink-eye from the moms, this sort of 'Who the hell are you and what are you doing here?' (Rochlen et al., 2008a:200)

Complete role reversal is rare. On the other hand, despite beliefs about essentialism and the pervading norm that men are providers and success objects, SAHFs have high levels of psychological well-being, adjustment, and life and relationship satisfaction (Rochlen et al., 2008b). However, the demeaning stereotypes of bumbling men who do not know how to hold a baby, soothe a sobbing child, or buy groceries persevere and serve to lower the skill level men need to succeed in domestic roles. Some men use the bumbling father stereotype as a strategy to get out of performing certain tasks:

- Getting the kids dressed—these buttons are so tiny—I can't do tiny buttons.
- Poor kids, they are always getting dressed backwards.
- When the kids hear daddy's going to make dinner they'd rather eat out. (Deutsch, 2004:470)

These men belittle their own efforts and at the same time praise their wives for succeeding where they have failed. This self-effacement also functions to maintain the traditional gendered division of labor in the household.

Regardless of whether he is "playing dumb" to get out of household work, masculinity's antifemininity norm bolsters his behavior. Men who freely choose to take care of their own children as househusbands or SAHFs, who take on equal partnering with their dual-earning or full-time homemaker wives, or who take care of others' children as early childhood educators are suspect in their masculinity. The exclusion of men from more meaningful participation in the lives of their children can devastate fathers who avidly desire these very roles.

Socialization. Although fathers have fewer expectations built into their roles regarding socialization of their children, the child-nurturing roles they do take on are extremely important. Strong father–infant attachment and involvement of fathers with their young children are linked to a child's personality adjustment, positive peer relationships, level of self-esteem, and overall sense of well-being. Fathers are the key figures in preventing the connection between violence and masculinity to be acted out by their sons (Pope and Englar-Carlson, 2001). Regardless of race or social class, in homes where fathers are absent or gone much of the time, children are at greater risk for maladaptive psychological, social, and development outcomes (Lamb, 2002). Increases in divorce and cohabitation undermine already fragile father–child relationships, reinforce masculinity norms about men's economic roles, and increase women's domination in child socialization (Goldscheider, 2000).

Decades of research on the aspirations fathers hold for their children remain remarkably consistent. In all socioeconomic classes fathers are stricter in gender-typed intentions of their children than mothers, and they give sons less latitude than daughters in experimenting with different gender role definitions. Fathers now believe that both their sons and daughters need to go to college, but that the college should provide a different option for sons. Fathers continue to pay close attention to the potential for their sons to be breadwinners and good providers but believe their daughters can use a degree "to fall back on." Whereas these patterns are more pronounced among working-class men compared to men in middle and upper classes, gender stereotypes surrounding masculinity norms invade socialization practices by fathers in all social classes (Chapter 3).

Parents as Partners

To make parenthood a true partnership for a couple, fathers and children need to be brought closer together. Research suggests this is what is highly desired by fathers, but as we saw in Chapter 8, it is eroded by images of masculinity that underscore the "good provider" image (success) of fathers to the neglect of a fledgling "involved-father" model. Fathers want to embrace new role definitions that rank nurturing equal to or higher than breadwinning but feel blocked by broader masculinity norms bolstering their advantage in the workplace but disadvantage at home. Fathers mention repeatedly that they want to be role models, teachers, companions, and playmates to their children (Gearing et al., 2001; Risman, 2001).

A father's participation in family life is enhanced when expanded role definitions are accepted on all fronts. Wives, children, other kin, friends, and coworkers can be supportive of men who take on a variety of not just child maintenance but also child-rearing responsibilities. Family-supportive workplace policies that allow flextime and paternity leave serve nurturing purposes as well. After his daughter was born with health problems, one father reported on his paternity leave experience where he took off two months and was working part-time for six months.

> I was just extremely fortunate to have the flexibility. I'm sure my co-workers would rather have had me back but I didn't get any pressure . . . (but) . . . I tried to keep up with what was going on . . . so there was kind of a self-regulating pressure. (Cooper, 2004:274)

Like the emerging tenderness masculinity norm, these comments suggest that men are in transition to gender role change. Involved fathers, for example, are not yet on equal par with provider-fathers. When paternity leave options are available, few fathers avail themselves of these opportunities. Because these are rarely paid options, many fathers cannot afford the time off work. The more common reason, however, is that employers and coworkers believe that men who take paternity leave are less serious about their careers. Corporate women who take time off from their careers for child-related responsibilities are frequently slotted into less-demanding and less-lucrative "mommy track" positions. A comparable "daddy track" for men may be destined for those who choose paternity leave. The rigidity of a masculinity image equating success in fatherhood in economic terms again intrudes.

Men in the Delivery Room. Another partnering mechanism is a father's inclusion in the childbirth experience—from training to be a labor coach and preparenting classes to the delivery room itself. Expectant fathers in Lamaze classes are quite aware that women control the class. A man may joke about the classes but he is frightened by the physical pain his wife will endure and by the isolation felt during his wife's pregnancy. Being present at childbirth offers a new father an incredibly powerful bond to his infant and to his wife or partner. After sharing in the birth of the child, the marriage is likely to be stronger, particularly if the father is highly involved in later child care.

The doors are open for contemporary expectant fathers who only a few decades ago were totally removed from the birthing process. Fathers were relegated to waiting rooms, where they nervously paced until the doctor brought news of the birth, upholding older images of men as appendages who get in the way. At childbirth, men are constrained by a double standard built into their role. They are encouraged today to actively participate, but at the same time they are seen as outsiders. Women dominate the moral discourse on childbirth. Expectant mothers are cast into positive, normative roles but there are no corresponding roles for expectant fathers. Except for his laughable nervousness, his fears are not addressed. Fear of his wife's death during childbirth and anxiety over new parenting roles and family responsibilities are major concerns of expectant fathers but are rarely discussed. With attention turned to motherhood, the transition to fatherhood is overlooked. When natural fears experienced by expectant fathers are discussed openly and unashamedly with their spouses, relationships are deepened.

Health-care communities need to be aware of their own stereotypes in working with expectant fathers. The evidence is clear that benefits will be realized for the marriage and for later parenting when this occurs.

Divorce

Divorced fathers who would like to be actively involved with their children must contend with restrictions on parenting tied to masculine gender roles that interfere with responsible parenting. Fathers who feel cut off from their children after a divorce have heightened levels of anxiety, depression, and stress. The bleak statistics on child support payments by fathers is well documented (Chapter 10). Joint custody may be less economically advantageous for ex-wives, but it increases contact and self-esteem for ex-husbands. Those fathers who absent themselves from their children after divorce and fail to pay child support often report that they were treated unfairly in the divorce settlement. They may view this as a legitimate strategy to maintain control over their former wives (Flood, 2008; Unger, 2008). These regrettable practices suggest that fathers may be locked in to a system shaped by gendered ideology that discourages positive postdivorce relationships for the ex-spouses and their children.

MEN AT MIDDLE AGE AND IN LATER LIFE

Sociological perspectives on the **life course** highlight the process of continuing socialization in the roles people play over a lifetime and the ages associated with those roles. The varied paths of the life course are shaped by individual experiences as well as broader social change, particularly related to gender.

Retirement

The transition to retirement requires major adjustments in all segments of life. It restructures daily living, alters family relationships and spending patterns, and can generate psychological stress. Yet retirement has become such a part of life's expectations that if financial security is ensured, workers prefer early retirement. Gender role beliefs are central to retirement adjustment. Men undergo a profound shift in identity that often requires a resculpting of their ideas about masculinity (McDaniel, 2003a). The provider-role script and success norms associated with masculinity sharpen an already strong American work ethic from which identity and self-esteem are gained.

The psychological investment in the world of paid employment for men predict that they would have a more difficult time with retirement than women. Available data, however, suggest that retirement satisfaction is based on the same factors for women and men. Like men, career women anticipate retiring at an earlier age, but they use the resulting free time differently. Women restructure their domestic lives that were constrained because of employment and spend more time with family and on home-related activities. Men take on more extradomestic roles and activities, but many of these activities are done with family members rather than friends or former coworkers. Egalitarian men do the same level of routine household work at retirement; egalitarian women invest more time in these tasks at retirement. Marital satisfaction for men and women increases as adjustments to a less time-driven life are made (Barnes and Parry, 2004; Solomon et al., 2004; Schmitt et al., 2007). Gender is less of a predictor of life satisfaction at retirement than are income and health. Both male and female workers are less satisfied if poor health forced them to retire or if fewer economic resources forced them to remain on the job.

Midlife as Crisis

Do men have a midlife crisis? Health-care professionals continue to debate the question in light of a configuration of physical and emotional symptoms that emerge for many men between the ages of 45 and 55. Variously referred to as the male climeractic, male menopause, or midlife crisis, men may present symptoms of night fears, sweats and chills, and depression. The psychological and social turmoil associated with these symptoms are linked to hormonal changes, such as a sharp drop in testosterone level for a few men and a slow but gradual change with considerable hormonal variation, including a rise in estrogen (Stengler, 2005). Unlike women who experience noticeable changes heralding the cessation of menses, in normal aging for men the changes are subtle. Older men retain their interest in sex, but sexual performance becomes less predictable. Gender scripts linking masculinity to sexual prowess remain. A fear of impotence may come true not because of hormones but because of the fear itself (the massive sales of drugs that enhance the sexual performance of men may be linked to this fear). Men perceive themselves and are perceived by others as men first; their elder status comes second. Men do not drift into a version of sexless androgyny at old age (Thompson, 2006). Biological changes must be seen in light of the social and psychological factors embedded in masculinity norms.

Professionals are starting to suggest that these symptoms are a normal part of the aging process, and although initially alarming, they are not debilitating. The appearance of symptoms prompts many men to engage in a review of their lives, make choices, and alter life paths. Others suggest that this stage is neither normal nor healthy and that it produces psychological turmoil for men who make unwise decisions that are maladaptive for themselves and their families. This latter view asserts that men at midlife become acutely aware of their own mortality and, in reviewing their accomplishments, focus on what they have not done rather than what they have done. Unmet goals founded on masculinity's success scripts create turmoil for the midlife man who is then said to be in crisis.

Women at Midlife. For women, the depression that supposedly occurs when the last child is launched, or moves away from home, is referred to as the empty nest syndrome. Research shows, however, that the empty nest syndrome is largely a myth. Contrary to the stereotype, women tend to experience an upturn in psychological well-being when children are launched. Marital satisfaction also increases, but "too much" time with their partners can decrease overall life satisfaction. Like good provider men, women who are identified according to motherhood roles must negotiate their cultural and personal identities. They generally feel good about this life stage but must contend with cultural beliefs suggesting otherwise (Gorchoff et al., 2008; Sheriff and Weatherall, 2009). Women tend to look to the empty nest stage of life as offering opportunities to pursue activities that were put on hold during child raising. Personality development for women at midlife is related to increases in competence, independence, and an age-related rise in androgyny (Kasen et al., 2006:955). They generally seek expanded roles in a society increasingly receptive to women like themselves, who are venturing outside the traditional confines of the home.

Men at Midlife. Men may have a more difficult time with the empty nest than women. Some evidence suggests that men's increased depression at midlife is linked to their regrets about career priorities that distanced themselves from their children. A positive life course path to recapture the lost parenting experience prompts many men to turn to grandchildren. Grandchildren provide a sense of biological continuity, emotional self-fulfillment, and a way for men to be free of the competition, arguments, and power struggles they experienced in their workplaces and when raising their own children. The stereotype of a grandfather as a stern, aloof, family patriarch counters the reality that grandparenting offers men rewarding and emotionally enriching experiences.

Men at midlife often begin to reintegrate the masculine and feminine traits that were separate for most of their lives. Traditional masculinity is tempered by a more well-rounded personality, which accounts for roles of husband, father, and breadwinner (Mann, 2007). Women approach midlife differently than men. Men seek greater interdependence at old age, whereas women seek greater autonomy. At this stage men become more nurturant and women more independent. Her capability of standing apart from him may help relieve him of the burden of responsibility he feels he has carried for the family. It is interesting that the woman who grows in assertiveness and independence provides the best source of support for a man in this phase of life. Each spouse may begin to loosen the bonds of restrictive gender roles as they make the transition from middle to old age.

Widowhood

Compared to widows, widowers are much more likely to remarry; thus among the elderly the large majority of widows reside alone. Although most older adults return to earlier levels of physical and emotional health within two years after the loss of their spouse, social isolation and loneliness are frequent outcomes of widowhood. The surviving spouse is at higher risk for physical illness and even death (Carr, 2001). If a caregiver–spouse dies, the already debilitated surviving spouse is left in an even more dependent and vulnerable position. Suicide rates among the elderly have increased since the 1980s, and they remain the highest of all age groups. Men account for the large majority of all suicides, and white males in their 80s have the highest suicide rates of all races and both genders. Suicide attempts by younger people (those under age 35) are likely to fail; suicide attempts rarely fail for the elderly, and the failure rate is smallest for elderly males. The suicide rate of older men, especially widowers, is a consistent trend since Emile Durkheim's analysis of suicide over a century ago.

Widows. The death of a spouse has a profound and devastating effect on the surviving partner, but becoming a widow is a qualitatively different experience than becoming a widower. Older women are more likely to form their identity around marriage, so losing a spouse literally means loss of a central life role. Widows are likely to experience a sudden decrease in standard of living, and for working-class women, widowhood can quickly result in poverty. Isolation increases and support networks decrease (Hungerford, 2001). These are worsened if the couple has moved away from her family for his career advancement. If a widow feels emotionally secure enough to venture into dating, prospects for male companionship and remarriage are limited.

On the other hand, widows are guided by many others with whom they can share experiences, memories, and activities. Due to their numbers alone, a variety of productive roles have been carved out for widows. Because married women know that widowhood is probable, they may begin to actually mentally rehearse it through anticipatory socialization. Their role choices may not be completely clear but most widows cope with the crisis reasonably well, adapt as necessary, and productively map out the rest of their lives in ways that contribute to their well-being.

Widowers. The role of widower is much more vague than that of widow. At first glance, it would seem that adjustment is difficult because men lose their most important source of emotional support and probably their major, if not their only, confidant. Wives typically take responsibility for maintaining the couple's social calendar and network of friendships. Masculinity norms earlier in life prevented interpersonal skill building. Lacking the strategies for either preserving or reestablishing intimate relationships, widowers find themselves with reduced social contacts. Traditional norms of masculinity may intrude again, preventing them from talking out their grief with others. Retirement increases social isolation. Widowhood intensifies it. The net result is a loss of significant personal relationships. Older men are also less likely to be prepared for the everyday domestic responsibilities necessary for taking care of themselves. When ongoing relationships and customary responsibilities are shattered, anomie (normlessness) can follow. This pattern helps explain the high suicide rate of elderly males.

On the other hand, marriage prospects remain bright for widowers, with many embarrassed by all the attention they receive from widows who want to "do" things for them. In addition to the number of women of their own age or younger who are available to widowers as potential dating and mating partners, men are better-off financially to actually support another spouse. Finally, men may have a stronger need to be remarried, so they quickly move through the dating stage to make remarriage a reality (Moore and Stratton, 2002). Overall, adjustment to widowhood may be different for men and women, but it remains unclear as to which gender fares better.

GENDERED VIOLENCE

It is abundantly evident that the acceptance of traditional masculine gender roles in a patriarchal society is closely connected with escalating violence toward women. Virtually all masculinity norms (antifemininity, toughness, self-reliance, aggression, and sexual conquest) reinforce this fact. Some of these norms are functional in societies such as the United States that value individualism and economic achievement through competition. But in other contexts these norms are highly maladaptive and dysfunctional, most vividly documented in overall patterns of male violence, specifically violence against women. When men are granted permission to subordinate women in patriarchal societies, sexual terrorism is a common result. Sexual terrorism includes sexual intimidation, threat of violence, and overt violence (Sheffield, 2007).

Rape

The threat of sexual terrorism and rape is so pervasive that firsthand experience is not needed to instill its fear in women. Representations of rape in the media serve to legitimize male aggression, reinforce gender stereotypes, and perpetuate rape myths (Table 9.2). Media lessons from the coverage of the Kennedy Smith and Mike Tyson rape trials, for example, provided a disciplinary function to women. Rape fear is heightened, and women's freedom of movement is restricted.

Recent press coverage has moved away from reports that exaggerated a woman's helplessness and her inability to fight back. In light of research that there are four rape attempts for every one completed, women are being taught

Table 9.2 Myths of Rape

Myth	Reality
1. Rape is a sexual act.	Rape is an act of violence to show dominance of the rapist and achieve submission by the victim.
2. Rapes are committed by strangers.	Rape more often occurs between acquaintances. Date rape is an example.
3. Most rapes are spontaneous, with the rapist taking advantage of the opportunity to rape.	Rape is likely to be preplanned. If spontaneity occurs, it may be part of another crime such as robbery.
4. Women wear provocative clothing or flirt with men.	This is the classic "blaming victim" myth. Since most rapes are preplanned, the rapist will strike regardless of appearance.
5. Women enjoy being raped.	The pain, violence, degradation, and psychological devastation experienced by the victim are overwhelming. She can also be killed.
6. Most rapists are psychopathic or sexually abnormal.	It is difficult to distinguish the rapist from other men in terms of personality or ideas about sexuality.
7. When she says "no" to sex she really means "yes."	When she says "no" she really means "no."

self-defense tactics and ways to avoid being raped (Bureau of Justice Statistics, 2009). The burden of responsibility, however, still falls on women to always protect themselves, to always be on the alert, and to always avoid places perceived to increase vulnerability. Because the general social norm is that male prerogative takes precedence, the antirape strategy is to change the woman rather than change the situation that creates the problem. Fear of rape shapes women's lives and curtails their freedom (Hirschmann, 2003).

Statistics. The staggering statistic is that 25–30 percent of all females are victims of sexual assault involving rape or attempted rape. Women do commit rape, but it is quite rare and is thought to account for less than one-half of 1 percent of cases. When males are raped the perpetrator is another male. Considering that definitions, perceptions, and legal standards vary considerably between states and between municipalities, between victims and perpetrators, and according to the context of occurrence, official figures on rape are probably underestimated. In addition, women who report a rape are likely to be demeaned and can be accused of false reporting. The reality is that false reports of rape are small (estimated between 2 and 8 percent) and much less than false reports of other crimes (Lonsway et al., 2008; Uniform Crime Reports, 2009). Sensationalist media coverage on rape involving famous men contributes to her secondary victimization as she relives the rape again. Today most municipalities incorporate counseling and more humane approaches in questioning victims of rape, and many courts will no longer allow the sexual history of the victim as part of the proceedings. Unfortunately, the victim herself is still often treated like the criminal. The reporting of rapes has steadily increased, but fewer than one-third of all rapes are reported.

Profile of the Rapist. Until recently rape was viewed as a crime committed by a few demented men of lower intelligence who have uncontrollable sexual impulses. These few psychotic men cannot be responsible for these staggering rape statistics. The reality is that there is no consistent personality type that reliably distinguishes rapists from men who commit other crimes and from men who do not commit crimes. Men are not psychotic at the time of the rape. Given the difficulty of getting accurate statistics on rape, the profile of the so-called typical rapist is a sketchy one. Rape is a crime perpetrated by a wide spectrum of men, but they do share some key characteristics (Robertiello and Terry, 2007; Gannon et al., 2008; Lord et al., 2008):

1. He has a high need for dominance and a low need for nurturance.
2. He deals with his perceived inadequacies by relying on traditional masculinity norms related to aggression and the sexual control of women. He may be defined as "hypermasculine" in his rigid acceptance of these norms.
3. He is socially insecure and interpersonally isolated.
4. He is likely to accept rape myths and justifies his behavior so that his victim is made to seem culpable (Table 9.2).
5. Sexual violence is used as a means of revenge or punishment, sometimes to specific women but more often to women in general, who he holds responsible for his sexual problems.
6. He presents rape in what he believes to be socially acceptable terms. His aggression is often followed by expressions of remorse.

The following comments by convicted rapists serve as examples of this profile:

> Rape gave me the power to do what I wanted to do without feeling I had to please a partner . . . I felt in control, dominant.

> I have never felt that much anger before. . . . The rape was for revenge. I didn't have an orgasm. She was there to get my hostile feelings off on.

> Rape is a man's right. If a woman doesn't want to give it, the man should take it. Women have no right to say no. (Scully and Marolla, 1990; Scully, 1993)

When men from all walks of life are presented with information about the motives of a rapist, they express disdain and horror about the victimization and anger that all men are tainted because a few men rape. Other men remain mystified about the motives of a rapist, as reported by a file clerk who heard about a woman who was beaten, raped, and hospitalized:

> That's beyond me. I can't understand why somebody would do that. If I were going to rape a girl I wouldn't hurt her. I might restrain her, but I wouldn't hurt her. (Beneke, 2004:411)

It is not difficult to understand why this profile is a sketchy one. It can fit many men.

Rape on College Campus. In the United States and Canada, between 25 and 35 percent of college women report a rape or attempted rape. The typical pattern reported by college women is that rape and pressured intercourse occur through the use of physical force, drugs, alcohol, and psychological intimidation (Hamilton, 2008).

Date or acquaintance rape is a fact of life on college campuses. About half of college men have engaged in some form of sexual aggression on a date; between one-fourth and one-half of college women report being sexually victimized. Despite these high numbers, when the victim and offender know one another and alcohol is involved, the incident is less likely to be reported to school officials or the police and even less likely to gain a criminal conviction. Date rape is also associated with alcohol and other drug use, for both the victim and the perpetrator, the belief that men are entitled to sex after initiating and paying for the date, fraternity parties, and length of time the couple has been dating (Benson et al., 2007; Girard and Senn, 2008; Maurer and Robinson, 2008). The so-called date rape drugs—colorless, odorless pills slipped into a drink causing a victim's sleepiness and vulnerability—are used to plan a rape and are widespread on college campuses. And despite substantial evidence to the contrary, male college students are more likely to accept the rape myths than female college students (McDonald and Kline, 2004; Castello et al., 2006; Black and Gold, 2008; Girard and Senn, 2008).

Pornography and Rape. Because of its link to sexual aggression, pornography has come under a great deal of scientific and legal scrutiny. Pornography can be categorized according to two major factors—degree of depiction of sexual acts and depictions of aggression in these acts. Hard-core pornography usually depicts genitalia openly and shows sex acts that are aggressive and violent. Women are uniformly the objects of the violence, and it is rare to see men portrayed in this manner. In experimental research, sexually suggestive but nonviolent soft-core pornography appears to have no direct effect on sex crimes or attitudes toward rape. However, aggressive sexual stimuli or hard-core pornography showing rape scenes heightens sexual arousal, increases acceptance of rape myths, desensitizes viewers to violent sexual acts, and leads them to see rape victims as less injured and less worthy (Milburn et al., 2000; Sharp and Joslyn, 2001). Although it is still unclear if the arousal actually leads to later aggression, some research shows that almost one-third of women who were sexually abused and/or raped reported that their abuser used pornography, and 12 percent said it was imitated during the abusive incident (Bergen and Boyle, 2000).

The issue of what constitutes pornography and whether it should be illegal is hotly debated (MacKay, 2001). One side of the debate focuses on pornography as implicitly condoning the victimization of women, arguing that sexual violence against women is increasing and pornography fuels the desensitization to sexual violence and rape. The other side contends that pornography may reduce sex crimes by providing a nonharmful release of sexual tension. Proponents of this view do not deny the association of pornography with women's degradation, but assert that campaigns against it obscure more urgent needs of women and denies income for women who are pornographic models and actresses. There is concern in both camps that banning pornography amounts to censorship in a free society. All factions do agree, however, that child pornography should be censored, and there is some consensus on the necessity of legally distinguishing pornography according to its degree of violent imagery.

People may not agree on the definition of pornography, and the empirical evidence of a causal link between pornography and sexual violence is debatable. This lack of agreement, however, does not justify ignoring the social issues surrounding pornography's role in socialization into masculinity and in reinforcing gender stereotypes. The effects of pornography will continue to be scientifically scrutinized to bolster or refute the claims of one side or the other in the debate.

Masculinity and Rape. Rape is a behavior learned by men through interaction with other men and is consistent in critical ways with socialization into masculinity norms related to antifemininity, toughness, sexual prowess, and aggression (O'Toole, 2007). Coupled with patriarchal beliefs about domination, these norms blend insecure and destructive masculinity with violence and sexuality, with rape as the end logic (Herbert, 2002).

Feminists and conflict theorists contend that power and patriarchy combine to spur rape and increasing sexual violence. Media representations often legitimize male aggression and reinforce gender stereotypes, especially in college life. Movies such as the classic *Animal House* serve to legitimate and dismiss men's sexual "antics," even if the behavior is a criminal offense that clearly harms women. Patriarchal norms that culturally condone relationships putting men in dominant and aggressive roles and women in passive and submissive ones are widely accepted (Anderson and Swainson, 2001). On a global scale, patriarchal norms regarding women as the sexual and economic property of men not only dismiss rape but often have few legal protections for its victims. Even if marital rape laws are in place, legal standards still largely treat rape not as a personal crime but as a property offense. Sex is viewed as part of the marriage agreement, whether the wife wants it or not. Both genders are socialized with these standards in mind. This view allows the victim to be blamed and in turn justifies the crime.

Domestic Violence and Battered Women

The dramatic increase in domestic violence makes the family home one of the most lethal environments in the United States. Intimate partner violence against women make up about one-fifth of all nonfatal violent crimes experienced by women. Although it cuts across all demographic groups, wife battering is more prevalent in families with low income and unemployment, isolation from kin and community, and alcohol use. It is spiking during the MR, particularly in cities with high job loss (Wexler, 2003; Human Rights Watch, 2008; Kohler and Cambria, 2009). When race is factored in, African-American women are twice as likely than white women to experience more violence and more severe violence. Privacy of the family, the reluctance of the police to get involved in family disputes, lack of consistent legal standards, and accepted masculinity norms make it difficult to get accurate statistics on all forms of family violence and abuse. Statistics on child abuse are more accurate because hospitals are now on the front line in investigations of possible cases. Wife battering is the most underreported of all crimes, and underreporting is linked with the persistent belief that wife beating is either not improper or a part of normal marriage (Buzawa and Buzawa, 2003).

Domestic violence encompasses a wide array of physical, sexual, and emotional abuse. Marital rape and wife beating have been commonplace throughout history, but until the mid-twentieth century, a husband's right to a wife's body was considered both as personal privilege and as amounting to legal right. Standards from English Common Law transported to the United States generally supported a man's right to beat his wife, even for such infringements as talking back to him. The infamous **rule of thumb** allowed a husband to beat his wife with a stick no bigger than his thumb.

All states now have laws against marital rape, but they vary considerably. A man may be prosecuted if there is obvious and sustained physical injury, the couple had separated or filed for divorce, or if his wife is physically or mentally incapacitated. He may be exempt if she fails to report it to the police within a specified period of time, if the couple is not legally married, or if there is a hint that she consented to intercourse. The vast majority of women raped by their spouses or partners do not report it, especially if no weapon was used or no physical injury was sustained.

The following overview suggests the extent and lethality of gendered domestic violence (Williams, 2003b; Dobash et al., 2004; McCue, 2008).

1. Over one-third of all women are victims of some type of sexual coercion with a husband or partner in their lifetime.
2. Domestic abuse is the leading cause of injury to women in the United States.
3. Both men and women assault one another in marriage, and mutual abuse is more common than either alone. However, a man's physical strength makes the consequences for a woman much more lethal.
4. One-third of all women who are murdered die at the hands of husbands or boyfriends.
5. Half of all homeless women and children are fleeing domestic violence.
6. Most family homicides are preceded by at least one call to the police for a domestic disturbance, often weeks before the murder.

Why Doesn't She Leave? When battering becomes public, many people express disbelief as to why women remain in abusive households. Referred to as **battered women's syndrome**, abused women often have a poor self-image, which contributes to their feelings of powerlessness and dependence. They may believe they are responsible for the violence against them and attempt to alter their behavior to conform to their husbands' expectations. Expressions of remorse by the batterer lead to a short-lived honeymoon period, followed by recurrence of the abuse, with the likelihood of its increasing in severity (Stahly, 2004). A pattern of *learned helplessness* emerges for these women: the beatings are endured, they feel guilty about them, and they are unlikely to confide to others about the situation. Battered women with small children often stay back because they are financially trapped and economically dependent. They fear for the lives of themselves and their children if they go to a shelter but are forced to return home. A woman is also at risk for increased violence if she threatens to leave, files for divorce, or calls the police, although attacks will most likely continue if she stays. The behaviors batterers use to control women are akin to hostage-taking. Women are held hostage (Stark, 2009; Walker, 2009a). To add insult to injury (literally), battered women may be denied health insurance because their lifestyles are considered too dangerous.

When abused women retaliate and kill their attackers, the courts are reluctant to use self-defense or battered women's syndrome as justifications for acquittal (Leonard, 2002). Many women do leave abusive husbands and partners, however, especially when they receive social support and legal help. Antistalking laws enacted to protect celebrities from deranged fans have been successfully used to protect battered women. More enlightened police responses to domestic violence calls, shelters for women and children, crisis hotlines, and self-defense classes also help (Jordan and Garlow, 2007). The murder of Nicole Brown Simpson elevated the issue of domestic violence to the public consciousness with clear evidence that she had been battered by her former husband, football star O. J. Simpson. This reminds us that battering happens not just in Hollywood but everywhere.

Sociological Perspectives. According to the functionalist perspective, the social organization of family life, with its intimacy and intensity of relationships, lays the groundwork for family violence. The functionalist perspective, however, does not hold up to cross-cultural evidence in cultures where domestic violence and rape are rare (Sanday, 2007). Feminist and conflict theorists argue that wife battering has not gained as much attention as child abuse, for example, because it remains subtly condoned by a social system that is inconsistent in enforcing the law (Dalton and Schneider, 2000). From these perspectives, the element of power offers the best explanation for all forms of family violence, rape, and partner battering. Violence is most common in societies where men hold power over the women and children in their families and least common in societies with high levels of gender equity. In all societies, egalitarian families have the lowest rates of domestic violence. The greater the power gap between partners, the greater the risk of violence against women. The underlying issue in almost all cases of men battering women is his perception that his position of dominance is threatened (Johnson, 2007). An interesting research finding also suggests that women who stray from traditional, feminine gender roles may be especially targeted for aggression by men (Reidy et al., 2009). These are the women who need to be "kept in their place." Men protect their masculinity and retaliate based on the perceived threat that their dominance is challenged.

THE MEN'S MOVEMENT IN THE UNITED STATES

Change cannot occur in a vacuum. As women take on new roles or expand old ones, changes inevitably occur for men, some of which they eagerly support, and others that they find unpalatable. The movement for male liberation originated on college campuses in the 1970s as a positive response to the feminist movement. Support for feminist causes and their involvement with feminist women as husbands, partners, and friends encouraged these men to reflect on how rigid conceptions about masculinity influenced their own self-image and their behavior toward other men. They were well aware, for example, that men who reject sexual bravado and oppressive behavior toward women are targets for ridicule and exclusion by other men and that definitions of masculinity disallowing expressions of vulnerability, nurturing, and caring undermined their overall well-being.

National Organization for Men Against Sexism

These men eventually formed the **National Organization for Men Against Sexism** (NOMAS) and have organized annual conferences on themes related to parenting, sexism, violence against women, sexuality, sexual orientation, and friendship. As a group to enhance men's lives under a banner of "pro-feminist, gay-affirmative, and anti-racist," this branch of the men's movement works on male liberation by consciousness-raising on the negative effects of striving for power and the disabling effects of unyielding masculinity (NOMAS, 2009). A key concern is how they can change a system in which violence against women is institutionalized. To this end, they have established counseling resources and support centers such as RAVEN (Rape and Violence End Now) and ALIVE (Alternatives for Living in Violent Environments) for men dealing with issues of masculinity and violence and for women seeking to escape violent relationships. NOMAS remains a viable presence on college campuses throughout the United States, attracting to their ranks students in a variety of disciplines and men who are clergy, academics, K-12 educators, and in the helping professions. Overall, however, NOMAS has not attracted working-class men and men of color from outside the student population. Neither has it attracted other professional men, particularly those representing the corporate, legal, or administrative elite.

Mythopoetic Men

The lack of public awareness of the first men's movement is revealed in how media publicized later men's movements. Media attention focused on poet Robert Bly's (1990) belief that men are caught in a toxic masculinity that demands efficiency, competition, and an emotional distance that separates them from one another. Rooted in a competitive work environment that keeps fathers absent from their families, Bly contends, boys turn to women to meet emotional needs. Using myths, art, and poetry as vehicles to access inner emotions, men must unearth and celebrate their lost natural birthright of righteous anger and primordial masculinity, which can be regained only in communion with men. Communication between men is encouraged, but the "soft male" who is out of touch with his masculinity and turns to women as authority figures as substitutes for absent or distant fathers is denounced. Through healing rituals at weekend retreats, men become aware of their animal instincts and come to embrace their full masculinity (Wilson and Mankowski, 2000).

Media were so swept away with Bly's ability to bring these men together that they referred to his following as *the* men's movement and erroneously reported it as the first social movement stemming from a general malaise of men (Adler, 1991:47). Currently it is referred to as the *mythopoetic* branch of the men's movement. The retreats are few and less attended, but its healing techniques are used by psychotherapists who believe that many men can be helped when they rediscover and repair the damage caused by father deprivation. Robert Bly continues to speak to large audiences. Unlike the profeminist NOMAS movement, which argues against men's privilege, the mythopoetic movement is promasculinist and seeks to heal men's pain by distancing them from women. However, mythopoetic men may reject rather than simply repackage patriarchy (Barton, 2006). The men attracted to the mythopoetic ranks tend to be powerful, straight, middle class, and white. They seek to change their lives by making success less a priority than emotional values and spiritual well-being (Magnuson, 2007, 2008). Economically successful men fill the mythopoetic ranks. Working-class men and men of color are virtually nonexistent.

African-American Men

Another branch of the men's movement focuses on the African-American male experience. Research shows that African-American males tend to construct definitions of masculinity in direct opposition to Euro-American male models (Harris et al., 1994). Feeling blocked in achieving masculine goals offered by mainstream society, these men may initially adopt the dominant hegemonic views of masculinity. Their values change, however, as they get older and recognize that the dominant model is deficient in light of the race and class cultural configurations of African-American men (Hunter and Davis, 1994). The 1997 "Million Man March" in Washington, D.C., organized by controversial Black Muslim leader Louis Farrakhan, was an effort to bring together African-American men in support of one another and to offer positive role models to young people and their communities.

Depending on the source of the evaluation, the effort got mixed reviews (Gabbidon, 2001). The media spotlighted positive role models, but the luster was tarnished by its antiwoman thrust and heavy infusion of patriarchy (West, 1999). Although all the national and international women's conferences welcomed men, the Million Man March did not invite women to join. And Farrakhan later applauded Iran for setting a shining example to the world on behalf of democratic principles. Iran's unquestionably brutal record regarding both women and democracy intensified any existing schism between men and women.

Promise Keepers

The Promise Keepers (PK), the newest branch of the men's movement, is the largest, drawing men tostadium events and to small group meetings for over two decades (Promise Keepers, 2009). Founded by Bill McCartney, former head football coach of the University of Colorado, PK is an evangelical Christian organization dedicated to reestablishing male responsibility in the family and overcoming racial divisions. Media coverage of PK has been so positive that some research suggests it is less like news and more like advertising (Claussen, 2000). Similar to both the mythopoetic and the African-American branches, PK sees the fatherless home as the source of America's problems. It is different, however, in that its foundation appears to resonate with many more men. To become a Promise Keeper, a man must pledge his commitment to seven "promises," including honoring Jesus Christ, practicing spiritual and sexual purity, and building strong marriages and families. PK is also founded on the goal to reconnect men to their families and to take back family leadership that "sissified men" abdicated, leaving women to fill the vacuum of leadership. As one PK leader suggests, men should not ask for their role back, but are urged to take it back (Healey, 2000:221). Although PK has distanced itself from political affiliation and its members, its goals for asserting Christianity into home and society closely parallel the agenda of the political right wing and the New Christian Right (Quicke and Robinson, 2000). This political avoidance but religious thrust has attracted many middle- and upper-class Protestant men to become involved with the movement (Lockhart, 2000).

Toward the Future

All branches of the men's movement believe women will be the ultimate beneficiaries of their agendas. New branches may be emerging but with more specific agendas, such as gay rights, father's rights, and Catholic-based men's spirituality (Crowley, 2008; Gelfer, 2008). Generally participants in the various branches know little about the other branches. When they do know about them, they tend to be lukewarm or wary about the motives. There is no sense of unity that brings all men together under an accepted banner (Fox, 2004). All the branches expect NOMAS share a promasculinist stance that supports traditional, nonoverlapping gender roles and largely exclude women from their ranks except as volunteers. In general, media have given high approval ratings to PK but have virtually ignored criticisms that the ultimate effect will be to subjugate women. PK leaders say that women need not be threatened because in the kingdom "there is no male or female." Feminists point out, however, that patriarchy and not partnership is the outcome. PK would agree.

Feminist men and women support men coming together in exclusive male groups for healing and sharing, but the promasculinist themes in all but NOMAS propose that women are responsible for the problems of men. Blaming serves to undermine dialogue, reinforce sexism, and distance men and women from one another.

Do these gatherings of men suggest that a mass-based men's movement—whether profeminist or promasculinist—has occurred? Four decades of evidence suggest that it has not. Although these are referred to as "branches" of a larger movement, there is virtually no overlap in membership, ideology, or goals. The first three do share prosmasculinist ideology but not in a way that would unite them under a common banner. Because of the small groups that come together outside the large stadium events, PK may be the most viable in its ability to attract large numbers of men in a sustainable way. It is not clear, however, if the numbers include many new recruits. In addition, membership and finances have fallen considerably since its 1996 peak, and unity is being eroded by differing beliefs about masculinity, evangelism, and religious inclusiveness (ecumenism). PK's racial unification goal has made little progress, failing to attract a significant number of men of color to its ranks. And it is difficult to assess the long-term effects of McCartney's admission that he had been unfaithful to his wife (Lundskow, 2002).

NOMAS has not received the level of publicity the compared to other three groups, but after almost 40 years it is still convening conferences and drawing together men who are supportive of partnering roles with women and who challenge masculinity norms. On college campuses across the country young men are dialoging with one another, sowing the seeds for a new generation of potential supporters. Latino men are gathering in small groups and discussing how the concept of machismo has harmed them and relationships with the women in their lives (Mena, 2000; Stasio, 2001). It remains to be seen if the other three groups will be as successful as NOMAS over the long run. The women's movement has touched the lives of millions of women; the same cannot be said for the men's movement.

Summary

1. Patriarchy and male domination dominate history. Historically, idealized masculinity is validated by war. The loss of employment during the Depression assaulted masculinity, but subsequent wars revitalized idealized older images. Sports is the contemporary way men use to validate masculinity.

2. Hegemonic masculinity offers versions of masculinity norms that vary by time and content. These norms include antifeminist, success, toughness, aggression, sexual prowess, and tenderness.

3. Homophobia, the fear and intolerance of homosexuals, is fueled by the antifeminine norm. Minority gay men are at higher risk of oppression and homophobia. Tolerance of gay men and lesbians is increasing; however, women are more tolerant than men.

4. The gay rights movement has helped men positively affirm their gay identity. One faction believes they share a common oppression with women; another faction believes it is better to capitalize on their advantage of being male, even if women are undermined.

5. Images of fatherhood are contradictory. The antifeminine norm and socialization for economic roles separate men from their children. Fathers desire roles that increase nurturing and involvement with their children. A father's inclusion in the childbirth experience and acknowledgement of his fears are examples.

6. Gender is less of a predictor of retirement satisfaction than are income and health. Most older men are concerned about sexual performance as they age, but few experience a midlife crisis. Whereas the empty nest syndrome is a myth for women, men whose

careers distanced them from children can have difficulty at this life stage. Grandfathering is particularly satisfying for men.

7. Roles for widows and widowers differ greatly, and data are unclear as to which gender fares better in these roles. Elderly widowers are more likely to remarry and have the highest risk for suicide of all age groups.

8. Traditional masculine gender roles are connected to increased violence against women. Media coverage heightens rape fears in women. Rape is perpetrated by a wide spectrum of men. Rapists do tend to have high needs for dominance, are isolated from others, use rape as revenge, and present rape in socially acceptable terms. Half of college men use some form of sexual aggression on a date; up to half of college women report sexual victimization.

9. Pornography as an influence in rape continues to be debated. There is agreement about its link to women's degradation and oppression. Hard-core pornography increases acceptance of rape myths and desensitizes viewers to violent sexual acts. Debates revolving around definitions of pornography, censorship, and the loss of income for women portrayed in pornography are unresolved.

10. Until the last half century marital rape and wife beating were seen as a husband's right. Marital rape laws exist but vary greatly in interpretation. Few women report marital rape.

11. Domestic abuse is the leading cause of injury to U.S. women, and one-third of murdered women are killed by husbands or boyfriends. Battered women's syndrome, learned helplessness, fear of retaliation, and economic dependence keep women in abusive relationships.

12. The men's movement in the United States is spearheaded by several groups, including National Organization of Men against Sexism (NOMAS), the mythopoetic branch, African-American men (Million Man March), and Promise Keepers. NOMAS is profeminist; all the others are promasculinist. NOMAS appears to be the most enduring.

Key Terms

battered women's syndrome 266	heterosexism 252	National Organization for Men Against Sexism 267
hegemonic masculinity 245	homophobia 252	
	life course 258	rule of thumb 265

Critical Thinking Questions

1. Identify the contemporary norms associated with hegemonic masculinity and document the consequences of these norms for men and their families and their relationships with women. What is the impact of gender socialization on reinforcing or challenging these norms?

2. Considering issues related to rape inside and outside marriage, domestic abuse, and pornography, what suggestions would you offer to policy makers seeking to reduce men's violence toward women? In your suggestions, account for legal issues related to men's rights and censorship and for the factors that may prevent women from escaping abusive relationships.

3. Compare the various "men's movements" in terms of their goals with specific reference to gender ideology, attitudes about masculinity, and gender roles in religion. Document the success of these movements according to their goals and prospects for longevity and sustained challenges to men's roles.

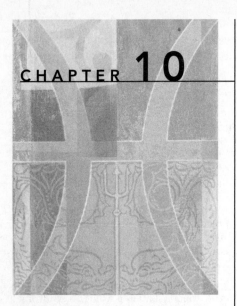

The devaluing of traits and activities stereotypically associated with women is deeply embedded in the economic rules and models. . . . So our hidden system of gendered values has shaped economic policies.

—Riane Eisler, 2007:36
The Real Wealth of Nations,

The adage that "a woman's place is in the home" no longer applies. Indeed, it never applied. Although it may express a nostalgic preference, historically it was never the norm and is not the current norm in the United States or globally. Women's unrelenting global march into the labor force in the twentieth century is associated with significant changes in the family and the workplace. Employed women are socially measured according to how their paid labor outside the home impacts their unpaid labor in the home. Their employers, however, measure them in the reverse—how their home-based labor impacts the manner in which they carry out their jobs. Sociologists are interested in the type of work men and women perform and why it is differentially valued. As we will see, the standards that women are expected to live up to in the home and the workplace routinely collide, and the choices they make relative to these standards are linked to all levels of economic disparity between men and women.

HISTORICAL OVERVIEW

Throughout history, women have made major economic contributions to their societies and families through their labor. Archaeological evidence from prehistory through to the written evidence of history clearly discounts the "nonworking" woman or "female frailty" myths that supposedly kept women from engaging in demanding work. Even today women grow and process over half the world's food, and in the developing world, women's subsistence agricultural activities are essential to feed their families (Chapter 6). To explain the world of work for women, sociologists focus on four major types of production in which women have traditionally engaged: producing goods or services for consumption within the household, producing goods or services at home for sale or exchange elsewhere (cottage industry), caregiving and volunteer work, and working for pay.

The Home as Workplace

Women's work roles traditionally have been closely tied to the home. For well over a century the United States had a family-based agricultural economy that required the services of all family members for a farm household to survive. Older children took care of their younger siblings so men and women could work together in the fields. In addition to cash crops, most family farms had gardens cultivated by women producing the family's food and allowing surpluses to be packaged for sale or exchange. Women produced cloth from raw material, and made soap, shoes, candles, and most other consumable items required for their households. In wealthier homes in the seventeenth and eighteenth centuries, female slave labor and paid female domestic servants produced the bulk of necessary items for their employers' households. In nonfarm households and family-owned businesses colonial women worked as paid and unpaid laborers, as innkeepers, shopkeepers, craftsworkers, nurses, printers, teachers, and child-care providers. In more remote areas, women also acted as dentists, physicians, and pharmacists. Married women were more likely to engage in home-related work activities, whereas widows and single women were more likely to work outside the home as paid employees. Regardless of marital status, immigrant girls and women often worked for pay, and were especially recruited for physically demanding jobs in agriculture. Like other women, however, a day of paid labor overlapped with the unpaid—but economically productive—labor at home (Chapter 5).

The Industrial Revolution. The Industrial Revolution indeed revolutionized the work worlds of men and women. First men and then women flocked from farms to factories as wage laborers in the burgeoning industrializing economy that desperately needed their services. With the advent of the water-powered textile factory in 1789, the Industrial Revolution made remarkable strides. Women and female children continued to be the producers of cloth, but now in the factory rather than at home. As exemplified by the famous Lowell Mills in Massachusetts, female employment in textile mills also reflected the lack of available male labor, which was still needed on the farm. The "Lowell girls" were well aware they were needed in the textile mills. They sometimes resorted to organized protests when the conditions under which they labored became intolerable (Dublin, 2009). Many of the other products women traditionally produced at home gradually switched to factory manufacturing. The transition of America and Western Europe from agrarian societies to urban industrial societies took about 150 years. When the family was transformed from a unit of production to a unit of consumption, a dramatic shift occurred in attitudes and norms surrounding the work roles of women.

Victorian Myths. By the end of the nineteenth century, Victorian norms ascended to define middle-class women as physically and mentally incapable of working in factories. The consequences of the myth of "feminine frailty" in the workplace that emerged during this era have not been eradicated. Among its negative effects, the myth created a class-based wedge between homemakers and women who either by choice or by necessity worked outside the home. Different from the young women who had a relatively sequestered existence during the Lowell era, later women factory workers were drawn from the ranks of recent immigrants, young girls from rural areas and mining towns who helped support their families, and widows with no other means of support. Their high illiteracy rates and farm backgrounds planted the seeds for stereotypes linking poor women as capable only for the physical labor required in factories. When paid work was available, these women did have one competitive advantage: They were white. In times of work surplus but worker shortage, women of color were employable in factories at lower wages and less desirable jobs than white women. Except as domestic workers and restaurant help, paid employment for women of color remained limited. Men of color who migrated off farms into the rapidly growing urban areas were employable as unskilled laborers in construction, as dockhands, and in other jobs requiring arduous physical labor. White women still had the advantage in factory work, especially textile production, over men of color. Service jobs demanded by an industrializing economy were open for white women with some education. The latter were deemed less frail than the robust factory women, but both groups garnered public disapproval for roles that put them in the public sphere outside the home.

In the western migration woman were valued for their nondomestic work and also expected to engage in it. For those who were literally tied to the home with child-care responsibilities, "homework" was an option, especially among poor immigrants. Mostly consisting of piecework, it was dependent on the whims of bosses and swings of a seasonal market and encouraged the exploitation of its dominantly female workers. The ideology of the time was that women's place was at home and, as exploitative as it was, "homework" allowed the ideology to be bolstered. However, most of these other groups, through necessity, were working outside the home. During the late nineteenth century the middle-class homemaker was the enviable standard to which women aspired. Poor women who worked outside the home were often demonized as unfit mothers who were neglecting their families (Broder, 2002). The statuses of full-time homemaker and employed woman have shifted considerably over time, but as we have seen, it is the homemaker status that continues to serve as the standard by which women are judged.

War and Jobs. In the nineteenth century women were establishing control in several occupations, including nursing and elementary school teaching. Although women began to enter the teaching profession by the beginning of the nineteenth century, the Civil War transformed teaching from a male to female profession. Women were able to retain their teaching jobs after the war not only because of the shortage of men, but because they could be paid less than the men they replaced. Rather than celebrating the care ethic that women brought to the profession—one that contrasted sharply with the physical discipline and harshness of male teachers of the time—teaching swiftly became viewed as an extension of motherhood. Women's biological qualities offered an advantage that required no special skill base. Historians of education trace the female takeover of teaching to the loss of pay and prestige that continue to plague the profession today (Edwards, 2002). Like teaching, clerical work was originally a male occupation. The invention of the typewriter in 1873 brought with it an increase in the number of clerical jobs and a large increase in female employment in those jobs. By the late 1920s, over half of all clerical workers were female, and even with upgraded skills demanded by word processing and a technologically driven workplace, today over 95 percent of secretarial and administrative assistant jobs are held by women (Coyle, 1929; U.S. Census Bureau, 2009). Like teaching, as women increasingly took over the male clerical positions, there was a marked decrease in the prestige and wages of these positions. Women remain concentrated in poorly paid **pink-collar jobs**, such as clerical and retail sales, associated with high competition, part-time work, lack of benefits, and few opportunities for advancement. Because such jobs continue to severely limit upward mobility both within and between jobs, women are said to be trapped in the "pink collar ghetto" (Mastracci, 2004). Over half of employed women are located there today.

The shortage of males in the labor force during the two World Wars again set the stage for the next wave of job opportunities open to women. During each war women replaced men in both factories and offices. World War I mainly reshuffled existing female workers into new areas rather than increasing overall participation rates and after the war women generally retreated back to their homes. As we saw in Chapter 5, the situation was different after World War II. Women were expected to return to hearth and home, but large numbers did not. They did lose the more lucrative industrial jobs, but a new trend developed—married women began entering the labor force in greater numbers—a trend that heralded major repercussions for all areas of American society.

BALANCING MULTIPLE WORK AND FAMILY ROLES

Social change and the specialization of functions that it brings inevitably create additional role responsibilities for both men and women. Demographic shifts account for many of these new or altered roles, such as increased numbers of dual-earner families, later and fewer marriages, fewer children, increased life expectancy, and the massive migration shifting employees across a nation and across the globe. For example, men who marry later are bringing a greater range of domestic skills into their marriages than the previous generation of men. Increased life expectancy has created an active and healthy aged population that is staying in the workplace longer and, especially among the poor, is taking on more child-care responsibilities in service to their own children. The rapidly increasing population of the oldest old, those aged 80 years and older, however, are at heightened risk for dependence. Job shifts that require a change of location for the family add to new role patterns in contemporary families. Whereas multiple roles are increasing for both genders, family responsibilities remain fundamentally women's tasks, regardless of whether she is a paid employee. But because the large majority of women *are* wage earners, compared to men, their enactment of the multiple roles is substantially different.

Employment and Health

Paid employment is a major determinant of good physical and mental health for men and women. In the United States and other societies where people are socialized into a strong work ethic, satisfying work enhances health, life satisfaction, and well-being (Theorell, 2001). The impact of work is evident in Sigmund Freud's answer to the question of what "normal" people should do well. For Freud, it is "to love and to work." Good psychological functioning emphasizes both one's work and one's family. The ideal is to create an environment where work and family are not opposed to one another.

Achieving this ideal is difficult, especially for women, whether in a dual-earner marriage or as a single parent. On the one hand, a rewarding job in general and a rewarding career in particular have beneficial effects for women's overall well-being. Work is not the brutal psychological jungle popularized in media accounts, and a rewarding career actually shields a woman against pressures encountered at home. Referred to as the *role enhancement hypothesis,* and contrary to what we might expect, multiple roles that include marriage, children, and satisfying work are associated with better health, enhanced self-esteem, and lower rates of depression. Women who are caregivers, who work, and who volunteer use multiple productive roles as sources of support that allow them to remain socially integrated. Balance at home and work is also important. Satisfying jobs and careers are optimized when marriages are egalitarian and domestic responsibilities are shared by spouses (Rozario et al., 2004; Barnett and Gareis, 2006; Chrouser and Ryff, 2006). Despite multiple roles, employed women are the healthiest and report feeling better about themselves than do full-time homemakers. An employed woman's income represents a huge mental health asset both on and off the job (Matthews and Powers, 2002; Elgar and Chester, 2007; Pearson, 2008). These studies suggest positive outcomes of multiple roles for women.

On the other hand, the mental health advantages of multiple roles are fewer for women compared to men, in part because work and family hold different gendered meanings. Women expect that their family roles will spill over to their jobs, but the life stage for this expectation is important. Wives and new mothers have more role balance but experience more job stress compared to husbands and new fathers (Etaugh, 2001; Marks et al., 2001). The *role overload hypothesis* suggests that women experience emotional distress when employment and the second-shift work of family and child-care roles put women into two full-time jobs. Employed women with children—whether married or not—report more health problems than women without children. The homemaker role by itself or the worker and single-parent roles in combination are the most stressful. Although income does not explain all the variation, it is an important factor in the poorer mental health associated with these roles. Single-parent women and single-earning men are less likely to have incomes that exceed household expenses (Gabe, 2003; He, 2007; Perry-Jenkins et al., 2007; Glynn et al., 2009). Role overload is also linked to unique stressors women face in the workplace, including gender discrimination, sexual harassment and stereotyping (Shrier, 2002).

Caregiving

Evaluation of multiple work and family roles must also account for caregiving to other than one's own children. The second shift of a woman's unpaid work is rapidly turning into a third shift for many homemakers and employed women who must care for the elderly who are part of their lives. Combined with the hours spent on housework, eldercare rather than child care is associated with more stress for women (MacDonald et al., 2005). A spouse is the first to provide care for his or her ailing partner. Because men become physically dependent and need extended care earlier in life than women, an elderly wife is much more likely to be the caregiver of her husband. The next level of responsibility falls on adult children. For the poor elderly, the next level is the network of extended family and kin. The final level is nonkin volunteers or paid caretakers who come to the home. When financial resources are depleted, they are moved to the extended care facilities (nursing homes) paid for with Medicaid funds. In these facilities, too, caretakers are virtually all female.

Although type of care and patterns of caregiving in families vary greatly, women are the primary caregivers to elderly parents, whether they are daughters or daughters-in-law. Referred to as the **sandwich generation**, they are caught between caring for the older and younger generations at the same time. Many of these women are middle aged, in the workforce, and still have children at home. Love, commitment, and responsibility describe caregivers. Other words to describe caregiving are guilt, burden, depression, and strain. Assistance to the elderly correlates with higher levels of caregiver strain and work interference than assistance to younger adults or children. The stress of the eldercare role for women is associated with compromises in both physical health and psychological well-being and is worsened for poor women who care for young children and parents with greater impairment at the same time (Stephens et al., 2001). Employed women report higher levels of job stress as their parents or grandparents become more debilitated and when one elderly parent can no longer take care of the other. Time away from spouse and children can negatively affect marriage and cause guilt when caregiving results in less affection to the parent (Rossi, 2001; Neal and Hammer, 2007). Although caregiving provides opportunities for adult children and elderly parents to grow closer, the positive psychological outcomes for both are often overshadowed by the demands of too little time to serve the needs of everyone—including the caretaker herself.

Unpaid Work

Women do the globe's unpaid second- and third-shift work of household tasks and caregiving. Economists have in effect ignored this productive work because it *is* unpaid. All work makes an economic contribution, but the unpaid work activities related to the home have been marginalized in economic rendering of production. According to Riane Eisler (2007:16),

> A much more sensible, and realistic, standard for what is given economic value is what supports and advances human survival and human development. By this standard, a *caring orientation*. . . . concern for the welfare and development of ourselves, others, and our natural environment is highly valued. So also is the work of caregiving and the creation of caring environments, whether in homes, business, communities, or governments.

In addition to the goods and services provided by the unpaid work of women discussed earlier, economic contributions include managing household resources, creating and maintaining the future labor force (children), and serving as an auxiliary labor force. In the United States the estimated yearly cost for services women provide for free—cooking, cleaning, shopping, child care, chauffeuring, repairing, counseling and therapeutic services, and sickness care—would cost well over $50,000. At the global level, if the unpaid work of women were added to the world's economy, it would expand by one-third. On the positive side, the economic reality of women's unpaid productive work is gaining public and governmental attention (Chapter 6).

Money and Mental Health. The better psychological health of an employed woman compared to a full-time homemaker is certainly associated with the income each receives. Dual-earning couples share spending decisions more equally than singe-earner couples (Lindsey, 1996c; Treas and de Ruijiter, 2008). When the husband is the sole wage earner, those wages are distributed in a variety of ways. Some wives receive their husband's paychecks and determine how the money will be apportioned; other wives receive "allowances" from their husbands that go toward household expenses. Regardless of how they determine the way the money will be spent, she has not "earned" it in the same way he has.

This perception contributes to the burden of dependency experienced by many housewives. A husband's economic leverage in the household is conducive to his wife's dependency. To a large extent, his paycheck becomes the controlling factor in her life. Many women who do not work outside the home find themselves in conflict-ridden, emotionally debilitating marriages but see no alternative but to remain where they are. Financial and psychological dependencies go hand in hand. Family dynamics change when a wife brings a paycheck into the home or when she outearns her husband. The shift to more egalitarian gender roles may also be traced to the fact that between one-third and one-half of married women now have incomes larger than their spouses (Labov, 2007; U.S. Census Bureau, 2009). Husbands may be threatened at the outset by the earning capability of their wives but are gratified when instrumental roles and financial household burdens are shared.

Summary. It is complicated to sort out all these variables to determine the specific sources of role strain. In combination with paid work, why are some caregiving roles more stressful than others? We can conclude, however, that the *number* of roles may be less stressful than the way women *perceive* the roles. Multiple family and work roles are most beneficial for women emotionally, physically, and financially when they perceive support from their partners or spouses at home, and from employers and colleagues at work (Greenglass, 2002; He, 2007; Henderson, 2008; Glynn et al., 2009). Research on multiple roles generally points to the benefits associated with the role enhancement hypothesis rather than the liabilities associated with the role overload hypothesis.

GENDERED INSTITUTIONS IN CHOICE OF WORK

Societies (cultures) are organized via *social institutions* to ensure that social needs are met in predictable ways (Chapter 3). It is difficult to separate out the impact of the various institutions on gender roles as related to work because the interaction effects are both complicated and powerful. As we saw in Chapter 8, there is a great deal of research on the influence of women's employment on their families. The focus here will be on the work–family connection in the other direction: the influence of women's family roles on their employment and workplace roles. A key issue in this connection is **work–family spillover**, the largely genedered attitudes and behaviors that carry over from roles in both social institutions. Economic effects reverberate throughout all the social institutions. Despite highly interdependent structures, sociologists agree that the economy is the key catalyst for shaping changes experienced in all the other social institutions.

The Influence of Family on Workplace

The transition from an agricultural to an industrialized economy profoundly altered the work roles of men and women and enlarged any existing gender gap between home and workplace. The outset of the transition for women led them from unpaid work on the farm to unpaid work in the family. Men were firmly established in their earner roles when women began to be tracked into the labor force in large numbers. These new female entrants quickly collided with cultural beliefs that viewed women disdainfully, suspiciously, or hostilely when they ventured out of their homes into paid employment. The instrumental–expressive schism that followed women into the workplace over a half century ago has not been eradicated.

Socialization. The family is the key force in gender socialization and primes children for later social roles, including the choices they make regarding work. The family can be further subdivided into two categories that differentially affect these choices. The first category, the **family of orientation**, is the family in which one grows up. In this first family a child gains a sense of self and a set of relative benefits based on the *social capital* the family offers to a child, such as material resources, housing, and education. Social capital is translated into opportunity structures for children. Because parents may be unable or unwilling to provide the same opportunity structures for all their children, social capital for boys is leveraged differently than social capital for girls. As discussed in Chapter 3, children receive gendered messages from parents related to, among others, clothing, toys, chores, dating, autonomy, and education. Children match these messages to attitudes about later job options. When fathers talk to their sons about the joys of caring for others and mothers talk to their daughters about the wonders of discovery and then actually see their dad as a preschool teacher or nurse and their mom as an engineer or scientist, then the seeds are planted for their children to select these job options.

The trend toward egalitarian marriages is challenging the gender messages children receive in the family of orientation that limit their horizons about the work choices they will make. Despite widespread messages about egalitarian gender roles, however, other agents of socialization counter them. The reality is that messages for girls continue to be focused on home and family taking precedence over paid work, and that for boys paid work takes precedence over family. Because the large majority of young women now say they desire a combination of family and career roles, the message that they hear is how to juggle, balance, and deal with these roles. Young men also expect to carry out both sets of roles, but they do not receive the "juggling" message received by young women. Their message is not how they will balance family and work but how they will pay for family through work.

The second category, the **family of procreation**, is the family established when one marries or establishes a long-term partnership. Because each partner brings a unique set of socialization experiences to this family and each has already lived through a generation of social change, this second family is more directly influenced by broader sociocultural factors regarding gender. As parents, both men and women will face a new set of family contingencies that impact roles in and out of the home. The family of procreation focuses on *continuing socialization*, since new parents must learn the skills in their struggle with the demands of raising children. There is little preparation for these roles, so the process appears to be one of trial and error. However, it is heavily influenced by the gender models of the family of orientation. Parents must reconcile personal desires for fulfillment and economic obligations to maintain the home, decisions that impact their children's quality of life. Although these factors affect parents' work-related issues, men do not have to face the struggle to "be employed or not be employed" as women do. Most partners opt for a dual-earning status before children arrive, and most women continue some level of paid work after they arrive. These decisions affect not only what happens to home-based roles, but also what happens to work roles.

The Child-Care Crisis. About two-thirds of all married women with children under the age of 6 are in the labor force (U.S. Census Bureau, 2009). Although the dual-earner family is the American norm, there is broad research agreement that women with children are significantly more likely to be employed if they have a college degree and if they have husbands who support their wives' choice to return to work. These households are likely to be child centered and generally egalitarian on attitudes about gender (see Chapters 7 and 8). Even in egalitarian marriages, however, wives spend significantly more time on child care and household tasks than husbands. Wives take the lead in organizing child-care arrangements for preschoolers and after-school activities for older children. When a child is sick, when there is an unexpected early dismissal from school, or when a day-care crisis arises, women are much more likely than men to accommodate their job schedule to resolve the problem. Work role quality and its rewards are reduced when women have children with temperamental or behavior problems (Daczo and Bianchi, 2003; Hyde et al., 2004; Beaujot and Liu, 2005). Care work—especially child care—is the determining factor for when and if a woman returns to paid work after the birth of her child.

Increased demands for child care come at a time when the supply of domestic help is shrinking, grandmothers (probable caretakers) are returning to the labor force, state budgets offering subsidized child-care vouchers have been slashed, and funding for preschool and after-school programs parents rely on heavily have been eliminated or, if retained, are unaffordable. As more women with young children join the labor force out of both desire and need, the child-care crisis must be addressed. This problem looms larger for single parents or women receiving public assistance who are required to work or be in work-training programs to preserve benefits. It is an issue that affects all working women and their families, regardless of the ability to pay for adequate care. Child-care issues have a major spillover effect on the career achievement of women.

Married with Children: The Demography of Career Achievement. Career achievement is also impacted by a host of other family-related variables including marital status, age at marriage, age at childbirth, and professional status when married. Women who marry after they have completed their education and began to ascend a career ladder bring more resources to their marriages and reduce the likelihood that their husbands expect them to give up their careers. Smaller family size and age of children also correlate with paid employment. The percentage of employed mothers decreases rapidly for families with five children or more and with at least two children under age 6. Compared to single women, married women have higher rates of interrupted job mobility—often to accommodate a career move for their husbands. Men report less satisfaction for their own work when they perform roles in support of their partners' careers. In addition, men's satisfaction at work is enhanced with relationship satisfaction; women satisfaction at work is enhanced with more egalitarian housework arrangements (Stevens et al., 2007). Interruption rates increase significantly for married women who stall careers or forego them altogether to raise children. Both groups of married women are likely to return to paid employment, but in less satisfying work situations and lower-paying jobs, rather than in more satisfying and higher-paying careers.

Opportunity structures in families encouraging a daughter's education have high payoffs in the workplace. The more education a woman has attained, the greater the likelihood that she will engage in paid employment. Conversely, the lower the educational attainment, the more likely a woman is a full-time homemaker. This pattern challenges the myth that those who have the choice would prefer exclusive domestic roles. By virtue of her education, she is the least likely to be financially dependent and the most likely to work outside the home. The combined impact of low education and a full-time homemaker role can have devastating financial consequences in the event of divorce or death of a spouse. Research on women who in the 1950s followed the "June Cleaver" stay-at-home model of marriage and motherhood with financial dependence on their husbands or sporadic work in low-paid jobs offering few benefits finds a significant number of them living in poverty or near poverty in their retirement years (Olson, 2003).

Career versus Job. Although all employed women have *jobs*, they do not necessarily have meaningful *careers*. Jobs interfere with family in a different way than careers. A career orientation is associated with men and women in the professions who have a high degree of commitment, personal sacrifice, and a planned developmental sequence (career path). In addition to the family factors noted earlier, career orientation for married women is compromised when a wife's career is viewed as less important than her husband's career. For example, she will relocate to benefit his career but his relocation for hers is unlikely. When he outearns her, his career takes on more importance and will be nurtured to gain higher income returns.

The success stories of women who "have it all"—great marriages, wonderful children, rewarding careers—are replete. Women are in a second wave of progress, moving up the corporate ladder or advancing through their own business enterprises. They have found ways to favorably reconcile problems between career and family, such as buying services for household tasks and high-quality child care, telecommuting from home, or staying on career tracks through flexible work time options. These women, however, are the exception to the rule. The rule is that women may combine work (jobs) and marriage successfully, but they are severely compromised in their quest for upward career mobility by marital and family obligations and traditional beliefs about his breadwinning role compared to hers. Young couples advocate the ideal that career satisfaction is important for both men and women, but they believe one partner should always be home with children (Pavalko and Henderson, 2006; Koski, 2007). That partner, of course, is a wife. Women's careers are put on hold, change directions, or abruptly end.

Employer Views. Employers are well aware of these trends. Highly educated women have greater leverage in the workplace because they are viewed as having higher commitment to their jobs. It is illegal for employers to overtly use marital status or age of children in hiring, but such decisions are routinely made covertly. Even married women with children who are in professional careers are often considered a liability because employers believe they will favor family over workplace when the inevitable juggling act occurs. For women, marriage may send a signal that she has a different set of priorities. As sexist as it is, an employer often interprets marriage and children as making a woman less reliable, dedicated, and permanent. Postponing children increases lifetime earnings for women. A single break in employment has immediate, adverse effects, which translates into lower wages and job status. Women in management, for example, are often tracked into two distinct groups: those with a career and family and those with only a career. The former may be "mommy track" women who are not expected to adhere to the same standards as corporate women choosing faster-track career options. Businesses justify this track by arguing that their investment in women managers is lost when careers are interrupted by family concerns. When they return to the corporate world, the dues they pay go beyond catching up on seniority or retooling their skill base. They are treated virtually as beginners. For those who scale back even one day a week, that one day keeps them behind in their careers in terms of salary, title, and responsibility. For women planning to "have it all," timing is everything (Hudson, 2003:C3).

Married men, on the other hand, are considered an asset if they are married with children. Employers view a man as more stable and committed to his job and job location if he has children in school and he and his family are involved in a range of community activities and organizations. From an employer view, another important criterion in judging the potential for the success of his male employee is that that he has "wifely support" for demanding work roles. The vast majority of the top corporate executives in the United States are not only married men but also include

> stay-at-home wives ever ready to journey with them and be at their sides in public. (For) corporate executives . . . she planned the dinner parties, kept house in fitting style and . . . kept pace with his rising social requirements. The duties of running a corporation are so varied and relentless that no rational man tries them solo if he can split them with a wife. (Walsh, 2001:3)

A reading of these trends may make it appear that an employer is justified about hiring preferences for married men with children over married women with or without children. Often overlooked factors, however, are that there are no significant gender differences in job commitment, loyalty to firm, leadership effectiveness, and most important, number of jobs over time held by professional men and women (Bureau of Labor Statistics, 2006; Dey and Hill, 2007). Any reading of the demographics of career achievement needs to account for the gender stereotypes that lurk behind differential hiring practices and promotion for men and women.

Economic Trends and the Family

Economic trends filtering down to the family reinforce the employment choices of men and women. Women are welcomed into the labor force during times of need, such as war, during periods of economic growth, such as the Industrial Revolution, and in transitions to new economic forms, such as the shift from advanced machine technology in a manufacturing economy to the information technology demanded in a knowledge-based service economy. During these times women function as a reserve labor pool to be called on or discarded as needs change. Women, therefore, could not rely on stable employment. Today's postindustrial era, however, requires workers with an education and skill base women are now more likely to possess. In this sense, women are catching up with men in opportunities for more stable employment.

Postindustrial societies are also unprecedented in their consumption orientation and target services and products to market niches based on household characteristics. The United States is a consumer society and the majority of consumption is done by women as they carry out their family roles related to daily household spending. Employed women have less time but more money available for consumption; the American economic system has responded to this reality. The retailing sector, in particular, caters to employed women by lengthening times they are open, by locating near homes and new housing developments, through the use of mail catalogs, and increasingly, through the web marketplace. Although the family exerts counterpressures on women in these consumer roles, they emerge overall in a position of strength. The resources offered by stable employment, combined with the traditional role of overseeing the daily household spending, make employed women a formidable economic force. Conflict theorists suggest that these combined roles offer them advantages that translate into more power in their families and the workplace.

The Legal System

Propelled by the equality goals of the women's movement and minority rights movement, an array of legal and political decisions have had a major impact on gender patterns of employment and women's work roles. This is discussed in detail in Chapter 14. This section overviews key legislative actions related to two of the most important gendered economic challenges: the work–family spillover and the wage gap.

Both directions of the work–family spillover are addressed in the **Family and Medical Leave Act (FMLA)**, passed in 1993. This act allows eligible employees to take 12 weeks of unpaid leave per year for the birth and care of a newborn or an adopted or foster child and to care for spouse, child, or parent with a serious health condition. In 2009, FMLA was expanded to 26 weeks of leave in a single 12-month period to care for a service member recovering from a serious injury or illness incurred while on active duty. FMLA is intended to be gender neutral, but it is apparent that it was written with women as caregivers in mind. How successful is FMLA and other workplace benefits that address workplace spillover, especially the crisis in child care?

On the positive side, women are more likely to take advantage of workplace flexibility and family leave policies than are men and these are associated with higher rates of retention for women. Both white women and men and women of color are likely to take family leave compared to white men. Men of all races take shorter leaves than women. In dual-earner couples a woman's unpaid leave does not have as severe economic consequences for the household. Perceived family-work balance is also linked to leave policies that benefit both men and women (Armenia and Gerstel, 2006; Noonan et al., 2007). On the other hand, FMLA does not address the child-care crisis in any meaningful way. Women continue to exit jobs when quality, affordable child care is unavailable (Gordon et al., 2008). Single parents and poor women use unpaid leave as the final option when their children are in crisis (Gault and Lovell, 2006; Gordon et al., 2008). Australia and the United States are the only two developed world nations without paid family leave. The influx of women in paid employment and, increasingly, in the military would appear to indicate that "separation of spheres" beliefs can no longer be sustained. FMLA, however, may have preserved this separation by its very limited substance and scope (Berggren, 2008).

On the wage gap issue, the *Equal Pay Act* (EPA), passed in 1963, is the first federal legislation that addressed the issue of equal pay for men and women. It allows for differences in pay based only on a nondiscriminatory seniority system, a merit-based system, or "piecework" basis. Although originally designed with minority men in mind, the most important legal prohibition against gender discrimination in employment is **Title VII of the 1964 Civil Rights Act**. The language is not gender neutral but the following two key provisions affecting women make discrimination and occupational segregation illegal.

1. To fail or refuse to hire or to discharge any individual, or otherwise discriminate against any individual with respect to his compensation, terms, conditions, or privileges of employment, because of such individual's race, color, religion, sex or national origin; or
2. To limit, segregate, or classify his employees in any way which would deprive or tend to deprive any individual of employment opportunities or otherwise adversely affect his status as an employee, because of such individual's race, color, religion, sex or national origin.

In 1972, Executive Orders extended the provisions of the Civil Rights Act legislation to all federal contracts. *Title IX* of the 1972 Educational Amendments further extended them to all educational programs or activities receiving federal funding. EPA and Title VII of the Civil Rights Act have allowed the "equal work for equal pay" doctrine to resound throughout the American economy, and it is difficult to formally circumvent them. However, both laws are vulnerable to the gendering of occupations and the informal systems that evolve in the workplace.

Recognizing the realities of a continuing gender and race wage gap, the legal approach was altered from simply barring discrimination to "preferential" treatment through **affirmative action** to women and minorities underrepresented in certain job categories. Affirmative action has had more positive effects for women entering professions (although not for women already there) and management positions. However, with the decline in skilled trade jobs and the limited number of women in these and other blue-collar categories, most employed women have not benefited from the job integration policy. The positive effect of affirmative action has not reached the bulk of women who work in lower-level jobs and has not redressed continuing wage inequalities that still exist a half century after these legislative efforts (Badgett and Lim, 2001; Wolf-Devine, 2002). And as we will see in Chapter 14, because affirmative action is intimately but erroneously linked in the public eye with quotas and reverse discrimination, it is on the political chopping block and may not survive in a viable form.

Comparable Worth. This is another strategy that carves a rocky path through legislative and judicial processes, and like affirmative action, the evidence is mixed in terms of its success (Hattiangadi, 2000). **Comparable worth** aims to upgrade the wage scales for jobs that employ large numbers of women. Because comparable worth arguments were successfully used in Washington and California when it was documented that women received far less pay in comparable jobs, such as police and fire dispatching, most states have taken some legislative action to deal with broadly based pay inequity.

The judicial thrust has been generally the same as the legislative by emphasizing that employers cannot discriminate on the basis of gender if a woman meets the necessary qualifications. Working with the *Equal Employment Opportunity Commission (EEOC)*, the judiciary oversees the thousands of gender discrimination cases that have arisen since the 1960s. A landmark case demonstrates the importance of these actions. The 1971 unanimous Supreme Court decision in *Reed v. Reed* ruled that an Idaho law giving males preference over females in selecting administrators of an estate was in violation of the Fourteenth Amendment. This was the first time the Court ruled that an arbitrary discrimination law against women was unconstitutional.

Political and legal mandates have helped remove barriers that unfairly limit or circumscribe women's potential employment choices. They cannot focus on the individual decision-making process that is viewed as the personal province of a woman and her family. Fueled by the Millennium Recession (MR), however, the political atmosphere has changed considerably.

Gender, Unemployment, and Recession. The employment advocacy of the 1970s gave way to the entrenchment of the 1980s, moderate backlash in the 1990s, and severe backlash in the first decade of the millennium. In tracking unemployment over time in the United States, the Bureau of Labor Statistics gathers data on unemployed job seekers. As recession moved into its second year in 2009, men's unemployment rose at a faster rate (2.8 percent) that the rate for women (1.6 percent); over two-thirds of rise in unemployment has been among men. Only once since World War II—in 1983—has men's unemployment been higher than that for women (Boushey, 2009). Unemployment data suggest, too, those women who are *not* employed, such as homemakers, rather than those who are *unemployed*, are gaining jobs because their husbands are out of work.

Gender differences in employment also need to account for the type of jobs that women are getting compared to the types of jobs men have lost. Given factors such as the wage gap and the pink-collar job options, itis clear that newly employed women will not make up the income deficit in their households. The Obama administration's stimulus package for job creation during the MR targets jobs traditionally held by men, such as road and bridge building. As of this writing, however, the package is shifting to jobs in health care and education that are traditionally jobs for women. Yes, a job is a job. But will it pay enough to keep families reasonably solvent until the recession wanes? It is unclear how these policies will fare in the short run, but a renewed commitment to gender fairness and social justice is needed to take legislative accomplishments well into the twenty-first century. It is important to carefully monitor gender trends in unemployment during the recession:

> Too many layoffs are based on gender-biased evaluations. . . . In this dire turndown, we can't allow the economy to be used as an excuse for gender bias and roll back progress we've made. (Neil, 2009)

WOMEN IN THE LABOR FORCE

The dramatic, consistent increase in the labor force participation of all categories of women is the most important economic trend of the last century. Almost 60 percent of all women 16 years and over are in the labor force and the participation rate of married women with children has tripled since 1960. About 70 percent of all mothers are employed and over half have children under one year of age. Female single parents (single, divorced, separated, or widowed) participate in even greater proportions: over 75 percent in 2009, a two-thirds increase just since 1965. The percent of middle-age (45–64), college-educated women in their peak earnings years has gradually increased since 1970 and shows a record of stable employment, but lower earnings than men with comparable education. As women's paid work has increased, men's labor force participation shows consistent declines, from a high of about 87 percent in 1947 to 74.7 percent in 2000 and projected to decrease another 2 percent by 2015. Women now represent half of *all employed people* in the United States (U.S. Bureau of the Census, 2009). If these trends continue, the proportion of women in the labor force may exceed that of men (Table 10.1).

Gender-Typing in Occupational Distribution

As would be expected, women are not equally distributed throughout the occupational structure. Although women make up almost half of top-level managerial and professional occupations and require requisite educational credentials even at the entry level, the jobs they hold are occupationally segregated. For example, the professional category includes accountants, architects, and engineers, who are largely male, and teachers, nurses, and social workers, who are largely female. Although all these occupations require high levels of education, the female occupations are far lower in degree of pay, prestige, authority, and other job-related reward criteria.

Occupational segregation by gender bolsters **gender-typing**—when the majority of the occupations are those of one gender, it becomes a normative expectation and, in turn, the job is associated with less pay and prestige. Referred to as the "devaluation thesis," gender-typing translates to a wage penalty for people working in occupations that are dominated by females (England et al., 2000). Gender-typing extends to the way a job is perceived. Nursing, social work, and teaching are "engendered" as feminine professions linked with caring and nurturing. Nursing, in particular, is

Table 10.1 Labor Force Participation by Gender, Race, and Marital Status, Selected Years and Projection

	Year						
	1980	1990	2000	2005	2007	2009*	2016
Gender							
Total Employed Women	51.5	57.5	59.9	59.3	59.3	59.5	59.2
Total Employed Men	77.4	76.4.	74.8	73.3	73.2	72.1	72.3
Female Employment by Marital Status							
Single	64.4	66.7	68.9	66.0	65.3	x	x
Married with spouse	49.8	58.4	61.1	60.7	61.0	x	x
Employment by Race and Gender							
White Female	51.2	57.4	59.5	58.9	60.4	60.5	58.4
White Male	78.2	77.1	75.5	74.1	74.0	75.4	72.9
African American Female	53.1	58.3	63.1	61.6	61.1	64.1	63.1
African American Male	70.3	71.0	69.2	67.3	66.8	70.4	67.1
Latino Female	47.4	53.1	57.5	55.3	56.5	x	57.8
Latino Male	81.4	81.4	81.5	80.1	80.5	x	70.0

*Mid-year average

Sources: U.S. Census Bureau, *Statistical Abstract of the United States, 2009*. Adapted from Tables 568 and 576; and A-4, www.bls.gov/web/cpseea4

increasing its professional status by successful challenges to the jurisdictional boundaries determined by physicians. Until recently, nursing as a female-dominated profession has been in virtual servitude to the male-dominated profession of medicine. Nurses are also finding allies in female physicians who are adopting morecare-oriented rather than compliance-oriented patient strategies that parallel nursing strategies. Upgrading the profession as a whole has challenged both the gender-based and the occupationally-based hierarchy of medicine and health care.

Men on the Escalator. These professions provide examples of what happens when men enter predominately female occupations. In tracing the trajectories of males in female-dominated occupations, although men face some disadvantages, they have more advantages than women in these jobs. In such jobs males are likely to hold the higher positions. They differentiate themselves from the devalued female work they do by dominating "that which is female." Males who cross over into nursing, social work, elementary school teaching, and librarianship face some prejudice from those outside the professions, but have clear advantages inside them. Both men and women employed in nontraditional occupations (as defined by gender) face discrimination, but the forms and consequences are different for males in female professions than the reverse. Both genders perceive that men are given fair, even preferential, treatment in hiring and promotion, are accepted by supervisors and colleagues, and are integrated into the subculture of the workplace. The subtle mechanisms that enhance a man's position in these professions are referred to as the *glass escalator effect* (Williams, 2003a).

Men take their gender privileges with them to female occupations and experience acceptance from their colleagues and upward mobility. However, men experience the glass escalator differently depending on factors such as the man's race and the type of women's profession he enters. In nursing, for example, recent research suggests that African-American men must contend with more unfriendly interaction from colleagues and patients regarding their "suitability" in a profession that is viewed not only as a female job, but as a *white* female job. As an African-American male nurse reports,

> . . . being a Black male is a weird position for me. . . . a white male patient (will say), "where's the pretty nurse? Where's the blonde nurse? (I say) . . . You don't have one. I'm the nurse. (Wingfield, 2009:18)

Older white women may flat out refuse treatment from a black male. On the other hand, white male nurses must routinely explain that they are nurses to patients who assume they are doctors. And male nurses of all races must contend with homophobia constructing them as gay, in turn exposing them to stigma from patients and coworkers (Harding, 2007).

More research is needed to determine how race, heterosexism, and gender intersect to buffer the glass escalator for men. We can conclude, however, that even when the occupation is designated female, regardless of race, most women are subordinate to the men who hold the most powerful supervisory and high-paying positions. This is referred to as *hierarchical segregation* and is a strategy that further prevents women from earning equal pay and exercising equal authority with men.

Women in the Professions. Women have significantly increased their numbers in the professions. There is now a higher percentage of women in management and professional occupations than there are men (Figure 10.1). Women are rapidly moving into elite professions such as law, medicine, and

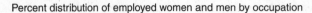

Percent distribution of employed women and men by occupation

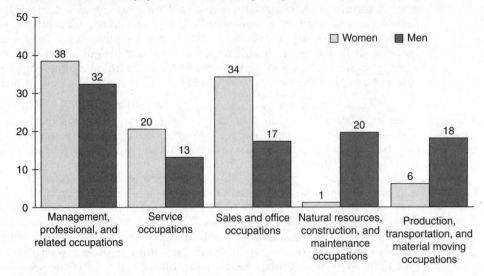

Figure 10.1 Women and Men in Selected Occupational Categories

Source: U.S. Department of Labor, Bureau of Labor Statistics. *Charting the U.S. Labor Market in 2006.* August, 2007. www.bls.gov/cps/labor2006

university teaching. About one-third of practicing physicians and lawyers are women, and they will represent over half of these professions by the next decade. Although these gains are impressive, gender-typing is pervasive. The majority of women professionals are in two categories, nursing and teaching, and command less pay than men in the other occupations making up the professions, such as engineering and computer science. In the "elite" professions, women are clustered in the overcrowded, less prestigious specialties that are considered more appropriate for women in male-dominated professions (Bagilhole, 2002). In medicine, for example, men make up large proportions of surgeons, cardiologists, and emergency medicine (EM) physicians; women make up large proportions of pediatricians, psychiatrists, and public health physicians. Women in EM do not report difficulty with balancing work and family time, but they do perceive less control over their work situation, see few leadership positions available, and perceive less organizational support. Job satisfaction decreases, and compared to men, they are less likely to stay in EM (Pachulicz et al., 2008). Males choosing female-dominated medical specialties are now likely to have completed much of their medical training in other countries. Thus physicians in less prestigious specialty areas are likely to be women and ethnic minority men.

Women attorneys are more likely to specialize in trusts, estates, family, and tax law and are more likely to be employed by the government or are in solo practice. Men are more likely to specialize in more lucrative trial, corporate, and international law and be employed in larger, prestigious, law firms. Women attain partnerships at slower rates than men. Women represent only 17 percent of partners in major law firms. Although this total is low, it does represent a four percent increase in less than a decade. Women of color are virtually invisible as law partners, representing only 4 percent of all women partners. Over 80 percent of minority female associates leave their law firms within five years of being hired (American Bar Association, 2006a, b). Women engineers make up about 10 percent of the total, and they are more likely to specialize in chemical and environmental engineering and work in manufacturing and service firms. Men are more likely to specialize in higher-paid aerospace and electrical engineering and work in consulting and service firms. The salaries of women in all science and engineering fields are lower than their male counterparts with similar levels of experience. Even as women are gaining math and science educational parity with men, the gender gap in engineering, especially in the more highly paid prestigious specialties, is increasing (Guizzo, 2008).

The increase of women throughout professional and managerial jobs is impressive, but to move from the periphery to the center of their professions they must gain access to the networks offering visibility, leadership mentoring, and the highest career mobility (Warren, 2009). The net result of these stubborn trends for professional women is less pay, less prestige, and less authority.

White-Collar Women. The many overlapping categories of white-collar occupations employing women do include those in the elite professions. Although many are college degree holders, compared to men, women represent the large majority of the nonmanagerial jobs clustered in less technical areas, especially in pink-collar jobs. Office jobs in particular exhibit strong patterns of gender-typing and are stratified according to gender. Lower-level clerical staff are managed by women who in turn are managed by both men and women. The higher-ranked white-collar jobs in offices are managed by men and at the highest ranks men manage the male executives directly under them.

Some change in these patterns is evident. White-collar women at all levels are reaping benefits in companies that promote from within and train workers in a variety of tasks that "cross over" to the other gender. Management streams are rapidly diversifying. Pink-collar women may be the last to benefit as these changes filter down, but research suggests that gendered management hierarchies are eroding (Ocon, 2006; Gatrell and Swan, 2008).

The lines between white-collar, pink-collar, and blue-collar jobs and between professional and nonprofessional jobs are blurry ones. Even when separating jobs by pay and level of education, categories overlap a great deal. The most common occupations for women include jobs in all categories (Table 10.2).

Blue-Collar Women. Women are most underrepresented in blue-collar, transportation, and nonfarm labor areas. Barriers have been legally lifted for women to pursue the skilled, elite blue-collar trades to become plumbers, electricians, machinists, carpenters, and craftspeople. However, they have not done so to any great degree. For those women who do enter the skilled trades, they remain in the female-dominant ones, such as dressmaker and electronic equipment assemblers. The resistance to women in the blue-collar trades remains strong. Even among lower-level semiskilled operative jobs, which can be learned quickly, women are underrepresented in those that are unionized. They have made their greatest strides in public sector operative jobs such as letter carrier and bus driver, where their numbers have more than doubled since 1980. Nevertheless, they are virtually invisible in the higher-paying skilled trades. Over 90 percent of precision production, craft, and repair occupations are held by men. The majority of women who hold blue-collar jobs perform those that require few skills, have poor working conditions, have high fluctuations in employment, and command low pay.

Table 10.2 Ten Leading Occupations of Employed Women

Occupation	Percent Women
Secretaries/administrative assistants	96.1
Child-care workers	95.6
Receptionist/information clerks	93.6
Registered nurses	91.7
Bookkeeping/accounting clerks	91.4
Maids/housekeeping cleaners	89.7
Nursing/psychiatric/health aides	88.7
Personal and home care aides	85.4
Elementary and middle school teachers	81.2
Cashiers	75.5

Source: U.S. Department of Labor, Women's Bureau, 2008. Adapted from *Leading Occupations of Employed Women* (2008 Annual Averages). www.dol.gov/wb/factsheets

Blue-Collar Men. Minority men are also likely to be in the lower paid blue-collar ranks but they are paid more than women. The skilled elite trades are reserved for white men, fewer men of color, fewer white women, and even fewer women of color. Occupational segregation persists, however, regardless of race. Auto mechanics earn almost double the annual salary of bank tellers. Perhaps more startling is the average salary comparisons between mid-career blue-collar men in the skilled trades and graduate level white-collar women professionals. Heating and air conditioning mechanics' earnings are 13 percent higher than that of reference librarians; bricklayers' earnings are 8 percent higher than that of social workers (Pay Scale, 2009). The skilled elite jobs are reserved for men.

Despite the gaps between pink-collar women and blue-collar men, the large majority of blue-collar workers hold the lowest-paid unskilled or semiskilled jobs. The gendered reality, however, is that blue-collar jobs for women are paid less than those for men (Table 10.3).

Jobs Ratios and Gender Beliefs. Gender-typing of occupations is a fundamental part of the U.S. economic system, though it violates one of capitalism's basic premises—obtaining the best person for the job—especially as it acts to limit or channel women's choice of jobs. Gender-typing links occupational roles with gender roles and tends to designate female occupations, such as nursing and social work, as those involving nurturing, helping, and high levels of empathy. Psychology and counseling are fast becoming female-dominated fields. Conversely, occupations associated with detachment, leadership, and outspokenness, like medicine and politics, are designated as masculine. When women do move into these fields, they tend to adopt the behavioral traits that retain the masculine qualities.

Although gender-typing is generally universal throughout the occupations, some jobs have changed their gender distribution, such as pharmacy and realty, and are now female dominated. And we have already seen that teaching and secretarial work were transformed from male to female. These patterns are important in countering the argument that gender-typing is based on the "naturalness" of one gender or another being suited for a given occupation. The exposure of flaws in the stereotype that "women take care" and "men take charge" in the workplace will benefit women and their employers (Catalyst, 2005).

Table 10.3 Ten Lowest-Paying Occupations and Earnings for Men and Women

Women's Occupations	Median Weekly Earnings
Counter/coffee shop attendants	$299
Food preparation workers	$338
Food serving workers/fast food	$341
Laundry/dry-cleaning workers	$345
Agricultural workers	$346
Cashiers	$349
Cooks	$363
Servers (waitresses)	$367
Hand packers/packagers	$368
Maids/cleaners	$371

Men's Occupations	Median Weekly Earnings
Dishwashers	$367
Food preparation workers	$368
Service station attendants	$378
Dining room attendants/bar helpers	$394
Cashiers	$399
Agricultural workers	$402
Cooks	$404
Hand packers/packagers	$410
Laundry/dry cleaning workers	$414
Grounds maintenance workers	$422

Source:Institute for Women's Policy Research. IWPR #C350a: April, 2009. Adapted from Table 3: Gender Wage Gap by Occupation. www.iwpr.org

The Wage Gap

As measured by median annual earnings of full-time employees, women earn less than men, a global pattern that holds across all racial and ethnic groups, all levels of education, and as we saw earlier, throughout occupations. The wage gap has profound consequences. If both men and women were paid equally, more than half of low-income households in the United States would be lifted over the poverty line.

The gender wage gap has been a persistent economic fact in the United States since records have been available (Figure 10.2). This pattern also holds globally in both the developed and the developing world and accounts for occupational segregation, initial salary, and family obligations. The gender earnings gap in affluent nations such as the United States and Britain endures even when powerful demographic variables are added to the picture, including age, type of job, seniority, and region. It holds for women who have continuous full-time employment, have no children, and express no desire for children (Aisenbrey and Brückner, 2008; Manning and Swaffield, 2008). The strong emphasis that Americans place on talent and achievement to pay off in the workplace cannot explain why at all educational levels males still outearn females, and why the gap widens at the higher educational levels. The gap is largest at the very *highest* education levels. The wage gap for a full-time woman worker costs her over $700,000 in her lifetime; women with advanced degrees employed in high-paying occupations can expect an astounding $2 million less than comparable men (Murphy, 2006; Compton, 2007; Black et al., 2008). The wage gap starts early in life, widens with age, and follows her into retirement. Median pension wealth, for example, is over

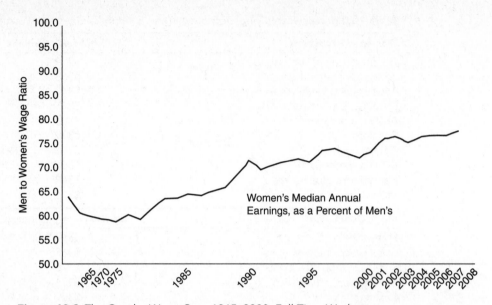

Figure 10.2 The Gender Wage Gap, 1965–2008, Full Time Workers

Source: Institute for Women's Policy Tesearch. IWPR #350: April, 2009. Adapted from *The Gender Wage Gap*. www.iwpr.org

three-fourths greater for men than women, a situation contributing to poverty of women at old age (Tamborini, 2007; Besen-Cassino, 2008; Hartmann, 2009).

With historical exceptions such as the Great Depression and World War II, the wage gap gradually narrowed during the twentieth century. We saw that economic recession hits women harder than men. Between 1967 and 1974, for example, the gap widened from 62 percent to less than 61 percent. In 1980 a woman employed full-time earned about 65 cents for every dollar a man employed full-time earned; that figure remained stagnant at 75 cents in the 1990s and is about 77.5 cents today. The narrowing of the wage gap in two decades by less than one cent per year is certainly debatable as a sign of progress. It is more important to note, however, that since the wage gap stagnated for 20 years, the current wage gap cannot be traced to the economic turndown. In addition, women's relative gains came largely because men are earning less, a trend that is expected to accelerate (Blau and Kahn, 2006; IWPR, 2006, 2008).

Triple Jeopardy: Gender, Race, and Social Class. Occupational distribution of minority women reflects changes in the labor force as well as gender inequality. After World War II, large numbers of African-American women moved into government white-collar and clerical jobs and the lowest-level private sector jobs, such as data entry or filing clerks. Wage levels of minority women are less than those of men of the same group. African-American, Asian-American, and white women earn two-thirds to four-fifths of what men earn, with the greatest disparity occurring between white men and white women. Rooted in a tradition valuing economic opportunities for women, African-American middle-class women moved into the professions earlier than white women. Like white women, they are steered into traditionally female occupations, but they have an added race liability. Concentrated in the public sector, such as teaching and social work, there is not only less discrimination but also less pay (Higginbotham,

2002). Although white women are also segregated in female-dominated professions, they are represented throughout the private sector where pay is higher. Overall, white women have not experienced as sharp a decline in earnings as have African-American women in the last two decades (Newsome and DoDoo, 2006).

Sexual Orientation: A Paradox? Pervasive heterosexism in the United States would predict another layer of economic jeopardy for gay men and lesbians compared to heterosexual men and women. This is not borne out by research. A number of research studies confirm that there is an earnings penalty for gay men relative to heterosexual men, but an earnings premium for lesbian women relative to heterosexual women (Schmitt, 2008). Lesbians are certainly "vulnerable to discrimination on the job," but they are viewed differently and more positively than heterosexual women in terms of career commitment. They are overrepresented in the highly skilled, better paid jobs typical of gendered occupational categories (Peplau and Fingerhut, 2004). Data are not abundant, but lesbian workers are found in favorable numbers at higher management corporate positions and higher prestige professional specialties dominated by men. Lesbian workers appear to be more successful in reconciling conflict between paid work and motherhood that nets a favorable balance. Lesbian families exhibit role flexibility and even in their child-centered homes biological parent is not given a higher rank over primary caregiver or wage earner (Stuart, 2007; Hadley and Stuart, 2007). Certainly lesbian parents struggle with the work–family spillover, but from an employer standpoint, these struggles are not viewed as detriments to the job.

The Human Capital Model. Capitalism is played out in the United States according to strongly held economic convictions related to the **human capital model**. With the United States as its lead, the model is also embraced by the rich, industrialized nations across the globe. According to this view, the gender gap in wages is due to personal, individual choices in matters of education, childbirth, and child-rearing decisions, and occupation. If women choose to interrupt schooling or careers for marriage and family reasons, experience and productivity are compromised and wages are lower. In support of this model, because women now demonstrate less discontinuous work patterns than in the past, their wages have increased, and the wage gap is decreased (Penner, 2008; Napari, 2009). In addition, the human capital model is consistent with the law of supply and demand. Women can be paid less because they choose occupations and work schedules offering part-time options and requiring less prior experience. These flexible approaches make fewer demands on women's family responsibilities and hours spent in home production (Kunze, 2008; Albanesi and Olivetti, 2009). In this supply side argument, these jobs are very competitive with an abundance of workers who can be paid less. If there is artificial intervention to make jobs equitable in terms of wages, such as setting quotas for certain jobs for men and women, the law of supply and demand will be violated (Becker, 1994; Jacobsen, 2007).

The human capital model is consistent with functionalism in two important ways. First, men and women may attach different meanings to work. Men may gain more self-esteem from their work and may view breadwinning as more central to their identity. Employers in turn justify pay differences by these qualities (Billitteri, 2008; Fortin, 2008; Judge and Livingston, 2008). They contend that gender *per se* is irrelevant: It is not an employer's responsibility to change attitudes about gender roles or how they may play out differently for men and women workers. Second, and more central to functionalism, the human capital argument suggests that gender equity in wages must be able to unfold gradually and in line with a capitalistic system believed to function best if left unfettered and unregulated. Interference with this process will put economic equilibrium at risk and, therefore, do more harm than good.

Symbolic Interaction and Conflict Theory. These two sociological theories in combination offer good explanations for the wage gap and focus on two factors: the power relationships between men and women in all work settings, and definitions of masculinity and femininity that are carried into the workplace. Their combined view suggests that men exercise power in the workplace to maintain their wage advantage. A good example is a protégé system, in which an already powerful member serves as a sponsor for entry and upward movement of a novice. An effective "old boy system" keeps power in the hands of a few men. This system also operates on norms that support cultural notions of masculinity and femininity that often bar women from meaningful participation in informal work groups. Women will not be accepted if they are "too masculine" but are taken less seriously if they are "too feminine." Mentors and role models are essential for upward corporate mobility (Cohen, 2007; Andreoni and Petrie, 2008). Until women's networks include people of high rank, the corporate advancement of women will be stalled.

Summary. Although there are merits to each of these explanations, there is broad consensus that the gender gap is clearly linked to three factors:

1. The work women do—regardless of content, skill, or functional necessity—is less valued overall than the work men do.
2. The higher the number of women in the occupation, the lower the wages; the converse is true for male-dominated occupations. One-third of the wage gap is correlated with gender segregation.
3. Regardless of the law, gender discrimination in the workplace endures.

The stereotypes about the suitability of a job for men or women are pervasive. Research concludes that men are paid more than women for what they do largely because they are men (Hesse-Biber and Carter, 2005; Hartmann, 2008). Women's patterns of employment are different from men's, but for equal work there is not equal pay.

Corporate Women

As women have increased their rate of labor force participation, they are also bringing in the education and expertise that make them excellent prospects for management-level positions. Education and expertise brought by women to their careers have translated into two important but paradoxical trends. They are steadily increasing their share of management positions in corporations, and they are starting their own businesses at record levels. Understanding how gender plays out at the corporate level helps explain these seemingly opposing trends.

Corporate Barriers. Women have made great strides in corporate advancements to middle management positions, but have stalled in their ascendance to upper management. To increase female representation in upper management in the 1980s many businesses originally adopted a strategy in the addition of one woman to their corporate board of directors. However, because the vast majority of business promotion ladders were, gender segregated, there were few women to draw from, a pattern that continues into the millennium. In viewing research on these trends, the

Feminist Research Center (2000) states that "the rate of increase has been so slow that parity with men on corporate boards will not be achieved until the year 2116."

The Glass Ceiling. Research demonstrates that for women at all ranks, but particularly women managers, barriers to upward mobility exist, including role conflict, gender stereotypes, lack of mentors, insufficient feedback and training, and isolation. Under Title VII of the 1964 Civil Rights Act, sexual harassment in the workplace is also illegal, but women throughout corporate America report that it continues to be pervasive. Issues of double standards in defining competence and isolation from powerful networks remain thorns in the side for corporate women. For example, high-echelon professional women in many occupations are likely to be judged differently than men in terms of their work performance, even when all characteristics except gender are the same (Johnson, 2008; O'Connell et al., 2008). Others report that they are denied entrance into the informal networks that allow them to understand the intricacies of the power structure that are the keys to corporate survival (Schipani et al., 2009). Encouraged to specialize in a small area of the corporate enterprise, women find themselves in networks that lack diversity and control and are removed from understanding the broader workings of the system. With job functions also specialized via gender, a kind of corporate purdah emerges (Lindsey, 1992).

Women globally continue to report gender discrimination as the most frequent barrier to their advancement. In the elite ranks of the most powerful companies, regardless of the law and the fact that women bring with them human capital comparable to men, traditional gender bias emerges that effectively thwarts a woman's move up the corporate ladder (Metz and Tharenou, 2001; Johnson, 2008; Singh et al., 2008). Many of these patterns converge in a pattern referred to as the **glass ceiling**, describing women's failure to rise to senior level positions because of invisible and artificial barriers constructed by male management. Although lateral movement is possible, women are not able to advance hierarchically. It may be unintentional, but executives hire and promote according to a stereotypical masculine model categorizing men as more capable, commanding, aggressive, and objective leaders than women. Women's other family roles, especially as mother, are viewed as detrimental to leadership qualities. The ideal corporate recruit also represents the "image" of those who hired them. Although this model virtually excluded men of color in senior management, this has fast declined in the last decade. The "white male model" is eroding but the "male model" remains firm. The patriarchal world of senior management is upheld (Broadbridge, 2008; Pichler et al., 2008). Whether the gender discrimination inherent in the glass ceiling is intentional or not, the effect is the same: Women are excluded from the ranks of upper management.

Toward Corporate Success. In cooperation with private enterprise, the federal government initiated a number of programs to counter the glass ceiling and provide incentives for businesses to encourage the upward track and thwart the mommy track agenda imposed on corporate women. Many programs focus on offering flexibility for women who are juggling career and family responsibilities. Although FMLA may be a foundation, many businesses offer a wider range of workplace benefits to retain and advance talented women (Compensation, 2008). These family-friendly policies also benefit men.

These initiatives are laudable, but there are criticisms. They are more beneficial for women moving from middle to upper management in companies that are already female friendly or who offer products and services geared to a female market. Figures fluctuate by a few percentage points up or down over the last decade, but in the golden *Fortune 500,* women represent 1–2 percent of CEOs, 16 percent of corporate offices, and 15 percent of members of boards of directors. Estimates from a decade ago that by 2020 women would hold almost one-third of all corporate office positions are unlikely to be realized (BPW, 2007; Werhane et al., 2008). The experiences of high-level women, single or married, with or without children, who follow their career path as passionately, competitively, and diligently as comparable corporate men are unable to crack the glass ceiling (Eagly and Carli, 2008; Eagly and Sczesny, 2009). Women not only represent half the labor force, but they make the majority of consumer purchasing decisions in their households. "The bottom line is if you want to serve the market, hire the market" (Perry, 2009). Unless "old style" gender bias is explicitly targeted, not only will barriers to advancement remain, but qualified women will also desert the ranks of corporations to go out on their own.

Women Business Owners

And indeed, they *are* going out on their own. Entrepreneurial women find that business formation is an alternative to management positions in large organizations. Research consistently demonstrates that the number one reason high achieving corporate women desert firms is that they are denied access to the higher level management positions and the decision-making power they believe they fully deserved. If they cannot achieve a larger role in running a company, they will start their own company. This trend is suggested in the following data (Center for Women's Business Research, 2008; NAWBO, 2009):

- Whether as partners with women or men, or as sole proprietors, women-owned business firms represent almost one-third of all businesses in the United States, with one-fifth owned by women of color.
- Five times more women started small businesses in the 1990s compared to men, and in the last decade the number of women-owned firms increased almost 20 percent.
- Sole proprietorships are increasing at double the rate of those owned by men; 40 percent of all sole proprietorships are owned by women.
- All firms owned by women increased employment by about 70,000. Firms owned by men lost 1 million employees. Despite the difficult economic challenges faced by all business owners today, women owners report no plans to reduce employment; close to one-fourth report they plan to add jobs.

The businesses women own may be grouped into two general categories. The first is a business enterprise developed around traditional areas of female work, such as services targeting women and retail trades. For example, women have businesses that do housecleaning, catering, closet organizing, and child care or they have small boutiques and stores offering specialty items and household products geared to women. They are likely to employ less than 10 people, most of whom are women working part-time. They are in peripheral economic niches that do not seriously compete with more powerful small companies owned by men. Women tend to be in competition more with other women in similar businesses than men. Women-owned businesses also tend to be concentrated in industries with low-volume sales that lack access to capital and government contracts and that are often in need of more management expertise. However, women view their small businesses as a way to be creative, gain autonomy and flexibility, and balance career with family responsibilities. They put in longer hours but express enjoyment of their work. They are associated not only with high commitments of time and energy, but also with a great deal of personal satisfaction (Bond, 2003; Wilmerding, 2006).

A second category of women business owners is comprised of those middle managers who encountered the glass ceiling and jumped into their own businesses before their "corporate clock" ran out. They astutely recognized the amount of career time needed to successfully build a new business. They are the stockbrokers, banking executives, and financial managers who capitalize on the expertise, insights, and corporate experiences gained from their previous employer. The message that this group of women sends is that companies will ultimately lose if they continue to limit the talent and ambition of their female employees. If women leave a company to start their own businesses or jump to another company, former employees will be competitors.

Companies are also acknowledging that profit and diversity go hand in hand. The human capital model may suggest that it is not the job of corporate boards to create cultural diversity. However, it *is* their job to create profit for shareholders, and diverse boards generate higher returns. As a result, companies are now more enthusiastic about seeking ways to shatter the glass ceiling and retain rather than thwart the upward mobility of their talented female executives (Peppers and Rogers, 2008; Zhang et al., 2009). In the organizational sense, the term *male corporate America* is redundant. Diversity is no longer a choice but a necessity for companies to be successful. It remains to be seen, however, if corporate women will gain parity with men before 2116.

Gendered Management Styles: The Partnership Alternative

Despite barriers to success, some research suggests that a woman's socialization pattern may offer an advantage to modern corporations. In sharp contrast to the traditional corporate hierarchy, women executives tend to develop leadership structures that fit with a workplace where innovation and creativity are necessary but where an authoritarian chain of command is obsolete (Helgesen, 1990:37). Women bring interpersonal skills gained outside the organization back into the organization. They form friendships in their workplace that endure after leaving a job. In contrast, men give up significant parts of their private lives for corporate success in traditional business hierarchies, a situation detrimental to themselves, their families, and their employers (Faludi, 2000). For companies more receptive to alternative visions of corporate life, the distinctive management styles of women are encouraged. Women managers tend to adopt styles compatible with overall gender socialization patterns of females, such as encouraging participation, mentoring, sharing power and information, and interacting with all levels of employees.

To some extent these patterns parallel culturally based *Japanese Style Management* (JSM). This management model encourages a sense of employee community, an interest in employees' lives outside the office, consensus building, socioemotional bonding between employees and between management and labor, and a flattened management structure that is more egalitarian than hierarchical (Ohtsu, 2002). Principles of JSM are compatible with important American gender role socialization patterns for females (Lindsey, 1992, 1998; Chen, 2004). JSM also fits with partnership models emerging in innovative corporations with participative leadership styles emphasizing teamwork (Eisler and Loye, 1990; Graham, 2003; Kantrowitz, 2005).

Critique. Partnership models work best in smaller firms or where close collaboration on projects is necessary, such as in companies carrying out scientific and technological work. It is likely that employee satisfaction is associated more with the type of task and the amount of teamwork required rather than the gender of the employee. In addition, JSM models are losing ground in a global economy with a "sweeping conquest of American-style capitalist principles," where powerful corporate hierarchy is the rule and partnership the fast-eroding exception (Tokoro, 2005). Remaining firms in Japan that continue to embrace traditional JSM cannot be separated from the powerful prescribed rules of behavior according to which all Japanese live. Gender roles are even more tightly controlled within Japanese companies and women executives in Japan are virtually nonexistent (Kimoto, 2005). Most important, the "celebration" of the female advantage in the workplace may lead to increased stereotyping and a reaffirmation of the differences between women and men. The image of women as nurturers who smooth over problems may be as stereotypical as the image of men who create the problems.

On the positive side, the multicultural workplace is the emerging norm, and businesses today recognize that "difference" does not mean better or worse or stronger or weaker. A partnership model is associated with a revision of the standard definition of success, for example, that acknowledges other employee roles, such as parent and caretaker, in the life of any employee.

Today's employees are more willing to trade compensation for quality of work life. When conflicts between work and family are resolved in favor of the job, it is usually—and initially—to the detriment of the worker and his or her family. But the detrimental effect carries over to the employer and to society (Cowan, 2007). Talented women often opt out of high-level positions not because of their lack or competitiveness or dedication but because of the brutality associated with the corporate climb that is the antithesis of the partnership model. What is the potential effect of a new success model?

> Sanity, balance, and a new definition of success . . . just might be contagious. And instead of women being forced to act like men, men are being freed to act like women. Because women are more willing to leave (corporations), men are more willing to leave, too. . . . It is about a door opened . . . by women that could usher in a new environment for us all. (Belkin, 2003:86)

The door is only cracked open. A paradigm shift is needed for a partnership approach to be institutionalized as a new workplace norm. Companies adopting a partnership approach can benefit by recognizing that employee job satisfaction is critically linked to quality of life—both on and off the job.

GLOBAL FOCUS: MICROENTERPRISE AND WOMEN

Propelled by NGOs advocating for the world's poor, the informal sector of the global economy has been made more visible (Chapter 6). Because large-scale development projects have largely ignored the informal sector where most of the poorest of the poor work and reside, **microenterprise programs** to address their needs have arisen. These programs consist of core segments of income-earning manufacturing or agricultural activities located in or around the household.

Microenterprise is linked to the buzzword in the development assistance community, **microcredit** or microenterprise lending, where groups of four or five borrowers receive small loans at commercial interest rates to start or expand small businesses and open their first savings accounts. Peer lending is the most important feature of microcredit so a group assumes responsibility for each other's loans: If one fails, they all fail (Anderson et al., 2002; Ahmed, 2007).

Microcredit began 30 years ago when economics professor Muhammad Yunus founded the Grameen ("village") bank of Bangladesh and extended credit to people too poor to qualify for loans at other banks. The first microcredit lending came from his own pocket. He lent $26 to a group of 42 workers who bought materials for a day's work weaving chairs and making pots. At the end of the first day as independent business owners they sold their wares, made a profit, and soon repaid the loan. The 62 cents per worker from the $26 loan began the microcredit movement. The Grameen program was astonishingly successful. Not only did 97 percent repay their loans at a 20 percent interest rate but their microenterprises also became sustainable and allowed their families to survive. The large majority of the workers in these successful microenterprise programs were women.

Women and Microcredit

Microcredit works better for the very poor because the very poor are usually women. Muhammad Yunus noticed very early that women used profits from microenterprise activities to feed their children and build their businesses, whereas men spent profits on electronics and personal goods. A growing body of research suggests that when women have disposable income, it is used in ways to sustain their family's long-term needs, such as nutrition, health care, and education. In addition, data on Grameen Bank borrowers show women's loan repayment rates above 98 percent. Because social and economic benefits are much greater when money is loaned to women, the Grameen Bank decided to concentrate on them. Approximately 4 million Grameen borrowers in Bangladesh are women. The impact on the lives of Bangladeshi women and their families through microcredit is largely responsible for the higher economic rankings the nation as a whole has experienced over the last two decades (Mahal and Lindgren, 2002; Islam, 2007; Lucy et al., 2008).

The successes of Grameen in Bangladesh have been replayed with microcredit schemes targeted at women in India, Egypt, Zambia, Bolivia, and other parts of the developing world (Navajas et al., 2000; Geloo, 2008; Moodie, 2008; Nader, 2008). It has been adapted to in the United States in development efforts in agricultural areas of the South and in poor inner city neighborhoods in the Midwest and Northeast. Microcredit is particularly effective in the developing world because they are likely to have collectivistic cultures. In addition, it capitalizes on gender socialization patterns that build cooperative networks among women from early in life.

Critique. Lending money to women through microcredit is not without a downside. Some research indicates that when women are lent money, men may gain control of the funds, making loan repayment difficult. These women repay their loans but often under intense pressure from their peers and bank, who may threaten public humiliation for failure to pay. Challenging cultural and religious norms about women's traditional roles may also increase household tension, and in turn domestic violence may escalate. Outside their homes, women's businesses have been targets of attacks (Blau et al., 2006; Kumari, 2008). However, other research suggests that microcredit lending does offer women a major step to empowerment, cultural obstacles can be overcome, and women and their families, including men, benefit as a result (Ahmed, 2008; DoDoo and Frost, 2008). As Grameen Bank founder Yunus notes,

> . . . . each individual is very important. *She* alone can influence the lives of others within communities, nations within and beyond her own time. We need to build enabling environments to discover the limits of our potential. (Adapted from *Countdown 2005*, 1997:2) (Italics mine)

For his efforts to create social and economic development for the world's poor using bottom-up approaches, Muhammad Yunus was awarded the Nobel Peace Prize in 2006.

Summary

1. The increase of women in the labor force is linked to major changes in home and workplace. Employers are interested in how a woman's home life affects her workplace life.

2. Women have always held economically productive work roles connected to their homes. The Industrial Revolution opened paid work for women but by the Victorian era middle-class women retreated to their homes. War encourages women to enter the labor force and has altered the gender composition of some fields, such as clerical work and teaching.

3. Employment is a major determinant of good health for both men and women. Multiple roles for women—the role accumulation view—including job, marriage, and children, have major health and emotional benefits. The role overload view argues that psychological problems occur when women are put into two full-time jobs. Poor, single-parent women are at most risk from role overload. Women in the sandwich generation who care for others are under added stress. Benefits of multiple roles outweigh liabilities.

4. Women make enormous contributions to the economy and families by their unpaid labor. When a woman has a paycheck of her own family dynamics change.

5. Both socialization into the family of orientation and that into the family of procreation influence workplace roles. Girls hear messages about juggling family and employment that boys do not hear. Even in egalitarian marriages wives spend much more time on child care and household tasks than husbands.

6. Career achievement for women is severely compromised by these tasks. Employers see women with children as a liability and often informally cast them into a mommy track in the workplace. Married men with children are seen as an asset. Gender stereotypes remain key factors in hiring and promotion.

7. The Equal Pay Act and Title VII of the 1964 Civil Rights Act, affirmative action, and comparable worth have helped gender equity in the workplace and reduced blatant workplace discrimination. Backlash against some of these provisions is occurring.

8. Women make up half of the professions but are distributed in those with less pay, power, and prestige, such as nursing and teaching for women and engineers and architects for men. Occupational segregation and gender-typing go hand in hand. Men in female-dominated fields have more advantages than women in male-dominated fields. Women are segregated in the lower-prestige specialties of elite fields such as medicine and law.

9. Women in white-collar jobs are clustered in clerical or in retail sales with male managers. Blue-collar women are largely absent from the skilled elite, such as electrician, carpenter, and plumber. Most blue-collar women are in low-level semiskilled jobs.

10. Men of all races outearn women regardless of age, occupation, seniority, and region. Gender, race, and class intersect to lower the wages of women of color. The human capital model, consistent with functionalism, explains the gender wage gap due to, individual choices in education and family decisions. Conflict theory and symbolic interaction explain it according to the power relations between men and women and cultural norms about masculine and feminine jobs.

11. Corporate women's advancement to top management stops when women hit the glass ceiling—the invisible barrier constructed by male management. Women who are thwarted in corporations may start their own businesses. Women-owned businesses are in two categories: traditional areas of female work in peripheral economic niches that compete with other women and high-level managers competing with former employers.

12. Women's socialization may offer an advantage to modern corporations in that their management styles are compatible with partnership and consensus approaches. These approaches are linked to the success of Japanese firms. Celebrating the female advantage, however, may increase gender stereotyping.

13. Microcredit peer lending programs for very poor women in the developing world to start their own businesses are highly successful. If cultural obstacles are removed, these programs offer women a major step in empowerment.

Key Terms

affirmative action 284

comparable worth 284

Family and Medical Leave Act (FMLA) 283

family of orientation 279

family of procreation 279

gender-typing 286

glass ceiling 295

human capital model 293

microcredit 299

microenterprise programs 298

pink-collar jobs 275

sandwich generation 277

Title VII of the 1964 Civil Rights Act 284

work–family spillover 278

Critical Thinking Questions

1. How do gender-typing in jobs and the gender wage gap violate assumptions about the economic system in the United States and the values associated with it? Evaluate policy approaches in this chapter on level of success in addressing these issues. Based on this evaluation, offer policy strategies that would be successful in minimizing gender-typing and the wage gap.

2. As an employer interested in maximizing the potential of your female employees, what benefit packages would you offer and what management tactics would you use? Demonstrate how these devices will also serve as advantages to your male employees.

3. Document the influence of women's unpaid work on their families, their jobs, and their societies according to functionalism and conflict theory and then determine whether and/or how public policy should address the unpaid work issue. Which framework provides the better foundation for policy? Justify your selection.

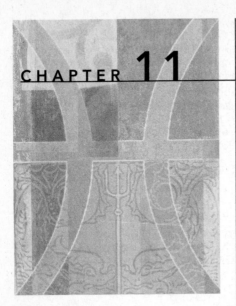

Math class is tough!
—"Teen Talk" Barbie™

Mattel pulled Teen Talk Barbie™ from the shelves in 1992 over public outrage about how the doll's utterance reinforced gender stereotypes regarding girls and math. Yet one of the hallmarks of the twentieth century has been the stellar educational achievement of girls and women. This achievement continues into the millennium at such a spectacular level that it may be difficult to deny assertions that any gender gap in education now favors girls over boys. Compared to boys, however, girls are more likely to be penalized for academic success, especially if it exceeds that of boys. When girls do not measure up to boys, explanations center on essentialism, especially the differences between male and female brains. Less than a decade after the demise of Teen Talk Barbie™ Mattel unveiled Barbie P.C.™ (a pink computer for girls) and Hot Wheels P.C.™ for boys. For the same price, Barbie's computer was loaded with half of the software of the Hot Wheels™ computer. Barbie's computer did not get programs related to human anatomy, three-dimensional visualization, and logical thinking games. The boys lost out on fashion and shopping. As one columnist plaintively asks, "can we please retire the claim that boy brains are hard-wired for math and girl brains are not?" (Headlam, 2000; Begley, 2008). This chapter examines varieties of educational gender gaps with an eye to debunking gender myths in education, particularly about the way boys and girls learn.

Compared to other social institutions, education is probably the most equitable. Like other nations in the developed world, the United States is oriented to *credentialism*—an individual's qualifications for a job or other position is based on completion of formal education or training. At a minimum, a college degree is the key credential for the most prestigious and financially rewarding positions. Parents are concerned about quality of teaching, curriculum, information technology, and the range of opportunities schools can provide. The issue of equity for parents often focuses on amount of public funds reserved for their school district. Regardless of funding, concerned parents would be dismayed to discover that their sons and daughters experience the educational process quite differently—even when seated in the same classroom. Education is a sorting process designed to benefit students and society, but gendered schooling brings benefits for some students and liabilities for others. In the most equitable of America's social institutions, the gender of the child becomes a key determinant in his or her educational journey.

A BRIEF LESSON IN HISTORY

The history of Western civilization demonstrates that education in general, and literacy in particular, was reserved for the elite. Until the eighteenth century the vast majority of all people—both men and women—were excluded from any formal learning. During the classical Greek and Roman era (dating from about the first century C.E.), the sons of the wealthy, and selected young men in other social classes, were taught reading, writing, and mathematics necessary for the economic, political, and military functioning of their homes and society. Certain upper-class women were educated in the arts, learned poetry, and were trained in music to entertain household guests. This tradition continued into the Middle Ages and served to reinforce the image of women as sources of diversion from a tedious world.

Christianity enveloped Europe during the Middle Ages and established a stronghold in all social institutions. Because literacy was necessary for women serving as nuns, convent schools were established. The few other wealthy women who attended these schools became part of a system in which learning was designed to produce socially proper behavior and ensure sexual purity. Functionalists suggest that even the mediocre education of this era supported social values that a woman's duty was to her husband or, if entering the convent, to the church. With church social and political domination, the family reinforced the religious values of a woman's piety, purity, and devotion to hearth and home. By the seventeenth century, however, even these few educational opportunities for women in convents deteriorated, fueled by the fear that communities of educated, semi-independent women might prove dangerous to absolute church authority. Whereas many convents worked to preserve their intellectual traditions, nuns were rendered powerless in church decisions affecting them. Thus despite the rise of universities in the twelfth and thirteenth centuries, and the profound impact of the Renaissance, education was aimed at the sons of nobility and the emerging bourgeoisie, who would engage in business, become scholars and clerics, or enter the professions of law and medicine.

The Enlightenment

Rumblings of education for both genders and all classes came with the Enlightenment. It was during this period that Jean-Jacques Rousseau published *Emile* (1762), a book destined to become one of the most influential works in the history of education. In describing a man, Emile, and a woman, Sophie, who would be Emile's wife, Rousseau suggested that men and women are inherently different in abilities. A man must be schooled or trained according to his natural talents and encouraged to cultivate his mind and spirit without restraint or coercion. A woman, however, is passive and weak and should be humbly submissive, accepting a man's judgment in all matters. Rousseau would not deny literacy to women, but he believed a woman's schooling should be practically oriented otherwise intellectual pursuits could wreak havoc on her naturally fragile temperament. Education for women must correspond to the roles they freely choose, those of wife and mother. Women have power over men because they have power over men's hearts. Men have power over women because they provide for women's economic upkeep. Women gain more from their dependence on men and less from education (Green, 1995:79). Rousseau justified gender inequality because he believed that the patriarchal family was a necessary precondition for modern society, founded on a woman's acceptance of her subservience to a man.

Progressive Education

Considered radical at the time, Rousseau's discourses on the education of boys from all social classes laid the foundation for the twentieth-century Progressive Education movement. His views on women were not as controversial because they reflected widespread convictions about a woman's nature. Because Progressive Education championed the idea of civic egalitarianism, the so-called leveling effects of the Enlightenment were directed at glaring social class differences. Rousseau's defense of civic egalitarianism, however, is weaker because he failed to account for the interdependent relationship between gender and class that perpetuates women's subordination and served to undermine efforts at social class equality. For sociological theory, an interesting contradiction results. Sounding like Marx and conflict theorists, Rousseau advocated social change that would increase class equality. But the final outcome was decidedly functionalist, in support of a patriarchal family considered to be the moral structure on which social order rests. Education for women, therefore, was not only impractical and unwise; it was detrimental to social stability.

Other voices also heard during the eighteenth century did call for gender equality in education. In France, the Marquis de Condorcet declared that government should provide education for all people, and that it had a duty to instruct both boys and girls in common. Equality and justice demanded it. Madame de Lambert advised women to study Latin, philosophy, and science to bolster their resources because other roads to success were closed to them. She bitterly lamented that women have but "coquetry and the miserable function of pleasing" as their wealth (Greard, 1893). The true spirit of the Enlightenment emerged in the late nineteenth century in Europe and the United States when policies advocating free and compulsory education for all children were adopted. A half century later, these principles were strengthened in the United States during the civil rights movement when the issue of equality of opportunity was seriously debated.

Americans wholeheartedly embrace the belief that education is the key vehicle for social mobility and economic success. Equality in education is assumed during the school years. Yet when the female kindergarten teacher removes Dick's mittens and helps Jane off with her coat, by virtue of gender alone, their educational journey will contain fundamental differences.

THE PROCESS OF EDUCATION

When children enter the classroom, earlier gender role patterns follow them (Chapter 3). These patterns are reinforced and reproduced throughout all educational levels and in all types of educational institutions. These gendered patterns are grounded in both the formal curriculum—such as textbooks, course requirements, grading scales, and standardized tests—and the powerful **hidden curriculum**, consisting of all the informal and unwritten norms that serve to control students, including expectations about gender.

Kindergarten and Early Childhood Education

Preschool is now normative, introducing children to their first educational expectations. Research clearly documents that gender segregation occurs swiftly in preschool and that it is reinforced by teacher expectations, gendered play and game activities, types of toys, and desires of the children themselves (Fromberg, 2005; Koch and Irby, 2005). The transition to more formal learning begins with kindergarten and follows from these preset patterns. Kindergarten classrooms are usually extensions of familiar household surroundings. Classes allow for the gradual structuring of the child's day so that ample time is set aside for play activities. Both boys and girls enjoy the time reserved for playing with the variety of toys and games available, many of which they have at home or have seen on television.

Jane. When play period begins, girls rush off to the minikitchen reserved for them. Here Jane can pretend to cook, set the table, and clean with miniature household devices that are designed for her small hands. This miniature house comes complete with dolls on which she can hone domestic skills. Because the doll corner is not designed for vibrant, rough-and-tumble play, Jane may be less restricted if she is wearing a dress or sandals. Girls are princesses, brides, models, and mothers in this part of the kindergarten world, fantasies easily acted out in the way the classroom is structured (Kuznets, 1999; Blakemore, 2005). But Jane also wears jeans and sneakers. This clothing does not prevent her from running with the other children and climbing on equipment in the playground. Girls may envy the boys as they display more power and freedom in their play behavior, but that envy is tempered by the teacher's obvious disapproval of the boys' boisterous classroom behavior. Jane gains more approval from classmates and teachers for her quiet demeanor and studiousness.

Although Jane may occasionally exchange the domestic roles of the doll corner for kickball and action oriented fantasy games during recess, the pull to the doll corner as a representation of home and babies is powerful and reigns supreme throughout kindergarten. Jane rarely plays with the boys and prefers playing house or, when outdoors, jumping rope with a few friends.

Kindergarten continues a process of self-selected gender segregation that increases throughout the school years. Gender of same age peers is a better predictor of choice of playmates than is race (Haynes, 2001; Hoffmann and Powlishta, 2001). Gender segregated play groups during early childhood education have powerful socialization outcomes (Wilgus, 2005). Children are acquiring distinctive interaction skills that can hamper cross-gender relationships later in life.

Dick. Meanwhile, Dick enters kindergarten more unprepared for the experience than Jane. His higher level of physical activity is incompatible with the sedate atmosphere of school. He is soon aware that his teacher approves of the quieter children—and the quieter children are usually the girls. Rather than gaining the teacher's attention by copying the girls and being labeled a sissy by the boys, he plays games that are physically vibrant and selects toys that reinforce these activities (Thorne, 1993, 2002). When Dick is expected to engage in quieter activities such as art, he chooses to draw gender-stereotyped pictures—such as those depicting outdoor scenes associated with fighting, building, and demolishing. Dick discovers that the teacher pays attention to the children who are more disruptive—and the more disruptive children are usually the boys. He may also feel it is better to be reprimanded than ignored.

Physical space in the early childhood classroom is highly gendered. When boys venture into the doll corner, they use the area and the toys differently than the girls. Boys use domestic-type toys to stage games based on fighting and destruction—turning plastic utensils into swords and plates into shields, for example. When boys play with Barbie™, they often "sexualize" her or even turn her into a weapon! (MacNaughton, 2007:266). Teachers who otherwise encourage imaginative play will not allow disruption and conflict in the classroom and boys are banished from the area (Jordan and Cowan, 2004).

Dick and his friends favor trucks, action figures, and building blocks as toys. These toys are more mechanical, complicated, computerized, and motorized than Jane's toys. Numerical board games and building blocks that boys prefer offer ways to hone spatial-visual and manipulative skills. Dick will have an early edge over Jane in experiences to better understand math and physical science (Polnick and Funk, 2005; Casey et al., 2008). Girls, too, enjoy building things. A girl may wander over and attempt to join in the louder and seemingly more interesting activities of the boys. She is likely to be discouraged from long-term participation, however, by their rough-and-tumble play and the very spiritedness of the activities to which she was originally attracted. In and outside the classroom, these activities reward boys for being independent, active, and assertive and punish them for engaging in behavior defined by their peers as sissy. Beliefs about masculinity are enforced even in early childhood education (Blaise, 2005). School norms call for docility and quietness, realms in which girls feel more at ease. It is understandable that boys often find their first school experiences unsettling.

Elementary and Middle School

For girls, elementary school and middle school are sites of achievement. They receive higher grades than boys, and they exceed boys in most areas of verbal ability, reading, and mathematics. Teachers also put a premium on being good and being tidy, which may account for fewer negative comments given to girls. High achievement coupled with low criticism would appear to be an ideal learning environment. Yet the message that is also communicated to girls early in their education is that they are less important than boys.

Jane and the Gendered Curriculum. Compared to boys, girls are called on less, have less overall interaction with teachers, and get less criticism but also receive less instructional time. When teachers criticize boys for inadequate academic work, they suggest that it is lack of effort rather than intelligence that is the cause (Burnett, 2002; Weinstein et al., 2007). Research demonstrates that elementary school teaches boys that problems are challenges to overcome; it often teaches girls that failure is beyond their control. As symbolic interactionists suggest, a self-fulfilling prophecy may be set into motion if girls internalize the notion that they have less intellectual ability, in turn discouraging them from tackling more difficult courses. Compliance in girls serves to weaken intellectual risk taking.

Although curricular material is more egalitarian today, stereotyped gender portrayals are prevalent. Decades of research on such material demonstrates that girls are depicted much less frequently than boys and, when depicted, are in marginalized, insignificant roles. Children's books may show girls as brave and adventuresome, but when they attempt to do exciting things, they have to be rescued by boys. Girls who are princesses often marry the boys who rescue them (Evans and Davies, 2000; Levstik, 2001).

Gender stereotyping in education has received national attention. It would be expected, therefore, that current instructional materials reflect more realistic and expanded roles for both genders. The research evidence is mixed. Children continue to read books with characters in traditional gender roles. Women and girls are portrayed as dependent, cooperative, submissive, and nurturing, whereas men and boys are portrayed as independent, creative, aggressive, competitive, and assertive. Research on textbooks that teach reading, social studies, and even mathematics demonstrate that less importance is attached to girls—especially girls of color—by the number of female characters represented and the stereotyped roles they play. On the other hand, numbers and types of female characters have increased, and less stereotyped portrayals are evident. Girls are now more likely to be shown in the world of paid work. They are more frequently depicted in sports, although in traditional female sports, such as gymnastics and ice skating rather than basketball or soccer. Although gender parity has not been reached, strides toward less stereotyped female portrayals are evident in textbooks at all school levels (Woyshner, 2006).

Dick and the Gendered Curriculum. Boys are experiencing elementary and middle school quite differently. They do not easily adjust to a classroom environment that emphasizes silence and inactivity, with teachers reprimanding them more. Boisterous, competitive boys are more likely to receive lower grades than quiet, cooperative girls. When boys learn that more effort and less disruptive classroom behavior will increase teacher approval, their self-esteem is protected. Teachers talk to them more about the subject matter, listen more to their complaints and questions, and praise them most for their intellectual competence. Although teachers maintain that they do not treat girls and boys differently, boys shout out answers to questions, whether right or wrong, and get attention. Girls raise their hands and get ignored (Sadker and Sadker, 1994, 2002) Guzzetti et al., 2002.

Textbooks and readers in elementary school are replete with male, main characters doing interesting and exciting things, both in occupational and in recreational activities. They see active and resourceful adult males who are jobholders and boys of their own age who build, create, and discover, as well as protect and rescue girls (Hunter and Chick, 2005; Porche, 2007). Men are scientists, firefighters, and police officers. They are involved in a variety of sports activities. Males are also cast into father roles, but these roles are given less coverage and less importance than bread-winner/career depictions. Joint father–children activities are rarely portrayed, including those involving father–son. Newer textbooks do show boys engaging in nontraditional roles, such as babysitting and household work, but the gendered curriculum bias for boys binds Dick to expectations for high achievement in career roles. The fact that he will also be a husband and father is disregarded.

In all these roles Dick is taught to be strong and tough. Emotional displays such as outward signs of fear, hardship, and sorrow are disapproved. Anger is the only emotion that is somewhat tolerated as long as it does not revert to bullying or fighting. Although Dick may find aspects of elementary school frustrating and confusing, curricular materials confirm his anticipated masculine role and serve to strengthen his identity as eventual wage earner.

Overall, research on the impact of gender-typed curricular materials concludes that gender role attitudes of elementary and middle school students are compromised. Instructional materials that perpetuate gender role stereotyping in turn reinforce gender-typed beliefs, with children in the younger grades being the most susceptible.

High School

Whereas in elementary school girls are confident and assertive, they experience a sharp drop in self-esteem in middle school, entering high school with a poorer self-image (Langlois, 2006). As measured by standardized tests and grades, achievement for girls in reading and writing tends to plateau and their middle school advantage in math begins to decline. On the other hand, boys experience consistent gains in self-confidence, and they believe they are good at a lot of things, but especially in math and physical sciences, where they are beginning to excel.

Gender and Mathematics. Research on the link between gender and math is abundant, complex, and often confusing. The data summarized below suggest this confusion.

A high school gender gap in math has disappeared:
- High school girls have caught up with boys in overall math performance. They take as many advanced math courses today as boys. Average scores on most standardized tests are virtually the same and girls do as well as boys on equally complex questions. Boys and girls appear to tap into different skill sets to solve the math questions but the different paths lead to the same results (Dar-Nimrod and Heine, 2007; McCormick, 2007; Hyde et al., 2008).
- Girls do as well or better than boys in advanced classes, in classes when girls equal or outnumber boys, and when classes are taught by women. Girls do better when "math-identified" adult female role models are available. Both boys and girls are greatly influenced by peers who have good grades. These friends are gauges to determine whether to take math classes at all and which ones to take. This peer connection is stronger for girls. When all these social and structural factors are controlled for, gender differences in math performance vanish (Quaiser-Pohl and Lehmann, 2002; Lesko and Corpus, 2006; Crosnoe et al., 2008).

A high school gender gap in math has not disappeared:

- When verbal processes are used in math questions, girls outperform boys. When spatial–visual processes are used, boys outperform girls. Boys do better on multiple-choice items and girls do better on extended response items, although these differences are slight (Beller and Gafni, 2000; Lichtenberger and Kaufman, 2007).
- Boys are more proficient at math when tests require more complex problem solving, such as the SAT taken by high school seniors. The SAT is the key standardized test that continues to show a significant gender gap in math. In overall math competency, boys enter college with better grades and the prerequisites needed for science- and math-based majors such as actuarial science and engineering (Gallagher et al., 2000).

The persistent pattern showing a slight male edge in math proficiency continues to be seized to conclude that there are biologically based sex differences in analytic ability, interest, *and* motivation to pursue math and science. The biology argument for gender differences in math and physical science uses everything from chromosomes, hormones, brain organization, evolutionary mandates, and genetic codes to explain the male edge (Berenbaum and Resnick, 2007; Geary, 2007; Haier, 2007). Some researchers focus on gender differences in the rate of development that may more or less favor one gender or the other from early childhood to young adulthood (Lubinski and Benbow, 2007). Biology may not be dismissed as *a* factor in exploring any gender gap in math proficiency but it is clearly not *the* factor. Refined measurement techniques are yielding results showing many more gender similarities rather than gender differences.

The better argument is that sociocultural factors propel boys but deter girls in mathematics as well as science (Orenstein, 2001; National Science Foundation, 2007). Perhaps the strongest evidence against natural differences favoring boys in math is that cross-cultural research now shows girls in some nations matching or exceeding math performance of boys not only within their own nations but also in the United States and Canada (Hyde, 2007). In more gender-equitable nations girls and boys perform equally well in math. In some countries the gender gap in math favors girls. If any gender gap can be said to exist, it is certainly mediated by culture (Ceci and Williams, 2007; Tsui, 2007; Guiso et al., 2008).

Despite continued weakening of the "innate differences" argument, the belief that math ability is grounded in unalterable biological factors remains very powerful. Highly motivated girls in advanced physics and math classes, for example, encounter both teachers and classmates who believe girls are not as bright as boys. As mentioned by one girl,

> . . . I guess I feel a little bit as a girl, kind of not taken as seriously sometimes . . . like my opinion doesn't count as much . . . Like in math and science . . . which is supposed to be harder (but), more people just kind of didn't listen to you. (Rodriguez, 2006:73)

Girls who accept the stereotype that they are not naturally (biologically) suited for math often track these beliefs to negative outcomes that include heightened math anxiety, poorer performance on timed tests, and avoidance of any courses based on "numbers." If they believe their abilities are shaped by the environment, and can be changed, their math performance improves dramatically; if they believe the stereotype that "girls can't do math," their performance scores decrease (Jordan and Lovett, 2007; Khoromi, 2007). Symbolic interactionists assert that untold damage is done when girls believe math ability is genetic gift and they can never be successful regardless of their amount of effort.

High-profile media accounts reinforce these beliefs. Lawrence Summers, economist and President of Harvard, unleashed an uproar for suggesting that women do not have the same "natural ability" as men for math. These innate sex differences explain the underrepresentation of women in math and science faculty and careers. Although acknowledging that discrimination may also be a factor, he suggested that behavioral genetics shows that "things people previously attributed to socialization weren't due to socialization at all" (Bombardieri, 2005; Pollitt, 2005). He was ultimately unseated for these remarks. Investigators need to carefully monitor how their results are interpreted, especially when stories about connections between genes and math ability are grossly simplified in the media (*Science Daily*, 2007). Any lingering gender gap in math competence is better explained by gender factors, due to culture, rather than sex factors, due to biology.

Social Class and Race. Research confirms that in both high school and college race and social class are better predictors for academic performance, including math and science, than is gender. White, middle-class children of both genders outperform children of other races as well as children from lower- and working-class backgrounds (Sacks, 2007; AAUW, 2008). In academic achievement overall, Britain has been successful in significantly narrowing the gender educational gap, but seemingly insurmountable social class inequalities persist (Plummer, 2000). African-American and Latino high school boys, who are disproportionately from poor families, are particularly vulnerable. Although gender differences in achievement are declining in all racial and ethnic groups, minority males are more likely to be at the academic bottom and to drop out of high school compared to girls of all races and white boys (Clarkwest, 2007). Adding to the social class vulnerability quotient, African-American boys tend to be rated academically and socially as less competent (Parks and Kennedy, 2007). Symbolic interactionists assert that such labels can severely compromise a student's motivation for academic success in high school.

Gender Diversity: Self-Esteem and Academic Achievement. Academic success, especially in math and science, is strongly related to level of self-esteem among high school girls. When a high school girl enjoys tackling difficult courses, she also feels good about herself and her schoolwork, sees herself as important, and feels better about her relationships. The drop in self-esteem girls experience by the time they enter high school is more pronounced for Latino girls, who start out with the highest level of self-esteem for girls of all races and end with the highest school dropout rates (Canedy, 2001; Guinn and Vincent, 2002; Mahaffy, 2004; Adams et al., 2006).

African-American girls receive the same messages other girls receive in high school—that girls are less important than boys. But African-American girls tend to retain their sense of self-esteem despite negative messages from teachers and difficulties with academic achievement. Bolstered by racial pride and perceived social support, self-esteem is maintained (Constantine et al., 2006). They listen to their own voices rather than accepting devaluing judgments from others (Brown and Gilligan, 1992; Gilligan et al., 1995).

Girls of color clearly understand the reality of racism and know that education will not translate into the economic rewards relative to whites with the same credentials. However, Jeanne Weiler's research on "at-risk" female students attending an alternative high school in New York suggests that young girls of color value academic achievement as the best route to improve their economic future. The achievement paradox is implied by a Puerto Rican girl:

> I'll either get a job or go to college. Well, this is really what I want to do after I get out of high school. I'm going to go into the army and I'll get the G.I. bill for college. . . . (Weiler, 2000:76)

This research also shows that girls of color are more likely to come from families where women are the sole or dominant wage earners and attach more importance to further schooling than do white girls; the latter bet more on marriage for economic security. Weiler speculates that although the high school offers compelling messages about a diploma or degree as the most important route to a good job, white girls internalize the louder gender message that marriage is the better economic guarantee. Weiler's research offers insight into the connections between race and class in patterns of female achievement in high school.

Gendered Tracking and Vocational Education. Historically committed to the less powerful of society, vocational education (VE) serves the noncollege bound. Although college attendance for racial and ethnic minorities and students from working-class backgrounds has skyrocketed, these are the groups largely enrolled in VE. Vocational education is sharply gender segregated and, contrary to perception, more girls than boys are enrolled. Girls from working-class families represent a large share of its students. Many of these girls do not see college as a realistic or desirable option and marriage looms as the alternative. Obtaining a marketable skill for employment immediately out of high school is needed until they marry and for supplementary household income later.

Girls are tracked into clusters of courses related to clerical skills, health assistance, beauty (cosmetology and manicuring), and retail sales. Boys are tracked into courses clustered in mechanical (electrical and plumbing) and automotive trades, and information technology. VE options for boys will have higher economic returns after high school. Girls are the overwhelming majority in vocational programs that are based on household skills. Despite the desire to earn a paycheck, such programs for girls mirror the cultural assumption—but not the economic reality—that working outside the home is optional for women. The myth of female dependence on males for income is not a benign one. When young women graduate from high school with severely restricted career options, it translates into poor economic outcomes that are worsened by divorce and single parenthood (Chapter 8). Overall, high school VE for girls is geared to the noncollege bound who marry and, when they do work outside the home, wind up in low-paying, dead-end jobs.

Recent federal legislation is helping to open VE for training in higher-paying fields, offered as options to both genders (Magnuson, 2005). Improving gender equity in vocational education empowers all students. But a remaining problem is that gender equity is hampered by high school gender codes that keep boys and girls from venturing too far off traditional paths.

Gender in the Hidden Curriculum. The confusion of earlier school years for boys begins to evaporate as they are rewarded more for their independence. Dick's grades have improved, and he is able to demonstrate his talents in courses (shop and automobile mechanics) and sports (wrestling and football) specifically geared to boys.

Enrollment by girls in courses traditionally designed for boys is exploding, but boys are less inclined to take courses associated with traditional feminine activities. When course titles do not reflect the so-called feminine content, such as "Bachelor Living" and "Home Mechanics" boys enroll more freely. Changing the title of a course to entice male enrollment may be pandering and serves to devalue courses that females take, but these courses provide boys with needed practical domestic skills, such as cooking, child care, home maintenance, and household organization.

Other school mechanisms help perpetuate the gendered high school system. For example, both genders take the same academic courses such as history, but as in elementary and middle school, these courses demonstrate that "boys do" and "girls don't." In history books, when women are mentioned, it is usually in the context of a traditional role—Betsy Ross for sewing and Florence Nightingale for nursing—or of becoming notable because of marriage to famous men—from Jackie Kennedy to Ivana Trump. The few women who are portrayed conform to a stereotypical image of what women are supposed to be. The content of history courses in college is beginning to reflect current ideas about diversity in general and women in particular, but this trend is lagging in high schools. Controversial men are portrayed. Controversial women are omitted.

The achievement and career interest tests taken by high school students also maintain a consistent androcentric bias, from the content to the pronouns used. College and career counseling in high school frequently continues this bias. Gender bias by counselors is a problem that can affect students' attitudes to career selection, choice of major, or even willingness to pursue a college education (Sciarra et al., 2007). Other staffing patterns demonstrate to students and community alike that males are the leaders. The male high school principal reports to the male school superintendent who regularly meets with a predominantly male school board. Even among lower-level school staff a gender hierarchy exists. In both pay and prestige, for example, female cafeteria workers are ranked lower than male janitors. Women are gaining higher-level administrative positions in education but not fast enough to change these patterns.

Acknowledging the insidious nature of these latent but powerful gendered codes, successful intervention strategies are widespread. Programs supported by the Gender Equity Education Act of 1995 fund initiatives designed to raise the gender consciousness of educators and help them to understand how cultural beliefs influence their work with students. Programs are in place to encourage girls in math and science and boys in reading and home economics. It is in high school athletics, however, where much progress is reported, but where many obstacles to gender equity remain.

Athletics and Masculinity. Achievement on the playing fields of high schools across the United States is strongly linked to community and school pride. How does this achievement affect those who strive for covered team sports? Girls who succeed in high school athletics feel good about themselves and are increasingly viewed favorably by their peers. Attractiveness and popularity with boys, however, remain the best gauges to judge prestige for girls. Athletic success provides the same function for boys. From early childhood, boys receive powerful messages that athletic accomplishment is a key barometer to judge a man's success (Suitor and Carter, 1999; Neu and Weinfeld, 2007). This is an accurate assessment. Because of the billion-dollar sports–media connection, these messages are in fact stronger than at any other time in history. Boys not only see the financial rewards and personal glory associated with sports, but also the athletes themselves who often emerge more lustrous by the injuries, fights, and general mayhem that occur on and off the football field, basketball court, or ice rink.

Sports demonstrate the importance of competition and allows participants to gain in confidence, concentration, and courage, all traits associated with successful American males (Chapter 9). These functions of sports, however, are tempered with a potential downside: relationships with coaches and teammates socialize boys to defer to a powerful male status hierarchy that supports the acceptance of pain and the denigration of women. Football especially perpetuates patriarchy and male privilege through bonding relationships with figures such as coaches who are more dominant than the athletes themselves (Sabo and Panepinto, 2001). Boys who gauge themselves by athletics and cannot measure up to their peers or achieve their personal best in the grueling hierarchy of high school athletics often feel inadequate and unpopular. Athletic failure is associated with a loss of self-confidence and poor educational outcomes for boys. These values will not accept academic achievement as a substitute for athletic rewards. A masculine gender identity is formed and polished by sports. This identity may be tarnished if a boy succeeds in coeducational sports, especially if a girl can outperform a boy in the same athletic competition. Such a belief not only discourages coed teams but provides ammunition that implicitly deprecates those activities where girls can succeed at an equal or better level than boys.

The importance attached to high school athletics is measured by the financial and organizational support given to male compared to female sports. At all levels of education, boys' teams have better equipment and facilities, more space for practice and competition, and higher-paid coaches than comparable girls' teams (Chapter 14). Both boys' and girls' teams are likely to be administered by men. Successful high school teams are routinely scrutinized by scouts representing major college and professional teams. It is understandable that athletics is viewed as a road to success for high school males. This is a gilded road for those boys who intend to pursue college on an athletic scholarship.

Higher Education

If high school has done its job well all qualified students will pursue a college education. For whites, African Americans, and Latinos, gender gaps favoring males in high school and college graduation rates largely disappeared by the 1990s; today the gender gap in both favors females (Table 11.1). A college degree is mostly equivalent to what a high school diploma was merely 20 years ago. Ideally, college should be the key educational institution that evaluates students largely on academic achievement and the potential for success. But the lessons of high school are not easily forgotten.

The Gendered College Classroom. Men find that academic life exemplifies a male mode of performance. The values of competition, individualism, and aggressive classroom debates are stronger than in high school. College men quickly learn the value of catching the attention of faculty who will be instrumental for later graduate work. Men's self-esteem continues to improve and soon outpaces their women classmates.

Table 11.1 High School and College Graduation Rates by Gender and Race, Selected Years

	Total			White		African American		Latino	
Year	Total	Male	Female	Male	Female	Male	Female	Male	Female
Percentage of 25 to 29 Year Olds who Completed High School									
1971	77.7	79.0	76.5	83.0	80.5	56.7	60.5	51.4	45.8
1981	86.3	86.5	86.1	89.7	89.9	78.8	76.6	59.1	60.4
1991	85.4	84.9	85.8	89.2	90.4	83.6	80.1	56.4	57.1
2001	87.7	86.9	88.6	93.0	93.6	87.5	86.7	59.4	67.2
2007	87.0	84.9	89.1	92.7	94.2	87.4	87.9	60.5	70.7
Percentage of 25 to 29 Year Olds with a Bachelor's Degree or Higher									
1971	17.1	20.4	13.8	22.4	15.4	6.9	6.6	8	2.6
1981	21.3	23.1	19.6	25.5	21.7	12.1	11.1	8.6	6.5
1991	23.2	23	23.4	26.5	26.9	11.5	10.5	8.1	10.4
2001	28.6	26.2	31.1	29.7	36.3	17.9	17.8	9.1	13.3
2007	29.6	26.3	33	31.9	39.2	19.9	20	8.6	15.4

Source: National Center for Education Statistics. U.S. Census Bureau, *Current Population Survey*, March Supplement, 1971–2007. Adapted from Tables 25-1 and 25-3.

Women entering college experience a small, but measurable drop in self-esteem. In addition to anxiety about major and career, college women express concern about career–family conflict as they plan their future (Chapter 7). Self-esteem is also threatened by their belief that the campus climate is a "chillier" one for them (Sandler, 2004). Women discover early that they receive less faculty encouragement for their work and will be listened to less and interrupted more than their male classmates. Almost half of women report instances of gender discrimination in their treatment in and outside the classroom by instructors, administrators, and classmates. This chilly climate can negatively affect a woman's personal and intellectual development.

Major and Career Paths. Women are rapidly entering male-dominated majors; men entering female-dominated majors is not nearly as evident. Graduate and professional school enrollments for women have soared and are projected to climb even further (Figure 11.1). Women earn almost 60 percent of graduate degrees overall and over half of doctorates in fields other than science and engineering. Biology is the exception: more than half of all biology degrees—B.S., M.A., and Ph.D.—are awarded to women. Gains in professional degrees have been steady; women have a slight majority in medicine and other health science professional programs (National Center for Education Statistics, 2009). Considering that opportunities for women to pursue higher education are relatively recent, these numbers are impressive.

Despite these advances, college women find it easier to choose the well-traveled gender road of majoring in the arts and humanities, in teaching, and in nursing. During the last decade the desegration of majors stalled not only because of women's slowdown in making less traditional choices, but also because men were disinclined to enter fields with "too many" women (England and Li, 2006:657). Almost half of women who enter college with interests in science, technology, engineering, and mathematics (STEM) switch to other majors. The math–gender link described earlier comes into play. Insufficient precollege preparation, gender stereotypes about women's suitability for math and science, few female role models and mentors, and

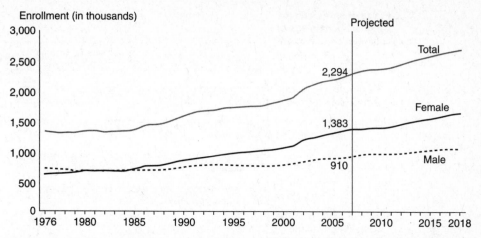

Figure 11.1 Graduate Enrollment by Gender, 1976 to 2009 and Projected to 2018

Source: U.S. Department of Education, National Center for Educational Statistics. *The Condition of Education, 2009.* http://nces.ed.gov/programs/ceo/2009/charts

lack of peers in the field are key factors in explaining these choices (Correll, 2001; National Research Council, 2006).

Most majors continue to demonstrate significant levels of gender segregation (Figure 11.2). Compared to women, men are distributed in a wider variety of majors and dominate the most competitive areas of architecture and STEM majors. The majority of noneducation doctorates and master's degrees in science are awarded to men. These majors lead to jobs in expanding, more lucrative fields such as engineering, biomedical technology, and computer science. The gender gap in starting-salary for new college graduates can be explained by the gender differences in college major (McDonald and Thornton, 2007). Men dominate the most influential fields where graduate work is required and are at the top of the prestige hierarchy within them. In medicine, men are surgeons and women are pediatricians. Men practice international law and women practice family law. Female nurses are in clinical roles and male nurses are in administrative roles.

Women are concentrated in nursing, literature, home economics, social work, education, and library science. Although these majors offer jobs that are vital to society, female-dominated fields garner less pay and more competition for the fewer job slots available (Chapter 10). For the behavioral sciences, almost 80 percent of B.A.'s in psychology are awarded to women, a number that is expected to increase. Sociology and history are among the few undergraduate majors and graduate fields with relative gender parity. The gender effects of the college experience largely accounts for these patterns. The culmination of college or graduate school—whether as holder of B.A., M.D., or Ph.D.—is also the end of an educational journey of attitudes and behaviors regarding gender.

Graduate School. Psychological roadblocks emerging at the undergraduate level are intensified in graduate and professional education as competition for grades and grants increase. Besides dealing with increasing career–motherhood pressures, women must cope with pervasive patterns of subtle gender bias existing in many graduate departments. Academic careers blossom, for example, through a

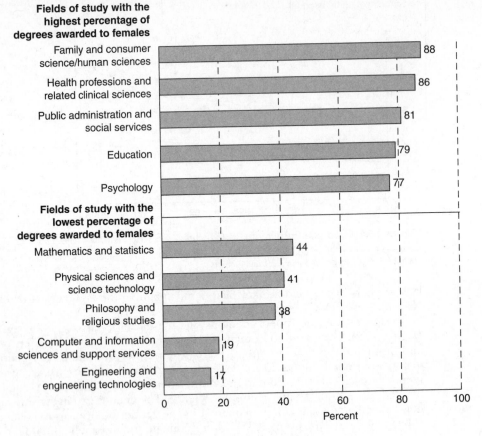

Figure 11.2 Gender Segregation in Undergraduate Major

Source: U.S. Department of Education, National Center for Educational Statistics. *The Condition of Education, 2009.* http://nces.ed.gov/programs/ceo/2009/charts

protégé system that matches a talented graduate student with a recognized, established faculty member. Through the informal networks reverberating through departments women quickly determine that, compared to their male colleagues, they are not as suitable as protégés. Although not overtly discriminatory, these pervasive patterns keep both faculty and graduate student men in control of the powerful subculture of graduate school. Faculty prefer protégés of their own gender and both students and faculty prefer mentors of their own gender. The fewer number of available female faculty and the gender segregation of the discipline, however, do not allow for these preferences. Such patterns are even more detrimental to female students of color (Cleveland, 2004). Based on both their gender and race they often feel isolated from informal networks and faculty contact. Restricted opportunities for networking in college and graduate school have a major impact on later careers.

Mentoring is one way to help women facing gender discrimination, especially when discrimination occurs covertly. Even given the lopsided faculty ratio favoring men, plentiful research suggests many ways that mentoring is used to address female graduate students' and female faculty concerns about gender discrimination (Johnson, 2003; Wasburn, 2007). Important recent research extends these mentoring success stories by focusing on the gender characteristics of the departments themselves. Departments with female chairs and with faculty engaged in research on gender- and feminist-related topics are more likely to have mentoring policies in place (Dua, 2008). It is likely that "gender-friendly" departments with mentoring programs are also "diversity-friendly departments." Mentoring can instill both gender consciousness and awareness of faculty and student diversity on campuses throughout the United States.

Academic Women. Female faculty are important for women students as role models and mentors. Women's progress in academia is not inevitable. Fueled by the MR and legal setbacks related to gender and diversity on campus, past progress appears to be eroding. Where does the academic path lead for women Ph.D.s? Most are in two- and four-year state colleges, usually satellite campuses, with heavy teaching loads and committee responsibilities. Community colleges do offer hospitable environments for both female students and faculty; half of the faculty in community colleges are women (Townshend, 2007). However, like their counterparts in other colleges and universities, they are clustered in less powerful, overcrowded disciplines and hold most adjunct and part-time faculty positions in these fields. If full-time, they are instructors and assistant professors. The pattern repeats itself throughout academia—the higher the rank, the fewer the women.

Tenure. Tenure explains the low number of female full professors. Approximately two-thirds of men on the faculties of four-year colleges have tenure compared to one-third of women, a pattern holding for two decades (National Center for Education Statistics, 2007). For highly qualified women faculty in STEM disciplines the tenure gap widens. Although women in these fields are equally competitive with men in research training, are successful grant recipients, and meet similar productivity qualifications, they represent roughly 15 percent of full professors in research universities (National Academy of Sciences, 2006; CPST, 2007). Women devote a greater amount of their time to teaching, and engage in more unpaid professional service than their male colleagues. Women's family roles—marriage and children—decrease their likelihood of advancing; for men these same roles increase it. Faculty men who are married and have dependents work fewer hours on noncareer activities such as housework and caregiving than their female counterparts (Perna, 2005; Ginther and Kahn, 2006). Students are more likely than faculty to have priority in university-based child-care facilities:

> I was going to put him in the daycare center but faculty was last on the list.
>
> We do really well because my husband is an undergraduate. . . . we get none of these things because I'm a faculty member. (Any) faculty benefits . . . are mostly geared towards older men. . . . (benefits) pay for tuition but not childcare. Faculty can be on the waiting list for years. (Armenti, 2004:74)

As evidenced by less success at gaining tenure, already tough higher education careers are tougher for females compared to males.

Research also shows the powerful impact of gender stereotypes for evaluating faculty performance. Faculty women are evaluated differently than faculty men by students, colleagues, and administrators in teaching and administrative roles. They are expected to be nice as well as competent, maintain a pleasant classroom atmosphere, be more responsive to students with personal needs, be overly accessible to students outside class, especially answering emails, and engage students using a variety of learning styles. Women are judged more harshly when they deviate from the gender-imposed model of a caring professor. Both men and women faculty adopt stereotyped gender role images that influence peer evaluation and, like graduate students, the informal networks in which female faculty are first assessed (Laube et al., 2007; Merchant et al., 2007; Spelke and Grace, 2007). Besides the clear inequity of such patterns, it is a sad comment on college education that good teaching, where women excel, is often not the basis for the reward of tenure.

Women faculty often find themselves pulled away from career goals by the same challenges faced by other bright, ambitious women—the multiple demands of family and university. Given the extremely competitive academic marketplace, Jane must make the difficult decision to uproot her life to seek employment elsewhere or find part-time work at other local colleges. The latter course will be her likely choice, especially if she has children and an employed spouse. She will remain in academia but in a marginal position, often as an "academic gypsy" migrating between part-time or temporary jobs, with little hope of advancement, influence, or tenure.

GENDER ISSUES IN EDUCATION

It is clear that gender bias in education is associated with restricted options for both male and female students and faculty. Given limited resources at all educational levels, strategies to address stubbornly persistent gender biases are often contentious and, as we will see, may succumb to the very stereotypes that originally fueled the gender gap in educational equity.

Shortchanged Students: Girls or Boys in Educational Crisis?

Spearheaded by the legal foundation of Title IX (discussed later) and landmark research documenting that the educational needs of girls lagged behind boys, programs related to gender equity in education have been instituted. Follow-up research suggests that public schools have made impressive educational gains in policies targeting gender equity (AAUW, 2008).

What about the Boys? Rather than celebrating these achievements, however, a backlash to attention paid to the gender gap in education has been launched, suggesting that the shortchanged group is not girls, but boys. This backlash centers on the belief that an advantaging of girls in classrooms throughout the United States has led to a "boy crisis," with boys lagging behind girls on major indicators of achievement. These indicators include grades, standardized test scores in elementary and high school, and high school graduation rates. The rationale for the boy crisis in education focuses on the contention that, under the guise of helping girls, boys are penalized in girl-friendly/boy-unfriendly classrooms. Favoritism for the sedate behavior of girls works against the physical vibrancy of boys. Boys fall prey to feminist pedagogy that is confusing and harmful to a boy's emerging masculinity. Such pedagogy is associated with consensus-style learning favoring girls rather than competitive-style learning favoring boys. This contention is augmented by essentialist beliefs that teachers not only overlook biological factors prompting typical masculine behavior but also utilize the cognitive and emotional attributes of girls as the classroom standard (Gurian, 2007; James, 2007).

These factors jeopardize academic success for boys at all levels of education. Boys take longer to complete high school and have higher dropout rates than girls. About three-fourths of all girls and two-thirds of all boys who start high school graduate four years later. Compared to boys, girls take more college prep courses in most subject areas and report higher career aspirations. In turn, within five years of being admitted to college, about 7–8 percent more women complete a bachelor's degree than men. Like in high school, men are more likely to drop out of college. Teachers may unwittingly create a classroom environment that, as one researcher direly claims, is literally toxic for boys (Sax, 2007).

Another troubling pattern is that boys are more likely to be held back, suspended, or expelled from school. Boys exhibit more discipline problems, including belligerence to teachers and classmates. Boys as a group are more likely to be labeled as "impaired" and are overrepresented in special education classes; African-American boys are significantly overrepresented in these patterns. Attention Deficit and Hyperactivity Disorder (ADHD) diagnoses—associated with short attention span, difficulty in concentration, and erratic behavior—are triple for boys (Williams, 2007; Weaver-Hightower, 2007).

The "boy crisis" label has gained a great deal of media attention and is largely offered to the public as a win-lose model. Inclusiveness, as a goal of gender equity, is couched in media accounts as a cause of boys falling behind girls. The achievement of girls, therefore, comes at the expense of boys. What is the research evidence for this contention?

Assessing the Boy Crisis. With a boy crisis theme as catalyst, a great deal of new research on shortchanged students at all levels of education was launched. In elementary and high school research suggests that gender differences in learning styles and teacher concern for a more sedate classroom with less disruption do tend to favor the behavior of girls over that of boys. On the other hand, teacher favoritism for girls is countered by research consistently showing that girls spend more time studying, doing homework, and reading than boys, and boys spend more time watching television, playing video games, partying, and exercising than girls. Pop culture and peers offer more distractions for boys than for girls (Fletcher, 2002; Lloyd, 2007). Empowering boys to succeed in school means tackling the gender stereotypes allowing them greater entitlement outside of school.

Girls receive higher grades than boys throughout elementary and middle school in most subjects, but by high school boys catch up and match or exceed girls in overall GPA. The data of the National Assessment of Education Progress (NAEP)—referred to as the "Nation's Report Card" taken in grades 4, 8, and 12—on average, shows a gender gap favoring girls in reading and writing, a pattern holding for almost 40 years. A less publicized pattern is that NAEP data *before* 1980 indicated a gender gap in math favoring girls, but by 1990 the gender gap in math and science on NAEP and other standardized tests favoring boys emerged. Initiatives to address the math and science aptitude of girls have paid off spectacularly. As discussed earlier, although the gender gap continues to decrease, boys still maintain a clear (but narrow) advantage in both areas by high school.

College Entrance Exams. Other data countering the assertion that education shortchanges males are scores on the critical standardized tests used for college admission and graduate and professional studies (Spelke and Grace, 2006; AAUW, 2008).

- Boys retain a narrow but consistent advantage on the SAT and ACT even as the population of test takers becomes more diverse. White students were three-quarters of test takers in 1987; students of color are now almost half of test takers.
- On the ACT, girls have an edge in reading and English, but boys have an edge on ACT composite. Girls began to lose their advantage in the verbal area on the SAT as early as the 1970s. They have not been able to regain the math advantage. This is despite the success girls demonstrate on standardized tests and advanced math courses in high school.
- On the average, boys score higher on both the SAT and the ACT, particularly in math, science, and composite. This holds for boys of all races and family incomes.
- Boys retain their advantage in tests used for admission to graduate and professional schools, including medicine, law, and business (GRE, MCAT, LSAT, GMAT). Similar to college entrance exams, the population taking these tests has increased, with women now the majority of test takers.

To understand these patterns, it is important to remember that the larger pool of women test takers includes those of all ability levels compared to the smaller pool of men test takers with higher ability levels. Another key point is that although men outperform women on standardized tests, the larger pool of women *still* generates a larger, qualified pool who will apply to college.

College Enrollment: Race, Social Class, and Age. The gender gap favoring women is widening in higher education. It is the pivotal intersection of race, social class, and age that largely explains this gap. Among students aged 18–24 there is a larger female share from low-income white and Latinos compared to the same categories of males. With fewer lower-income males enrolling in college, the male share—especially among traditional age, higher income white males—decreases further. Adding race to the picture, we find the largest gender gap among African Americans, even as African-American males increased their share of college enrollment over the last two decades. Latino and African-American women are more likely to be enrolled in college than comparable men, regardless of social class. Asian-American men and women are at parity (King, 2006; Lederman, 2006; Lewin, 2006a).

Age is another key factor explaining the gender profile of current college students. Women are much more likely to be in the ranks of returning students; women over 25 outnumber men by a 2-to-1 margin, and among African Americans, women account for nearly 70 percent of older students. Nontraditional age women are more likely than men to be enrolled in community colleges; traditional age men are more likely to be enrolled in four-year colleges, especially in highly selective elite universities. The *number* of men enrolled in all colleges is steadily increasing but not fast enough to narrow "the 57% female majority in *total* enrollment" (King, 2006; Lewin, 2006b). Propelled by a gradual, but continuing influx of nontraditional-age women who attend community colleges part time, the percentage of women in all colleges should be near 70 percent within a decade (Figure 11.3).

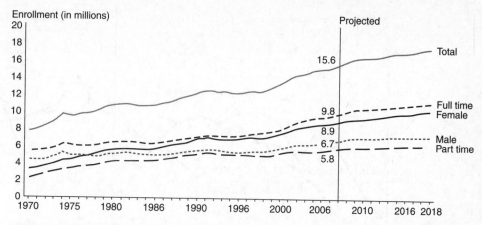

Figure 11.3 Undergraduate Enrollment by Gender and Full-Time/Part-Time Enrollment 1970 to 2009 and Projected to 2018

Source: U.S. Department of Education, National Center for Educational Statistics. *The Condition of Education, 2009.* http://nces.ed.gov/programs/ceo/2009/charts

What a Degree Buys? Another compelling argument against the belief that educational institutions systematically harm boys is that at all educational levels men continue to significantly outearn women (Figure 11.4). For undergraduate degrees, compared to women, men's degrees garner work in more highly paid fields. Women employed full-time on average earn 77 percent of what a man earns. Ten years out of college the pay gap widens to 69 percent (Chapter 10). This pattern holds true even after controlling for factors known to affect earnings, such as seniority, demographics, type of job, amount of education, and personal choice, including parenthood (AAUW, 2008:64). If education is the ticket to financial success, the success translates differently according to gender.

Critique. Multiple sources of educational data do not show boys doing worse. Both boys and girls have improved on educational performance. Boys' test scores have improved alongside that of girls and the proportion of boys graduating from high school and earning B.A.'s is at an all-time high. Despite media panic, the truth is that "the real story is not the bad news about boys doing worse, but good news about girls doing better." Girls have made outstanding progress in narrowing education gaps that previously favored boys. Nevertheless, other long-standing gaps favoring girls have widened, especially college enrollment, leading to the belief boys are falling behind (Mead, 2006:1). Suggesting that boys as a group are jeopardized by these patterns more than girls as a group is not justified. Implying that boys *should* be doing better than girls also devalues the achievement of girls. There was quiet public acceptance when boys began outperforming girls in math and for the continuing math gap favoring boys. Only when reports highlighted the gap, and focused on strategies to help girls, did the "girls versus boys" scenario gain media attention.

Although it cannot be said that boys as a group are in educational crisis relative to girls, it *is* valid to say that some categories of boys are in crisis compared to other

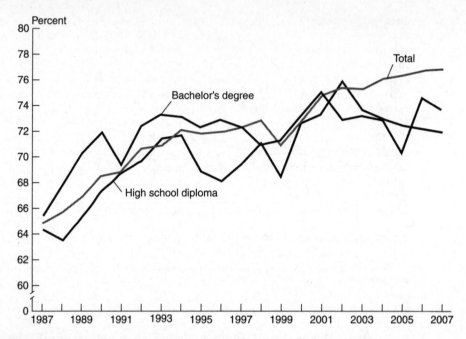

Figure 11.4 Women's Median Income as a Percentage of Men's Median Income by Educational Attainment, 1987 to 2007

Note: Includes full-time year-round workers, aged 25 and over

Source: Educational attainment in the United States: 2007. *Current Populations Reports*. January, 2009. U.S. Census Bureau

categories of boys and most girls. The "real" crisis is that children from poor families, who are disproportionately nonwhite, are less likely to attend college or to graduate once they are admitted. Girls have higher graduation rates but race and poverty are the real culprits explaining the gap (Barnett, 2007). Educational achievement is much more influenced by poverty than by gender (Petrovich and Wells, 2005). Despite the clear, pivotal role in educational outcomes, however, social class and race are glossed over in favor of gender in explaining the patterns. The race–class link is very significant since, compared to women, young men in the highest-income groups of all races are more likely to be attending college.

The focus on existing gender gaps in selected areas of educational attainment is a simplistic way of viewing the issue. The data are complicated and show disappearing and reappearing gender and social-class gaps in achievement, especially in math. Many studies do not account for race. Scientific research may eventually sort out the complexities between race, class, and gender in explaining these patterns, but as we will see, social policy fueled by a political agenda will decide which group, if any, is shortchanged overall.

Single-Gender Education

Until the Nineteenth Century females were discouraged from attending high school and virtually denied access to higher education in the United States. Since coeducation was nonexistent, educational spaces for female students from middle-class families were created by founding women's colleges, many providing excellent programs that rivaled male-only institutions. Bringing together unlikely partners who support the "shortchanged girls or boys in crisis" theme, precollegiate single-gender education is making a comeback. It is offered as a strategy for dealing with a host of issues related to gender-based restrictions in schools, including gender gaps in achievement and sexual harassment. If boys and girls learn differently, mature at different paces, and are distracted by one another in classrooms, then perhaps they should be schooled separately.

Schools may offer single-gender courses for either boys or girls, so long as the *Equal Protection Clause* of the 14th Amendment in the Constitution is upheld. Districts must make available courses that are "comparable" for students of the other gender. This section will assess evidence suggesting that single-gender education—either in separate classrooms or in separate schools—is better or worse than coeducation.

Girls in Single-Gender Classrooms. Liabilities for female students decline when women outnumber men in high school and college classrooms or when female faculty represent a larger proportion of overall faculty, particularly in math and science. When girls become the sole group of learners, on measures of scholarship, academic aspirations, attitudes toward studies, leadership, and self-confidence, the research is quite favorable for single-gender education for girls of all races. Among high school students, African-American and Latino girls score higher on measures of leadership and self-esteem (Campbell and Sanders, 2002; Riordan, 2002). Single-gender education for girls is linked to later academic and career success. Girls from single-gender high schools are more likely to attend better colleges, to outperform girls who attend coed colleges, and to go on to graduate or professional schools (U.S. Department of Education, 2005; Clarke, 2007; Salomone, 2007a).

Females who make a transition the other way—from a single-gender educational environment to a coeducational one—indicate they experience a "clash of cultures" and report discomfort and dissatisfaction with the coed format (Sadovnik and Semel, 2002). Women express concern that friends could become competitors when men are a regular part of campus life. Qualitative research by Janice Streitmatter (1999:87, 105) on middle and high school girls attending single-gender schools or taking girls-only classes in coed schools points to the benefits of single-gender formats. For example, girls describe fewer distractions from learning. They are aware that in coed classes boys receive most of the teacher's attention: "In a mixed class . . . you're like off in the background—you're quieter about what you know." In the single-gender format, girls ask and answer questions without the risk of "feeling stupid."

A powerful message to girls in single-gender classes is that they are intellectually strong and are not limited in their aspirations just because they are girls.

Boys in Single-Gender Classrooms. With research attention on how boys fare in single-gender classrooms, a number of trends are now suggested. Boys do appear to be as successful as girls in achievement tests and there is evidence that boys in single-gender classrooms have higher career aspirations and choose more humanities-related subjects than boys in coeducational classrooms. When race is factored in, minority males appear to benefit more than white males (James, 2003; U.S. Department of Education, 2005).

In terms of classroom atmosphere, learning outcomes appear to be enhanced for boys in classrooms encouraging competition, technical skill building, and mechanical expertise. Plentiful "boy friendly" books on topics such as war, spaceships, and pirates, and biographies of famous athletes encourage reading. Male teachers in single-gender classrooms for boys tend to allow for more physical movement. Regardless of the gender of the teacher, however, there are limits to boy "vibrancy" in the classroom. Research on teachers evaluating single-gender classes for boys believes that both behavior and academic performance deteriorated in this format (Gray and Wilson, 2006). The irony of the belief that "boys can't sit still" is that single-gender classrooms for boys in turn impose stricter discipline and more rigid, formal classroom procedures similar to schools of the past.

Single-gender education for boys is likely to be based on even stronger androcentric pedagogy than in either girls' schools or coeducational institutions. Elementary school on the surface appears to favor girls' passivity rather than boys' activity but it, too, is largely based on a male-centered approach to learning, a pattern that is heightened in high school. Although consensus style activities are normative, coed high school classrooms are structured around hierarchy, domination, and win-lose grading and pedagogy. Masculinity norms are strongly reinforced and rarely questioned in boys' schools by the formal and hidden curriculum. Girls in single-gender schools hold less rigid gender stereotypes; boys hold more (Karpiak et al., 2007).

Critique. In evaluating the impact of precollegiate single-gender instruction—either in separate classrooms or in separate schools—most studies report generally "positive" effect on achievement tests in all subjects for both males and females and for both elementary and high school students. The benefits of single-gender education appear to be the greatest for students determined as "at risk" for a variety of academic, social, and emotional reasons. This should not be construed to mean, however, that coeducation is *worse* than single-gender education in achievement, but only that it is not significantly better (Cooper, 2006; Weil, 2008).

However, both boys and girls in coeducation settings place high importance on having the other gender in their classes and, as expected, report a more appealing social climate. In terms of school culture, both boys and girls attending single-gender schools place higher values on "grades and leadership and less on attractiveness and money" (U.S. Department of Education, 2005). Schools are the settings offering the best atmosphere for primary contact necessary to reduce both racism and sexism in young people.

Opponents of single-gender schools argue that single-gender education represents "benevolent sexism." It can be used for emancipation or oppression but either way an outcome is not guaranteed (Datnow and Hubbard, 2005). Appearing to be a panacea for problems in schools, single-gender schooling discourages understanding between the genders, may reproduce damaging gender stereotypes, and diminish respect for women (Salomone, 2007c). In both high school and college, single-gender education may serve to reinforce negative effects of an already pervasive gender-segregated society (Hubbard and Datnow, 2002; Baskin, 2004). Some critics charge that it heralds retreats from gender inclusiveness to gender resegregation and to the days of "separate but unequal" classrooms (Davis, 2006; Salomone, 2007b). A strong case can be made that single-gender schools for boys discourage egalitarian beliefs about gender roles and may actually increase the propensity for sexual harassment when males and females do come together in other settings. Throughout socialization, within-gender solidarity is enhanced through gender segregation, but between-gender understanding is diminished (Chapter 3). A powerful message to boys in single-gender settings is that they are better than girls.

Perhaps the most compelling challenge is, as we have seen, the rate of student success is class based more than gender based. Single-gender schools are likely to be private schools attended by more affluent students, and that have better facilities, higher-paid teachers, and smaller student–teacher ratios. Private single-gender schools can also expel disruptive students who then retreat to public coeducational schools that must accept them.

It is unlikely that single-gender education will be able to compete with coeducation for all but a small subset of students. Even with the upsurge of single-gender classrooms, mostly with boys in mind and the solid evidence that high school girls are the greatest beneficiaries of single-gender instruction, the coeducation norm will not be significantly altered. High achieving girls are less likely to enter women's colleges than even a decade ago (Salomone, 2007b). The premium of coeducation in college is growing. It is also responsible for the difficulty women's colleges face in attracting students.

Coeducation can certainly provide a major channel for reducing gender segregation and, with attention to gender-equitable instruction, gender stereotyping is also likely to be reduced. If there is a problem of male dominance in the coed classroom that is detrimental to girls, an argument can be made that it is also detrimental to boys. Rather than retreating into gender-segregated schools, the classroom atmosphere can be altered to reflect a more gender-sensitive school culture that is beneficial to both females and males. Schools are microcosms of the real world, so they need to model that world. Regardless of which side of the debate one is on, classroom environments can be modified to capitalize on successful learning strategies provided by single-gender education. Such modifications may also reduce sexual harassment, including sexualized bullying and gender-related violence.

Sexual Harassment in Schools

Sexual harassment legally includes physical or verbal conduct that is sexual in nature, is unwanted, and creates a hostile environment that interferes with school or work activities. Despite the fact that sexual harassment is illegal, it is so widespread at all levels in schools—from elementary through graduate school—that it is considered a part of everyday life for students (AAUW, 2001; Stein, 2007a).

Sexual harassment, ranges from so-called "joking" about a girl's body, pinching, physical contact and groping, demeaning images, negative remarks, and sexist comments, to unwanted advances, demands for sexual favors, and sexual aggression or victimization. When race is factored in, some research reports higher rates of sexual harassment for girls and women of color compared to white women. How common is sexual harassment in schools? (AAUW, 2002, 2006; Boland, 2002; Walker, 2008)?

- About 80 percent of both boys and girls in elementary and middle school experience sexual harassment.
- Almost 40 percent of teachers and school staff in high schools have been harassed by students.
- Almost half of teachers and school staff have been harassed by each other.
- Two-thirds of both male and female college students have been harassed at their university but fewer than 10 percent of victims report it; dorms are the sites for about 40 percent of the cases.

- Over one-third of college students do tell anyone about sexual harassment.
- Among college students, approximately half of the men and one-third of the women admit to sexually harassing someone on campus.

Approximately one-fourth of all students at all levels who admit to sexual harassment repeat it, either occasionally or often.

Bullying. The most virulent forms of bullying usually occur in middle school. For these students, bullying commonly consists of sexualized comments and actions acting as weapons of humiliation. In cross-gender bullying, boys may call girls "sluts," "pussies," or "bitches"; girls may be humiliated through staring, touching, and ridiculing the size of their breasts. Girls report avoiding crowded school hallways known as places where boys intentionally brush up against girls, pinching and fondling them as they pass by. Although much less common, girls do harass boys, usually through taunting that implicitly derides assumptions about masculinity (wuss, geek, loser).

Same-gender bullying behavior is common and growing. Boys are not only more likely to be the perpetrators of bullying but they are also more likely to be the victims of it (Stein, 2007b). Boys especially fear being mocked with derisive name-calling associated with homosexuality (fag, queer, pervert). Any perceived deviation from stereotypical male images and norms can turn into such derision. Sexualized bullying between boys is likely to be ignored, but when teachers fail to act on it, consequences can be deadly, especially for gay and lesbian students. In reporting research on sexual harassment, for example, an openly gay student attempted suicide after classmates assaulted him by kicking him in the face while screaming "faggot" (Sandler and Stonehill, 2005).

Although girl-to-girl bullying is less frequent, it is escalating and in ways that mimic male-to-male bullying. Like boys, girls use sexually degrading names for other girls (whore, cunt) and harass each other about their appearance, mostly to do with their clothing and their bodies. Like boys, the psychological warfare perpetrated on girls who do fit popularity norms about femininity are most vulnerable to bullying (Simmons, 2003; Gardner et al., 2008). Under a cloak of anonymity, Internet sexual harassment, bullying, and sexual solicitation have exploded (Ybarra et al., 2007).

For fear of being discovered, called a "snitch," and subject to ridicule or isolation by classmates, and branded a "troublemaker" by teachers, both boys and girls are not likely to report bullying. Bullying decreases with age but bullies and their allies are often difficult to topple in middle school. The perceived assault on a boy's gender identity begun in elementary school makes boys reluctant to report bullying at all, but especially if they are bullied by girls. Whether referred to as bullying or not, the reporting pattern repeats itself in college. College students do not report sexual harassment, and sexual violence such as date rape is underreported (Chapter 9). Reprisals for college women include the "troublemaker" brand or being frozen out by faculty, staff, and classmates.

Military Schools. In military schools cadets are subject to various rites of passage including hazing and training designed to cement a class and plant unquestioned obedience to military authority (Manegold, 2000). Hazing includes use of sexualized language and demeaning stereotypes related to gender roles. Such training represents the extreme forms of bullying, but in the case of military schools, it is legitimized and usually encouraged.

Bullying is not considered sexual harassment. Cadets of both genders are viewed the "same." Sameness means that men and women adhere to powerful masculinity norms that include derogatory beliefs about women. Female cadets must walk a fine line of supporting cadet bonding but without denigrating other women. Male cadets can be accused of sexual harassment—and expelled—only if bullying becomes sexualized so that the "hidden gender" of the female cadets is revealed and acted upon in denigrating words and deeds.

The sameness–difference issue has haunted us throughout this text. Symbolic interactionists maintain that once admitted to "uncontaminated" all-male military schools new female cadets are tokens and must constantly negotiate gender differences and similarities—always "doing" gender. "When they stressed sameness they were seen as different; when they stressed difference, they were treated the same." Both male and female cadets believe that equal means the same, and standards of training should reflect that sameness. But as Michael Kimmel (2000:505, 507) suggests, not acknowledging important differences that do exist—treating unlikes alike—is also a form of discrimination.

Disproving stereotypes of women as incapable of withstanding the rigorous training for later military roles is fairly easy. Both men and women cadets achieve higher levels of success related to leadership, preparation for team diversity, and physical endurance when trained together (Diamond, 2007). Close physical contact between women and men does not distract them from the performance of their military duties. Women have been admitted to West Point and all the elite service academies for over 30 years and the ability to wage war has not been compromised by their presence. The sexism in arguments that rely on notions of one gender being more or less inherently capable, especially in the face of massive evidence to the contrary, makes it difficult for any public figure to support such arguments today.

Sexual Harassment or Bullying? Educators are quite aware of the difference between benign teasing and bullying. But the distinction between sexual harassment and bullying is a blurry one. Bullying behavior among middle school and military school students is clearly harassment, but it is usually not defined as "sexual" harassment unless it involves cross-gender behavior, regardless of the derogatory language used about women.

Sexual harassment involving bullying behavior of boys to girls, although illegal, is largely ignored—accepted by the boys, tolerated by the girls, and ignored by the teachers. When adults and teachers hear comments but do not intervene, both boys and girls believe that the behavior is appropriate (Stein, 2007b; AAUW, 2008). Whereas racial comments are swiftly censured, sexually harassing ones are usually dismissed unless physical harm results.

Educators are calling for a wider definition of sexual harassment that encompasses all forms of bullying, whether it is cross-gender or not. Since bullying is associated with sexual derogatory language and behaviors demeaning to both genders, the legal power behind the label of "sexual harassment" makes it easier to censure—and hopefully reduce—both sexual harassment and bullying. Schools that tolerate sexual harassment and bullying are associated with negative outcomes for everyone (Gruber and Fineran, 2007; Ormerod et al., 2008).

Females and males do not differ in intelligence and capability. However, because educational institutions, like all social institutions, are gendered, the results of the gendering should not be ignored in school policies. Gender needs to be considered, for example, in terms of who gets accepted to selective and competitive schools—whether as a female cadet or a male nursing student.

Gender Parity in College

The most important emerging gender issue in education has to do with the very successes girls have achieved at all educational levels. Women have made remarkable strides in educational achievement, but college admissions offices are dealing with the results of these strides in an unforeseen way.

College Admissions. High school females are at parity with, or outperforming, males on criteria indicative of success in college, such as GPA, standardized tests on reading and writing literacy, and paid work and volunteer experiences. Women are tackling and achieving in formerly male-dominated areas, such as law, medicine, and biology. Women with superior academic credentials continue to ascend in athletics, and colleges are more actively recruiting female athletes. The pool of scholar-athletes is increasing for women but shrinking for men. Women are described as more intensely motivated in the admissions process, work harder than men on their applications, and apply to more schools (Lewin, 2006a). From the end of World War II to the 1970s most universities had larger acceptable gender imbalances favoring men. Today most universities have increasingly unacceptable gender imbalances favoring women. This pattern is repeated in the United States, Canada, and England (Evers et al., 2006).

How are colleges dealing with the ever increasing pool of highly qualified women applicants compared to a smaller pool of less qualified men? Many colleges are admitting less qualified men and acknowledging they are doing so. Accomplished women face much higher rejection rates. "Maintaining gender equity on some campuses appears to require a thumb on the scale in favor of boys" (Kingsbury, 2007). Many admissions officers believe that a 60/40 ratio of female to male is the "tipping point" that will hurt the coeducational climate on campus. Some research indicates that college women prefer a gender-equitable 50–50 split. College men, however, see the larger ratio of women to their (men's) advantage in the sexual scripts played out in campus life. It is unlikely that men will continue to find it acceptable if the imbalance tips beyond the 60 percent level, especially at more prestigious colleges. If a campus is perceived as too "feminized" because of the number women students, men may retreat to other campuses (Whitmire, 2008).

Admissions policies are complicated and secretive, especially in highly selective private institutions. Although the legalities are unclear and rulings are inconsistent (Fletcher, 2002), the Supreme Court has endorsed race as a factor that, under some circumstances, can be used in decision making; it has not "directly addressed gender targeting in admissions" (Kingsbury, 2007). The higher rejection rate of accomplished females is not only legally questionable but it implies that girls are penalized for their success.

It is doubtful that complacency of this issue will continue and advocates for women will begin to challenge the system. The question becomes how to provide strategies that do not pit males and females against one another and allow gender balance on campus without compromising other forms of diversity.

THE LESSONS OF TITLE IX

Virtually all of the education issues discussed in this chapter have legal implications that, in effect, can be addressed at some level by **Title IX of the 1972 Educational Amendment Act**. Since this act prohibits sex (gender) discrimination in any school receiving federal assistance, the majority of educational institutions fall under its mandate. At the overt, formal level Title IX has ushered in school policies reducing glaring gender discrimination. It has had a huge impact on athletics, for example, and is directly responsible for major increases in the sports participation of female students at all school levels (Chapter 14).

Title IX has been most successful in tackling issues of gender discrimination viewed as detrimental to *both* females and males. Policies related to single-gender education and sexual harassment are two such issues. Under Title IX, the U.S. Department of Education provided the green light for public schools to offer single-gender alternatives under certain conditions. Title IX also forbids sexual harassment of students, and a school may be liable if authorities know it is occurring but fail to act on it (Raskin, 2008). However, the courts have been inconsistent in rulings related to both single-gender schooling and sexual harassment about specific circumstances that can be used to hold a school liable.

At the informal level, discriminatory practices that are difficult to eradicate through legal means persist throughout the educational process. The gender gap in career aspirations has largely disappeared and women's participation in traditional male-dominated majors continues to climb. Women continue to be discouraged, however, from the very majors offering the most lucrative job options, such as engineering and chemistry (Burge, 2007). Math and science are the glass ceiling academic equivalents for women.

Gender segregation exists throughout all levels of education. Kindergarten girls are princesses and play with dolls; boys are pirates and play with trucks. Girls take home economics in middle school and boys take shop in high school. In college, men major in physics and women in literature. A male Ph.D. teaches engineering. A female Ph.D. teaches French. He is paid more than she is. Even the more progressive world of the university remains gender role oriented and gender separated. And despite Title IX, gender discrimination in college admissions is making a comeback.

Curricular revisions aimed at gender inclusiveness are slow to implement, teachers retreat to gendered beliefs about classroom behavior that may punish boys and overlook girls, and the hidden curriculum stubbornly persists. When children self-select school activities by gender, teachers are reluctant to resist these choices. With seeming approval for voluntary gender segregation for twelve years, it is difficult to alter the resulting gender segregation of academic fields, at either the student or the faculty level.

Title IX has enormous potential to change practices that restrict educational opportunities because of gender, especially in a political environment where gender equity again becomes an important agenda item. A more receptive political climate appears to be on the forefront. Although gender segregation in education is normative, this chapter documents encouraging signs that gender stereotypes are gradually being reduced. The good news is that gender discrimination may disappear by the time Jane and Dick reach college. But gender prejudice is likely to linger for their children and grandchildren.

GLOBAL FOCUS: THE DEVELOPING WORLD'S GENDER GAP IN EDUCATION

One of greatest returns on all development investments is to teach girls to read. A girl's education is linked to decreased child death rates, dramatic drops in infant mortality, delayed marriage, and poverty reduction. Even lower rates of HIV infection and higher crop yields are correlated to every year a girls remains in school. Children of a literate mother have a better chance of survival than the children living in the same place at the same level of income of a mother who is illiterate.

Among the most important global demographic trends, a woman's education level is the strongest predictor of fertility rate. This is true among countries and among women in the same country. Females with more education marry later, want fewer children, and have only the number of children they want. Birth rates and child death rates decline fastest where there is access to family planning, health services, and educational opportunities for girls. Thailand and Sri Lanka represent family planning success stories. Compared to other parts of developing Asia, these countries also have higher levels of female education and literacy (World Health Organization, 2003; Herro, 2007). The simple correlation between education and fertility masks its enormous, positive impact on the lives of individual women and their families, and also on the world as a whole. It is clear that the ripple effect of a girl's education is both powerful and productive.

Throughout the developing world the enrollment of girls at all levels of education continues to improve. Gross enrollment rates for girls in some poor countries have doubled in three decades. These rates are perhaps more remarkable because girls carry a heavier workload both at home and at school and have less leisure time than boys, especially during adolescence (Lloyd et al., 2008). Despite these improvements, the United Nations Millennium Development Goal of gender parity in primary and secondary education by 2005 was not met in most developing regions. There is a large and persistent global education and literacy gap (Table 11.2). China

Table 11.2 Youth Female (Aged 15–24) Literacy Rates, Selected Developing World Regions and Countries

Region	Overall % Youth Female Literacy Rate
Latin America and Caribbean	97
Middle East and North Africa	86
South Asia	74
Sub-Saharan Africa	67

Country	Under 70% Youth Female Literacy
India	67.8
Zambia	66.2
Morocco	60.5
Nepal	60.2
Pakistan	54.1
Haiti	53.8
Senegal	40.9
Liberia	38.6
Ethiopia	34.1
Bangladesh	33.2
Mozambique	31.7
Chad	23.3
Niger	23.2
Afghanistan	18.4
Mali	16.9

Note: Latest figures available, 2006–2008.

Source: World Bank, 2008, 2009. *World Development Indicators*. International Bank for Reconstruction and Development. Washington, D.C.: World Bank.

has made spectacular gains in reducing adult illiteracy to less than 10 percent, but women make up the large majority of the illiterate population. Even with a world-wide drop in illiteracy, two-thirds of the world's people who cannot read are female, and in any part of the world, an illiterate adult is likely to be a woman. The largest education gap is between the developed and developing world (Chapter 6). In the developing world the largest gap is in Africa. Almost all of the world's children not enrolled in primary school are in the developing world. For every 100 boys not in primary school there are 270 girls in Yemen, 316 in Iraq, 426 in India, and 257 in Benin who are not enrolled (World Bank, 2008). For all out-of-school children, most live in Sub-Saharan Africa and South and West Asia. Most of these children are in poverty, most are in rural areas, and most of them are girls.

Investing in women's education brings high returns globally. Despite the fact that elimination of the gender education gap is in the best interest of a thriving global economy, reducing the gap in the developing world loses priority during global economic downturn. As conflict theorists remind us, altering gender role norms to bring about social change brings both benefits and liabilities, depending on how various social groups are affected. The paradox of the globe's gender gap is that women and girls have not amassed the power to challenge these norms in part because of their lack of education.

Summary

1. Historically when women were first granted the right of education, it was to be in line with their wife and mother roles.

2. The process of education is highly gendered and operates through a hidden curriculum. Gender segregation in kindergarten is reinforced by toys and games that provide high levels of activity for boys and quietness for girls.

3. Girls in elementary school have higher achievement levels and receive less criticism but less instructional time than boys. Boys adjust less easily to school but gain more attention from teachers. Children read textbooks that underrepresent girls and cast males and females into stereotyped roles.

4. Boys gain in self-confidence and achievement in high school; girls decline in both, especially Latino girls. The math gender gap has virtually disappeared. Existing differences are best explained by cultural factors, due to gender, rather than biological factors, due to biology. Social class and the race–SES link are better predictors of math performance and school achievement than is gender.

5. Tracking puts more girls than boys in all vocational courses and in academic courses like English. Textbooks in high school are gender stereotyped, and an androcentric bias exists in standardized achievement tests.

6. Popularity for boys in high school is tied to athletics; for girls it is attractiveness and popularity with boys. Athletics for boys provides powerful gender identity messages; boys who cannot perform in sports can lose self-esteem, and more so if they do coeducational sports. More money and facilities are given to sports for males.

7. Fueled by women over 35 attending part-time, women are enrolled in college at higher numbers than men. Women are undermined in college achievement and career orientation by issues related to marriage and motherhood. Men are more consistent with predictions about career in their future plans.

8. Women are distributed in majors that translate into less lucrative jobs. Men are concentrated in science and engineering and dominate fields requiring graduate work. Women in graduate school have fewer mentors of their own gender and spend less time with all faculty.

9. Female college faculty are more likely to be part-time, in nontenure tracks, and at lower ranks than males. Compared to faculty men, faculty women are evaluated differently and in line with gender stereotypes by students, colleagues, and administrators.

10. Boys or girls in educational crisis have received research attention. Boys retain narrow leads in the SAT and ACT; girls have ACT leads in reading. Men's degrees pay higher economic returns than women's degrees. The boy crisis belief is not borne out by data.

11. Single-gender education for females is associated with higher self-confidence, leadership, and achievement. Single-gender education for boys is associated with strong androcentric pedagogy. When males and females are schooled separately, understanding between men and women may be further decreased. Coed classrooms can be modified for the strengths of single-gender classrooms.

12. Sexual harassment of girls by boys in elementary schools is often in the form of bullying. Research on whether women of color are harassed more is unclear. Sexual harassment of males is growing. In military schools girls are bullied, but it is not sexual harassment unless sexualized terms are used. Boys use these terms to bully other boys. Female cadets must negotiate how much they are the same and how much they are different from male cadets. Single-gender schools are not substantially better than co-ed schools.

13. Women outnumber men on campus but colleges want to retain gender balance. Less-qualified men are being admitted.

14. Title IX—which prohibits sex discrimination in schools—has dealt with blatant discrimination and has greatly aided sports programs for females. But is has had limited effect in altering gender segregation in academic fields.

15. Literacy for females is one of the best ways to make development a success. When girls are taught to read, family size shrinks, child death rates decrease, and wages increase. Despite advances, a global gender gap in education persists. Women make up the vast majority of illiterate adults worldwide.

Key Terms

hidden curriculum 305

sexual harassment 325

Title IX of the 1972
  Educational Amendment
  Act 328

Something went terribly wrong with Christianity's original gospel of love.

—*The Chalice and the Blade,*
Riane Eisler, 1995

The transformation of ancient spirituality into modern religion came with a heavy price. Religious imagery is used to maintain injustice, suffering, and oppression—of nation against nation, men against men, and men against women. Institutionalized religion—whether pagan, Hebrew, Christian, or Islamic—not only helped maintain hierarchies of domination and oppression but also functioned to alleviate part of the suffering caused by these very hierarchies (Eisler, 1995a:203). In many ancient spiritual and religious traditions and in the societies in which they were practiced, women held influential and esteemed partnership roles with men. As religions became more formal and moved toward institutionalization, the spirituality and the partnership on which many are based receded into the background. Net gains in overall gender equality in all social institutions are recorded across the globe, but organized religion lags behind in the amount of religious authority granted to women compared to men. Religion is the one institution that should offer the most potential for freedom of expression through liberating spirituality, but the undeniably sexist interpretations and practices—and human rights violations—in the name of religion seriously impede its liberating potential (Eisler, 1995b; Nussbaum, 2000). We will see, however, revised interpretations provide opportunities to release patriarchy's religious stranglehold and open the doors of churches, temples, and mosques to the empowering messages religions offer to both women and men.

REDISCOVERING THE FEMININE FACE OF GOD

The image of God as a woman is probably quite startling to those who identify with any of the major world religions. The explosion of research on the role and status of women in these religions reveals that these early religions were infused with notions of gender interdependence rather than gender separation. Based on archaeological evidence found in both prehistoric and historic societies, research now offers a view of the first civilizations as exhibiting **gynocentrism**, with an emphasis on female and feminine interests (Gimbutas, 1991, 2001; Sered, 1994; Eisler, 1995a; Gross, 2009). Whereas androcentrism translated to patriarchy in some ancient societies, gynocentrism did not translate to matriarchy in others. Instead, it translated into partnership. As Riane Eisler (1995b) points out, the terms *patriarchy* and *matriarchy* refer to a ranking of one part of humanity over the other. She asserts that partnership is the third, overlooked alternative that characterized much of early civilization. Unlike patriarchy or matriarchy, *partnership* is based on the principle of linking and relating rather than domination and separateness. Males and females may be different, but these differences are not associated with either inferiority or superiority. Given the powerful influence of religion in the structure of ancient civilizations, evidence for gynocentric societies offers important messages to contemporary theologians as they struggle with issues related to gender role change in their respective religions.

Goddess Images

The most ancient human image we have of the divine is a figure of a female. When gynocentrism was replaced by androcentrism in partnership-oriented societies, the millennia of goddess prehistory and history were relegated to academic oblivion or dismissed by scholars as incidental to the span of humanity (Gimbutas, 2001). From a conflict perspective, when spirituality began the road to institutionalized religion, goddess images were suppressed because their power was threatening to an emerging male-dominated religious status quo. For contemporary women, rediscovering the goddess heritage can affirm their sense of religious well-being. Contrary to the conflict perspective, however, a partnership approach does not create a new hierarchy of religious images that would serve to empower women but disenfranchise men. From Eisler's partnership viewpoint, both men and women can share in and celebrate the principles rooted in the goddess heritage and use these principles as standards as they work together for religious reform.

The emerging picture, then, demonstrates a religious portrait of ancient civilizations where women played a central role, where female deities were worshipped, and where religious life was a partnership between men and women, much more than modern institutionalized religion would have us believe. The intent here is to provide a brief chronicle of some images of women as they appear in the mythology and religious heritage of people in the ancient world. Such an account is important for grasping the significance of attitudes toward women in modern world religion that is the focus of the latter part of this chapter.

Women's Religious Roles. Compelling evidence for a continuous, influential goddess heritage and the significance of women's ancient religious roles in this heritage abounds (Roller, 1999; Berger, 2000; Cleary and Aziz, 2000). The cult of the mother-goddess was one of the oldest, most widespread, and longest-surviving religions throughout the Paleolithic to Neolithic periods in sites from Western Europe, through the Mediterranean world, and into India. The cult of the mother-goddess provides images of women in roles as leaders, healers, artists, music makers, and food providers. In an early effort to document women's dominance of prehistoric civilization, Elizabeth Davis's (1971:16) then controversial book, *The First Sex*, states not only that there is massive evidence for the matriarchal origins of human society but also that the "further back one traces *man's* history, the larger loomed the figure of woman." She maintains that in all myth, the goddess is synonymous with gynocracy so when the goddess reigned, women ruled. Although scholars continue to debate the amount of actual power women held in goddess-dominated societies, abundant archaeological evidence on goddess worship does suggest gynocentric (rather than matriarchal) origins of civilization (Eller, 2000; Christ, 2003b).

Archaeological evidence attesting to gynocratic religious and artistic traditions has been uncovered in the world's best-preserved and oldest Neolithic sites in Catal Huyuk, what is now modern Turkey. These traditions span 800 years, from 6500 to 5700 B.C.E., and are vividly represented by numerous goddess figurines, all emphasizing worship of a female deity. The artifacts of prehistoric European peoples demonstrate representations of the goddess as a symbol of life, fertility, creativity, and regeneration. Although the vast majority of the symbols are associated with life images rather than death images, they all speak to the veneration and powerful sacredness of women (Gimbutas, 2001).

Goddess as Creator. The goddess image is carried through to the idea of the creator when examining accounts from ancient Native America, Sumer, Babylon, Assyria, Greece, Egypt, India, and China. Nammu is the Summerian goddess who gives birth to heaven and earth, Tiamet is the Babylonian "Creator of All," the mother of gods, and in Greek mythology, Metis, loosely translated as the creative power of female intelligence, brings the world into being without a male partner. In the *Tao te ching*, creation is the reproduction of all matter from the womb of the Mother. Paleolithic peoples saw the original source of life on earth not as a divine Father but as a divine Mother, and the creative sexual power of women as a miracle of nature, to be revered and blessed. In Chinese Buddhism the goddess of compassion is Kuan Yin; in Hinduism the goddess of destruction is Kali, the consort of Siva, who is revered both as a giver and as a destroyer of life. The twenty-one representations of the female Tibetan deity Tara symbolize compassion, the easing of human suffering, and the guidance to wisdom and salvation. The goddess as the first creator is associated with mythology and religious principles in all corners of the world. It is only in later myth that she is replaced by a god (Ruether, 2006; Weaver, 2006; Mabbett and Bapat, 2008).

With the Babylonian empire's dominance in the emerging urban–agricultural world, the warrior-champion Marduk arises as the god of the new city–state. The Marduk–Tiamet story tells of the defeat of Tiamet and her consort, who represent the power of chaos, by the new god Marduk and his followers, who represent the power of order (Ruether, 1983:50). The emergence of the new gods, however, did not erase female names and memories. Marduk molded the cosmos out of Tiamet's body, so she retained her place as the creator. Siva in India, Atea in Polynesia, and Ea in Syria are also names of goddesses carried over to the male gods who replaced them. Goddess worship was not eradicated but many practices were driven underground by later religious persecution (Cleary and Aziz, 2000; Lightfoot, 2003). Perhaps the female names given to male gods were, and still are, the vestiges of such practices.

Africa. The oldest record of human habitation is in Africa, and it is there where perhaps the best examples of the goddess as the Mother of All are found. On a continent with an incredible diversity of peoples, customs, and religious symbolism, images of the goddess throughout Sub-Saharan Africa vary as well, from Mawu, creator of the world, to the Goddess as the Moon, to the Goddess as "She Who Sends Rain" (Stone, 1990). In Ghana, Nigeria, and other parts of west and central Africa, tribal religions recognize a divinity that may be male or female. Other cults have primarily female spirit beings. Even given such diversity, the symbolism that emerges most consistently among African indigenous religions involves the concerns for honesty, courage, sympathy, hope, and humanitarianism, which the goddesses represented and the peoples who worshipped them revered. The roots of this heritage are expressed in the many female-dominated religious cults and secret societies that give meaning to African women's lives and continue today to affirm their power (Sered, 1994; Amadiume, 1997; Nkulu-N'Sengha, 2001).

Asia. The ancient texts of China and India also speak clearly to the goddess image. Taoism, the indigenous religious tradition of China, is illustrated by the *Chuang Tzu,* written in the third century B.C.E. Part of this account is a description of the Era of the Great Purity, a utopian matrilineal society, where life was characterized by happiness, harmony, and spontaneity and where women held influential and venerated family and extradomestic roles. Most of the symbols in this and other Taoist (Daoist) works are explicitly female and highlight fertility and abundant, unqualified motherly love (Wong, 2002; Despeux and Kohn, 2003). It is interesting that women's spiritual power and social influence found in Taoist societies developed and coexisted in a region dominated by Confucian principles, which were highly patriarchal and hierarchical and viewed women as inferior by nature. Although Confucianism remained the dominant religion, Taoist elements could be discovered within other parts of ancient Chinese culture. Contemporary Taoism upholds the positive principles of the feminine and of mutuality in beliefs and rituals (Xiaogan, 2001).

In India, ancient Buddhist traditions supported women's quest for enlightenment (Gross, 2009). Taoism shares with Buddhism less restrictive and more positive images of women compared with many other Eastern and Western traditions (Coleman, 2001; Puntarigvivat, 2001). In the few Chinese regions where Taoist and Buddhist principles intersected, some evidence suggests that women had such high degrees of power that matriarchal societies were said to exist. More research is needed to support this suggestion, but contemporary women in these areas hold positions associated with more esteem and power than women in other regions of China (Lindsey, 1999).

The Principle of Gender Complementarity

Beyond the goddess images that dominated many ancient practices and beliefs, some religious systems also incorporated principles of balance where, in principle, neither gender was superior. Most notable among these is the ancient Chinese concept of *Yin and Yang*. Although Western interpretation often misrepresents the female principal of Yin as being passive and dominated by the active and aggressive male principal of Yang, this is a distortion of the ancient belief, which emphasized equilibrium, complementarity, and a portion of each principle being incorporated into the other. The Yin–Yang ideal of harmonious balance remains central to the Chinese value system. Much of the original intent of balance was lost as patriarchy extended its influence to all cultural elements, including religion.

Tantric Buddhism in medieval India and Tibet was amenable to both male and female *siddhas*—accomplished ones—whose gender was considered irrelevant to the ultimate Buddhist goal of enlightenment. Buddha's disciples included both men and women, and spiritual paths to enlightenment were open to both men and women. Women could be ordained as nuns just as men could become monks, practices that continue today. In Native American spiritual traditions the complementarity of men and women was evident, with the genders performing unique spiritual practices or sharing others. The matrilineal Iroquois tribes of eastern North America participated in religious ceremonies where both the male and the female dimensions were needed, such as rites to encourage the male activity of hunting or the female activity of agriculture. It is difficult to generalize about such diverse Native American cultures, but they were likely to be holistic and organized their worldviews according to the interdependence of natural forces and human forces (Jocks, 2001; Staeger, 2003). With male and female powers balancing each other, social equilibrium was said to be maintained.

Critique. In ancient and contemporary societies, religious traditions incorporating notions of male and female complementarity and balance did not inevitably carry over into other realms. If Tantric Buddhism was a path open to both genders, the Indian and Tibetan cultures made it very difficult for women to pursue such a path, given their restrictions in other institutional settings. Women who wished to follow the path as nuns had to submit to rigid standards of male control established by the monks, practices which carry through to today. Buddhism is shifting in response to feminist interpretations and to global politics, and contemporary nuns are challenging the gender hierarchy giving monks predominant power (Gutschow, 2004; Hooks et al., 2008). For Native Americans, the Iroquois also denied public expression of women in a variety of settings. Gender complementarity does not necessarily translate into gender equity. Complementarity assumes males and females are "designed to make up for one another's deficiencies, rather than inspiring one another to overcome them" (Webster, 1995:194).

Regardless of the inequality that doubtlessly existed in other parts of the society, these accounts of goddess images and male–female complementarity in early religious traditions do provide an alternative, clearly positive view of women. This view can help offset contemporary religious interpretations about women's submissiveness, subordination, and powerlessness that impact three-quarters of the world's 6 billion people who identify with a world religion.

ISLAM

Islam is the second largest and fastest-growing religion, representing about one-fifth of the world's population. The word *Islam* translates into submission, and Muslims, the adherents of Islam, are ones who have "submitted" to the will of God, or Allah. Founded in the first century, Islam is based on the teachings of Muhammad (570–632), the greatest among God's prophets whose revelations are recorded in the *Qur'an* (Koran), the holy book of Islam. Islam emerged in response to unique Arab needs and circumstances, including Muhammad's desire to aid the poor and provide economic resources for those who were not under the care and protection of others, including widows, orphans, and unmarried women. Islam introduced changes that were advantageous to women in the areas of marriage, divorce, and inheritance, although other Islamic practices served to disempower women (Brooks, 2002b; Hassan, 2002). In the pre-Islamic Arab world, women had esteemed roles as soothsayers, priestesses, and queens, but it is clear that these images had been swept away once Islam became entrenched in Arab cultures. By the third century, women were more secluded and degraded than anything known in earlier Islamic decades (Minai, 1991; Shehadeh, 2007).

Muslims vary considerably in how they interpret the Qur'an in regard to the roles of contemporary women (Moosa, 2003; Wadud, 2005). Much of what is expected of women is based on short narratives about the sayings and deeds of Muhammad's many wives that were passed down orally. These stories are part of the commentaries on the Qur'an that have since become authoritative sources for Islamic teaching. The accuracy of these thousands of narratives is questionable and each period interprets them according to prevailing cultural standards. They have been used to validate a wide range of contradictory attitudes and practices concerning Islamic women. Women are seen as ideal, obedient, and gentle as well as jealous, conspiratorial, and having imperfect minds (Ahmed, 2002; Hotaling, 2003; Hammer, 2008). One of the most controversial passages of the Qur'an (4:34) has been used to justify corporal discipline against women:

As to those women on whose part you fear disloyalty and ill-conduct, admonish them (first), (next), refuse to share their beds, (and last) beat them (lightly).

Although contemporary Islam defines men and women as complementary rather than equal, passages from the Qur'an emphasizing inequality over complementarity are favored, such as another part of the passage above: "men are in charge of women, because God hath made the one of them to excel the other" (Qur'an, 4:34). Since men are a step above women and the protectors of women, God gives preference and authority to men over women. For centuries the verse was used to condone women's oppression and abuse. Muslim feminist scholars, however, are challenging these interpretations, suggesting that human rights and equality are the expression of true Islam (Scott, 2009:60–61).

Islamic law is nurtured by a code of ethics that views a woman's key role as providing male heirs. This role may be compromised if women are not restricted in their activities, especially during childbearing years. Muhammad himself was awed by woman's power and what he saw as a mysterious, unlimited sexual drive that, if left unfettered, could wreak social havoc by casting doubt on the legitimacy of the husband's heirs. From a functionalist perspective, the practices involving purdah arose as a response to these attitudes (chapter 6). Women have less freedom outside their homes in Islamic nations where the law is based on interpretations of the Qur'an and where there are high levels of female illiteracy.

Feminist Views of Islam

Numerous restrictions on women in the name of the Qur'an are much more likely the result of a nation's history and politics rather than its religion. When women are educated in Islamic history and empowered to interpret the Qur'an, they not only offer more positive messages, but also balance the distorted ones regarding the role and status of Islamic women (Ali, 2004; Badran, 2009).

Scholarship on the role of women in Islam written by Muslim women is providing alternative interpretations of the Qur'an and transforming the women of the holy texts into feminist role models (Cooke, 2001). Sufism, the mystical school of Islam, is replete with women saints. Their shrines exist throughout North Africa, India, and the Middle East and are visited by women in search of special needs connected with their family life. Both men and women could follow a religious path and live the life of an itinerant Sufi traveler or as a mystic in their own communities (Hutson, 2005; Pemberton, 2005). Another example is in regard to the wives of Muhammad, who hold powerful places as the "Mothers of Believers." These women are venerated for the roles they played in Muhammad's household during the emergence of Islam.

> When we listen here to these women who surrounded the Prophet and whose words and actions held his attention . . . we hear a very present-day message. . . . Do not these wives, Mothers of Believers, remind us . . . that a society of progress and justice takes place through the restoration of women, to all women, of the dignity and the position which the religion award them? (cited in Ascha, 1995:107)

Islamic Women in the United States

With the global spotlight on the Taliban after 9/11, attention was riveted on Islamic women in the United States, which enlarged the existing dialogue among Muslims regarding women's contribution to the formation of American Islam. Muslim women are altering as well as affirming the traditional values of their religion. Although women are denied the opportunity to be *imams*—religious leaders and administrative officers of mosques—there is strong support for the belief that Islam provides equal rights and responsibilities for women. Most Muslim women earn or expect to earn college degrees, and most work outside the home. But like women of other faiths, there is a debate about how women can successfully reconcile employment and family roles, especially concerning child care (Akhtar, 2007; Jamil, 2009; Zakaria, 2009). Another debate concerns the proper dress of Muslim women in certain settings and how much of her body should be veiled (Gehrke-White, 2006). Reflecting the rapid gains in education among Muslim women and the unique American stamp on Islam, women are actively engaged in these debates and have more influence than their Islamic sisters in the Arab world in resolving them.

HINDUISM

Dating 4,500 years ago Hinduism is the oldest of the world's major religions, with almost 800 million followers, most of whom live in India. As Islam is to Arab cultures, Hinduism is incorporated into the cultural fabric in so many ways that it is impossible to visualize what India would be like without it. Because Hinduism is based in one of the most ethnically diverse regions in the world, and its practices have been adapted to suit such a wide variety of cultural circumstances, contradictory images of women may be expected.

The Feminine in Hindu Scripture

The oldest Hindu scriptures, the *Vedas* and *Upanishads* (1800–500 B.C.E.), provide images of women that have been interpreted in many ways. Some condemn women for selfishness, energy, and ambition, especially if they forsake their "higher" level of womanhood and neglect to serve their families (Jacobson and Wadley, 1995; Weisgrau, 2000). An influential work written over a half century ago describes such women:

> (They) take pride in proving that they never developed a talent for domesticity . . . (and) society will have to allow for them. Such "masculine" women do not reach the highest of which womanhood is capable. (Radhakrishnan, 1947:142)

These beliefs are fostered by interpretations of the ancient *Ramayana* and *Mahabharata* epics, which describe many Hindu ideals related to the proper role of men and women in their families. Combined with the Hindu scriptures, these popular epics offer children authoritative messages supporting traditional beliefs about gender roles. Women are violent ogresses and loving saints. Other interpretations dating to Hinduism's spiritual, preinstitutionalized era are much more positive (Doniger, 2009). These demonstrate an esteem for femininity and complementarity between spouses.

The Hindu ideal is that male and female are balanced, with man as the creator and woman as the lover, and with a woman's sexual tendencies being as varied and erotic as a man's. Hindus celebrate a number of female goddesses, saints, and deities, the most prominent of whom are linked to symbols of fertility, creation, and hope (Gupta, 2000; Khanna, 2000). Unlike Muslims in India, where males control religious practice and where virtually all significant religious figures are male, Hindus allow women to serve in temples and lead religious rituals (Narayanan, 2002). Hinduism has the longest-continuing goddess heritage in the world and offers models for men and women to follow and revere.

Despite the variety of religious images offered to Hindu women, it is safe to conclude that they practice rituals congruent with their roles as mothers, wives, and homemakers. These customs exemplify the domestic sphere of life, the only one known to most Hindu women. In many Indian villages, for example, childbirth involves an elaborate series of rituals lasting from pregnancy until the child ventures outside the home. Many North Indian Hindu women practice rituals expressing their concerns for family and household. Observed only by women, although these ceremonies do not require the services of male priests, they reflect a strong patriarchal society. Some practices involve the direct worship of husbands and brothers for the purpose of obtaining their protection whereas others offer prayers and supplications for the happy marriages of daughters and for the joys of being blessed with male offspring (Younger, 2002; McDaniel, 2003b).

Sati

"The greatest misfortune that can befall a (Hindu) wife is to survive her husband" (cited in Jarman, 2002:2). Hindu religious rituals reinforce women's roles as mothers, wives, and homemakers and connections to men for their well-being. When women became "unconnected" to men by widowhood, the widow, referred to as a **sati**, was frequently expected to be buried alive with her dead husband or, more commonly, self-immolated on his funeral pyre. This section ends with a historical glimpse at this infamous ritual.

The widow-burning ritual originated during the ancient Vedic period, where the widow performed a symbolic self-immolation on her husband's death. In later centuries the symbol became the reality. The practice and veneration of the practice speak to centuries of women's subordinate status in India.

Literally translated to mean "virtuous woman," satis were largely confined to the aristocracy and courts. During wartime, however, widow burning occurred on a massive scale among widows of soldiers who were spared the humiliation of surrendering to the victors. Becoming a sati was considered the most auspicious moment of her existence. She was given the "supreme opportunity for self-sacrifice that consummates her life of dedication to her dead husband." A sati brought dignity and honor to her family and her community. A living widow was seen as "not only unfortunate but positively inauspicious, an ogress who ate her husband with karmic jaws" (Young, 1987:83). She would feel guilty the rest of her life that her husband died before her. This sense of guilt was heightened by the Hindu belief that a sin in her previous life was responsible for his earlier death. In principle, this was a voluntary rite on the part of the widow. In practice, her grief was often used by relatives who desired the honor associated with a sati ceremony. Only faithful wives could be honored as a sati, so a widow's refusal could be taken as an admission of infidelity (Fisch, 2006; Yang, 2008). In a culture where widow remarriages were discouraged, where women were identified only in connection to their husbands, and where widows occupied the lowest rung on the social hierarchy, widowhood magnified a woman's dependence, subservience, and fear of sexual exploitation and abandonment. Given these dire circumstances, a woman consumed with grief and guilt may believe "that the brief agony of sati was better than the long agony of widowhood" (Jarman, 2002:2). When India was ruled by Muslim Mughals, attempts were made to abolish the practice, and the British outlawed it as early as 1829. British lack of success in eliminating it altogether shows the intransigence of Hindu religious beliefs and their intimate connection to the social order.

India is rapidly modernizing, though many villages and rural areas are basically untouched by this trend. It speaks to the extraordinary power of socialization that sati is still associated with the image of virtue for numerous Hindu women. No longer do dying husbands extract oaths to be a sati from grieving wives, but the practice has not died out. In the last several decades 40 recorded cases of the sati ritual are documented, but it is likely that others occur that remain hidden and uncounted. In rural areas of Rajasthan there is evidence that the practice is symbolically resurging (Pinney, 2001; Sen, 2002). The concern is that the symbol may again become the reality.

JUDAISM

The ancient biblical world of Judaism was a powerful patriarchal world. The two most important documents governing the conduct of Jewish life for both men and women are the *Torah* (law), the first five books of the Hebrew Bible, providing the whole of God's teaching as revealed to the Jewish people, and the *Talmud*, a collection of rabbinic interpretations of scripture transmitted around the middle of the first century. Because the Hebrew Bible and the Old Testament of the Christian Bible contain these five books, the Torah is the shared heritage of both peoples. Interpretation of scripture has been fairly flexible to account for the varying circumstances and cultural challenges faced by the Jewish people, but views of women and their approved roles have remained remarkably stable (Nadell and Sarna, 2001; Raphael, 2002). A strict gendered division of labor dictated family and religious life. Men's duties were to lead, teach, and legislate, and women's were to serve and to follow.

Family Life

Men's family responsibilities included being a breadwinner and instructing their children in the history and religious obligations demanded by their faith. Women's duties were confined to the household, including overseeing domestic religious rituals, such as preparing Sabbath meals. A woman required permission from her husband to engage in any outside activities, and she could divorce him only if he granted it. Ancient customs prescribed daily, rigorous religious duties for men from which women were exempt. If a wife was fulfilling her household responsibilities, including those religious functions centered in the household, then her husband was able to concentrate on his religious obligations, patterns that continue today. Throughout Jewish history a woman was described, defined, and judged by her roles as wife and mother (Goldberg, 2003; Taitz et al., 2003; Ilan, 2006). However, women did venture outside their homes to connect with other women and to engage in some community activities, so the image of seclusion and isolation is not the whole portrait of their lives (Meyers, 2009). Most of Judaism's 4,000-year heritage is marked by intense prejudice and anti-Semitism, including the Nazi Holocaust. Survival of Judaism itself depended on growth; hence motherhood meant that a woman individually sacrificed for children and family as well as for religious identity.

Sexuality and Social Control. This concern for stability in family life resulted in excessive control over women's sexuality. The ancient Hebrews severely punished infidelity on the part of a wife, but a husband was punished for infidelity only if he violated another man's rights by consorting with his wife (Daly, 1991:139). The right of a husband to own his wife kept her sexuality under control because she was regarded as a piece of property. An example of this control is found in the following verse:

> I took this woman and . . . . . . did not find the tokens of virginity. . . . The father of the young woman shall say to the elders . . . "he has made shameful charges against her . . . these are the tokens of my daughter's virginity" . . . then the elders . . . shall take the man and whip him . . . But if the thing is true, that the tokens of virginity were not found in the young woman, the . . . the men of the city shall stone her to death. (Deuteronomy, 22:14–21)

Women were denied access to the goddess religions that coexisted with Judaism during early biblical times. The goddess religions threatened Jewish monotheism, the religiously based political structure, and the sexual control of women. Patriarchal social order could be assaulted if women took advantage of the freedoms associated with these pagan religions.

The goddess religions are gone but beliefs about controlling women, especially their sexuality, in the name of social order continue (Keshet-Orr, 2003; Ariel, 2006). However, even conservative women are not passive recipients of these beliefs. Research on orthodox Jewish Israeli women suggests that they orchestrate marital sexuality according to a range of cultural contexts provided by their religion (Avishai, 2008). In this sense, they do not "comply" with "regulations" but are agents in acting out their religious identity in marriage.

The Texts of Terror

The **Texts of Terror**, parts of four books of the Torah that include the Old Testament of the Christian Bible that document abuse and sexual violence against women, were often used as justifications for restricting women's lives (Trible, 1984, 2003). These texts (*Genesis*, 16:1–16 and 21:9–21; II *Samuel*, 13:1–22; *Judges*, 19:1–30, and *Judges*, 11:29–40) testify to rape, murder, human sacrifice, and the widespread abuse of women and girls. In *Judges* 19:1–30, a concubine flees from her Levite master back to her father's house, where he is entertained by her father and then prepares to return with her to his own home. Along the way he is invited into the home of a man from Ephraim when the home is besieged. In pleading for the safety of the Levite, the Ephraimite host says,

> Behold, here are my virgin daughter and his concubine; . . . . Ravish them and do with them what seems good to you; but against this man do not do such a vile thing. So the man seized his concubine, and put her out to them; and they knew her and abused her all night . . . . And as the dawn began to break they let her go . . . then he put her upon the ass . . . and went away to his home. And when he entered his house, he took a knife, and laying hold of his concubine he divided her, limb by limb, into twelve pieces, and sent her throughout all the territory of Israel.

Virgin daughters and concubines are treated as property to be used at will by fathers or masters to entertain male guests.

Other biblical references could be included in these texts of terror. They serve as testimony to justify rape of virgins, abandonment of wives, and sexual violence against slave girls and women taken as prisoners of war.

Contemporary Images

All branches of Judaism are engaged in making its religious heritage more palatable to contemporary women (Heschel, 2002). Much of this effort is focused on reinterpreting Talmudic legislation and demonstrating the variety of roles Jewish women assumed throughout their religious history. For instance, positive countervoices exist throughout scripture that confirm God's high regard for women. In first-century documents Eve is visioned as a woman who may have been naive but certainly not wicked—an unselfish woman whose good character Satan abused. Throughout the Diaspora Jewish women lived their lives as wives and mothers and as earners, organizers, and entrepreneurs. They sought and gained opportunities to climb to prestigious positions and to assume leadership roles in Jewish communities. Jewish women confront the misogyny of their own religious traditions; the rediscovered positive images of women are eroding the negative and hostile ones (Raphael, 2002; Mirkin, 2004).

CHRISTIANITY

From its origins 2,000 years ago as a Middle Eastern cult rooted in Judaism, Christianity developed as a result of the life events of its charismatic leader, Jesus of Nazareth, who was born a Jew. Christianity is the largest of the world's religions, representing about one-third of the world's population. Christianity's phenomenal growth rate is in part due to its early focus on class and ethnic inclusiveness (Stark, 1996). Gender inclusiveness highlighted the ministry of Jesus but remained unacknowledged for centuries.

The Bible and Patriarchy

Religious socialization of the young often proceeds from the teaching of biblical stories replete with colorful pictures of David confronting Goliath or Moses parting the sea in the escape from Egypt. These childhood images are nurtured by interpretations that perpetuate gender role stereotypes. The Bible is frequently evoked as the final authority in settling disputes in many areas but in particular those involving women and men.

Because the Bible expresses the attitudes of the patriarchal cultures in which it was written, it is logical that its most popular texts would be representative of those cultures. Historically the androcentric passages have been emphasized. Positive views of women and the partnerships forged between men and women exist throughout the Bible but scripture pointing to the subordination of women is favored, in part because it is more known.

The following examples, often repeated from the pulpit, demonstrate how androcentric ideology permeates the Bible. It is appropriate to begin with the version of the creation story that is most accepted as representing the traditional view of both Christianity and Judaism.

> And the rib which the Lord God had taken from man, made the woman and brought her unto the man. And Adam said, This is now bone of my bones, and flesh of my flesh; she shall be called Woman, because she was taken out of Man. (*Genesis*, 2:20–23)

Contrary to all subsequent natural law, woman is made from man. Her status as helpmate and server to man (read "males") is confirmed. The idea that Eve was not only created out of Adam's rib, but also that she was created second, is used to justify the domination of man-husband over woman-wife. This view of Eve is stubbornly persistent. As one writer contends, the biblical text refers to God's "curse" of Eve and woman being a "helper" to Adam; "Adam dominates Eve sexually and otherwise from the very moment of Eve's creation" (Gellman, 2006:319). The *order* of creation, however, is not an issue in supremacy when considering that animals were created before humans.

The Writings of Paul. In supporting this perspective, Paul has the dubious honor of formulating views, or having writings attributed to him, that continue reinforce contemporary Christian images of women. On the one hand, Paul is closely linked with a "Christianity of female subordination," and his proclamations are used to keep women out of the ministry and confined to religious roles that are home based or, if outside the home, have a charitable basis. Perhaps Paul was concerned about the scandal and ridicule directed at the fledgling Christian sect if women were encouraged to venture into roles that could challenge existing patriarchy. On the other hand, he accepted the beliefs and practices of earlier inclusive charismatic Christianity, "the theology of equivalence of women." This form of Christianity incorporated women as local leaders, evangelists, and prophets (Ruether, 2001a). Paul acknowledged the idea of equality but insisted on the divinely given quality of sexual differences. Paul's contradictory beliefs about women are evident in the *Pauline* texts, consisting of those biblical passages attributed to Paul that contain striking misogyny as well as more gender egalitarian treatment (Adams, 2000). However, it is the former that are the most well known and frequently used to justify the subordination of Christian women.

> For a man ought not to cover his head since he is the image and glory of God; but woman is the glory of man. For man was not made from woman, but woman from man. Neither was man created for woman but woman for man. (I *Corinthians*, 11:7–11)

> Let a woman learn in silence with all submissiveness. I permit no woman to teach or have authority over men; she is to keep silent. (I *Timothy*, 2:11–12)

> Wives be subject to your husbands, as to the Lord. For the husband is the head of the wife as Christ is the head of the Church. As the Church is subject to Christ, so let wives also be subject in everything to their husbands. (*Ephesians*, 5:22–24)

Women are repeatedly viewed in terms of their status as possessions of men. The Ten Commandments list a neighbor's wife, along with his house, fields, manservant, ox, and ass as property not to be coveted (*Exodus*, 20:17). Lot offers his daughters to the male guests in his house.

> Behold, I have two daughters who have not known man. Let me bring them out to you and do to them as you please. (*Genesis*, 19:8)

Contemporary compilations of stories about biblical women continue these images. On the surface it would seem that older works like Edith Deen's *Wisdom from Women in the Bible* (1978) are focusing on women's accomplishments in a period of history in which liberating religious interpretation occurred. Yet Deen presents narratives of women that provide ammunition reinforcing stereotypes about women. For example, Jochebed, the mother of Moses, is praised for her role in recognizing exceptional promise in their children. The heroic efforts in carrying out this role are ignored. Selfish and possessive women—like the wife of Potiphar, who was responsible for the unfair imprisonment of Joseph—are admonished for their wickedness and deceit. Deen asserts that women are different but not inferior to men, but the images she presents are consistently in line with women's traditional or "acceptable" roles. Those women who either refuse or challenge such roles are chastised, negatively portrayed, or cast into historical oblivion (Lindsey, 1979:793).

Biblical Men. The Christian tradition portrays men as both rational and irrational. They are warriors, leaders, teachers, builders, and cultivators whose minds, talents, and strength are recruited in the service of God. But they are also driven by sexual desires and are irrational in their inability to resist the lure of women. Even in their irrational moments, they are portrayed as multifaceted beings who adapt to and thrive in a variety of roles. In contrast, women are dualistically cast with no room for deviation. Eve may be the mother of humanity, but she is also the temptress responsible for the fall of humanity. Because Eve yielded to the serpent, women thereafter are incapable of leadership. Adam succumbs to Eve's feminine wiles but is largely exempt from blame. On the other hand, Mary as the mother of Christ is the idealized image of the perfect woman—a humble, submissive virgin. Joseph is Mary's husband and Jesus' earthly father, but compared to Mary, he is relegated to only a few biblical references. Some biblical scholars may suggest that his "ordinary" roles as carpenter and supporter of the family do not elevate him to the same biblical importance as Christianity's political or religious leaders. In this sense, the Bible tends to neglect unexceptional men—those who for better or worse do not deviate from their roles—but focuses attention on exceptional women—those who for better or worse do deviate from their roles.

Alternative Views of Biblical Women

Numerous biblical alternatives to traditional views document the stories, images, and metaphors demonstrating a range of interpretive options related to women. Paul's forceful passage (from the Pauline texts) speaks directly to the idea of equality of the genders under God:

> there is neither Jew nor Greek, there is neither slave nor free, there is neither male nor female, for you are all one in Jesus Christ. (Galatians, 3:28)

On the heels of the equality issue is the rediscovery of the nontraditional roles women played in biblical times. Mary Magdalene and the women who went to Jesus' tomb hold the credibility of Christianity in their hands. Jesus first appeared to them and they were instructed to gather the disciples. Mary Magdalene can be elevated as the first prophet and the first Christian of the new religion (Griffith-Jones, 2008). Deborah, in the book of Judges, is an arbitrator, queen, and commander of the army that she led in the defeat of the Canaanites. In Exodus it is the women who first disobeyed Pharaoh, with his own daughter adopting Moses as her child. Women are wives and mothers as well as leaders, prophetesses, teachers, and tillers of the soil. Even Mary's humility and submissiveness are being taken to task by feminists, who argue that Mary submitted to God alone and not to Joseph or other male authority figures. She was an independent actor when she affirmed the course of her life (Ostling, 1991:64).

It is a rereading of the Gospels with an examination of the life and teachings of Jesus that provides the best message in recasting biblical imagery concerning women. Jesus' open attitude toward women is found throughout the Gospels. His acceptance of women was so uncharacteristic of the times that it could not be seen as anything short of scandalous (Magli, 2003). Women were prominent in Jesus' ministry from the beginning. They recognized him early on as the Messiah, they witnessed his death and resurrection, they conversed with him on theological topics, and they were faithful followers through even the lethal portions of his ministry.

Women of biblical times would have been the major beneficiaries of Jesus' ministry. Examples are numerous: He preached that divorce should be forbidden at a time when only husbands had the right of divorce and wives were often abandoned to a life of poverty; he rejected the double standard of sexual morality, helping to absolve women of their temptress image that previously made them solely responsible for sexual misdeeds; and he opened a religious path and monastic life for both men and women. He demonstrated that women could join men in spiritual quests and that men and women could interact in radically different ways than suggested by the patriarchy of the times. By these standards, Jesus can be counted as feminist (Graetz, 2003a; Swidler, 2007).

Gender Roles and American Christians

Religious pluralism is a hallmark of the United States and there are numerous religions, branches of religions, denominations, cults, and new religious movements in various stages of, growth, decline, and emergence. Of all the groups that comprise the religious salad bowl in the Unites States, the largest in number are under the Christian umbrella. Over three-fourths of the U.S. population identify themselves as Christian, and of these about half are Protestant and one-fourth are Catholic. American Christians share basic theological beliefs, but diverge sharply on key gender related issues.

American Protestants. Protestants are divided into many denominations and independent churches but some generalizations about their attitudes regarding gender roles can be made. Mainstream denominations including Methodists, Lutherans of the Evangelical Church in America (ELCA), Presbyterians, and Episcopalians are more inclusive and liberal in their theology, accommodating a variety of interpretations. These denominations are likely to have women in key leadership roles, including ordained ministers. Women take up visible, active roles in weekly services and share in church functions with men. Special services spotlighting alternative images of women are conducted. Sunday schools provide children with images of biblical men and women in an array of roles.

Conservative mainstream denominations, including Lutheran Church—Missouri Synod, some Baptist branches, Pentecosts, and small Protestant churches not otherwise affiliated with any specific Protestant groups are more absolutist in their beliefs, viewing the Bible as the literal, unerring word of God. These Protestants are at the core of fundamentalist religious trends in the United States. Bolstered by literal theological interpretations favoring traditional biblical views noted earlier, male and female adherents hear the message that egalitarian or companionate-style families and gender roles are contrary to God's plan for the world. Patriarchal families are godly, wise, desirable, necessary, and in the best interests of family and society (Hoffmann and Bartkowski, 2008).

Many support the agenda of the **New Christian Right (NCR)**, a fundamentalist political movement composed largely of conservative, Protestant groups that promotes a specific Christian brand of morality based on the Bible and God's will as the ultimate source for political and social life. Issues related to sex and gender are the core of NCR's agenda in its call for restrictions on sex education and opposition to homosexual rights, abortion rights, and the Equal Rights Amendment (Chapter 14).

American Catholics. Probably the most important issues dividing contemporary U.S. Catholics from the authority of the broader Roman Catholic Church are attitudes regarding sex and gender. This division shows up among both clergy and laypeople. For example, various orders of nuns have removed themselves from traditional patterns of Catholic hierarchy and worship; they take a distinctly female-centered view of religion, preferring to pray to "Her" rather than "Him." Other parishes allow altar girls, nuns as campus ministers, and women leading "priestess parishes" in rural areas where there are shortages of male priests. Among laypeople, a majority of American Catholics practice birth control other than the rhythm method, support the use of condoms and sex education in schools, believe priests should be allowed to marry, do not believe political candidates should be judged solely on the abortion issue, believe that divorced Catholics need to be welcomed back into the Church, and are receptive to women's ordination, all in direct contradiction to Vatican authority (Stange, 2002; Maher et al., 2006; Wald and Calhoun-Brown, 2007; Ruether, 2008). Because so many Catholics have beliefs and practices that directly counter Vatican teaching, the Church is reluctant to dismiss them from church rosters.

Issues related to women and sexuality have been in the forefront of Catholic controversy for decades. However, a new twist to the sexuality issue exploded in the media when widespread sexual abuse by Catholic priests perpetrated on children was revealed. The shock that priests engaged in "serial, predatory and sexual abuse of minors" was magnified when it was learned that Roman Catholic officials who knew of abuse routinely shuffled "problem priests" to other parishes, ignored the problem, or swept it under the rug. These cover-ups were as disturbing to many Catholics as the original abuse, and most people believed that the Church did a poor job in handling the scandal (Roane, 2002; Dale and Alpert, 2007). Through the United States Conference of Catholic Bishops (USCCB), the Church offered official apologies, counseling, and monetary compensation for victims and the removal from the priesthood and criminal charges for perpetrators as short-term solutions. Surveys of Catholic priests toward the USCCB response showed that they believed the media's portrayal of the bishops engaging in cover-up. However, they also believed that the USCCB response was inadequate, ill-conceived, and designed to satisfy public pressure. They also believed the bishops had abandoned their priests (Kane, 2008:579). Regardless of the success of these solutions, the sex scandal will certainly magnify the existing split in the Church and refocus attention on another issue it prefers to ignore—the issue of women's ordination into the Catholic priesthood.

GENDER, RELIGIOSITY, AND LEADERSHIP

Religion is a powerful agent of gender socialization as well as a major source of a person's overall well-being. Degree of religiosity is correlated with lower support on a number of attitudes related to sex and gender including women's ordination, women working outside the home, reproductive choice, contraceptive use, homosexuality, and the Equal Rights Amendment (Chapter 14). Stronger religiosity translates to less gender egalitarianism, stronger beliefs about essentialism, and female submissiveness in marriage and higher fertility, a pattern that cuts across all religions. Level of religiosity is a better predictor of beliefs about gender equality than is a particular religious affiliation (Gallagher, 2004; Anderson and Hall, 2005; Hayford and Morgan, 2008; NORC, 2008). Although measures of religiosity vary, it is safe to conclude that a strong religious commitment in conservative religions, especially fundamentalist Protestantism, predicts a preference for highly traditional gender roles (Marsh, 2009). Some suggest that secular laws protecting religious freedom allow religions to be exempt from gender discrimination that would not be tolerated in other institutions (Skjeie, 2007). Preference for traditional gender roles discourages many women from seeking positions of leadership in those very religious organizations from which they derive a strong sense of well-being.

Gender and Religious Orientation

The issue of women as religious leaders is perhaps even more significant since abundant sociological research suggests that women have a greater degree of religious orientation than men, a pattern that straddles the globe (Stark, 2002). Compared to men, women report higher levels of need for a religious dimension in their daily lives and believe that religion is an answer to contemporary problems. Women pray and read scripture more than men and have higher rates of church and synagogue attendance and practice. Religious orientation is reinforced by women's responsibility for the religious socialization of the children. Women ensure that children receive religious instruction, attend services, and practice the rituals important to their religion.

Sociological Perspectives. All sociological perspectives highlight the link between family and religion in explaining gender differences in the level of religious orientation. Functionalists maintain that social cohesion is strengthened when families and communities share the same beliefs derived from the moral communities established by their religion. Traditional gender roles in the home are bolstered by similar messages from the pulpit about the proper place of men and women. Feminists also suggest that church and family are consistent, because they both share similar patriarchal structures. For feminists, however, the social cohesion functionalists highlight reinforces patriarchy and benefits its male leaders, but does a disservice to women who are excluded from religious leadership.

Because traditional gender roles and patriarchy go hand in hand, inclusiveness and partnership roles sought by men and women congregants are discouraged.

Conflict theorists use classical Marxism to explain women's religious orientation for Christian women. Religion acts as an opiate, discouraging people from challenging the religious status quo. Christianity's belief that heavenly rewards come to those who lead humble, pious, and self-sacrificing lives bolsters women's acceptance of an "other worldly" ideology. Marx suggested that religion lulls people into a *false consciousness,* the tendency for oppressed people to accept the ideology of the dominant class, in this sense, church patriarchy. These beliefs are transmitted via religious socialization in families and are largely unchallenged. The overall result is that oppression, in the name of God, is legitimized. Conflict theorists support biblical interpretations challenging these beliefs and calling for people to use their religions in the active pursuit social justice. Advanced initially by Catholic clergy in Latin America, **liberation theology** calls for redistribution of wealth and economic equality grounded in biblical messages about God's concern for the poor and oppressed. Liberation theology's messages about oppression of economic inequality can also be brought to bear on the oppression of gender inequality. Opening up the religious leadership structure to women is a key mechanism challenging gender oppression perpetrated in the name of God and religion.

The Issue of Ordination

Seminaries are rapidly being feminized. Among all religions that allow women to be ordained, 60–70 percent of seminary students are women and their numbers continue to grow. The feminization of divinity schools should translate into a pulpit with women's voices offering alternative views and explanations of women from the Bible and the holy texts from other religions. These views are necessary when contemporary women seek equal footing with men as leaders in their religious organizations, whether in churches, synagogues, temples, or mosques.

Confucianism and Islam. In outlining women's roles in the world religions, the religions that stand out as the most restrictive in terms of women's leadership roles are Islam, the second largest religion in the world and on track to become the largest, and Confucianism, the smallest of the world religions. Neither religion can be described as "hierarchal" in leadership structure. In Confucianism a variety of men may organize and lead rituals, although women often ensure that appropriate rituals are conducted in their households. Men are the arbitrators and interpreters of Confucian texts as they pertain to family, business, and politics. Confucian ideals consign women to their family and household roles (Woo, 2002). Islam does not have priests but imams are powerful figures, especially in religious states such as Iran and Saudi Arabia, where imams serving large mosques have a great deal of political clout. They have the right to choose and interpret passages from the Qur'an. Muslim women are restricted from becoming imams and as a result are denied an important public opportunity to provide alternative interpretations of the Qur'an.

Judaism. When Jews began to enter modern, Western society in the late nineteenth century, attitudes toward women shifted dramatically. Patriarchy was evident, but the flexible, adaptive quality of Jewish beliefs and practices is again demonstrated in accommodating women's greater independence and higher levels of education. This accommodation is reflected in the increased number of women rabbis in most branches of Judaism. Each of its three main branches—Orthodox, Conservative, and Reform—varies according to the degree to which theology is literally interpreted and acted on in daily life. Orthodox Jews, for example, have the strictest interpretation, viewing the Torah as the absolutely binding word of God. Those who identify as Conservative are less strict, allowing interpretation of the Torah in the context of modern life. Reform Jews, the most liberal and assimilated branch, accept the Torah's ethical guidelines and general religious precepts, but are open to alternative interpretations of the Torah, especially related to gender roles. As the least strict branch, Reform Judaism was the first to make possible rabbinical ordination, with Sally Priesand becoming the first female rabbi in 1972. A year later ordination was open to women in the Conservative branch but the first Conservative rabbi was not ordained until 1985. Among Orthodox Jews, although ordination for women is still forbidden, there is a growing movement to achieve increased participation in synagogue ritual and in religious authority. The ultimate objective of this movement is rabbinical ordination of Orthodox women (Israel-Cohen, 2008).

Christianity. Three major Christian faiths do not ordain women: Lutheran Church–Missouri Synod, Eastern Orthodox, and Roman Catholic. In 1972, after a long and bitter struggle that culminated in a controversial ceremony in 1974 in Philadelphia, 11 women were ordained as Episcopal priests. Two years later the Episcopal Church gave its legal, institutional blessing for the right of women to become priests. Twelve years later, by a margin of two votes, that right to become a priest was extended to women in the Church of England. This came about despite a warning by the Anglican Archbishop of Canterbury that women's ordination would hurt dialogue with the Roman Catholic Church. Episcopalians and Anglicans across the globe show higher levels of acceptance for women priests, but decades later the dust from the first controversial ordinations has not settled.

Catholicism. Although the Catholic Church may quietly overlook theological principles in accepting the large number of divorced Catholics in its parishes, regarding the issue of women in the priesthood, the Church will not budge. The Second Vatican Council (1963–1965) monumentally changed the Catholic Church and opened up new roles for men and women to serve the Church, but women's ordination was not one of them. A pastoral letter addressing issues raised by Catholic women, including their place in the Church, that took nine years to prepare was rejected by U.S. bishops in 1992. This was the first time in history that a pastoral letter proposed for a final vote was defeated. For every proclamation reasserting the Vatican's position that women can never be ordained, a worldwide outcry centered in the United States against the position occurs. Despite the Church's acknowledgment that ordaining women could alleviate the serious shortage of priests in many parts of the world, the issue is dealt with by encouraging married men to become priests under certain conditions. The Vatican believes allegiance of Catholics can be maintained without women's ordination. Others take the view that this issue will cause an irrevocable split in the Church (Weaver, 1999; Anderson, 2006).

The priest sex scandal provides more ammunition for ordaining women. Feminists contend that the Church fails to recognize the incredible power held by an all-male priesthood that not only heightens the potential for abuse in all areas, whether related to sex, love, money, or politics, but also covers up the abuse by rallying around the priestly brotherhood to protect its own interests. As noted by one feminist scholar,

> The argument for female priests has never been stronger as a result of this scandal . . . women have no stake in protecting the interests of errant male colleagues. The presence of women (as priests) would inevitably transform the Men's Club of power and privilege the priesthood has become. (Stange, 2002:13A)

Jewish and Lutheran women have the option of shifting to other branches without changing their religion, but for those Catholic women who seek the priesthood, their choices are limited. Some convert to seek ordination in other denominations (Perl, 2005). Others assume leadership roles as lay members of the Church, or they can become nuns. This is not to minimize the leadership roles nuns assume or the other vital services they provide. But compared to priests, these roles are more restrictive and secondary. They are excluded from the position that allows the greatest authority on both doctrinal and parish matters—that of priest. The tradition of nuns as helpmates is also impacting their very livelihood. Unlike priests of a diocese, they are not employees of the local bishop; hence they receive no pension. In addition, there are far fewer young women entering the convent today, forcing some convents to close. Although nuns are better educated than most women and seldom retire from work unless their health fails, they face grim financial prospects in old age because there are fewer younger nuns to support them.

Protestantism. American Protestantism has fared better in terms of women in positions of authority, with many women preachers emerging from the ranks of Quakers during the colonial era. America's first successful religious commune, the Shakers, was founded by Ann Lee, who preached that God is both male and female. Although the Shakers had no formal ordination process, all adherents, regardless of gender, were permitted complete freedom in teaching and preaching. This is also generally true of other religious sects and churches where women are credited as founders or proved to be the dominant influence in their establishment. Included here are the Seventh Day Adventists, the Spiritualist Church, and the Christian Science Church. By the middle of the twentieth century most mainstream Protestant denominations, including the Methodist and Presbyterian Churches, the United Church of Christ, and the merged ELCA granted full ordination rights to women. Ordination also allows for women to begin the climb to significant positions of administrative leadership offering high levels of decision making within their religious groups.

Clergy Women as Leaders

For those leaders who are clergy, do women differ in their approach to their ministries compared to men? The answer depends on the type of minister one has in mind and the type of ministry. In general, male and female ministers differ in their willingness to exercise power over congregations, with women more willing to give the congregation the power over its own affairs. Men and women do not differ in desire for positions of formal authority, approach to preaching, and involvement in social issues beyond the congregation (Lehman, 1993). Gender socialization encourages women to adopt styles of interaction that are relational, open, nonconfrontational, and consensual. These characteristics can serve congregations well when adopted by both male and female clergy. Women and men have different paths to the ministry, but when they arrive and gain acceptance among their parishioners, the differences are muted (Lehman, 2002).

Although women are gradually assuming new roles within the hierarchy of their religions, the battle is far from won. Ordination does not guarantee a call to lead a congregation. Some parishes still refuse to accept female ministers, rabbis, or priests, whether ordained or not, which propels many of them into more peripheral leadership positions. The large majority of ordained women serve as associate pastors, youth ministers, educational directors, or in some other institutional capacity. Women clergy are more likely than their male counterparts to be heads of religious coalitions or leaders of campus churches or temples.

The crux of the clergy issue can be traced back to interpretations of doctrine embodied in a religion's sacred texts. It is the exclusivity of the male image of God in these texts that makes it difficult to see women as representing this image. Although theologians uniformly reject the notion that God is a "male being," centuries of religious patriarchy, institutional sexism, and linguistic convention are barriers to those women and men who support women's ascendance to more authoritative ranks of their respective religions.

TOWARD AN INCLUSIVE THEOLOGY

From this account of religious misogyny, it might seem that feminism and the patriarchal vision of the Church cannot be reconciled. Feminists are unwilling to equate religion with oppression. They believe it is not real liberation to sever ties with a religion that is one of the most important elements of their heritage, belief system, and well-being. They choose to work at reform in a number of areas, especially in providing a historical account of women's roles in ancient religions and reevaluating scripture according to that account, whether it be in the Qur'an, Talmud, Vedas, or Bible. Even if religious experience is filtered through misogynous cultural traditions, religion should transcend gender. Every adherent should have the right to fully participate in her or his religion in a manner that best enhances individual well-being and community service. Feminists contend that only when women become aware of the root causes of their religious status and the sociopolitical nature of religious doctrine can they truly experience their religion. Historical reanalysis of world religions provides meaningful consciousness-raising for women coming to grips with their religious identity.

The Language of Religion

Language is a powerful force in socialization, and nowhere is this more apparent than in the language of religion (Chapter 4). Altering the written words of sacred texts to make it more gender inclusive, more palatable, or more understandable to contemporary readers may be accompanied by bitter controversy (Ellis, 2003; Johnson, 2003). "Radical" feminists, for example, are blamed for altering the word of God to suit political correctness. According to this view, God's word should "speak for itself", and the generic "he" has been used for so long that "the average person *instinctively* senses that the feminist claim is not valid" (italics mine)

(Clason, 2006:28, 30). Clearly this criticism ignores the fact that once language is learned via socialization, it is perhaps the most powerful taken-for-granted way we organize our perceptions.

The language of religion can be subdivided into *religious* language, which uses imagery and symbols appealing to emotion and imagination and readily incorporates female imagery, and *theological* language, which uses abstractions evolving out of formal, critical appraisals of religious experience and readily incorporates male imagery. Because theological language is the language of written texts, bestowed with authority, credibility, and importance, female imagery is largely excluded. Theological language is viewed as more legitimate but is a "creation of a male specialist group, whether Brahmans, priests, rabbis, or monks" (King, 1989:44–45).

Male imagery is evoked when conceptualizing God, and in turn such images are used to support the subordination of women. Christians and adherents of other religions who firmly believe that men and women are equal under God confront a theological language that contradicts this belief. God and god-language is associated with male imagery and masculine traits (Johnson, 2003; Wiley, 2003). Women are portrayed as distracting men from godliness, as Eve did when she tempted Adam. The language is clear: There are "Sons of God" but "Daughters of Eve." Theologians do agree that the use of the generics *man* and *he* impedes our understanding of God's view of the genders. Yet when congregations begin the arduous task of altering liturgy, hymns, and prayers to conform to nonsexist, inclusive language, resistance runs very high. The old argument reappears: One is not only tampering with tradition but, more importantly, the "language of God."

Supported by trends in *ecumenism*—promoting practices that bring churches together, such as through joint worship and communion—mainstream Christian denominations are making headway incorporating inclusive language in the written material used in religious services. Here is a portion of the Nicene Creed, recited by many Christians, demonstrating that a one-word change suggests a meaningful difference in imagery.

Who for us *men*, and for our salvation, came down from heaven. . . .

to

For *us* and for our salvation He came down from heaven. . . .

Though it is inappropriate to remove the word *He* from the second version because it refers directly to Jesus, the word *men* is now deleted. A hymn titled "Good Christian *Men*, Rejoice and Sing" in older hymnals was changed to "Good Christian *Friends*, Rejoice and Sing." Seemingly subtle changes can have a profound impact on images of men and women.

Reinterpretation of Scripture

Reinterpretation of scripture is an important mode of reform, especially if coupled with changes in linguistic reference. By pointing out alternative translations of key words, introducing nonsexist, inclusive language that minimizes the powerful aspects of male imagery, and highlighting lesser-known biblical texts and religious writing that demonstrate both gender equity and nontraditional roles of women, a gradual shift in religious awareness regarding gender roles and relationships is occurring. In Christianity, for example, because theology and preaching are so strongly oriented to masculine images and symbols of God— such as *king, father,* and *shepherd*—the feminine corollary of God goes unrecognized. In *Matthew* 13:31, although it is acknowledged that the man who sowed the mustard seed is God, most miss the parallel image that immediately follows in *Matthew* 13:33, where God is presented as a woman hiding leaven in meal.

We have already seen that most world religions emerged out of spiritual heritages that were more gender egalitarian than what exists today. But the esoteric and mystical schools of Christian Gnosticism, Islamic Sufism, and the Kabbalah movement of Judaism show a continuous heritage of men and women in equitable partnership (McKechnie, 2001; Buehrens, 2003). This is pointed out by Elaine Pagels (1979) in her classic work recounting the archaeological discovery in Upper Egypt, now referred to as the *Gnostic Gospels,* offering evidence that the early Christians viewed women in very different terms than what is implied by the practices of many contemporary churches. In the *Gospel of Mary* (Magdalene), for example, we find a view of Mary as an "apostolic leader" and as part of an inclusive ministry that is not strictly divided by gender (De Boer, 2004). The texts on which these views are based are providing important alternative perspectives concerning women.

Many biblical writings can be reevaluated with these standards of reform in mind. Consider the lesser quoted of the Judeo-Christian creation stories:

> So God created man in his own image, in the image of God he created him; male and female he created them. (*Genesis,* 1:27)

God is still named as "he," but this version clearly does not have the implication that God's image of people is different depending on gender. Even Paul's most restrictive passages may be reevaluated with the idea that the Gospel liberates people to stand equally before God. Reread *Ephesians* 5:22–24 with the idea that the words *be subject* were not in the original biblical text. Religious scholars suggest that Paul is calling for mutual submission of the genders within marriage and not the superiority of the husband (Schüssler-Fiorenza, 1984; Groothuis, 1997; Perriman, 1998; Carey, 2001). Paul's writings must be scrutinized carefully with an eye toward context, taking into account the historical setting and the gospel of Jesus (Megill-Cobbler, 1993). Given these new directions, Paul's misogyny continues to fade.

Feminist Theology

Religious reform related to gender is perhaps best expressed by a rapidly growing **feminist theology**, which draws on women's experience as a basic source of content previously shut out of theological reflection. Feminist theology makes theological knowledge visible, understandable, inclusive, and acceptable to all who believe in the liberating power of religion. It may also be viewed as an example of liberation theology in that it interprets the Bible from the perspective of an oppressed group. In this sense, female experience is an appropriate metaphor for the divine. Feminist theology is necessary when the female experience is excluded from traditional theology and when women are excluded from institutionalized religious structures (Maynard, 2001; Ruether, 2001b). Articulating with the female experience in any of the world's major religions, feminist theology is also ecumenical from its origins and borrows models from a wide range of disciplines. Although it accepts the idea that a major critique of god-symbolism is called for, there is much disagreement on the solutions to the problems resulting from such a critique. Views of religious tradition advocated by feminist theologians may be grouped in three categories (Christ, 1987:144):

Type 1: Tradition is essentially nonsexist in vision that becomes clear through proper interpretation.

Type 2: Tradition contains both sexist and nonsexist elements; nonsexist elements must be affirmed as revelation and the sexist elements rejected. Nonsexist visions must account for the contemporary experience of all women and embrace their full humanity.

Type 3: Tradition is essentially sexist and must be rejected. New traditions must be created on the basis of both past experience and/or nonbiblical religion.

Depending on which viewpoint is subscribed to, god symbolism would be altered. For example, those subscribing to the third position would likely advocate female symbolism for God found both inside and outside of biblical tradition. Since God is best symbolized by dual male–female imagery, outside sources might include the goddess symbolism of non-Western religions (Pui-Lan, 1988; Christ, 2003a). Those subscribing to Type 2 would agree with the words of a Peruvian Christian leader.

> Christian women have developed theological reasons not to have rights. So we are dedicated to resolving a fundamental problem: how to convince that there is equality with men by means of the Bible whose vision is patriarchal. (Basye, 2005:17)

Feminist theology takes on many forms. Regardless of the position held by any one person, feminist theology has been the major source of new research, scholarship, and critiques on gender as related to religious tradition. Feminist theology serves to infuse institutionalized religion with the inclusive spirituality of its heritage and is the key catalyst reopening religion's liberating potential for both women and men.

Summary

1. When spirituality became institutionalized as religion, women lost prestige and influence. The first civilizations probably had more partnership-based spiritual traditions and social institutions. In these gynocratic—female-centered—societies, a goddess heritage provided significant religious roles for women. The goddess as creator and powerful female deities existed throughout Africa and Asia. Many societies exhibited balance and complementarity where in principle neither gender was superior.

2. Muslims vary considerably in interpreting the Qur'an in terms of the role of women. Gender roles are mainly defined as complementary but inequality and women's task to provide male heirs are favored. Feminist Muslims are providing alternative interpretations based on the powerful and esteemed roles of the Prophet's wives. U.S. Muslim women are altering as well as affirming the traditional values of their religion.

3. Interpretations from Hindu scripture are contradictory: Women are idealized as submissive and serving their families and condemned if too ambitious; other views see male and female as balanced and emphasize the continuing goddess heritage of Hinduism. Historically, both the low and idealized opinion of women was seen when at widowhood she became a sati and immolated herself on her husband's funeral pyre.

4. In Judaism, scripture has been interpreted to ensure a strict gender division of labor in family and religious life. Contemporary Jewish women must deal with the separation between family and their religious lives outside the home. The Texts of Terror, four books of the Torah and Christian Bible, document sexual violence against women. Today all branches of Judaism are finding positive countervoices in scripture for women.

5. The Christian Bible's images of patriarchy and androcentric ideology have been favored, especially writings of St. Paul. Alternative views are offered by reformists demonstrating nontraditional and vital roles of women, especially Mary Magdalene. American Christians, both Protestants and Catholics, vary considerably in attitudes about women's roles and rights.

6. Women have a greater degree of religious orientation than men. The link between family and religion explains this, specifically related to women's role in the religious socialization of children.

7. Ordination and other leadership roles for women vary by religion and how each religion interprets scripture. Confucianism and Islam are the most restrictive for any public religious roles for women. All branches of Judaism except Orthodox ordain women. Most Christian religions ordain women. The notable exceptions of large groups are Lutheran Church–Missouri Synod and Catholics. The priest shortage and sex scandals in the Catholic Church provide fuel for women's ordination.

8. Female clergy are more willing to share power with congregations and have more consensual interaction styles than male clergy; otherwise there are few differences between them. Ordained women are less likely than men to receive a call to lead a congregation.

9. To make theology more inclusive in all religions, feminists and scholars are providing historical accounts of women in ancient religions, inclusive language is being adopted, ecumenism is encouraged, and scripture is being reinterpreted.

10. Feminist theology is an interdisciplinary field drawing on women's experience previously shut out of theological reflection. Religious tradition contains both sexist and nonsexist elements that may or may not be rejected.

Key Terms

feminist theology 355

gynocentrism 334

liberation theology 350

New Christian Right (NCR) 348

sati 341

Texts of Terror 343

Critical Thinking Questions

1. Demonstrate how women lost prestige and influence and misogyny increased when spirituality became institutionalized to religion. Specifically reference Hinduism, Judaism, Christianity, and Islam in this discussion. What strategies are used by feminist adherents to deal with the misogyny of their respective religions?

2. Why would functionalism be the dominant theoretical perspective explaining the persistence of gender inequity related to religion? How does feminist theology counter this perspective?

3. Based on your understanding of gender and religious socialization, how can women who are of faiths that restrict ordination and other leadership roles of women work for gender equity in their respective religions?

CHAPTER 13

Chick Flicks? Are you nuts? Director Kathryn Bigelow makes movies that go right to the gut. . . . She is a great female director of muscular action movies . . . But here's a radical thought: She is, simply, a great film director.

—(Dargis, 2009:AR1)

MEDIA

The influence of mass media on our lives is profound. The columnist above offers a backhanded compliment to a woman who defies stereotypes by making movies that, despite "two X chromosomes," shows "an occasional fist in the face, a knee to the groin" and "gets into your head even as it sends shock waves throughout your body." The perception that women are interlopers in mass media controlled by men is pervasive. Gender must be explained away in order to attract male audiences for date movies and female audiences for "blood and guts" action movies.

We are bombarded by media sights and sounds daily. We are subjected to music, news, and advertising at our office desks, in elevators, while jogging or driving to and from school or work. Advertisements crop out at virtually every site we encounter from the usual billboards and subway ads, to computer pop-ups and shopping cart ads in supermarkets. They shout out the newest, best, modern, and most efficient products and services available. Film and television offerings allow for every conceivable programming taste. With the advent of extraordinary, convenient technology, we can choose our entertainment specialties without ever leaving home.

As documented in Chapter 3, gender socialization occurs via multiple agents. Parents provide the earliest source, but beginning at about age 3, television becomes another potent socializer. We rely more and more on the mass media, especially television, to filter the enormous amount of information we receive. This filtering process has a major impact on our ideas about gender. Indeed, one of the most documented, consistent findings is that for both males and females, and in all age and racial categories, heavy television viewing is strongly associated with adherence to traditional and stereotyped views about gender.

Television is strengthened by advertisements, magazines, movies, and other media that present the genders in stereotyped ways. It is easy to see why, even at an early age, we form relatively rigid beliefs about what is considered appropriate behavior for boys and girls, women and men. Though media representatives may argue that what is presented merely reflects the reality of gendered beliefs, the question of reinforcing an already sexist society cannot be easily dismissed. After reviewing the media's record on how the genders are portrayed, we will return to this question.

PRINT MEDIA

Of all types of print media, magazines and newspapers are powerful in presenting views about gender roles. Gender stereotypes persist and thrive in print media across the globe, regardless of how media content is adapted to a culture's values and norms (Al-Olayan and Karande, 2000; Munshi, 2001). Early research about the impact of print media on attitudes about women and gender came from the source that was also a founding document of the women's movement.

Magazines

The publication of Betty Friedan's *Feminine Mystique* in 1963 challenged notions about contented American women in their homebound roles. Friedan was one of the first to look at the role of the print media, in this case popular women's magazines, in the formation of attitudes about women.

Fiction. Concentrating on the fiction that was the staple of women's magazines until recent decades, Friedan traced the images of women from the emancipated views in the 1930s and 1940s to the "happy housewife" and glorified mother of the 1950s and early 1960s. This beginning led to a great deal of research on gender stereotypes in magazines. Data over the next two decades confirmed the earlier patterns, but with some new twists: The ideal woman of magazine fiction was a housewife with one or two children ("homemaker" was the less common label). These women may experience psychological difficulties raising a family and attending to their husbands' needs, but they carried out their roles in exemplary manners. Employed women were unfeminine and posed threats to otherwise happy marriages. The baby boom accelerated in the 1950s, and so did the birth rate in magazines. Having a baby was a good bet for saving a floundering marriage. Married women who remained childless and spinsters who remained childless and husbandless were pitied for their wasteful, unhappy lives. Fiction of this period cheered on heroines who, through virtue and passivity, won the hearts of the men they would marry. Widows and divorcees were portrayed as unable to cope without a man. The overall conclusion: The happy housewife was even happier.

Articles. By the 1970s magazine fiction was being gradually replaced with other material targeted to women. But dramatic changes affecting gender roles were occurring that eventually impacted magazine images as well. The birth rate was leveling off, thousands of women moved into the paid labor force, and the feminist movement was making headlines. Magazines focusing on the challenges of women working outside the home emerged, some with explicitly feminist orientations, such as *Ms. Magazine.* Older, more traditional magazines such as *Ladies Home Journal* and *McCall's* began to include articles about educational opportunities, employment options, and women's rights. Magazines such as *Savvy, New Woman,* and *Working Woman,* geared to single women or employed married women, also appeared, offering advice to those coping with increased role responsibilities. Nonetheless, compared to the social upheaval in the real world of women, the magazine world of women has been minimally affected. After flirting with themes related to self-development, establishing one's identity, and expanded opportunities, the 1980s witnessed a return to more antiquated images, a situation that remains today. Magazines promote a traditional motherhood ideology. Homemakers with children may be shown as confused, overwhelmed, and focused only on their households, but products, services, and advice offered through the magazines help the frazzled women (Johnston and Swanson, 2003).

Most important, educated women with children who opt out of careers in order to be full-time homemakers are emerging in magazines as the new model of the feminine mystique. Reinforced by daytime television (think *Dr. Phil*), magazines offer advice to women who contemplate how to abandon careers to become stay-at-home moms. The newly minted homemakers emphasize their preference for the homemaker rather than career road. They continue to be high-achieving at home: "raising children is as challenging as anything else they've ever done" (Peters, 2008). Although articles in newspapers portray these women as heralding a return-to-the-hearth revolution, labor force trends do not match the media images. Highly educated mothers are more likely to be employed than less-educated mothers, a pattern virtually unchanged for over cades (Hesse-Biber and Carter, 2005; Kuperberg and Stone, 2008). Clearly, the reality is that for most women opting out is neither a simple choice nor a choice at all (Chapter 8).

With a half century of magazines showing a standard of femininity associated with domestic life, appearance, romance, and dating, it is not surprising that in the millennium the two dominant themes in magazines such as *Cosmopolitan, Glamour,* and *Essence* are, first, how to be more beautiful, and, second, relationships with men (how to get and keep them). The subtext in the relationship message is sexual. To keep their men from straying, women must develop sexual skills; they must be aware that his needs are met, but so are hers (Farvid and Braun, 2006). Advice about beauty, relationships, and sex are found in the same article. Magazine advertisers are happy to oblige women who want all of these.

Advertising

Articles about women in magazines related to beauty, romance, and home-making are reinforced through advertisements testifying to the power of makeovers and weight loss and the glories of spotless floors, soft toilet tissue, and antiseptic children. Extensive research has documented the fact that even with some improvement over time, advertising images of women continue to be based on these traditional gender role norms.

Stereotypes. An early major study on gender stereotyping in advertising analyzed magazines according to the number of males and females and the gender of adults, the occupations and activities in which they were presented, and the kinds of products being promoted (Courtney and Lockeretz, 1971). Despite the explosion of women in the labor force, the data showed that women's place is in the home, they do not make important decisions, and they are dependent on men, who in turn regard them as sex objects. Women are only interested in buying cosmetics and cleaning aids. A number of studies quickly followed. Ads were beginning to depict women in more occupational roles, but the vast majority of women were still pictured exclusively in the home. There was a decline in the blatantly sexist ads, but advertisers continued to be insensitive to the real world. Women's concerns centered on appearance, men, and simple decisions revolving around domestic roles (Should I cook turkey or beef for dinner?). Advertisements spanning two decades rarely showed women in nontraditional situations, even in magazines oriented to a wider audience, such as *Newsweek, Look*, and *Sports Illustrated* (Courtney and Whipple, 1983). Since it was first published, the swimsuit issue of *Sports Illustrated* maintains the same content of ideally beautiful and sexy women who are available to men.

Not only do advertisements today maintain these stereotyped images but in important ways gender-stereotyped and biased portrayals of white, African-American, and Asian women have increased. Highly stereotyped ads appear in general interest and fashion magazines and in mainstream magazines aimed at African-American women (Lindner, 2004; Kim and Chung, 2005; Hazell and Clark, 2008). Preteen, teenage, and young adult females are the targets. With nudity and near-nudity now the norm in mainstream magazines, it is common to see undressed or scantily dressed women selling all kinds of products. Car and boat ads typically show women in bathing suits draped over fenders and on cabin decks.

Products sold primarily to men, such as machine tools and industrial equip-ment, use a similar format. In gun magazines women in lingerie or evening gowns clutch men who are holding handguns and rifles. Advertising campaigns for popu-lar brands of clothing and fragrances routinely show near nude women or women and men in sexually provocative scenes—but do not show the items they are selling—only the logo of the company. This content often includes messages related to aggression and violence. When sex is used to sell a product, the ad is usually aimed at men (Monk-Turner et al., 2008). Advertisers in magazines such as *Vogue, Cleo, Elle, GQ*, and *Esquire* typically portray women who are helpless, passive, bound, or are being maimed and abused by men or animals. Men are shown as independent, rugged, sexually risky and dominant over women and other men (Wolf, 2002; Hirschman, 2003; Stankiewicz, 2008).

Subtlety and Subliminals. It is relatively easy to analyze ads according to general themes and images. Ads also sell products and reinforce attitudes in ways that are often unrecognized by the casual reader. Advertisers may embed *subliminal* messages at a subconscious level to prompt consumers to buy a product. Whether subliminal messages actually increase sales is debatable, but it is a standard tool in advertising. The pioneering work of Erving Goffman (1979) concentrated on the subtleties of posture and relative size and positioning of hands, eyes, knees, and other parts of the body in ads. A man is pictured taller than a woman unless he is socially inferior to her. Men and boys are shown instructing women and girls. A woman's eye is averted to the man in the picture with her, but a man's eye is averted only to a superior. Women's hands caress or barely touch. They are rarely shown grasping, manipulating, or creatively shaping. Women have faraway looks in their eyes, especially in the presence of men. Women act like children and are often depicted with children. Factoring in race—and counter to the contradictory stereotypes of sexualized or strong African-American women—black models are posed less sexually and more submissive than white models. Female models have fairer complexions then male models of the same race, images that are largely unchanged over time (Doring and Poschl, 2006; Millard and Grant, 2006; Baumann, 2008).

Such depictions are reinforced by how much of the body is shown in an ad. Males represent "face-isms," in that their faces are photographed more often than their bodies. Females represent "body-isms" or "partial-isms," in that their bodies or parts of their bodies are more often shown. Women, for example, appear much more in swimwear than do men. Data continue to confirm these depictions.

Face-ism ads still dominate for men as do body-ism ads for women. When accounting for occupation of the model, men depicted in intellectual occupations (accountant, executive) have higher face-to-body ratios than women in similar occupations (Matthews, 2007). The face is associated with qualities such as character and intellect whereas the body is associated with qualities such as weight and emotion, thus contributing to beliefs about what is deemed important for men and women (Shields, 2002). Women make desperate efforts to conform to a beauty ideal by manipulating their faces and bodies to achieve an impossible standard. Adolescent girls and older women are particularly vulnerable to such advertising and are its prime targets. Ads targeted to young girls play on their insecurities and wishes to be older and more sexually appealing (Willemsen, 1998; Kitch, 2001).

Age and Gender. Age and gender stereotypes combine in ads targeted to older women and play on their insecurities and desires to stop the aging clock and maintain their sex appeal. Older women are portrayed much less frequently than men and women in all age groups. Despite the demographic shift favoring longer and healthier lives for women, they are portrayed even less frequently than in the past. Throughout mainstream magazines aimed at all age groups, young women advertise products to older women (McConatha et al., 1999; Miller et al., 1999). The fear-of-aging theme increased cosmetics sales dramatically for the over-50 baby boomers. There are almost no older models, however, who sell these products. Whereas younger women sell lipstick and hair color to older women, when older women are used in ads at all, it is for products and medications signaling body decline and loss of independence, such as adult diapers, dentures, bone-strengthening drugs, and emergency alert devices.

Besides beauty products, clothing represents another method to attain the beauty standard by manipulating the body. The most successful models are paid millions to reinforce unnatural images of womanhood, which keep women chained to seasonal, changing, and expensive fashion trends. There is a growing market for seductive clothing designs aimed at little girls. Childhood is sexualized. From Barbie™ to Bratz™, advertisers tell girls that it is never too young to be sexy (Levin and Kilbourne, 2008).

Considering the avalanche of physical appearance messages women receive in advertising, symbolic interaction correctly predicts the self-fulfilling prophecies that follow. These are demonstrated in everything from self-esteem, cigarette smoking, eating disorders, and mental health, as well as a range of attitudes related to gender. Advertising artificially creates images that become the reality. In addition, as predicted by symbolic interaction's end-point fallacy, new labels about attractiveness will produce new behavior in an ongoing process. Beauty standards will continue to change, and consumers will adapt to these standards and change their behavior accordingly in a never-ending cycle.

The Business of Beauty. What is remarkable about such findings is that women—and increasingly men—are very critical of the images. If the people to whom the ads are directed find them distasteful and irritating, how can a double standard continue? From a pure business viewpoint, sexism is disadvantageous in that a product's market potential is not realized. Another problem is that advertisers are the lifeblood of magazines and make concessions to receive their business. Advertisers demand that a "supportive editorial atmosphere" or "complementary copy" appear with their ads. This means that an article about beauty to support or complement an ad about a beauty product must be included on the same page. In this way advertisers literally control the editorial content of the entire magazine (Steinem, 1995:316).

The minimal changes that have occurred are depicting women in more diverse occupational roles and in more general interest magazines. Older women are a huge potential market. While proclaiming that older women are (still) beautiful, advertisers are offering images of fitness, vitality, and blazing new trails associated with aging. Regardless of age, she is active, involved in an array of projects, and enjoys her home but is not monopolized by it. Some advertisers are only beginning to recognize that women are diverse, lead successful lives, and can balance home and career. The impact of this remains to be seen. The caution here is that another artificial creation emerges along with yet another set of standards women are expected to adhere to.

Advertisers must be aware of trends affecting products and services. The moment an improvement is made on a particular product, campaigns begin to sell the public on its virtues. To sell means to change. Yet advertising is stubbornly persistent in the manner in which this is done. Gender-based ads have not kept up with changes in the real world of families, of relationships, and of economics (Levy, 2006/2007; Robinson and Hunter, 2007). What is ironic is that ad agencies ignore the research documenting the fact that consumers react negatively to advertising that is sexist and desire campaigns that portray both men and women in nonstereo-typed ways. Men have been slower to lobby for these changes than women, but with the rapid increase in print ads and other media showing men as sex objects and portraying perfect male bodies that are just as unattainable for men, men are joining forces with women to protest sexism in advertising (Nathanson and Young, 2001). Considering this research and the numerous instances of public outrage over certain advertisements, the adage that "sex (and sexism) sells" must be questioned (Parker and Furnham, 2007).

FILM

Compared to other media, women have enjoyed a more central position in the film industry. Director and producer largely remain the province of men, but women have succeeded as screenwriters, editors, costume designers, critics, and actors. In the early days of film when the studio system was at its height, women dominated the star spotlight. This was reflected in popularity polls and the billings female leads received. Although the contract system allowed studios to literally own actors, women had influence in determining their careers and the parts they received. The female stars of this era were offered roles showing them to be articulate, self-reliant, and independent (Tirohl, 2003). It has only been since the 1940s that female stars have been overshadowed by males. With a few exceptions, this continues to the present. In contrast to the reality of women's diverse contemporary roles, current film portrayals are sorely lacking in depth and authenticity.

Screen History

Reflected in screen images, World War II encouraged the independence and initiative of women. They were portrayed as efficient homemakers who could make the transition from kitchen to the war industry smoothly, without severely disrupting family life. Or they were shown as nurses serving overseas and at times as combatants who, like men, died for their country. Movies were a critical part of the war effort and emphasized the need for self-sacrifice to ensure victory. Women on the home front were necessary for this effort. The double-duty woman who worked in a defense plant was symbolized by *Rosie the Riveter,* who became the home-front heroine.

Although women on the World War II screen possessed self-confidence and strength, a certain ambiguity was also evident. The taken-for-granted functional balance of home and workplace was upset. Both men and women left home to engage in the unlikely occupations of soldier and defense worker. They were fighting to save the American home, and films reassured audiences that after the war women would be as eager as men to return to the natural order of things. True to this message, by the 1950s films reaffirmed the domestic subservience of women.

Good Women and Bad Women. Whereas the war years presented women as multifaceted, after the war they were portrayed as one dimensional, as either good or bad. The "good" woman embodied the feminine mystique. She remained virtuous throughout courtship. Her premarital virginity was never questioned. She might have a successful career, but Mr. Right would change her priorities and definitions of success. After marriage she became the ideal wife and mother. Doris Day and Debbie Reynolds represented this image. Indeed, Doris Day became the national emblem of the perfect, sanitary, All-American girl next door (Kaufman, 2008). The "bad" woman, on the other hand, was the sexpot, who could entice a man away from his faithful wife and loving family. Marilyn Monroe and Ava Gardner represented this image. Regardless of the good–bad dichotomy screen actresses had to endure, these movies were awash with sexual innuendo and hinted broadly at the enticements of immorality. The difference between this era and those to follow, however, was that sexual desires were actualized on the functionalist screen only when it was normative to do so. Just in his fantasies did married Tom Ewell succumb to Marilyn Monroe in the *Seven Year Itch* (1955), and Doris Day would not surrender to Cary Grant in a *Touch of Mink* (1962) until they were married.

Although the films of the 1950s display a concern for domestic righteousness, they also reflected the disenchantment women faced in their struggle with narrowly defined gender roles. This period combined both conventional and progressive expressions of the difficulty women faced as they made the transition between domestic roles and newer alternatives. Screen actresses portrayed women torn between desire for security, symbolized by the customary and comfortable lifestyle of home, and desire for adventure and challenge beckoning to them outside home. These conflicts and contradictions of the transitional women helped set the stage for the changes of the next two decades.

If the early days of film romanticized women and put them on a pedestal, the 1960s and 1970s quickly compensated. Blatant sexuality laced with violence became the staple of the era. The new women of this era were loosened from the constraints of family life, but with the breaking of the bonds, an attitude of "they deserve what they get" arose. Women who ventured outside the home were portrayed negatively, suffered, and were usually punished as a result. The favorable images of the war years disintegrated, and women were accorded fewer roles than ever before. Male speaking roles outdistanced female by twelve to one. This period has been referred to as the most disheartening in the screen history for women on the screen and the women they represented off the screen. As the women's liberation movement gained momentum and women were asserting themselves in new realms, a backlash occurred in commercial film (Haskell, 1987, 1997).

James Bond and "His Girls". By the 1970s sex and sexual violence became explicit enough to create a rating system to determine the level of suitability for audiences below a certain age. The system is more concerned with sex than violence so that love scenes are more apt to get the film a restricted rating than rape scenes. The rating system also helps perpetuate the idea that rape is inconsequential. Rapists are often portrayed heroically when their victims love them at the time of the rape or fall in love with them later. In four decades of James Bond films, for example, women are depicted enjoying rape. Bond is the suave, charismatic good guy—the supposed fantasy of every woman and enviable role model of every man. James Bond gets to play out men's fantasies—he drives fast cars, fights ruthless villains, wears a nice suit, and has sex with any "girl" he desires, all who eventually say "*yes*" to him. Bond films are a composite of sex, spectacle, and menace (Wilson, 2002). Once raped, women are then ignored by the male star, sometimes murdered by him, and often murdered by someone else.Bond must always be free of women. If he inadvertently falls in love with her, she is doomed to die before the end of the picture.

As Bond ages, his girls do not. The most enduring Bonds—Sean Connery, Roger Moore, and Pierce Brosnan—were often 30 years older than their leading ladies. The women are as sleek and young as ever, picture after picture. As the newest Bond, Daniel Craig is merely 11–12 years older than Eva Green and Olga Kurylenko, the Bond girls of two recent films. It is likely that if Craig continues in the role—and ages with it—the age difference will again widen.

To maintain a female audience, producers acknowledge the flagrant abuse of women in past Bond films. Newer Bonds are more often paired with strong, intelligent (always beautiful) lead women in both heroine and villainess roles who match his wit, confidence, and resourcefulness. Partnership rather than submission is touted as the newer thrust of the Bond films, with leading ladies as supposedly sexually liberated as Bond is himself (Chapman, 2000). In an effort at emancipation from Bond, the female leads are publicized as the Bond "women" rather than the Bond "girls" (but still *his* females). Although not as overtly misogynous, the James Bond mystique endures. In a review of Halle Berry's portrayal of Jinx, Pierce Brosnan's Bond girl in *Die Another Day*, resourceful Halle Berry is pictured in an orange bikini with a dagger in a white belt. Pictured also is the movie poster of Ursula Andress in the identical outfit she wore in 1962's *Dr. No*. The ironic, even astonishing, caption reads, "Halle Berry is less of a sex symbol than a female equivalent to Bond" (Wilson, 2002:F1).

Pairing Sex and Violence

Despite the occasional spurts of romantic comedies like *You've Got Mail* and *Sleepless in Seattle*, referred to somewhat disdainfully as "chick flicks"—not suitable for male audiences or only if men are coerced by their female partners—film romance has been replaced with sexuality, violence, and their pairing in contemporary mainstream movies. Romantic movies of the past often had bold and capable females paired with males (Fred Astaire/Ginger Rogers; Katherine Hepburn/Spencer Tracy). These couples are gone, with prostitutes and girlfriends of questionable morals filling the void. The most typical occupation for women in the last three decades of movies is prostitute or ex-prostitute. Themes of love and adultery are infused with violence and murder.

Mainstream films are often more violent than pornographic films. Movies with comparable sex and violence that received an "X" rating a generation ago (*Exorcist, Midnight Cowboy*) would receive an "R" rating today. "Slasher" movies appealing to adolescent males regularly send the message that sexual violence is normal and acceptable. The higher the exposure to sexually violent media, the more likely the viewer will accept rape myths (Emmers-Sommers et al., 2006). Movies routinely portray scenes of graphic violence against passive female victims. Stalking and its often violent conclusion are associated with comedy and romance in mainstream cinema (*Basic Instinct, Fatal Attraction*). Love and violence coincide. Females are victims in movies of horror, murder, and especially rape, in which film directors seem to have a macabre interest. During the past three decades movies with a central rape theme increased dramatically. Although women as rape victims are more sympathetically depicted than in the past, moviegoers are also becoming more desensitized to the issue, reinforcing the notion that the possibility of rape is an inescapable burden women must face.

Aging Females, Ageless Males

Unlike men, women must be young and show high levels of physical strength to be seriously considered for romantic leads and the action-oriented roles of sexy heroines (*Crouching Tiger, Hidden Dragon, Miss Congeniality, Charlie's Angels*) in emerging action films appealing to both young men and women. In Hollywood young translates to under 30. The hottest stars of the 1930s–1960s were women in powerful, multidimensional roles—Bette Davis, Joan Crawford, Kathryn Hepburn, and Rosalind Russell—and were often playing romantic leads well into their 40s and 50s. Today these women would have long before been consigned to obscure roles or relegated to made-for-TV cable movies. After a certain age, women are destined to play shrews, jealous housewives, lonely executives, or kooky aunts. Only 8 percent of roles for women in the top 250 films go to women over 40 (Waxman, 2002). Younger female faces are sought to replace aging stars. Distinguished female actors such as Faye Dunaway, Shirley MacLaine, and Meryl Streep get old; Robert Deniro, George Clooney, and Richard Gere get distinguished. Harrison Ford's reprise as Indiana Jones is played as an Indie who was older than Sean Connery, who played Indie's father in an earlier Jones movie.

Gender Parity and Film Portrayal

Over 75 percent of feature-film roles go to men, a figure that increased over the last decade (Gibbons, 2009). The so-called wholesome roles for women, although devoid of the sexual content that may demean women, signals doom in Hollywood. It is a sign she is an aging bygone. A rather cynical comment on the paucity of either featured or supporting parts for mature, skilled actresses came in 1993 when the theme for the Academy Awards was "Oscar Celebrates Women in the Movies." Six of the ten nominees for Best Actress and Best Supporting Actress came from Australia, England, and France because Hollywood studios simply did not offer enough meaningful roles for women to even get nominated for the award. Hollywood greeted the millennium with the gendered Hollywood staples of the previous decades.

There are a few positive signs suggesting a return of women to movies that offer greater role latitude and countering stock Hollywood formulas related to gender. Although not immune to gender stereotypes critically acclaimed, popular films not resting on a male lead attracting male and female audiences are in evidence. They highlight sensitive issues related to friendship and loyalty among women. These include W*aiting to Exhale, A League of their Own, Sisterhood of the Traveling Pants,* and perhaps, *Friends with Money.* Success for some female friendship movies is bittersweet. *Fried Green Tomatoes* and *Silkwood* were criticized for lesbian overtones. *Thelma and Louise* was charged with male-bashing; the subtext of violence against women was ignored (Welsch, 2001).

While countering masculinist bias in some movies that portray lesbians, other stereotypes persist to make the films more palatable to a wider audience. Filmmakers believe an injection of violence satisfies this criterion. Sharon Stone's portrayal of a bisexual murderer in *Basic Instinct* drew storms of protest from gay men and lesbians. It is apparent that film critics, too, subscribe to a gender-stereotyped world that is suspicious of loving and cooperative relationships between women. It reveals much about the tenacity of gendered society when decades of movies routinely show females who are mutilated, maimed, murdered, and raped film after film, but when a successful movie reverses the scenario, a charge of man-bashing is leveled against it. The issue is not so much that turnabout is fair play but that violence is viewed as an acceptable mode of conflict resolution.

With limited roles and limited meaty roles going to women, it is not surprising that female stars and superstars far outnumber their female counterparts. A cursory look at film offerings in your local paper testifies to the scarcity of female stars— strong, multidimensional, or otherwise. Barbra Streisand was the only bankable female lead for a decade. Jessica Lange, Diane Keaton, Susan Sarandon, Demi

Moore, Meg Ryan, Helen Hunt, and Halle Berry occupy star status. Superstardom will elude them more as they age. Julia Roberts and Meryl Streep are superstar frontrunners; they endure the Hollywood roller coaster for women. There is less tolerance for box-office bombs starring women. Jack Nicholson, Al Pacino, or Kevin Costner may emerge relatively unscathed from bad reviews and bad movies, but studios are reluctant to offer parts to women who have fallen victim to the critics' axe. Women are almost hidden among the faces of numerous male actors who endure as superstars. Although complaints abound that women are held hostage by Hollywood, the bottom line is male domination of movie marquees.

The film industry offers a number of excuses for portraying women in limited and stereotyped roles that emphasize their sexuality. Male studio executives often maintain that the public disdains "macho" women and that television offers a diverse range of female roles for free. This may suggest that men create inappropriate images for female roles simply because their feedback from women is limited. Roles emerge from male fantasies, the fear men express in dealing with women as allies rather than as adversaries, and the tenacious belief that men must dominate and control women. They cite statistics that the average moviegoer is a young male, and it is his fantasies that are being catered to. The male disdain for female- or feminine-oriented content is reflected in the following:

> The noise you hear when the weather and the movies get hot—is the tumbling of actresses, as male stars push them aside into big action films. Out of the way, ladies. Summer is men's work. (Corliss, 2003:57)

Critique. There are challenges to these views. Box-office advertising is increasingly directed at women. Filmmakers will continue to focus on the key age demographic (young—between 14 and 24); male and female are almost at parity in the moviegoing public. To make movies that ignore or demean a large portion of the audience does not make good marketing sense. Two decades of Hollywood's service to teenage boys may be matched with offerings geared to teenage girls (*Freaky Friday, Bend It Like Beckham, Whale Rider*). Because these movies also spotlight rebellious teens who succeed in challenges to parents, teachers, and adults, they also attract the necessary number of males to ensure the movies' profit. Such movies do not do much to dissuade gender or age stereotypes about teenage girls, but they can offer young women alternatives from the typical female bashing movies they usually see.

The dilemma faced by film producers concerned with the image of women is how to successfully combine the elements of fantasy and realism attracting people to movies in the first place. Mainstream cinema continue to represent women as either "idealized objects of desire or as threatening objects to be tamed" (Pribram, 1993). The limited range of female characters finds them in the same roles: as madonnas, whores, bimbos, psychotics, and bitches (Silvas et al., 1993). On the other hand, should women be portrayed as victims of patriarchy, conquerors against mighty odds, or burnt out employees and soccer moms? Will romance be crushed by realism? Movies can still have the requisite fantasy and magic without accepting a narrow range of behaviors from female actors. In Oscar winner Emma Thompson's view, women have to debrief themselves to resist the messages that they have no history or no heroines and to unlearn the stereotypes that chip away at their sense of self-esteem (Italie, 1993).

Filmmakers are only beginning to deal with the struggles facing contemporary women, and few directors are willing to confront the issues. So movies retreat into an unrealistic stereotyped world. The majority of the viewing public believes that movies demean women, but gender stereotypes remain an American film staple. Movies may be creations of male fantasies, but women need to invent and portray their own fantasies as well.

MUSIC

Media cater to a public always demanding innovative sights and sounds to satisfy an unending thirst for entertainment. Music is increasing its already powerful role in gender socialization. Nowhere is this more apparent than in the world of popular music. Whatever niche is defined—country, rock, pop, rap, hip-hop, alternative, or heavy metal—the quest for musical notoriety, as evidenced by the volume of CD sales, continues unabated. Although the music industry is diverse, it recognizes that a significant portion of the record market is controlled by teens and young adults. Compared to music depicted on television a generation ago, producers of contemporary music and television videos are ruthless in competing for the teen dollar.

Music is always at the vanguard of change. Protest movements are fired by songs that unify members against a common foe. Rock musicians take conventional morality to the limits. Their music challenges the traditional and creates the conditions for further change. Because many genres of contemporary music defy social norms, it would appear to be the one medium where traditional gender roles are also challenged. Evidence counters this assumption. Popular music is the most stereotyped and misogynistic of all media in its gender portrayals.

A half century of popular music sings to the conquest of women by men. The conquest theme shows males objectifying women and using sexual violence as a means of control. The dependent women theme in turn emerges—women assess their self-worth by the men in their lives (Bretthauer et al., 2006). On the other hand, beauty and sex appeal are used by women to manipulate unsuspecting, naive men. A beautiful woman can use supposed submissiveness to her advantage. Country music in particular stereotypes women in two categories: They are temptresses as well as wives who wait patiently for their two-timing husbands to return. No matter what the consequences, "stand by your man" is the response for the long-suffering woman.

Rock Music

For popular music, rock claims artistic supremacy. Rock is and the creative force behind all popular music (Regev, 1994:97). This claim to supremacy serves to legitimize whatever musical representation it offers to its public, including the portrayal of men and women and how gender is racialized in rock music. Popular music may be gender stereotyped, but its rock niche exceeds all others in these portrayals.

Since the 1950s, images of women in rock music have become increasingly associated with sexual violence. The misogyny in the lyrics of many categories of music that can be regarded as rock—"cock rock," heavy metal, rap, R&B, hip-hop—is unconcealed, with little attempt to be subtle. Some images of women in rock are positive, but these exist side by side with overriding, blatant misogyny. Women are cast into rigid categories determined by their perceived gender role characteristics. These images are expanded by CD covers depicting women being brutalized by men and animals. Computer images allow these depictions to be acted out. The love–hate dichotomy is featured, where men are kissing and killing women at the same time. Boycotts of records showing violent themes against women on CD covers have generally failed. As rock lyrics have become more sexually explicit, however, some record companies have agreed to put a warning label on their album covers indicating that the words may be unsuitable for younger audiences. Like in the film rating system, it is a significant social comment that sexual themes are considered more offensive than violence against women.

The Women of Rock. Before the advent of rock in the 1950s, female singers occupied one-third of the positions on singles charts, but by 1985 that figure had decreased dramatically to 8 percent (Groce and Cooper, 1990:221). A number of female entertainers—such as Patti Page, Rosemary Clooney, and the Andrews Sisters—were popular before World War II and were commercially successful for decades later by combining music and film careers. With the emergence of rock music and its appeal to teenagers, younger male entertainers moved into the spotlight. Only the "girl groups" of the 1960s and 1970s—such as the Supremes, Ronnettes, and Shangri-Las—charted any real successes for female singers during this era.

In the 1960s Janis Joplin broke into the rock culture and emerged as a unique, controversial, and often-contradictory symbol for young women caught in the middle of a confusing period of history. She was viewed not only as a floozy as well as one who sang of the pains of womanhood, but also as a feminist symbol who paved the way for other women destined to enter the sacred realm of the male rock kingdom (Hirshey, 1997). As rock musician Melissa Etheridge attests,

> In 1967, Janis was strange and freakish. Today she would be hip and alternative. Because of her drive to be true to her soul, girls like me in 1976 didn't feel so strange wanting to sing rock 'n' roll. Because she wrote, "either take the love I offer or let me be," I didn't feel so different for wanting power in my life. We didn't have to be secretaries or housewives; we could be rock stars. (Cited in Levins, 1995)

A number of rock bands either led by women or with female and male lead singers and musicians have emerged. Only a few steps behind superstars Madonna, Gloria Estefan, Christina Aguilera, and Britney Spears are other leading women of rock, including Alicia Keyes, Kelly Clarkson, Shakira, Missy Elliot, and Ashanti. Many of these women are African American or have Latino roots, and are hugely successful among the music-buying public of the Americas. They have garnered the music industry's most prestigious awards. It cannot be said, however, that their songs substantially differ from, or offer challenges to, stereotyped representations of women. Like pop and country singers they, too, sing mostly of love and pain and chant about vulnerable women being abandoned by men.

Challenges to Misogyny. Until recently, female rock artists have produced few popular songs depicting women in a sympathetic light and have had little power in altering the sexist material of their bands while remaining commercially successful. Resurgent sexism on the rock scene may also counter efforts at change. With the rise of the female superstars of rock, however, even if the lyrics do not reflect much change now, it may happen in the near future. Women rock artists are creating new identities that challenge male domination in mainstream rock culture and are gaining control over their own images (Katovich and Makowski, 1999; Grajeda, 2002; Schippers, 2002). A major result of attaining economic independence is that they can seriously challenge rock's misogyny.

Madonna may be the exception to this pattern, but she is also an enigma. Her music frequently counters traditional feminine ideals of dependency and reserve, presenting a postmodern feminist image that shatters all gender barriers. Others condemn her for sending potent messages to teens about the glamour of sex and pregnancy through a fantasy world she creates (cited in Brown and Schulze, 1990:92). She remains an inveterate gender rule breaker but is still judged by different standards than males. Her videos have been banned by MTV and mainstream video networks for sexual and violent content that men would have likely escaped (Gundersen, 2001). But because she has transitioned successfully into film, her multidimensional talents are receiving high marks. Janis Joplin died early in her career. It will be interesting to see if Madonna becomes the feminist role model that may have been Joplin's destiny.

MTV and Music Videos

MTV was introduced to cable subscribers in 1981 and soon catapulted to become one of the most widely consumed forms of popular culture for adolescents in the United States. A wave of cable programming devoted to niche music videos for various age groups and genres followed on MTV's successful heels, including VH1 for adult contemporary music, BET geared to African Americans, and CMT for country music fans. Under the umbrella of MTV Networks, music channels throughout the globe play 24-hour music videos in the native language of the country where they are aired. On MTV and television channels around the world, males appear on the videos twice as often as females. Despite these quite diverse niches, three patterns are clear: adolescents and young adults are the largest music video consumers; these two age groups are the target market for its most sexualized and violent content; and music videos are highly gendered and misogynistic.

Gender Ideology. "Generic" rock videos, hip-hop, and rap—whether performed by male or female artists—provide a visual extension and support a gender ideology of male power and dominance reinforcing misogyny. Videos routinely depict women as emotional, illogical, deceitful, fearful, dependent, and passive and men as adventuresome, domineering, aggressive, and violent. Sexual imagery has increased steadily in all genres of music videos and today almost three-quarters of all music videos depict sexual images. The most disheartening fact is that *most* videos combine sexual images with acts of violence; these acts usually depict rape imagery.

Heavy metal and rap display the most violent and sexually violent lyrics and images. Whereas heavy metal uses more double entendres and symbolic allusions to refer to sexual acts and male domination of women, rap and gangsta rap makes these acts more graphic and explicit. Typical of rape and sexual violence in songs are: *Stripped, Raped and Strangled* by Cannibal Corpse, "Smack My Bitch Up by Prodigy," and "Balla Baby" by Chingy. The lyrics in Poison's "I Want Action" leave no room to doubt the message: "I want action tonight. If I can't have her, I'll take her and make her." Routine exposure to such images desensitizes viewers to erotica and sets the stage for more graphic and sexually violent portrayals on "mainstream" television.

Since males of all races not only consume more sexualized videos than females and prefer more violent content, they are more likely to view women as sex objects and to accept rape myths (Selah-Shayovits, 2006; Peter and

Valkenburg, 2007; Colley, 2008). Consistent with symbolic interaction theory, gender is a social construction shaped by social myths articulated in popular culture. Publicity surrounding the graphic portrayals of sexual themes is exactly what some performers desire. In addition to CD sales, cable subscribers will pay extra for premium channels that show controversial videos that other networks refuse to air.

Race and Gender. With misogyny as the ever-present backdrop, music videos portray gender in highly racialized ways, especially for African Americans. Even counting videos by black artists, white women outnumber African-American women almost three to one. When they are portrayed, however, African-American women are increasingly taking on the roles white women traditionally assume in videos. A decade ago black women were shown in more active, foreground roles, such as dancing or playing an instrument; white women were shown more in the background for decoration (Smith and Boyston, 2002; Smith, 2005). Today women of all races are depicted in roles that are more passive and decorative. African-American women, however, are the most sexualized and represented as "porno chicks" throughout the world of music videos.

Most telling is that African-American women are, literally, looking more and more like white women. They are thinner, have lighter complexions, have longer and straighter hair, and have features that are generally Eurocentric. African-American girls are fast succumbing to the white beauty and appearance norms that they had long resisted. African-American men, whether as the musical artists or in the background, have darker complexions and more natural hair. Black gangsta rappers are likely to have liberally tatooed and pierced bodies. All varieties of male rappers and hip-hop artists are associated with criminality, supposedly appealing to African-American women who desire a thug in their lives (Gordon, 2008; Zhang et al., 2008; Conrad et al., 2009). These videos conceptualize African-American masculinity as evolving out of gangs and ghettos (Kubrin, 2005; Balaji, 2009). They do untold harm in reinforcing gender and race stereotypes.

How images are differentially embraced by men and women remains unclear. Women may read the female images in videos as powerful or vulnerable. Men may read the female images as teasing and playing hard to get or as submissive (Milburn et al., 2000). Young African Americans who readily consume a diet of hip-hop and rap videos are aware of the masculinist, misogynistic images but may not consider them disempowering (Sharpley-Whiting, 2007). The majority of young African-American men consuming the same videos are more likely to be socialized into accepting its misogynistic content rather than its violent content (Ward et al., 2005; McQuillar, 2007; Oliver, 2007). Nonetheless, music video content depicting African-American women as sexually promiscuous and African-American men as criminals remain largely unchallenged in the African-American community or in the larger corporate culture (Littlefield, 2008).

Regardless of race, women popular culture musical artists do break out of the mold in which they are embedded by the broader rock culture, but in turn find themselves in a no-win situation. From a conflict theory perspective, they may have a financial stake in maintaining the racialized, misogynistic images they disdain. Only when they reach superstardom or own their own studios can they be somewhat immune to the power of record producers. Indeed, few can act as role models and challenge rock's misogynous lyrics. With notable exceptions such as semi-retired Tina Turner, who reemerged in rock, and catapulted to the superstar category, alternative views of women that are both popular and empowering are rarer today than in the 1960s.

TELEVISION

Television is not only by far the most influential of all media, television watching is at an all-time high. In the United States virtually all households have at least one TV; the average number of sets per home is 2.24, one of which is turned on seven hours per day. Approximately three-quarters of households pay or have access to cable programs. Although people over age 55 watch television the most, preschoolers and young children may spend up to one-third of the day in front of the set.

Television plays a central role in the lives of children and is a powerful agent of socialization (Chapter 3). Television for children is much more gender stereotyped than the shows adults watch. In the early stages of identity formation, young children from all races in the United States use television for role modeling (Huston et al., 2007; Schmidt and Anderson, 2007). Seventy percent of day-care centers use television on a typical day. Children from poor homes watch television more than those from affluent homes, working- and lower-class children more than those whose parents have higher education and income, and African Americans and Latinos more than European Americans (Comstock, 2008; Nielsen, 2009).

Gendered Violence

More than 2,000 studies conducted over four decades document a clear and consistent correlation between amount of television viewing and aggression. Viewing violence increases the potential for violence and desensitizes the viewer to subsequent violence. The more violent the content, the more aggressive the child or adolescent. Consider the following facts on the aggression–media–television link (Pecora, 2007; Rich, 2007; Comstock, 2008; Murray, 2008; Nagle, 2009).

- Two out of three TV programs contain violence that threatens or actualizes hurt and killing.
- By sixth grade the average child has witnessed at least 8,000 TV murders and 100,000 other violent acts.
- Nearly 70 percent of children's programs contain physical aggression—an average of 14 violent acts per hour of typical programming.

Although the number of violent acts may have plateaued on television, the violence that is shown is more graphic and realistic. Other forms of media violence repeat and exaggerate many of the patterns found on television. Exposure to video game violence is linked to increases in aggressive behavior, particularly in boys (Anderson and Bushman, 2001; Signorielli, 2003). Because of the ability to manipulate characters, violent video games have a stronger connection to aggression in children and adolescents. Attracting over 9 million players, "America's Army" is a collection of sophisticated, realistic, and extremely violent video games developed by the U.S. army. Players are taken on virtual missions from basic training to waging war and fighting terrorists. Players are entertained as well as enticed to enlist (Bica, 2009).

Television violence is directed toward women. Overall, men kill and women get killed. Men kill more than twice as often as they are killed. White adult males and attractive white boys are more likely to perpetrate violence and to get away with it, with girls and women of color, older women, and foreign women the most likely victims (Smith et al., 2002; Hetsroni, 2007). Children learn though gendered media messages that men are aggressive and women are vulnerable. These messages may be altered, but they are not erased in adulthood.

Prime Time

Women's prime-time presence continues to increase and women now account for over 40 percent of all characters. On-screen presence, however, does not predict plot or importance of character. Television prime time revolves around men. Leading male characters outnumber females about two to one, a consistent trend since the early days of television. Highlighted in this section, a great deal of research focuses on the continuing unrealistic, stereotyped portrayals of both television men and women (Comstock and Scharrer, 2007; Kircher, 2008; Shanahan et al., 2008).

Gender Profiles in Drama. Men dominate dramatic shows, especially those involving action, adventure, and crime. In lead roles they play tough and emotionally reserved characters who are unmarried but have beautiful female companions. The profile of prime-time men includes the following: He is in his 30s, single, white, handsome, smart, middle class, and sexy. We do not know much about his family, his leisure life, or his interests outside of work. He may be attracted to a coworker but usually fails in his attempts to hide it from others.

Compared to men, women have far fewer leading roles. Their increase in on-screen presence is attributed to minor roles. However, minor roles where ongoing characters have speaking parts are expanding for women. Female characters are attractive bystanders in background shots but are less attractive than females who are named as specific characters. The sex appeal of background females cannot outshine those with more important roles. The profile of prime-time women includes the following: She is unmarried, under 30, employed outside the home, more likely to be in a professional occupation than in the past, cares for children if she is a single mother, and is not involved in, but looking for, a romantic relationship. Their lives are more complicated than those of male characters. Marriage rates of prime-time women are increasing. They often delay marriage until their mid-30s, with subthemes revolving around their quest for pregnancy before their biological clocks time out.

Invisible Women. Older women are invisible in prime time. If seen at all, they are marginalized and subordinated, lacking prestige and leadership. A few powerful women may have minor roles, but their on-screen presence is minimal (*Boston Legal*). Gone are Jessica Fletcher (*Murder She Wrote*) and the older, powerful women of *Dynasty* and *Falcon Crest*. Often representing the serious side of comedy, shows such as the *Golden Girls* have also disappeared. Viewers today are most likely to see characters in their 30s and least likely to see characters in their 60s (Lauzen and Dozier, 2005; Grant and Hundley, 2007; Lauzen et al., 2007). Age is also not kind to older men on prime-time TV, but men still represent almost three-fourths of all age 60 plus characters. Prime time sends powerful messages about what the general population thinks about aging in general and older women in particular (Signorielli, 2004).

The mismatch of age and gender on prime-time television is puzzling. Older women are the heaviest viewers of television and the fastest growing age group in the United States and globally. They remain healthy and active well into old age. Baby Boomer women are the first generation with the largest proportion of women working full time throughout their lives. Advertisers have yet to recognize the enormous returns by providing more images, and more positive images, of older women on television. To date, however, older women remain invisible.

Intersecting Gender, Race, and Ethnicity. Although network television is dominated by white males, African-American characters are increasing rapidly, with males outpacing females. Compared to their population numbers, TV today is overrepresented by African-American characters. and underrepresented by Latinos, now the largest minority group in the United States. A range of research documents the following trends that intersect gender with race and ethnicity (Chin et al., 2006; Shek, 2006; Comstock and Scharrer, 2007; Greenberg and Worrell, 2007).

- African-American boys and men are leads, costars, with white partners, and have an array of major supporting roles. Criminals and bad guys are no longer exclusively African American.
- African-American girls are cast as leads and in key supporting roles (*Sister Sister, That's So Raven*).
- African-American women are less likely to be leads. They are cast in a more limited range of roles; the most frequent portrayals are of overweight, asexual mothers and aunts; second are the sexually alluring girlfriends and unmarried temptresses.
- Asians are very under represented on prime time television. Asian males have more starring roles than Asian females but both, however, are depicted as professionals. Asian women in background roles are exoticized often portraying prostitutes.
- Of all races, Latinos are most underrepresented. With the notable exception of the *George Lopez Show*, few men are in starring roles. Unlike the music industry, Latinas are virtually nonexistent. The few roles they do play are as domestics, waitresses, and low-level hospital workers. Rare starring roles are highly stereotyped by race and gender. Although she effectively satirizes the "stereotype of the Latina sexpot," Sofia Vergara plays a trophy wife in *Modern Family* (Bellafante, 2009:MT3). Gabrielle, of *Desperate Housewives* is strong and willful but her role model status is undermined by Latina stereotypes of a "flesh-flashing, promiscuous, cantina girl" (Merskin, 2007).

The popularity of these shows, however, may signal a trend for prime-time television to become more female friendly and less gender stereotyped.

Comedy. In comedies, women now appear in about the same frequency as men. The completely dependent housewife role in early comedy series like *Leave it to Beaver* and *I Love Lucy* have all but disappeared. The "liberated" women of the 1970s, such as *Maude* and *Rhoda* paved the wave for this trend. The immense popularity of the long-running *Mary Tyler Moore Show* is linked to the fact that this was the only show in which a single career woman was depicted without a steady boyfriend or any major story line revolving around her unmarried and nonmotherhood status. Some suggest that *Ally McBeal* was the new Mary Richards, but her ditzy character, self-absorption, inappropriate dress, and obsession with romance counters this view. Homemakers may have disappeared, but there are virtually no comedy or dramas that have the equivalent of a Mary Richards.

Beauty, Age, and Reality TV. Issues related to appearance permeate prime-time comedy and reality shows. Women and girls are laughed at when they are too heavy—the heavier the woman the more negative the comments about them, especially comments made by men (Fouts and Burggraf, 2000; Barriga et al., 2009). These images continue despite increases in shows featuring female leads. Younger women are particularly vulnerable to stereotyping and are depicted as empty headed and obsessed with beauty, clothes, shopping, materialism, and dating. The character of Kelly in the old *Married With Children* series is the teenage/young adult caricature of this portrayal. Other examples include Phoebe of *Friends*, London Tipton of *Suite Life of Zack and Cody*, and Amber in *Hannah Montana*.

The huge success of reality TV combines elements of comedy and drama, often with ruthless competition. These shows include *America's Next Top Model, The Biggest Loser, Entertainment News* (how celebrities maneuver the red carpet), and *Dancing with the Stars*. Reality TV offers instruction to audiences about how to manage their lives, their homes, and especially their personal appearance. If they cannot succeed, it is their own fault (Ouellette and Hay, 2008). The obsession with adhering to a rigid beauty standard affects both men and women, but young women are its most likely prey.

Television's beauty obsession collided with gender, age, and class stereotypes when Susan Boyle, an overweight, middle-aged woman from a working-class background appeared on Britain's version of *American Idol*. Prejudged to fail by an appearance completely at odds with TV beauty standards, she stunned audiences with her magnificent voice. In popular culture media, the belief that feminine beauty equates to talent, goodness, and social acceptance is extremely difficult to dislodge. Rather than newspaper accounts admonishing us about the harm, injustice, and inaccuracy of sexist and ageist stereotypes, scientists astonishingly suggested that, from an evolutionary perspective, snap judgments are "only natural" (Belluck, 2009). The "only natural" argument is routinely used to sustain gender role stereotypes that are individually and socially damaging (Chapter 3).

Employed Women. The explosion of women in the workplace translated to prime-time television. In the rush to capture the female 20–50 age group, television shows depicting employed women mushroomed. By the millennium, employed women comprised over three-fourths of prime-time female characters, about 15 percent more than those who worked outside the home in real life. Regardless of what they do in their TV workplaces, however, their roles revolve around finding or holding on to romantic relationships, marriage, and family. In *Cougar Town*, Courtney Cox plays divorced mom Jules, a successful real estate agent. The show features her desperate quest "to find a hunk, not a home buyer (Stanley, 2009:MT1,4). Female characters are likely to be identified by their marital status; male characters are likely to be identified by their occupation. Compared to men, women's occupations are less prestigious and less powerful. The powerful woman in some shows are shadows, remaining in the background with less airtime. They maintain a "now you see them, now you don't" shadow existence.

Employed women may be married and have children, but few experience work–family conflicts. Prime-time drama and comedy revolve around what happens at work or after work—but not both. Research reflects television's continual lack of attention to the real-world experiences of women (Asher and Lederer, 2000; Signorielli and Kahlenberg, 2003).

Soap Operas

Directed at a daytime female audience, soap operas have more female than male lead characters. Soaps are ludicrous in their distortion of reality but are popular because of it. Soaps provide the daytime opportunity for women to escape into a fantasy world of romance and adventure. Soap opera women seek one another for advice on family and sexual matters. Soap opera women are schemers, victims, bed-hoppers, and idealistic romantics. Family relationships equate women with motherhood, but lust and adultery lurk in the background. The soap opera family is a dominant concern of the women. The family suffers because of affairs that children learn about. The forgiving wife holds the family together until her errant husband returns and temporarily makes amends.

Despite these portrayals, however, the women of soaps are intelligent, self-reliant, and articulate. Soaps appear to both engage and distance their viewers while keeping them entertained. Some strong soap opera women question the gender status quo and challenge patriarchy. However, with new television niches geared to women who work outside the home, the traditional daytime soap opera may be on the verge of extinction.

TV's Gendered Exceptions

Standout exceptions in past and current television programming can serve as cues to predict future trends. Debuting in 1982, *Cagney and Lacey* was the first prime-time drama featuring two female leads as police partners. Deviating from the prime-time television norm, crime plots intertwined sensitively with issues rarely addressed on police shows of this era, including breast cancer, domestic violence, abortion, and child neglect. Police women, like all women, faced career and family conflict, misogyny and prejudice, and ambition and hope at midlife. These compassionate yet entertaining portrayals created a loyal male and female audience for its six-year run. The Cagney and Lacey roles were reprised in the 1990s by the original stars in a series of popular made-for-television movies.

Recent exceptions to the stock gender-role television drama formula include 50ish Detective Superintendent Jane Tennison (Helen Mirren) in the British series *Prime Suspect* and the brilliant forensic anthropologist Dr. Temperence Brennan (Emily Deschanel) in *Bones*. In *The Good Wife*, 40-something Jenny Sanford (Julianna Margulies) is a respected defense attorney who must reclaim her life and identity after her philandering political husband lands in jail (Chozick, 2009). These new type of heroines lead diverse casts of men and women who solve complicated crimes, deftly defend their clients, and thoughtfully struggle with issues related to family, friendship, and motherhood. Gender stereotypes do lurk in the background. Their careers offer fulfillment, but their personal lives are in a state of disarray. The message that women can't have it all—rewarding career and loving family—remains as a subtext.

For high school girls and young women the success of *Xena: Warrior Princess,* and *Charmed* is attributed to the nonstereotyped traits associated with the characters—confidence, strength, and the ability to match and outwit male villains—as well as loyalty and friendship among young women. With the action, fantasy, and adventure of these series, young males crossed over to a show that could have been directed to an exclusively female audience. *Buffy the Vampire Slayer,* another crossover show with a strong and heroic female lead, continues to attract a legion of viewers for its reruns (Stabile, 2009). The beauty subtext and sexism vestige for all the female characters in these shows are certainly evident. It may or may not overshadow the shows' other messages.

It is now common to see more gender-related social issues on entertainment-focused dramas, on talk shows, and increasingly on comedy series. Despite enduring stereotyped portrayals, women and men are pursuing a diversity of nontraditional roles in real-world living arrangements and occupations far removed from Beaver Cleaver's family. Consider *The Cosby Show, Will & Grace,* and *Designing Women* of the past, and more recent, *The Office, The New Adventures of Old Christine,* and *Ellen.* These shows demonstrate that class, race, age, sexual orientation, and gender diversity can be successfully portrayed without the demeaning stereotypes often associated with these categories. In 1992, the *Murphy Brown* series became a political football when Vice President Dan Quayle argued that it glorified motherhood for unmarried women. The producers countered by using the controversy in the series itself. The show spotlighted families that did not fit the traditional form, a tactic that enhanced the show's popularity.

These exceptions need to be considered in light of overall programming, including cable TV and the market for reruns dating back a half century. Even with women in lead roles in a few popular series, they still do not typically include major roles, especially for minority women. Gender role diversity has had minimal impact on the stereotypes embedded within the very programs that are often promoted as representing more realistic gender images. As shows enter the rerun market, *Roseanne* competes with *Charlie's Angels* (Whose angels are they?) and *Cheers,* the bar owned by womanizer Sam Malone. Intent to make programming less gender stereotyped is often countered by reruns.

Commercials

Television advertising reinforces the hundreds of print images we encounter daily. Nonverbals in print ads can be used effectively, but their use is limited compared to what can be done with television commercials. Television uses hundreds of techniques to create a particular view of a product. Lighting, camera angle, tone of voice, body movement, animation, and color, to name a few, can be infinitely manipulated to provide the ideal sales mix.

Research on thousands of commercials determines the extent and change of gendered content television advertising. For network and cable television, the results are similar to print advertisements. Gender stereotypes also far outweigh racial stereotypes. As judged by location of the commercial, the single largest occupation for a female is homemaker. She is usually shown at home testifying to the merits of bathroom and kitchen products. Though she is selling products to other women, a man's voice in the background tells her what to do. The large majority of voice-overs are male. She is portrayed in dependent, subordinate, and helping roles to her husband, her children, and her male employer if she works outside the home. If she is African American, this pattern intensifies. Consistent with print ads, television commercials emphasize that women must first and foremost be attractive to be acceptable. About one in every three commercials presents a message about attractiveness to women through a male voice-over. Women and men are now at parity in prime-time commercials, but they are shown in domestic situations as wife or mother; when shown with men outside the home, they are portrayed as less assured and more foolish and immature. These trends are consistent over time (Hentges et al., 2007; Messineo, 2008; Yoder et al., 2008).

Children's Commercials. Of all forms of television advertising, commercials for children are the most gender stereotyped. Because a child typically views about 20,000 commercials annually, the potential impact on gender attitudes is enormous. Commercials depicting children are strictly gender segregated. Girls are shown in more passive activities and dependent on another person or a doll for entertainment. They learn how to help their mothers, assist in household tasks, serve men and boys—especially where food is concerned—and see how to become beautiful or stay cute. The ads focus on passive and quiet play and use dreamy content, soft music, and fades or dissolves for sequencing. Commercials do not teach independence or autonomy for young girls. The opposite characteristics are depicted in commercials for boys and focus on aggression, action, control, completion, and independence, most in scenes outside the home (Kunkel, 2001; Larson, 2003; Palmer and Young, 2003).

Changing these patterns is not encouraging. Females still need males to tell them what to do or buy, even for products like window cleaner, deodorant, or hair color. Gender stereotypes in children's commercials have actually increased. Only a tiny portion of alternative gender possibilities are imaged in children's advertisements. Advertisements continue to picture children in settings that are unrealistic and in roles that are nonoverlapping and oppositional: boys will be boys and girls will be girls. Overall, television advertisers speak in male voices to female consumers.

MEN'S IMAGES IN MEDIA

Given their varied roles in the real world, women have not fared well in media. Men star in more television series, sell more records, make more movies, and are paid more than female media counterparts. But men, too, pay a price for that power and popularity. From the media's standpoint, a man is a breadwinner who cheats on his wife, has no idea how to wash clothes or vacuum a rug, is manipulated by his children, and uses force to solve problems. How do media contribute to these images?

Advertising

Advertisers divide products according to their emotional appeal; hence, some are seen as masculine and some as feminine. Cars, life insurance, and beer are masculine, so men do the selling to other men. Men also sell women's products, such as cosmetics and pantyhose. In fact, men do most of the selling on television, as evidenced by the use of male voice-overs in both daytime and prime-time television. Male voice-overs have decreased slightly over time but in over three-fourths of all commercials the voice of men is heard (Bartsch et al., 2000). Advertising puts men in positions where they direct what all people buy. A man's voice is the voice of authority.

Commercials shown on television, usually during sports events, are almost exclusively male oriented. Often laced with violent images that endorse the sexual objectification of women, men respond positively to these ads, but women do not (McDaniel et al., 2007; Hust and Ming, 2008). Advertisers intensify their marketing of beer to males rather than alter content to make beer ads more palatable to women. Traditional images of masculinity surrounding beer commercials on television and products in print ads directed to males are camping, cowboys, competition, and camaraderie. Men are the good old boys who are adventurous, play hard at sports, exercise vigorously, and have a country spirit. Compared to television, print ads with male models deviate sharply from those of only a decade ago. Men who read male-directed magazines (*Maxim, Men's Health*) are more likely to value thinness in women and muscularity for men (Hatoum and Belle, 2004). *Playgirl* centerfolds depict idealized versions of muscular men supposedly desired by women (Leit et al., 2001). Capitalizing on men's concerns about being underweight or undermuscular, advertisers aggressively market dietary supplements, sports equipment, and weight-lifting CDs to men and boys. Eating disorders in men are correlated with the increasing objectification of men's bodies (Chapter 2). Underweight males on television series' and in film are often portrayed as insecure, shy, and unappealing as friends. Overweight male, however, are still potrayed in a range of positive roles.

For other products and for both print ads and television commercials, women are increasingly shown in activities outside the home and men increasingly shown in family roles. Men inhabit nondomestic worlds of workplace, gym, and sports bar, and are portrayed as mature, wise, successful, competitive, and powerful. The competent man image shifts greatly when men are shown doing housework and child care. In their homes they are depicted as more foolish than women, bumbling in the kitchen and inept with infants and children. The audience is meant to laugh at men who create havoc when doing chores typically performed by women. His ineptness, lack of success, and less time devoted to the task at hand characterizes him as "hardly working" rather than "working hard" (Scharrer et al., 2006). Men may be doing more in-home work in today's commercials, but stereotypes about his incompetence in a woman's sphere persist.

Film

Fueled by advertisers, films contribute to the images of men as invulnerable, decisive, and increasingly as sex objects. Films routinely portray men in two thematic ways. The first is the hero theme. Heroes are the hard living and adventurous tough guys and superheroes engaged in action–adventure plots. Pure fantasy exists in movies where the hero escapes unscathed from the jaws of death. The twist for some movies is that the hero starts out insisting he is not brave, really cowardly at heart. Circumstances prove otherwise as he rescues the maiden, finds the gold, or saves the world from destruction. John Wayne, Gary Cooper, and Clint Eastwood of the past have been replaced by Antonio Banderas, Will Smith, Brad Pitt, and Matt Damon. Unlike women appearing as leads in either romantic or adventure films, these men will maintain their hero qualities well into later life.

Often men are linked in "buddy" movies. The plot makes them initially suspicious and competitive on the surface and then they gradually move toward genuine—if begrudging—respect and camaraderie. Heroes move in and out of relationships with women. Romance is short-lived, not enough to keep the men from their carefree but dangerous escapades. They learn to admire one another for traits they see lacking in themselves. *Die Hard, Lethal Weapon, 48 Hours,* and *Men in Black* are examples of heroic buddy movies.

The sex object subtext of the hero theme suggests that action motion picutures of the last several decades are increasingly portraying men as leaner and meaner. The gaunt heroes of the past (Clark Gable, James Stuart) are replaced by aggressive, muscular men who achieve positive outcomes, including romance, by the end of the movie (Morrison and Halton, 2009). Like TV, film allows men to be older and larger and still be admired by men and desirable to women. Weight gains by Russell Crowe, John Travolta, and Denzel Washington do not disqualify them as heroes or as romantic leads in adventure movies (Cieply, 2009). The next generation of aging male actors may not be as fortunate, however, if men's bodies continue to be objectified.

Second is the violence theme. Both heroes and villains are violent, and violence is needed to end violence. The kill-and-maim plots of the *Friday the Thirteenth, Halloween,* and *Prom Night* movies, the *Star Wars* and *Lord the Rings* epics, and a multitude of graphically violent movies where drug lords and organized crime are toppled, attest to revenge, killing, and violence in the name of justice and honor. Male characters who refuse to abide by this formula to resolve the problem are portrayed as unintelligent, egotistical, and cowardly.

Violence is normative in all genres of movies, increasing most rapidly for films aimed at younger audiences. The escalation of violence and the graphic display of sexual violence in action–adventure films are associated with the financial success of movies released to international audiences. In the global economy, high-profit films need minimal editing for non-English speakers or for audiences who cannot read subtitles. The next time you watch a film, note the length of time of a scene that has no dialogue. Chances are it is an action–adventure sequence consisting of heroic males in chase scenes, explosions, and nonstop escapades related to violence and destruction.

Television

Television reinforces other images of media masculinity. In prime-time dramas men are portrayed as active, independent, less tied to relationships, and in control. Men acknowledge that power is a double-edged sword, and it may bring adversity as well as rewards, but they are willing to accept the consequences. Shows such as *Law and Order, House, and CSI* suggest this pattern. Less favorable portrayals of men are connected to their use of violence and force to deal with ongoing relationships. Whether as heroes or villains, television equates male strength with lack of emotion (other than anger), self-reliance, and ability to fight out of a difficult spot.

Situation Comedies: Men in Families. The key exception to the image of masculine independence is the situation comedy, where men in their homes take on a childlike dependence on their wives*(The Simpsons, Home Improvement; Family Guy).* It is also rare to find men in loving and nurturing relationships with their television children without a woman hovering in the background. A half century of television refuses to allow men to be shown as competent fathers who are capable of raising young children on their own. In the *Andy Griffith Show,* there was Aunt Bee; in the *Courtship of Eddie's Father,* there was Mrs. Livingston; and in *Family Affair,* there was Mr. French. Past shows like *Full House* and recent shows like *Two and a Half Men* portray single dads in amazingly nontraditional living arrangements where there are other adults always present Unlike series' featuring women as single parents, almost ludicrous circumstances must be invented to accommodate single fathers.

An interesting twist on fathers with children is the "mockumentary" series, *Modern Family,* featuring a clan of families including a gay couple raising a baby daughter. Two gay fathers rather than one father—gay or not—are surrounded by an army of female friends and kin who aid them in child rearing. Of all shows featuring males as single parents or as guardians of children, there are only two exceptions. From the early days of television, the *Rifleman* portrayed a father raising his son alone. In *Hannah Montana* a single father is raising a teenage son and daughter alone. In examining 60 years of television, it is virtually impossible to find a father raising an infant or very young child alone The media allow men to display a greater range of roles than women, but stereotypes lurk in most men's imagery as well.

TV's Gender, Race, and Class Link

Like *Mr. Rogers' Neighborhood*, until the mid-1960s, prime-time television was mainly inhabited by white middle-class professional and managerial men of generic northern European background. They were married to women of similar backgrounds who were depicted as full-time homemakers. When male people of color were seen, they usually fell into three categories: African-American chauffeurs and bodyguards, Asian cooks and gardeners, and Latino desperadoes and drug lords. However, the next two decades saw a marked shift for people of color in both numbers as well as types of roles, a pattern that continues today. After African-American and Asian men, however, portrayals by Latino men remain a distant third. Latino men are largely supporting players and background figures and are much more likely to be portrayed as poor, deviant, or criminal compared to all other racial and ethnic groups (Greenberg and Worrell, 2007).

A gradual but steady blurring of racial differences among men is occurring on prime-time television. However, as racial differences steadily decrease, a corresponding increase in class differences is occurring. Gone are the struggling working-class African-American families of 1970s television. The laborers, servants, and junk collectors of the Evans family (*Good Times*) and *Sanford and Son* were replaced by the 1980s with business owners, attorneys, and other professionals (*The Jeffersons, The Cosby Show*). Now into the millennium, leading roles for African-American secret agents, doctors, lawyers, and police officers are common (*NYPD Blue, Scrubs, Criminal Minds*). For the white working class, a similar pattern occurred, especially for women. The struggling waitresses of *Alice* and assembly-line workers of *Laverne and Shirley* have been supplanted by the professionals of *Friends* and *Sex in the City*.

As men from all races moved up in social class, they left their working-class counterparts behind. Television is a virtual haven for the middle class, with middle-class men dominating television in number of series, number of roles, and number of starring roles (*Monk, 30 Rock, White Collar. The Mentalist*). Most middle-class men on prime-time television are college educated, lead interesting and productive lives, and have disposable income to travel and buy expensive artifacts for their tastefully decorated homes. Advertisers desiring to show a full range of products used by glamorous people are often catered to. The result is television shows built around affluent middle-class characters. The psychiatrist brothers of *Frasier* represent the middle-class standard of prime-time television for males. Racial stereotypes are still apparent, but class stereotypes are on the fast track in overtaking them. Gender stereotypes, however, remain intact.

Working-Class Men. In the real world, people in the working class are those who lift, bend, drive, keyboard, clean, load, unload, provide physical care for others, cook, and serve (Ehrenreich, 1998). They are high school graduates working for a wage rather than a salary and employed in blue-collar positions, retail sales, and lower level white-collar clerical jobs. Although they represent over two-thirds of employed Americans and include well paid workers in the skilled trades, (Chapter 10), the working class of prime-time television is largely unseen. In over a half century of situation comedies, working-class households with blue-collar families are the most underrepresented. The large majority of sitcom families are in the middle class and above, with the working class relegated to a vague, marginalized category of "other" (Leistyna and Alper, 2005). During the Millennium Recession TV plot lines accounted for the harder times faced by American families. However, rather than making hardship too obvious by spotlighting the plight of the working class, the focus was on the middle class—especially upper-middle-class men —who successfully reinvent themselves after their economic slide into a more "average" lifestyle (*Bored to Death, Brothers*) (Angelo, 2009). "Average" does not translate into "working class." New shows featuring working-class families confronting an even greater economic slide are invisible on TV.

Prime-time television's construction of men from this small group of working-class families is a vastly different reality than that of television's middle class. Blue-collar men are depicted as needing supervision, and it is up to middle-class professionals to provide it. Working-class characters have few starring roles and are usually depicted as friends or relatives of the main characters in situation comedies (*Everybody Loves Raymond*) or as unsavory characters lurking in the background of police precincts, courtrooms, schools, and hospital waiting rooms in prime-time drama (*NCIS, Grey's Anatomy, Fringe*).

Unlike racial portraits of men, comparable working-class portraits have remained virtually the same throughout television's history. Ralph Cramden, Fred Flintstone, and Archie Bunker have been replaced by Homer Simpson. The few shows that portray working-class or even lower-middle-class men in lead roles have prototype characters: They are now men of all races depicted as lovable but incompetent with parochial, poor, or questionable taste in all things. They hide behind a thin veil of exaggerated masculinity that is easily unwoven by their ever-suffering wives (*Tyler Perry's House of Payne, Roc, King of Queens*). Male household heads of television families in situation comedies over 50 years are not only portrayed more foolishly than in shows featuring middle- to upper-class families, but the pattern has increased over time. Reality TV featuring working-class families who swap wives, have extreme makeovers on their bodies and their clothing, and redecorate tasteless homes into tasteful ones offers a venue for the middle class to exoticize their less fortunate brothers and sisters (Scharrer, 2001a; Lyle, 2008).

The significant holdouts to this pattern were *Roseanne*, which for a decade was one of the most popular shows on television, and the five-year run of *Grace Under Fire*. Both shows deviated from the working-class norm by showing family members in diverse roles dealing sensitively with a range of difficult issues all families face. Comedy was not sacrificed in these portrayals.

Changing Images. Cable reality television may be doing a better job portraying working class positively. High-rated shows follow men in their dangerous work as loggers in Oregon, long-haul drivers, and fishers, all who battle the elements to carry out their work (Poniewozik, 2008). Others are the paramedics, firefighters, and police offers who routinely lead risky lives in the service of others. Framing working-class men as capable because of the risks they take and the physical strength needed for their jobs is a double-edged sword. Working-class men are defined by images of masculinity drawing on physical capability that few can attain. Since these are "reality" shows, stereotypes equating masculinity with physical strength and action are more difficult to dislodge (Chapter 9).

Like media-created women, men cannot be all that they are meant to be, or all that they are. Men increasingly disdain their sex object and success object media portrayals. They want to be identified more for their lives as fathers and husbands and less as sexual exploiters of women and ruthless competitors of men. Tom Hanks and Robin Williams demonstrate this; Howard Stern and Donald Trump do not. Until we see men consistently portrayed as loving fathers, compassionate husbands, and household experts, attitudes about masculinity will not be significantly altered.

GENDER AND MASS MEDIA INDUSTRIES

The lack of women in creative and decision-making positions in media industries helps explain the pervasive gender typing throughout the mass media (Table 13.1). Except as secretarial staff, for example, women are numerically underrepresented in all phases of advertising. Because advertising is the medium with the power to quickly alter the pervasive and consistent stereotyping it now supports, an influx of women into managerial positions may provide the industry with more realistic images of women.

Television

The same can be said for television. In 1980 about 30 percent of the employees at network headquarters and network-owned stations were women, but only 10 percent were at the managerial level. Ten years later almost 20 percent of directors of commercial television in news and entertainment shows stations were women. Women make up over one-third of news professionals but few are news directors (Media Report to Women, 2008a; Gibbons, 2009). Although women account for almost half of TV characters, as actors in commercials, soap operas, and prime-time television, their representation in leadership roles in production, management, and news is much more limited.

The major qualifications for entry into these positions are advanced, specialized education and experience. Although women have very similar educational profiles, their experience is less favorable when compared to male counterparts. Most women managers in television entered the industry within the last decade. As they move up the hierarchy, they will in turn create opportunities for those women who follow. Until then, like in most jobs, gendered occupational segregation in the television industry is the norm.

Table 13.1 Percentages of Males and Females in Selected Media Forms

Media Form	% Males	% Females
Sports Editors	90	10
TV Characters Age 40 and over	89	11
Cable News Hosts	83	17
Saturday Morning TV Programs	73	27
Movie Reviewers	70	30
Music Videos	63	37
Commercials During Children's Programs	63	37
Prime-Time Network TV Programs	62	38
Prime-Time TV characters	57	43

Source: Adapted from Comstock and Scharrer, 2007:87; *Media Report to Women*, 2008a; Gibbons, 2009.

Broadcast Journalism

Compared to overall television programming, women appear to be making the greatest strides in TV news and commentary, at least gaining more on-screen visibility. Katie Kouric, Rachel Maddow, Barbara Walters, and Diane Sawyer demonstrate the professionalism and integrity of women broadcasters. Using her popular daytime talk show as a springboard, Oprah Winfrey is moving into broadcast journalism with prime-time specials on topics such as drugs, domestic violence, and child abuse. Until recently the few women seen during news programs were billed as "weather girls" and held third-rate positions on the news teams. Today female meteorologists are responsible for preparing and broadcasting the weather. Metropolitan areas have male–female news teams that vie with one another for ratings. Inroads have been made by women in the news and weather departments, but it is likely that the sports anchor is a man.

Does increased visibility in news and information programs mean that gender barriers are eroding? The answer is both yes and no, and a look at morning television news helps explain why. The three major networks produce a morning show described as combining news with entertainment. Currently, each of these shows is hosted by a male and female team. Commercial ratings indicate that this format is now necessary for success. No longer can a man or completely male news team expect to carry the show. Yet the networks insist that audiences favor the male over the female, which justifies more money, more air time, and better stories being given to the male.

On the other hand, women are increasing their numbers rapidly as foreign/war correspondents. In 1970 only 6 percent of women were foreign correspondents; today over one-third fill this slot. They have more control over what they report and how they report war news. They tend to focus more on the human toll of war related to civilian populations and highlight the issues faced by women and children in war-torn areas (Gibbons, 2002). In high visibility positions reporting from war zones, they are in harm's way. Public acceptance of these women and their reporting is at an all-time high.

Compared to other areas of broadcast news, the large number of foreign correspondents is startling. The scarcity of women in the other news media is associated with the way feminism is portrayed in television news coverage. Although there is overwhelming support for feminist goals, the news media consistently represent feminism as an unpopular fringe movement and exclude serious feminist comment from the airwaves (Zimmerman, 2003; Gill, 2007).

Film

The golden days of film coincided with the Depression. Ironically, this period was the golden age for women actors but the dark age for women directors. The position of director is the apex of the film industry. In the silent screen and pre–World War I eras, there were over 30 female directors, more than at any other time in film history. The rise of the studio system and its vertical monopoly model consolidated the production, distribution, and exhibition of films in individual companies and forced many independent filmmakers out of work.

Directors. In this early era where film norms were still emerging, Dorothy Arzner was the only woman directing for a studio (1927–1943). During the next two decades Ida Lupino was the only woman directing major feature films, and she established herself even before World War II. Actors including Penny Marshall, Kathy Bates, Sally Field, Jodie Foster, and Barbra Streisand emerged as acclaimed directors by the millennium. For all films released, women comprise about 25 percent of the combined total of directors, executive producers, writers, and cinematographers. Men direct nine out of ten films in the United States. Women's share of these positions is increasing, but they still hold only a handful of prized director slots. The number of female directors can be correlated with the number of parts for female actors. There are three speaking males for every one speaking female, a consistent trend for 40 years. In the past 30 years there has been "no improvement in gender balance" for Academy Award nominated films in the best picture category (Lauzen, 2003; Media Report to Women, 2008b).

Whereas the position of director remains a male bastion, the number of women producers, editors, and screenwriters is rapidly increasing. Although less likely in major studios that produce box-office blockbusters, they are entering areas offering creative work in newer cinematic forms. Art, documentary, educational, experimental, and emerging "alternative" cinema are especially hospitable to women eager to demonstrate their talents. Women film critics do hold influential positions in the industry, so efforts outside mainstream filmmaking are not ignored. Feminist film theory is emerging from these efforts. Prominent female critics review films from perspectives male critics usually dismiss, such as how women are portrayed, the quality of the roles women are being offered, and the degree to which films reflect social reality.

These achievements are impressive, but they account mostly for films outside the mainstream and in lesser known studios. These are not the studios producing movies people will line up outside on a cold Saturday night to see. Money and fame are reserved for commercially successful films. Although alternative cinema may provide creative, though not lucrative, outlets for women filmmakers, a male monopoly in the established film industry makes the switch from one system to the other difficult.

MEDIA AND SOCIAL CHANGE

Media present views of women and men far removed from the reality of our everyday lives. Men are portrayed as more multidimensional and more positive than women, but still in highly stereotypical ways. Based on tactics for over three decades, the advertising industry's willingness to reduce gender stereotyping is not very encouraging (Craig, 2003). Advertisers argue that their images reflect society, and these are images the public wants to see. They acknowledge that advertising images may reinforce an already existing sexist society, but they did not create it. From their viewpoint, altering advertising patterns simply to counter sexism risks both public acceptance and profit. Moral responsibility for gendered media messages is rarely an issue.

Changing for Profit and Social Progress

Media are powerful because of our thirst for entertainment, our demand for continually updated news and information and our needs to be moved from the mundane to a world of fantasy and excitement. Is it possible for media to provide the entertainment and information, maintain public acceptance, increase profits, and simultaneously provide alternatives to the sexist portrayals of men and women? Because people are uncomfortable with what they see, and research indicates that gender role shifts are associated with financial profits, the answer to this question is affirmative. An irony of media and advertising is that they thrive on change, yet are barely beginning to shift away from rigid patterns regarding gender. When convinced that success can be profitable when packaged differently, media change will likely accelerate.

Finally there is the issue of moral responsibility. The issue is usually addressed when sexual and violent content of the media consumed by children and teens is examined. Little attention is paid to gender role portrayals such as the blatant misogyny of the 2008 presidential election or the ongoing, taken-for-granted hidden misogyny that casts women in a different light because of gender (Chapter 14). Consider the following comments about Dr. Margaret Chan, the director of the World Health Organization and the most powerful international public health official in history.

> All of this authority is packed into a diminutive woman with large glasses who does not drive, type or cook, is fond of sharp suits and silver pins, and may be among the most qualified people in the world to lead the global response to the threat of a pandemic flu. (Harris and Altman, 2009)

The media cannot be absolved of moral responsibility for any of these portrayals. By addressing the sexual content of violent media, however, a latent function regarding gender stereotyping may also occur. Because all gender role portrayals are intertwined, attention to sexually violent media forms can carry over into consciousness-raising about the damaging effects of misogyny in other media.

Women as Media Executives

Women hold a minimum of influential positions within mass media industries. As women gain positions of power and prestige, gender-stereotyped images will be altered. But the media are entrenched in a broader social system that supports the notion of female subordination. When advertisers are singled out for blatant sexist portrayals, for example, they defend themselves by saying they are trend followers, not trend setters. They ignore the mountains of research indicating that heavy diets of gender stereotypes in all media forms are associated with higher levels of intolerance and prejudice, lower acceptance of gender and racial equality, and lower self-esteem for both females and males. In dealing with diversity and equity, mass media industries subordinate gender issues to racial and ethnic issues. With the acclaim and public acceptance of movies like *Brokeback Mountain* (2006), issues of sexual orientation are also gaining more positive attention from leaders in all media forums (Boucher and Pinto, 2007). Subordination in any area harms efforts of equity in the others. For the voices of women in media industries to be heard, they need to be in significant decision-making roles (Wilson et al., 2003; Widestedt, 2008).

The media are formidable socializers and provide images that both reflect and reinforce gender stereotypes. Whether they acknowledge it or not, media do have the power and responsibility to alter stereotypes. Evidence indicates they are slowly moving in this direction. As the public continues to demand entertainment, news, and advertising that offer positive images of their gendered lives in line with social reality, the media will respond accordingly.

Summary

1. Mass media, particularly television, is a major agent of gender socialization. Heavy television viewing is strongly linked to traditional and stereotyped views about gender.

2. Decades of research on magazines show women linked to home and family and interested in beauty and relationships with men. Highly stereotyped advertising showing beautiful women available to men reinforces these images. Symbolic interaction emphasizes sexual subliminals in ads. Age and gender stereotypes in ads play on the insecurities of women as they age. Both men and women are critical of advertising images, but only minimal changes have occurred.

3. In the early days of film women held more powerful and diverse positions. Films during World War II depicted independent, multifaceted women, but after the war women were dichotomized as good (feminine mystique) or bad (sexual and immoral). Sexual violence in films continues to increase. Mainstream films now routinely pair sex and violence. Females are offered fewer diverse roles and, as they age, fewer roles than males.

4. The film industry claims that stereotypes of gender are what moviegoers want. But female teens and young women represent the newest market, and demeaning this group in film counters this claim.

5. Popular music is highly gender stereotyped, with rock music and its heavy metal segment the most misogynistic. There have been many successful female groups and rock bands led by females, but they have had little power in altering sexist material. Janis Joplin of the past and Madonna may be feminist role models.

6. Rock videos of heavy metal and rap display the most violent lyrics and images related to sexual violence. Men and women receive the messages differently.

7. Gendered violence on television is routine. Amount of television viewing is clearly linked to attitudes and behaviors related to aggression. Television violence is directed toward women.

8. In prime-time television drama, leading male characters outnumber females two to one. Prime-time women are unmarried, professional, and looking for romance. In comedies men and women are about equal in numbers. In soap operas female leads outnumber male leads. Portrayals of independent, single women without a story line revolving around her relationship with a man are absent from television. Employed women in comedies do not experience work–family conflict. Heavy women and girls obsessed with shopping are laughed at by males and popular characters.

9. The majority of television commercials portray women as homemakers and mothers in helping roles with male voice-overs telling them what to do. One in three commercials has an attractiveness message for women. Children's commercials are the most gender stereotyped: Girls are shown inside their homes in passive, quiet, and dependent roles; boys are shown outside their homes as aggressive, active, in control, and independent. Efforts at changing these portrayals are not encouraging.

10. Men in media are portrayed as competent, wise, and successful breadwinners outside the home but inept in their households. Men do most of the selling on television, to women and to other men. Commercials during sports events are exclusively male oriented.

11. Men in film are portrayed in two thematic ways: as heroes and in violent scenarios. In prime-time dramas men are powerful and independent; in comedies about families men are portrayed with a childlike dependence on their wives and as incompetent in raising children without other adults present. Racial differences in portrayals of men are decreasing, but class differences are increasing. Working-class men have fewer lead roles and are portrayed as laughable or bumblers.

12. Women are underrepresented as mangers in all mass media industries. They are gaining in broadcast journalism, especially as foreign correspondents. Women directors have decreased in numbers; men direct nine of ten films. Women producers, editors, and screenwriters are increasing in number but in less mainstream studios. Female decision makers in films are necessary to counter gender-stereotyped portrayals of women.

13. Although advertisers are reluctant to reduce gender stereotyping, they will do so if they become convinced that success can be packaged differently. Media do have the power and responsibility to alter stereotypes and will respond to a public desiring more positive images of their gendered lives.

Critical Thinking Questions

1. Based on your knowledge of media's influence in gender socialization, why do gender stereotypes persist in advertising when both men and women are critical of the images?

2. Analyze two prime-time television series and two movies that represent stereotypical and nonstereotypical content regarding gender content. What gender features contribute to their success? How can the stereotyped content be altered in ways that still maximize the success of the portrayals?

3. Discuss how the double standard for male and female movie directors, actors, and broadcasters serves to limit opportunities for the advancement of women in mass media industries and also limits the profit of these very industries. How can this double standard be altered in a manner that benefits women and still caters to the programming tastes of the audiences served by mass media?

CHAPTER **14**

POWER, POLITICS, AND THE LAW

The oppression of women worldwide is the human rights cause of our time. And their liberation could help solve many of the world's problems, from poverty to child mortality to terrorism.

—(Kristof and WuDunn, 2009:28)

Formed in 1966, the National Organization of Women (NOW) embraced as key goals the achievement of equality for women in America and a "fully equal partnership of the sexes." Networking with NGOs globally, a half century later NOW's efforts continue through the worldwide revolution that recognizes human rights abuse as the "cause of our time." These efforts focus on the legal and political interventions necessary to not only liberate women from oppression but provide them with a true sense of empowerment (Chapter 1).

Laws reflect the values of any society. The political institution and its legal foundation provide the critical lens through which all gender relations are viewed. In the United States the "equal justice for all" principle around which the law functions is embraced. This gap between principle and practice, however, is a large one. Cultural definitions related to gender, race, social class, religion, age, and sexual orientation often determine how justice will be served. Power is a basic element in the social fabric and people possess it in varying degrees according to the social categories they occupy. Max Weber (1864–1920), one of the founders of sociology, defined *power* as the likelihood a person may achieve personal ends despite resistance from others. Because this definition views power as potentially coercive, Weber also considered ways in which power can be achieved through justice. *Authority,* he contended, is power that people determine to be legitimate rather than coercive. When power becomes encoded into law, it is legitimized and translated into the formal structure of society. In Weber's terms, this is known as *rational–legal authority* (Weber, 1946). Women as a group are at a distinct legal disadvantage when both power and authority are considered.

We have already seen how this is economically true. In virtually all job categories women are rewarded less than men in terms of money and prestige. Interpersonal power is also compromised, even in the family, where women may have more weight in terms of decision making. To this list can be added the limited political and legal power that women wield. Social stratification is based on differential power, which in turn underlies all inequality. Inequality between the genders persists because the power base women possess is more circumscribed than that of men. Restrictions in terms of political power and legal authority are at the core of inequality.

THE LAW

Key assumptions about gender that permeate the law and provide the basis for how the law is differentially applied in the United States are as follows.

1. Women are incompetent, childlike, and in need of protection.
2. Men are the protectors and financial caretakers of women.
3. Husband and wife are treated as "one" under the law. The "one" is the husband.
4. Males and females are biologically different, giving them differing capabilities and differing standards on which to judge their actions (Richardson, 1988:104).

These assumptions are taken for granted and rarely questioned. When formally developed into law, they become sacrosanct.

Law serves to perpetuate yet also alter traditional gender roles. At all levels of government, laws are enacted that may offer one or the other gender certain advantages or disadvantages. There is considerable variation on how laws are interpreted and how they are enforced. Even strong, constitutionally based federal legislation is inconsistently applied. What will become clear is that, regardless of beliefs about equality and justice, the law is not gender-neutral, much less gender-equal. Although efforts to remedy this situation are ongoing, we will see the difficulty of the task ahead. Note, too, that most legal statutes use the word *sex* rather than *gender* in written law and in most discussions concerning it. This designation will generally be retained when discussing the gendered impact of politics and the law on females and males.

Employment

One of the most important pieces of legislation to prohibit discrimination in employment based on sex is *Title VII of the 1964 Civil Rights Act* making it unlawful to refuse to hire, discharge, discriminate against an employee with respect to "compensation, terms, conditions, or privileges of employment" because of "race, color, religion, sex, or national origin."

Bona Fide Occupational Qualification. The only way that Title VII can be legally circumvented is through the **bona fide occupational qualification (BFOQ)**, which allows hiring an employee on the basis of one sex, thereby "discriminating" against the other, if it is deemed critical for carrying out the job. For example, a woman can be hired over a man as an actor for a specific part in a movie to establish "authenticity or genuineness" of the role. If characteristics of one sex are necessary for the job, a person of that sex is hired, such as for a job modeling men or women's clothing. The courts have also rejected "customer preference" arguments to hire women over men as flight attendants and "job preference" beliefs that exclude women from working night shifts. With few exceptions, the BFOQ rule is very narrowly interpreted by the courts and is seldom used as a defense for charges of sex discrimination.

Disparate Impact. Another accomplishment of Title VII has been the elimination of policies that may appear to be neutral but can have a "disparate impact" on one or the other gender. When employees have to be within certain height or weight limits, a large proportion of males or females may be excluded. Women, who on the average weigh less than men, have been systematically denied employment opportunities in areas such as law enforcement, security, paramedical fields, mining, and construction by setting such limits. Men, who on the average have larger hands than women, are less likely to be denied factory work where small components must be hand tooled. Employers must now demonstrate that such policy is a business necessity without which the job could not be safely or efficiently carried out. A strength test, for example, can determine if an employee is suitable for jobs where a specified amount of lifting is required. The test would have less disparate impact on women, as well as some men.

Equal Pay Act. Because Title VII mandates the elimination of sex as a basis for hiring, the corollary should be an end to wage discrimination on the same basis. In 1963 the **Equal Pay Act (EPA)**, requiring that females and males receive the same pay for the same job, became federal law. We have seen, however, that even when controlling for educational level and occupational classification, women earn less on the average than men, an earnings gap that has only slightly improved over the last two decades. This disparity in pay continues even with EPA because, as we have seen, women and men typically hold different jobs, and women's jobs are undervalued and underpaid in comparison to those held by men (Chapter 10). Occupations are gender segregated and become gender stratified. The challenge, then, becomes how to assess jobs on the basis of skill level, effort, and responsibility. According to this argument, equal pay should be judged in terms of equal worth.

Comparable Worth. To be interpreted through the provisions of Title VII, *comparable worth* was initiated to deal with the persistent gender gap in pay. In a suit against the state of Washington, a hospital secretary charged that she was being paid much less than men employed by the state, even though her job was "worth" much more. The same case brought evidence showing that laundry workers, who are mostly female, earned $150 less per month than truck drivers, who are mostly male. In 1983, a federal court ordered the state of Washington to raise the wages of 15,500 employees in predominantly female occupations, which amounted to almost $1 billion in back pay. Two years later a higher court overturned the decision with the argument that market forces created the inequity, and the government has no responsibility to correct them.

Critique. Even if objective measurements for comparable worth can be established, the perception that the government should not interfere with supply and demand in a free-market economy is strong. If the wage gap between males and females is a true reflection of market forces, then there must be other reasons for it. The market-driven pay system is perceived to be so neutral that if women get paid less, they must either prefer less demanding jobs or are less productive in the jobs they do get (Chapter 10). This not only justifies the wage gap, but eliminates gender discrimination as another reasonable explanation for it. In this context, comparable worth is seen as a radical departure from traditional economic beliefs. If implemented on a large scale, it would create unnecessary bias in an already fair and neutral system.

On the other hand, comparable worth issues a challenge to reevaluate all the work that women do, and questions the existing gender-based hierarchy that systematically denies comparable earnings to women. Employers typically use gender to assign people to jobs. In the public sector, women are assigned to jobs with less pay and shorter career ladders. In the private sector, women are assigned to already overcrowded female-dominated jobs, which in turn creates an oversupply of labor. Organizations may hire an abundance of women professionals, for example, and justify paying them less. Recruitment strategies thus limit a woman's access to positions of authority.

Comparable worth can be used to redress not only the gender wage gap, but also the damage to overall market productivity. Although it departs from the traditional model, functionalists would applaud comparable worth if the market system becomes more efficient and productive. Comparable worth is used to counter a powerful economic argument that supports an institutional theory of wage discrimination and sex discrimination in employment (Hattiangadi and Habib, 2000). The courts are inconsistent in decisions regarding comparable worth. Title VII and EPA notwithstanding, laws are interpreted according to rigid textbook standards about market economics. Comparable worth will be short-changed if it means "interfering" in economic principles that allow employers to determine salary structures.

Affirmative Action. Also discussed in Chapter 10, another bulwark of federal policy is *affirmative action*, the generic term for an employment policy that takes some kind of voluntary or involuntary initiative (under the compulsion of the law) to increase, maintain, or alter the number or position of people, usually defined by their race or sex. Affirmative action calls for a fairer distribution of social benefits, a constitutionally accepted principle applied throughout U.S. history. Devised primarily to promote the economic status of African-American men, other people of color and ethnic minorities can fall under its scope. In the involuntary situation though the courts, the Civil Rights Act can justify ordering employers found guilty of discrimination to create and implement an affirmative action plan. Public perception and media portrayals notwithstanding, affirmative action policies are *not* the opposite of policies based on merit; neither are they efforts at "reverse" or "inverse" discrimination (Cowan, 2002; Pincus, 2003; Kellough, 2006).

The Gender–Race Link. As a program that is also assumed to benefit women, affirmative action has mixed results. In compliance reviews, African-American males and other minority males have been advanced more than African-American females and significantly more than white females. On the other hand, women's overall economic progress is upgraded by affirmative action. For example, women's employment has increased in male-dominated occupations that are organized by race as well as gender, such as construction and the skilled trades (Price, 2002). Because women of color have clearly benefited directly, affirmative action's gender repercussions benefit all women indirectly.

Prompted by partisan politics, affirmative action is paraded as a wedge issue during elections. Ideology and perception take precedence over data and experiences in shaping public support for affirmative action. Although preferential treatment and affirmative action are not the same, the media have perpetuated this belief. The more the public knows about affirmative action, the more support it receives. Most people believe that affirmative action programs should set objectives, but not rigid quotas (the *Q-word*), to allow opportunities for women and minorities to get hired. It is clear that public opposition increases when affirmative action is associated with quotas and preferential hiring, whether to do with race or gender (Kowalski, 2007).

As would be expected, support for affirmative action also varies considerably by demographic category. Although support remains generally dependent on a person's race and gender, age and educational background are becoming key factors. Whites and men are less supportive than people of color and women. Whites are more influenced in their perception by ideology, and people of color are more influenced by their experiences (Kleugel and Bobo, 2001). Support appears to be declining for younger people overall, regardless of race. Minority college students, like their white counterparts, generally oppose racial preference, especially on college campuses that have higher numbers of African-American but not Asian-American enrollments (Rothman et al., 2003). Gender is less of a predictor of level of support for gender-based affirmative action than is race for comparable race-based programs (Baunach, 2002). Gender is less salient than race in overall perceptions about affirmative action.

The Courts. Given the history of misperception and contentious debate on affirmative action, two decades of Supreme Court rulings offer confusing and inconsistent messages about it. Rulings generally have not made a clear distinction between equal opportunity and discrimination, but tougher standards for federal affirmative action programs have been enacted. In a high profile case, the George W. Bush White House filed a brief with the Supreme Court against the University of Michigan, opposing their affirmative action policy which used a point system based on a number of admission factors, including test scores, grade point average, and race. The admissions policy was previously upheld by lower courts. The Supreme Court later ruled that race cannot be an overriding factor in admissions but can still be a "less prominent" factor. In the language that fueled misperceptions, the Bush administration cited the ruling as a victory for "diversity without using racial quotas." Opponents cited the narrower use of affirmative action as a retreat from progress related to equalizing opportunity for people of color and, by extension, for women.

Women who disagree with affirmative action assert that when women receive special assistance, it reinforces stereotypes about gender roles and stigmatizes those women who gain jobs through it. They are put in a double bind. They may be in a work environment where suspicion abounds because others believe they got the job over better qualified people. When they succeed in the job, the preferential treatment they receive at the outset will tend to devalue their performance. Self-esteem can also be endangered when everyone, including the recipient, believes that being awarded a privilege overrides being given an opportunity to achieve. Sometimes referred to as "twofers," woman of color are more vulnerable to these messages because they fill two minority categories at the same time.

Affirmative action lost political clout over the last decade. Decline in support for affirmative action is linked to resegregation in higher education and loss of gender and ethnic diversity in corporations. Businesses originally opposed to affirmative action, however, find themselves struggling to compete in a global market hit hard by the Millinnium Recession (MR). They are keenly aware of the benefits and profitability of a workforce that not only represents diversity, but values it (Ryan et al., 2002; Wood, 2003b). They may join with supporters of affirmative action to gain back losses of diversity and equality of opportunity. The Obama administration advocates strengthening affirmative action, but without quota restrictions.

Equal Employment Opportunity Commission. The viability of law depends on how earnestly it is enforced. Although the **Equal Employment Opportunity Commission (EEOC)** was created to ensure that Title VII mandates are carried out, enforcement is primarily aimed at protecting minorities, particularly African-American men, rather than women. EEOC often ignores the sex provision because there is fear it would dilute enforcement efforts for racial minorities. Fortunately, the National Organization for Women was formed in part to protect women's rights and directed its initial efforts at changing EEOC guidelines. These efforts were seriously hampered during the Reagan years, when cases of sex discrimination filed by EEOC dropped by over 70 percent. As discussed later, this figure would not have changed significantly during the Bush presidency if Anita Hill had not presented a major challenge at the Clarence Thomas confirmation hearings. EEOC's fortunes continue to be buffeted by political agendas. The Clinton presidency revived and strengthened EEOC, placing importance on civil rights legislation for minorities and women. Accused of deciding that equalizing the field of opportunity for women and people of color is no longer a priority, the subsequent George W. Bush presidency reduced EEOC's prominence (Dervarics, 2003). Returning to constitutional mandates to ensure equal rights, within weeks of taking office, President Obama strengthened the work of EEOC.

Education and Title IX

Title IX of the Educational Amendments Act of 1972 was enacted to prohibit sex discrimination in any school receiving federal assistance (Chapter 11). The key provision of Title IX states that

> No person in the United States, shall, on the basis of sex, be excluded from participation in, be denied the benefits of, or be subjected to discrimination under any educational program or activity receiving federal financial assistance.

This legislation is very comprehensive and has helped alter, and in many instances eliminate, blatant sex discriminatory practices in schools. These include dismantling gender barriers in relation to admissions, promotion, and tenure of faculty. Different standards related to health care, dress codes, counseling, housing, sex segregated programs, financial aid, and organizational membership have also eroded. Policies are devised for equitable treatment that are compatible with the local conditions and the culture of the educational institutions involved.

The Courts. The courts allow for exceptions to the law. Fraternities and sororities may still be gender segregated, as can sex education classes. Housing and living arrangements can also be restricted by gender as long as comparable facilities are available for both men and women. The most notable exception concerns educational institutions exempt from Title IX provisions—those that do not receive federal funds as well as public institutions that have historically always been gender segregated. When considering all schools, those that fall under the Title IX mandate include previously integrated public schools and universities and most vocational, professional, and graduate schools. A number of private, religious, and military schools remain excluded. If by choice or legal mandate any single-gender school does begin to admit the other gender, equal admissions requirements must be followed.

Issues involving equity for women are at the forefront of Title IX enforcement, but in *Mississippi University v. Hogan,* the case related to a violation of men's rights, the U.S. Supreme Court narrowed the scope of gender-based classifications by holding that an all-female state institution that excluded qualified males from its nursing program was in violation of the equal protection clause of the Fourteenth Amendment. Both men and women have benefited from gender equity legislation originally formulated for women.

Athletics. Title IX has had a huge impact on athletic programs. Until Title IX, money allocated to female athletics had been negligible in comparison to money provided for male athletics. Fearing that an equal redistribution of financial resources would hamper men's programs, the National Collegiate Athletic Association (NCAA) strongly opposed any federal intervention under Title IX mandates. In a compromise to the storm of controversy generated by potential interference in untouchable men's sports, the final regulations did not insist on equal spending. Title IX instead called for both sexes to be offered equitable opportunities to participate in college sports. Schools were not required to offer identical athletic teams for males or females or identical numbers of opportunities for athletic participation (NCAA, 2008). Big-ticket men's sports were protected but improvements were made to support women's athletics and opportunities for women to receive athletic scholarships.

Benefits to Females. Before Title IX, few colleges offered female athletes adequate facilities or training, and no institution of higher education offered athletic scholarships to women. Participation in athletics is not benign in its effects. It is associated with better grades, higher graduation rates, and enhanced self-esteem for women (Rishe, 2003). Budgets for female athletics in schools have steadily increased as well, which may account for the dramatic increase from one in thirty, to half of high school girls now participating in interscholastic athletics. Before Title IX 10–15 percent of college women participated in athletics; today half of them participate. Scholarship aid is reaching gender parity. Impressive as these figures are, in 1972 women's athletic programs at 90 percent of all colleges were administered by females, but by 2000 the figure had plummeted to under 20 percent (Acosta and Carpenter, 2002).

Title IX may be responsible for eliminating overt discrimination, but beliefs about the place of men and women in athletics and sport organizations prevail (NCAA, 2009). The power behind Title IX lies in potential funding cuts to schools not in compliance. Many programs that practice some form of gender discrimination, intentional or not, are allowed to continue, even in direct violation of the intent of Title IX. This is particularly true of athletic programs that can exist independent of school budgets because they are supported by revenue from sports events and contributions from parents and alumni.

Partisan politics, inconsistent court rulings, and inaccurate media accounts about quotas have hampered Title IX enforcement. Like affirmative action, if a school is found to be discriminatory, a formal plan must be submitted to rectify the problem. Until recently, most schools ignored this provision. The partisan political pattern is repeated. The situation improved during the Clinton administration, and compliance reviews increased fourfold, with Title IX complaints doubling. A return to the conservative political climate during the Bush administration hampered Title IX enforcement. In the Obama administration Title IX enforcement is again a priority.

Critique. In replaying the affirmative action backlash theme, critics suggest that Title IX hurts women and is discriminatory to men, specifically minority men. Gender equity is seen as robbing racial equity in sports programs such as basketball and football that have high concentrations of minority participation. Like affirmative action, these criticisms suggest that race is more important than gender in athletics. Also, although some schools are adding women's teams, such as soccer and tennis, they are eliminating men's teams, such as gymnastics and swimming. Critics of Title IX use the inflammatory "quota" label, associated with public disapproval, whether in employment, education, or sports. They also assert that in women's sports, hard work and dedication are not rewarded when talent is "shackled" to federal mandate (Gavora, 2003). This latter argument mysteriously suggests that women are hurt and the women's movement loses ground when Title IX is viewed as responsible for female athletic accomplishments.

Title IX is the major federal effort dealing with gender inequity in education. Political maneuvering and charges of reverse sexism, however, damage consensus building. Since Title IX is a formal, legal approach, it must also be assessed in light of the informal biases in education, particularly higher education. If discouraged from pursuing athletics in high school, scholarship opportunities for college athletics are unavailable. There are far fewer women than men in the higher ranks in academic institutions, and even fewer women have decision-making authority in athletics. Women have limited exposure and influence in serving as role models for aspiring female athletes. Legal approaches need to account for sources of bias from informal sources.

Sexual Harassment

Sexual harassment is a form of sex discrimination that is prohibited under Title VII of the 1964 Civil Rights Act (Chapter 11). In 1980 the EEOC adopted the following definition of sexual harassment:

Unwelcome sexual advances, requests for sexual favors, and other verbal or physical conduct of a sexual nature constitute sexual harassment when

1. submission to such conduct is made either explicitly or implicitly a term of condition of an individual's employment;
2. submission to or rejection of such conduct by an individual is used as a basis for employment decisions affecting such individuals; or
3. such conduct has the purpose or effect of unreasonably interfering with an individual's work performance or creating an intimidating, hostile, or offensive working environment.

Although sexual harassment is a pervasive problem existing throughout schools, government, and workplaces, until fairly recently it had been an area with a noteworthy lack of interest, reporting, and enforcement.

The Thomas–Hill Controversy. The event that swiftly and dramatically brought the issue to the attention of the public was the 1991 Senate Judiciary hearings on the confirmation of Clarence Thomas for Supreme Court Justice. The nation was riveted to the television during Professor Anita Hill's testimony that Clarence Thomas had sexually harassed her on numerous occasions. Hill's testimony centered on Thomas's comments regarding sex and sexual matters, her personal appearance, and pressure for dates when she worked as his assistant at the Department of Education and later with the Equal Employment Opportunity Commission. The intensity of this testimony transformed the hearing into a trial where, "regardless of the confirmation, the public decided who was telling the truth." As Hill stated,

> It would have been more comfortable to remain silent . . . I took no initiative to inform anyone. But when I was asked by a representative of this committee to report my experience I felt I had to tell the truth. I could not keep silent. (Cited in Norton and Alexander, 1996:502)

Impact of Sexual Harassment. The Thomas confirmation hearings allowed a firsthand view of the extent of sexual harassment. Research continues to demonstrate that sexual harassment remains pervasive. It is estimated that in workplaces, between 15 and 20 percent of men claim they have been sexually harassed by women but between 60 and 75 percent of women claim they have been sexually harassed by men. It is safe to conclude that three-fourths of all women have experienced it in some form at school or work in their lifetimes (EEOC, 2009).

Sexual harassment is linked to emotional trauma, compromised work productivity, absenteeism from work and school, lower grades, a deterioration in morale, and long-term depression, all of which can seriously impact a person's work and private life. Although its effects are serious, most employees, both men and women alike, do not report sexual harassment, fearing retaliation by employers and coworkers that can amount to career suicide. Recent court rulings strengthened approaches by schools and workplaces to combat sexual harassment, but as a taken-for-granted fact of social life, it is difficult to dislodge (Montemurro, 2003; Bergman and Henning, 2008; Young and Ashbaker, 2008; *School Law News*, 2009).

Despite the fear of backlash, however, the Hill–Thomas confrontation resulted in a massive increase in sexual harassment lawsuits, prompting companies to adopt more rigorous policies to protect employees. The turnabout of the courts has been dramatic. Earlier instances of blatant abuses of power by supervisors were likely to be disregarded, with the belief that attraction by supervisor to employee was natural and unrelated to the job situation. Employer defenses of sexual harassment continue to erode. For example, a woman does not forfeit her right to be free of sexual harassment when she chooses a work setting that traditionally allowed openly antifemale behavior, vulgar and obscene language, and pornographic material on display. The courts challenged the belief that women at school or in the workplace could *expect* to be sexually harassed. In a straightforward and unanimous Supreme Court ruling, Justice Sandra Day O'Connor stated that targets of sexual harassment do not need to show they suffered psychological damage to win their suits. The court upheld the notion that sexual harassment violates workplace equality (Bennett-Alexander and Hartman, 2007). From a feminist perspective, women should be able to enjoy sexual freedom, but sexual harassment is sexism—not sex (Chaucer, 1998).

The Social Construction of Sexual Harassment. Despite court rulings, confusion still exists about what is acceptable or not in behavior that has sexual overtones. Men polled about sexual harassment report sympathy, but are often bewildered by sexual harassment claims made by women. Women are angry and fearful when they are sexually harassed. Men and women talk about and construct sexual harassment differently. Reinforced by institutional sexism, both men and women are socialized into powerful beliefs that define women largely in terms of their sexuality (Clason, 2000; MacKinnon, 2000a,b). We have seen how this kind of sexism plays out at school and work, regardless of legal protection. As symbolic interaction theorists assert, sexual harassment will be dislodged through its social reconstruction from an acceptable social condition to an unacceptable social problem. Feminist and conflict theorists assert that institutional sexism will stall the process of reconstruction until women increase their sense of empowerment in their schools, workplaces, and families. Sexual harassment is so hard to identify and resolve because of accepted definitions of sexuality that disguise and dismiss sexual domination and exploitation of men over women.

There is a final note on the Hill–Thomas case. In 1991 the public and Congress split on whether they believed Anita Hill lied and perjured herself during the hearings. Clarence Thomas' confirmation by the narrowest margin ever for a Supreme Court Justice (52–48) clearly indicated this split (Anderson, 2001). By 1997, over 80 percent of the public believed Anita Hill told the truth. In 2001 new information emerged that allegedly confirms her testimony (Brock, 2001).

Domestic Relations

Perhaps more than any other area, it is in domestic law where gender inequity is most evident. Legal statutes regarding expected wife–husband marital roles are based on three models (McBride-Stetson, 2004).

1. Unity—husband is dominant, and the wife has few rights and responsibilities.
2. Separate but equal—husband is breadwinner and wife is companion and nurturer of children, but they share similar legal rights. Also known as the reciprocity model, this is the functionalist assumption of nonoverlapping, complementary responsibilities.
3. Shared partnership—husband and wife have equal rights and overlapping responsibilities.

Historical circumstances dictate whether one model dominates at any point in time. Because contemporary law is comprised of elements from each theory, with each state having its own pattern, reform in family law is an exceedingly complicated task.

Divorce. Chapter 8 documented the impact of divorce on women and the failure of the law to do much about collecting child support or alimony when it is awarded. The fact that women gain custody of children who are minimally, or not, supported by their fathers propels many divorced women into poverty.

Property division at the dissolution of the marriage also contributes to women's poverty. Although the trend is to have individual attorneys work out the details of the divorce, these details must be considered in light of overriding state laws. In a **community property** state, all property acquired during the marriage is jointly owned by the spouses, so in the event of divorce, each partner is entitled to half of the said property. Community property recognizes the value of the homemaker role. Residing in a community property state, however, is not a panacea. Equal division of property, which originally was intended to help women, can actually hurt them. A woman is forced to sell her home, often the couple's only "real" property, and she and her children find themselves in less than desirable rental property, often in a new location. They are dislocated from home, friends, school, and neighborhood at the very time these are most needed for emotional support.

The other states are referred to as **common law** states, with property belonging to the spouse in whose name it is held. Any property acquired during the marriage belongs to each spouse individually. Unless a house or car is also in the wife's name, the husband can lay claim to it in a divorce. Because the common law system has severely restricted and penalized women economically, most states have also passed equitable distribution laws. Rather than viewing property solely on the basis of whose name it is in, courts now consider a number of factors, including length of the marriage, amount of time parties spend on child care and household tasks, earnings ability, age, health, and resources available from friends and kin. Most important, this accounts for marriage as an economic partnership where both wage earning and unpaid homemaking should be considered as contributions. It at least attempts to redress past abuses where the legal system put women at a major disadvantage in divorce. Nonetheless, regardless of more recent equitable distribution laws, women still get well under half of marital property in divorce. Many divorced women who are also single parents were not covered by such laws when their divorces were finalized, and community property is the exception rather than the rule.

Confusion reigns in divorce law. Punitive and sexually biased legislation results in uncertainty over issues such as sale of the family home, rights to the ex-spouse's future income, and revising child-support orders to reflect changes in income and inflation. Conflicting interpretations in family law, therefore, increase. Gender bias becomes entrenched as a major influence in decisions, contributing to an adversarial relationship to men's and women's positions. Although changes in family form and functioning will add to this confusion, a positive sign is that there is some shift from lethal patriarchy to partnership.

Family Economics. With regard to Social Security, the housewife role is an economic liability. Women are unpaid for this role and do not contribute to disability or retirement funds for ensuring their future. If a woman is married less than ten years before divorce from or the death of her husband, she is not eligible for his benefits. All the years she put into child rearing and domestic duties are ignored (Hartmann, 1999). Social Security policies were originally based on a division of labor and family life that do not exist today. In 1984, the **Retirement Equity Act (REA)** was passed to deal with some of these issues and to make pension benefits fairer to women. Under REA, an employer is required to get the spouse's approval before an employee is permitted to waive any spousal benefits offered through the employer, such as pensions or health insurance. Of key importance is that REA allows for pensions to be included as part of property settlements in divorces.

Statistics are dismal in indicating how poverty has become feminized, particularly for elderly and African-American women (see Chapter 8). Inequity related to Social Security, the main source of income for unmarried women over 65, is responsible for this trend. The "separate but equal" theory of the marital relationship, establishing that husbands and wives have reciprocal but not equal rights, is still strongly evident in domestic law. A husband is required to support his wife and children, and in return a wife must provide services as companion, housewife, and mother. It is left up to the individual couple to determine how these requirements are actualized. In some families the wife controls all household expenses and decides on how one or both salaries are apportioned. In others, husbands provide their wives with allowances and to take care of household or personal needs. She may file for divorce if there is evidence of gross financial neglect, or he may do so for unkempt children, a dirty house, or if she refuses to have intercourse. As discussed earlier, until recently spouses have been excluded from charges of rape because sexual intercourse has traditionally been viewed as "his right and her duty." This exemption had also included separated, divorced, and cohabiting couples. Today, there are more provisions for prosecution if the couple is legally divorced or separated, but because of questions concerning consent, most states allow for spousal exemptions.

Domestic Abuse and the Courts. Given the doctrine of reciprocity and the huge differences in legal definitions of domestic violence, the courts are inconsistent in efforts to prosecute cases of wife abuse (Buzawa, 2007). The most disheartening evidence about continuing gender bias in the courts is in the area of "domestic relations," which is also the most life threatening. We have seen how history reflects the belief that wives are expected to be controlled by their husbands, and that physical force is an often acceptable means of control. Feminists have publicized the issue of wife abuse, and awareness of its incidence and lethality has grown. This awareness has led to police training programs in family violence and the establishment of hotlines to provide emergency help and counseling. Although more judges are ensuring that the rights of abused wives are enforced, a significant number remain unwilling to implement newer legislation protecting battered women.

Gendered Rights and Liabilities. Justification for this unwillingness is also tied to how a judge determines which laws are the more important ones to enforce. Barring a husband from his home through civil protection orders and antistalking laws may be interpreted that his due process rights are more important than his wife's right to be protected from assault. The abusive husband is protected over the wishes of the victim. At the police level, mandatory arrests are now more likely to include dual arrests of both the man and the woman. Judges and police often accept the stereotype that it is the wife's behavior that caused the battering anyway, the classic "blaming the victim" ideology. A wife is penalized by being arrested with her husband, even when the charges of her alleged abuse of him are found to be untrue (Tjaden, 2007; Alvarez and Bachman, 2008).

With powerful constitutional mandates, the criminal justice system in the United States protects the rights of alleged perpetrators; victim rights are not legally guaranteed. Domestic abuse legislation is of enormous benefit to women but it "is about promises made—their implementation is about promises kept" (Beatty, 2003:22).

Reproductive Rights

From the colonial era to the nineteenth century, a woman's right to an abortion could be legally challenged only if there was "quickening"—when she felt the first movements of the fetus. In 1800, not only were there no known statutes concerning abortion, but also drugs to induce abortion were widely advertised in virtually every newspaper. By 1900, every state banned abortion except to save the life of the mother.

Americans are about equally divided in general support for abortion rights. The numbers shift acording to how questions are asked and under what conditions abortions might be performed. A majority of both men and women believe that abortion should be legal and safe, but the percentage for men is higher. Adolescent males have the highest percentage of pro-choice supporters of all age groups of males. These numbers mask the complexity of the issue. For example, whites are more supportive of abortion rights than African Americans or Latinos, but there are no significant differences between the races for females of childbearing age. Abortion rates are at the lowest level since 1974 for all women, including teens. However, even with less support for abortion among Latino and African-American women, the abortion rate for these women is three to five times higher than for whites. African-American women have a 70 percent unintended pregnancy rate compared to 49 percent among all other racial and ethnic groups (Henshaw and Kost, 2008).

Regardless of race, over three-fourths of people approve of abortion when the mother's life is endangered, in cases of incest, or when pregnancy resulted from rape. Severe fetal deformity is also a major reason for women to elect abortion (Greenberg, 2001a; Roberts et al., 2002; Caron, 2008). As we will see, religion is the key variable dividing those who do or do not support abortion rights. Catholics, for example, are historically likely to oppose abortion rights, but a significant minority are pro-choice (Dombrowski and Deltete, 2000; Cochran, 2008). Americans are deeply ambivalent about abortion. A majority believe that some restrictions should be placed on abortion but do not want it outlawed.

Legal History. On January 22, 1973, with two landmark decisions by the Supreme Court—**Roe v. Wade** and *Doe v. Bolton*—the Supreme Court voted seven to two in support of the right to privacy of the women involved in the abortion cases. The states in question, Texas and Georgia, had failed to establish "any compelling interest" that would restrict abortion to the first trimester of pregnancy. Abortion in this instance would be between a woman and her physician. In the second trimester, when an abortion is deemed more dangerous, the state could exert control to protect the health of the mother. Although these cases concluded that women did not have the absolute Constitutional right to abortion on demand, a broadening of the legal right to an abortion was established. The right to an abortion has been challenged ever since.

In 1983 the Supreme Court reaffirmed the 1973 decisions by ruling that second trimester abortions may be performed in places other than hospitals. A city ordinance requiring a physician to inform the woman that "the unborn child is a human life from the moment of conception" was also struck down because Roe v. Wade held that a "state may not adopt one theory of when life begins to justify its regulation of abortion." The ordinance was also unacceptable because it intruded into the physician–patient relationship.

Although this ruling was a victory for reproductive rights, a setback occurred in 1977 with the enactment of the *Hyde Amendment,* which restricts funding for abortions for women who also receive Medicaid (unless the pregnancy is considered life threatening). **Medicaid** is a health insurance program jointly funded through state and federal governments for qualifying people of any age who are unable to pay medical expenses. Low-income women and their children are the large majority of Medicaid recipients. Because Medicaid is publically funded, supporters of the Hyde Amendment argued that the government should not be in the business of funding abortions. In 1980, a federal judge in New York ruled that a denial of Medicaid funds for medically necessary abortions was unconstitutional and violated a woman's right to privacy. Although he ordered the state government to resume funding, two weeks later the Supreme Court overturned this ruling, thereby upholding the constitutionality of the Hyde Amendment.

In 1989, Roe v. Wade was tested in *Webster v. Reproductive Health*. The Supreme Court upheld a Missouri law stating that life begins at conception and requires physicians to conduct viability tests on fetuses of 20 weeks or more before an abortion could be performed. But Roe v. Wade was not overturned. Sandra Day O'Connor, a Reagan appointee and the first woman on the Supreme Court, voted with the majority to retain the constitutionality of legal abortions. Three years later the Supreme Court ruled in *Planned Parenthood v. Casey* that a state cannot place substantial obstacles in the path of a woman's right to choose an abortion prior to fetal viability—the ability of the fetus to survive outside the womb. States can still restrict previability abortions as long as the health of the mother and fetus are promoted. As of this writing, in 32 states and Washington, DC, Medicaid covers abortion (after consultation with health care professionals) only in cases of rape, incest, or life endangerment of the mother. Seventeen states use Medicaid funds to cover most "medically necessary" abortions. Approximately 80 percent of employer sponsored health plans include abortion related services. Health care reform legislation currently will certainly impact all these options, regardless of whether they are public or private.

President Clinton was elected to office on a platform that included a pro-choice plank. On the twentieth anniversary of Roe v. Wade, less than two weeks after his inauguration, he issued an executive order rescinding the so-called gag rule that had prohibited the discussion of abortion as an alternative in clinics receiving public funds. The George W. Bush administration reinstituted the gag rule and reversed many of Clinton's reproductive health and abortion rights initiatives, many previously available to poor women. Taking away a poor woman's right to an abortion carried over to abortions for other women.

The higher rate of unintended pregnancy and abortion for African-American women compared to white women is largely explained by lack of health insurance and lack of access to contraceptives. Half of all states require that if an insurer covers prescription drugs, contraceptives must be part of that coverage. President Obama was elected on a platform that supports abortion rights and universal health care. It is likely that health care reform will include expanded contraceptive coverage in overhauling all public and private plans. Changes in existing abortion rights, however, are much more uncertain. Abortion rights remain at the center of continuing health care reform debate. The federal ban on public funding for abortions stands as a key obstacle for the expanded role of government in health care and may mean even more restrictions on legal abortions for poor women who would otherwise be eligible under current public plans, however limited they already are. Circumventing the ban may also increase costs and reduce coverage for abortion services among private health insurance plans (MacGillis, 2009). The Obama administration is credited with passing historic health care legislation to reduce the ranks of the insured and loosening the insurance industry's stranglehold on determining cost and coverage for health care in the United States. Despite Obama's pro-choice platform, ironically, the compromises necessary to get any health-care reform passed may be the forum that reduces all women's abortion rights.

Until the George W. Bush administration, the political discourse of reproductive health and abortion was not openly framed in religious language. But allied with the New Christian Right (Chapter 12), and despite the separation of the church and state cornerstone of the Constitution, *the* White House routinely blurred the distinction. Like Clinton, Obama was elected on a platform that includes pro-choice. Reproductive rights will not be the issue dividing the public into two opposing camps under pro-life and pro-choice banners, but it will remain on the political burner in the foreseeable future.

Pro-Life. Bolstered by the reaffirmation of divinely ordained sex and gender differences, the New Christian Right has been effective in challenging abortion rights. The association of their moral stance with religion is clear by the term *pro-life*, adopted as a label for their group. Stronger religiosity for the pro-life group is a key element separating them from the general public. In the United States, Canada, and Europe, a higher degree of religious fundamentalism is strongly associated with lower support for reproductive rights (Wolbrecht, 2000; Kuttner, 2001; NORC, 2008).

With religion as the factor that distinguishes pro-life activists from others, it is understandable that their antiabortion work is viewed as "God's work." As one pro-life activist said after her arrest for illegally blocking entrance to a clinic that performed abortions, "I know murder is against God's commandments . . . . These children we 'rescue' are the children of God. It's God's will" (cited in Ruth, 2001:272). Antiabortion activists lobby tirelessly against funding for any national or international agencies offering abortion counseling, even if such counseling is only a small part of a broader program of family planning. Tactics to limit or eliminate abortion rights have ranged from gruesome antiabortion films and television commercials, boycotting facilities where abortions are performed, to death threats, bombing of abortion clinics, attempted murder, and finally to murder. Nine people have been murdered in the name of antiabortion linked to religion, including five physicians, three clinic employees, and a clinic escort. After the murder of physicians in the 1990s, antiabortion activists were quick to point out that these tactics are neither advocated nor supported. At that time a small number of extremists in their ranks condoned the killings, publicly stating that it was justifiable homicide (Poppema, 1999; Samuels, 1999a).

It is apparent that these tactics are garnering more support. Unlike in the past, many antiabortion organizations do not keep as wide a distance between themselves and the extremists. The president of Operation Rescue, the most visible antiabortion organization in the United States, issued a statement following the murder of Dr. George Tiller, a women's health care physician who also performed abortions, condemning the act as a cowardly act of vigilantism. The organization's founder, however, stated that Dr. Tiller was a "mass murderer" and "reaped what he sowed." He is grieved because "he did not have time to properly prepare his soul to face God." Other antiabortion leaders issued statements that included the following: they were cheered by his death; all abortionists are desiring of death; the killing was absolutely justified; and any politician and judge supporting abortion desire the same penalty (Barnes, 2009; CNN, 2009; PBS, 2009; Terkel, 2009).

Despite the condemnation of violent tactics by other national antiabortion organizations, and the call to focus on legal, nonviolent means to thwart abortions in the United States, the extremists at this point may have the upper hand in antiabortion activities. The irony of tactics that have been described as "domestic terrorism" is that they are successful from the extremist view. Not only do abortion providers fear for the lives of themselves and their families, but also the large numbers of antiabortion activists who condemn these tactics do not speak out for similar reasons.

Pro-Choice. On the other side, and just as tireless and now perhaps more determined, are *pro-choice* activists, who cite public and legislative support for abortion rights by a spectrum of people. Women legislators are more likely than male counterparts to oppose overturning Roe v. Wade (Carroll, 2003). Pro-choice advocates note that throughout history women sought abortions—and will continue to seek them—whether they are legal or not. The death rate of illegal abortions far exceeds risk of dying from a legal abortion or dying from complications due to pregnancy and childbirth. Safe abortions are associated with lower maternal mortality globally (UNFPA, 2009). The pro-choice camp affirms men who want to stay with women throughout the procedure and during recovery. These men support the decision of their pregnant partners, but their needs for counseling and assurance in the process are generally ignored by the health industry. Others argue that abortion rights is a referendum on women's rights to control their own bodies (Luker, 1984; Cannold, 2000; Shostak, 2008).

Although the abortion issue is presented to the public as two intractable sides, there is agreement that preventing unwanted pregnancy is a desirable option to abortion. People on both sides of the issue are discussing positive alternatives to abortion, such as sex education, easier access to birth control, and better financial support for parents. Theological debates are also yielding common ground (Cannold, 2000; Chesler, 2001). The RU-486 pill that can terminate a pregnancy within a week of unprotected intercourse has gained widespread acceptance. How these goals are to be achieved relates to the intersection of gender, religion, and politics. Antiabortion activists argue that life begins at conception, so they promote abstinence for the unmarried and limited types of contraception for the married. Feminists suggest that sex education and availability of contraception should be expanded for young people, married or not. By beginning with the idea that abortion is not in anyone's best interests, there may be a glimmer of hope for consensus. It is unclear, however, whether the upsurge of antiabortion violence will destroy this effort.

Crime

Crime is a highly gendered activity and the criminal justice system reflects this fact. Statistics from official sources and self-reports indicate that about 90 percent of all serious crimes—murder, assault, violent personal crime, and robbery—and virtually 100 percent of rapes are committed by males, a pattern in the United States and globally. The 10 percent of crime committed by females is mostly in the nonserious/nonviolent category and includes prostitution, shoplifting, forgery, petty larceny, and for juvenile offenders, truancy and alcohol consumption. The male–female arrest ratio is approximately four male offenders to one female offender (Bureau of Justice Statistics, 2008; NCVS, 2008). Both males and females commit substance abuse related crimes but males are much more likely than females to engage in violence to support a drug habit. Since males comprise the criminal rosters, until recently there has been lack of attention paid to issues of female criminality.

Rising rates of female crime changed this situation. Female crime and arrest rates grew slowly in the 1970s, plateaued in the 1980s, and have again grown slowly since. This growth includes more arrests for violent crimes, especially connected with gang behavior and drug use. In explanation for the gender patterns of crime, criminologists focus on three general areas differentiated by gender: socialization, economic background, and the manner in which the criminal justice system treats offenders.

Socialization. As detailed in Chapter 3, the impact of gendered socialization is profound. In explaining the gender gap in delinquency and crime, social learning and cognitive development theorists focus on early socialization patterns that allow boys to be more autonomous, impulsive, rebellious, and physically aggressive and expect girls to be more "ladylike," nice, protected, monitored, and expressive (Crosnoe et al., 2000; Mason and Windle, 2002). Such traits become part of a gendered core of self-image, which are reinforced by peers and other agents of socialization later in life (Laundra et al., 2002; Jensen, 2003). Socialization patterns preparing girls for lives connected to the home and boys for lives outside the home also provide boys more opportunities for criminal activity.

Economics. Landmark feminist research highlighting the economic disparity between men and women, challenged the socialization model (Adler, 1975; Simon, 1975, 2002b). These researchers asserted that traditionally lower rates of female crime can be traced to attitudes and behaviors associated with women's lower SES. Women may be engaging in criminal activities because they need to bolster their economic security but also because social change allows them more latitude to engage in nondomestic activities. Since increases in female crime are largely due to property crime, the economic explanation is compelling. In the long run, therefore, the lifestyles and criminality of men and women may be comparable. The rising subset of "new" female criminals—younger, more violent and with higher rates of recidivism (the return to incarceration)—reflects these changes.

Criminal Justice. The third explanation focuses on crime in relation to patterns favoring the arrest of males over females. The *chivalry hypothesis* suggests that police are reluctant to arrest women and judges are reluctant to incarcerate women precisely because they are female. By virtue of gender, they are treated less harshly and are less severely punished than males in the criminal justice system. This differential treatment serves to mask levels of female criminality. Empirical support for the chivalry hypothesis and its gender-disparate effects in arrest, incarceration, and punishment is weak (Kempf-Leonard and Sample, 2000; Atwell, 2002; Harper et al., 2002). Research suggests that females are treated more—not less—harshly than males for delinquency and crimes related to deviations from gendered behavior. The most common reason that brings a girl to the attention of the courts is referred to as "precocious sexuality," which is seen as more dangerous and immoral for girls compared to boys. Increases in arrest and incarceration rates for the subset of females engaged in violent crime and gangs are linked to changes in criminal law that impose stiffer penalties and less latitude ("three strikes you're out") for all perpetrators, regardless of gender (Atwell, 2002; Chesney-Lind, 2004). In addition, beliefs about equality under the law are making their way into the criminal justice system for both perpetrator and victim.

Prostitution: A Case Study. As a case study, prostitution provides insights into all three explanations. Prostitution, a subset of *sex work*, is fundamentally a female occupation. Historically, poverty-stricken women turned to prostitution as a means of survival, a pattern that continues today. Some women work occasionally as prostitutes as an aside to their roles as hostesses and adult entertainers. Others derive their total income from prostitution. At the global level children are much more likely to be prostitutes than in the United States. Of the estimated 2 to 3 million children with an average age of 13–14 working as prostitutes, between 200,000 and 300,000 are in the United States. Young girls are recruited, sold, or forced into prostitution by poverty-stricken parents. In parts of the developing world, girls are often abducted from their villages by owners of brothels dotting sprawling urban slums. Another pattern is recruiting migrant women for jobs as nannies, maids, or dancers that serve as covers for sex work. The "legitimate" job does not exist, they owe money to the recruiters who paid their way, and they are left stranded in a foreign country with no means of support. Sex work is presented as the solution (Ehrenreich and Hochschild, 2004; UNICEF, 2008). Although arrest rates of men who engage the services of prostitutes is increasing, female sex workers are more likely to be arrested than their male clients.

Critique. Feminists condemn prostitution when women and girls are exploited as sexual objects for the sexual pleasure of men. There is disagreement about the reasons women become sex workers. Do they offer their services because of financial desperation or as a freely chosen occupation? One faction argues that prostitution exists due to male demand and a need to subordinate women to male sexuality. She is vulnerable to rape, sexual violence, and exposure to HIV infection, especially in war-torn areas with a history of human and civil rights abuses (Beyrer, 2001). If a woman chooses prostitution because of economic needs, then it is not a free choice; child prostitutes have no choice. Sex traffickers and buyers, therefore, should be criminalized and prostitution eliminated. Women need to be retrained for meaningful work offering them a living wage and an enhanced sense of self-worth (Whisnant and Stark, 2005; Agnes, 2008; Elleschild, 2008).

The other faction argues that sex workers are free agents who choose the best job they can of the gendered work available. They question the term *sex work* as being equivalent to prostitution—sex work suggests agency, prostitution does not. The sexism in prostitution is no different than sexism in the rest of society. Although the feminization of poverty may be a factor in a woman's choice to become a prostitute, women should not be further impoverished by denying them income from prostitution. Like other service industries, prostitution and its traffickers and buyers can be regulated, but laws against prostitution oppress sex workers the most. Prostitution, therefore, should be decriminalized (Ditmore, 2006; Oakley, 2007; Della Giusta et al., 2008).

Explanations for criminal activity such as prostitution remain unresolved. Changes in criminal law and in the justice system it is supposed to represent have not kept pace with gender role changes in larger society.

POLITICS

Changing the law to reflect equality and justice regarding gender is linked to two key factors: understanding how gendered perceptions influence voters, and increasing the number of women in office who address women's concerns through social policy. Once the law is changed, interpretation and enforcement must be consistent with gender equality. This also assumes that the women who serve in their political roles view issues related to gender differently than men. Voting behavior, therefore, should mirror such differences. This assumption has been confirmed.

Women legislators have a major impact on the extent to which women's interests are represented in state policy. Compared to their male colleagues, women legislators are more supportive of policies providing access to services for traditionally disadvantaged groups in American society, including women and minorities (Carroll, 2004). However, women represent only a small percentage of political elites who wield power in the United States. In global rankings the United States ranks 58 out of 186 countries for its percentage of women in national legislatures (PBS, 2008). Women are rapidly being elected to public office, but not in the numbers necessary for achieving parity with men.

The Gender Gap

The **gender gap** concept was first used to describe male–female differences in a political context, including votes for candidate and party, and policy preferences. When women gained the right to vote in 1920 it was widely believed that women's political opinions differed considerably from those held by men, and these differences would be evident in voting behavior. For over half a century, this belief remained unfounded; women, like men, tended to vote along class, ethnic, and regional lines. In the 1980s, however, a new political trend emerged. A higher percentage of males voted for Ronald Reagan in 1980 than did females. By 1982 the gap widened, this time accounting for party identification and policy issues: 55 percent of women and 49 percent of men identified themselves as Democrats; 34 percent of women identified themselves as Republican compared to 37 percent of men. Women increasingly opposed Reagan's policies regarding the economy, foreign relations, environmental protection, and gender equity. Women have shifted to the Democratic side at a faster rate than men. The political "gender gap" was born (Figure 14.1).

Presidential Voting Patterns. In 1988, George H.W. Bush received 50 percent of women's votes and 57 percent cast by men. Despite the overwhelming defeat of Democratic contender Michael Dukakis, the Republican Party clearly recognized the need to address a widening gender gap on issues identified with women's

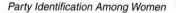

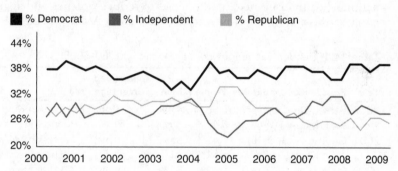

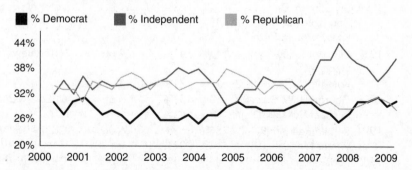

Figure 14.1 Gender Gap in Party Identification, 2000–2009.

Source: Jones, 2009. Adapted from Gallup Poll. May 6 www.gallup.com/poll/118207

stronger support, such as parental leave, child care, educational equity, and women's employment. The military bravado of the Reagan years was substituted for rhetoric focusing on a domestic agenda in a "kinder, gentler" nation. In the 1992 election, the gender gap was formidable. Not only did women cast more votes than men, but 47 percent of women and 41 percent of men voted for Bill Clinton; 36 percent of women and 37 percent of men voted for George Bush. A gender gap persisting since 1980 continued in the 2008 election with women favoring Obama by 7 percentage points over McCain (Table 14.1). Republicans, much more divided on gender-based issues, have been slower to respond to the split. As indicated, too, by the Republican gender deficit in higher public office, the perception that the Republican Party is "antiwoman" needed to be addressed (Parker, 2009). Discussed later, Election 2008 was the unparalleled Republican strategy to do exactly that.

Gendered Issues. The gender gap widens on issues that have a differential impact on women. Until the 1970s, except for women's higher opposition to war and to capital punishment, it would have been difficult to separate the way men and women viewed social and political issues. Any gender gap before 1980 could be summed up with the phrase that "men were more likely to be hawks and women more likely to be doves." This statement holds today, but the gender gap has broadened. A significant gap exists in a number of areas including stronger support by women for women's rights (Equal Rights Amendment and reproductive freedom), human compassion (assistance to the poor, minority and gay rights, child care, and national health insurance), and policies to reduce violence and aggression (stricter gun control, ending the Iraq War) (NORC, 2008; AMGOV, 2009).

Table 14.1 Gender Gap in Presidential Elections, 1980–2008

Year	Presidential Candidates	Women	Men	Gender Gap (Percentage Pts.)	Source
2008	Barack Obama (D)	56%	49%	7 pts.	Edison Media Research
	John McCain (R)	43%	48%		and Mitofsky International
2004	George W. Bush (R)	48%	55%	7 pts.	Edison Media Research
	John Kerry (D)	51%	41%		and Mitofsky International
2000	George W. Bush (R)	43%	53%	10 pts.	Voter News Service
	Al Gore (D)	54%	42%		
	Ralph Nader (Green)	2%	3%		
1996	Bill Clinton (D)	54%	43%	11 pts.	Voter News Service
	Bob Dole (R)	38%	44%		
	Ross Perot (Reform)	7%	10%		
1992	Bill Clinton (D)	45%	41%	4 pts.	Voter News Service
	George Bush (R)	37%	38%		
	Ross Perot (Reform)	17%	21%		
1988	George H. W. Bush (R)	50%	57%	7 pts.	CBS News/*New York Times*
	Michael Dukakis (D)	49%	41%		
1984	Ronald Reagan (R)	56%	62%	6 pts.	CBS News/*New York Times*
	Walter Mondale (D)	44%	37%		
1980	Ronald Reagan (R)	46%	54%	8 pts.	CBS News/*New York Times*
	Jimmy Carter (D)	45%	37%		
	John Anderson (I)	7%	7%		

Source: Adapted from CAWP Fact Sheet. The Gender Gap: Voting Chioces in Presidential Elections. Center for American Women and Politics, 2008. www.cawp.rutgers.edu/fast_facts/voters/gender_gap.php

Whether women vote as a block on any one issue is debatable. Age, SES, race, education, and religiosity may be as important as gender on some issues. There is less support among older women and religiously conservative men and women for reproductive rights and the Equal Rights Amendment; there is more support for both issues among younger men and women. Older African-American women with higher levels of religiosity mirror conservative white women on some issues. Regardless of age and race, women are much more likely to support social programs that can have a direct impact on them, such as funding for day care, and are sympathetic to programs helping the poor and disadvantaged.

Gender and Public Office

As expected, the gender gap in voting patterns of the electorate extends to voting patterns of officeholders. The gender gap may widen or narrow depending on certain factors.

Political Party. Men and women are closing ranks on a number of issues that favor feminist attitudes. Although the gender gap is smallest at the municipal level and largest at the state level, women and men in public office and at all levels differ in attitudes within their own political parties. At the national level, in the George W. Bush administration, Republican women *appointees* were highly conservative, matching the levels of their male colleagues. But Republican women *elected* to state or national offices express more progressive attitudes than comparable Republican men—including on some issues that feminists support. With the notable exception of attitudes toward abortion rights, regardless of party, women tend to be more liberal than men. It can be speculated that conservative women officeholders become more sympathetic to feminist issues as they, too, confront the male stronghold of politics. By their gender alone, they find themselves hindered in political effectiveness.

With more coalition building, the gender gap may begin to close. Both political parties understand that women have the potential for voting as a bloc if the right mix of issues and circumstances are present. Women are not a homogeneous group, but mobilization around issues of gender may occur. Political strategists cannot afford to ignore existing gender differences and will attempt to leverage them to the benefit of their respective parties.

Women in Office. To influence long-term gender equity, elected women must increase their numbers at all levels of government—municipal, state, and federal. There are eight states with women governors; of the 100 largest cities in the United States, 11 have women mayors, including three African Americans and one Latina (CAWP, 2009a). Between 1979 and 2009 the number of women elected to state legislatures dramatically increased from 10 percent to 24.3 percent, with the fastest gains between 1980 and 1991 (CAWP, 2009b). Although the first decade of the millennium marked a downturn in gains, statewide elected positions are also increasing. In 2008 New Hampshire became the first state in history with a female majority in the senate; 13 of the 24 members are women and all but two are Democrats (Snow and Milberger, 2008). At the Congressional level, except for a slight decline in the 1960s, women have steadily increased their numbers (Table 14.2).

The 1992 election was heralded as the "Year of the Woman," with sharp increases in women being elected officials throughout the United States and leading to optimistic predictions about women's continued gains in elected national political slots. Note, too, that women who filled Congressional seats in the past were likely to have completed the unexpired terms of their late husbands. Recently elected senators and representatives are definitely a new breed of Congressional women who have

Table 14.2 Women in U.S. Congress, Selected Years

	Senate	House	Total
1921–23	1	3	4
1941–43	1	9	10
1951–53	1	10	11
1961–63	2	18	20
1971–73	2	13	15
1981–83	2	21	23
1991–93	4	28	32
2001–03	13	59	73
2003–05	14	60	74
2005–07	14	68	82
2007–09	16	72	88
2009–11	17	73	90

Source: Compiled from "Women in Congress: Women Representatives and Senators by Congress." http://womenincongress.house.gov/data/wic-by-congress

carved out stellar professional and political careers in their own right. Because of the seniority system in Congress, however, it will be some time before this small group gains prominence on important committees and exerts the influence necessary to see goals realized. The political glass ceiling for women is slowly cracking (Palmer, 2008). The current cohort of Congressional women are in a position to challenge the old boy network of "politics as usual."

Appointments. The pattern of women's appointments to high administrative positions is inconsistent, indicating both gains and losses. Reagan was criticized for being the first president in a decade who failed to appoint more women to high-level federal posts than his immediate predecessor. Nonetheless, Reagan can be credited as the first president to appoint a woman, Sandra Day O'Connor, as a justice to the Supreme Court. Her appointment came long after the public was willing to accept a female in this position. Although female appointees under Republican presidents were less than under Democratic presidents, women's number of mid- to high-level appointments increased during the last three decades. Women who received political appointments during Republican administration were more likely to represent the New Right, often appointed to positions with little authority.

Compared to the terms by both Bush administrations, Clinton made auspicious moves in countering the tokenism that was the hallmark of presidential top-level appointees for women. He appointed four women to cabinet-level positions, including Attorney General Janet Reno and Secretary of State Madeline Albright, two of the most powerful posts in the nation. Perhaps more significant is that he appointed Ruth Bader Ginsberg, a longtime advocate for women's rights, to the Supreme Court. Jimmy Carter was the first president to stress diversity on the bench, with 34 percent of judicial appointees being women and minority males. Reflecting the belief that the federal judiciary should mirror the life experiences of a wide spectrum of society, Clinton surpassed Carter in such appointments. During the first year of the George W. Bush administration, of all potential appointees requiring Senate confirmation, 25 percent were women, down sharply from 37 percent in the first year of Clinton administration (Tessier, 2002). Bush's most prominent woman appointee was Condoleezza Rice, first as National Security Advisor and later as Secretary of State.

As of this writing, the Obama administration already surpasses that of any president in history for 16 top-level appointments of women, including four cabinet-level positions, the U.N. Ambassador, administrators of the Small Business Administration and Environmental Protection Agency, chairs of the powerful Council of Economic Advisors and Securities and Exchange Commission, and perhaps most important, a justice of the Supreme Court.

Barriers to Female Candidates

Public support for qualified women in public office at all levels has skyrocketed. Elected and appointed female officials are proven competent, decisive, and fair in how they conduct their political roles and in the issues they confront in carrying out these roles. The top-level election of women and their appointments by both Republican and Democratic administrations ensured that women would no longer be relegated to behind-the-scenes positions. As clearly demonstrated in Election 2008, however, women face major hurdles when entering the political arena (Chapter 1).

Women in public service may still be defined as pioneers in terms of their achievement and leadership in areas traditionally assigned to men. They continue to face different obstacles than those encountered by men in politics. Once they attain office, women must do politics differently. According to Madeleine Kunin, the former Democratic Governor of Vermont, gender is a huge issue in how the rules are played and how power is distributed. Women endure the experience of intimidation, being demeaned, and being ignored. She suggests that women officeholders must "invent" themselves continuously and must adjust to a male-defined space (Kunin, 2008). Leadership styles are defined by gender expectations. Women are criticized for being too strident or aggressive and for being too ambivalent or tentative (Bligh and Kohles, 2008). Political effectiveness for women in high political office is linked to successfully maneuvering the language barriers imposed by gender.

Socialization Factors. Socialization into gender roles may impede political participation for women. If politics demands a self-serving style and a high degree of competitiveness to be effective, men have the advantage. Women in public office appear to be more public spirited and oriented to broader principles rather than to narrower issues. Although politicians are expected to have higher moral standards than those who elected them to public office, women are expected to be higher than men in this regard. Although both men and women must run a gauntlet to counter the rumors and smear campaigns now routinely associated with political life, women have a more difficult time overcoming the hurdles. Gender stereotypes may put women at an advantage or disadvantage for public office. Female politicians are often viewed as interlopers in a political realm dominated by men. Others believe that women will be elected to public office because of disillusionment with morally corrupt male politicians (Smith and Fox, 2001). Although in the long run it works more to women's political disadvantage, the stereotype of the trustworthy woman may be used to gain political office. It is ironic that to be successful, strategies in masculine politics are less likely to serve broader public interest.

Beliefs about Women's Roles.   Another barrier to women in politics is beliefs about marriage and motherhood. Women must contend with potential disapproval if the public believes children and husbands are being neglected in the quest for public office. This is consistent with the weighty research that gender equity in the workplace does not translate into gender equity in sharing domestic tasks (Chapter 7). Male candidates begin their political ascent sooner in their careers than women.

Motherhood and Husbands.   Even high profile women often wait until their children are grown to reduce the risk of being labeled "neglectful mothers." In Election 2008, Hillary Clinton was absolved of the motherhood mandate in the media; Sarah Palin was not. By earnestly embarking on political careers later in life, women as a group have a difficult time catching up with men in seeking higher public offices. A woman must also be mindful of the relationship with her husband, who may be unwilling or unprepared to deal with his wife's candidacy. Husbands play vital, supportive roles in promoting their wives' campaigns, but cultural beliefs about masculinity and dominance may prevent men from enthusiastically carrying out such activities. Irrespective of political party, women must face questions about their appearance, marital status, and household responsibilities that are rarely asked of men. Reporters reinforce the notion that women are exceptions: How does she balance kids with Congress (Layton, 2007)? As detailed in Chapter 1, the discourse of the media frames women as different beings than men in politics. Press secretaries attempt to counter such discourse by directing the public to websites portraying the women they represent in a nonstereotypical manner, highlighting their political clout and diversity of interests. These efforts, however, are easily countered by the enormous power media hold in fueling the gendered stereotypes of political women.

After Sarah Palin was chosen by John McCain as his running mate, a headline in a major newspaper read, "McCain, new sidekick, a hit" (Schlinkmann and Munz, 2008). Never would a man picked to run for any office, much less the office of Vice President, be labeled a "sidekick." Another example is from a headline reading, "It was a big night for Bay Area women," when Barbara Boxer and Diane Feinstein won Senate seats. Was it not also a big night for Bay Area men who favored these candidates (Jamieson, 1995:167)? When Bill Clinton was attempting to gain support for his first two female candidates for Attorney General, the defining qualification for these women became the manner in which child care and household help were arranged and paid for. Male nominees for any office were not subjected to such questions. The persistent place of "woman" in polically oriented headlines and news indicates that gender is a category of evaluation for women but not for men.

The generation of women now seeking office have pioneers behind them who helped pave the way. Marginality can be psychologically debilitating, but activist women have honed their psychological skills in confronting their own professional careers, so the jump into the political arena may be less stressful. Socialization into the female gender role may initially be an inhibiting factor for women entering politics, but one that can be adequately dealt with to achieve political success.

Structural Barriers.   Educational barriers have all but disappeared in women's quest for public office. Women in office have the same, or slightly higher, educational credentials as men. Limits, imposed by age, social class, and occupation, however, remain formidable. Age is a factor because, as mentioned earlier, women's political careers start later than men's. Compared to men, women are also less likely to have the economic resources needed to run for public office (Clift and Brazaitis, 2003). Women are often denied even the foot in the door expected of realistic and eligible candidates. Male candidates not only have more money, but are also much more likely to be bankrolled in campaigns by affluent wives. Celebrities in the fields of sports (Senator Bill Bradley, Governor Jesse Ventura) and entertainment (President Ronald Reagan, Governor Arnold Schwarzenegger) have risen to high political offices. Such occupations offer visibility, flexibility, opportunities for developing communication skills, and substantial income, thus serving as training grounds for future politicians. We have seen the financial and social effects of occupational segregation on women. Politically, such segregation hampers women from being recruited as candidates. On the positive side, women have made significant progress in the legal profession, a key source of political eligibility. In the last decade alone the number of women seeking public office who are drawn from these ranks has rapidly increased.

Race and Gender in Election 2008

The remarkable Presidential election in 2008 offers important insights regarding gender roles. Specifically, the election allowed a rare view of how the pivotal gender–race intersection unfolded during the campaign. This view provides clues in predicting the success of candidates for high public office.

Media's already powerful influence in the political process was magnified during the election (Chapter 1). Throughout the campaign, pundits selected by the media talked to one another about representations of the race and gender of the candidates; scholars and specialists who study how media frame content were largely absent from the discourse (Monaghan, 2008). Hillary Clinton's post-primary support of Barack Obama again catapulted her (and Bill Clinton) into the election spotlight. While purporting to be color-blind and gender-blind, available research suggests that media continued to overrepresent gender and race characteristics related to Clinton, Palin, and Obama; McCain's white, Irish ancestry was ignored. For the fundamental race and gender profile, John Mc Cain was the presumed "natural" candidate (Coates, 2008; Major and Coleman, 2008).

In line with a symbolic interactionist explanation, network and print news reinforced normative, cultural representations about race and gender by which the candidates were judged. Attractive and articulate, Obama was on par with—or above—white candidates of the past (Walker, 2008). Even as an insurgent, however, Obama was recast to fit the media mold that allowed beliefs about white, masculine domination of politics to remain unchallenged. In this sense, race was nullified and Obama slipped into the "natural" candidate category (Eargle et al., 2008; Walsh, 2009). In another twist in this remarkable campaign, Obama was (and is) always referred to in the media as African American, rather than "biracial," even if the latter label may have speeded up the recasting to benefit his campaign.

The Primary Election. Demographic variables remain powerful predictors of voting behavior. Despite the ongoing gender gap in politics, in the multiple identities of voters (including age and SES), race generally trumped other categories as the most salient association in the primary battle between Obama and Clinton. Exit polls of voters who are Democrat showed that Clinton was more favorable for white, female, older voters (age 65 plus); Obama was more favorable for African-American women and older African Americans regardless of gender. Most important, he also had more support from both African American and white men, young adults, and people under age 65 who voted in historically high numbers (Stockley, 2008). In the absence of specific information, people vote for those who they see as similar to themselves (Abramson et al., 2007). In this sense, race was highly salient for African Americans but less salient for whites. The complicated pattern has yet to be thoroughly researched, but we can conclude that in the primary election, race could be recast in a manner that advantaged Obama; gender could not be recast and worked to the disadvantage of Clinton.

The General Election. Whereas race was the salient issue in the primary election, gender was the salient issue in the general election. As the only other woman nominated to run for office on a major ticket, Geraldine Ferraro in 1984 paved the way for Sarah Palin in 2008. Sarah Palin's choice as vice-presidential nominee was founded on two strategies: to bolster support from the conservative base of the Republican arty and to gain votes from disaffected women who supported Hillary Clinton. For the first strategy, Palin received mixed support from conservative women. She represented the conservative stand on issues such as support for abstinence-based education, and opposition to abortion rights, gun control, same-sex marriage, and the withdrawal from Iraq. On the other hand, conservative women criticized Palin for stepping outside of the traditional roles expected of women. She was first and foremost a mother, and however admirable public service might be, it could wait until after her children were grown. With traditional gender roles as a backdrop, the McCain–Palin ticket lost votes from the conservative women they reached out to.

The second strategy to gain votes from disaffected women who supported Clinton in the primary was a considerable failure. It is astonishing that the McCain–Palin strategists failed to review the hefty research on gender and politics suggesting that women vote on shared issues rather than on gender per se; they will not vote for any candidate who advocates policies that diminish rather than enhance gender equity and gender justice. Although less articulated among conservatives, this pattern holds for women in both the conservative and the progressive camps (Calmes, 2008; Chozick, 2008; Jack, 2008). Views of the progressive Democratic women who supported Clinton were diametrically opposed to views of conservative Republican men and women represented by the McCain–Palin ticket. Despite media propaganda, very few Clinton supporters retreated to the Republican ticket. Women as a group have more liberal gender role and political attitudes (Simon and Hoyt, 2008). Obama gained votes from moderate Republican women disillusioned with the Palin nomination and her obsolete messages to women, and about women. These women criticized McCain for not choosing from an array of respected conservative, female politicians with more substance and more experience. The choice of Sarah Palin to redress the "antiwoman" bias in the Republican Party failed.

HRC: The Hillary Factor. With Eleanor Roosevelt as the pioneer, Hillary Rodham Clinton (HRC) is considered the first First Lady to break the mold of expected roles of women in this position, and continued to do so as senator from New York and presidential contender. Although presidential wives exert a great deal of behind-the-scenes influence, she assumed an unprecedented leadership role in the Bill Clinton administration. She spoke frequently to young women, challenging them to shun gender role stereotypes, aspire to political heights, and become activists. She advocated for poor women globally and sought legislation to benefit women in their career and family roles. Her confidence and ability won her not only high praise but also severe, relentless criticism about the "proper place" of the First Lady. During the media-feeding frenzy concerning her husband's affair, she was accused of keeping too silent (showing her support for him) and speaking too much (showing her lack of support for him). As honorary head of the U.S. delegation to the United Nations Conference on Women, she received high marks for criticizing China's record on human rights on its own turf in Beijing (Chapter 6).

Clinton's Senate election and viability as a candidate for President indicate much more positive public reaction today than only a generation ago. When Clinton graduated from Wellesley College in 1969, just over half of the public said they would support a well-qualified woman for president; today that number is close to 90 percent (Kohut, 2007). On the other hand, gendered expectations about women and leadership intrude. Progressive attitudes do not fully translate into voting behavior. On advice from aides, Clinton accommodated gender role norms by "softening" her image; at the same time she challenged gender stereotypes, forging new definitions of women in the political sphere. The closer to the nomination goal, the stronger were the attacks—for her gender as much as for her politics. Even as she prepared for the presidential bid, she was criticized for using her position as senator to poise for the campaign. Critics ignored the fact that this is the common, acceptable, and expected pattern to forge ahead in public office—apparently for men but not for women. HRC carved the path for women aspiring to climb the political ladder and, as Secretary of State, continues as a model for the next generation of politically ambitious women.

THE EQUAL RIGHTS AMENDMENT

Although the Equal Rights Amendment (ERA) (see below) to the U.S. Constitution was first introduced in Congress in 1923 and proposed yearly after that, Congress did not pass it until almost half a century later. The House of Representatives passed it with a vote of 354 to 23; the Senate approved it with a vote of 84 to 8. After passage by the Senate on March 22, 1972, the Ninety-Second Congress submitted it to the state legislatures for the three-fourths vote needed for ratification. The original deadline for ratification was 1979, but ERA proponents mustered support to get this extended until 1982. Despite ratification by 38 states, three additional votes were needed before the 1982 deadline. Since then, the ERA has been reintroduced yearly into Congress. History seems to be repeating itself, but ERA proponents remain optimistic. The battle for ratification has enhanced their political sophistication and understanding in dealing with the forces that challenge ratification.

The complexity of issues surrounding the ERA is shrouded by its deceptively simple language. The complete text of the **Equal Rights Amendment** is as follows:

Section 1. Equality of rights under the law shall not be denied or abridged by the United States or by any state on account of sex.
Section 2. The Congress shall have the power to enforce, by appropriate legislation, the provisions of this article.
Section 3. This Amendment shall take effect two years after the date of ratification.

Once ratified, it will become the Twenty-Seventh Amendment to the Constitution. It remains unclear, however, if the text will be modified so that the word "gender" replaces the word "sex" in the final version.

Support for the ERA is wide, and passage is favored by a majority of both men and women. ERA has been supported by Republicans and Democrats and Presidents as diverse as Eisenhower, Kennedy, Johnson, and Nixon. Almost 500 major organizations (with well over 60 million members) representing men and women with different interests and philosophies support it. This broad base of support is evident with organizations that include the National Education Association, the International Union of Electrical Radio and Machine Workers, the American Public Health Association, and the United Presbyterian Church.

Ratification's Rocky Path

During the ten-year ratification process, a number of factors combined to defeat the ERA. It is not simply a matter of saying who is in favor of equality and who is not. Few would argue against the principle of equality, but many are suspicious of how equality is to be implemented. The death of the ERA was related to two other key changes occurring in American political attitudes: increased legislative skepticism concerning the U.S. Supreme Court's authority to review legislation and fear that the Supreme Court would unduly interfere in state efforts to implement it.

The New Christian Right. The perception that ERA would interfere with the state's rights was a rallying cry that fueled the power and organization of the political New Right and its allies in the Christian Coalition. Strong beliefs about women's traditional role and status are at the nucleus of the New Christian Right (NCR) political platform. NCR adherents seek to reverse the tide of gender equity, which they believe has eroded the divinely inspired moral order, and to return the United States to its patriarchal roots (Bendroth, 1999). Similar to fundamentalists worldwide, NCR focuses on the traditional role of women because women's emancipation is seen as a hallmark of modernity and secularization (Armstrong, 2001).

Where the "old" radical right targeted issues of national defense and communism, the ERA became a focus for new attacks. For the first time personal issues related to family, children, sexuality, religion, and women's roles coalesced with a political agenda that resonated with many conservative Americans. Aligned with fundamentalist churches, conservative politicians highlighted the religious and political rhetoric making traditional homemakers sympathetic to the anti-ERA cause. Anxious to retrieve what homemakers believed was a lost status, NCR mounted a massive effort against ratification. Opponents like Phyllis Schlafly fueled "nonissues" (nonsense issues) like unisex bathrooms, absolving men from sex crimes, and an end to alimony. By generating enough fear and innuendo on nonissues, debate on substantive issues, such as the rapid rise in women's poverty, were curtailed. Scare tactics were not only used against ERA ratification but also served to heighten and reinforce conventional suspicion between the genders.

Issues of Interpretation

The ratification process generated much confusion over what ERA would actually change, augment, or accomplish. Whereas anti-ERA groups capitalized on this lack of understanding to help sow the seeds for its defeat, interpretations among supporters were often inconsistent. What would a Constitutional ERA mean for

19 states that already have equal rights guarantees in their constitutions? For example, although both parents are required in Texas to provide child support, the services of a housewife (*sic*) are counted in kind. Texas recognizes the value of a mother's services not just in terms of financial contributions. Pennsylvania has a similar specification under its equal rights amendment, interpreted so that a divorced mother is not required to work outside the home because her value as a homemaker is recognized. When Medicaid money for abortion was curtailed, Massachusetts and Connecticut ordered funding on privacy and equal protection grounds. These examples give some indication of how equal rights have been carried out in states already affirming equal rights. For a federal ERA, groups such as Common Cause, the National Organization for Women, and The Equal Rights Campaign provide some reasonable answers to the unsettling questions regarding ERA. These include the following:

1. Women will not be deprived of alimony, child custody, or child support. Men will be eligible for alimony and child custody under the same conditions as women, as they are already in most states.
2. Individual circumstances and need will determine domestic relations and community property. ERA does not require both spouses to contribute equal financial support to the marriage. The law will recognize a homemaker's contribution to the support of the family, whether the homemaker is a man or a woman.
3. ERA will fit into existing constitutional structures regarding privacy. The sexes will continue to be segregated in public restrooms, sleeping quarters at coeducational colleges, prison dormitories, and military barracks.
4. It will be illegal to enact "protective" labor regulations, such as limiting work hours for one sex or the other.
5. ERA will allow meaningful choices to men and women in terms of family and careers. Those who choose to be homemakers will not be economically deprived for this choice.
6. ERA will not invalidate state laws on abortions that are otherwise constitutional.
7. ERA will nullify state laws that have greater penalties for one sex or the other when committing the same crime.
8. ERA will require that all the benefits of publicly supported education be available to women and men on an equal basis.

The Draft. A critical issue related to the defeat of ERA had to do with military service and the draft at a time when the United States was barely recovering from the psychological wounds of the Vietnam War. Would ERA require women to register for Selective Service at age 18 as men already must do? Congress already has the power to draft women and historically has been prepared to do so, such as the nurse draft during World War II that was halted when the tide turned in the war. It is unlikely that the draft will be resurrected. Currently, with almost two decades of war and no college deferments, serious discussion in Congress about the draft is quickly tabled. ERA would eliminate the barriers to women's full participation in the armed services. Women will no longer be discriminated against in terms of assignment or promotion and would be entitled to the same benefits as men, such as in education and health care, when they leave active duty. Like in Israel, virtually the only country in the world to conscript women, this is unlikely to translate into a gender-neutral armed force (Chapter 6). Gender differences between men and women in the armed forces can be muted, compensated for, and even exploited to enhance military performance, but they cannot be ignored.

Military service remains voluntary for both men and women and today women are over 15 percent of all enlistments. Nonetheless, the issue of the draft will be a key point in the ratification campaign. Until Selective Service registration for men is eliminated, the ERA would likely require the same registration for women. Exempting women from a potential draft also exempts them from equal rights in the Constitution. As one columnist thoughtfully notes, "It is high time our government declare gender discrimination unconstitutional as it has nobly done with race" (Cook, 2009). Sending a clear message that the United States stands for full equality for *all* its citizens, ERA invests in women's progress and the nation's progress.

ERA Campaign Network. A renewed ERA campaign has been launched. The ERA was ratified with 35 of the necessary 38 states. The new campaign is using two strategies to achieve ratification: focusing on three of the remaining 15 states that offer the best chances for ratification and using constitutional justification for nullifying deadlines that require new referendums from states that already ratified the ERA. Representing a spectrum of NGO networks with thousands of organizations and millions of individuals, the campaign capitalizes on political lessons learned in the first campaign. It highlights the wage gap and the issues employed mothers face, with NOW's slogan "every mother is a working mother," an affirmation of the valuable work all women perform, whether as homemakers or employed outside the home. The new campaigners are acutely aware that their political learning curve may be matched by that of the opposition. ERA supporters, however, represent a much wider spectrum of women and men that is unmatched by opponents. The unprecedented number of women and men who supported a pro-women platform in Election 2008 suggests that opposition to ERA continues to decline.

Feminism in the Twenty-First Century

NCR hailed the defeat of the ERA as a defeat for feminism, a morality lesson to women admonishing them about their proper place. Women would be returned to a pedestal free of the trials and tribulations of the world of men. The inability to garner enough support in the last three states pointed out not only NCR's power but also internal problems hampering the feminist movement. The movement of the 1960s and 1970s focused on the root causes of gender inequality, yet in doing so, issues surrounding motherhood and family were given less priority. Many women of color felt overlooked in the quest for economic parity with men and the lack of diversity in the movement's leadership. The movement itself was spawned by women who wanted to escape the shackles of the feminine mystique and gain a new sense of independence. To a great extent, this has been accomplished. The challenge ahead is to integrate this newfound independence with issues related to marriage, motherhood, parenting, and employment. The early movement was most vulnerable on the family issue and the failure to account for the multiple challenges women face because of class, color, ethnicity, disability, age, or sexual orientation. Feminists in the new ERA campaign and in the movement at large are taking new messages to the media and to legislators at all government levels. As we have seen throughout this text, key issues related to employment and family shape women's experiences. These are at the forefront of the feminist agenda in the twenty-first century. The agenda is also one of inclusiveness and embraces the politics of accommodation, which are starkly different from the former politics of separatism.

The movement clearly understands that women do not have to be in full agreement with one another to work for feminist goals. The decentralized structure provides the catalyst for feminists to work on an array of issues. Local feminist groups target issues most relevant for their communities. They lobby businesses for maternity leave or day care for employees; they testify for smoking bans and healthy, safe workplaces where large numbers of young women are employed; they do media campaigns spotlighting domestic violence and the need for safe houses and shelters for abused and homeless women and their children. The movement today is more politically savvy and skilled in media usage, especially in dealing with opponents (Freedman, 2002). The backlash to feminism at the end of the twentieth century attempted to thwart the concerns of women by calling for outdated solutions that separate the home from outside the home that cannot possibly work today. The winds of political change have again shifted toward a more favorable outlook for a feminist agenda. The success of the women's movement suggests that this agenda has widespread support. People no longer question the right of women to achieve their fullest individual potential, whether inside or outside the home. The earlier movement was characterized by mass mobilization and confrontation. The current movement is less visible but more powerful.

Feminism at the millennium is diverse in programs, tactics, and goals. The United Nations Conference on Women in Beijing was a watershed for women. By encouraging open dialogue, inclusiveness, and consensus building, it attested to the ability of women to work toward goals of sisterhood, female empowerment, and partnering with men. With a heightened degree of political sophistication, that very diversity will contribute to the strength of the movement.

Summary

1. Assumptions about gender in the law include the following: women need protection, men are protectors, spouses are treated as "one" under the husband, and biological differences between men and women justify different legal standards.

2. Title VII of the 1964 Civil Rights Act can only be circumvented by claiming a BFOQ. Regardless of the Equal Pay Act, a gender wage gap exists. Comparable worth strategies to deal with the gap are difficult to measure but call attention to lost market productivity. Originally designed to promote status of African-American men, women have been helped by affirmative action. It is inaccurately portrayed in the media as reverse discrimination, but the more the public understands the policy the more they support it. The EEOC enforces Title VII, but its strength under Clinton had been reduced under the Bush administration.

3. Title IX prohibits sex discrimination in schools receiving federal funds. It has been most successful for gender equity in athletic programs, such as offering athletic scholarships for females. Backlash, conservative politics, and inconsistent court rulings hurt its enforcement.

4. Sexual harassment is prohibited under Title VII. Anita Hill's testimony of sexual harassment leveled at Clarence Thomas during his confirmation hearings opened the issue to the public, showing its extent and negative effects. Symbolic interaction highlights how sexual harassment has been reconstructed from acceptable to unacceptable; however, it is still seen as a fact of social life.

5. Marital roles are based on three legal models: unity—husband is dominant; separate but equal based on breadwinning and nurturing roles; shared partnership—spouses have equal rights and responsibilities.

6. In a divorce, state law determines property divisors: in community property states, spouses jointly own property; in common law states, property belongs to spouse in whose name it is held. To deal with inequities other factors such as length of marriage, age, health, and earning abilities are now considered. Social Security rules have hurt homemakers in a divorce. The 1984 Retirement Equity Act was passed to make pensions fairer to women.

7. Many judges do not implement newer legislation designed to protect battered women. Enforcement is hampered because judges maintain a stereotyped traditional image of a husband–wife relationship.

8. Until the nineteenth century, women had a general right to an abortion. In 1973 with Roe v. Wade and Doe v. Dalton women again obtained this right under certain conditions. Level of religiosity separates pro-life and pro-choice groups. Challenges to abortion rights led by the pro-life groups has taken an extreme turn with murders of abortion providers. Pro-choice activists cite maternal health, women's rights to control their bodies, and support from a spectrum of people for abortion rights. Under certain conditions most people believe abortion should be legal and safe.

9. About 90 percent of serious crimes are committed by men, and four males are arrested for every one female. Socialization allowing more aggression for boys and more dependence for girls helps explains the gender gap in crime. Feminist researchers explain the gap according to women's lower SES and need for money. Empirical support for the chivalry hypothesis that police are reluctant to arrest women is weak. Prostitution reflects all these explanations. Debate continues on whether sex work should be legalized.

10. The number of women in office continues to increase, but more rapidly at the state level. Top-level female appointments under Clinton were followed with a sharp decrease under Bush. Obama already has appointed more women in top positions than any President in history. Support to elect qualified women is strong but is impeded by traditional beliefs about women's roles.

11. The gender gap in political attitudes shows more women identifying as Democrats than Republicans. Women have more support for issues related to women and children and less support for capital punishment and military involvement and war than men.

12. Support for the ERA is favored by a majority of men and women. Opposition from the New Christian Right and confusion of its provisions, hampered ratification. A renewed ERA is much more politically astute.

13. Election 2008 provides insights about the intersection of gender and race. Media overrepresented gender and race characteristics related to Clinton, Obama, and Palin. Symbolic interactionists suggest Obama was recast to minimize race; Clinton and Palin were cast according to gender stereotypes. Palin's selection did not increase her choice by women voters, including those who voted for Clinton in the primary election. HRC continues as a role model for women aspiring to high public office.

14. Feminism in the twenty-first century capitalizes on consensus building among diverse groups of women, a greater understanding of the family–employment dilemma, and greater political skill.

Key Terms

bona fide occupational qualification (BFOQ) 392

common law 401

community property 400

Equal Employment Opport-
unity Commission (EEOC)
396

Equal Pay Act (EPA) 393

Equal Rights Amendment 417

gender gap 409

Medicaid 403

Retirement Equity Act (REA)
401

Roe v. Wade 403

Critical Thinking Questions

1. Provide evidence for the gender inequity that persists in the legal and criminal justice systems and evaluate the negative differential gender consequences that result. Suggest specific alternatives to make these systems more just related to gender. Can a system be gender-just if it is not gender equitable?

2. Given the increasing number of women officeholders and the concern politicians are expressing related to a gender gap in politics, how do you think public policy will be altered to account for these realities over the next decade?

3. Based on your understanding of gender in the political process, what strategies can feminists use to maximize success in campaigns related to gender equity in employment and education and in garnering support for reproductive rights and ratification of the ERA?

References

AARP (American Association of Retired Persons). 2003. "Women get more bad news about hormone therapy." *AARP Bulletin* July–August:19.

AAUW (American Association of University Women). 2001. *Hostile Hallways: Bullying, Teasing, and Sexual Harassment in Schools*. Washington, DC: Association of University Women Educational Foundation.

———. 2006. *Drawing the Line: Sexual Harassment on Campus*. Washington, DC: American Association of University Women Educational Foundation.

———. 2008. *Where the Girls Are: The Facts about Gender Equity in Education*. Washington, DC: American Association of University Women Educational Foundation.

Abraham, William Todd, Robert Ervin Cramer, Ana Maria Fernandez, and Eileen Mahler. 2003. "Infidelity, race, and gender: An evolutionary perspective on asymmetries in subjective distress to violations of trust." In Nathaniel J. Pallone (ed.), *Love, Romance, Sexual Interaction: Research Perspectives from Current Psychology*. (pp. 211–44). New Brunswick, NJ: Transaction.

Abramson, P., J. Aldrich, and D. Rhode. 2007. *Change and Continuity in the 2004 and 2006 Elections*. Washington, DC: CQ Press.

Acosta, R.V., and L.J. Carpenter. 2002. *Women in Intercollegiate Sport: A Twenty-Five Year Update: A Longitudinal Study, 1977–2002*. Brooklyn, NY: Brooklyn College, Department of Physical Education.

Adams, Abigail. 1776. "Remember the ladies letters." In Mary Beth Norton and Ruth M. Alexander (eds.), *Major Problems in American Women's History*. Lexington, MA: D. C. Heath.

Adams, Edward. 2000. *Constructing the World: A Study in Paul's Cosmological Language*. Edinburgh, Scotland: T & T Clark.

Adams, Michele A. 2006. "Framing contests in child custody disputes: Parental alienation syndrome, child abuse, and fathers' rights." *Family Law Quarterly* 40(2):315–38.

Adams, Sue K., Jennifer Kuhn, and Jean Rhodes. 2006. "Self-esteem changes in the middle school years: A study of ethnic and gender groups." *Research in Middle Level Education* 29(6):1–9.

Addley, Esther. 2009. "Zahra Rahnavard: Wife who urges protesters on." June 15. www.guardian.co.uk

Addis, Michael E. 2008. "Gender and depression in men." *Clinical Psychology: Science and Practice* 15(3):153–68.

Adler, Freda. 1975. *Sisters in Crime: The Rise of the New Female Criminal*. New York: McGraw-Hill.

Adler, Jerry. 1991. "Drums, sweat and tears." *Newsweek* June 24:48–51.

Adriaanse, Johanna, and Janice J. Crosswhite. 2008. "David or Mia? The influence of gender on adolescent girls' choice of sport role models." *Women's Studies International Forum* 31(5):383–89.

Afifi, Walid A., and Sandra L. Fulkner. 2000. "On being 'just friends': The frequency and impact of sexual activity in cross-sex friendships." *Journal of Personal and Social Relationships* 17(2):205–22.

Agnes, Flavia. 2008. "The bar dancer and the trafficked migrant: Globalisation and subaltern existence." In Gayle Letherby et al. (eds.), *Sex as Crime*. (pp. 99–117). Cullompton, UK: Willan.

Agosto, Denise. E. 2004. "Design vs. content: A study of adolescent girls' behavior." *International Journal of Technology and Design Education* 14:245–60.

Aguinis, Herman, and Christine A. Henle. 2001. "Effects of nonverbal behavior on perceptions of a female employee's power bases." *Journal of Social Psychology* 141(4):537–49.

Ahluwalia. Lisa A., and Madeeha Mir Suzuki. 2009. "Dating, partnerships, and arranged marriages." In Nita Tewari and Alvin N. Alvarez (eds.), *Asian American Psychology: Current Perspectives*. (pp. 273–94). New York: Psychology Press.

Ahmed, Akbar S. 2002. "Muhammad." In John Miller and Aaron Kenedi (eds.), *Inside Islam: The Faith, the People, and the Conflicts of the World's Fastest-Growing Religion*. (pp. 11–26). New York: Marlowe.

Ahmed, Fauzia Erfan. 2007. "Microcredit, segmentation, and poverty alleviation strategy for women: Who are the customers." In V. Kasturi Rangan et al. (eds.), *Business Solutions for the Global Poor: Creating Social and Economic Values*. San Francisco: Jossey-Bass.

Ahmed, Fauzia Erfan. 2008. "Microcredit, men, and masculinity." *NWSA Journal* 20(2):22–55.

Aikau, Hokulani K., Karla A. Erickson, and Jennifer Pierce. 2007. "Introduction: Feminist waves, feminist generations." In H.K. Aikau, K.A. Erickson, and J.L. Pierce (eds.), *Feminist Waves, Feminist Generations: Life Stories from the Academy*. (pp. 1–45). Minneapolis: University of Minnesota.

Aisenbrey, Silke, and Hannah Brückner. 2008. "Occupational segregation and the gender gap in wages." *European Sociological Review* 24(5):633–49.

Aitchison, Cara Carmichael. 2006. *Sport and Gender Identities: Masculinities, Femininities, and Sexualities*. New York: Routledge.

Akhtar, Mohammad (ed.). 2007. *Muslim Family in a Dilemma: Quest for a Western Identity*. Lanham, MD: University Press of America.

Albanesi, Stefania, and Claudia Olivetti. 2009. "Home production, market production, and the gender wage gap: Incentives and expectations." *Review of Economic Dynamics* 12(1):80–107.

Alderman-Swain, Wanda, and Juan Battle. 2000. "The invisible gender: Educational outcomes for African American females in father-only versus mother-only households." *Race and Society* 3(2):165–82.

Ali, Syed Mohammed. 2004. *The Position of Women in Islam: A Progressive View.* Albany, NY: State University of New York.

Al-Olayan, Fahad S., and Kiran Karande. 2000. "A content analysis of magazine advertisements from the United States and the Arab world." *Journal of Advertising* 29(3):69–82.

Alvarez, Alex, and Ronet Bachman. 2008. *Violence: The Enduring Problem.* Thousand Oaks, CA: Sage.

Amadiume, Ifi. 1997. *Reinventing Africa: Matriarchy, Religion and Culture.* New York: Zed.

Amare, Nicole. 2007. "Where is she? Gender occurrences in online grammar guides." *Research in the Teaching of English* 42(2):163–87.

Amato, Paul R. 2007. "Transformative processes in marriage: Some thoughts from a sociologist." *Journal of Marriage and the Family* 69:305–9.

Amato, Paul R., Alan Booth, David R. Johnson, and Stacy J. Rogers. 2007. *Alone Together: How Marriage in America is Changing.* Cambridge, MA: Harvard University.

Amato, Paul R., and Denise Previti. 2003. "People's reasons for divorcing: Gender, social class, the life course, and adjustment." *Journal of Family Issues* 24(5):602–26.

Amato, Paul R., David R. Johnson, Alan Booth, and Stacy J. Rogers. 2003. "Continuity and change in marital quality between 1980 and 2000." *Journal of Marriage and the Family* 65(1)1–22.

Amba, Joyce C., and Freya L. Sonenstein. 2002. "Sexual activity and contraceptive practices among teenagers in the United States, 1988 and 1995." *Vital and Health Statistics.* Series 23(21): May. Centers for Disease Control and National Center for Health Statistics.

Ambwani, Suman, and Jaine Strauss. 2007. "Love thyself before loving others? A qualitative and quantitative analysis of gender differences in body image and romantic love." *Sex Roles* 56(1/2):13–21.

American Bar Association. 2006a. "Charting Our Progress: The Status of Women in the Profession Today." Commission on Women in the Profession. Chicago: American Bar Association. www.abanet.org

———. 2006b. "Visible Invisibility: Women of Color in Law Firms: Executive Summary." Commission on Women in the Profession. Chicago: American Bar Association. www.abanet.org

AMGOV. 2009. *Public Opinion: Listening to Citizens.* New York: McGraw-Hill.

ANAD. 2009. "Excerpts from ANAD's letter to Viacom/MTV; Facts about eating disorders." National Association of Anorexia Nervosa and Associated Eating Disorders. www.anad.org

Anastaskos, Kiki. 2002. "Structural adjustment policies in Mexico and Costa Rica." In Rekha Datta and Judith Kornberg (eds.), *Women in Developing Countries: Assessing Strategies for Empowerment.* (pp. 113–27). Boulder, CO: Lynne Rienner.

Andersen, Peter A. 2008. *Nonverbal Communication: Forms and Functions.* Long Grove, IL: Waveland.

Anderson, C.A., and Brad J. Bushman. 2001. "Effects of violent video games on aggressive behavior, aggressive cognition, aggressive affect, physiological arousal, and prosocial behavior: A meta-analytic review of the scientific literature." *Psychological Science* 12(5):353–9.

Anderson, C. Leigh, Laura Locker, and Rachel Nugent. 2002. "Microcredit, social capital, and common pool resources." *World Development* 30(1):95–105.

Anderson, Irina, and Victoria Swainson. 2001. "Perceived motivations for rape: Gender differences in beliefs about female and male rape." *Current Research in Social Psychology* 6(8):np.

Anderson, Margaret. 2001. "A nation's downward spiral into cynicism: Revisiting Clarence Thomas and Anita Hill. *SWS Network News* 28(4):20–21.

Anderson, Mary Jo. 2006. "Women should not be ordained as priests." In Mary E. Williams (ed.), *The Catholic Church.* Detroit: Greenhaven.

Anderson, Tamara L., and Elizabeth Lewis Hall. 2005. "Introduction to the special issue on gender and Christianity." *Journal of Psychology and Theology* 33(3):163–65.

Andersson, Gunnar, Karsten Hank, and Andres Vikat. 2007. "Understanding parental gender preferences in advanced societies: Lessons from Sweden and Finland. *Demographic Research* 17(July/December):135–55.

Andersson, Gunnar, Karsten Hank, Marit Ronsen, and Andres Vikat. 2006. "Gendering family composition: Sex preferences for children and childbearing behavior in the Nordic countries." *Demography* 43(2):255–67.

Andreoni, James, and Ragan Petrie. 2008. "Beauty and gender stereotypes: Evidence from laboratory experiments." *Journal of Economic Psychology* 29(1):73–93.

Andryszewski, Tricia. 2000. *Gay Rights.* Brookfield, CT: Twenty-First Century Books.

Angelo, Megan. 2009. "Reinventing TV as viewer reinvent life." *New York Times* September 20:MT4.

Aranat, Elizabeth, and Guy Michaels. 2008. "The effect of marital breakup on the income distribution of women with children." *Journal of Human Resources* 43(3):611–29.

Ariel, Yaakov. 2006. "Can Adam and Eve reconcile?" *Nova Religio: The Journal of Alternative and Emergent Religion.* 9(4):53–78.

Aries, Elizabeth. 2006. "Sex differences in interaction." In Kathryn Dindia and Daniel J. Canary (eds.), *Sex Differences and Similarities in Communication.* (pp. 21–36). Mahwah, NJ: Lawrence Erlbaum.

Armenia, Amy, and Naomi Gerstel. 2006. "Family leaves, the FMLA and gender neutrality: The intersection of race and gender." *Social Science Research* 35(4):871–91.

Armenti, Carmen. 2004. "Women faculty seeking tenure and parenthood: Lessons from previous generations." *Cambridge Journal of Education* March 34(1):71.

Armstrong, Karen. 2001. "Cries of rage and frustration." *New Statesman* September 24. 17–18.

Arnot, Madeleine, Miriam David, and Gaby Weiner. 1999. *Closing the Gender Gap: Postwar Education and Social Change.* Cambridge, UK: Polity.

Arnstein, Aassve, Gianni Betti, Stefano Mazzuco, and Letizia Mencarini. 2007. "Marital disruption and economic well-being: A comparative analysis." *Journal of the Royal Statistical Society* 170(3):781–99.

Ascha, Ghassan. 1995. "The 'Mothers of the Believers': Stereotypes of the Prophet Muhammad's wives." In Ria Kloppenborg and Wouter J. Hanegraaff (eds.), *Female Stereotypes in Religious Traditions.* Leiden, Netherlands: Brill.

Asher, Lauren, and Lisa Lederer. 2000. *Work/Family Conflicts Still Largely Absent from Entertainment.* Common Dreams Progressive Newswire February 9. www.commondreams.org/news2000/0209-o1

Ashwin, Sarah (ed.). 2005. *Adapting to Russia's New Labour Market: Gender and Employment Behaviour.* London: Routledge.

Athanases, Steven S., and Tess A. Comar. 2008. "The performance of homophobia in early adolescent's everyday speech." *Journal of LGBT Youth* 5(2):9–32.

Atkins, David C., and Neil S. Jacobson. 2001. "Understanding infidelity: Correlates in a national random sample." *Journal of Family Psychology* 15(4):735–49.

Atkins, David C., Sona Dimidjian, and Neil Jacobson. 2001. "Why do people have affairs? Recent research and future directions about attributions for extramarital involvement." In Valerie Manusov and John H. Harvey (eds.), *Attribution, Communication Behavior, and Close Relationships.* (pp. 305–19). Cambridge, UK: Cambridge University.

Atwell, Mark Welek. 2002. *Equal Protection of the Law? Gender and Justice in the United States.* New York: P. Lang.

Auerbach, Carl F., and Louise Bordeaux Silverstein. 2006. "Further thoughts on 'paternal involvement.'" *Journal of Feminist Family Therapy* 18(4):99–101.

Avellar, Sarah, and Pamela J. Smock. 2005. "The economic consequences of the dissolution of cohabiting unions." *Journal of Marriage and the Family* 67:315–27.

Avishai, Orit. 2008. "'Doing religion' in a secular world: Women in conservative religions and the question of agency." *Gender & Society* 22(4):409–33.

Azmitia, Margarita, Catherine R. Cooper, and Jane R. Brown. 2009. "Support and guidance from families, friends, and teachers in Latino early adolescents' math pathways." *Journal of Early Adolescence* 29(1):142–69.

Badgio, Peter C., and Blaise L. Worden. 2007. "Women, aging, and alcohol use disorders." In Victor J. Malatesta (ed.), *Mental Health Issues of Older Women: A Comprehensive Review for Health Care Professionals.* Binghamton, NY: Haworth.

Badran, Margot. 2009. *Feminism in Islam: Secular and Religious Convergence.* Oxford: Oneworld.

Bagilhole, Barbara. 2002. *Women in Non-Traditional Occupations: Challenging Men.* Houndmils, Basingstoke, Hampshire, UK: Palgrave Macmillan.

Baharke, Michael. 2007. "Muscle enhancement substances and strategies." In J. Kevin Thompson and Guy Cafri (eds.), *The Muscular Ideal: Psychological, Social, and Medical Perspectives.* Washington, DC: American Psychological Association.

Bailenson, Jeremy N., and Nick Yee. 2007. "Virtual interpersonal touch and digital chameleons." *Journal of Nonverbal Behavior* 31:225–42.

Baillargeon, R.H. et al. 2007. "Gender differences in physical aggression: A prospective population - based survey of children before and after 2 years of age." *Developmental Psychology* 43:13–26.

Baird, Julia, Pat Wingert et al. 2008. "From Seneca Falls to . . . Sarah Palin?" *Newsweek* September 22:30–36.

Baker, Christina. 2000. "Telling our stories: Feminist mothers and daughters." In Andrea O'Reilly and Sharon Abbey (eds.), *Mothers and Daughters: Connection, Empowerment and Transformation.* (pp. 203–12). Lanham, MD: Rowman & Littlefield.

Baker, Kathleen, Carol Ann Beck et al. 2003. "The relationship between maternal employment and perceptions of child, spouse, and self." ERIC, *Resources in Education.* Accession No.: ED472514.

Baker, Peter, and Jeff Zeleny. 2009. "Obama hails judge as 'inspiring.'" *New York Times* May 27. www.nytimes.com/2009/05/27

Balaji, Murali. 2009. "Owning black masculinity: The intersection of cultural commodification and self-construction in rap music videos." *Communication, Culture, and Critique* 2(1):21–38.

Balanoff, Elizabeth. 1990. "The American woman and the labor movement: Bitter fruit in the economy of profit." In Frances Richardson Keller (ed.), *Views of Women's Lives in Western Tradition.* Lewiston, NY: Edwin Mellen.

Ball, Philip. 2008. "Where have all the flowers gone?" *Nature* 454 (July 24):374–5.

Bandura, A., and Bussey, K. 2004. "On broadening the cognitive, motivational, and sociostructural scope of theorizing about gender development and functioning: Comment on Martin, Ruble, and Szkrybalo (2002)." *Psychological Bulletin* 130; 691–701.

Bandura, Albert, and Richard H. Walters. 1963. *Social Learning and Personality Development.* New York: Holt, Rinehart & Winston.

Banner, Lois W. 2005. *Women in Modern America: A Brief History.* Belmont, CA: Thomson/Wadsworth.

Bardsley, Sandy. 2007. *Women's Roles in the Middle Ages.* Westport, CT: Greenwood.

Barriga, Claudia, Michael Shapiro, and Rayna Jhaveri. 2009. "Media context, female body size and perceived realism." *Sex Roles* 60(1/2):128–41.

Barlow, Rebecca. 2008. "Women's rights in the Islamic Republic of Iran: The contributions of secular-oriented feminism." In Shahram Akbarzadeh and Benjamin MacQueen (eds.), *Islam and Human Rights in Practice: Perspectives across the Ummah.* London: Routledge.

Barnes, Helen, and Jane Parry. 2004. "Renegotiating identity and relationships: Men and women's adjustment to retirement." *Ageing and Society* 24(2):213–33.

Barnes, Robert. 2009. "Abortion provider shot dead in church." *Washington Post* June 1. www.washingtonpost.com/wp-dyn/content/article/2009/5/31

Barnett, Rosalind Chait, and Karen C. Gareis. 2006. "Role theory perspectives on work and family." In Marcie Pitt-Catsouphes, Ellen Ernst Kossek, and Stephen Sweet (eds.), *The Work and Family Handbook: Multi-disciplinary Perspectives.* (pp. 209–21). Mahwah, NJ: Lawrence Erlbaum.

Barnett, Rosalind Chait. 2007. "Separating boys and girls: A debate on the benefits of single-sex education" *Teacher Magazine* 18(4):12.

Baron-Cohen, Simon. 2007. "Sex differences in mind: Keeping science distinct from social policy." In Stephen Ceci and Wendy Williams (eds.), *Why Aren't More Women in Science? Top Researchers Debate the Evidence.* (pp. 159–72). Washington, DC: American Psychological Association.

Barrett, Jennifer B., and Cynthia Buckley. 2009. "Gender and perceived control in the Russian Federation." *Europe-Asia Studies* 61(1):29–49.

Barry, Herbert, III, and Aylene S. Harper. 2000. "The last three letters identify most female last names." *Psychological Reports* 87(1):48–54.

Bartley, Sharon J., Priscilla W. Blanton, and Jennifer L. Gilliard. 2005. "Husbands and wives in dual-earner marriages: Decision-making, gender role attitudes, division of household labor, and equity." *Marriage and Family Review* 37(4):69–94.

Barton, Edward Read. 2006. "Are mythopoetic men's support groups repackaged patriarchy?" *International Journal of Self Help and Self Care* 4(1–2):99–117.

Bartsch, Robert A., Teresa Burnett, and Tommye Diller. 2000. "Gender representation in television commercials: Updating and update." *Sex Roles* 43(9/10):735–43.

Baskin, Kara. 2004. "Singled out." *New Republic* March 22. 230(10).

Bassani, Cherylynn. 2003. "A look at changing parental ideologies and behaviors in Japan." *Sociological Research Online.* http://www.socresonline.org.uk

Basye, Anne. 2005. "Discovering bold women in blue." *Lutheran Women Today* June:16–17.

Batalova, Jeanne A., and Philip N. Cohen. 2002. "Premarital cohabitation and housework: Couples in cross-national perspective." *Journal of Marriage and the Family* 64(3):743–55.

Batten, Mary. 1992. *Sexual Strategies.* New York: Jeremy P. Tarcher/Putnam.

Baum, Nehami. 2007. " 'Separation guilt' in women who initiate divorce." *Clinical Social Work Journal* 35(1):47–55.

Baumann, Shyon. 2008. "The moral underpinnings of beauty: A meaning-based explanation for light and dark complexions in advertising." *Poetics* 36(1):2–23.

Baunach, Dawn Michelle. 2002. "Progress, opportunity, and backlash: Explaining attitudes toward gender-based affirmative action." *Sociological Focus* 35(4):345–62.

Baunach, Dawn Michelle. 2001. "Gender inequality in childhood: Toward a life course perspective." *Gender Issues* 19(3):61–86.

Bauserman, Robert. 2002. "Child adjustment in joint-custody versus sole-custody arrangements: A meta-analytic review." *Journal of Family Psychology* 16(1):91–102.

Baxter, Janeen, Belinda Hewitt, and Michele Haynes. 2008. "Life course transitions and housework: Marriage, parenthood, and time on housework." *Journal of Marriage and the Family* 70(2):259–72.

Baxter, Janeen. 2000. "The joys and justice of housework." *Sociology* 34(4):609–31.

Baxter, Leslie A., Tim Dun, and Erin Sahlstein. 2001. "Rules for relating communicated among social network members." *Journal of Personal and Social Relationships* 18(2):173–99.

Bazelon, Emily. 2009. "2 kids + 0 husbands family." *New York Times Magazine* February 1:30–35.

Beatty, D. 2003. "Stalking legislation in the United States." In M. Brewster (ed.), *Stalking: Psychology, Risk Factors, Interventions, and Law.* (pp. 1–55). Kingston, NJ: Civic Research Institute.

Beauchamp, Tom L. et al. (eds.). 2008. *The Human Use of Animals: Case Studies in Ethical Issues.* Oxford, UK: Oxford University.

Beaujot, Roderic, and Jianye Liu. 2005. "Models of time use in paid and unpaid work." *Journal of Family Issues* 26(7):924–46.

Becker, Gary S. 1994. "Working women's staunchest allies: Supply and demand." In Susan F. Feiner (ed.), *Race and Gender in the American Economy: Views from Across the Spectrum.* Englewood Cliffs, NJ: Prentice Hall.

Bedard, Kelly, and Olivier Deschenes. 2005. "Sex preferences, marital dissolution, and the economic status of women." *Journal of Human Resources* 40(2).

Beddoe, Deirdre. 1989. *Back to Home and Duty: Women Between the Wars, 1918–1939.* London: Pandora.

Bedolla, Lisa Garcia, Jessica L. Lavariega, and Adrian D. Pantoja. 2006. "A second look: Is there a Latina/o gender gap?" *Journal of Women, Politics, and Policy* 28(3/4):147–71.

Beek, Yolanda and Judith Dubas. 2008. "Age and gender differences in decoding basic and non-basic facial expressions in late childhood and early adolescence." *Journal of Nonverbal Behavior* 32(1):37–52.

Begley, Sharon. 2008. "Math is hard, Barbie said." *Newsweek* October 27. www.newsweek.com/id/164523

Behling, Laura. 2001. *The Masculine Woman in America, 1890–1935*. Urbana: University of Illinois.

Behm-Morawitz, Elizabeth, and Dana E. Mastro. 2008. "Mean girls? The influence of gender portrayals in teen movies on emerging adults' gender-based attitudes and beliefs." *J&MC Quarterly* 85(1):131–46.

Behnke, Andrew O. Shelley M. MacDermid et al. 2008. "Family cohesion in the lives of Mexican American and European American parents." *Journal of Marriage and the Family* 70(4):1045–59.

Beier, Margaret E., and Philip L. Ackerman. 2003. "Determinants of health knowledge: An investigation of age, gender, abilities, personality and interests." *Journal of Personality and Social Psychology* 84(2):439–48.

Bellafante, Ginia. 2009. "Face to Watch: Sofia Vergara." *New York Times* September 20:MT3.

Belkin, Lisa. 2003. "The opt-out revolution." *New York Times Magazine* October 26:42–47, 58, 85–86.

Bell, Linda, Celine Goulet et al. 2007. "Mothers' and fathers' view of the interdependence of their relationships with their infant: A systems perspective on early family relationships." *Journal of Family Nursing* 13(2):179–200.

Beller, Michal, and Naomi Gafni. 2000. "Can item format (multiple choice vs. open-ended) account for gender differences in mathematics achievement?" *Sex Roles* 42(1/2):1–21.

Belluck, Pam. 2009. "Yes, looks do matter." *New York Times* April 26(Sunday Styles):1,8.

Bem, Sandra Lipsitz. 1981. "Gender schema theory: A cognitive account of sex-typing." *Psychological Review* 88:354–64.

———. 1983. "Gender schema theory and its implications for child development: Raising gender-aschematic children in a gender-schematic society." *Signs* 8:598–616.

———. 1985. "Androgyny and gender-schema theory: A conceptual and empirical integration." In T.B. Sonderegger (ed.), *Nebraska Symposium on Motivation 1984: Psychology and Gender* 32:179–226. Lincoln: University of Nebraska.

———. 1987. "Gender schema theory and the romantic tradition." In Phillip Shaver and Clyde Hendrick (eds.), *Sex and Gender.* (pp. 251–71). Thousand Oaks, CA: Sage.

———. 1993. *The Lenses of Gender: Transforming the Debate on Sexual Inequality*. New Haven, CT: Yale University.

———. 1996. "Transforming the debate on sexual inequality: From biological difference to institutionalized androcentrism." In Joan C. Chrisler, Carla Golden, and Patricia D. Rozee (eds.), *Lectures on the Psychology of Women*. New York: McGraw-Hill.

Bem, Sandra Lipsitz, and Daryl J. Bem. 1970. "Case study of a nonconscious ideology: Training the woman to know her place." In Daryl J. Bem (ed.), *Beliefs, Attitudes and Human Affairs*. Belmont, CA: Brooks and Cole.

Bendroth, M.L. 1999. "Fundamentalism and the family: Gender, culture, and the American profamily movement." *Journal of Women's History* 10(4):35–53.

Beneke, Tim. 2004. "Men on rape." In Michael S. Kimmel and Michael A. Messner (eds.), *Men's Lives*. (pp. 195–208). Boston: Allyn & Bacon.

Benjamin, Jessica. 1988. *The Bonds of Love: Psychoanalysis, Feminism and the Problem of Domination*. New York: Pantheon.

Bennett-Alexander, Dawn, and Laura P. Hartman. 2007. *Employment Law for Business*. Boston, MA: McGraw-Hill/Irwin.

Benson, Brenda, Carol Gohm, and Alan Gross. 2007. "College women and sexual assault: The role of sex-related alcohol expectancies." *Journal of Family Violence* 22(6):341–51.

Berenbaum, Sheri, and Susan Resnick. 2007. "The seeds of career choices: Gender abilities and sociocultural factors." In Stephen J. Ceci and Wendy M. Williams (eds.), *Why Aren't More Women in Science? Top Researchers Debate the Evidence.* (pp. 147–58). Washington, DC: American Psychological Association.

Bergen, Raquel Kennedy, and Kathleen A. Boyle. 2000. "Exploring the connection between pornography and sexual violence." *Violence and Victims* 15(3):227–34.

Berger, Helen A. 2000. "High priestess: Mother, leader, teacher." In Wendy Griffin (ed.), *Daughters of the Goddess: Studies of Healing, Identity, and Empowerment.* (pp. 103–18). Walnut Creek, CA: AltaMira.

Berggren Heidi M. 2008. "US family-leave policy: The legacy of 'separate spheres.' " *International Journal of Social Welfare* 17(4):312–23.

Bergman, Mindy E., and Jaime B. Henning. 2008. "Sex and ethnicity in the sexual harassment phenomenon: A revision and test of Fitzgerald et al. 1994." *Journal of Occupational Health Psychology* 13(2):152–67.

Bergman, Solvieg. 2009. Collective organizing and claim making on child care in Norden: Blurring the boundaries between the inside and the outside." In Christine E. Bose and Minjeong Kim (eds.), *Global Gender Research: Transnational Perspectives.* (pp. 315–20). New York: Routledge.

Bergner, Daniel. 2009. "What do women want?: A new generation of postfeminists sexologists is trying to discover what ignites female desire." *New York Times Magazine* January 25:26–33; 46, 51.

Bergqvist, Christina, and Anita Nyberg. 2002. "Welfare state restructuring and child care in Sweden." In Sonya Michel and Rianne Mahon (eds.), *Child Care Policy at the Crossroads: Gender and Welfare State Restructuring.* (pp. 287–308). New York: Routledge.

Berkowitz, Dana. 2007. *Maternal Urges, Biological Clocks, and Soccer Moms: Gay Men's Procreative and*

Fathering Narratives. American Sociological Association. New York.

Berkowitz, Dana, and William Marsiglio. 2007. "Gay men: Negotiating procreative, father, and family identities." *Journal of Marriage and the Family* 69:366–81.

Berlin, Steve. 2006. "Boys aren't testing badly – but girls are testing well." *Education Daily* 39(June 27):3.

Bernard, Neal D. 2003. "Nutritional factors in menstrual pain and premenstrual syndrome." *PCRM Clinical Research.* Physician's Committee for Responsible Medicine. www.perm.org/research/mentrual.html

Bernhard, Blythe. 2008. "Estrogen paradox can fight tumors." *St. Louis Post-Dispatch* December 12:A1, A10.

Bernstein, Robert, and Tom Edwards. 2008. "An older and more divorced nation by midcentury." *U.S. Census Bureau News* August 14.

Besen-Cassino, Yasemin. 2008. "The cost of being a girl: Gender earning differentials in the early labor markets." *NWSA Journal* 20(1):146–60.

Better, Alison. 2005. *Best of Two Worlds: An Exploration of Identity Issues Among Gay Fathers.* American Sociological Association. Philadelphia.

Beynon, John. 2002. *Masculinities and Culture.* Buckingham, UK: Open University Press.

Beyrer, Chris. 2001. "Shan women and girls in the sex industry in Southeast Asia: Political causes and human rights implications." *Social Science and Medicine* 53(4):543–50.

Bialik, Joyce. 2008. "Men dealing with fatherhood and poverty." *Dissertation Abstracts International Section A: Humanities and Social Sciences* 68(5-a):1984.

Bianchi, Suzanne M. 1999. "Feminization and juvenilization of poverty: Trends, risks, causes, and consequences." *Annual Review of Sociology* 25:307–33.

Bianchi, Suzanne M., John P. Robinson, and Melissa A. Milkie. 2006. *Changing Rhythms of American Family Life.* New York: Russell Sage Foundation.

Bica, Camillo Mac. 2009. "Deadly games." *Truthout Perspective.* May 5. www.truthout.org/050509J

Billitteri, Thomas J. 2008. "Gender pay gap." *CQ Researcher* 18(11):243–50.

Bio-Medicine. 2008. "Breast cancer in men: Mammography and sonography findings." *Bio-Medicine News.* December 1. www.bio-medicine.org/medicine-news-1

Bjerk, David. 2009. "Beauty vs. earnings: Gender differences in earnings and priorities over spousal characteristics in a matching model." *Journal of Economic Behavior and Organization* 69(3):248–59.

Björkqvist, Kaj, and Pirkko Niemelä. 1992. "New trends in the study of female aggression." In Kaj Björkqvist and Pirkko Niemelä (eds.), *Of Mice and Women: Aspects of Female Aggression.* San Diego, CA: Academic Press.

Björkqvist, Kaj. 1994. "Sex differences in physical, verbal and indirect aggression: A review of recent research." *Sex Roles* 30:177–88.

Black, Dan A. Amelia M. Haviland, Seth G. Sanders, and Lowell J. Taylor. 2008. "Gender wage disparities among the highly educated." *Journal of Human Resources* 43(3):630–59.

Black, Donald W. 2007. "Antisocial personality disorder, conduct disorder, and psychopathy." In Jon E. Grant and Marc N. Potenza (eds.), *Textbook of Men's Mental Health.* Washington, DC: American Psychological Association.

Black, Katherine A., and David J. Gold. 2008. "Gender differences and socioeconomic status biases in judgments about blame in date rape scenarios." *Violence and Victims* 23(1):115–28.

Blackwell, Judith C., Murray E.G. Smith, and John S. Sorenson (eds.). 2003. "Feminism and the women's movement." Part 6 in *Culture of Prejudice: Arguments in Critical Social Science.* Peterborough, Ontario, CA: Broadview.

Blaise, Mindy. 2005. *Playing it Straight: Uncovering Gender Discourse in the Early Childhood Classroom.* New York: Routledge.

Blakemore, Judith E. (2005) "Characteristics of boys' and girls' toys." *Sex Roles* 53(9/10):619–33.

Blakemore, Judith E. Owen, and Renee E. Centers. 2005. "Characteristics of boys' and girls' toys." *Sex Roles* 53(9/10):618–33.

Blakemore, Judith E., and Craig Hill. 2008. "The child gender socialization scale: A measure to compare traditional and feminist parents." *Sex Roles* 58(3/4):192–207.

Blanco, Carlos, and Oriana Vesga Lopez. 2007. "Psychiatric disorders in men: Assessment and treatment-Anxiety disorders." In Jon E. Grant and Marc N. Potenza (eds.), *Textbook of Men's Mental Health.* Washington, DC: American Psychological Association.

Blau, Francine, and Lawrence M. Kahn. 2006. "The U.S. gender pay gap in the 1990s: Slowing convergence." *Industrial and Labor Relations Review* 60(1):45–66.

Blau, Francine, Marianne A. Ferber, and Anne E. Winkle. 2006. "Microcredit for women: Lifeline or mirage?" From Chapter 11, *The Economics of Women, Men, and Work.* Upper Saddle River, NJ: Pearson/Prentice Hall.

Bleske, April L., and Todd K. Shackelford. 2001. "Poaching, promiscuity, and deceit: Combating mating rivalry in same-sex relationships." *Personal Relationships* 8(4):407–24.

Bligh, Michelle C., and Jeffrey C. Kohles. 2008. "Negotiating gender role expectations: Rhetorical leadership and women in the U.S. Senate." *Leadership* 4(4):361–402.

Blood, Robert O., Jr., and Donald M. Wolfe. 1960. *Husbands and Wives: The Dynamics of Married Living.* New York: Free Press.

Blumen, Orna. 2002. "Criss-crossing boundaries: Ultraorthodox women go to work." *Gender, Peace and Culture* (2):133–51.

Blumer, Herbert. 1969. *Symbolic Interactionism: Perspective and Method.* Englewood Cliffs, NJ: Prentice Hall.

Blumstein, Philip, and Pepper Schwartz. 1983. *American Couples.* New York: Pocket Books.

Bly, Robert. 1990. *Iron John.* Reading, MA: Addison-Wesley.

Bock, Gisela. 2003. "Challenging dichotomies in women's history." In Mary Beth Norton and Ruth M. Alexander (eds.), *Major Problems in American Women's History.* Boston: Houghton Mifflin.

Bock, Gisela. 2002. "The French Revolution: The dispute is resumed." Part 2 in *Women in European History.* Oxford, UK: Blackwell.

Bodrova, V.V. 2002. "Reproductive behavior as a factor of depopulation in Russia." *Sotsiologicheskie Issledovaniya* (abstract) 28(6):96–102.

Boekhout, Brock, Susan S. Hendrick, and Clyde Hendrick. 2000. "The loss of loved ones: The impact of relationship infidelity." In John H. Harvey and Eric D. Miller (eds.), *Loss and Trauma: General and Close Relationship Perspectives.* (pp. 358–74). New York: Brunner-Routledge.

Bokker, Paul. 2006. "Factors that influence the relationships between divorced fathers and their children." *Journal of Divorce and Remarriage* 45(3/4):157–72.

Boland, Mary L. 2002. *Sexual Harassment: Your Guide to Legal Action.* Naperville, IL: Sphinx.

Bombardieri, Marcella. 2005. "Summers' remarks on women draw fire." *Boston Globe* January 17.

Bond, James T. 2003. *Highlights of the National Study of the Changing Workforce.* New York: Families and Work Institute.

Book, Angela, S., K.B. Starzyk, and V.L. Quinsey. 2001. " The relationship between testosterone and aggression: A meta-analysis." *Aggression and Violent Behavior* 6:579–99.

Boone, Jon. 2009. "Taliban shoot dead Afghan politician who championed women's rights." *The Guardian UK* April 13.

Booth, Alan, Douglas A. Granger, Alan Mazur, and Katie T. Kivlighan. 2006. "Testosterone and social behavior." *Social Forces* 85(1):167–91.

Boserup, Ester. 1970. *Women's Role in Economic Development.* London: Allen and Unwin.

Bosmajian, Haig. 1995. "The language of sexism." In Paula S. Rothenberg (ed.), *Race, Class and Gender in the United States: An Integrated Study.* New York: St. Martin's.

Boucher, Leigh, and Sarah Pinto. 2007. "I ain't queer': Love, masculinity and history in Brokeback Mountain." *The Journal of Men's Studies* 15(3):311–30.

Boushey, Heather. 2009. "Equal pay for breadwinners: More men are jobless while women earn less for equal work." *Center for American Progress* January. www.americanprogress.org

Boustany Nora. 2002. "Up from the underground, Russia's feminists speak out." *Washington Post* November 1:A28.

Bowerbank, Sylvia. 2001. "Of mice and women: Early modern roots of ecological feminism." *Women and Environments International Magazine* 52/53(Fall):27–9.

Boyko, Olga V. 2002. "How social issues were represented in the Russian press in the 1990s." *Sotsiologicheskie Issledovaniya* (abstract) 28(6):120–28.

Boyle, Elizabeth Heger. 2008. "The evolution of debates over female genital cutting." In Frank J. Lechner and John Boli (eds.), *The Globalization Reader.* (pp. 268–73). Malden, MA: Blackwell.

BPW. 2007. "101 facts on the status of working women." Business and Women's Professional Foundation. October. http://wusa.org/i4a/pages/index.cfm

Brainerd, Elizabeth. 2000. "Women in transition: Changes in gender wage differentials in Eastern Europe and the former Soviet Union. *Industrial and Labor Relations Review* 54(1):138–62.

Brand, Madeleine, and Alex Cohen. 2007. "Research links wealth, marriage." *Day to Day Show, NPR News* July 6.

Brandsma, Lynn. 2007. "Eating disorders across the lifespan." In Victor J. Malatesta (ed.), *Mental Health Issues of Older Women: A Comprehensive Review for Health Care Professionals.* Binghamton, NY: Haworth.

Brannon, Robert. 1976. "The male sex role: Our culture's blueprint of manhood and what it's done for us lately." In D. David and Robert Brannon (eds.), *The 49% Majority.* Reading, MA: Addison-Wesley.

Bratter, Jenifer L., and Rosalind B. King. 2008. "But will it last? Marital instability among interracial and same-race couples." *Family Relations* 57(2):160–71.

Braudy, Leo. 2003. *From Chivalry to Terrorism: War and the Changing Nature of Masculinity.* New York: Alfred A. Knopf.

Brausch, Amy M., and Peter M. Gutierrez. 2009. "The role of body image and disordered eating as risk factors for depression and suicidal ideation in adolescents." *Suicide and Life Threatening Behavior* 39(1):58–71.

Bregar, Louis. 2000. *Freud: Darkness in the Midst of Vision.* New York: John Wiley.

Breines, Winifred. 2006. *The Trouble Between Us: An Uneasy History of White and Black Women in the Feminist Movement.* New York: Oxford University.

Brescoll, V.L., and E.L. Uhlmann. 2005. "Attitudes toward traditional and nontraditional parents." *Psychology of Women Quarterly* 29:436–55.

Bretthauer, Brook, Toni Schindler, Zimmerman, and James H. Banning. 2006. "A feminist analysis of popular music: Power over, objectification of, and violence against women." *Journal of Feminist Family Therapy* 18(4):29–51.

Briggs, Robin. 2002. *Witches and neighbours: The Social and Cultural Context of European Witchcraft.* Oxford, UK: Blackwell.

Brinamen, Charles E., and Valory Mitchell. 2008. "Gay men becoming fathers: A model of identity expansion." *Journal of GLBT Studies* 4(4):521–41.

Brizendine, Louann. 2006. *The Female Brain.* New York: Morgan Road.

Broadbent, Kaye. 2002. "Gender and part-time work in Japan." *Equal Opportunities International* 21(3):57–74.

Broadbridge, Adelina. 2008. "Barriers to ascension to senior management in retailing." *Service Industries Journal* 28(9):1225–245.

Brock, David. 2001. *Blinded by the Right: The Conscience of an Ex-Conservative.* New York: Crown.

Brod, Harry. 2003. "Scholarly studies on men: The new field is an essential complement to women's studies." In Estelle Disch (ed.), *Reconstructing Gender: A Multicultural Anthology.* (pp. 411–14). New York: McGraw-Hill.

Broder, Sheri. 2002. *Tramps, Unfit Mothers, and Neglected Children: Negotiating the Family in Nineteenth Century Philadelphia.* Philadelphia: University of Pennsylvania.

Brooke, James. 2005. "Fighting to protect her gift to Japanese women." *New York Times* May 28. International.

Brooks, Fred. 2002a. "Impacts of child care subsidies on family and child well-being." *Early Childhood Research Quarterly* 17(4):498–511.

Brooks, Geraldine. 2002b. "Women in Islam." In John Miller and Aaron Kenedi (eds.), *Inside Islam: The Faith, the People, and the Conflicts of the World's Fastest-Growing Religion.* (pp. 213–34). New York: Marlowe.

Brown, Barbara A. 2008. "Student perceptions regarding gender-related learning differences and their correlation to achievement outcomes." *Dissertation Abstracts International Section A: Humanities and Social Sciences* 68(10-A):41–46.

Brown, Dorothy M. 1987. *Setting a Course: American Women in the 1920s.* Boston: Twayne.

Brown, Edna, Terri L. Orbuch, and Jose A. Bauermeister. 2008. "Religiosity and marital stability among black American and white American couples. *Family Relations* 57(2):186–97.

Brown, Jane D., and Laurie Schulze. 1990. "The effects of race, gender and fandom on audience interpretations of Madonna's music videos." *Journal of Communication* 40(2):88–102.

Brown, Lyn Mikel, and Carol Gilligan. 1992. *Meeting at the Crossroads: Women's Psychology and Girls' Development.* Cambridge, MA: Harvard University.

Brown, Susan L., Jennifer Roebuck Lee, and Gary R. Lee. 2005. "The significance of nonmarital cohabitation: Marital status and mental health benefits among middle-aged and older adults." *Journals of Gerontology Series B: Psychological Sciences and Social Sciences* 60B(1):S21–S29.

Browne, Kingsley R. 2002. *Biology at Work: Rethinking Sexual Equality.* New Brunswick, NJ: Rutgers University.

Bruch, Monroe A. 2006. "Cognitive bias in men's processing of negative social information: The role of social anxiety, toughness as a masculine role norm, and their interaction." *Cognitive Therapy and Research* 30(3):273–89.

Brumm, Walter. 2008. "Putting Sodus Shaker village on the map." *American Communal Societies Quarterly* 2(4):153–88.

Bryant, Joanne. 2007. "Feminine sexual subjectivities: Bodies, agency, and life history." *Sexualities* 10(3):321–40.

Buckley, Tamara R., and Robert T. Carter. 2005. "Black adolescent girls: Do gender role and racial identity impact their self-esteem?" *Sex Roles* 53(9/10):647–62.

Buehrens, John A. 2003. *Understanding the Bible: An Introduction for Skeptics, Seekers, and Religious Liberals.* Boston: Beacon.

Bulcroft, Richard, and Jay Teachman. 2004. "Ambiguous construction: Development of a childless or child free life course." In Marilyn Coleman and Lawrence H. Ganong (eds.), *Handbook of Contemporary Families.* Newbury Park, CA: Sage.

Bumiller, Elisabeth. 1995. *The Secrets of Mariko.* New York: Times Books.

Bumpus, Matthew F., Ann C. Crouter, and Susan M. McHale. 2001. "Parental autonomy granting during adolescence: Exploring gender differences in context." *Development Psychology* 37(2):163–73.

Bunch, Charlotte. 1993. "Prospects for global feminism." In Alison M. Jaggar and Paula S. Rothenberg (eds.), *Feminist Frameworks: Alternative Theoretical Accounts of the Relations Between Women and Men.* (pp. 249–52.). New York: McGraw-Hill.

Bunster-Bunalto, Ximena. 1993. "Surviving beyond fear: Women and torture in Latin America." In Alison M. Jaggar and Paula S. Rothenberg (eds.), *Feminist Frameworks: Alternative Theoretical Accounts of the Relations Between Women and Men.* New York: McGraw-Hill.

Burchinal, Margaret R., Frank Porter Graham, and Lauren Nelson. 2000. "Family selection and child care experience: Implications for studies of child outcomes." *Early Childhood Research Quarterly* 15(3):385–411.

Bureau of Justice Statistics. 2002. "Rape and sexual assault: Reporting to police and medical attention, 1992–2000. Washington, DC: U.S. Department of Justice, Office of Justice Programs. www.ojp.usdoj.gov/bjs/abstract/rsarp00

Bureau of Justice Statistics. 2008. *Sourcebook of Criminal Justice Statistics.* Washington, DC: U.S. Department of Justice, Bureau of Justice Statistics.

Bureau of Labor Statistics. 2006. *Women in the Labor Force: A Databook.* Washington DC. www.bls.gov/wlf-databook2005

Burge, Stephanie Woodham. 2007. "Academic majors." In Barbara J. Bank (ed.), *Gender and Education: Volume I.* (pp. 381–87). Westport, CT: Praeger.

Burgoon, Judee K., and Norah E. Dunbar. 2006. "Nonverbal expressions of dominance and power in human relationships." In Valerie Manusov and Miles L. Patterson (eds.), *The Sage Handbook of Nonverbal Communication.* (pp. 279–97). Thousand Oaks, CA: Sage.

Burleson, Brant R., and Adrianne W. Kunkel. 2006. "Revisiting the different cultures thesis: An assessment of sex differences and similarities in supportive communication." In Kathryn Dindia and Daniel J. Canary (eds.), *Sex Differences and Similarities in Communication*. (pp. 137–60). Mahwah, NJ: Lawrence Erlbaum.

Burnett, Paul C. 2002. "Teacher praise and feedback and student's perceptions of the classroom environment." *Educational Psychology* 22(1):1–16.

Burwell, Bryan. 2009. "Jack Clark is willing to take on the cheats." *St. Louis Post- Dispatch* May 12:B1,5.

Bussey, Kay, and Albert Bandura. 1999. "Social cognitive theory of gender development and differentiation." *Psychological Review* 106(4):676–713.

Buunk, Bram P., and Pieternel Dijkstra. 2004. "Gender differences in rival characteristics that evoke jealousy in response to emotional versus sexual infidelity." *Personal Relationships* 11:395–408.

Buzawa, Eve. 2007. "Victims of domestic violence." In Robert C. Davis, Arthur J. Lurigio, and Susan Herman (eds.), *Victims of Crime*. (pp. 55–74). Thousand Oaks, CA: Sage.

Buzawa, Eve S., and Carl G. Buzawa. 2003. *Domestic Violence: The Criminal Justice Response*. Thousand Oaks, CA: Sage.

Byron, Kristin. 2007. "Male and female managers' ability to 'read' emotions: Relationships with supervisor's performance ratings and subordinates' satisfaction ratings." *Journal of Occupational and Organizational Psychology* 80:713–33.

Cagatay, Nilufer. 2001. *Gender, Poverty and Trade*. United Nations Development Program. New York: United Nations. www.undp.org/rbap/Trade/Gender

Callister, Lynn Clark, and Ana Birkhead. 2008. "Mexican immigrant childbearing women: Social support and perinatal outcomes." In D. Russell Crane and Tim B. Heaton (eds.), *Handbook of Families and Poverty*. (pp. 181–197). Thousand Oaks, CA: Sage.

Calmes, Jackie. 2008. "Palin gets women's attention, not necessarily their support." *New York Times* August 31:1,10.

Campbell, Anne, Louisa Shirley, and Julia Candy. 2004. "A longitudinal study of gender-related cognition and behaviour." *Developmental Science* 7(1):1–9.

Campbell, Patricia B., and Jo Sanders. 2002. "Challenging the system: Assumptions and data behind the push for single-sex schooling." In Amanda Datnow and Lea Hubbard (eds.), *Gender in Policy and Practice: Perspectives on Single-Sex and Coeducational Schooling*. New York: Routledge/Falmer.

Canary, Daniel J., and Marianne Dainton (eds.). 2003. *Maintaining Relationships Through Communication: Relational, Contextual and Cultural Variations*. Mahwah, NJ: Lawrence Erlbaum.

Canary, Daniel L., and Jodi Wahba. 2006. "Do women work harder than men at maintaining relationships?" In Kathryn Dindia and Daniel J. Canary (eds.), *Sex Differences and Similarities in Communication*. (pp. 359–78). Mahwah, NJ: Lawrence Erlbaum.

Canedy, Dana. 2001. "Troubling label for Hispanics: 'Girls most likely to drop out.' " *New York Times* March 25:1, 20.

Cantor, Joanne L., L. Rowell Huesmann, Jo Groebel, Neil M. Malamuth, Emily A. Impett, Edward Donnerstein, Stacy Smith, and Brad J. Bushman. 2001. "Some hazards of television viewing: Fears, aggression and sexual attitudes." In Dorothy G. Singer and Jerome L. Singer (eds.), *Handbook of Children and the Media*. (pp. 207–307). Thousand Oaks, CA: Sage.

Cancian, Francesca. 2003. "The feminization of love." In Michael S. Kimmel (ed.), *The Gendered Society Reader*. New York: Oxford University.

Cannold, Leslie. 2000. *The Abortion Myth: Feminism, Morality, and the Hard Choices Women Make*. Hanover, NH: Wesleyan University.

Caplan, Leslie J., and Carmi Schooler. 2006. "Household work complexity, intellectual functioning, and self-esteem in men and women." *Journal of Marriage and the Family* 68:883–900.

Caputo, Marc. 2008. "Voting falls along gender lines." *Miami Herald* March 20.

Carey, Philip. 2001. "One role model for all: The biblical meaning of submission." In Rita Halteman and Kari Finger Sandhaas (eds.), *The Wisdom of Daughters; Two Decades of the Voice of Christian Feminism*. Philadelphia: Innisfree Press.

Carlson, Douglas W. 1990. "Discovering their heritage: Women and the American past." In June Steffensen Hagen (ed.), *Gender Matters: Women's Studies in the Christian Community*. Grand Rapids, MI: Zondervan.

Caron, Simone M. 2008. *Who Chooses? American Reproductive History Since 1830*. Gainesville, FL: University of Florida.

Carpenter, Laura M., Constance A. Nathanson, and Young J. Kim. 2009. "Physical women, emotional men: Gender and sexual satisfaction in midlife." *Archives of Sexual Behavior* 38(1):87–107.

Carpenter, Siri. 2001. "Does estrogen protect memory?" *Monitor on Psychology* 32(1): January. American Psychological Association. www.apa.org/monitor/jan01/estrogen/html

Carr, Deborah. 2001. "Widowhood: Research dispels some common myths." Population Association of America. http://www.umich.edu/~newsinfo/Releases/2001/Mar01

Carrington, Christopher. 1999. *No Place Like Home: Relationships and Family Life Among Lesbians and Gay Men*. Chicago: University of Chicago.

Carroll, Susan J. 2003. *Are U.S. Women State Legislators Accountable to Women? The Complementary Roles of Feminist Identity and Women's Organizations*. Winnipeg, Canada: Gender and Social Capital Conference, May.

Carroll, Susan J. 2004. "Women in state government: Historical overview and current trends." Center for American Women and Politics. From *Book of the States, 2004.* Lexington, KY: Council of State Governments. www.cawp.rutgers.edu/Research/Reports/BookofStates

Cartier, Carolyn L. 2001. *Globalizing South China.* Oxford, UK: Blackwell.

Casey, Beth M., Nicole Andrews, Holly Schindler, and Joanne E. Kersh. 2008. "The development of spatial skills through interventions involving block building activities." *Cognition and Instruction,* 26(3):269–309.

Caspi, Avner, Eran Chajut, and Kelly Saporta. 2008. "Participation in class and online discussions: Gender differences." *Computers and Education* 50(3):718–24.

Castello, Jennifer, Christina Coomer, and Jamie Stillwell, and Kelly Leach Care. 2006. "The attribution of responsibility in acquaintance rape involving ecstasy." *North American Journal of Psychology* 8(3):411–19.

Catalyst. 2005. "Women 'take care,' men 'take charge': Stereotyping of U.S. business leaders exposed." October. www.catalyst.org/publication/94

Cauley, Jane A. et al. 2003. "Effects of estrogen plus progestin on risk of fracture and bone mineral density." *Journal of the American Medical Association* 290(13):1729–38.

CAWP. 2009a. "Women in elective office 2009." *Fact Sheet. Center for American Women and Politics.* www.cawp.rutgers.edu

———. 2009b. "Women of color in elective office 2009: Congress, statewide, state legislature." *Fact Sheet: Center for American Women and Politics.* www.cawp.rutgers.edu

Ceci, Stephen J., and Wendy M. Williams. 2007. "Are we moving closer and closer apart?" In Stephen Ceci and Wendy Williams (eds.), *Why Aren't More Women in Science? Top Researchers Debate the Evidence.* (pp. 213–35). Washington, DC: American Psychological Association.

Center for Women's Business Research. 2008. "New study shows women own 20% of businesses with revenues exceeding $1 million." December 3. www.women'sbusinessresearchcenter.org

Centers for Disease Control. 2008a. "Subpopulation estimates from the HIV incidence surveillance system – United Sates, 2006." *Morbidity and Mortality Weekly Report (MMWR)* October 3. www.cdc.gov/mmwr

———. 2008b. "HIV prevalence estimates – United States, 2006." *Morbidity and Mortality Weekly Report (MMWR)* September 12. www.cdc.gov/mmwr

———. 2009. "QuickStats: Death rates for human immunodeficiency virus (HIV) disease among women, by race and age group – United States, 1987–2005." *Morbidity and Mortality Weekly Report (MMWR)* March 27. www.cdc.gov/mmwr

Chafetz, Janet Saltzman. 1988. *Feminist sociology: An Overview of Contemporary Theories.* Itasca, IL: F. E. Peacock.

Chang, Chingching, and Jacqueline C. Bush Hitchon. 2004. "When does gender count? Further insights into gender schematic processing of female candidates' political advertisements." *Sex Roles* 51(3/4):197–208.

Chao, Y. May, Emily M. Pisetsky et al. 2008. "Ethnic differences in weight control practices among U.S. adolescents from 1995 to 2005." *International Journal of Eating Disorders* 41(2):124–33.

Chapman, David, Laura Dales, and Vera Mackie. 2008. "Minority women will change the world! Perspectives on multiple discrimination in Japan." *Women's Studies International Forum* 31(3):192–99.

Chapman, James. 2000. *License to Thrill: A Cultural History of James Bond Films.* New York: Columbia University.

Chapple, Constance L., and Katherine A. Johnson. 2007. "Gender differences in impulsivity." *Youth Violence and Juvenile Justice* 5(3):221–34.

Chaucer, L.S. 1998. *Reconcilable Differences: Confronting Beauty, Pornography and the Future of Feminism.* Berkeley: University of California.

Chen, Grace A. 2009. "Managing multiple social identities." In Nita Tewari and Alvin N. Alvarez (eds.), *Asian American Psychology: Current Perspectives.* (pp. 173–92). New York: Psychology Press.

Chen, Min. 2004. "Japanese management style." From *Asian Management Systems: Chinese, Japanese, and Korean Styles of Business.* (pp. 151–77). London: Thompson Learning.

Cherney, Isabelle, and Kamala London. 2006. "Gender-linked differences in the toys, television shows, computer gains, and outdoor activities of 5-to-13-year-old children." *Sex Roles* 54(9/10):717–26.

Cherney, Isabelle. 2005. "Children's and adults' recall of sex-stereotyped toy pictures: Effects of presentation and memory task." *Infant and Child Development* 14:11–27.

Cheshire, Tamara. 2001. "Cultural transmission in urban American Indian families." *American Behavioral Scientist* 44(9):1528–35.

Chesler, Ellen. 2001. "New options, new politics." *American Prospect* Fall:A12–A14.

Chesney-Lind, Meda. 2004. *The Female Offender: Girls, Women and Crime,* Thousand Oaks, CA: Sage.

Chick, Kay A., Rose Ann Heilman-Houser, and Maxwell W. Hunter. 2002. "The impact of child care on gender role development and gender stereotypes." *Early Childhood Education Journal* 29(3):149–54.

Chin, Christina, Meera E. Deo et. al. 2006. *Asian Americans in Prime Time: Setting the Stage.* Washington, DC: Asian American Justice Center.

Chodorow, Nancy. 1978. *The Reproduction of Mothering: Psychoanalysis and the Sociology of Gender.* Berkeley: University of California.

———. 1993. "Family structure and feminine personality." In Stevi Jackson et al. (eds.), *Women's Studies Essential Readings.* New York: New York University.

———. 2001. "The sexual sociology of adult life." In Roberta Satow (ed.), *Gender and Social Life.* (pp. 4–25). Needham Heights, MA: Allyn & Bacon.

Chozick, Amy. 2008. "Palin pick fails to charm Clinton backers." *Wall Street Journal* September 9:A11.

———. 2009. "A macho man's quiet heroine." *Wall Street Journal* November 13:W2.

Christ, Carol P. 1987. *Laughter of Aphrodite: Reflections on a Journey to the Goddess.* San Francisco: Harper & Row.

———. 2003b. "Why women need the goddess: Phenomenological, psychological, and political reflections." In Philip E. Divine and Celia Wolf-Devine (eds.), *Sex and Gender: A Spectrum of Views.* (pp. 358–62). Belmont, CA: Wadsworth/Thomson.

Chrouser Ahrens, Christina J., and Carol D. Ryff. 2006. "Multiple roles and well-being: Sociodemographic and psychological moderators" *Sex Roles* 55(11/12):801–15.

Churchill, Ward. 2007. "Crimes against humanity." In Margaret L. Anderson and Patricia Hill Collins (eds.), *Race, Class, and Gender: An Anthology.* (pp. 376–83). Belmont, CA: Thompson Wadsworth.

Ciabattari, Teresa. 2002. "Are cohabiters sharing the housework? Mixed evidence from the NSFH." Paper at the Southern Sociological Society, New Orleans, LA. April.

Cieply, Michael. 2009. "What's the skinny on the heftier stars?" *New York Times* April 18:C1.

Clark, Catherine L., Phillip R. Shaver, and Matthew F. Abrahams. 1999. "Strategic behaviors in romantic relationship initiation." *Personality and Social Psychology Bulletin* 25(6):707–20.

Clarke, Suzanne. 2007. *Single-Sex Schools and Classrooms.* Alexandria, VA: Educational Research Service.

Clarkwest, Andrew. 2007. *School Characteristics, Family Background, and Variation in the Gender Gaps on College Graduation among African Americans.* University of Michigan: Institute for Social Research March 1.

Clason, Marmy A. 2006. "Feminism, generic 'he,' and the TNV Bible translation debate." *Critical Discourse Studies* 3(1):23–35.

Clason, Marmy. 2000. "The social construction of sexual harassment." *Women & Language* 23(2):56.

Claussen, Dane S. 2000. " 'So far, news coverage of Promise Keepers has been more like advertising': The strange case of Christian men and the print mass media." In Dane S. Claussen (ed.), *The Promise Keepers: Essays on Masculinity and Christianity.* (pp. 281–307). Jefferson, NC: McFarland.

Clearfield, Melissa W., and Naree M. Nelson. 2006. "Sex differences in mothers' speech and play behavior with 6-, 9-, and 14-month-old infants." *Sex Roles* 54(1/2):127.

Cleary, Thomas, and Sartaz Aziz. 2000. *Twilight Goddess: Spiritual Feminism and Feminine Spirituality.* Boston: Shambhala.

Clements, Barbara Evans, Rebecca Friedman, and Dan Healey (eds.). 2002. *Russian Masculinities in History and Culture.* Houndmills, Hampshire, UK: Palgrave.

Cleveland, Darrell (ed.). 2004. *A Long Way to Go: Conversations about Race by African American Faculty and Graduate Students.* New York: P. Lang.

Clift, Eleanor, and Tom Brazaitis. 2003. *Madame President: Women Blazing the Leadership Trail.* New York: Routledge.

Clift, Eleanor. 2003. *Founding Sisters and the Nineteenth Amendment.* Boston: Wiley.

Cloninger, C. Robert. 2004. *Feeling Good: The Science of Well-Being.* Oxford, UK: Oxford University.

Clum, John M. 2002. *He's all Man: Learning Masculinity, Gayness and Love from American Movies.* New York: Palgrave.

CNN. 2009. "Clinic worker chased off suspect before doctor's slaying." June 1. www.cnn.com/2009/CRIME/06/01

Coates, Jennifer. 2003. *Men Talk: Stories in the Making of Masculinities.* Malden, MA: Blackwell.

———. 2007. "Men's language." In Peter Stockwell (ed.), *Sociolinguistics: A Resource Book for Students.* (pp. 176–83). London: Routledge.

Coates, Rodney D. 2008. "Preserving the illusion of inclusion or investigating a matrix of identity." *Race, Gender and Class* 15(3–4):110–16.

Cobb, Nathan P., Jeffry H. Larson, and Wendy L. Watson. 2003. "The development of the attitudes about romance and mate selection scale." *Family Relations: Interdisciplinary Journal of Applied Family Studies* 52(3):222–31.

Cochran, Clarke E. 2008. *The Catholic Vote: A Guide for the Perplexed.* Markyknoll, NY: Orbis.

Cofer, Judith Ortiz. 1995. "The myth of the Latin woman: I just met a girl named Maria." In Paula S. Rothenberg (ed.), *Race, Class, and Gender in the United States: An Integrated Study.* New York: St. Martin's.

Cohen, Philip N. 2007. "Working for women? Female managers and the gender wage gap." *American Sociological Review* 72(5):681–704.

Cohler, Bertram J., and Galatzer-Levy, Robert M. 2000. *The Course of Gay and Lesbian Lives: Social and Psychological Perspectives.* Chicago: University of Chicago.

Cohn, Amy, and Amos Zeichner. 2006. "Effects of masculine identity and gender role stress on aggression in men." *Psychology of Men and Masculinity* 7(4):179–90.

Colapinto, John. 2000. *As Nature Made Him: The Boy Who was Raised as a Girl.* New York: HarperCollins.

Cole, Elizabeth R., Toby Epstein Jayaratne, Laura A. Cecchi, Merle Feldbaum, and Elizabeth M. Petty. 2007. "Vive la difference? Genetic explanations for perceived gender difference in nurturance." *Sex Roles* 57:211–22.

Cole, J.B., and B. Guy-Shetfall. 2003. *Gender Talk: The Struggle for Women's Equality in African American Communities.* New York: Ballantine.

Cole, Marcy Leslie. 2000. "The experience of never-married women in their thirties who desire marriage and children." *Dissertation Abstracts International, A: The Humanities and Social Sciences* 60(9):3526-A.

Coleman, James William. 2001. *The New Buddhism: The Western Transformation of an Ancient Tradition.* Oxford, NY: Oxford University.

Coles, Roberta L. 2006. *Race and Family: A Structural Approach.* Thousand Oaks, CA: Sage.

College Board. 2007. *Total Group Profile Report: 2007 College-Bound Seniors.* www.collegeboard.com

Colley, Ann, Todd Zarie et al. 2004. "Style and content in e-mails and letters to male and female friends." *Journal of Language and Social Psychology* 23(3):369–78.

Colley, Ann. 2008. "Young people's musical tastes: Relationship with gender and gender-related traits." *Journal of Applied Social Psychology* 38(8):2039–55.

Collins, Patricia Hill. 2009. "Bloodmothers and othermothers, and women-centered networks." In Estelle Disch (ed.), *Reconstructing Gender: A Multicultural Anthology.* (pp. 318–24). Boston: McGraw-Hill.

———. 2004. *Black Sexual Politics: African Americans, Gender, and the New Racism.* New York: Routledge.

Collins, Randall. 1975. *Conflict Sociology.* New York: Academic Press.

Collins, Randall. 1979. *The Credential Society: An Historical Sociology of Education and Stratification.* New York: Academic Press.

Coltrane, Scott, and Michele Adams. 2008. *Gender and Families.* Lanham, MD: Rowman and Littlefield.

Coltrane, Scott, Ross D. Parke et al. 2008. "Mexican American families and poverty." In D. Russell Crane and Tim B. Heaton (eds.), *Handbook of Families and Poverty.* (pp. 161–180). Thousand Oaks, CA: Sage.

Colwell, Malinda J., Gregory S. Pettit, Darrell Meece, John E. Bates, and Kenneth A. Dodge. 2001. "Cumulative risk and continuity in nonparental care from infancy to early adolescence." *Merrill-Palmer Quarterly* 47(2):207–34.

Comerford, Lynn. 2006. "Power and resistance in U.S. child custody mediation." *Atlantic Journal of Communications* 14(3):173–90.

Compensation. 2008. "Why women leave and what it means to retention initiatives." *Compensation and Benefits for Law Offices* 8(10):5–7.

Compton, Michele. 2007. "The gender pay gap." *Women in Business* 59(6):32–34.

Comstock, George. 2008. "A sociological perspective on television violence and aggression." *American Behavioral Scientist* 51(8):1184–211.

Comstock, George, and Erica Scharrer. 2007. *Media and the American Child.* Burlington, MA: Elsevier.

Connolly, Colleen M., and Mary Kay Sicola. 2006. "Listening to lesbian couples: Communication competence in long-term relationships." In Jerry J. Bigner (ed.), *An Introduction to GLBT Family Studies.* New York: Haworth.

Connor, Daniel F. 2002. *Aggression and Antisocial Behavior in Children and Adolescents: Research and Treatment.* New York: Guilford.

Conrad, Kate, Travis Dixon, and Yuanyuan Zhang. 2009. "Controversial rap these, gender portrayals and skin tone distortion: A content analysis of rap music videos." *Journal of Broadcasting and Electronic Media* 53(1):134–56.

Constantine, Madonna G., Vanessa L. Alleyne, Barbara C. Wallace, and Deidre C. Jackson. 2006. "Africentric cultural values: Their relation to positive mental health in African American adolescent girls." *Journal of Black Psychology* 32(2):141–54.

Constantine-Simms, Delroy. 2001. *The Greatest Taboo: Homosexuality in Black Communities.* Los Angeles: Alyson.

Conze, Susanne. 2001. "Women's work and emancipation in the Soviet Union, 1941–50." In Melani Ilic (ed.), *Women in the Stalin Era.* (pp. 216–35). Houndmills, Hampshire, UK: Palgrave.

Cook, Carolyn. 2009. "ERA would end women's second-class citizenship." *The Philadelphia Inquirer* April 12. www.truthout.org/041309WA

Cooke, Miriam. 2001. *Women Claim Islam: Creating Islamic Feminism through Literature.* New York: Routledge.

Coolidge, Shelley Donald. 1997. "Honey, will I see you on Labor Day?" *Christian Science Monitor* August 26. http://csmonitor.com/durable/1998/08/26/econ/econ.l.html

Coonan, Clifford. 2008. "900 party cadres pay for breaking one-baby rule." *Irish Times* January 8.

Coontz, Stephanie. 1997. *The Way We Really Are: Coming to Terms with America's Changing Families.* New York: Basic Books.

———. 2000. *The Way We Never Were: American Families and the Nostalgia Trap.* New York: BasicBooks.

———. 2005. *Marriage, A History: From Obedience to Intimacy or How Love Conquered Marriage.* New York: Viking.

———. 2008. "Mind the marriage gap." *Cato Unbound* January 23. www.cato-unbound.org/2008/01/23

Cooper, J. 2006. "The digital divide: The special case of gender." *Journal of Computer Assisted Learning* 22(5):320–34.

Cooper, Kenneth J. 2006. "Scholars debate effectiveness of single-sex classes." *Diverse Issues in Higher Education.* November 30. 23(21).

Cooper, Marianne. 2004. "Being the 'go-to guy': Fatherhood, masculinity, and the organization of work in Silicon Valley." In Michael S. Kimmel and Michael A. Messner (eds.), *Men's Lives.* (pp. 268–88). Boston: Allyn & Bacon.

Corey, Shana. 2003. *Players in Pigtails.* New York: Scholastic.

Corliss, Richard. 2003. "Movies have the same old reliable guys and a crop of brand-new gals. It must be summer." *Time* July 14:57–58, 61.

Correll, Shelley J. 2001. "Gender and the career choice process: The role of biased self-assessments." *American Journal of Sociology* 106(6):1691–730.

Countdown 2005. 1997. "USAID takes initiative." *Newsletter of the Microcredit Summit Campaign* 1(2):10–11.

Couric, Katie. 2008. "One-on-one with Sarah Palin." *CBS Evening News.* September 24. www.cbsnews.com/stories/2008/09/24/eveningnews

Courtney, Alice E., and Sarah Wernick Lockeretz. 1971. "A woman's place: An analysis of the roles portrayed by women in magazine advertisements." *Journal of Marketing Research* 8:92.

Courtney, Alice E., and Thomas W. Whipple. 1983. *Sex Stereotyping in Advertising*. Lexington, MA: Lexington Books.

Cowan, J.L. 2002. "Inverse discrimination." In Stephen Cahn (ed.), *The Affirmative Action Debate*. (pp. 5–7). London: Routledge.

Cowan, Kristina. 2007. "Taking time off: Can it hurt your market values?" *Pay Scale*. http://blogs.payscale.com/content/2007/05

Cowley, Geoffrey, and Karen Springen. 2002. "The end of the age of estrogen?" *Newsweek* June 22:38–41.

Coyle, Grace. 1929. "Women in the clerical occupations." *Annals of the American Academy of Political and Social Science* 143(May):180, 87.

CPST. 2007. "Despite progress in degree attainment, women chemists gain little ground in academia." *CPST Comments* January-February. www.cpst.org

CPST. 2007. American Chemical Society. 2007. "Despite progress in degree attainment, women chemists gain little ground in academia." *CPST Comments* (January-February). Washington, DC: Commission on Professionals in Science and Technology. www.cpst.org

Craig, Lyn. 2006. "Does father care mean fathers share? A comparison of how mothers and fathers in intact families spend time with children." *Gender & Society* 20(2):259–81.

Craig, Steve. 2003. "Madison Avenue versus the feminine mystique: The advertising industry's response to the women's movement." In Sherrie A. Inness (ed.), *Disco Divas: Women and Popular Culture in the 1970s*. (pp. 24–38). Philadelphia: University of Pennsylvania.

Cramer, Ervin, Jeffrey T. Schaefer, and Suzanne Reid. 2003. "Identifying the ideal mate: More evidence for male-female convergence." In Nathaniel J. Pallone (ed.) *Love, Romance, Sexual Interaction: Research Perspectives from Current Psychology*. (pp. 61–74). New Brunswick, NJ: Transaction.

Crick, Nicki R. et al. 2009. "Aggression and peer relationships in school-age children: Relational and physical aggression in group and dyadic contexts." In Kenneth H. Rubin, William M. Bukowski, and Brett Laursen (eds.), *Handbook of Peer Interactions, Relationships, and Groups*. New York: Guilford.

Crockett, Lisa J., Jill Brown, Stephen T. Russell, and Yuh-Ling Shen. 2007. "The meaning of good parent-child relationships for Mexican-American adolescents." *Journal of Research on Adolescence* 17(4):639–68.

Crosnoe, Robert, Catherine Riegle-Crumb, Sam Field, Kenneth Frank, and Chandra Muller. 2008. "Peer group contexts of girls' and boys' academic experiences." *Child Development* 79(1):139–55.

Crosnoe, Robert, Kristan G. Erickson, and Sanford M. Dornbusch. 2000. "Protective functions of family relationships and school factors on the deviant behavior of adolescent boys and girls: Reducing the impact of risky relationships." *Youth and Society* 33(4):515–44.

Crowley, Donna Annyce. 2001. "Gender-linked differences in the use of references to location in written language: A gender schema approach." *Dissertation Abstracts International: Section B: Sciences and Engineering* 62(2-B):1107.

Crowley, Jocelyn Elise. 2008. *Defiant Dads: Fathers' Rights Activists in America*. Ithaca, NY: Cornell University.

Crowley, Kathleen. 2006. "Where the twain meets: Similarities in Communication." *PsycCritiques* 51(34): Review of Kathryn Dindia and Daniel J. Canary (eds.). 2006. *Sex Differences and Similarities in Communication* Mahwah, NJ: Lawrence Erlbaum..

Cullen, Lisa Takeucki. 2003. "I want your job, lady!" *Time* May 12:52–56.

Cunningham, Mick. 2007. "Influences of women's employment on the gendered division of household labor over the life course: Evidence from a 31 year panel study." *Journal of Family Issues* 28(3):422–44.

Curran, Laura, and Laura S. Abrams. 2000. "Making men into dads: Fatherhood, the state, and welfare reform. *Gender & Society* 14(5):662–78.

Curry, Timothy Jon. 2004. "Fraternal bonding in the locker room: A profeminist analysis of talk about competition and women." In Michael S. Kimmel and Michael A. Messner (eds.), *Men's Lives*. (pp. 204–17). Boston: Allyn & Bacon.

Curzan, Anne. 2003. *Gender Shifts in the History of English*. Cambridge, UK: Cambridge University.

Cussins, Charis M. Thompson. 2000. "Primate suspect: Some varieties of science studies." In Shirley C. Strum and Linda M. Fedigan (eds.), *Primate Encounters: Models of Science, Gender and Society*. (pp. 329–57). Chicago: University of Chicago.

D'Souza, Neila, and Ramani Natarajan. 1986. "Women in India: The reality." In Lynn B. Iglitzin and Ruth Ross (eds.), *Women in the World, 1975–1985: The Women's Decade*. Santa Barbara, CA: ABC-Clio.

Daczo, Zsuzsa, and Suzanne Bianchi. 2003. *Weekly time use in middle class, two parent families with children*. Atlanta: American Sociological Association.

Dagg, Anne Innis. 2005. *Love of Shopping is Not a Gene: Problems with Darwinian Psychology*. Montreal: Black Rose.

Dahan-Kalev, Henriette. 2003. "Mizrahi feminism: The unheard voice." In Kalpana Mira and S. Rich (eds.), *Jewish Feminism in Israel: Some Contemporary Perspectives*. (pp. 96–112). Hanover, NH: University Press of New England.

Dahl, Edgar, Ruchi S. Gupta et al. 2006. "Preconception sex selection demand and preferences in the United States." *Fertility and Sterility* 85(2):468–73.

Dahl, Gordon B., and Enrico Moretti. 2008. "The demand for sons." *Review of Economic Studies* 75(4):1085–120.

Dahrendorf, Ralf. 1959. *Class and Class Conflict in Industrial Society*. Stanford, CA: Stanford University.

Dale, Kathryn, and Judith L. Alpert. 2007. "Hiding behind the cloth: Child sexual abuse and the Catholic church." *Journal of Child Sexual Abuse* 16(3):59–74.

Dalton, Claire and Elizabeth M. Schneider. 2000. *Battered Women and the Law.* New York: Foundation Press.

Daly, Frederica Y. 1994. "Perspectives of Native American women on race and gender." In Ethel Tobach and Betty Rosoff (eds.), *Challenging Racism and Sexism: Alternatives to Genetic Explanations.* New York: The Feminist Press.

Daly, Mary. 1991. "I thank thee, Lord, that thou has not created me a woman." In Evelyn Ashton-Jones and Gary Olson (eds.), *The Gender Reader.* Boston: Allyn & Bacon.

Daniels, Katherine C., Kathryn D. Rettig, and Robert delMas. 2006. "Alternative formulas for distributing parental income at divorce." *Journal of Family and Economic Issues* 27(1):4–26.

Dar-Nimrod and Steven J. Heine. 2007. *Science.* October 20. 314(4798):435.

Dargis, Manohla. 2009. "Action!" *New York Times* Arts & Leisure June 21:AR1.

Daswani, Kavita. 1999. "Second wives club." *South China Morning Post Magazine,* November 28:7–14.

Datnow, Amanda and Hubbard, Lea. 2005. "School choice in the foreground, gender equity in the background." In Janet Petrovich and Amy Stuart Wells (eds.), *Education Reform Since the 1980s.* (pp. 195–218). New York: Teachers College Press.

Daugstad, Gunnlaug, and Toril Sandes. 2008. "Gender and migration: Similarities and disparities among women and men in the immigrant population." Oslo: Statistics Norway. www.ssb.no/english

David, Grainger. 2003. "Alpha romeos." *Fortune* August 11:48, 50.

Davies, Sharyn Graham. 2007. *Challenging Gender Norms: Five Genders among the Bugis in Indonesia.* Belmont, CA: Thomson Wadsworth.

Davis, Elizabeth Gould. 1971. *The First Sex.* New York: Penguin.

Davis, Michelle. 2006. "New Title IX amendments boost single-sex schooling." *Education Week.* November 1.

Davis, Shannon N., and Lisa Pearce. 2007. "Adolescents' work-family gender ideologies and educational expectations." *Sociological Perspectives* 50(2):249–71.

Davis, Shannon N., Theodore N. Greenstein, and Jennifer P. Gerteisen Marks. 2007. "Effects of union type on division of household labor: Do cohabiting men really perform more housework?" *Journal of Family Issues* 28(9):1246–272.

Davison, Kevin G. 2007. *Negotiating masculinities and Bodies in School: The Implications of Gender Theory for the Education of Boys.* Lewiston: Edwin Mellen.

Davidson, Samuel Marc. 2006. "Exploring sociocultural borderlands: Journeying, navigating, and embodying queer identity." *The Journal of Men's Studies* 14(1):13–26.

Dawson, Jane. 2002. "Egalitarian responses in post-communist Russia." In Craig N. Murphy (ed.), *Egalitarian Politics in the Age of Globalization.* (pp. 96–123). Houndmills, Hampshire, UK: Palgrave.

De Boer, Esther A. 2004. *The Gospel of Mary: Beyond a Gnostic and a Biblical Mary Magdalene.* London: T &T Clark International.

De Brauw, Alan, Jikun Huang, and Scott Rozelle. 2002. "The evolution of China's rural labor markets during the reforms." *Journal of Comparative Economics* 30(2):329–53.

De Hart, Jane Sherron, and Linda K. Kerber. 2003. "Introduction: Gender and the new women's history." In Linda K. Kerber and Jane Sherron De Hart (eds.), *Women's America: Refocusing the Past.* New York: Oxford University.

De Luce, Dan. 2009. "US army base shuts down after rise in suicides." *Agency France-Presse* May 29. www.truthout.org/052909A

De Marneffe, Daphne. 2004. *Maternal Desire: On Children, Love, and the Inner Life.* New York: Little, Brown.

De St. Croix, Geoffrey. 1993. "The class struggle in the ancient Greek world." In Stevi Jackson et al. (eds.), *Women's Studies Essential Readings.* New York: New York University.

De Waal, Frans B. M, and Peter L. Tyack (eds.). 2003. *Animal Social Complexity: Intelligence, Culture, and Individualized Societies.* Cambridge, MA: Harvard University.

DeBeauvoir, Simone. 1953. *The Second Sex.* H. M. Parshey (trans.). New York: Knopf.

Deckard, Barbara Sinclair. 1983. *The Women's Movement: Political, Socioeconomic and Psychological Issues.* New York: Harper & Row.

Deen, Edith. 1978. *Wisdom from Women in the Bible.* San Francisco: Harper & Row.

Della Giusta, Marina, Maria Laura Di Tommaso, and Steinar Strom. 2008. *Sex Markets: A Denied Industry.* London: Routledge.

Dement'eva, I.F. 2001. "Negative factors of childrearing in a single-parent family." *Sotsiologicheskie Issledovaniya* (abstract) 27(11):108–13.

Demos, John Putnam. 1996. "The poor and powerless witch." In Mary Beth Norton and Ruth M. Alexander (eds.), *Major Problems in American Women's History.* Lexington, MA: D. C. Heath.

Dempsey, Kenneth C. 2001. "Feelings about housework: Understanding gender differences." *Australian Journal of Marriage and the Family* 7(2):141–59.

Denizet-Lewis, Benoit. 2008. "Young gay rites: Why would gay men in their 20s rush to the altar?" *New York Times Magazine* April 27:28–35,58–62.

Denner, Jill, and Biana L. Guzman (eds.). 2006. *Latina Girls: Voices of Adolescent Strength in the United States.* New York: New York University.

Denzin, Norman. 1993. "Sexuality and gender: An interactionist/poststructural reading." In Paula England (ed.), *Theory on Gender/Feminism on Theory.* New York: Aldine De Gruyter.

DePaulo, Bella. 2006. *Singled Out: How Singles are Stereotyped, Stigmatized, and Ignored, and Still Live Happily Ever After.* New York: St. Martin's.

DePaulo, Bella, and Kay Trimberger. 2008. "Single women." *Fact Sheet. Sociologists for Women in Society Newsletter.* Winter:17–20.

Dervarics, Charles. 2003. "Educators, activists criticize Bush's position on affirmative action." *Black Issues in Higher Education* February 13.

Desai, Manisha. 2001. "India: Women's movement from nationalism to sustainable development." In Ly Walter (ed.), *Women's Rights: A Global View.* (pp. 99–112). Westport, CT: Greenwood.

Desmond, Roger, and Rod Carveth. 2007. "The effects of advertising on children and adolescents." In Raymond W. Preiss et al. (eds.), *Mass Media Effects Research: Advances through Meta-Analysis.* Mahwah, NJ: Lawrence Erlbaum.

Despeux, Catherine, and Livia Kohn. 2003. *Women in Daoism.* Cambridge, MA: Three Pines.

Deutsch, Francine. 2004. "Strategies men use to resist." In Michael S. Kimmel and Michael A. Messner (eds.), *Men's Lives.* (pp. 469–74). Boston: Allyn & Bacon.

Deutsch, Francine M. 2007. "Undoing gender." *Gender & Society* 21(1):106–27.

Deutscher, Irwin and Linda Lindsey. 2005. *Preventing Ethnic Conflict: Successful Cross-National Social Strategies.* Lanham, MD: Rowman & Littlefield.

Devens, Carol. 1996. "Resistance to Christianity by the native women of New France." In Mary Beth Norton and Ruth M. Alexander (eds.), *Major Problems in American Women's History.* Lexington, MA: D.C. Heath.

Dey, Judy Goldberg, and Catherine Hill. 2007. *Behind the Pay Gap.* Washington DC: American Association of University Women Foundation.

Diamond, Diane. 2007. "Military colleges and academies." In Barbara J. Bank (ed.), *Gender and Education; Volume I.* (pp. 193–200). Westport, CT: Praeger.

Diamond, Lisa M. 2004. "Emerging perspectives on distinctions between romantic love and sexual desire." *Current Directions in Psychological Science* 13(3):116–19.

———. 2008. *Sexual Fluidity: Understanding Women's Love and Desire.* Cambridge, MA: Harvard University.

Diamond, Milton. 1982. "Sexual identity, monozygotic twins reared in discordant sex roles and a BBC follow-up." *Archives of Sexual Behavior* 11:181–86.

Diamond, Milton, and H.K. Sigmundson. 1997. "Management of intersexuality: Guidelines for dealing with people with ambiguous genitalia." *Archives of Pediatric and Adolescent Medicine* 151:1046–50.

Diamond-Smith, Nadia, Nancy Luke, and Stephen Garvey. 2008. "Too many girls, too much dowry: Son preference and daughter aversion in rural Tamil Nadu, India." *Culture, Health, and Sexuality* 10(7):697–708.

Diaz, Rafael M., George Ayala, and Edward Bein. 2001. "The impact of homophobia, poverty, and racism on the mental health of gay and bisexual Latino men: Findings from three U.S. cities." *American Journal of Public Health* 91(6):927–32.

Diekman, Amanda B., and Wind Goodfriend. 2006. "Rolling with the changes: A role congruity perspective on gender norms." *Psychology of Women Quarterly* 30:369–83.

Dindia, Kathryn. 2006. "Men are from North Dakota, Women are from South Dakota." In Kathryn Dindia and Daniel J. Canary (eds.), *Sex Differences and Similarities in Communication.* (pp. 2–20). Mahwah, NJ: Lawrence Erlbaum.

Ding, Qu Jian, and Therese Hesketh. 2006. "Family size, fertility preferences, and sex ratio in China in the era of the one child family policy: Results from national family planning and reproductive health survey." *British Medical Journal* 333:371–73.

Ditmore, Melissa Hope. 2006. *Encyclopedia of Prostitution and Sex Work.* Westport, CN: Greenwood.

Dobash, Russell P., R. Emerson Dobash, Margo Wilson, and Martin Daly. 2004. "The myth of sexual symmetry in marital violence." In Michael S. Kimmel (ed.), *The Gendered Society Reader.* Oxford, NY: Oxford University.

Dodge, K.A., J.D. Coie, and D. Lynam. 2006. "Aggression and antisocial behavior in youth." In W. Damon, R.M. Lerner, and N. Eisenberg (eds.), *Handbook of Child Psychology, Volume 3. Social, Emotional and Personality Development.* (pp. 719–88). Hoboken, NJ: Wiley.

DoDoo, F. Nii-Amoo, and Ashley E. Frost. 2008. "Gender in African population research: The fertility/reproduction health examples." *Annual Review of Sociology* 34(1):431–52.

Dombrowski, Daniel A., and Robert Deltete. 2000. *A Brief, Liberal, Catholic Defense of Abortion.* Urbana: University of Illinois.

Doniger, Wendy. 2009. *The Hindus: An Alternative History.* New York: Penguin.

Dorfman, Daba C. 2001. "The impact of mother's work on the life choices and sense of self of the young adult daughter during motherhood." *Dissertation Abstracts International, A: The Humanities and Social Sciences* 62(1):327-A.

Döring, Nicola, and Sandra Poschl. 2006. "Images of men and women in mobile phone advertisements: A content analysis of advertisements for mobile communication systems in selected popular magazines." *Sex Roles* 55:173–85.

Douglas, Susan J, and Meredith W. Michaels. 2009. "The new momism." In Estelle Disch (ed.), *Reconstructing Gender: A Multicultural Anthology.* (pp. 235–47). New York: McGraw-Hill.

Doyle, James A. 1995. *The Male Experience.* Dubuque, IA: Brown & Benchmark.

Dua, Priya. 2008. "The impact of gender characteristics on mentoring in graduate departments of sociology." *American Sociologist* 39(4):307–23.

Dublin, Thomas. 2009. "Women, work, and protest in the early Lowell mills: 'The oppressing hand of avarice would enslave us.' " In Kathryn Kish Sklar and Thomas Dublin (eds.), *Women and Power in American History.* (pp. 60–70). Upper Saddle River, NJ: Prentice Hall.

Duncombe, Jean, Kaeren Harrison, Graham Allan, and Dennis Marsden (eds.). 2004. *State of Affairs: Explorations in Infidelity and Commitment.* Thousand Oaks, CA: Sage.

Duran-Aydintug, Candan, and Kelly A. Causey. 2001. "Child custody determination: Implications for lesbian mothers." In Jennifer M. Lehmann (ed.), *The Gay and Lesbian Marriage and Family Reader: Analyses of Problems and Prospects for the 21st Century.* (pp. 47–64). New York: Gordian Knot.

Dweck, Carol. S. 2007. "Is math a gift? Beliefs that put females at risk." In Stephen Ceci and Wendy Williams (eds.), *Why Aren't More Women in Science? Top Researchers Debate the Evidence.* (pp. 47–56). Washington, DC: American Psychological Association.

Dworkin, Shari L., and Lucia F. O'Sullivan. 2007. "It's less work for us and it shows she has good taste: Masculinity, sexual initiation, and contemporary sexual scripts." In Michael Kimmel (ed.), *The Sexual Self: The Construction of Sexual Scripts.* Nashville, TN: Vanderbilt University.

Dyke, Karen D., and Denise L. Johnson. 2003. "Asian American women and racialized femininities: 'Doing gender' across cultural worlds." *Gender & Society* 17(1):33, 53.

Eagly, Alice H., and Linda L. Carli. 2008. *Through the Labyrinth: The Truth about How Women Become Leaders.* Boston, MA: Harvard Business School.

Eagly, Alice H., and Sabine Sczesny. 2009. "Stereotypes about women, men, and leaders: Have times changed?" In Manuela Barreto, Michelle K. Ryan, and Michael T. Schmitt (eds.), *The Glass Ceiling in the 21st Century: Understanding Barriers to Gender Equity.* (pp. 21–47). Washington DC: American Psychological Association.

Eargle, Lisa A., Ashraf M. Esmail, and Jas M. Sullivan. 2008. "Voting the issues or voting the demographics? The media's construction of political candidates' credibility." *Race, Gender and Class* 15(2/4):8–31.

Eckert, Penelope, and Sally McConnell-Ginet. 2003. *Language and Gender.* Cambridge, UK: Cambridge University.

Economist. 2001. "Third person singular: Finding substitutes for 'he' and 'his.' " April 14:20.

Edin, Kathryn. 2005. *Promises I Can Keep: Why Poor Women Put Motherhood Before Marriage.* Berkeley, CA: University of California.

Edwards, June. 2002. *Women in American Education, 1820–1955: The Female Force and Educational Reform.* Westport, CT: Greenwood.

Edwards, Tamala. 2000. "Flying solo." *Time* August 28:47–53.

EEOC. 2009. "Sexual harassment." The U.S. Equal Employment Opportunity Commission. www. eeoc.gov/types/sexual_harassment

Ehrenreich, Barbara. 1998. "The silenced majority: Why the average working person has disappeared from American media and culture." In Margaret

L. Andersen and Patricia Hill Collins (eds.), *Race, Class and Gender: An Anthology.* (pp. 147–49). Belmont, CA: Wadsworth.

Ehrenreich, Barbara, and Arlie Russell Hochschild (eds.). 2004. *Global Women: Nannies, Maids, and Sex Workers in the New Economy.* New York: Metropolitan/Henry Holt.

Eichstedt, Julie A., Lisa A. Serbin, Diane Poulin-Dubois, and Maya G. Sen. 2002. "Of bears and men: Infants' knowledge of conventional and metaphorical gender stereotypes." *Infant Behavior & Development* 25(3):296–310.

Eisler, Riane Tennenhaus. 1995a. *The Chalice and the Blade: Our History, Our Future.* San Francisco: HarperSanFrancisco.

_____. 1995b. *Sacred Pleasure: Sex, Myth, and the Politics of the Body.* San Francisco: HarperSanFrancisco.

_____. 2007. *The Real Wealth of Nations.* San Francisco: Berrett-Koehler.

Eisler, Riane, and David Loye. 1990. *The Partnership Way.* New York: HarperSanFrancisco.

El Guindi, Fadwa. 1999. *Veil: Modesty, Privacy and Resistance.* Oxford, UK: Berg.

Elgar, K., and A. Chester. 2007. "The mental health implications of maternal employment: Working versus at-home mothering identities." *Australian e-Journal for the Advancement of Mental Health* 6(1):1–9.

Eller, Cynthia. 2000. *The Myth of Matriarchal Prehistory: Why an Invented Past Won't give Women a Future.* Boston: Beacon.

Elleschild, Lyvinia Rogers. 2008. "Why do 'young people' go missing in 'child prostitution' reform?" In Gayle Letherby et al. (eds.), *Sex as Crime.* (pp. 199–219). Cullompton, UK: Willan.

Elliott, Brian. 1994. "Biography, family history and the analysis of social change." In Michael Drake (ed.), *Time, Family and Community: Perspectives on Family and Community History.* Oxford, UK: Open University.

Ellis, E. Earle. 2003. "Dynamic equivalence theory, feminist ideology and three recent Bible translations." *Expository Times* 114(12):7–12.

Ellison, Christopher, and John P. Bartkowski. 2002. "Conservative Protestantism and the division of household labor among married couples." *Journal of Family Issues* 23(8):950–85.

Elliston, Deborah. 1999. "Negotiating transnational sexual economies: Female and same-sex sexuality in 'Tahiti and Her Islands.' " In Evelyn Blackwood and Saskia Wieringa (eds.), *Female Desires: Same-Sex Relations and Transgender Practices across Cultures.* New York: Columbia University.

Ely, Robin J, and Debra Meyerson. 2008. "Unmasking manly men" *Harvard Business Review* July-August:20.

Embrick, David G., Carol S. Walther, and Corrine M. Wickens. 2007. "Working class masculinity: Keeping gay men and lesbians out of the workplace." *Sex Roles* 56:757–66.

Emmers-Sommers, Tara M., Perry Pauley, Alesia Hanzai, and Laura Triplett. 2006. " Love, sex, and violence: Men's and women's film predilections, exposure to sexually violent media, and their relationship to rape myth acceptance." *Sex Roles* 55:311–20.

Endo, Orie, and Janet S. Shibamato Smith. 2004. "Women and words: The status of sexist language in Japan as seen through contemporary definitions and media discourse." In Shigeko Okamato and Janet S. Shibamoto Smith (eds.), *Japanese Language, Gender, and Ideology: Cultural Models and Real People*. (pp. 166–86). Oxford, UK: Oxford University.

Engel, Gina, Kenneth R. Olson, and Carol Patrick. 2002. "The personality of love: Fundamental motives and traits related to components of love." *Personality and Individual Differences* 32(5):839–53.

Engels, Friedrich. 1942 (original 1884). *The Origin of the Family, Private Property, and the State*. New York: International.

England, Paula, Joan A. Hermson, and David A. Cotter. 2000. "The devaluation of women's work: A comment on Tam." *American Journal of Sociology* 105(6):1741–51.

England, Paula, and Su Li. 2006. "Desegregation stalled: The changing gender composition of college majors, 1971–2002." *Gender & Society* 20(50):657–77.

Erickson, Rebecca J. 2005. "Why emotion work matters: Sex, gender, and the division of household labor." *Journal of Marriage and the Family* 67(May):337–51.

Ericson, Gwen. 2009. "Estrogen can benefit women with metastatic breast cancer." *The Record* January 15. Washington University in St. Louis.

Esch, L., and K.J. Zullig. 2008. "Middle school students' weight perceptions, dieting behaviors, and life satisfaction." *American Journal of Health Education* 39(6):345–52.

Espiritu, Yen Le. 2008. *Asian American Women and Men: Labor, Laws, and Love*. Lanham, MD: Rowman and Littlefield.

Etaugh, Claire. 2001. "Attitudes of employed women towards parents who choose full-time or part-time employment following their child's birth." *Sex Roles* 44(9/10):611–19.

Evans, Jodie. 2009. "Hiding behind the skirts of women." *Common Dreams* May 21. www.commondreams.org/view/2009/05/21-9

Evans, Lorraine, and Kimberley, Davies. 2000. "No sissy boys here: A content analysis of the representation of masculinity in elementary school reading textbooks." *Sex Roles* 42(3/4):255–70.

Evans, Sara. 2000. "The first American women." In Linda K. Kerber and Jane Sherron De Hart (eds.), *Women's America: Refocusing the Past*. (pp. 30–38). New York: Oxford University.

Evers, Fred, John Livernois, and Maureen Mancuso. 2006. "Where are the boys? Gender imbalance in higher education." *Higher Education Management and Policy* 18(2):1–25.

Ezawa, Aya Elise. 2003. "Motherhood, family and inequality in contemporary Japan." *Dissertation Abstract International, A: The Humanities and Social Sciences* 63,11:4113–4114-A.

Ezazi, Shala. 2009. "Women's studies in Iran: The roles of activists and scholars." In Christine E. Bose and Minjeong Kim (eds.), *Global Gender Research: Transnational Perspectives*. (pp. 110–24). New York: Routledge.

Fagot, Beverly I., and Leslie Leve. 1998. "Gender identity and play." In Doris Pronin Fromberg and Doris Bergen (eds.), *Play from Birth to Twelve and Beyond: Contexts, Perspectives, and Meanings*. New York: Garland.

Fagot, Beverly I., and Leslie Leve. 2000. *Stiffed: The Betrayal of the American Man*. San Francisco: HarperCollins.

Fan, Cindy C., and Ling Li. 2002. "Marriage and migration in transitional China: A field study of Gaozhou, Western Guangdong." *Environment and Planning* A 34:619–38.

Faragher, John Mack. 1996. "The separate worlds of men and women on the Overland Trail." In Mary Beth Norton and Ruth M. Alexander (eds.), *Major Problems in American Women's History*. Lexington, MA: D. C. Heath.

Farley, Reynolds, and Richard Alba. 2002. "The new second generation in the United States." *International Migration Review* 36(3):669–701.

Farris, Coreen, Teresa A. Treat, Richard J. Vicken, and Richard M. McFall. 2008. "Perceptual mechanisms that characterize gender differences in decoding women's sexual intent." *Psychological Science* 19(4):348–54.

Farvid, Pantea, and Virginia Braun. 2006. "Most of us guys are raring to go anytime, anyplace, anywhere: Male and female sexuality in Cleo and Cosmo." *Sex Roles* 55(5/6):295–310.

Fasteau, Marc F. 1974. *The Male Machine*. New York: McGraw-Hill.

Fausto-Sterling, Anne. 1992. *Myths of Gender: Biological Theories about Women and Men*. New York: Basic Books.

———. 1993. "Hormonal hurricanes: Menstruation, menopause and female behavior." In Laurel Richardson and Verta Taylor (eds.), *Feminist Frontiers III: Rethinking Sex, Gender and Society*. New York: McGraw-Hill.

———. 2000. *Sexing the Body: Gender Politics and the Construction of Sexuality*. New York: Basic Books.

Feeney, Judith A. 2001. *Becoming Parents: Exploring the Bond between Mothers, Fathers, and their Infants*. Cambridge, UK: Cambridge University.

Feminist Research Center. 2000. "Empowering women in business." Feminist Majority Foundation. www.feministorg/research/ewb_toc.html

Feng, Wang. 2005. "Can China afford to continue its one-child policy?" *AsiaPacific Issues*. Analysis from the East-West Center March:

Fenstermaker, Sarah, and Candace West (eds.). 2002. *Doing Gender, Doing Difference: Inequality, Power and Institutional Change*. New York: Routledge.

Ferguson, Dianne L., Audrey Desjarlais, and Gwen Meyer. 2000. *Improving Education: The Promise of Inclusive Learning*. Education Development Center. Newton, MA: National Institute for Urban School Improvement.

Fernea, Elizabeth Warnock. 1998. *In Search of Islamic Feminism.* New York: Doubleday.

Fetto, John. 2000. "Be mine." *American Demographics* 22(2):11–12.

Filkins, Dexter. 2003. "Either take a shot or take a chance." *New York Times* March 29:5. www.nytimes.com/2003/03/29/international/world-special

———— 2009. "Afghan women protest new restrictive law." *New York Times.* The World. April 15.

Fisch, Jorg. 2006. *Burning Women: A Global History of Widow Sacrifice from Ancient Times to the Present.* Rekha Kamath Rajan (trans.). London: Seagull.

Fischer, Kirsten. 2005. "The imperial gaze: Native American, African American, and colonial women in European eyes. In Nancy A. Hewitt (ed.), *A Companion to American Women's History.* Oxford, UK: Blackwell.

Fivush, Robyn, Melissa A. Brotman, Janine P. Buckner, and Sherryl H. Goodman. 2000. "Gender differences in parent-child emotion narratives." *Sex Roles* 42(3/4):233–53.

Flaherty, Mary. 2001. "How a language gender system creeps into perception." *Journal of Cross-Cultural Psychology* 32(1):18–31.

Flanigan, Kathy. 2008. "Being a mom isn't easy in Facebook era." *Milwaukee Journal Sentinel* April 11.

Fletcher, Michael A. 2002. "Degrees of separation: Gender gap among college graduates has educators wondering where the men are." *Washington Post* June 25:A1, A10.

Flood, Michael. 2008. "What's wrong with father's rights?" In Shira Tarrant (ed.), *Men Speak Out: Views on Gender, Sex, and Power.* (pp. 206–11). New York: Routledge.

Forbes, Gordon B., Leah E. Adams-Curtis, Kay B. White, and Nicole R. Hamm. 2002. "Perceptions of married women and married men with hyphenated surnames." *Sex Roles* 46(5/6):167–75.

Forste, Renata. 2003. "Maybe someday: Marriage and cohabitation among low income fathers." In Lori Kowaleski-Jones and Nicholas Wolfinger (eds.), *Fragile Families and the Marriage Agenda.* New York: Springer.

Fortin, Nicole M. 2008. "The gender gap among young adults in the United States." *Journal of Human Resources* 43(4):884–918.

Foucault, Michael. 1990. "The uses of pleasure," Volume II of Robert Hurley (trans.), *The History of Sexuality.* New York: Vintage.

Fouts, Gregory, and Kimberley Burggraf. 2000. "Television situation comedies: Female weight, male negative comments. Audience reactions." *Sex Roles* 42(9/10):925–32.

Fox, John. 2004. "How men's movement participants view each other." *The Journal of Men's Studies* 12(2):103–118.

Frankfort-Nachmias, Chava. 2001. "Israel: The myth of gender equality." In Lynn Walter (ed.), *Women's Rights: A Global View.* (pp. 127–40). London: Greenwood.

Freedman, Estelle. 2002. *No Turning Back: The History of Feminism and the Future of Women.* New York: Ballantine.

Freedman, Marcia. 2003. "Theorizing Israeli Feminism, 1970–2000." In Kalpana Misra and Melanie S. Rich (eds.), *Jewish Feminism in Israel: Contemporary Perspectives.* (pp. 1–16). Hanover, NH: Brandeis University.

Freedman, Rita. 2001. "Myth America grows up." In Sheila Ruth (ed.), *Issues in Feminism: An Introduction to Women's Studies.* (pp. 138–47). Mountain View, CA: Mayfield.

Freeman, Nancy K. 2007. "Preschoolers' perceptions of gender appropriate toys and their parents' beliefs about genderized behaviors: Miscommunication, mixed messages, or hidden truths?" *Early Childhood Education Journal* 34(5):357–66.

French, Adrianne, and Kristi Williams. 2007. "Depression and the psychological benefits of marriage." *Journal of Health and Social Behavior* 48(June):149–63.

French, Howard. 2007. "China: One-child policy spurred gender gap." *New York Times* (International) January 24.

———— 2001. "Diploma at hand, Japanese women find glass ceiling reinforced with iron." *New York Times* January 1.

Freud, Sigmund. 1962. *Three Contributions to the Theory of Sex.* A.A. Brill (trans.). New York: E. P. Dutton.

Frey, Sylvia R., and Marion J. Morton. 1986. *New World, New Roles: A Documentary History of Women in Pre-industrial America.* Westport, CT: Greenwood.

Friedan, Betty. 1963. *The Feminine Mystique.* New York: W.W. Norton.

Friedman, Carly Kay, Campbell Leaper, and Rebecca S. Bigler. 2007. "Do mothers' gender-related attitudes predict young children's gender beliefs?" *Parenting Science and Practice* 7(4):357–66.

Friedman, Cary. 2007. "First comes love, then comes marriage, then comes baby carriage: Perspectives on gay parenting and reproductive technology." *Journal of Infant, Child, and Adolescent Psychotherapy* 62(2):111–23.

Friedman, Elisabeth. 2002. "Getting rights for those without representation: The success of conjunctural coalition-building in Venezuela." In Nikke Craske and Maxine Molyneux (eds.), *Gender and the Politics of Rights and Democracy in Latin America.* (pp. 57–78). Houndmills, Hampshire, UK: Palgrave.

Frisco, Michelle L., and Kristi Williams. 2003. "Perceived housework equity, marital happiness, and divorce in dual-earner households." *Journal of Family Issues* 24(1):51–73.

Fromberg, Doris Pronin. 2005. "The power of play: Gender issues in early childhood education." In Janice Koch and Beverly J. Irby. (eds.), *Gender and Schooling in the Early Years.* (pp. 1–28). Greenwich, CT: IAP.

Fu, Xuanning. 2007. "Interracial marriage and family socio-economic status: A study among white, Filipinos, Japanese, and Hawaiians in Hawaii." *Journal of Comparative Family Studies* 38(4):533–54.

———. 2008. "Interracial marriage and family socio-economic well-being: Equal status exchange or caste status exchange?" *Social Science Journal* 45(1):132–55.

Fuertes-Olivera, Pedro A. 2007. "A corpus-based view of lexical gender in written Business English." *English for Specific Purposes* 26(2):219–34.

Fugere, Madeleine A., Carlos Escoto. Alita J. Cousins, Matt L. Riggs, and Paul Haerich. 2008. "Sexual attitudes and double standards: A literature review focusing on participant gender and ethnic background." *Sexuality and Culture* 12(3):169–82.

Fulghum, Robert. 1997. *True Love.* New York: HarperCollins.

Fuller, Bonnie. 2008. "Election shows this generation of women that sexism is still alive." *Advertising Age* September 15. 79(34):4, 90.

Fuller, Patricia Anne. 2001. "Living single: A phenomenological study of the lived experiences of never-married professional African American women." *Dissertation Abstracts International, A: The Humanities and Social Sciences* 62(4):1592–93-A.

Fur, Gunlog. 2002. "Some women are wiser than some men: Gender and native American history." In Nancy Shoemaker (ed.), *Clearing a Path: Theorizing the Past in Native American Studies.* (pp. 75–106). New York: Routledge.

Gabbidon, Shaun L. 2001. "African American male college students after the million man march: An exploratory study." *Journal of African American Men* 15–26.

Gabe, Thomas. 2003. *Trends in Welfare, Work and the Economic Well-Being of Female-Headed Families with Children.* New York: Novinka.

Gadalla, Tahany. 2008. "Gender differences in poverty after marital dissolution: A longitudinal study." *Journal of Divorce and Remarriage* 49(3/4):225–38.

Gagne, Isaac. 2008. "Urban princesses: Performance and 'women's language' in Japan's Gothic/Lolita subculture." *Journal of Linguistic Anthropology* 18(1):130–50.

Galambos, Nancy L. 2004. "Gender and gender role development in adolescence." In Richard M. Lerner and Laurence Steinberg (eds.), *Handbook of Adolescent Psychology.* (pp. 233–62). Hoboken, NJ: John Wiley & Sons.

Gallagher, Ann. M., Richard DeLisi, and Patricia C. Holst. 2000. "Gender differences in advanced mathematical problem solving." *Journal of Experimental Child Psychology* 75(3):165–90.

Gallagher, Sally K. 2004. "The marginalization of evangelical feminism." *Sociology of Religion* 65(3):215–37.

Galvin, Christina Osen. 2008. "A gay couple's journey through surrogacy: Intended fathers." *Family Journal* 16(4):402–403.

Gambone, Kirsten, Jordan Arena et al. 2002. "Change in attitudes toward maternal employment during the past decade." *ERIC Resources in Education,* CG031648.

Gangoli, Geetanjali. 2007. *Indian Feminisms; Law, Patriarchies and Violence in India.* Aldershot, UK: Ashgate.

Gannon, Theresa A., Rachael M. Collie, Tony Ward, and Jo Thakker. 2008. "Rape: Psychopathology, theory and treatment." *Ageing and Society* 24(2):213–33.

Garasky, Steven, Elizabeth Peters et al. 2007. "Measuring support to children by nonresident fathers. In Sandra L. Hofferth and Lynne M. Casper (eds.), *Handbook of Measurement Issues in Family Research.* (pp. 399–426). Mahwah, NJ: Lawrence Erlbaum.

Gardiner, Judith Kegan. 2002. *Masculinity Studies and Feminist Theory.* New York: Columbia University.

Gardner, Olivia, Emily Buder, and Sarah Buder. 2008. *Letters to a Bullied Girl.* New York: HarperCollins.

Garey, Anita Ilta, and Terry Arendell. 2001. "Children, work and family: Some thought on 'mother-blame.' " In Rosanna Hertz and Nancy Marshall (eds.), *Working Families: The Transformation of the American Home.* (pp. 293–303). Berkeley: University of California.

Garside, Rula Bayrakdar, and Bonnie Klimes-Dougan. 2002. "Socialization of discrete negative emotions: Gender differences and links with psychological distress." *Sex Roles* 47(3/4):115–28.

Gatrell, Carline, and Elaine Swan. 2008. *Gender and Diversity in Management: A Concise Introduction.* Thousand Oaks, CA: Sage.

Gault, Barbara, and Vicky Lovell. 2006. "The costs and benefits of policies to advance work/life integration." *American Behavioral Scientist* 49(9):1152–164.

Gavora, Jessica. 2003. *Tilting the Playing Field: Schools, Sports, Sex, and Title IX.* San Francisco: Encounter Books.

Gavron, Daniel. 2000. *The Kibbutz: Awakening from Utopia.* Lanham, MD: Rowman and Littlefield.

Gearing, Robin, Nilco Zand, and Georgie Colvin. 2001. "Engaging fathers: A point of entry in promoting a culture of peace." *Journal of the Association for Research on Mothering* 3(2):57–73.

Geary, David C. 2007. "An evolutionary perspective on sex differences in mathematics and the sciences." In Stephen Ceci and Wendy Williams (eds.), *Why Aren't More Women in Science? Top Researchers Debate the Evidence.* (pp. 173–188). Washington, DC: American Psychological Association.

Geary, Patrick J. 2006. *Women at the Beginning: Origin Myths from the Amazons to the Virgin Mary.* Princeton, NJ: Princeton University.

Gehrke-White, Donna. 2006. *The Face Behind the Veil: The Extraordinary Lives of Muslim Women in America.* New York: Citadel.

Gelb, Joyce. 2000. "The Equal Opportunity Law: A decade of change for Japanese women?" *Law & Policy* 22(3–4):385–407.

Gelfer, Joseph. 2008. "Identifying the Catholic Men's Movement." *The Journal of Men's Studies* 16(1):41–56.

Gellman, Jerome. 2006. "Gender and sexuality in the Garden of Eden." *Theology and Sexuality* 12(3):319–36.

Geloo, Zarina. 2008. "Women breaking the cycle of poverty." *New African* 477(October):26–29.

Gender Equality Bureau. 2003. *Women in Japan Today.* Tokyo: Cabinet Office. www/gender.go.jp/english_contents/women2003/index

German, Miguelina, Nancy A. Gonzales, and Larry Dumka. 2009. "Familism values as a protective factor for Mexican-American adolescents exposed to deviant peers." *Journal of Early Adolescence* 29(1):16–42.

Gerschick, Thomas J., and Adam Stephen Miller. 2004. "Coming to terms: Masculinity and physical disability." In Michael S. Kimmel and Michael A. Messner (eds.), *Men's Lives.* (pp. 349–62). Boston: Allyn & Bacon.

Gerson, Kathleen. 2009. "Dilemmas of involved fatherhood." In Estelle Disch (ed.), *Reconstructing Gender: A Multicultural Anthology.* (pp. 325–34). New York: McGraw-Hill.

Getzinger, Donna. 2009. *The Triangle Shirtwaist Factory Fire.* Greensboro, NC: Morgan Reynolds.

Gibbons, Sheila. 2002. "Female war correspondents changing war coverage." *Women's Enews,* September 10. www.womensenews.org/article.cfm?aid=1074

Gibbons, Sheila. 2008. "Coverage of Clinton and Palin: What's your plan for America – and where did you get that jacket." *Media Report to Women* 36(4 Fall):24–26.

Gibbons, Sheila. 2009. "Women pursuing media careers." Industry Statistics (February) *Media Report to Women* www.mediareporttowomen.com/statistics

Gill, Rosalind. 2007. *Gender and the Media.* Cambridge, UK: Polity.

Gilligan, Carol, J.M. Taylor, and A. Sullivan. 1995. *Between Voice and Silence: Women and Girls, Race and Relationship.* Cambridge, MA: Harvard University.

Gimbutas, Marija. 1991. *The Civilization of the Goddess: The World of Old Europe.* San Francisco: HarperSanFrancisco.

———. 2001. *The Language of the Goddess: Unearthing the Hidden Symbols of Western Civilization.* London: Thames & Hudson.

Gimenez, Martha E. 2001. "Marxism, and class, gender, and race: Rethinking the trilogy." *Race, Gender & Class* 8(2):23–33.

Ginther, Donna, and Shulamit Kahn. 2006. "Does science promote women? Evidence from academia, 1973–2001." Washington, DC: National Bureau of Economic Research. June 10.

Girard, April, and Charlene Y. Senn (2008). "The role of the new 'date rape drugs' in attributions about date rape." *Journal of Interpersonal Violence* 23(1):2–20.

Glass, Christy M., and Sandra T. Marquart-Pyatt. 2008. "The politics of welfare in transition: Gender or back to class?" *International Journal of Sociology* 38(1):38–57.

Glazer, Deborah F., and Jack Drescher (eds.). 2001. *Gay and Lesbian Parenting.* New York: Haworth.

Gleason, Jean Berko, and Richard Ely. 2002. "Gender differences in language development." In Ann McGillicuddy-De Lisi and Richard De Lisi (eds.), *Biology, Society and Behavior: The Development of Sex Differences in Cognition.* Westport, CT: Ablex.

Glynn, Keva, Heather Maclean, Tonia Forte, and Marsha Cohen. 2009. "The association between role overload and women's mental health." *Journal of Women's Health* 18(2):217–23.

Goel, Rachna. 2008. *Family Court's Perception of Best Interests: Meeting the Needs of Children in Custody Disputes.* Honor's thesis. Washington University in St. Louis. March 8.

Goffman, Erving. 1959. *The Presentation of Self in Everyday Life.* New York: Anchor.

Goffman, Erving. 1963. *Behavior in Public Places.* New York: Free Press.

———. 1971. *Relations in Public.* New York: Basic Books.

———. 1979. *Gender Advertisements.* New York: Harper & Row.

Goldberg, Harvey E. 2003. *Jewish Passages: Cycles of Jewish Life.* Berkeley: University of California.

Goldberg, Linn, and Dianne Elliot. 2007. "The prevention of anabolic steroid use among adolescents." In J. Kevin Thompson and Guy Cafri (eds.), The Muscular Ideal: Psychological, Social, and Medical Perspectives. Washington, DC: American Psychological Association.

Goldman, Debra. 2000. "Consumer republic: Boys' names have become the province of girls." *AdWeek Midwest* 61(47):22.

Goldscheider, Frances K. 2000. "Men, children and the future of the family in the third millennium." *Futures* 32(6):525–38.

Goldscheider, Frances, and Gayle Kaufman. 2006. "Willingness to stepparent: Attitudes about partners who already have children." *Journal of Family Issues* 27(10):1415–436.

Gomez, Alan. 2009. "Suicide numbers rise with combat stress." *USA Today* March 25:1.

Gonzalez, Alexei Quintero, and Richard Koestner. 2006. "What Valentine announcements reveal about romantic emotions of men and women." *Sex Roles* 55:767–73.

Goodman, Ellen. 1999. "TV gives Fiji new look at self." *St. Louis Post-Dispatch* June 1.

Goodwin, Robin, and Tatiana Emelyanova. 1995. "The perestroika of the family: Gender and occupational differences in family values in modern day Russia." *Sex Roles* 32(5/6):337–51.

Gorchoff, Sara M., John P. Oliver, and Ravenna Helson. 2008. "Contextualising change in marital satisfaction during middle age: An 18-year longitudinal study." *Psychological Science* 19(11):1194–200.

Gordon, Maya K. 2008. "Media contributions to African American girls' focus on beauty and appearance: Exploring the consequences of sexual objectification." *Psychology of Women Quarterly* 32(3):245–56.

Gordon, Rachel A., Robert Kaestner, and Sanders Korenman Cuny. 2008. "Child care and work absences: Trade-offs by type of care." *Journal of Marriage and the Family* 70(1):239–54.

Gottfried, Adele Eskeles. 2005. "Maternal and dual-earner employment and children's development: Redefining the research agenda." In Diane F. Halpern and Susan Elaine Murphy (eds.), *From Work-Family Balance to Work-Family Interaction: Changing the Metaphor.* (pp. 197–217). Mahweh, NJ: Lawrence Erlbaum.

Graetz, Naomi. 2003a. *S/he Created Them: Feminist Retellings of Bible Stories.* Piscataway, NJ: Gorgias.

———. 2003b. "Women and religion in Israel." In Kalpana Misra and Melanie S. Rich (eds.), *Jewish Feminism in Israel: Contemporary Perspectives.* (pp. 17–56). Hanover, NH: Brandeis University.

Graham, Fiona. 2003. *Inside the Japanese Company.* London: Routledge/Curzon.

Grajeda, Tony. 2002. "The 'feminization' of rock." In Roger Beebe, Denise Fulbrook, and Ben Saunders (eds.). *Rock Over the Edge: Transformations in Popular Music Culture.* (pp. 233–54). Durham, NC: Duke University.

Granger, Dorothy. 2002. "Friendships between black and white women." *American Behavioral Scientist* 45(8):1208–13.

Grant, Jo Anna, and Heather L. Hundley. 2007. "Myths of sex, love, and romance of older women in Golden Girls." In Mary-Lou Galician and Debra L. Merskin (eds.), *Critical Thinking about Sex, Love, and Romance in Mass Media.* Mahwah, NJ: Lawrence Erlbaum.

Gravener, Juie A., Alissa A. Haedt, Todd F. Heatherton, and Pamela K. Keel. 2008. "Gender and age differences in associations between peer dieting and drive for thinness." *International Journal of Eating Disorders* 41(1):57–63.

Graves, Lucia. 2007. "The perils and perks of helicopter parents." *U.S. News and World Report* December 18.

Gray, Colette, and Joanne Wilson. 2006. "Teachers expectations of a single-sex initiative in a co-educational school." *Educational Studies* 32(3):285–98.

Gray, J. Glenn. 1992. "The enduring appeals of battle." In Larry May and Robert Strikwerda (eds.), *Rethinking Masculinity: Philosophical Explorations in Light of Feminism.* Lanham, MD: Rowman & Littlefield.

Greard, Octavia. 1893. *L'Education des Femmes par les Femmes.* Paris: Librairie Hachette.

Green, Carin. M.C. 2007. *Roman Religion and the Cult of Diana in Aricia.* Cambridge, UK: Cambridge University.

Green, Karen. 1995. *The Woman of Reason: Feminism, Humanism and Political Thought.* New York: Continuum.

Green, Vaness A., Rebecca Bigler, and D. Catherwood. 2004. "The variability and flexibility of gender-typed toy play: A close look at children's behavioral responses to counterstereotypical models." *Sex Roles* 51(7/8):371–86.

Greenberg, Anna. 2001a. "Will choice be aborted?" *American Prospect* Fall:A25–A28.

Greenberg, Sarah. 2001b. "Spousal caregiving: In sickness and in health." *Journal of Gerontological Social Work* 35(4)69–82.

Greenberg, Bradley S., and Tracy R. Worrell. 2007. "New faces on television: A 12 season replication." *The Howard Journal of Communication* 18:277–90.

Greenglass, Esther R. 2002. "Work stress, coping, and social support: Implications for women's occupational well-being." In Debra L. Nelson and Ronald J. Burke (eds.), *Gender, Work Stress, and Health.* Washington, DC: American Psychological Association.

Greenhalgh, Susan. 2001. "Fresh winds in Beijing: Chinese feminists speak out on the one-child policy and women's lives." *Signs* 26(3):847–886.

Greenwood, Dara, and Linda M. Isbell. 2002. "Ambivalent sexism and the dumb blonde: Men's and women's reactions to sexist jokes." *Psychology of Women Quarterly* 26(4):341–50.

Griffith-Jones, Robin. 2008. *Beloved Disciple: The Misunderstood Legacy of Mary Magdalene, the Woman Closest to Jesus.* New York: HarperOne.

Griffiths, Catherine, Rebecca S. French, Hansa Patel-Kanwal, and Greta Rait. 2008. "Always between two cultures: Young British Bangladeshis and their mothers' views on sex and relationships." *Culture, Health, and Sexuality* 10(7):709–23.

Groce, Stephen B., and Margaret Cooper. 1990. "Just me and the boys? Women in local-level rock and roll." *Gender & Society* 2(4):220–28.

Grogan, Sarah, and Helen Richards. 2002. "Body image: Focus groups with boys and men." *Men & Masculinities* 4(3):219–32.

Groothuis, Rebecca Merrill. 1997. *Good News for Women: A Biblical Picture of Gender Equality.* Grand Rapids, MI: Baker Books.

Gross, Rita M. 2009. *A Garland of Feminist Reflections: Forty Years of Religious Exploration.* Berkeley, CA: University of California.

Grote, Nancy K., Kristen E. Naylor, and Margaret S. Clark. 2002. "Perceiving the division of family work to be unfair: Do comparisons, enjoyment, and competence matter?" *Journal of Family Psychology* 16(4):510–22.

Gruber, James E., and Susan Fineran. 2007. "The impact of bullying and sexual harassment on middle and high school girls." *Violence Against Women* 13(6):627–43.

Guendouzi, Jackie. 2006. " 'The guilt thing': Balancing domestic and professional roles." *Journal of Marriage and the Family* 68(4):901–9.

Guerrero, Laura K., Susanne M. Jones, and Renee Reiter Boburka. 2006. "Sex differences in emotional communication." In Kathryn Dindia and Daniel J. Canary (eds.), *Sex Differences and Similarities in Communication.* (pp. 241–62). Mahwah, NJ: Lawrence Erlbaum.

Guilamo-Ramos, Vincent, Patricia Dittus et al. 2007. "Parenting practices among Dominican and Puerto Rican mothers." *Social Work* 52(1):17–30.

Guilbert, Douglas E., Nicholas A. Vacc, and Kay Pasley. 2000. "The relationship of gender role beliefs, negativity, distancing, and marital instability." *Journal of Counseling and Therapy for Couples & Families.* 8(2):124–32.

Guiller, Jane, and Alan Durndell. 2007. "Students' linguistic behaviour in online discussion groups: Does gender matter?" *Computers in Human Behavior* 23(5):2240–2255.

Guinn, Bobby, and Vern Vincent. 2002. "Determinants of coping responses among Mexican American adolescents." *Journal of School Health* 72(4):152–6.

Guiso, Luigi, Ferdinando Monte, Paola Sapienza, and Luigi Zingales. 2008. "Culture, gender, and math." *Science* 320(May 30):1164–1165.

Guizzo, Erico. 2008. "The EE gender gap is widening." *IEEE Spectrum* 45(12):23.

Gundersen, Edna. 2001. "Madonna hits an MTV/VH1 wall." *USA Today* March 22:2D.

Gupta, Samjukta Gombrich. 2000. "The goddess, women, and their rituals in Hinduism." In Mandakranta Bose (ed.), *Faces of the Feminine in Ancient, Medieval, and Modern India.* (pp. 87–108). New York: Oxford University.

Gurian, Michael. 2007. *The Minds of Boys: Saving our Sons from Failing in School and Life.* San Francisco: Jossey-Bass.

Guryan, Jonathan, Erik Hurst, Melissa Kearney. 2008. "Parental education and parental time with children." *Journal of Economic Perspectives* 22(3):23–46.

Gutschow, Kim. 2004. *Being a Buddhist Nun: The Struggle for Enlightenment in the Himalayas.* Cambridge, MA: Harvard University.

Guzzetti, B., J. Young et al. 2002. *Reading, Writing, and Talking Gender in Literacy Learning.* Newark, DE: International Reading Association.

Gygax, Pascal, Ute Gabriel et al. 2008. "Generically intended, but specifically interpreted: When beauticians, musicians, and mechanics are all men." *Language and Cognitive Processes* 23(3):464—85.

Hacker, Andrew. 2003. *Mismatch: The Growing Gulf Between Women and Men.* New York: Scribner.

Hadley, Erin, and Jennifer Stuart. 2009. "The expression of parental identifications in lesbian mothers' work and family arrangements." *Psychoanalytic Psychology.* 26(1):42–68.

Hagewen, Rachel E. 2002. "Division of household labor in same-sex families." Southern Sociological Society, New Orleans, LA.

Haier, Richard J. 2007. "Brains, bias, and biology: Follow the data." In Stephen J. Ceci and Wendy M. Williams (eds.), *Why Aren't More Women in Science? Top Researchers Debate the Evidence.* (pp. 113–20) Washington, DC: American Psychological Association.

Hall, Christine C, Iijima. 2009. "Asian American women: The nail that sticks out is hammered down." In Nita Tewari and Alvin N. Alvarez (eds.), *Asian American Psychology: Current Perspectives.* (pp. 193–210). New York: Psychology Press.

Hall, Edward T. 1966. *The Hidden Dimension.* Garden City, NY: Doubleday.

Hall, Judith A. 2006a. "Women and men's nonverbal communication: Similarities, differences, stereotypes, and origins." In Valerie Manusov and Miles L. Patterson (eds.), *The Sage Handbook of Nonverbal Communication.* (pp. 201–18). Thousand Oaks, CA: Sage.

———. 2006b. "Nonverbal behavior, status, and gender: How do we understand their relations." *Psychology of Women's Quarterly* 30:384–91.

Hall, Judith A., Lavonia Smith LeBeau, Jeanette Gordon Reinoso, and Frank Thayer. 2001. "Status, gender, and nonverbal behavior in candid and posed photographs: A study of conversations between university employees." *Sex Roles* 44(11/12):677–92.

Hall, Judith A., Nora A. Murphy, and Marianne Schmidt Mast. 2006. "Recall of nonverbal cues: Exploring a new definition of interpersonal sensitivity." *Journal of Nonverbal Behavior* 30:141–55.

Hall, Scott S. 2005. "Changes in paternal involvement from 1977 to 1997: A cohort analysis." *Family and Consumer Sciences Research Journal* 12(1):127–40.

Halpern Diane F. 2007. "Science, sex, and good sense: Why women are underrepresented in some areas of science and math." In Stephen Ceci and Wendy Williams (eds.), *Why Aren't More Women in Science? Top Researchers Debate the Evidence.* (pp. 121–30). Washington, DC: American Psychological Association.

Hamilton, Christopher J., and James R. Mahalik. 2009. "Minority stress, masculinity, and social norms predicting gay men's health risk behaviors." *Journal of Counseling Psychology* 56(1):132–41.

Hamilton, Jill (ed.). 2008. *Date Rape.* Detroit, MI: Thomson/Gale.

Hammer, Juliane. 2008. "Identity, authority, and activism: American Muslim women approach the Qur'an." *Muslim World* 98(4):443–64.

Hammond, Wizdom Powell, Kira Hudson Banks, and Jacqueline S. Mattis. 2006. "Masculine ideology and forgiveness of racial discrimination among African American men: Direct and interactive relationships." *Sex Roles* 55:679–92.

Han, Shin-Kap, and Phyllis Moen. 2001. "Coupled careers: Pathways through work and marriage in the United States." In Hans-Peter Blossfeld and Sonja Drobnic (eds.), *Careers of Couples in Contemporary Societies: From Male Breadwinner to Dual Earner Families.* (pp. 201–31). Oxford, UK: Oxford University.

Harden, Jeni. 2001. " 'Mother Russia' at work: Gender divisions in the medical profession." *European Journal of Women's Studies* 8(2):181–99.

Harding, Rosie. 2007. "Sir Mark Potter and the protection of the traditional family: Why same sex marriage is (still) a feminist issue." *Feminist Legal Studies* 15:223–34.

Harding, Thomas. 2007. "The construction of men who are nurses as gay." *Journal of Advanced Nursing* 60(6):636–44.

Harper, Catherine. 2007. *Intersex.* New York: Berg/Palgrave Macmillan.

Harper, Rosalyn L., Gemma C. Harper, and Janet E. Stockdale. 2002. "The role and sentencing of women in drug trafficking crime." *Legal and Criminological Psychology* 7(1):101–14.

Harragan, Betty Lehan. 1977. *Games Mother Never Taught You.* New York: Rawson.

Harris, A.H.S., and C.E. Thoresen. 2005. "Forgiveness, unforgiveness, health, and disease." In Everett L. Worthington, Jr. (ed.). *Handbook of Forgiveness.* (pp. 321–34). New York: Brunner-Routledge.

Harris, Gardiner, and Lawrence K. Altman. 2009. "Managing a flu threat with seasoned urgency." *New York Times* May 10:A1.

Harris, Ian, Jose B. Torres, and Dale Allender. 1994. "The responses of African American men to dominant norms of masculinity within the United States." *Sex Roles* 31(11/12):703–19.

Harris, Sandy, Sandra Lowery, and Michael Arnold. 2002. "When women educators are commuters in commuter marriages." *Advancing Women in Leadership* Winter. www.advancingwomen.com/awl/winter2002/harris.html

Harris-Lacewell, Melissa. 2009. "Michelle Obama, mom-in-chief." *The Nation* May 5. www.thenation.com

Harsch, Herta E. 2006. "Motherhood and work." In Alcira Mariam Alizade (ed.), *Motherhood in the Twenty-First Century.* (pp. 123–33). London: Karnac.

Hart, Donna, and Robert W. Sussman. 2009. *Man the Hunted: Primates, Predators, and Human Evolution.* Boulder, CO: Westview.

Hartmann, Heidi. 1993. "The unhappy marriage of Marxism and feminism." In Stevi Jackson et al. (eds.), *Women's Studies Essential Readings.* New York: New York University.

Hartmann, Heidi. 2008. "Still a man's market: The long-term earnings gap: A report on the wage gap and its implications for women, families, and the labor market." Research-in Brief #C2366: February. Institute for Women's Policy Research. www.iwpr.org

———. 2009. "Women and entitlements." Fact Sheet #D485. Institute for Women's Policy Research. February. www.iwpr.org

———. 1999. "Strengthening Social Security for women." *Report from the Working Conference on Women and Social Security.* Washington, DC: Institute for Women's Policy Research.

Harvey, Elizabeth. 1999. "Short-term and long-term effects of early parental employment on children of the National Longitudinal Survey of Youth." *Developmental Psychology* 35(2):445–59.

Hashmi, Taj ul-Islam. 2000. *Women and Islam in Bangladesh: Beyond Subjection and Tyranny.* Houndmills, Hampshire, UK: Palgrave.

Haskell, Molly. 1987. *From Reverence to Rape: The Treatment of Women in the Movies.* New York: Holt, Rinehart and Winston.

———. 1997. *Holding My Own in No Man's Land: Women and Men and Film about Feminists.* New York: Oxford University.

Hassan, Riffat. 2002. "Islam." In Arvind Sharma and Katherine K. Young (eds.), *Her Voice, Her Faith: Women Speak on World Religions.* (pp. 215–242). Boulder, CO: Westview.

Hatoum, Ida Jodette, and Deborah Belle. 2004. "Mags and abs: Media consumption and bodily concerns in men." *Sex Roles* 51(7/8):397–407.

Hattery, Angela J., and Earl Smith. 2007. *African American Families.* Thousand Oaks, CA: Sage.

Hattiangadi, Anita U. 2000. *A Closer Look at Comparable Worth.* Washington DC: Employment Policy Foundation.

Hattiangadi, Nita U., and Amy M. Habib. 2000. *A Closer Look at Comparable Worth.* Washington, DC: Employment Policy Foundation.

Hawkins, Daniel N., and Shawn D. Whiteman. 2004. "Balancing work and family: Problems and solutions for low-income families." In Ann C. Crouter and Alan Booth (eds.), *Work-Family Challenges for Low-Income Parents.* Mahwah, NJ: Lawrence Erlbaum.

Hayford, Sarah, and S. Philip Morgan. 2008. "Religiosity and fertility in the United States." *Social Forces* 86(3):1163–188.

Haynes, Gladys Verneal Oosting. 2001. "Playmate selections of preschool children." *Dissertation Abstracts International Section A: Humanities & Social Sciences.* September. 62(3-A):907.

Hayslett, Carrianne H. 2008. "Women's and men's language in moderated online course discussions." *Dissertation Abstracts International Section A: Humanities and Social Sciences* 69(3-A):947.

Hazell, Vanessa, and Juanne Clark. 2008. "Race and gender in the media: A content analysis of advertisements in two mainstream black magazines." *Journal of Black Studies* 39(1):5–21.

He, Wei. 2007. *Role transformation: Re-socialization and psychological stress.* American Sociological Association, New York.

Headlam, Bruce. 2000. "Barbie PC: Fashion over logic." *New York Times* January 20.

Healey, Kevin. 2000. "The irresolvable tension: Agape and masculinity in the Promise Keepers movement." In Dane S. Claussen (ed.), *The Promise Keepers: Essays on Masculinity and Christianity.* (pp. 215–25). Jefferson, NC: McFarland.

Heard, Holly E. 2007. "Fathers, mothers, and family structure: Family trajectories, parent gender, and adolescent schooling." *Journal of Marriage and the Family* 69:435–50.

Hearn, Jeff, and Michael Kimmel. 2006. "Changing studies on men and masculinities." In Kathy Davis, Mary Evans, and Judith Lorber (eds.), *Handbook of Gender and Women's Studies.* (pp. 53–70). London: Sage.

Heaven, Catherine P., and Kathleen McCluskey-Fawcett. 2001. "Intergenerational attitudes toward maternal employment." Society for Research in Child Development, Minneapolis.

Hegarty, Peter. 2002. " 'It's not a choice, it's the way we're built': Symbolic beliefs about sexual orientation in the U.S. and Britain." *Journal of Community & Applied Social Psychology* 23(3):153–66.

Heine, Katherine. 2003. "AIDS moves beyond 'high risk' groups in India." AlterNet: Reuters Foundation: December 13. www.alternet.org/thefacts

Helgesen, Sally. 1990. *The Female Advantage: Women's Ways of Leadership.* New York: Doubleday.

Henderson, Angela Cameron. 2008. "Caring for older family members: Testing the role strain and the role accumulation perspectives." *Dissertation Abstracts International Section A: Humanities and Social Sciences* 68(12-A):5212.

Henehan, David, Esther D. Roseblum, Sandra E. Solomon, and Kimberly. 2007. "Social and demographic characteristics of gay, lesbian, and heterosexual adults with and without children." In Fiona Tasker and Jerry J. Bigner (eds.), *Gay and Lesbian Parenting: New Directions.* Binghamton, NY: Haworth.

Henley, Nancy M. 1977. *Body Politics: Power, Sex and Nonverbal Communication.* Englewood Cliffs, NJ: Prentice Hall.

———. 1989. "Molehill or mountain: What we know and don't know about sex bias in language." In Mary Crawford and Margaret Gentry (eds.), *Gender and Thought: Psychological Perspectives.* New York: Springer-Verlag.

———. 2002. "Body politics and beyond." *Feminism & Psychology* 12(3):295–310.

Henshaw, Stanley K., and Kathryn Post. 2008. "Trends in the characteristics of women obtaining abortions." August. New York: Guttmacher Institute. www.guttmacher.org

Hentges, Beth A., Jo A. Meier, and Robert A. Bartsch. 2007. "The effect of race, gender, and bias on liking of commercials with perceived stereotypes." *Current Research in Social Psychology* 13(6):64–78.

Hepler, Juanita B. 2000. "Joining the 'in crowd': The social interactions and peer relations of preadolescent youth." *Journal of School Social Work* 11(1):67–84.

Hequembourg, Amy L., and Michael P. Farrell. 2001. "Lesbian motherhood: Negotiating marginal-mainstream identities." In Jennifer M. Lehmann (ed.), *The Gay and Lesbian Marriage and Family Reader: Analyses of Problems and Prospects for the 21st Century.* (pp. 126–48). New York: Gordian Knot.

Herbert, T. Walter. 2002. *Sexual Violence and American Manhood.* Cambridge, MA: Harvard University.

Herro, Alana. 2007. "Literacy improved worldwide." WorldWatch Institute. *Population and society.* November 8. www.worldwatch.org/node/5478

Herzog, Hanna. 2008. "Re/visioning the women's movement in Israel." *Citizenship Studies* 12(3):265–82.

Heschel, Susannah. 2002. "Judaism." In Arvind Sharma and Katherine K. Young (eds.), *Her Voice, Her Faith: Women Speak on World Religions.* (pp. 145–68). Boulder, CO: Westview.

Hesketh, Therese, Li Lu, and Zhu Wei Xing. 2005. "The effect of China's one-child family policy after 25 years." *The New England Journal of Medicine* 353:1171–176.

Hesli, Vicki L., Ha-Lyong Jung, William M. Reisinger, and Arthur H. Miller. 2001. "The gender divide in Russian politics: Attitudinal and behavioral considerations." *Women & Politics* 22(2):41–80.

Hess, Ursula, Sylvie Blairy, and Robert E. Kleck. 2000. "The influence of facial emotion displays, gender, and ethnicity on judgments of dominance and affiliation." *Journal of Nonverbal Behavior* 24(4):265–83.

Hesse-Biber, Sharlene Nagy, and Gregg Lee Carter. 2005. *Working Women in America: Split Dreams.* New York: Oxford University.

Hetsroni, Amir. 2007. "Four decades of violent content on prime-time network programming: A longitudinal meta-analytic review." *Journal of Communication* 57:759–84.

Hickey, Chris. 2008. "Physical education, sport, and hyper-masculinity in schools." *Sport, Education, and Society* 13(2):147–61.

Hicks, Stephen. 2005. "Is gay parenting bad for kids? Responding to the 'very idea of difference' in research." *Sexualities* 8(2):153–68.

Higginbotham, Elizabeth. 2000. "Women and employment: Obstacles and prospects." Women's History Month Presentation at Maryville University of St. Louis. March 16.

———. 2002. "Black professional women: Job ceilings and employment sectors." In Roberta Satow (ed.), *Gender and Social Life.* Needham Heights, MA: Allyn & Bacon.

Higginbotham, Evelyn Brooks. 2003. African American women in history." In Mary Beth Norton and Ruth M. Alexander (eds.), *Major Problems in American Women's History.* Boston: Houghton Mifflin.

Higham, James P., Stuart Semple, Ann MacLarnon, Michael Heisterman, and Caroline Ross. 2009. "Female reproductive signaling, and male mating behavior, in the olive baboons." *Hormones and Behavior* 55(1):60–67.

Hill, Shirley. 2005. *Black Intimacies: A Gender Perspective on Families and Relationships.* Walnut Creek, CA: AltaMira.

Hilton, Jeanne M., and Karen Kopera-Frye. 2004. "Patterns of psychological adjustment among divorced custodial parents." *Journal of Divorce and Remarriage* 41(3/4):1–30.

Hines, Melissa. 2004. *Brain Gender.* Oxford, UK: Oxford University.

———. 2008. "Early androgen influences on human neural and behavioural development." *Early Human Development* 84(12):805–7.

Hines, Paulette Moore, and Nancy Boyd-Franklin. 2005. "African American Families." In Monica McGoldrick, Joe Giordano, and Nydia Garcia-Preto (eds.), *Ethnicity and Family Therapy.* (pp. 87–100). New York: Guilford.

Hirschman, Elizabeth C. 2003. "Men, dogs, guns, and cars." *Journal of Advertising* 32(10):9–22.

Hirschmann, Nancy J. 2003. *The Subject of Liberty: Toward a Feminist Theory of Freedom.* Princeton, NJ: Princeton University.

Hirshey, Geri. 1997. "Women of rock." *Rolling Stone* 773:November 13.

Hochschild, Arlie Russell. 2003. *The Second Shift* (with new introduction). New York: Penguin.

Hoff, Joan. 2003. "The negative impact of the American Revolution on white women." In Mary Beth Norton and Ruth M. Alexander (eds.), *Major Problems in American Women's History*. Boston: Houghton Mifflin.

Hofferth, Sandra L. 2003. "Race/ethnic differences in father involvement in two-parent families: Culture, context, or economy?" *Journal of Family Issues* 24(2):185–216.

Hoffman, Lois W. 2000. "Maternal employment: Effects of social context." In Ronald D. Taylor and Margaret C. Wang (eds.). *Resilience across Contexts: Family, Work, Culture, and Community*. (pp. 147–76). Mahwah, NJ: Lawrence Erlbaum.

Hoffman, Lois W., and Lise M. Youngblade. 1999. *Mothers at Work: Effects on Children's Well-Being*. Cambridge, UK: Cambridge University.

Hoffmann, John E., and John E. Bartkowski. 2008. "Gender, religious tradition and biblical literalism." *Social Forces* 86(3):1245–72.

Hoffmann, Melissa L., and Kimberly K. Powlishta. 2001. "Gender segregation in childhood: A test of the interaction style theory." *Journal of Genetic Psychology* 162(3):298–313.

Hoffnung, Michele. 1995. "Motherhood: Contemporary conflict for women." In Jo Freeman (ed.), *Women: A Feminist Perspective*. Mountain View, CA: Mayfield.

Hogeland, Lisa Maria. 2007. "Fear of feminism: Why young women get the willies." In Barbara J. Balliet (ed.), *Women, Culture, and Society: A Reader*. (pp. 77–80). Dubuque, IA: Kendall/Hunt.

Hollingworth, Leta S. 2000. "Leta S. Hollingworth on coercive pronatalism. Reprint from the June 1916 edition of *American Journal of Sociology* titled 'Social devices for impelling women to bear and rear children.' " *Population and Development Review* 26(2):353–63.

Holmes, Janet, and Miriam Meyerhoff (eds.). 2005. *The Handbook of Language and Gender*. Malden, MA: Blackwell.

Honig, Alice S. 2002. "Choosing childcare for young children." In Marc H. Borstein (ed.), *Handbook of Parenting; Volume 5 – Practical Issues in Parenting*. Mahwah, NJ: Lawrence Erlbaum.

Hooks, Bell, Sharon Suh, Karma Lekshe Tsomo, and Susanne Mrozik. 2008. "Women changing Buddhism: Feminist perspectives." In Peter N. Gregory and Susanne Mrozik (eds.), *Women Practicing Buddhism: American Experiences*. (pp. 67–90). Boston: Wisdom Publications.

Hoover, Eric, and Beckie Supiano. 2008. "Surveys of students challenge 'helicopter parents' stereotypes." *Chronicle of Higher Education*. February 1. 54(21):A22.

Hori, Haruhiko. 2009. "Labor market segmentation and the gender wage gap." *Japan Labor Review* 6(1):5–20.

Hossain, Ziarat. 2001. "Division of household labor and family functioning in off-reservation Navajo Indian families." *Family Relations* 50(3):255–61.

Hotaling, Edward. 2003. *Islam without Illusions: Its Past, its Present, and its Challenge for the Future*. Syracuse, NY: Syracuse University.

Houvouras, Shannon, and Carter J. Scott. 2008. "The f-word: College students' definition of a feminist." *Sociological Forum* 23(2):234–56.

Howitz, Jeannine O. 2001. "Reflections of a feminist mom." In Susan E. Chase and Mary F. Rogers (eds.), *Mothers and Children: Feminist Analyses and Personal Narratives*. (pp. 81–85). New Brunswick, NJ: Rutgers University.

Hrdy, Sarah Blaffer. 1999. *The Woman that Never Evolved*. Cambridge, MA: Harvard University.

Hubbard, Lee, and Amanda Datnow. 2002. "Are single-sex schools sustainable in the public sector?" In Amanda Datnow and Lea Hubbard (eds.), *Gender in Policy and Practice: Perspectives on Single-Sex and Coeducational Schooling*. New York: Routledge/Falmer.

Hudson, Repps. 2003. "Fed researchers find that timing is everything for women who want to have it all." *St. Louis Post-Dispatch* April 15:C1, C3.

Hughes, Patrick. 2005. "Baby, it's you: International capital discovers the under threes." *Contemporary issues in Early Childhood* 6(1):30–40.

Human Rights Watch. 2008. "US: Soaring rates of rape and violence against women." December 18. www.hrw.org/12/18

Humphreys, T. 2007. "Perceptions of sexual consent: The impact of relationship history and gender." *Journal of Sex Research* 44(4):307–15.

Hungerford, T.L. 2001. "The economic consequences of widowhood on elderly women in the United States and Germany." *Gerontologist* 41(1):103–11.

Hunt, M. 1974. *Sexual Behavior in the 1970s*. Chicago: Playboy.

Hunter, Andrea G., and James Earl Davis. 1994. "Hidden voices of black men: The meaning, structure and complexity of manhood." *Journal of Black Studies* 25(1):20–40.

Hunter, Cameron. 2006. "Women are a growing factor in the peace process." *Palestine-Israel Journal of Politics, Economics, and Culture*. 13(4):117–19.

Hunter, Maxwell W., and Kay A. Chick. 2005. "Treatment of gender in basal readers." *Reading Research and Instruction* 44(3):65–76.

Hust, Stacey J.T., and Lei Ming. 2008. "Sexual objectification, sports programming and music television." *Media Report to Women* 36(1):16–23.

Huston, Aletha C., David S. Bickham et al. 2007. "From attention to comprehension: How children watch and learn from television." In Norma Pecora and John P. Murray (eds.), *Children and Television: Fifty Years of Research*. (pp. 41–64). Mahwah, NJ: Lawrence Erlbaum.

Hutson, Alaine S. 2005. "African Sufi women and ritual change." In Pamela J. Stewart and Andrew

Strathern (eds.), *Contesting Rituals: Islam and Practices of Identity-Making.* (pp. 101–25). Durham, NC: Carolina Academic.

Hutt, Rebecca. 2008. "Dance floor dialogue: A symbolic interaction study of contemporary social dancing." *Washington University Undergraduate Research Digest* 4(1):8–16.

Hyde, Janet S. 2007. "Women in science: Gender similarities in abilities and sociocultural forces." In Stephen Ceci and Wendy Williams (eds.), *Why Aren't More Women in Science? Top Researchers Debate the Evidence.* (pp. 131–46). Washington, DC: American Psychological Association.

Hyde, Janet S., Sara M. Linder, Marcia C. Linn, Amy B. Ellis, and Caroline C. Williams. 2008. Gender similarities characterize math performance." *Science* 321(July 25):494–95.

Hyde, Janet Shibley, Nicole Else-Quest, H.H. Goldsmith, and Jeremy C. Biesanz. 2004. "Children's temperament and behavior problems predict their employed mothers' work functioning." *Child Development* 75(2):580–94.

Hymowitz, Kay S. 2006. *Marriage and Caste in America: Separate and Unequal Families in a Post-Marital Age.* Chicago: Ivan R. Dee.

Iarskaia, Valentina, and Elena R. Iarskaia-Smirnova. 2002. "Ain't men's business: Gender analysis of employment in social work." *Sotsiologicheskie Issledovaniya* (abstract) 28(6):74–82.

Ibhawoh, Bonny. 2000. "Between culture and constitution: Evaluating the cultural legitimacy of human rights in the African state." *Human Rights Quarterly* 22(3):838–60.

Ilan, Tal. 2006. "Women in Jewish life and law." In Steven T. Katz (ed.), *The Cambridge History of Judaism: Volume 4, The Late Roman-Rabbinic Period.* Cambridge, UK: Cambridge University.

Ingraham, Chrys. 2008. *White Weddings: Romancing Heterosexuality in Popular Culture.* New York: Routledge.

Intons-Peterson, Margaret Jean. 1988. *Children's Concepts of Gender.* Norwood, NJ: Ablex.

Irmen, Lida. 2007. "What's in a (role) name? Formal and conceptual aspects of comprehending personal nouns." *Journal of Psycholinguistic Research* 36:431–56.

Islam, Tazul. 2007. *Microcredit and Poverty Alleviation.* Aldershot, UK: Ashgate.

ISR. 2002. "U.S. husbands are doing more housework while wives are doing less." *Institute of Social Research.* University of Michigan. www.umich.edu/newsinfo/Releases/ 2002/Mar02

Israel-Cohen, Yael. 2008. "Between feminism and orthodoxy in Israel." *Jewish Journal of Sociology* 50(1/2):51–66.

Italie, Hillel. 1993. "Emma Thompson: Fame, feminist, forster." *St. Louis Post-Dispatch* January 3:6C.

Ito, Kinko. 2002. "The world of Japanese ladies' comics: From romantic fantasy to lustful perversion." *Journal of Popular Culture* 36(1):68–85.

IWPR. 2006. "Running faster to stay in place?" *Institute for Women's Policy Research News.* December 20. www.iwpr.org

IWPR. 2008. "The gender wage gap: 2007." *IWPR Fact Sheet:* No. C350. Institute for Women's Policy Research. www.iwpr.org

Jack, Lenus Jr. 2008. "Post election reflection – An opportunity for change: A consensus for economic and social stability." *Race, Gender and Class* 15(3–4):117–26.

Jackson, Anita P., Ronald P. Brown, and Karen E. Patterson-Stewart. 2000. "African Americans in dual-career commuter marriages: An investigation of their experiences." *Family Journal-Counseling and Therapy for Couples and Families* 8(1):22–36.

Jackson, T., Therese Hesketh, and Z.W. Xing. 2006. "China's one-child family policy." *New England Journal of Medicine* 354:877.

Jacobsen, Joyce P. 2007. *The Economics of Gender.* Malden, MA: Blackwell.

Jacobson, Doranne, and Susan S. Wadley. 1995. *Women in India: Two Perspectives.* New Delhi, India: Manohar.

Jacobson, Linda. 2004. "Child-care centers have positive impact, study concludes." *Education Week* 23 February 18:22.

Jaquette, Jane S., and Gale Summerfield (eds.). 2006. *Women and Gender Equity in Development Theory and Practice: Institutions, Resources, and Mobilization.* Durham, NC: Duke University.

Jalilvand, Mahshid. 2000. "Married women, work, and values." *Monthly Labor Review* 123(8):26–31.

James, Abigail Norfleet. 2003. "Escaping stereotypes: Educational attitudes of male alumni of single-sex and coed schools." *Psychology of Men and Masculinity* 4(2):136–48.

James, Abigail Norfleet. 2007. *Teaching the Male Brain: How Boys Think, Feel, and Learn in School.* Thousand Oaks, CA: Corwin.

Jamieson, Kathleen Hall. 1995. *Beyond the Double Bind: Women and Leadership.* New York: Oxford University.

Jamil, Selina. 2009. "The interconnecting humanity: Connections between our spiritual and secular world." In Anjana Narayan, and Bandana Purkayastha (eds.), *Living Our Religions; Hindu and Muslim South Asian American Women Narrate their Experiences.* Sterling, VA: Kumarian.

Jandt, Fred, and Heather Hundley. 2007. "Intercultural dimensions of communicating masculinities." *Journal of Men's Studies* 15(2):216–31.

Jarman, Francis. 2002. "Sati: From exotic custom to relativist controversy." *CultureScan.* December. 2(5).

Jayson, Sharon. 2007. "Helicopter parents appear to defy socioeconomic pegging." *USA Today* April 4:5D.

Jeffrey, Julie Roy. 1998. *Frontier women: "Civilizing the West? 1840–1880.* New York: Hill and Wang.

Jensen, Gary F. 2003. "Gender variation in delinquency: Self-images, beliefs, and peers as mediating mechanisms." In Ronald L. Akers and Gary F. Jensen (eds.),

Social Learning Theory and the Explanation of Crime. (pp. 151–78). New Brunswick, NJ: Transaction.

Jensen, Joan M. 1994. "Native American women and agriculture: A Seneca case study." In Vicki L. Ruiz and Ellen Carol DuBois (eds.), *Unequal Sisters: A Multicultural Reader in U.S. Women's History.* New York: Routledge.

Jensen, Robert. 2007. *Getting off: Pornography and the End of Masculinity.* Cambridge, MA: South End.

Jepsen, Lisa K., and Christopher A. Jepsen. 2002. "An empirical analysis of the matching patterns of same-sex and opposite-sex couples." *Demography* 39(3):435–53.

Jewett, Christina. 2007. "Teaching teen boys to tame aggression." *Sacramento Bee* February 3.

Jocks, Christopher Ronwaniente. 2001. "A Native American perspective: To protect the ground we walk on." In John C. Raines and Daniel C. Maguire (eds.), *What Men Owe to Women: Men's Voices from World Religions.* (pp. 259–80). Albany: State University of New York.

Johns, Donald A. 2003. "Understanding the controversy over gender language in bible translation." *Journal of Religious and Theological Information* 6(1):43–53.

Johnson, Allan. 2005. "Here's what you're thinking in the shower." *Chicago Tribune.* September 10. www.chicagotribune.com

Johnson, Elizabeth. 2003. "Basic linguistic options: God, women, and equivalence." In Philip E. Divine and Celia Wolf-Devine (eds.), *Sex and Gender: A Spectrum of Views.* (pp. 363–68). Belmont, CA: Wadsworth/Thomson.

Johnson, Hortense. 1943/1996. "Hortense Johnson on black women and the war effort, 1943." In Mary Beth Norton and Ruth M. Alexander (eds.), *Major Problems in American Women's History.* Lexington, MA: D.C. Heath.

Johnson, H. Durell. 2004. "Grade, gender, and relationship differences in emotional closeness within adolescent friendships." *Adolescence* 39:243–56.

Johnson, H. Durell, Evelyn Brady et al. 2007. "Identity as a moderator of gender differences in the emotional closeness of emerging adults' same- and cross-sex friendships." *Adolescence* 42(165):1–23.

Johnson, Kathy Love. 2008. *Skirt! Rules for the Workplace: An Irreverent Guide to Advancing Your Career.* Guilford, CT: Skirt! Magazine (Morris).

Johnson, Michael P. 2007. "Domestic violence: The intersection of gender and control." In Laura O'Toole, Jessica R. Schiffman, and Margie L. Kiter Edwards (eds.), *Gender Violence: Interdisciplinary Perspectives.* (pp. 257–68). New York: NYU Press.

Johnson, Pamela, and Jennifer A. Johnson. 2001. "The oppression of women in India." *Violence Against Women* 7(9):1051–68.

Johnson, Suzanne M, and Elizabeth O'Connor. 2002. *The Gay Baby Boom: The Psychology of Gay Parenthood.* New York: New York University.

———. 2005. "The children of gay parents develop normally." In Kate Burns (ed.), *Gays and Lesbians.* Farmington Hills, MI: Greenhaven.

Johnson, W. Brad. 2003. *Getting Mentored in Graduate School.* Washington, DC: American Psychological Association.

Johnston, Deidre D., and Debra H. Swanson. 2003. "Invisible mothers: A content analysis of motherhood mythologies and myths in magazines." *Sex Roles* 49(1/2):21–33.

Jones, Jeffrey. 2009. "Republicans face steep uphill climb among women." *Gallup Poll* May 6. www.gallup.com/poll/118207

Joos, Kristin E. 2003. "LGBT parents and their children." *SWS Network News* 20(4):9–14.

Jordan, Alexander H., and Benjamin J. Lovett. 2007. "Stereotype threat and test performance: A primer for school psychologists." *Journal of School Psychology* (45)1:45–59.

Jordan, Ellen and Angela Cowan. 2004. "Warrior narratives in the kindergarten classroom: Renegotiating the social contract." In Michael Kimmel and Michael Messner (eds.), *Men's Lives.* (pp. 103–15). Boston: Allyn & Bacon.

Jordan, Lisae C., and Bette Garlow. 2007. In Rebecca Henry (ed.) *The Domestic Violence Civil Law Manuel Protection Orders and Family Law Cases.* Chicago: American Bar Association, Commission on Domestic Violence.

Joseph, Miriam. 2001. *Perceived Cultural Influences on Generativity Identified by Childless Women.* Dissertation, St. Louis University.

Joyce, Rosemary A. 2008. *Ancient Bodies, Ancient Lives: Sex, Gender, and Archaeology.* New York: Thames and Hudson.

Joyner, Kara, and Richard J. Udry. 2000. "You don't bring me anything but down: Adolescent romance and depression." *Journal of Health and Social Behavior* 41(4):369–91.

Judge, Timothy A., and Beth A. Livingston. 2008. "Is the gap more than gender? A longitudinal analysis of gender, gender role orientation, and earnings." *Journal of Applied Psychology* 93(5):994–1012.

Julé, Allyson. 2004. *Gender, Participation, and Silence in the Language Classroom: Sh-shushing the Girls.* Houndsmills, UK: Palgrave Macmillan.

Juntti, Scott A., Jennifer K. Coats, and Nirao M. Shah. 2008. "A genetic approach to dissect sexually dimorphic behaviors." *Hormones and Behavior* 53(5):627–37.

Kaba, Amadu Jacky. 2008. "Race, gender, and progress: Are black women the new model minority?" *Journal of African American Studies* 12(4):309–35.

Kaiser Family Foundation. 2008. "Women and HIV/AIDS in the United States." *HIV/AIDS Policy Fact Sheet* October. www.kff.org

Kaiser Family Foundation. 2009. "The global HIV/AIDS epidemic." *U.S. Global Health Policy Fact Sheet* April. www.kff.org

Kalbfleisch, Pamela J., and Anita L. Herold. 2006. In Kathryn Dindia and Daniel J. Canary (eds.), *Sex Differences and Similarities in Communication.* (pp. 299–317). Mahwah, NJ: Lawrence Erlbaum.

Kaledin, Eugenia. 1984. *Mothers and More: American Women in the 1950s.* Boston: Twayne.

Kalmijn, Matthijs, and Henk Flap. 2001. "Assortive meeting and mating: Unintended consequences of organized settings for partner choices." *Social Forces* 79(4):1289–312.

Kamen, Paula. 2000. *Her Way: Young Women Remake the Sexual Revolution*. New York: New York University.

Kane, Michael. 2008. "Investigating attitudes of Catholic priests toward the media and the U.S. Conference of Catholic Bishops response to the sexual abuse scandal." *Mental Health, Religion, and Culture* 11(6):579–95.

Kaneda, Toshiko. 2006. "China's concern over population aging and health." *Population Reference Bureau.* June. www.prb.org/Articles/2006

Kantor, Jodi. 2008. "Gender issue lives on as Clinton's hopes dim." *New York Times* May 19.

Kantor, Martin. 2009. *Homophobia: The State of Bigotry Today*. Westport, CT: Praeger.

Kantrowitz, Barbara. 2005. "When women lead." *Newsweek* October 24:46–76.

Karakhanova, T.M. 2003, "Working women's value orientations and paid work time use." *Sotsiologicheskie Issledovaniya* (abstract) 29(3):74–81.

Karant-Nunn, Susan C., and Merry E. Wiesner-Hanks. 2003. *Luther on Women: A Source Book*. Cambridge, UK: Cambridge University.

Karlsen, Carol F. 2004. "The devil in the shape of a woman: The economic basis of witchcraft." In Linda K. Kerber and Jane Sherron De Hart (eds.), *Women's America: Refocusing the Past*. New York: Oxford University.

Karpiak, Christie O., James P. Buchanan, Megan Hosey, and Allison Smith. 2007. "University students from single-sex and coeducational high schools: Differences in majors and attitudes at a Catholic university." *Psychology of Women Quarterly* 31:282–289.

Kasen, Stephanie, Henian Chen, Joel Sneed, Thomas Crawford, and Patricia Cohen. 2006. "Social role and birth cohort influences on gender-linked personality traits in women: A 20-year longitudinal analysis." *Journal of Personality and Social Psychology* 91(5):944–58.

Kashiwagi, Keiko, and Sono Hasuka. 2000. "Attitude and emotion toward mother-child separation (sending a child to day-care center) in working mothers and non-working mothers." *Japanese Journal Family Psychology* 14(1):61–74.

Katovich, Michael A., and Marya S. Makowski. 1999. "Music periods in the rock and post rock eras: The rise of female performers on a provocative stage." *Studies in Symbolic Interaction* 23:141–66.

Kaufman, David. 2008. *Doris Day: The Untold Story of the Girl Next Door*. New York: Virgin Books.

Kawaguchi, Akira. 2009. "Corporate governance by investors and the role of women." *Japan Labor Review* 6(1):72–90.

Kawaguchi, Daiji. 2009. "Introduction: The gender gap in the Japanese labor market." *Japan labor Review* 6(1):2–4.

Kay, Rebecca. 2006. *Men in Contemporary Russia: The Fallen Heroes of Post-Soviet Change?* Aldershot, UK: Ashgate.

Kazakova, Elena. 2007. "Wages in a growing Russia: When is a 10 percent rise in the gender wage gap good news?" *Economics of Transition* 15(2):365–92.

Kazemzadeh, Masoud. 2002. *Islamic Fundamentalism, Feminism, and Gender Inequality in Iran under Khomeini*. Lanham, MD: University Press of America.

Kazerounian, Kazem. 2009. "Forgive Mousavi, but never foget his name." *American Chonicle* June 26. www.americanchronicle.com

Kelle, Helga. 2000. "Gender and territoriality in games played by nine- to twelve-year old schoolchildren." *Journal of Contemporary Ethnography* 29(2):164–97.

Keller, James R. 2002. *Queer (Un)friendly Film and Television*. Jefferson, NC: McFarland.

Kellough, J. Edward. 2006. *Understanding Affirmative Action: Politics, Discrimination, and the Search for Justice*. Washington, DC: Georgetown University.

Kelly, Janice R., Julie D. Murphy, Traci Y. Craig, and Denise M. Driscoll. 2005. "The effect of nonverbal behaviors associated with sexual harassment proclivity on women's performance." *Sex Roles* 53(9/10):689–701.

Kemkes, Ariane. 2006. "Does the sex of firstborn children influence subsequent fertility behavior? Evidence from family reconstitution." *Journal of Family History* 31(2):144–62.

Kempf-Leonard, K., and Lisa L. Sample. 2000. "Disparity based on sex: Is gender specific treatment warranted?" *Justice Quarterly* 17(1):89–128.

Kendall, Shari. 2007. "Father as breadwinner, mother as worker: Gendered positions in feminist and traditional discourses of work and family." In Deborah Tannen, Shari Kendall, and Cynthia Gordon (eds.), *Family Talk: Discourse and Identity in Four American Families*. New York: Oxford University.

Kennison, Sheila M., and Jessie L. Trofe. 2003. "Comprehending pronouns: A role for wordspecific gender stereotype information." *Journal of Psycholinguistic Research* 32(3):355–78.

Kerr, Mary Margaret, and C. Michael Nelson. 2002. *Strategies for Addressing Behavior Problems in the Classroom*. Upper Saddle River, NJ: Merrill/Prentice Hall.

Keshet-Orr, Judi. 2003. "Jewish women and sexuality." *Sexual and Relationship Therapy* 18(2):215–24.

Kessler-Harris, Alice. 1991. "Where are the organized women workers?" In Linda K. Kerber and Jane Sherron De Hart (eds.), *Women's America: Refocusing the Past*. New York: Oxford University.

Keuls, Eva. 1993. *The Reign of the Phallus: Sexual Politics in Ancient Athens*. Berkeley: University of California.

Khanna, Madhu. 2000. "The goddess woman equation in Sakta Tantras." In Mandakranta Bose (ed.), *Faces of the Feminine in Ancient, Medieval, and Modern India*. (pp. 109–23). New York: Oxford University.

Khasbulatova, O.A., and L.S. Egorova. 2002. "Social feeling among women and men in medium sized

Russian cities." *Sotsiologicheskie Issledovaniya* (abstract) 28(11):48–54.

Khoromi, Farnaz. 2007. "The nature of gender differences in science, mathematics and engineering education: A literature review of stereotype threat and its underlying mechanisms." *Dissertation Abstracts International: Section B: The Sciences and Engineering* 68(1-B):625.

Kielty, S. 2008. "Working hard to resist a 'bad mother' label: Narratives of non-resident motherhood" *Qualitative Social Work* 7(3):363–79.

Kim Janna L., C. Lynn Sorsoli et al. (2007). "From sex to sexuality: Exposing the heterosexual script on prime time network television." *Journal of Sex Research* 44(2):145–57.

Kim, Bryan S.K. 2009. "Acculturation and enculturation of Asian Americans: A primer." In Nita Tewari and Alvin N. Alvarez (eds.), *Asian American Psychology: Current Perspectives.* (pp. 97–112). New York: Psychology Press.

Kim. Minjeong, and Angie Y. Chung. 2005. "Consuming orientalism: Images of Asian/American women in multicultural advertising." *Qualitative Sociology* 28(1):67–91.

Kim, Sonja de Groot. 2008. "Girls on the sidelines: 'Gendered' development in early childhood classrooms." In Bert van Oers, Wim Wardekker et al. (eds.)., *The Transformation of Learning: Advances in Cultural-History Activity.* New York: Cambridge University.

Kimmel, Michael S. 2000. "Saving the males: The sociological implications of the Virginia Military Institute and the Citadel." *Gender & Society* 14(4):494–16.

———. 2008. "Abandoning the barricades: Or how I became a feminist." In Shira Tirrant (ed.), *Men Speak Out: Views on Gender, Sex, and Power.* (pp. 171–81). New York: Routledge.

———. 2008. *Guyland: The Perilous World Where Boys Become Men.* New York: HarperCollins.

Kimoto, Kimiko. 2005. *Gender and Japanese Management.* Melbourne: Trans Pacific Press.

Kimura, Doreen. 2007. "Under-representation or misrepresentation?" In Stephen Ceci and Wendy Williams (eds.), *Why Aren't More Women in Science? Top Researchers Debate the Evidence.* Washington DC: American Psychological Association.

Kinelski, Kristin, Jessie Markowitz, and Catherine Chambliss. 2002. "The effects of maternal employment on the attitudes, work expectations, and self-esteem of urban and suburban middle school parents." ERIC: *Resources in Education,* CG031601.

King, Jacqueline E. 2006. *Gender Equity in Higher Education: Are Male Students at a Disadvantage?* Washington, DC: American Council on Education.

King, Ursula. 1989. *Women and Spirituality.* New York: New Amsterdam.

Kingsbury Alex. 2008. "Admittedly unequal." *U.S. News and World Report* June 25. 142(23).

Kinsey, Alfred E., Wardell B. Pomeroy, and Clyde E. Martin. 1948. *Sexual Behavior in the Human Male.* Philadelphia: Saunders.

Kinsey, Alfred E., Wardell B. Pomeroy, Clyde E. Martin, and H. Gephard. 1953. *Sexual Behavior in the Human Female.* Philadelphia: Saunders.

Kippen, R., A. Evans, and E. Gray. 2007. "Parental preferences for sons and daughters in a Western industrial setting: Evidence and implications." *Journal of Biosocial Science* 39(4):583–97.

Kircher, Jan Carolyn. 2008. "Another look at gender roles in prime-time television." *Dissertation Abstracts International Section A: Humanities and Social Sciences* 68(11-A):4883.

Kiselica, Mark S., Matt Englar-Carlson, Arthur M. Horne, and Mark Fischer. 2008. "A positive psychology perspective on helping boys." In Mark Kiselica, Matt Englar-Carlson, and Arthur Horne (eds.), *Counseling Troubled Boys: A Guidebook for Professionals.* (pp. 31–48). New York: Routledge.

Kitano, Harry H.L., and Roger Daniels. 1995. *Asian Americans: Emerging Minorities.* Englewood Cliffs, NJ: Prentice Hall.

Kitch, Carolyn. 2001. *The Girl on the Magazine Cover: The Origins of Visual Stereotypes in American Mass Media.* Chapel Hill: University of North Carolina.

Kleugel, James R., and Lawrence D. Bobo. 2001. "Perceived group discrimination and policy attitudes: The sources and consequences of the race and gender gaps." In Alice O'Connor, Chris Tilly, and Lawrence D. Bobo (eds.), *Urban Inequality: Evidence from Four Cities.* (pp. 163–213). New York: Russell Sage.

Kline, Galena, Scott M. Stanley et al. 2004. "Timing is everything: Pre-engagement cohabitation and increased risk for poor marital outcomes." *Journal of Family Psychology,* 18:311–318.

Knapp, Kiyoko Kamio. 1999. "Don't awaken the sleeping child: Japan's gender equality law and the rhetoric of gradualism." *Columbia Journal of Gender & Law* 8(2):178–83.

Knickmeyer, Nicole, Kim Sexton, and Nancy Nishimura. 2002. "The impact of same-sex friendships on the well-being of women: A review of the literature." *Women & Therapy* 25(1):37–59.

Knight, Jennifer, Michelle R. Hebl, and Miriam Mendoza. 2004. "Toy story: Illustrating gender differences in a motor skills task." *Teaching of Psychology* 31(2):101–103.

Knoblauch, Ann-Marie. 2007. "Promiscuous or proper? Nymphs as female role models in ancient Greece." In Alexandra Cuffel and Brian Britt, (eds.), *Religion, Gender, and Culture in the Pre-Modern World.* (pp. 47–62). New York: Palgrave Macmillan.

Knox, David, Mary Zusman, and Andrea McNeely. 2008. "University student beliefs about sex: Men vs. women." *College Student Journal* 42(1):181–85.

Koch, Janice, and Beverly J. Irby. (eds.). 2005. *Gender and Schooling in the Early Years.* Greenwich, CT: IAP.

Kodama, Naomi, Kazuhiko, and Yoko Takahashi. 2009. "Why does employing more females increase corporate profits? Evidence from Japanese panel data." *Japan Labor Review* 6(1):51–71.

Kogure, Tetsuo. 2007. "A preference for boys is causing massive headaches in India and China." *Asahi Shimbun* June 21:26.

Kohlberg, Lawrence. 1966. "A cognitive-developmental analysis of children's sex role concepts and attitudes." In Eleanor Maccoby (ed.), *The Development of Sex Differences.* Stanford, CA: Stanford University.

Kohler, Jeremy, and Nancy Cambria. 2009. "Family violence spikes here." *St. Louis Post-Dispatch* April 17:A1, A4.

Kohut, Andrew. 2007. "Are Americans ready to elect a female President?" Pew Research Center Publications. May 9. http://pewresearch.org/pubs/474/female-president

Koropeckyj-Cox, Tanya, and Gretchen Pendell. 2007. "The gender gap in attitudes about childlessness in the United States." *Journal of Marriage and the Family* 69(4):899–915.

Kosberg, Robert L., and Andrew S. Rancer. 1999. "Enhancing argumentativeness and argumentative behavior: The influence of gender and training." In Linda Longmire and Lisa Merrill (eds.), *Untying the Tongue: Gender, Power, and the Word.* Westport, CT: Praeger/Greenwood.

Koski, Jessica. 2007. *Kids, careers, and gender norms: Evaluating the potential for new choice.* New York: American Sociological Association.

Kowalski, Kathiann M. 2007. *Affirmative Action.* New York: Marshall Cavendish Benchmark.

Kowtko, Stacy. 2006. *Nature and the Environment in Pre-Columbian American Life.* Westport, CT: Greenwood.

Kramer, Heinrich, and Jacob Sprenger. 2000. "Methods of the devil." In Elaine G. Breslaw (ed.), *Witches of the Atlantic World: A Historical Reader and Primary Sourcebook.* (pp. 21–27). New York: New York University.

Kraus, Vered. 2002. *Secondary Breadwinners: Israeli Women in the Labor Force.* Westport, CT: Praeger.

Krauss, Daniel A., and Bruce D. Sales. 2000. "Legal standards, expertise, and experts in the resolution of contested child custody cases." *Psychology, Public Policy and Law* 6(4):843–79.

Kristiansen, Jan Erik, and Toril Sandnes. 2006. *Women and Men in Norway: What the Figures Say.* Oslo: Statistics Norway. www.ssb.no/english

Kristof, Nicholas D, and Sheryl WuDunn. 2009. "The women's crusade." *New York Times Magazine* August 23:28–39.

Kroska, Amy. 2004. "Divisions of domestic work: Revising and expanding theoretical explanations." *Journal of Family Issues* 25(7):900–32.

Krumhuber, Eva, Antony S.R. Manstead, and Arvid Kappas. 2007. "Temporal aspects of facial displays in person and expression perception: The effects of smile dynamics, head-tilt, and gender." *Journal of Nonverbal Behavior* 31:39–56.

Kubrin, C. 2005. "Gangstas, thugs, and hustlas: Identity and the code of the street in rap music." *Social Problems* 52(3):360–78.

Kukulin, Il'ia. 2008. "The strange adventures of feminism in Russia." *Russian Studies in Literature* 44(3):6.

Kulik, Liat. 2000. "The impact of education and family attributes on attitudes and responses to unemployment among men and women." *Journal of Sociology and Social Welfare* 27(2):161–83.

Kumari, Valsala. 2008. "Microcredit and violence: A snapshot of Kerala." In *Violence and Gender in the Globalized World: The Intimate and the Extimate.* Sanja Bahun-Radunovic and V.G. Julies Rajan (eds.). (pp. 41–46). Aldershot, UK: Ashgate.

Kunin, Madeleine. 2008. Pearls, *Politics and Power: How Women Can Win and Lead.* White River Junction VT: Chelsea Green.

Kunkel, Adrianne, Mary Lee Hummert, and Michael Robert Dennis. 2006. "Social learning theory: Modeling and communication in the family context." In Dawn O. Braithwaite and Leslie A. Baxter (eds.), *Emerging Theories in Family Communication: Multiple Perspectives.* Thousand Oaks, CA: Sage.

Kunkel, D. 2001. "Children and television advertising." In Dorothy Singer and Jerome L. Singer (eds.), *Handbook of Children and the Media.* Thousand oaks, CA: Sage.

Kunze, Astrid. 2008. "Gender wage gap studies: Consistency and decomposition." *Empirical Economics* 35(1):63–76.

Kuperberg, Arielle, and Pamela Stone. 2008. "The media depiction of women who opt out." *Gender & Society* 22(4):497–517.

Kuppens, S., H. Grietens, P. Onghena, D. Michiels, and S.V. Subramanian. 2008. "Individual and classroom variables associated with relational aggression in elementary-school aged children: A multilevel analysis." *Journal of School Psychology* 46(6):639–60.

Kurtz, Demie. 2002. "Caring for teenage children." *Journal of Family Issues* 23(6):748–67.

Kuttner, Robert. 2001. "Body politics." *American Prospect* Fall:A1.

Kuznets, Lois R. 1999. "Taking over the doll's house: Domestic desire and nostalgia in toy narratives." In Beverly Lyon Clark and Margaret R. Higonnet (eds.), *Girls, Boys, Books, Toys: Gender in Children's Literature and Culture.* (pp. 142–53). Baltimore: Johns Hopkins.

Labov, Teresa. 2007. *Gender or ethnicity? Patterns in U.S. intermarriage: 2000, 1990, 1980.* New York: American Sociological Association.

LaFrance, Marianne, and Jennifer L. Harris. 2004. "Gender and verbal and nonverbal communication." In Michele A. Paludi (ed.), *Praeger Guide to the Psychology of Gender.* (pp. 133–54). Westport, CT: Praeger.

LaFrance, Marianne, and Marvin A. Hecht. 2000. "Gender and smiling: A meta-analysis." In Agneta H. Fischer (ed.), *Gender and Emotion: Social Psychological Perspectives.* New York: Cambridge University.

LaFrance, Marianne, Marvin A. Hecht, and Elizabeth Levy Paluck. 2003. "The contingent smile: A meta-analysis of sex differences in smiling." *Psychological Bulletin* 129(2):305–34.

Lakoff, Robin. 1975. *Language and Woman's Place.* New York: Colsphon.

Lakoff, Robin. 2005. "Language, gender, and politics: Putting 'women' and 'power' in the same sentence." In Janet Holmes and Miriam Meyerhoff (eds.), *The Handbook of Language and Gender.* Malden, MA: Blackwell.

Lamb, Michael. 2002. "Nonresidential fathers and their children." In Catherine S. Tamis-LeMonda and Natasha Cabrera (eds.), *Handbook of Father Involvement: Multidisciplinary Perspectives.* Mahwah, NJ: Lawrence Erlbaum.

Lambdin, Jennifer R., Kristen M. Greer, and Kari Selby Jibotian. 2003. "The animal=male hypothesis: Children's and adults' beliefs about the sex of non-specific stuffed animals." *Sex Roles* 48(11/12):471–82.

Lance, Larry M. 2007. "College student sexual morality revisited: A consideration of pre-marital sex, extra-marital sex, and childlessness between 1940 and 2000–2005." *College Student Journal* 41(3):727–33.

Landry, Bart. 2000. *Black Working Wives: Pioneers of the American Family Revolution.* Berkeley: University of California.

Lang, Theo. 1971. *The Difference Between a Man and a Woman.* New York: John Day.

Langley, Winston E., and Vivian C. Fox (eds.). 1998. "Employed mothers and child care during the Depression and World War II." Document 93. In *Women's Rights in the United States: A Documentary History* (255–57). Westport, CT: Praeger.

Langlois, Carol. 2006. "The effects of single-gender versus coeducational environments on the self-esteem development and academic competence of high school females." *Dissertation Abstracts International: Section A: Humanities and Social Sciences* 66(12-A):4363.

Lareau, Annette. 2002. "Invisible inequality: Social class and childrearing in black families and white families." *American Sociological Review* 67(5):747–76.

Larson, Mary Strom. 2003. "Gender, race and aggression in television commercials that feature children." *Sex Roles* 48(1/2):67–75.

Laube, Heather, Kelley Massoni, Joey Sprague, and Abby L. Ferber. 2007. "The impact of gender on the evaluation of teaching: What we know and what we can do." *NWSA Journal* 19(3 Fall).

Laumann, Edward O., and Jenna Mahay. 2002. "The social organization of women's sexuality." In Gina M. Wingood and Ralph J. DiClemente (eds.), *Handbook of Women's Sexual and Reproductive Health: Issues in Women's Health.* (pp. 43–70). New York: Kluwer Academic/Plenum.

Laundra, Kenneth H., Gary Kiger, and Stephen J. Bahr. 2002. "A social development model of serious delinquency: Examining gender differences." *Journal of Primary Prevention* 22(4):389–407.

Lauzen, Martha M. 2003. *The Celluloid Ceiling: Behind-the-Scenes and On-Screen Employment of Women in the Top 250 Films of 2002.* San Diego, CA: School of Communication, San Diego State University.

Lauzen, Martha M., and David M. Dozier. 2005. "Recognition and respect revisited: Portrayals of age and gender in prime-time television." *Mass Communication and Society* 83:241–56.

Lauzen, Martha M., David M. Dozier, and Barbara Reyes. 2007. "From adultescents to zoomers: An examination of age and gender in prime-time television." *Communication Quarterly* 55(3):343–57.

Lawler-Row, Kathleen A., Johan C. Karremans, Cynthia Scott, Meirav Edlis-Matityahou, and Laura Edwards. 2008. "Forgiveness, physiological reactivity and health: The role of anger." *International Journal of Psychophysiology* 68(1):51–58.

Lawrence, Anne. E. 2003. "Factors associated with satisfaction or regret following male-to-female sex reassignment surgery." *Archives of Sexual Behavior* 32(4):299–315.

———. 2006. "Patient-reported complications and functional outcomes of male-to-female sex reassignment surgery." *Archives of Sexual Behavior* 35(6):717–27.

Lawton, Carol A., Judith E. Owen Blakemore, and Lesa Rae Vartanian. 2003. "The new meaning of Ms.: Single, but too old for Miss." *Psychology of Women Quarterly* 27:215–20.

Layton, Lyndsey. 2007. "Mom's in the House, with kids at home: For Congresswomen with young children, a tough balance." *The Washington Post* July 19:A1,A6.

Leaper, Campbell, and Carly K. Friedman. 2007. "The socialization of gender." In J. Grusec and P. Hastings (eds.), *The Handbook of Socialization.* (pp. 561–87). New York: Guilford.

Leaper, Campbell, and Melanie M. Ayres. 2007. "A meta-analytic review of gender variations in adults' language use: Talkativeness, affiliative speech, and assertive speech." *Personality and Social Psychology Review* 11(4):328–63.

Leaper, Campbell, Lisa Breed, and Laurie Hoffman. 2002. "Variations in the gender-stereotyped content of children's television cartoons across genres." *Journal of Applied Social Psychology* 32(8):1653–62.

Lebra, Takie Sugiyama. 2007. *Identity, Gender, and Status in Japan: Collected Papers of Takie Lebra.* Folkstone, UK: Global Oriental.

Lebsock, Suzanne. 1990. " 'No obey': Indian, European, and African women in seventeenth-century Virginia." In Nancy A. Hewitt (ed.), *Women, Families, and Communities: Readings in American History, Volume One: To 1877.* Glenview, IL: Scott, Foresman.

Lederman, Doug. 2006. "Gender gap grows." *Inside Higher education* July 12. www.insidehighered.com/news/2006/07/12/gender

Lee, Grace O.M. 2002. "The challenges of global capitalism: Unemployment and state workers' reactions and responses in post-reform China." *International Journal of Human Resources Management* 13(3):399–415.

Leeb, Rebecca T., and F. Gillian Rejskind. 2004. "Here's looking at you, kid! A longitudinal study of perceived gender differences in mutual gaze behavior in young infants." *Sex Roles* 50(1/2):1–14.

Lehman, Edward C., Jr. 1993. *Gender and Work: The Case of the Clergy.* Albany: State University of New York.

———. 2002. *Women's Path into Ministry: Six Major Studies.* Durham, NC: Duke Divinity School.

Lehman, Peter. 2004. "In an imperfect world, men with small penises are unforgiven: The presentation of the penis/phallus in American films of the 1990s." In Michael S. Kimmel and Michael A. Messner (eds.), *Men's Lives.* (pp. 522–32). Boston: Allyn & Bacon.

Leit, R.A., H.G. Pope, and J.J. Gray. 2001. "Cultural expectations of muscularity in men: The evolution of Playgirl centerfolds." *International Journal of Eating Disorders* 29:90–93.

Lemons, Mary, and Monica Parzinger. 2007. "Gender schemas: A cognitive explanation of discrimination of women in technology." *Journal of Business and Psychology* 22(1):91–98.

Leonard, Elizabeth Dermody. 2002. *Convicted Survivors: The Imprisonment of Battered Women who Kill.* Albany: State University of New York.

Leppänen, Jukka M., and Jari K. Hietanen. 2001. "Emotion recognition and social adjustment in school-aged girls and boys." *Scandinavian Journal of Psychology* 42(5):429–35.

Lerner, Gerda. 1996. "Placing women in history." In Mary Beth Norton and Ruth M. Alexander (eds.), *Major Problems in American Women's History.* Lexington, MA: D. C. Heath.

Lesko, Alexandra C., and Jennifer Henderlong Corpus. 2006. "Discounting the difficult: How high math-identified women respond to stereotype threat." *Sex Roles* 54(1/2):113–25.

Letherby, Gayle. 2002. "Childless and bereft? Stereotypes and realities in relation to 'voluntary' and 'involuntary' childlessness and womanhood." *Sociological Inquiry* 72(1):7–20.

Leistyna, Pepi, and Loretta Alper. 2005. *Class Dismissed: How TV Frames the Working Class.* Videorecording. Northhampton, MA: Media Education Foundation.

Letich, Larry. 1991. "Do you know who your friends are?: Why most men over 30 don't have friends and what they can do about it." *Utne Reader* May–June:85–87.

Levin, Diane, and Jean Kilbourne. 2008. *So Sexy So Soon: The new Sexualized Childhood, and What Parents Can Do to Protect Their Kids.* New York: Ballantine.

LeVine, Robert A. 1990. "Gender differences: Interpreting anthropological data." In Malkah T. Notman and Carol C. Nadelson (eds.), *Women and Men: New Perspectives on Gender Differences.* Washington, DC: American Psychiatric Press.

Levine, Stephen, and Jay Weissman. 2007. "Anxiety disorders and older women." In Victor J. Malatesta (ed.), *Mental Health Issues of Older Women: A Comprehensive Review for Health Care Professionals.* Binghamton, NY: Haworth.

Levins, Harry. 1995. "People" column. *St. Louis Post-Dispatch* March 19:2A.

Levstik, Linda S. 2001. "Daily acts of ordinary courage: Gender-equitable practice in the social studies classroom." In Patricia O'Reilly and Elizabeth M. Penn (eds.), *Educating Young Adolescent Girls.* (pp. 189–211). Mahwah, NJ: Lawrence Erlbaum.

Lev-Wiesel, Rachel. 2000. "The effect of children's sleeping arrangements (communal vs. familial) on fatherhood among men in an Israeli kibbutz." *Journal of Social Psychology* 140(5):580–8.

Levy, Jane C. 2006/2007. "Advertising to women: Who are we in print and how do we reclaim our image?" *Journal of Creativity in Mental Health* 2(4):75–86.

Lewin, Tamar. 2006a. "At colleges, women are leaving men in the dust." *New York Times* July 9:1,18. www.nytimes.com/2006/07/09/education/09college

———. 2006b. "A more nuanced look at men, women and college." *New York Times* July 12:C13. www.nytimes.com/2006/07/12/education/12gender

Lewis, Jan E. 2002. "A revolution for whom? Women in the era of the American Revolution." In Nancy A. Hewitt (ed.), *A Companion to American Women's History.* Oxford, UK: Blackwell.

Lewis, Karen Gail. 2001. *With or Without a Man: Single Women Taking Control of Their Lives.* Boulder, CO: Bull.

Li, Hongbin, and Junsen Zhang. 2007. "Do high birth rates hamper economic growth?" *Review of Economics and Statistics* 89(1):110–17.

Li, Jianghong, and William Lavely. 2003. "Village context, women's status, and son preference among rural Chinese women." *Rural Sociology* 68(1)87–106.

Lichtenberger, Elizabeth O., and Alan S. Kaufman. 2007. "Intelligence tests." In Barbara J. Bank (ed.), *Gender and Education: Volume I.* (pp. 421–25). Westport, CT: Praeger.

Lichtenstein, Bronwen. 2000. "Secret encounters: Black men, bisexuality, and AIDS in Alabama." *Medical Anthropology Quarterly* 14(3):374–93.

Lichter, Daniel T., and Nancy C. Landale. 1995. "Parental work, family structure, and poverty among Latino children." *Journal of Marriage and the Family* 57:346–54.

Liddle, Joanna, and Sachiko Nakajima. 2000. *Rising Suns, Rising Daughters: Gender, Class and Power in Japan.* London: Zed.

Lien, Pei-te, M. Margaret Conway, and Janelle Wong. 2004. *The Politics of Asian Americans: Diversity and Community.* New York: Routledge.

Lightfoot, J.L. (trans.). 2003. *On the Syrian Goddess.* New York: Oxford University.

Lincoln, Anne E. 2008. "Gender, productivity, and the marital wage premium." *Journal of Marriage and the Family* 70(3):806–14.

Lindberg, Carter. 2008. *Love: A Brief History through Western Christianity.* Malden, MA: Blackwell.

Linden, Wolfgang et al. 2003. "There is more to anger coping than 'in' or 'out.'" *Emotion* 3(1):12–29.

Lindgren, Elaine H. 1996. *Land in her Own Name: Women as Homesteaders in North Dakota.* Norman: University of Oklahoma.

Lindner, Katharina. 2004. "Images of women in general interest and fashion magazine advertisements from 1955 to 2002." *Sex Roles* 51(7/8):409–21.

Lindsey, Linda L. 1975. "Language and race: A sociolinguistic view of conflict". Ohio Academy of Science. Denison, Ohio: Denison University. April.

———. 1979. Book review of *Wisdom from Women in the Bible* by Edith Deen. *Review for Religious* 38(5):792–93.

———. 1984. "Career paths in pharmacy: An exploration of male and female differences." Midwest Sociological Society, Chicago.

———. 1988. "The health status of women in Pakistan: The impact of Islamization." Midwest Sociological Society, Minneapolis.

———. 1992. "Gender and the workplace: Some lessons from Japan." Midwest Sociological Society, Kansas City.

———. 1995. "Toward a model of women in development." Midwest Sociological Society, Chicago.

———. 1996a. "Women and agriculture in the developing world." In Paula J. Dubeck and Kathryn Borman (eds.), *Women and Work: A Handbook*. New York: Garland.

———. 1996b. "Gender equity and development: A perspective on the U.N. Conference on Women." Midwest Sociological Society, Chicago.

———. 1996c. "Full-time homemaker as unpaid laborer." In Paula J. Dubeck and Kathryn Borman (eds.), *Women and Work: A Handbook*. New York: Garland.

———. 1997. "Smoking out the gender connection." *Chicago Tribune* March 28:Sect. 1(11).

———. 1998. "Gender issues in Japanese style management: Implications for American corporations." Asian Studies Development Program National Conference, Baltimore.

———. 1999. "The politics of cultural identity and minority women in China." Mid-Atlantic Region for Asian Studies, Gettysburg, PA.

———. 2002a. "Gender segregation in a global context: Focus on Afghan women." Midwest Sociological Society, Milwaukee.

———. 2002b. "Globalization and human rights: Focus on Afghan women." In *September 11 and Beyond*. (pp. 62–67). Upper Saddle River, NJ: Prentice Hall.

———. 2004. "The paradox of women and economic development in China." Midwest Sociological Society, Kansas City.

———. 2007. "Impact of globalization on women in China." Midwest Sociological Society, Chicago.

———. 2006. "Globalization and development: Focus on women in China." East-West Center Association. Hanoi, Viet Nam.

———. 2010. "Glimpses of gender in Japan: Equity issues at the millennium." Japan Studies Association, Honolulu.

Lindsey, Linda L., and Stephen Beach. 2004. *Sociology*. Upper Saddle River, NJ: Prentice Hall.

Linnenberg, Kathryn D. 2007. "#1 father or fathering 101? Couple relationship quality and father involvement when fathers live with their children." In Paula England and Kathryn Edin (eds.), *Unmarried Couples with Children*. New York: Russell Sage Foundation.

Lipovskaya, Olga. 1994. "The mythology of womanhood in contemporary 'Soviet' culture." In Anastasia Posadskaya and the Moscow Gender Centre (eds.), *Women in Russia: A New Era in Russian Feminism*. London: Verso.

Lippa, Richard. 2005. *Gender, Nature, and Nurture*. Mahwah, NJ: Lawrence Erlbaum.

——— 2007. "The preferred traits of mates in a cross-national study of heterosexual and homosexual men and women: An examination of biological and cultural influences." *Archives of Sexual Behavior* 36(2):193–208.

Lips, Hilary M. 2001. *Sex & Gender: An Introduction*. Mountain View, CA: Mayfield.

Litosseliti, Lia. 2006. *Gender and Language: Theory and Practice*. London: Hodder Arnold.

Littlefield, Marci Bounds. 2008. : The media as a system of racialization: Exploring images of African American women and the new racism." *American Behavioral Scientist* 51(5):675–85.

Liu, Melinda. 2008a. "China's new empty nest." *Newsweek* March 10:41.

Liu, Tessie. 2008b. "Teaching the differences among women from a historical perspective: Rethinking race and gender as social categories." In Vickie L. Ruiz and Ellen Carol DuBois (eds.), *Unequal Sisters: An inclusive Reader in U.S. Women's History*. (pp. 28–40). New York: Routledge.

Lloyd, Cynthia, Monica Grant, and Amanda Ritchie. 2008. "Gender differences in time use among adolescents in developing countries: Implications of rising school enrollment rates." *Journal of Research on Adolescence* 18(1):99–120.

Lloyd, Elisabeth A. 2005. *The Case of the Female Orgasm: Bias in the Science of Evolution*. Cambridge, MA: Harvard University.

Lloyd, Sterling C. 2007. "Gender gap in education." *Education Week* July 6. www.edweek.org/rc/articles/2007

Lockhart, William. H. 2000. " 'We are one in life,' but not of one gender ideology: Unity, ambiguity and the Promise Keepers." *Sociology of Religion* 61(1):73–92.

Lonsway, Kimberly A., Joanne Archambault, and David Lisak. 2008. "False reports: Moving beyond the issue to successfully investigate and prosecute non-stranger sexual assault." *The Voice* 3(1). National Center for the Prosecution of Violence against Women.

Loraux, Nicole. 1998. *Mother in Mourning: With the Essay of Amnesty and its Opposite*, Corinne Pache (trans.). Ithaca, NY: Cornell University.

Lord, Vivian B., Boyd Davis, and Peyton Mason. 2008. "Stance-shifting in language used by sex offenders: Five case studies." *Psychology, Crime, and Law* 14(4):357–79.

Loscocco, Karyn, and Glenna Spitze. 2007. "Gender patterns in provider role attitude and behavior." *Journal of Family Issues* 28(7):934–54.

Loukas, Alexandra, Stephanie K. Paulos, and Sheri Robinson. 2005. "Early adolescent social and overt aggression: Examining the roles of social anxiety and maternal psychological control." *Journal of Youth and Adolescence* 34(4):335–45.

Low, Alaine, and Soraya Tremayne (eds.). 2001. *Sacred Custodians of the Earth: Women, Spirituality and the Environment.* New York: Berghahn.

Lubinski, David S., and Camilla Persson Benbow. 2007. "Sex differences in personal attributes for the development of scientific expertise." In Stephen Ceci and Wendy Williams (eds.), *Why Aren't More Women in Science? Top Researchers Debate the Evidence.* (pp. 79–100). Washington, DC: American Psychological Association.

Luciak, Ilja A. 2001. *After the Revolution: Gender and Democracy in El Salvador, Nicaragua, and Guatemala.* Baltimore: Johns Hopkins University.

Lucy, Denise M., Jayati Ghosh, and Edward Kujawa. 2008. "Empowering women's leadership: A case study of Bangladeshi microcredit business." *SAM Advanced Management Journal* 73(4):31–50.

Luker, Kristin. 1984. *Abortion and the Politics of Motherhood.* Berkeley, CA: University of California.

Lundskow, George N. 2002. *Awakening to an Uncertain Future: A Case Study of the Promise Keepers.* New York: Peter Lang.

Luo, Baozhen. 2008. "Striving for comfort: 'Positive' construction of dating cultures among second-generation Chinese American youths." *Journal of Social and Personal Relationships* 25(6):867–88.

Lyle, Samantha A. 2008. "(Mis)recognition and the middle-class/bourgeois gaze: A case study of Wife Swap." *Critical Discourse Studies* 5(4):319–30.

Lynn, David B. 1969. *Parental and Sex Role Identification: A Theoretical Formulation.* Berkeley, CA: McCutchan.

Lystra, Karen. 1989. *Searching the Heart: Women, Men and Romantic Love in Nineteenth Century America.* New York: Oxford University.

Mabbett, Ian and Jayant Bhalchandra Bapat. 2008. "Contextualising the goddess." In J. Bapat and I. Mabbett (eds.), *The Iconic Female: Goddesses of India, Nepal, and Tibet.* Clayton (Victoria). AS: Monash University.

Macatee, Tara Colleen. 2007. "Psychological adjustment of adult children raised by a gay or lesbian parent." *Dissertation Abstracts International: Section B: The Sciences and Engineering* 68(3-B):1983.

Maccoby, Eleanor E. 1998. *The Two Sexes: Growing up Apart, Coming Together.* Cambridge, MA: Belknap/Harvard University.

———. 2000. "Perspective on gender development." *International Journal of Behavioral Development* 24(4):398–406.

Maccoby, Eleanor Emmons, and Carol Nagy Jacklin. 1974. *The Psychology of Sex Differences.* Stanford, CA: Stanford University.

MacDonald, Martha, Shelley Phipps, and Lynn Lethbridge. 2005. "Taking its toll: The influence of paid and unpaid work on women's well-being." *Feminist Economics* 11(1):63–94.

MacGillis, Alec. 2009. "Health care reform and abortion coverage." Questions and answers. *Washington Post* November 15. http://washingtonpost.com/health-care-reform

MacKay, Judith. 2001. "Global sex: Sexuality and sexual practices around the world." *Sexual & Relational Therapy* 16(1):71–82.

MacKinnon, Catharine A. 2000a. "The social causes of sexual harassment." In Edmund Wall (ed.), *Sexual Harassment, Confrontation and Decisions.* (pp. 141–56). Amherst, NY: Prometheus.

———. 2000b. "Sexual harassment as sex discrimination." In Edmund Wall (ed.), *Sexual Harassment, Confrontation and Decisions.* (pp. 157–66). Amherst, NY: Prometheus.

———. 2003. *Sex Equality: Lesbian and Gay Rights.* New York: Foundation Press.

MacLean, Ian. 1980. *The Renaissance Notion of Woman: A Study in the Fortunes of Scholasticism and Medical Science in European Intellectual Life.* Cambridge, UK: Cambridge University.

Macleitch, Gail D. 2007. "Native American women: Gender and early American history." In S. Jay Kleinberg and Vicki L. Ruiz (eds.), *The Practice of U.S. Women's History: Narratives, Intersections, and Dialogues.* New Brunswick, NJ: Rutgers University.

MacNaughton, Glenda. 2007. "Early childhood education." In Barbara J. Bank (ed.), *Gender and Education; Volume I.* (pp. 263–67). Westport, CT: Praeger.

Madson, Laura, and Robert M. Hessling. 2001. "Readers' perceptions of four alternatives to masculine generic pronouns." *Journal of Social Psychology* 141(1):156–8.

Magli, Ida. 2003. *Women and Self Sacrifice in the Christian Church: A Cultural History from the First to the Nineteenth Century.* Janet Sethre (trans.). Jefferson, NC: McFarland.

Magnuson, Eric. 2007. *Changing Men, Transforming Culture: Inside the Men's Movement.* Boulder, CO: Paradigm.

———. 2008. "Rejecting the American dream." *Journal of Contemporary Ethnography* 37(3):255–90.

Magnuson, Katherine A., and Christina Gibson-Davis. 2007. "Child support among low-income noncustodial fathers." In Paula England and Kathryn Edin (eds.), *Unmarried Couples with Children.* New York: Russell Sage Foundation.

Magnuson, Stew. 2005. "Programs make inroads toward gender parity in voc ed." *Education Daily* 38–118(June 23):2.

Magovcevic, Mariola, and Michael E. Addis. 2008. "The masculine depression scale: Development and psychometric evaluation." *Psychology of Men and Masculinity* 9(3):117–32.

Mahaffy, Kimberley A. 2004. "Girls' low self-esteem: How it is related to later socioeconomic achievements." *Gender & Society* 18(3):309–27.

Mahal, Montarin, and Elaine Lindgren. 2002. "Microfinance and women's empowerment in rural Bangladesh." Midwest Sociological Society, Milwaukee.

Mahalik, James R., and Aaron B. Rochlen. 2006. "Men's likely responses to clinical depression: What are they and do masculinity norms predict them?" *Sex Roles* 55:659–67.

Mahalik, James R., Shaun M. Burns, and Matthew Syzdek. 2007. "Masculinity and perceived normative health behaviors as predictive of men's health behaviors." *Social Science and Medicine* 64(11):2201–9.

Maher, Michael J., Linda M. Sever, and Shaun Pichler. 2006. "The priest sex scandal and its effects on trust and respect: How Catholic college students think about Catholic leadership." *Journal of Religion and Abuse* 8(3):35–62.

Maher, Michael J., Linda M. Sever, and Shaun Pichler. 2007. "Beliefs versus lived experience: Gender differences in Catholic college students' attitudes concerning premarital sex and contraception." *American Journal of Sexuality Education* 24(4):67–87.

Major, Lesa Hartley, and Renita Coleman. 2008. "The intersection of race and gender in election coverage: What happens when the candidates don't fit the stereotypes?" *Howard Journal of Communications* 19(4):315–33.

Malesta, Victor J. 2007. "Sexual problems, women, and aging: An overview." *Journal of Women and Aging* 19(1/2):139–54.

Maley, William. 2008. "Human rights in Afghanistan." In Shahram Akbarzadeh and Benjamin MacQueen (eds.), *Islam and Human Rights in Practice: Perspectives across the Ummah*. London: Routledge.

Malley, Maeve, and Damian McCann. 2002. "Family therapy with lesbian and gay clients." In Adrian Coyle and Celia Kitzinger (eds.), *Lesbian and Gay Psychology: New Perspectives*. (pp. 198–218). Oxford, UK: BPS Blackwell.

Mandara, Jelani, Carolyn B. Murray, and Toya N. Joyner. 2005. "The impact of fathers' absence on African American adolescents' gender role development." *Sex Roles* 53(3/4):207–20.

Mandelbaum, Jenny. 2003. "Interactive methods for constructing relationships." In Phillip J. Glenn, Curtis D. LeBaron, and Jenny Mandelbaum (eds.), *Studies in Language and Social Interaction*. (pp. 195–206). Mahwah, NJ: Lawrence Erlbaum.

Mandziuk, Roseann M. 2008. "Dressing down Hillary." *Communication and Critical/Cultural Studies* 5(3):312–16.l

Manegold, Catherine S. 2000. *In Glory's Shadow: Shannon Faulkner, The Citadel and a Changing America*. New York: Alfred A. Knopf.

Mann, Robin. 2007. "Out of the shadows?: Grandfatherhood, age, and masculinities." *Journal of Aging Studies* 21(4):281–91.

Manning, Alan, and Joanna Swaffield. 2008. "The gender gap in early-career wage growth." *Economic Journal* 118(530):983–1024.

Manning, Wendy D., and Nancy S. Landale. 1996. "Racial and ethnic differences in premarital child-bearing." *Journal of Marriage and the Family* 58(1):63–77.

Manson, JoAnn E. et al. 2003. "Estrogen plus progestin and the risk of coronary heart disease." *New England Journal of Medicine* 349(6):523–34.

Mapes, Diane (ed.). 2007. *Single State of the Union: Single Women Speak Out on Life, Love, and the Pursuit of Happiness*. Emeryville, CA: Seal.

Marano, Hara. 2004. "A nation of wimps." *Psychology Today* 37(6):58, 103, 110.

Marklein, Mary Beth. 2008. "Study: Colleges shouldn't fret over hands-on parents." *USA Today* January 23.

Marks, Stephen R., Ted L. Huston, Elizabeth M. Johnson, and Shelley M. MacDermid. 2001. "Role balance among white married couples." *Journal of Marriage and the Family* 63(4):1083–98.

Marmion, Shelly, and Paula Lundberg-Love. 2004. "Learning masculinity and femininity: Gender socialization from parents and peers across the life span." In Michele A. Paludi (ed.), *Praeger Guide to Psychology of Gender*. (pp. 1–26). Westport, CT: Praeger/Greenwood.

Marsh, Betsa. 2007. "Helicopter parents hover over campus." *Miamian Magazine* Spring. Miamian Online www.miami.muohio.edu/University_Advancment /MiamiAlum/news

Marsh, Robert M. 2009. "Civilizational diversity and support for traditional values." *Comparative Sociology* 8(2):267–304.

Martin, Carol Lynn, and Diane N. Ruble. 2004. "Children's search for gender cues: Cognitive perspectives on gender development." *Current Directions in Psychological Science* 13:67–70.

Martin, Carol Lynn, Diane N. Ruble, and Joel Szkrybalo. 2002. "Cognitive theories of early gender development." *Psychological Bulletin* 128(6):903–33.

Martin, Carol Lynn, Diane N. Ruble, and Joel Szkrybalo. 2004. "Recognizing the centrality of gender identity and stereotype knowledge in gender development and moving toward theoretical integration: Reply to Bandura and Bussey." *Psychological Bulletin* 130(5):702–710.

Marx, Karl, and Friedrich Engels. 1964. *The Communist Manifesto*. Samuel Moore (trans.). New York: Washington Square.

Marx, Karl. 1967 (original, 1867–95). *Das Capital*. New York: International.

Mason, W. Alex, and Michael Windle. 2002. "Gender, self-control, and informal social control in adolescence: A test of three models of the continuity of delinquent behavior." *Youth and Society* 33(4):479–514.

Massey, Douglas S., and Garvey Lundy. 2001. "Use of Black English and racial discrimination in urban housing markets: New methods and findings." *Urban Affairs Review* 36(4):452–69.

Massey, Sean G. 2007. "Sexism, heterosexism, and attributions about undesirable behavior in children of gay, lesbian, and heterosexual parents." In Fiona Tasker and Jerry J. Bigner (eds.), *Gay and Lesbian Parenting: New Directions*. Binghamton, NY: Haworth.

Mast, Marianne Schmid. 2007. "On the importance of nonverbal communication in the physician-patient relationship." *Patient Education and Counseling* 67(3):315–18.

Masters, William H., and Virginia Johnson. 1966. *Human Sexual Response.* Boston: Little, Brown.

Masters, William H., and Virginia Johnson. 1970. *Human Sexual Inadequacy.* Boston: Little, Brown.

Mastracci, Sharon H. 2004. *Breaking Out of the Pink-Collar Ghetto: Policy Solutions for Non-College Women."* Armonk, NY:M.E. Sharpe.

Mather, Mark, Kerri L. Rivers, and Linda A. Jacobsen. (2005). "What the American Community Survey Tells Us About Marriage and the Family." *PRB Population Bulletin* April. *Population* 60(3):1–24 Reference Bureau.

Matthews, Justin L. 2007. "Hidden sexism: Facial prominence and its connections to gender and occupational status in popular print media." *Sex Roles* 57:515–25.

Matthews, Rebecca, and Victor Nee. 2000. "Gender inequality and economic growth in rural China." *Social Science Research* 29(4):606–32.

Matthews, Sharon, and Chris Powers. 2002. "Socioeconomic gradients in psychological distress: A focus on women, social roles and work-home characteristics." *Social Science & Medicine* 54(5):799–810.

Maurer, Trent, and David Robinson. 2008. Effects of attire, alcohol, and gender on perceptions of date rape." *Sex Roles* 58(5/6):423–34.

Maushart, Susan. 1999.*The Mask of Motherhood: How Becoming a Mother Changes Everything and Why We Pretend it Doesn't.* New York: New Press.

Mayer, Ann Elizabeth. 2008. "The reformulation of Islamic thought on gender rights and roles." In Shahram Akbarzadeh and Benjamin MacQueen (eds.), *Islam and Human Rights in Practice: Perspectives across the Ummah.* London: Routledge.

Maynard, Mary. 2001. "Beyond the 'big three': The development of feminist theory into the 1990s." In Darlene M. Juschka (ed.), *Feminism in the Study of Religion: A Reader.* (pp. 292–313). London: Continuum.

Mayo Clinic. 2002. "Premenstrual syndrome." Women's Health Center. www.mayoclinic.com

McAndrew, Francis T., Emily K. Bell, and Contita Maria Garcia. 2007. "Who do we tell and whom do we tell on? Gossip as a strategy for status enhancement." *Journal of Applied Social Psychology* 37(7):1562–1577.

McAndrew, Frank T. 2008. "Can gossip be good?" *Scientific American* 19(5):26–33.

McBride, James. 1995. *War, Battering, and Other Sports: The Gulf between American Men and Women.* Atlantic Highlands, NJ: Humanities Press.

McBride-Stetson, Dorothy E. 2004. *Women's Rights in the U.S.A: Policy Debates and Gender Roles.* New York: Routledge.

McCaughey. 2008. *The Caveman Mystique: Pop-Darwinism and the Debates over Sex, Violence, and Science.* New York: Routledge.

McConatha, Jasmin T., Frauke Schnell, and Amy McKenna. 1999. "Description of older adults in magazine advertisements." *Psychological Reports* 85(3):1051–6.

McCormick, Theresa. 2007. "Strong women teachers: Their struggles and strategies for gender equity." In David M. Sadker and Ellen S. Silber (eds.), *Gender in the Classroom: Foundations, Skills, Methods, and Strategies.* Mahwah, NJ: Lawrence Erlbaum.

McCorry, Timothy. 2006. "Adolescents' perceptions of monitoring and supervision in patriarchal and non-patriarchal households." American Society of Criminology, Los Angeles.

McCue, Margi Laird. 2008. *Domestic Violence: A Reference Handbook.* Santa Barbara, CA: ABC-CLIO.

McDaniel, Susan. 2003a. "Hidden in the household: Now it's men at midlife." *Ageing International* 28(4):326–44.

McDaniel, June. 2003b. *Making Virtuous Daughters and Wives: An Introduction to Brata Rituals in Bengali Folk Religion.* New York: State University of New York.

McDaniel, Stephen R., Choonghoon, and Joseph E. Manan. 2007. "The role of gender and personality traits in response to ads using violent images to promote consumption of sports entertainment." *Journal of Business Research* 60(6):606–12.

McDonald, Judith A., and Robert J. Thornton. 2007. "Do male and female college graduates receive unequal pay?" *Journal of Human Resources* 42(1):32–48.

McDonald, Kristina L., Martha Putallaz, and Christina L. Grimes. 2007. "Girl talk: Gossip, friendship, and sociometric status." *Merrill-Palmer Quarterly* 53(1)3:381–411.

McDonald, Theodore W., and Linda M. Kline. 2004. "Perceptions of appropriate punishment for committing date rape: Male college students recommend lenient punishments." *College Student Journal* 38(1):44–56.

McElhinny, Bonnie. 2005. "Theorizing gender in sociolinguistics and linguistic anthropology." In Janet Holmes and Miriam Meyerhoff (eds.), *The Handbook of Language and Gender.* Malden, MA: Blackwell.

McGinn, Susan Killenberg. 2002. "Friend or foe? Aggressiveness in primates rare; most social behavior affiliated. *The Record* 26(3):1,6. Washington University in St. Louis.

McHale, Susan M., Ann C. Crouter, and Shawn D. Whiteman. 2003. "Topic Review: The family contexts of gender development in childhood and adolescence." *Social Development* 12(1):125–48.

McKechnie. 2001. *The First Christian Centuries: Perspectives on the Early Church.* Downers Grove, IL: InterVarsity.

McLeod, Glenda. 1991. *Virtue and Venom: Catalogues of Women from Antiquity to the Renaissance.* Ann Arbor: University of Michigan.

McManus, Patricia A., and Thomas A. DiPrete. 2001. "Losers and winners: The financial consequences of separation and divorce for men." *American Sociological Review* 66(2):246–68.

McNulty, James K., and Terri D. Fisher. 2008. "Gender differences in response to sexual expectancies and changes in sexual frequency: A short-term longitudinal study of sexual satisfaction in newly married couples." *Archives of Sexual Behavior* 37(2):229–40.

McQuillar, Tayannah Lee. 2007. *When Rap Music had a Conscience: The Artists, Organizations, and Historic Events that Inspired and Shaped the 'Golden Age' of Hip-Hop from 1987 to 1996*. New York: Thunder's Mouth Press.

Mead, Margaret. 2001 (orig. 1935). *Growing up in New Guinea*. New York: HarperCollins.

Mead, Sara. 2006. *The Truth about Boys and Girls*. Sector Spotlight: June 12. Washington, DC: Education Sector. www.EducationSector.org

Mealey, L. 2000. *Sex Differences: Developmental and Evolutionary Strategies*. San Diego: Academic Press.

Media Matters. 2009. "Some media reject claims that Sotomayor is a liberal activist." *Media Matters for America* May 27. http://mediamatters.org/research/200905270045

Media Report to Women. 2008a. "Movie criticism dominated by male newspaper reviewers." *Media Report to Women* 36(3):Summer.

———. 2008b. "No Oscar for gender balance in Academy Award Best Picture." *Media Report to Women* 36(2):Spring.

Megill-Cobbler, Thelma. 1993. "Reading Paul on women." *Lutheran Women Today* 6(January):12–15.

Mellen, Henry S. 2002. "Rough-and-tumble between parents and children and children's social competence." *Dissertation Abstracts International: Section B: Sciences and Engineering* 63(3-B):1588.

Melli, Marygold, and Patricia R. Brown. 2008. "Exploring a new family form: The shared-time family." *International Journal of Law, Policy, and the Family* 22(2):231–69.

Melton, Willie, and Linda L. Lindsey. 1987. "Instrumental and expressive values in mate selection among college students revisited: Feminism, love and economic necessity." Midwest Sociological Society, Chicago. April.

Mena, Jennifer. 2000. "Men's groups delve into the concept of 'machismo.'" *St. Louis Post-Dispatch* December 31:EV8.

Mendoza, Isabella. 2005. "Moving to America to escape poverty." In C.J. Shane (ed.), *The Mexicans*. Detroit: Greenhaven.

Menninger, Sarah Wheeler. 2006. "The impact of rising women's salaries on marital and relationship satisfaction." *Dissertation Abstracts International Section A: Humanities and Social Sciences* 66(11-A):3940.

Merchant, A., A. Bhattacharya, and M. Carnes. 2007. "Can the language of tenure criteria influences women's academic advancement?" *Journal of Women's Health* 16(7):998–1003.

Merkin, Daphene. 2008. "The bitch and the airhead: Blatant women-bashing makes a gut-wrenching comeback." *The Daily Beast*. November 20. www.alternet.org

Merli, M. Giovanna, and Herbert L. Smith. 2002. "Has the Chinese family planning policy been successful in changing fertility preferences?" *Demography* 39(3):557–72.

Mernissi, Fatima. 1987. *Beyond the Veil: Male-Female Dynamics in Modern Muslim Society*. Bloomington: Indiana University.

Merry, Sally Engle. 2009. *Gender Violence: A Cultural Perspective*. Oxford, UK: Wiley-Blackwell.

Merskin, Debra. 2007. "Three faces of Eva: Perpetuation of the hot-Latina stereotype in *Desperate Housewives*." *The Howard Journal of Communication* 18:133–51.

Messineo, Melinda J. 2008. "Does advertising on Black Entertainment Television portray more positive gender representations compared to broadcast networks?" *Sex Roles* 59(9/10):752–64.

Meston, Cindy M., and David M. Buss. 2007. "Why humans have sex." *Archives of Sexual Behavior* 36(4):477–507.

Metz, Isabel, and Phyllis Tharenou. 2001. "Women's career advancement: The relative contribution of human and social capital." *Group & Organization Management* 26(3):312–42.

Meyerowitz, Joanne. 1990. "The roaring teens and twenties reexamined: Sexuality in the furnished room districts of Chicago." In Nancy A. Hewitt (ed.), *Women, Families and Communities: Readings in American History, Volume Two: From 1865*. Glenview, IL: Scott, Foresman.

Meyerowitz, Joanne. 2005. "Rewriting postwar women's history, 1945–69." In Nancy A. Hewitt (ed.), *A Companion to American Women's History*. Oxford, UK: Blackwell.

Meyers, Carol. 2009. "In the household and beyond." *Studia Theologica* 63(1):19–41.

Meyers, Diana T. 2002. *Gender in the Mirror: Cultural Imagery and Women's Agency*. Oxford, UK: Oxford University.

Mikulincer, Mario, and Gail S. Goodman (eds.). 2006. *Dynamics of Romantic Love: Attachment, Caregiving, and Sex*. New York: Guilford.

Milburn, Michael A., Roxanne Mather, and Sheree D. Conrad. 2000. "The effects of viewing R-rated movie scenes that objectify women in perceptions of date rape." *Sex Roles* 43(9/10):645–64.

Miles, Rosalind. 1989. *The Women's History of the World*. Topsfield, MA: Salem House.

Milkman, Ruth. 2003. "Gender at work: The sexual division of labor during World War II." In Linda K. Kerber and Jane Sherron De Hart (eds.), *Women's America: Refocusing the Past*. New York: Oxford University.

Mill, John Stuart. 1869/2002. *The Basic Writings of John Stuart Mill: On Liberty, The Subjection of Women and Utilitarianism*. New York: Modern Library.

Millard, Jennifer E., and Peter R. Grant. 2006. "The stereotypes of black and white women in fashion magazine photographs: The pose of the model and the impression she creates." *Sex Roles* 54:659–73.

Miller, Andrea J., Everett L. Worthington, Jr., and Michael McDaniel. 2008. "Gender and forgiveness: A meta-analytic review and research agenda." *Journal of Social and Clinical Psychology* 27(8):843–76.

Miller, Casey, and Kate Swift. 1993. "Who is man?" In Anne Minas (ed.), *Gender Basics: Feminist Perspectives on Women and men.* Belmont, CA: Wadsworth.

Miller, Cindy Faith, Hanns Martin Trautner, and Diane N. Ruble. 2006. "The role of gender stereotypes in children's preferences and behavior." In Catherine S. Tamis-MeMonda (ed.), *Child Psychology: A Handbook of Contemporary Issues.* (pp. 293–323). New York: Psychology Press.

Miller, Cristanne. 1994. "Who says what to whom." In Camille Roman, Suzanne Juhasz, and Cristanne Miller (eds.), *The Women and Language Debate: A Sourcebook.* New Brunswick, NJ: Rutgers University.

Miller, Eleanor M., and Carrie Yang Costello. 2001. "The limits of biological determinism: Comment on J.R. Udry." *American Sociological Review* 66(4):592–98.

Miller, Kathleen E. 2008. "Wired: Energy drinks, jock identity, masculine norms, and risk taking." *Journal of American College Health* 56(5):481–89.

Miller, Patricia N., Darryl W. Miller, and Eithne M. McKibbin. 1999. "Stereotypes of the elderly in magazine advertisements, 1956–1996." *International Journal of Aging and Human Development* 49(4):319–37.

Millett, Kate. 1995. "Sexual politics." In Stevi Jackson et al. (eds.), *Women's Studies Essential Readings.* New York: New York University.

Million, Joelle. 2003. *Woman's Voice, Woman's Place: Lucy Stone and the Birth of the Woman's Rights Movement.* Westport, CT: Praeger.

Mina, Maria. 2008. "Figurin' out Cretan Neolithic society: Anthropomorphic figurines, symbolism, and gender dialectics." In Valasia Isaakidou and Peter D. Tomkins (eds.), *Exploring the Labyrinth: The Cretan Neolithic in Context.* Oxford, UK: Oxbow.

Minai, Naila. 1991. "Women in early Islam." In Carol J. Verburg (ed.), *Ourselves among Others: Cross-Cultural Readings for Writers.* Boston: Bedford Books.

Mir-Hosseini, Ziba. 2001. "Iran: Emerging feminist voices." In Lynn Walter (ed.), *Women's Rights: A Global View.* (pp. 113–25). Westport, CT: Greenwood.

Mirkin, Marsha. 2004. *The Women Who Danced by the Sea: Finding Ourselves in the Stories of our Biblical Foremothers.* New York: Monkfish.

Mirowsky, John, and Catherine E. Ross. 2003. *Social Causes of Psychological Distress.* Hawthorne, NY: Aldine de Gruyter.

Mischel, W.A. 1966. "A social learning view of sex differences in behavior." In E.E. Maccoby (ed.), *The Development of Sex Differences.* Stanford, CA: Stanford University.

Mishori, Ranit. 2007. "The truth about hormones." Women' Health – A Special Report. *Parade Magazine.* October 14:4–5.

Misra, Joya. 2002. "Class, race, and gender and theorizing welfare states." *Research in Political Sociology* 11:19–52.

Missildine, Whitney, Gideon Feldstein, Joseph C. Punzalan, and Jeffrey T. Parsons. 2005. "S/he loves me, s/he loves me not: Questioning heterosexist assumptions of gender differences for romantic love and sexually motivated behaviors." *Sexual Addiction and Compulsivity* 12(1):65–74.

Mitchell, Juliet. 2000. *Psychoanalysis and Feminism.* New York: Basic Books.

Mitter, Sara S. 1991. *Dharma's Daughters: Contemporary Indian Women and Hindu Culture.* New Brunswick, NJ: Rutgers University.

Moallem, Minoo. 2005. *Between Warrior Brother and Veiled Sister: Islamic Fundamentalism and the Politics of Patriarchy.* Berkeley, CA: University of California.

Moen, Phyliss. 2003. *It's about Time: Couples and Careers.* Ithaca, NY: ILR Press.

Moghadam, Valentine M. 2002. "Islamic feminism and its discontents: Toward a resolution of the debate." *Signs* 27(4):1135–71.

Mojab, Shahrzad. 1998. "Muslim women and Western feminists: The debate on particulars and fundamentals." *Monthly Review-New York* 50(7):19–30.

Molina, Olga. 2000. "African American women's unique divorce experiences." *Journal of Divorce & Remarriage* 32(3/4):93–9.

Monaghan, Peter. 2008. "Going with the "Flow." *Chronicle of Higher Education* 55(11):B16.

Money, John. 1995. *Gendermaps: Social Constructionism, Feminism and Sexosophical History.* New York: Continuum.

Money, John, and Anke A. Ehrhardt. 1972. *Man and Woman, Boy and Girl.* Baltimore: Johns Hopkins University.

Money, John, and P. Tucker. 1975. *Sexual Signatures.* Boston: Little, Brown.

Mongeau, Paul A., Mary Claire Morr Serewicz, Mary Lynn Miller Henningsen, and Kristin Leigh Davis. 2006. "Sex differences in the transition to a heterosexual romantic relationship." In Kathryn Dindia and Daniel J. Canary (eds.), *Sex Differences and Similarities in Communication.* (pp. 337–58). Mahwah, NJ: Lawrence Erlbaum.

Monk-Turner, Elizabeth, Kristy Wren et al. 2008. "Who is gazing at whom? A look at how sex is used in magazines." *Journal of Gender Studies* 17(3):201–9.

Montagne, Renee. 2008. "Palin's nomination fuels working-moms debate." Morning Edition (NPR). September 8.

Montagu, Ashley. 1999. *The Natural Superiority of Women.* Lanham. MD: Altamira.

Montemurro, Beth. 2003. "Not a laughing matter: Sexual harassment as 'material' on workplace-based situation comedies." *Sex Roles* 48(9/10):433–45.

Montgomery, Marilyn J. 2005. "Psychosocial intimacy and identity: From early adolescence to emerging adulthood." *Journal of Adolescent Research* 20(3):346–74.

Montrie, Chad. 2008. Making *a Living: Work and the Environment in the United States.* Chapel Hill, NC: University of North Carolina.

Moodie, Megan. 2008. "Enter microcredit." *American Ethnologist* 35(3):454–65.

Moore, Alinde J., and Dorothy C. Stratton. 2002. *Resilient Widowers: Older Men Speak for Themselves.* New York Springer.

Moore, Valerie Ann. 2000. "Comparing kids' constructions of race and gender." American Sociological Association, San Francisco.

Moosa, Ebrahim. 2003. "The debts and burdens of critical Islam." In Omid Safi (ed.), *Progressive Muslims: On Justice, Gender and Pluralism.* Oxford, NY: Oneworld.

Morgan, Patricia. 2008. *The War between State and the Family: How Government Divides and Impoverishes.* New Brunswick, NJ: Transaction.

Morgen, Sandra. 2002. *Into Our Own Hands: The Women's Health Movement in the United States, 1969–1990.* New Brunswick, NJ: Rutgers University.

Morris, Lois B. 2001. "She feels sick. The doctor can't find anything wrong." *New York Times* June 24. Sect. 15:4.

Morrison, Todd G., and Marie Halton. 2009. "Buff, tough, and rough: Representations of muscularity in action motion pictures." *The Journal of Men's Studies* 17(1):57–74.

Morrongiello, Barbara A., and Kerri Hogg. 2004. "Mothers' reactions to children misbehaving in ways that can lead to injury: Implications for gender differences in children's risk-taking and injuries." *Sex Roles* 50(1/2):103–18.

Motzafi-Haller, Pnina. 2000. "Reading Arab feminist discourses: A postcolonial challenge to Israeli feminism." *Hagar: International Social Science Review* 1(2):63–89.

———. 2001. "Scholarship, identity, and power: Mizrahi women in Israel." *Signs* 26(3):697–734.

Moynihan, Daniel P. 1965. *The Negro Family: The Case for National Action.* Office of Policy Planning and Research, U.S. Department of Labor. Washington, DC: U.S. Government Printing Office.

Mullen, Ann L. 2005. "Major differences: Gender and curricular choice at an elite American university." American Sociological Association, Philadelphia.

Mullen, Kenneth, Jonathan Watson, Jan Swift, and David Black. 2007. "Young men, masculinity, and alcohol." *Drugs, Education, Prevention, and Policy* 14(2):151–65.

Mundy, L.A. 2006. "Men's heterosexual initiation: Sexual agency and empowerment in Post-World War II American culture." *Journal of Men's Studies* 14(2):173–89.

Munn, Mark Henderson. 2006. *The Mother of the Gods, Athens, and the Tyranny of Asia: A Study of Sovereignty in Ancient Religion.* Berkeley, CA: University of California.

Munoz-Laboy, Miguel, Hannah Weinstein, and Richard Parker. 2007. "The hip-hop club scene: Gender, grinding, and sex," *Culture, Health and Sexuality* 9(6):615–28.

Munshi, Shoma (ed.). 2001. *Images of the Modern Woman in Asia: Global Media, Local Meanings.* Richmond, Surrey: Curzon Press.

Murphy, Evelyn F. 2006. *Getting Even: Why Women Don't Get Paid Like Man and What To Do About It.* New York: Simon and Schuster.

Murphy, Suzanne, and Dorothy Faulkner. 2000. "Learning to collaborate: Can young children develop better communication strategies through collaboration with a more popular peer?" *European Journal of Psychology and Education* 15(4):389–404.

Murray, John. P. 2008. "Media violence: The effects are both real and strong." *American Behavioral Scientist.*" 51(8):1212–230.

Murray, Stephen O. 2000. *Homosexualities.* Chicago: University of Chicago.

Muse, Dahabo Ali. 2000. "Feminine pain." Cited in "Female genital mutilation also known as female circumcision" by Comfort Momoh. Pamphlet from the African Well Women's Clinic of the Guy's & St. Thomas Hospital Trust. London.

Myers, Steven Lee. 2003. "Haunting thoughts after a battle." *New York Times* March 29:5. www.nytimes.com/2003/03/29/international/worldspecial

Nadell, Pamela S., and Jonathan D. Sarna (eds.). 2001. *Women and American Judaism: Historical Perspectives.* Hanover, NH: University Press of New England.

Nader, Yasmine. 2008. "Microcredit and the socio-economic wellbeing and their families in Cairo." *Journal of Socio-Economics* 37(2):644–56.

Nagle, Jeanne. 2009. *Violence in Movies, Music, and the Media.* New York: Rosen.

Najafizadeh, Mehrangiz. 2003. "Women's empowering carework in Post-Soviet Azerbaijan." *Gender & Society* 17(2):293–304.

Nanda, Serena. 1997. "The hijras of India." In Martin B. Duberman (ed.), *A Queer World: The Center for Lesbian and Gay Studies Reader.* New York: Center for Lesbian and Gay Studies, City University.

Napari, Sami. 2009. "Gender differences in early-career wage growth." *Labour Economics* 16(2):140–48.

Narasimhan, Sakuntala. 2000. "Special report: A married women's right to live." *Ms.* 10(6):76–81.

Narayanan, Vasudha. 2002. "Hinduism." In Arvind Sharma and Katherine K. Young (eds.), *Her Voice, Her Faith: Women Speak on World Religions.* (pp. 11–58). Boulder, CO: Westview.

Nathanson, Amy I., Jocelyn McGee, and Barbara J. Wilson. 2002. "Counteracting the effects of female stereotypes on television via active mediation." *Journal of Communication* 52(4):922–37.

Nathanson, Paul, and Katherine K. Young. 2001. *Spreading Misandry: The Teaching of Contempt for Men in Popular Culture.* Montreal: McGill Queens University.

National Academy of Sciences. 2006. *Beyond Bias and Barriers: Fulfilling the Potential of Women in Academic Science and Engineering.* Washington, DC: National Academies press.

National Center for Health Statistics. 2009. *Health, United States, 2008.* (Chartbook). Hyattsville, MD: NCHS.

National Center for Education Statistics. 2007. "Employees in postsecondary institutions, Fall,

2005 and salaries of full-time instructional faculty, 2005–06." NCES 2007-150. March. Washington, DC: U.S. Department of Education.

———. 2009. *The Condition of Education, 2009.* Washington, DC: U.S. Department of Education.

National Institute on Alcohol Abuse and Alcoholism. 2008. *Alcohol: A Woman's Health Issue.* Washington, DC: National Institutes of Health.

National Institute on Drug Abuse. 2008. "Prescription drugs: Abuse and addiction." *Research Report Series* July. National Institutes of Health. www.nida.nih.gov

National Research Council. 2006. *To Recruit and Advance: Women Students and Faculty in Science and Engineering.* Washington, DC: National Academies Press.

National Science Foundation. 2007. "Back to school: Five myths about girls and science." Division of Science Resources Statistics. Press release 07-108.

Navajas, Setgio et al. 2000. "Microcredit and the poorest of the poor: Theory and evidence from Bolivia." *World Development* 28(2):333–46.

NAWBO. 2009. "Survey finds women business owners holding their own amid economic downturn." National Association of Women Business Owners. www.nawbo.org

NCAA. 2008. "Gender equity in intercollegiate athletics: A practical guide for colleges and universities." National Collegiate Athletic Association. www.ncaa.org

———. 2009. "Gender equity in college coaching and administration." Perceived Barriers Report. January. National Collegiate Athletic Association. www.ncaa.org

NCVS. 2008. *National Crime Victimization Survey.* Washington, DC: U.S. Department of Justice.

Neal, Margaret B., and Leslie B. Hammer. 2007. *Working Couples Caring for Children and Aging Parents: Effects on Work and Well-Being.* Mahwah, NJ: Lawrence Erlbaum.

Negy, Charles, and Cliff McKinney. 2006. "Application of feminist therapy: Promoting resiliency among lesbian and gay families." In Anne M. Prouty Lyness (ed.), *Lesbian Families' Challenges and Means of Resiliency: Implications for Family Therapy.* New York: Haworth.

Neil, Martha. 2009. "Too many firm layoffs are gender-biases, ABA leader says." *ABA Journal Law News Now* March 18. www.abajournal.com/news

Nelson, Adia. 2000. "The pink dragon is female: Halloween costumes and gender markers." *Psychology of Women Quarterly* 24(2):137–44.

Nemoto, Kumiko. 2008. "Postponed marriage: Exploring women's views of matrimony and work in Japan. *Gender & Society* 22(2):219–37.

Nepomnyaschy, Lenna. 2007. "Child support and father-child contact: Testing reciprocal pathways." *Demography* 44 (1):93–112.

Neu, Terry W., and Rich Weinfeld. 2007. *Helping Boys Succeed in School: A Practical Guide for Parents and Teachers.* Waco, TX: Prufrock Press.

Newbart, Dave. 2005. "College students: Mom will fix it." *Chicago Sun Times* December 27.

Newman, Matthew L., Carla J. Groom, Lori D. Handelman, and James W. Pennebaker. 2008. "Gender differences in language use: An analysis of 14,000 text samples." *Discourse Processes* 45(3):211–36.

Newsome, Yvonne D., and F. Nii-Amoo DoDoo. 2006. "Reversal of fortune: Explaining the decline in black women's earnings." In Marlese Durr and Shirley A. Hill (eds.)., *Race, Work, and Family in the Lives of African Americans.* (pp. 159–84). Lanham, MD: Roman & Littlefield.

Nielsen, Francois. 1994. "Sociobiology and sociology." *Annual Review of Sociology* 20:267–303.

Nielsen. 2009. "Television, internet and mobile usage in the (U.S.) *A2.M2 Three Screen Report: 4th Quarter, 2008.* http://en-us.nielsen.com

Nilsen, Alice Pace. 1993. "Sexism is English: A 1990s update." In Virginia Cyrus (ed.), *Experiencing Race, Class, and Gender in the United States.* Mountain View, CA: Mayfield.

Nishimura, Junko. 2001. "The uneasiness of housewives and the housewife as an institution: From the analysis of life stories of midlife women in contemporary Japan." *Japanese Journal of Family Sociology* 12(2):223–35.

Nkulu-N'Sengha, Mutombo. 2001. "Bumuntu paradigm and gender justice: Sexist and antisexist trends in African traditional religions." In John C. Raines and Daniel C. Maguire (eds.), *What Men Owe to Women: Men's Voices from World Religions.* (pp. 69–108). Albany: State University of New York.

NOMAS. 2009. National Organization for Men Against Sexism. www.nomas.org

Noonan, Mary C., Sarah Beth Estes, and Jennifer L. Glass. 2007. "Do workplace flexibility policies influence time spent in domestic labor?" *Journal of Family Issues* 28(2):263–88.

NORC. 2008. *General Social Survey Cumulative Codebook, 2008.* Chicago: National Opinion research Center, University of Chicago. www.norc.org/GSS+Website/Documentation

Norton, Mary Beth. 2003. "The positive impact of the American Revolution on white women." In Mary Beth Norton and Ruth M. Alexander (eds.), *Major Problems in American Women's History.* Boston: Houghton Mifflin.

Norton, Mary Beth, and Ruth M. Alexander (eds.). 1996. "Anita Hill's testimony before the Senate Judiciary Committee, 1991." In Mary Beth Norton and Ruth M. Alexander (eds.), *Major Problems in American Women's History.* Lexington, MA: D. C. Heath.

Notter, David. 2002. "Towards a cultural analysis of the modern family: Beyond the revisionist paradigm in Japanese family studies." *International Journal of Japanese Sociology* 11:88–101.

NOW. 2009. "Abortion providers under siege. Is this the new face of domestic terrorism? PBS :NOW show." Airtime: June 12.

NSTA. 2007. "Dads can influence daughters' interests in math, science." Discussion of research by Pamela Davis-Kean. *NSTA Reports* 19(2):12. National Science Teachers Association.

Nussbaum, Martha Craven. 2000. *Women and Human Development: The Capabilities Approach.* Cambridge, UK: Cambridge University.

O'Beirne, Kate. 2006. *Women Who Make the World Worse.* New York: Sentinel.

O'Connell, David J., Eileen McNeely, and Douglas T. Hall. 2008. "Unpacking personal adaptability at work." *Journal of Leadership and Organizational Studies* 14(3):248–59.

O'Keefe, Abigail Tuttle. 2002. "It's not what mothers do but the reasons they do it: Mothers' reasons for their employment decisions and mothers' well-being." *Dissertation Abstracts International: Section B: The Sciences & Engineering* 63(1-B):568.

O'Neil, Robert Paul. 2002. "Sexual profanity and interpersonal judgment." *Dissertation Abstracts International: Section A: The Humanities and Social Sciences* 63(2):781-A.

O'Neill, Adrian. 2009. "Married? with children?: Same-sex couples in Britain." *Commonweal* January 16:12–13.

O'Reilly, Andrea. 2000. "Feminist thought on motherhood, the motherline, and the mother-daughter relationship." In Andrea O'Reilly and Sharon Abbey (eds.), *Mothers and Daughters: Connection, Empowerment and Transformation.* (pp. 143–60). Lanham, MD: Rowman & Littlefield.

O'Reilly, Patricia. 2001. "Learning to be a girl." In Patricia O'Reilly and Elizabeth M. Penn (eds.), *Educating Young Adolescent Girls.* (pp. 11–27). Mahwah, NJ: Lawrence Erlbaum.

O'Toole. Laura. 2007. "Subcultural theory of rape revisited." In Laura O'Toole, Jessica R. Schiffman, and Marge L. Kiter Edwards (eds.), *Gender Violence: Interdisciplinary Perspectives.* (pp. 214–22). New York: New York University.

Oakley, Annie (ed.). 2007. *Working Sex: Sex Workers Write about a Changing Industry.* Emeryville, CA: Seal.

Ocon, Ralph. 2006. *Issues on Gender and Diversity in Management.* Lanham, MD: University Press of America.

Off-Centre. 2001. "Matchmakers have their work cut out." *Financial Times* May 5/6.

Ogawa, Naohiro, Robert D. Retherford, and Yasuhiko Saito. 2003. "Caring for the elderly and holding down a job: How are women coping in Japan?" *Asia-Pacific Population & Policy* April. 65.

Ogletree, Shirley Matile, Marc G. Turner, and Victoria Vickers. 2006. "Developing an attitudes toward housecleaning scale: Gender comparisons and counseling applications." *The Family Journal* 14(4):400–407.

Ohara, Yumiko. 2000. *A Critical Discourse Analysis: Ideology of Language and Gender in Japanese.* Ph.D. Dissertation. University of Hawaii at Manoa.

———. 2001. "Finding one's voice in Japanese: A study of the pitch levels of L2 users." In Aneta Pavlenko, Adrian Black-ledge, Ingrid Piller, and Marya Teutsch-Dwyer (eds.), *Multilingualism, Second Language Learning, and Gender.* (pp. 231–54). Berlin: Mouton de Gruyter.

———. 2004. "Prosody and gender in workplace interaction: Exploring constraints and resources in the use of Japanese." In Shigeko and Janet Shibamato Smith (eds.), *Japanese Language, Gender, and Ideology: Cultural Models and Real People.* (pp. 222–39). New York: Oxford University.

Ohara, Yumiko, and Scott Saft. 2003. "Using conversation analysis to track gender ideologies in social interaction: Toward a feminist analysis of a Japanese phone-in consultation TV program." *Discourse & Society* 14(2):153–72.

Okamoto, Dina G., and Lynn Smith-Lovin. 2001. "Changing the subject: Gender, status, and the dynamics of topic change." *American Sociological Review* 66(6):852–73.

Olivardia, Robert. 2007. "Body image and muscularity." In Jon E. Grant and Marc N. Potenza (eds.), *Textbook of Men's Mental Health.* Washington, DC: American Psychological Association.

Oliver, William. 2007. "Hip-hop culture: An alternative site for gender socialization in the African-American community." In Letha A. Lee (ed.), *Human Behavior in the Social Environment from an African-American Perspective.* (pp. 365–91). New York: Haworth.

Ollenburger, Jane C., and Helen A. Moore. 1992. *A Sociology of Women: The Intersection of Patriarchy, Capitalism and Colonization.* Englewood Cliffs, NJ: Prentice Hall.

Olson, Laura Olson. 2003. "Whatever happened to June Cleaver? The fifties mom turns eighty." *Race, Gender and Class* 10(1):129–43.

Ono, Hiromi, and James M. Raymo. 2006. "Housework, market work, and 'doing gender' when marital satisfaction declines." *Social Science Research* 35(4):823–50.

Opplinger, Patricia. 2007. "Effect of gender stereotyping on socialization." In Raymond W. Preiss et al. (eds.), *Mass Media Effects Research: Advances through Meta-Analysis.* Mahwah, NJ: Lawrence Erlbaum.

Oransky, Matthew, and Celia Fisher. 2009. "The development and validation of the meanings of adolescent masculinity scale." *Psychology of Men and Masculinity* 10(1):57–72.

Orenstein, Peggy. 2001. "Unbalanced equations: Girls, math, and the confidence gap." In Roberta Satow (ed.), *Gender and Social Life.* Needham Heights, MA: Allyn & Bacon.

———. 2006. "What's wrong with Cinderella?" *New York Times* 156(December 24):34–39.

Ormerod, Alayne J., Linda L. Collinsworth, and Leigh Ann Perry. 2008. "Critical climate: Relations among sexual harassment, climate, and outcomes for high school girls and boys." *Psychology of Women Quarterly* 32:113–25.

Orzeck, Tricia, and Esther Lung. 2005. "Big-five personality differences of cheaters and non-cheaters." *Current Psychology: Developmental, Learning, Personality, Social* 24(4):274–86.

Osawa, Mari. 2000. "Government approaches to gender equality in the mid-1990s." *Social Science Japan Journal* 3(1):3–19.

Ostling, Richard N. 1991. "The search for Mary: Handmaid or feminist?" *Time.* December 30:62–66.

Ouellette, Laurie, and James Hay. 2008. *Better Living through Reality TV: Television and Post-Welfare Citizenship.* Malden, MA: Wiley-Blackwell.

Ousley, Louise, Elizabeth Diane Cordero, and Sabina White. 2008. "Eating disorders and body image of undergraduate men." *Journal of American College Health* 56:617–21.

Oygard, Lisbet, and Stein Hardeng. 2001. "Divorce support groups: How do group characteristics influence adjustment to divorce?" *Social Work with Groups* 24(1):69–87.

Pachulicz, Sarah, Neal Schmitt, and Goran Kuljanin. 2008. "Models of career success: A longitudinal study of emergency physicians." *Journal of Vocational Behavior* 73(2):242–53.

Pagels, Elaine. 1979. *The Gnostic Gospels.* New York: Random House.

Palgi, Michal. 2003. "Gender equality in the kibbutz— From ideology to reality." In Kalpana Misra and Melanie S. Rich (eds.), *Jewish Feminism in Israel: Contemporary Perspectives.* (pp. 76–95). Hanover, NH: Brandeis University.

Pallone, Nathaniel J. (ed.). 2003. *Love, Romance, Sexual Interaction: Research Perspectives from Current Psychology.* New Brunswick, NJ: Transaction.

Palmer, Barbara. 2008. *Breaking the Glass Ceiling: Women and Congressional Elections.* New York: Routledge.

Palmer, Edward L., and Brian M. Young (eds.). 2003. *The Faces of Televisual Media: Teaching, Violence, Selling to Children.* Mahwah, NJ: Lawrence Erlbaum.

Palomares, Nicholas A. 2008. "Explaining gender-based language use: Effects of gender identity salience on references to emotion and tentative language in intragroup and intergroup contexts." *Human Communication Research* 34(2):263–86.

Pappas-Deluca, Katina. 1999. "Transcending gendered boundaries: Migration for domestic labour in Chile." In Janet H. Momsen (ed.), *Gender, Migration, and Domestic Service.* (pp. 98–114). London: Routledge.

Park, Yong S., Leyna P. Vo., and Yuying Tsong. 2009. "Family affection as a protective factor against the negative effects of perceived Asian values gap on the parent-child relationship for Asian American male and female college students." *Cultural Diversity and Ethnic Minority Psychology* 15(1):18–26.

Parke, Ross D. 2002. "Parenting in the new millennium: Prospects, promises, and pitfalls." In James P. McHale and Wendy S. Grolnick (eds.), *Retrospect and Prospect in the Psychological Study of Families.* (pp. 65–93). Mahwah, NJ: Lawrence Erlbaum.

Parker, Ellie, and Adrian Furnham. 2007. "Does sex sell? The effect of sexual Programme content on the recall of sexual and non-sexual advertisements." *Applied Cognitive Psychology* 21:1217–228.

Parkerm Kathleen. 2009. "Politics: The GOP's gender deficit in high public office reflects a broader assumption that Republicans oppose women's rights." *St. Louis Post-Dispatch* September 16:A15.

Parks, Felicia R., and Janice H. Kennedy. 2007. "The impact of race, physical attractiveness, and gender on education majors' and teachers' perceptions of student competence." *Journal of Black Studies* 37(6):936–43.

Parr, Patricia, Rebecca A. Boyle, and Laura Tejada. 2008. "I said, you said: A communication exercise for couples." *Contemporary Family Therapy: An International Journal* 30(3):167–73.

Parrott, Dominic J., John L. Peterson, Wilson Vincent, and Roger Bakeman. 2008. "Correlates of anger in response to gay men: Effects of male gender role beliefs, sexual prejudice, and masculine gender role stress." *Psychology of Men and Masculinity* 9(3):167–78.

Parsons, Talcott, and Robert F. Bales (eds.). 1955. *Family, Socialization, and Interaction Process.* Glencoe, IL: Free Press.

Parsons, Talcott. 1966. *Societies: Evolutionary and Comparative Perspectives.* Englewood Cliffs, NJ: Prentice Hall.

Pascoe, C.J. 2007. *Dude, You're a Fag: Masculinity and Sexuality in High School.* Berkeley, CA: University of California.

Pasley, Kay, and Carmelle Minton. 2001. "Generative fathering: After divorce and remarriage: Beyond the 'disappearing dad.' " In Theodore F. Cohn (ed.), *Men and Masculinity: A Text Reader.* (pp. 239–48). Belmont, CA: Wadsworth.

Passet, Joanne Ellen. 2003. *Sex Radicals and the Quest for Women's Equality.* Urbana: University of Illinois.

Patterson, Charlotte J. 2006. "Children of lesbian and gay parents." *Current Directions in Psychological Science* 15(5):241–44.

Pauwels, Anne, and Joanne Winter. 2006. "Gender inclusivity or 'Grammar rules, OK'? Linguistic Sprescriptivism vs. linguistic discrimination in the classroom." *Language and Education* 20(2):128–40.

Pavalko, Eliza K., and Kathryn A. Henderson. 2006. "Combining care work and paid work." *Research on Aging* 28(3):359–74.

Pavelka, Mary S. McDonald. 1998. "The nonhuman primate perspective: Old age, kinship, and social partners in a monkey society." In Jeanette Dickerson-Putman and Judith K. Brown (eds.), *Women among Women: Anthropological Perspectives on Female Age Hierarchies.* (pp. 89–99). Urbana: University of Illinois.

Pay Scale. 2009. "Who makes more?" http://blogs.payscale.com/content/2009/02

Payne, Kaye E. 2001. *Different but Equal: Communication between the Sexes.*Westport, CT: Praeger/Greenwood.

PBS. 2008. "Ladies first map: Global gender balance." *Wideangle* July 22. www.pbs.org/wnet/wideangle/episodes

———. 2009. "Abortion providers under siege. Is this the new face of domestic terrorism?" NOW on PBS. Aired: June 12.

Pearson, Quinn M. 2008. "Role overload, job satisfaction, leisure satisfaction, and psychological health among employed women." *Journal of Counseling and Development* 86(1):57–63.

Pecora, Norma. 2007. "The changing nature of children's television: Fifty years of research." In Norma Pecora and John P. Murray (eds.), *Children and Television: Fifty Years of Research.* (pp. 1–40). Mahwah, NJ: Lawrence Erlbaum.

Pedrovska, Tetyana, and Deborah Carr. 2008. "Psychological adjustment to divorce and widowhood in mid- and later life: Do coping strategies and personality protect against psychological distress?" In Heather H. Turner and Scott Schieman (eds.), *Stress Processes and the Life Course: Introduction and Overview.* Oxford, UK: Elsevier JAI.

Pellegrini, Anthony D., Jeffrey D. Long et al. 2007. "A shirt-term longitudinal study of preschoolers, (Homo sapiens) sex segregation: The role of physical activity, sex, and time." *Journal of Comparative Psychology* 121(3):282–89.

Pemberton, Kelly. 2005. "Muslim women mystics and female spiritual authority in South Asian Sufism." In Pamela J. Stewart and Andrew Strathern (eds.), *Contesting Rituals: Islam and Practices of Identity-Making.* (pp. 3–40). Durham, NC: Carolina Academic.

Penner, Andrew M. 2008. "Race and gender differences in wages: The role of occupational sorting at the point of hire." *Sociological Quarterly* 49(3):597–6145.

Peplau, Letitia, and Adam Fingerhut. 2004. "The paradox of the lesbian worker." *Journal of Social Issues* 60(4):719–35.

Peppers, Don, and Martha Rogers. 2008. *Rules to Break and Laws to Follow: How Your Business Can Beat the Crisis of Short-Termism.* Hoboken, NJ: John Wiley.

Perl, Paul. 2005. "Are former Catholic women overrepresented among Protestant clergy?" *Sociology of Religion* 66(4):359–79.

Perna, Laura. 2005. "Sex differences in faculty tenure and promotion." *Research in Higher Education* 46(3):277–307.

Perriman, Andrew. 1998. *Speaking of Women: Interpreting Paul.* Leicester, UK: Apollos.

Perry, Alex. 2001. "Crossing the line." *Time* May 7:18–21.

Perry, Ann. 2009. "Women climbing corporate ranks: Study." *Toronto Star* March 6.

Perry-Jenkins, Maureen, Abbie E. Goldberg, Courtney P. Pierce, and Aline G. Sayer. 2007. "Shift work, role overload, and the transition to parenthood." *Journal of Marriage and the Family* 69(1):123–38.

Peter, Jochen, and Patti M. Valkenburg. 2007. "Adolescents' exposure to a sexualized media environment and their notions of women as sex objects." *Sex Roles* 56:381–95.

Peters, Brad, and Marion Ehrenberg. 2008. "Father-child relationships." *Journal of Divorce and Remarriage* 49(1/2):78–109.

Peters, Christine. 2003. *Patterns of Piety: Women, Gender and Religion in Late Medieval and Reformation England.* Cambridge, UK: Cambridge University.

Peters, Joan K. 2008. "Women's work: Dismantling the maternal wall." *Women's Studies* 37:17–33.

Petrovich, Janice, and Amy Stuart Wells (eds.). 2005. *Bringing Equity Back: Research for a New Era in American Educational Policy.* New York: Teachers College.

Pettigrew, John. 2007. *Brutes in Suits: Male Sensibility in America, 1890–1920.* Baltimore: Johns Hopkins University.

Phillips, April. 2006. "Reactions to infidelity: Gender differences and relative mate value." *Dissertation Abstracts International: Section B: The Sciences and Engineering* 66(8-B):4536.

Phillips, L.E. 1999. "Love, American style." *American Demographics* 21:56–57.

Phipps, Shelley, Peter Burton, and Lars Osberg. 2001. "Time as a source of inequality within marriage: Are husbands more satisfied with time for themselves than wives?" *Feminist Economics* 7(2):1–21.

Piaget, Jean. 1950. *The Psychology of Intelligence.* London: Routledge.

———. 1954. *The Construction of Reality in the Child.* New York: Basic Books.

Pichler, Shaun, Patricia A. Simpson, and Linda K. Stroh. 2008. "The glass ceiling in human resources: Exploring the link between women's representation in management and the practices of strategic human resource management and employee involvement." *Human Resource Management* 47(3):463–79.

Pike, Jennifer J., and Nancy A. Jennings. 2005. "The effects of commercials on children's perceptions of gender appropriate toy use." *Sex Roles* 52(1/2):83–91.

Pimentel, Ellen Efron. 2006. "Gender ideology, household behavior, and backlash in urban China." *Journal of Family Issues* 27(3):341–65.

Pincus, Fred. 2003. *Reverse Discrimination: Dismantling the Myth.* Boulder, CO: Lynne Rienner.

Pinney, Christopher. 2001. "Fueling the fire of the sati debate." *Times Higher Educational Supplement* August 10:30.

Pinto, Katy M. 2006. *Taking out the Trash: Racial and Gender Differences in the Effect of Marital Status on Housework.* American Sociological Association, Montreal.

Pitt, Richard N., and Elizabeth Borland. 2008. "Bachelorhood and men's attitudes about gender roles." *Journal of Men's Studies* 16(2):140–58.

Pittman, LaShawnda L. Wells. 2005. *Creating 'Psychological Hygiene' from the Ground Up: African American Women and Psychological Well-Being.* Philadelphia: American Sociological Association.

Plant, E. Ashby, Janet Shibley Hyde, Dacher Keltner, and Patricia G. Devine. 2000. "The gender stereotyping of emotions." *Psychology of Women Quarterly* 4(1):81–92.

Plante, Ellen M. 1997. *Women at Home in Victorian America: A Social History.* New York: Facts on File.

Plonski, Sharri. 2005. "Developing agency through peacebuilding in the midst of intractable conflict." *Compare: A Journal of Comparative Education* 35(4):393–409.

Plotnick, Robert d. 2007. "Adolescent expectations and desires about marriage and parenthood." *Journal of Adolescence* 30(6):943–63.

Plummer, Gillian. 2000. *Failing Working-Class Girls.* London: Trentham.

Pollitt, Kathy. 2005. "Summers of our discontent." *Nation*. February 21. 280(7):10.

Polnick, Barbara, and Carole Funk. 2005. " Early mathematics learning in the block center." In Janice Koch and Beverly J. Irby (eds.). *Gender and Schooling in the Early Years*. (pp. 99–112). Greenwich, CT: IAP.

Pomerantz, Eva M., Florrie Fei-Yin Ng, and Qian Wang. 2004. "Gender socialization: A parent x child model." In Alice H. Eagly, Anne E. Beall, and Robert J. Sternberg (eds.), *The Psychology of Gender*. (pp. 120–44). New York: Guilford.

Pomerantz, Eva, and Missa Murry Eaton. 2001. "Maternal intrusive support in the academic context: Transactional socialization processes." *Developmental Psychology* 37(2):174–86.

Pound, Nicholas, Ian S. Penton-Voak, and Alison K. Surridge. 2009. "Testosterone responses to competition in men are related to facial masculinity." *Proceedings: Biological Sciences* 276(January):153–59.

Poniewozik, James. 2008. "Reality TV's working class heroes." *Time*. May 22.

Pope, Mark, and Matt Englar-Carlson. 2001. "Fathers and sons: The relationship between violence and masculinity." *Family Journal* 9(4):367–73.

Popenoe, David. 2003. "Modern marriage: Revising the cultural script." In Michael S. Kimmel (ed.), *The Gendered Society Reader*. New York: Oxford University.

Popp, Danielle, Roxanne A. Donovan, and Mary Crawford. 2003. "Gender, race, and speech style stereotypes." *Sex Roles* 48(7/8):317–25.

Poppema, Suzanne. 1999. "The future of *Roe v. Wade: Medical*." In Patricia Ojea and Barbara Quigley (eds.), *Women's Studies* (Annual Editions) (pp. 117–18). Guilford, CT: Dushkin/McGraw-Hill.

Porche, Michelle V. 2007. "Reading." In Barbara J. Bank (ed.), *Gender and Education; Volume I*. (pp. 443–48). Westport, CT: Praeger.

Potts, Malcolm. 2006. "China's one child policy: The policy that changed the world." *British Medical Journal* 333:361–62.

Povey, Elaheh Rostami. 2001. "Feminist contestations of institutional domains in Iran." *Feminist Review* 69:44–72.

Powell, Kimberley A., and Lori Abels. 2002. "Sex role stereotypes in TV programs aimed at the preschool audience: An analysis of Teletubbies and Barney & Friends." *Women & Language* 25(1):14–22.

Powers, Bill. 2001. "Quiet! Dad is dusting his G.I. Joes." *New York Times*. December 30:Section 9:1.

Press, Julie E., and Eleanor Townsley. 1998. "Wives' and husbands' housework reporting: Gender, class, and social desirability." *Gender & Society* 12(2):188–218.

Press, Julie, Janice Johnson-Dias, and Jay Fagin. 2005. "Welfare status and child care as obstacles to full-time work for low-income parents." *Journal of Women, Politics, and Policy* 27(5):55–79.

Pribram, E. Deidre. 1993. "Female spectators." In Stevi Jackson et al. (eds.), *Women's Studies Essential Readings*. New York: New York University.

Price, Vivian. 2002. "Race, Affirmative action, and women's employment in U.S. highway construction." *Feminist Economics* 8(2):87–113.

Prior, Mary. 1994. "Freedom and autonomy in England and the Netherlands: Women's lives and experience in the seventeenth century." In Els Kloek, Nicole Teeuwen, and Marijke Huisman (eds.), *Women of the Golden Age: An International Debate on Women in Seventeenth-Century Holland, England and Italy*. Amsterdam: Hilversum Verloren.

Promise Keepers. 2009. www.promisekeepers.org

Puentes, Jennifer, David Knox, and Marty E. Zusman. 2008. "Participants in 'friends with benefits' relationships. *College Student Journal* 42(1):176–80.

Pugh, Allison. 2005. "Selling compromise: Toys, motherhood, and the cultural ideal." *Gender & Society* 19(6):729–49.

Pui-Lan, Kwok. 1988. "Mothers and daughters, writers and fighters." In Letty M. Russell et al. (eds.), *Inheriting our Mother's Garden: Feminist Theology in Third World Perspective*. Philadelphia: Westminster.

Puntarigvivat, Tavivat. 2001. "A Thai Buddhist perspective." In John C. Raines and Daniel C. Maguire (eds.), *What Men Owe to Women: Men's Voices from World Religions*. (pp. 211–38). Albany: State University of New York.

Punyanunt-Carter, Narissa Maria. 2006. "Love on television: Reality perception differences between men and women." *North American Journal of Psychology* 8(2):269–76.

Purkayastha, Bandana, Mangala Subramanium, Menisha Desai, and Sunita Bose. 2009. "The study of gender in India: A partial review." In Christine E. Bose and Minjeong Kim (eds.), *Global Gender Research: Transnational Perspectives*. (pp. 92–109). New York: Routledge.

Putallaz, Martha, and Karen L. Bierman. 2004. *Aggression, Antisocial Behavior, and Violence Among Girls: A Developmental Perspective*. New York: Guilford.

Quaiser-Pohl, Claudia, and Wolfgang Lehmann. 2002. "Girls' spatial abilities: Charting the contributions of experiences and attitudes in different academic groups." *British Journal of Educational Psychology* 72(2):245–60.

Quicke, Andrew, and Karen Robinson (ed.). 2000. "Keeping the promise of a moral majority: A historical/critical comparison of the Promise Keepers and the Christian Coalition, 1989–98." In Dane S. Claussen (ed.), *The Promise Keepers: Essays on Masculinity and Christianity*. (pp. 7–19). Jefferson, NC: McFarland.

Quindlen, Anna. 2008. "Can you say sexist?" *Newsweek*. September 15:104.

Quinn, Beth A. 2002. "Sexual harassment and masculinity: The power and meaning of 'girl watching.'" *Gender & Society* 16(3):386–402.

Radcliffe, Sarah A. 1999. "Race and domestic service: Migration and identity in Ecuador." In Janet H. Momsen (ed.), *Gender, Migration, and Domestic Service*. (pp. 83–97). London: Routledge.

Radford, M.J., and V. Vaccarino et al. 2001. "Sex differences in cardiac catheterization: The role of physician gender." *Journal of the American Medical Association* 286:2849–56.

Radhakrishnan, Sarvepalli. 1947. *Religion and Society*. London: Allen and Unwin.

Raffaelli, Marcela, and Lenna K. Ontai. 2001. "She's sixteen years old and there's a boy calling over to the house: An exploratory study of sexual socialization in Latino families." *Culture, Health, and Sexuality* 3:295–310.

Raffaelli, Marcela, and Lenna K. Ontai. 2004. "Gender socialization in Latino/a families: Results from two retrospective studies." *Sex Roles* 50(5/6):287–99.

Rainer, Goldfrad et al. 2002. "Influence of patient gender on admission to intensive care." *Journal of Epidemiology and Community Health* 56(4):418–23.

Rainey, Amy. 2006. "Parents of college students today, often referred to as 'helicopter parents' . . . . . are in frequent contact with their children . . . . ." *Chronicle of Higher Education* April 14. 52(32):A39.

Raley, Sara, Suzanne Bianchi, Karen S. Cook, and Douglas S. Massey. 2006. "Sons, daughters, and family processes: Does gender of children matter?" *Annual Review of Sociology* 32(1):401–21.

Raphael, Marc Lee. 2002. *Gendering the Jewish Past*. Williamsburg, VA: College of William and Mary.

Rapoport, Tamar, Yoni Garb, and Anat Penso. 1995. "Religious socialization and female subjectivity: Religious-Zionist adolescent girls in Israel." *Sociology of Education* 68(1):48–61.

Raskin, Jamin B. 2008. *We the Students : Supreme Court Cases For and About Students*. Washington, DC: CQ Press.

Raymo, James M., Jr. 2003. "Educational attainment and the transition to first marriage among Japanese women." *Demography* 40(1):83–103.

Reddy, Gayatri. 2006. *With Respect to Sex: Negotiating Hijra Identity in South India*. New Delhi: Yoda.

Regan, Pamela C. 2000. "Love relationships." In Lenore Szuchman and Frank Muscarella (eds.), *Psychological Perspectives on Human Sexuality*. (pp. 232–82). New York: Wiley.

Regan, Pamela C., Ramani Durvasula, Lisa Howell, Oscar Ureno, and Martha Rea. 2004. "Gender, ethnicity, and the developmental timing of first sexual and romantic experiences." *Social Behavior and Personality* 32(7):667–76.

Regev, Motti. 1994. "Producing artistic value: The case of rock music." *Sociological Quarterly* 35(1):85–102.

Reid, Scott A., Natasha Keerie, and Nicholas A. Palomares. 2003. "Language, gender salience, and social influence." *Journal of Language and Social Psychology* 22(2):210–33.

Reidy, Dennis E., Steven D. Shirk, Colleen A. Sloan, and Amos Zeichner. 2009. "Men who aggress against women: Effects of feminine gender role violation on physical aggression in hypermasculine men." *Psychology of Men and Masculinity* 10(1):1–12.

Reimer, Susan. 2008. "Advice women should not skirt." *Baltimore Sun* January 22.

Reineke, Martha J. 1995. "Out of order: A critical perspective on women in religion." In Jo Freeman (ed.), *Women: A Feminist Perspective*. Mountain View, CA: Mayfield.

Renk, Kimberly, Reesa Donnelly et al. 2006. "The development of gender identity: Timetables and influences." In Kamshing Yip (ed.). *Psychology of Gender Identity: An International Perspective*. (pp. 49–68). Hauppauge, NY: Nova Science.

Retherford, Robert D., Naohiro Ogawa, and Rikiya Matsukura. 2001. "Late marriage and less marriage in Japan." *Population and Development Review* 27(1):65–102.

Rhoades, Galena Kline, Scott M. Stanley, and Howard J. Markman. 2006. "Pre-engagement cohabitation and gender asymmetry in marital commitment." *Journal of Family Psychology* 20(4):553–60.

Rhoades, Helen. 2002. "The 'no-contact mother': Reconstructions of motherhood in the era of the 'new father.' " *International Journal of Law, Policy and the Family* 16(1):71–94.

Rhodes, Angel R. 2002. "Long-distance relationships in dual-career commuter couples: A review of counseling issues." *Family Journal-Counseling and Therapy for Couples and Families* 10(4):398–404.

Rhonda, James P. 1996. "The attractions of Christianity for the native women of Martha's Vineyard." In Mary Beth Norton and Ruth M. Alexander (eds.), *Major Problems in American Women's History*. Lexington, MA: D. C. Heath.

Rich, Michael. 2007. "Is television healthy?" In Norma Pecora and John P. Murray (eds.), *Children and Television: Fifty Years of Research*. (pp. 183–204). Mahwah, NJ: Lawrence Erlbaum.

Richardson, D.S., and G.S. Hammock. 2007. "Social context of human aggression: Are we paying too much attention to gender?" *Aggression and Violent Behavior* 12:417–26.

Richardson, Laurel. 1986. "Another world." *Psychology Today*. February. 23–27.

———. 1988. *The Dynamics of Sex and Gender: A Sociological Perspective*. New York: Harper & Row.

Ridgeway, Celia L., and Shelley J. Correll. 2004. "Motherhood as a status characteristic" *Journal of Social Issues* 60:683–700.

Riley, Glenda. 2007. *Inventing the American Woman: An Inclusive History. Volume I: To 1877*. Wheeling, IL: Harlan Davidson.

Riley, Naomi Schaefer. 2008. "Sarah Palin Feminism." *Wall Street Journal*. September 5:W11.

Riley, Pamela, and Gary Kiger. 1999. "Moral discourse on domestic labor: Gender, power and identity in families." *Social Science Journal* 36(3):541–48.

Rimashevskaia, Natal'ia. 2008. "Gender stereotypes and the logic of social relations." *Russian Social Science Review* 49(3):35–48.

Rinderle, Susana, and Danielle Montoya. 2008. "Hispanic/Latino identity labels: An examination of cultural values and personal experiences." *Howard Journal of Communications* 19(2):144–64.

Riordan, Cornelius. 2002. "What do we know about the effects of single-sex schools in the private sector? Implications for public schools." In Amanda Datnow and Lea Hubbard (eds.), *Gender in Policy and Practice: Perspectives on Single-Sex and Coeducational Schooling.* New York: Routledge/Falmer.

Rishe, Patrick James. 2003. "A reexamination of how athletic success impacts graduation rates: Comparing student-athletes to all other undergraduates." *American Journal of Economics and Sociology* 62(2):407–27.

Riska, Elianne. 2001. *Medical Careers and Feminist Agendas: American, Scandinavian, and Russian Women Physicians.* Hawthorne, NY: Aldine de Gruyter.

Riska, Elianne. 2006. *Masculinity and Men's Health: Coronary Heart Disease in Medical and Public Discourse.* Lanham, MD: Rowman and Littlefield.

Risman, Barbara J. 2001. "Necessity and the invention of mothering." In Roberta Satow (ed.), *Gender and Social Life.* (pp. 26–31). Needham Heights, MA: Allyn & Bacon.

Risman, Barbara J., and Kristin Myers. 2006. "As the twig is bent: Children reared in feminist households." In Gerald Handel (ed.), *Childhood Socialization.* (pp. 65–88). Brunswick, NJ: Aldine Transaction.

Risman, Barbara J., and Pepper Schwartz. 2002. "After the sexual revolution: Gender politics in teen dating." *Contexts* 1(1 Spring):16–24.

Risman, Barbara. 2009. "From doing to undoing: Gender as we know it." *Gender & Society* 23(1):81–4.

Risman, Barbara J. 2001. "Calling the bluff of value-free science: Comment on J.R. Udry." *American Sociological Review* 66(4):605–11.

Roane, Kit R. 2002. "The long arm of abuse: Problem priests cross not just states but oceans as well." *U.S. News & World Report* May 6:26–29.

Robb, Amanda. 2008. "Look! It's a bird! It's a plane! It's . . . supermom!" *O, The Oprah Magazine* July 9(7):210–32.

Robertiello, Gina, and Karen J. Terry. 2007. "Can we profile sex offenders. A review of sex offender typologies." *Aggression and Violent Behavior* 12(5):508–18.

Roberts, Christy D., Laura M. Stough, and Linda H. Parrish. 2002. "The role of genetic counseling in the elective termination of pregnancies involving fetuses with disabilities." *Journal of Special Education* 36(1):48–55.

Roberts, Sam. 2007. "51% of women are now living without spouse." *New York Times* January 16. www.nytimes.com2007/01/16/us/16census

Robertson, Brian C. 2003. *Day Care Deception: What the Child Care Industry isn't Telling Us.* San Francisco: Encounter.

Robinson, Bryan, and Erica Hunter. 2007. "Is mom still doing it? Reexamining depictions of family-work in popular advertising." New York: American Sociological Association.

Robles, Barbara J. 2008. "Latina entrepreneurship in the borderlands: Family well-being and poverty reduction policies." In Raquel R. Marquez and Harriett D. Romo (eds.), *Transformations of La Familia on the U.S. Mexican Border.* Notre Dame, IN: University of Notre Dame.

Rochlen, Aaron B., Marie-Anne Suizzo, and Ryan A. McKelley. 2008a. "I'm just providing for my family: A qualitative study of stay-at-home fathers." *Psychology of Men and Masculinity* 9(4):193–206.

Rochlen, Aaron B., Ryan A. McKelley, Marie-Anne Suizzo, and Vanessa Scaringi. 2008b. "Predictors of relationship satisfaction, psychological well-being, and life satisfaction among stay-at-home fathers." *Psychology of Men and Masculinity* 9(1):17–28.

Rodman, Aronson, Kimberley M. Bucholz, and Ester Schaeler. 2001. "The post-feminist era: Still striving for equality in relationships." *American Journal of Family Therapy* 29(2):109–24.

Rodriguez, Alicia P. 2006. "The role gender plays." In Pedro A. Noguera and Jean Yonemura Wing (eds.), *Unfinished Business: Closing the Racial Achievement Gap in our Schools.* (pp. 68–75). San Francisco: Jossey-Bass.

Roen, Katrina. 2002. "'Either/or and 'both/neither': Discursive tensions in transgender studies." *Signs* 27(2)501–22.

Rogers, Stacy J., and Danelle D. DeBoer. 2001. "Changes in wives' income: Effects on marital satisfaction, psychological well-being, and the risk of divorce." *Journal of Marriage and the Family* 63(2):458–72.

Roller, Lynn E. 1999. *In Search of God the Mother: The Cult of Anatolian Cybele.* Berkeley: University of California.

Rong, Jiaojiao. 2005. "When little emperors become parents." *China Daily* March 18:5.

Rose, Barbara. 2007. "Barbara Rose Your Space Column: Gen Y's parents staying at helm." *Chicago Tribune* April 23.

Rose, Jacqueline. 2005. "Femininity and its discontents." *Feminist Review* 80:24–43.

Rossi, Alice S. 2001. "The impact of family problems on social responsibility." In Alice S. Rossi (ed.), *Caring and Doing for Others: Social Responsibility in the Domains of Family, Work and Community.* (pp. 321–47). Chicago: University of Chicago.

Rothman, Stanley, Seymour Martin Lipset, and Neil Nevitte. 2003. "Racial diversity reconsidered." *The Public Interest* 151:25–38.

Roxburgh, Susan. 2006. "I wish we had more time to spend together": The distribution and predictors of perceived family time pressures among married men and women in the paid labor force." *Journal of Family Issues* 27(4):529–53.

Roy, Ranjan. 1994. "AIDS explosion feared in India's prostitute towns." *St. Louis Post-Dispatch* March 27:67G.

Rozario, Phillip A. James E. Hinterlong, and Nancy Morrow-Howell. 2004. "Role enhancement or role strain." *Research on Aging* 26(4):413–28.

Rozelle, Scott, Xiao-Yuan Dong, Linxiu Zhang, and Andrew Mason. 2002. *Gender Wage Gaps in Post-reform Rural China.* Development Research Group/Poverty Reduction and Economic Management Network. World Bank, May.

Ruble, Diane N., Carol Lynn Martin, and Sheri A. Berenbaum 2006. "Gender development." In Nancy Eisenberg, William Damon, and Richard M. Lerner (eds.), *Handbook of Child Psychology: Volume 3: Social, Emotional, and Personality Development.* (pp. 358–92). Hoboken, NJ: John Wiley & Sons.

Rudd, Jane. 2001. "Dowry-murder: An example of violence against women." *Women's Studies International Forum* 24(5):513–22.

Ruether, Rosemary Radford. 1983. *Sexism and Godtalk: Toward a Feminist Theology.* Boston: Beacon.

———. 2001a. "Christian feminist theology: History and future." In Yvonne Yazbeck and John L. Esposito (eds.), *Daughters of Abraham: Feminist Thought in Judaism, Christianity, and Islam.* (pp. 65–80). Gainesville: University Press of Florida.

———. 2001b. "Feminist theology in a global context." In Rita Halteman and Kari Finger Sandhaas (eds.), *The Wisdom of Daughters; Two Decades of the Voice of Christian Feminism.* Philadelphia: Innisfree Press.

———. 2005. *Integrating Ecofeminism. Globalization, and World Religions.* Lanham, MD: Rowman and Littlefield.

———. 2006. *Goddesses and the Divine Feminine: A Western Religious History.* Berkeley: University of California.

———. 2008. *Catholic Does Not Equal Vatican: A Vision for Progressive Catholicism.* New York: New Press.

Ruiz, Vicki L. 2008. "Introduction." In Vicki L. Ruiz and Ellen Carol DuBois (eds.), *Unequal Sisters: An Inclusive Reader in U.S. Women's History.* (pp.xiii–xviii). New York: Routledge.

Ruth, Sheila. 2001. *Issues in Feminism: An Introduction to Women's Studies.* Mountain View, CA: Mayfield.

Ryan, John, James Hawden, and Allison Branick. 2002. "The political economy of diversity: Diversity programs in Fortune 500 companies." *Sociological Research Online* 7(1):May. www.socresonline.org.uk

Ryan, Scott. 2007. "Parent-child interaction styles between gay and lesbian parents and their adopted children." In Fiona Tasker and Jerry J. Bigner (eds.), *Gay and Lesbian Parenting: New Directions.* Binghamton, NY: Haworth.

Sabo, Donald F. 2004. "Masculinities and men's health: Moving toward post-superman era prevention." In Michael S. Kimmel and Michael A. Messner (eds.), *Men's Lives.* (pp. 321–34). Boston: Allyn & Bacon.

Sabo, Donald F., and Joe Panepinto. 2001. "Football ritual and the social reproduction of masculinity." In Theodore F. Cohen (ed.), *Men and Masculinity: A Text Reader.* (pp. 78–86). Belmont, CA: Wadsworth.

Sacks, Peter. 2007. *Tearing Down the Gates: Confronting the Class Divide in American Education.* Berkeley: University of California.

Sadker, David M., and Karen Zittleman. 2007. Practical strategies for detecting and correcting gender bias in your classroom." In David M. Sadker and Ellen S. Silber (eds.),*Gender in the Classroom: Foundations, Skills, Methods, and Strategies.* Mahwah, NJ: Lawrence Erlbaum.

Sadker, David M., and Myra Sadker. 2002. "The miseducation of boys." In Susan M. Bailey (ed.), *The Jossey-Bass Reader on Gender and Education.* (pp. 182–203). San Francisco: Jossey-Bass.

Sadker, Myra, and David Sadker. 1994. *Failing at Fairness: How America's Schools Cheat Girls.* New York: Charles Scribner's.

Sadovnik, Alan R., and Susan F. Semel. 2002. "Transition to coeducation at Wheaton College: Conscious coeducation and gender equity in higher education." In Amanda Datnow and Lea Hubbard (eds.), *Gender in Policy and Practice: Perspectives on Single-Sex and Coeducational Schooling.* New York: Routledge/Falmer.

Safa, Helen. 2003. "Changing forms of U.S. hegemony in Puerto Rico: The impact on the family and sexuality." *Urban Anthropology* 32(1):7–40.

Safi, Omid (ed.). 2003. *Progressive Muslims: On Justice, Gender and Pluralism.* Oxford, UK: OneWorld.

Saginak, Kelli A., and M. Alan Saginak. 2005. "Literature review – Research: Balancing work and family: Equity, gender, and marital satisfaction." *Family Journal* 13(2):162–66.

Salmela-Aro, Katariina, Jari-Erik Nurmi, Terhi Saisto, and Erja Halmesmäki. 2000. "Women's and men's personal goals during the transition to parenthood." *Journal of Family Psychology* 14(2):171–86.

Salmivalli, Christina, and Katlin Peets. 2009. "Bullies, victims, and bully-victim relationships in middle childhood and early adolescence." In Kenneth H. SRubin, William M. Bukowski, and Brett Laursen (eds.), *Handbook of Peer Interactions, Relationship, and Groups.* New York: Guilford.

Salomone, Rosemary. 2007a. "Separating girls and boys: Should school districts offer single-sex public schools and classes?: Yes. *Teacher Magazine* January/February 18(4).

———. 2007b. "Public single-sex and coeducational schools." In Barbara J. Bank (ed.), *Gender and Education; Volume I.* (pp. 217–25). Westport, CT: Praeger.

———. 2007c. "A place for women's colleges." *Chronicle of Higher Education.* February 16. 53(24).

Samuels, David. 1999. "The making of a fugitive." (Anti-abortion odyssey). *New York Times* March 21:47–53, 62.

Samuels, Patrice D. 1999. "Back at work but never far from family." *New York Times* October 10:10.

Sanasarian, Eliz (ed.). 1982. *The Women's Rights Movement in Iran: Mutiny, Appeasement and Repression from 1900 to Khomeni.* Westport, CT: Greenwood.

Sanchez, Diana T., and Amy K. Kiefer. 2007. "Body concerns in and out of the bedroom: Implications for sexual pleasure and problems." *Archives of Sexual Behavior* 36(6):808–20.

Sanchez, Patricia. 2008. "Coming of age across borders: Family, gender, and place in the lives of second-generation transnational Mexicanas." In Raquel R. Marquez and Harriett D. Romo (eds.), *Transformations of La Familia on the U.S. Mexican Border*. Notre Dame, IN: University of Notre Dame.

Sanday, Peggy Reeves. 2007. "The socio-cultural context of rape: A cross-cultural study." In Laura O'Toole, Jessica R. Schiffman, and Marge L. Kiter Edwards (eds.), *Gender Violence: Interdisciplinary Perspectives*. (pp. 56–72). New York: New York University.

Sandler, Bernice R. 2004. "The chilly climate: Subtle ways in which women are often treated differently at work and in classrooms." In Joan Z. Spade and Catherine G. Valentine (eds.), *The Kaleidoscope of Gender: Prisms, Patterns and Possibilities*. (pp. 187–190). Belmont CA: Wadsworth.

Sandler, Bernice, and Harriett Stonehill. 2005. *Student-to-Student Sexual Harassment K-12: Strategies and Solutions for Educators to Use in the Classroom, School, and Community*. Maryland: Rowman & Littlefield.

Sano, Shinpei. 2009. "Testing the taste-based discrimination hypothesis. Evidence from data on Japanese listed firms." *Japan Labor Review* 6(1):36–50.

Sapolsky, Robert M. 2002. *A Primate's Memoir*. New York: Simon and Schuster.

Sarkar, Tanika. 2001. *Hindu Wife, Hindu Nation: Community, Religion, and Cultural Nationalism*. London: Hurst.

Sarkisian, N., and Naomi Gerstel. 2008. "Till marriage do us part: Adult children's relationships with their parents." *Journal of Marriage and the Family* 70:360–76.

Sarlo, Chris. 2000. "Single-parent families: Then and now—what are the consequences for the children." *Fraser Forum* July. www.theinvoledfather.com

Sassler, Sharon, Sarah Favinger, and Amanda Miller. 2006. "From sexual involvement to coresidential unions: New findings from the 2002 NSFG." Montreal: American Sociological Association.

Sasson-Levy, Orna. 2003. "Feminism and military gender practices: Israeli women soldiers in 'masculine' roles." *Sociological Inquiry* 73(3):440–63.

Sato, Barbara Hamill. 2003. *The New Japanese Woman: Modernity, Media, and Women in Interwar Japan*. Durham, NC: Duke University.

Sato, Satoru, Kalynn M. Shulz, Cheryl L. Sisk, and Ruth I. Wood. 2008. "Adolescents and androgens, receptors and rewards." *Hormones and Behavior* 53(5):647–58.

Saules, Karen K., James C. Tate, and Cynthia S. Pomerleau. 2008. "Weight control smoking in women." In Katherine P. Tolson and Emily B. Veksler (eds.). *Research Focus on Smoking and Women's Health*. New York: Nova Biomedical.

Sawhill, Isabel V. 2006. "Teenage sex, pregnancy, and nonmarital births." *Gender Issues* 23(4):48–59.

Sax, Leonard. 2007. *Boys Adrift: Five Factors Driving the Growing Epidemic of Unmotivated Boys and Underachieving Young Men*. New York: Basic Books.

SBA. 2006. "Women in business: A demographic review of women's business ownership." *Small Business Research Summary* No. 280: August. Office of Advocacy, U.S. Small Business Administration. www.sbc.gov/advo

Scharrer, Erica, and George Comstock. 2003. "Entertainment televisual media: Content patterns and themes." In Edward L. Palmer and Brian M. Young (eds.), *The Faces of Televisual Media: Teaching Violence, Selling to Children*. (pp. 161–93). Mahwah, NJ: Lawrence Erlbaum.

Scharrer, Erica, D. Daniel Kim, Ke-Ming Lin, and Zixu Liu. 2006. "Working hard or hardly working? Gender, humor, and the performance of domestic chores in television commercials." *Mass Communications and Society* 9(2):215–38.

Scharrer, Erica. 2001a. "From wise to foolish: The portrayal of the sitcom father, 1950s–1990s." *Journal of Broadcasting and Electronic Media* 45(1):23–40.

———. 2001b. "Men, muscles, and machismo: The relationship between television exposure and aggression and hostility in the presence of hypermasculinity." *Media Psychology* 3(2):159–88.

Schifter, Jacobo, and Johnny Madrigal. 2000. *The Sexual Construction of Latino Youth: Implications for the Spread of HIV/AIDS*. New York: Haworth.

Schipani, Cindy A., Terry M. Dworkin, Angel Kwolek-Folland, and Virginia G. Maurer. 2009. "Pathways for women to obtain positions of organizational leadership: The significance of mentoring and networking." *Duke Journal of Gender Law and Policy* 16(1):89–106.

Schippers, Mimi. 2002. *Rockin' Out of the Box: Gender Maneuvering in Alternative Hard Rock*. New Brunswick, NJ: Rutgers University.

Schlafly, Phyllis. 2003. *Feminist Fantasies*. Dallas, TX: Spence.

Schlinkmann, Mark, and Michele Munz. 2008. (Photographer) "McCain, new sidekick a hit at O'Fallon rally." *St. Louis Post-Dispatch* September 1:A1.

Schmidt, Lucie. 2008. "Risk preferences and the timing of marriage and childrearing." *Demography* 45(2).

Schmidt, Marie Evans, and Daniel R. Anderson. 2007. "The impact of television on cognitive development and educational achievement." In Norma Pecora and John P. Murray (eds.), *Children and Television: Fifty Years of Research*. (pp. 65–84). Mahwah, NJ: Lawrence Erlbaum.

Schmitt, David P. 2006. "Evolutionary and cross-cultural perspectives on love: The influence of gender, personality, and local ecology on emotional investment in romantic relationships." In Robert J. Sternberg and Karin Weiss (eds.), *The New Psychology of Love*. (pp. 249–73). New Haven, CT: Yale University.

Schmitt, Ed. 2008. "Discrimination versus specialization: A survey of economic studies on sexual orientation, gender, and earnings in the United States. *Journal of Lesbian Studies* 12(1):17–30.

Schmitt, M., M. Kliegel, and A. Shapiro. 2007. "Marital interaction in middle and old age: A predictor of marital satisfaction?" *International Journal of Aging and Human Development* 65(4):283–300.

Schmookler, T., and K. Bursik. 2007. "The value of monogamy in emerging adulthood: A Gendered perspective." *Journal of Social and Personal Relationships* 24(6):819–35.

Schnittker, Jason, Jeremy Freese, and Brian Powell. 2002. "Who's a feminist and what do they believe? Age ideology and feminist self-identification." Southern Sociological Society, New Orleans, LA. April.

School Law News. 2009. "Law shields employee from reprisal for opposing sexual harassment." 37(3)March:9–10.

Schopp, Laura H., Glenn E. Good, Micah O. Mazurek, Katharine B. Barker, and Renee C. Stucky. 2007. "Masculine role variables and outcomes among men with spinal cord injury." *Disability and Rehabilitation* 29(8):625–33.

Schüssler-Fiorenza, Elizabeth. 1984. *The Challenge of Feminist Biblical Interpretation.* Boston: Beacon.

Schwartz, Pepper 2002. "Maintaining relationships at the millennium." In John H. Harvey and Amy Wenzel (eds.), *A Clinician's Guide to Maintaining and Enhancing Close Relationships.* (pp. 303–12). Mahwah, NJ: Lawrence Erlbaum.

Sciarra, Daniel T., Kerri Keegan, and Bridget Sledz (2007). "School counseling." In Barbara J. Bank (ed.), *Gender and Education, Volume II.* (pp. 563–69). Westport, CT: Praeger.

Science Daily. 2007. Cited in *Off our Backs* October, 2007. 36(3). www.offourbacks.org

Scott, Betsy. 2007. "That's the way the courtship crumbles." *News-Herald* (Northeast Ohio) March 24.

Scott, Kimberly A. 2000. "Selfhood developed: Verbal and nonverbal expressiveness in firstgrade African-American girls' play." American Sociological Association, San Francisco.

Scott, Rachel M. 2009. "A contextual approach to women's rights in the Qur'an: Readings 4:34." *Muslim World* 99(1):60–85.

Scully, Diana. 1993. "Understanding sexual violence." In Stevi Jackson et al. (eds.), *Women's Studies Essential Readings.* New York: New York University.

Scully, Diana, and Joseph Marolla. 1990. "Riding the bull at Gilley's: Convicted rapists describe the rewards of rape." In James M. Henslin (ed.), *Social Problems Today: Coping with the Challenges of a Changing Society.* Englewood Cliffs, NJ: Prentice Hall.

Scully, Diana, and Pauline Bart. 2003. "A funny thing happened on the way to the office: Women in gynecology textbooks." *Feminism & Psychology* 13(1):11–16.

Seifert, E. 2000. "Strategies for a successful long-distance marriage: The story of two administrators." In A. Pankake, G. Schroth, and C. Funk (eds.), *Women as School Executives: The Complete Picture.* (pp. 214–18). Austin, TX: Texas Council of School Executives.

Selah-Shayovits, Revital. 2006. "Adolescent preferences for violence in television shows and music video clips." *International Journal of Adolescence and Youth* 13(1–2):99–112.

Sen, Mala. 2002. *Death by Fire: Sati, Dowry Death, and Female Infanticide in Modern India.* New Brunswick, NJ: Rutgers University.

Sered, Susan Starr. 1994. *Priestess, Mother, Sacred Sister: Religions Dominated by Women.* New York: Oxford University.

Serriere, Stephanie Cayot. 2008. "The making of 'masculinity:' The impact of symbolic and physical violence on students, pre-k and beyond." *Democracy and Education* 18(1):18–27.

Shakib, Sohalla, and Michele D. Dunbar. 2004. "How high school athletes talk about maternal and paternal sporting experiences: Identifying modifiable social processes for gender equity physical activity interventions." *International Review for the Sociology of Sport* 39(3):275–99.

Shanahan, James, Nancy Signorielli, and Michael Morgan. 2008. "Television and sex roles 30 years hence: A retrospective and current look from a cultural indicators perspective." Conference paper. Mass Communications Division of the International Communication Association.

Sharp, Edlaine B., and Mark Joslyn. 2001. "Individual and contextual effects on attributions about pornography." *Journal of Politics* 63(2):501–19.

Sharpley-Whiting, T. Denean. 2007. *Pimps Up, Ho's Down: Hip Hop's Hold on Young Black Women.* New York: New York University.

Shattuck, Anne M. 2005. "What's their real problem with gay marriage? (It's the Gay Part)." *New York Times Magazine* July 3:13.

Shearer, Cindy. 2008. "Gender socialization in the family." *Dissertation Abstracts International: Section B: The Sciences and Engineering* 68(10-B):7004.

Sheffield, Carole J. 2007. "Sexual terrorism." In Laura O'Toole, Jessica R. Schiffman, and Margie L. Kiter Edwards (eds.), *Gender Violence: Interdisciplinary Perspectives.* (pp. 111–320). New York: NYU Press.

Shehadeh, Lamia Rustum. 2007. *The Idea of Women in Fundamentalist Islam.* Gainesville, FL: University Press of Florida.

Shek, Yen Ling. 2006. "Asian American masculinity: A review of the literature." *The Journal of Men's Studies* 14(3):379–91.

Shellenbarger, Sue. 2005. "Helicopter parents: The emotional toll of being too involved in your kid's life." *Wall Street Journal: Eastern Edition* April 14. 245(73):D1.

———. 2006. "Helicopter parents go to work: Mom and dads are now hovering at the office." *Wall Street Journal: Eastern Edition* March 16. 247(62):D1.

———. 2007. "Helicopter parenting: A breakdown." *Wall Street Journal: Eastern Edition* 250(74)September 27:D1.

Shelton, Beth Anne. 2000. "Understanding the distribution of housework between husbands and wives." In Linda J. Waite and Christine Bachrach et al (eds.), *The Ties that Bind: Perspectives on Marriage and Cohabitation.* (pp. 343–55). New York: Aldine de Gruyter.

Shelton, Beth Anne, and Ben Agger. 1993. "Shotgun wedding, unhappy marriage, non-fault divorce? Rethinking the feminism–Marxism relationship." In Paula England (ed.), *Theory on Gender/Feminism on Theory.* New York: Aldine De Gruyter.

Sheriff, Michelle, and Ann Weatherall. 2009. "A feminist discourse analysis of popular press accounts of post-maternity." *Feminism and Psychology* 19(1):89–108.

Sherman, Donald K. 2005. "Child custody and visitation." *Georgetown Journal of Gender and the Law: Annual Review* 6(3):691–718.

Shields, Vickie Rutledge. 2002. *Measuring Up: How Advertising Affects Self-Image.* Philadelphia: University of Pennsylvania.

Shikakura, Hisayo, and Gavin W. Hougham. 2000. "High school education for girls in Japan: Do traditional gender-role values still matter?" American Sociological Association, Washington DC.

Shiller, Virginia. 2007. "Science and advocacy issues in research on children of gay and lesbian parents." *American Psychologist* 62(7):712–13.

Shirane, Haruo (ed.). 2008. *Envisioning the Tale of Genji: Media, Gender, and Cultural Production.* New York: Columbia University.

Shirazi, Faegheh. 2003. *The Veil Unveiled: The Hijab in Modern Culture.* Gainesville, FL: University Press of Florida.

Shostak, Art. 2008. "Men, me, and abortion." *Men and Masculinities* 10(3):360–66.

Shrier, Diane K. 2002. "Career and workplace issues." In Susan G. Kornstein and Anita H. Clayton (eds.), *Women's Mental Health: A Comprehensive Textbook.* (pp. 527–41). New York: Guilford.

Shumaker, Sally A. 2003. "Estrogen plus progestin and the incidence of dementia and mild cognitive impairment in postmenopausal women." *Journal of the American Medical Association* 289(20):2673–84.

Shuto, Wakana. 2009. "Occupational sex segregation and the Japanese employment model: Case studies of the railway and automotive industries." *Japan Labor Review* 6(1):21–35.

Sidanius, Jim, and Yesilernis Pena. 2003. "The gendered nature of family structure and group-based anti-egalitarianism: A cross-national analysis." *Journal of Social Psychology* 143(2):243–51.

Sidnell, Jack. 2005. "Constructing and managing male exclusivity in talk-in-interaction." In Janet Holmes and Miriam Meyerhoff (eds.), *The Handbook of Language and Gender.* Malden, MA: Blackwell.

Sify. 2003. "India no longer shying away from AIDS." *Sify News* December 31. http://sify.com/news/fullstory

Signorella, Margaret, and Irene Hanson Frieze. 2008. "Interrelations of gender schemas in children and adolescents: Attitudes, preferences, and self-perceptions." *Social Behavior and Personality* 36(7):941–54.

Signorielli, Nancy. 2004. "Aging on television: Messages related to gender, race, and occupation in prime time." *Journal of Broadcasting & Electronic Media* 48(2):279–301.

———. 2003. "Prime-time violence 1993–2001: Has the picture really changed?" *Journal of Broadcasting & Electronic Media* 47(1):36–57.

Signorielli, Nancy, and Susan Kahlenberg. 2003. "Television's world of work in the nineties." In Toby Miller (ed.), *Television: Critical Concepts in Media and Cultural Studies, Volume 2.* London: Routledge.

Silvas, Sharon, Barbara Jenkins, and Polly Grant. 1993. "The overvoice: Images of women in the media." In Jodi Wetzel, Margo Linn Espenlaub, Monys A. Hagen, Annette Bennington McElhiney, and Carmen Braun Williams (eds.), *Women's Studies Thinking Women.* Dubuque, IA: Kendall/Hunt.

Simmons, Rachel. 2003. *Odd Girl Out: The Hidden Culture of Aggression in Girls.* San Diego, CA: Harcourt.

Simon, Rita James. 1975. *The Contemporary Woman and Crime.* Washington, DC: U.S. Government Printing Office.

———. 2002a. "Revisiting the relationships among gender, marital status, and mental health." *American Journal of Sociology* 107(4):1065–96.

———. 2002b. "Women and violent crime." In Wendy McElroy (ed.), *Liberty for Women: Freedom and Feminism in the Twenty-First Century.* (pp. 231–38). Chicago: Ivan R. Dee.

Simon, Stefanie, and Crystal L. Hoyt. 2008. "Exploring the gender gap in support for a woman for President." *Analyses of Social Issues and Public Policy* 8(1):157–81.

Simpson, Jeffry A., W. Stevens Rholes, and Lorne Campbell. 2003. "Changes in attachment orientations across the transition to parenthood." *Journal of Experimental Social Psychology* 39(4):317–31.

Singh, Pradeep. 2007. "Domestic violence against women – Etiology and legal regime in India." *Caribbean Journal of Criminology and Social Psychology* 12(1&2):114–54.

Singh, Val, Siri Terjesen, and Susan Vinnicombe. 2008. "Newly appointed directors in the boardroom: How do women and men differ?" *European Management Journal* 26(1):48–58.

Skaine, Rosemarie. 2004. *The Cuban Family: Custom and Change in an Era of Hardship.* Jefferson, NC: McFarland.

Skelton, Christine. 2006. "Boys and girls in the elementary school." In Christine Skelton, Becky Francis and Lisa Smulyan (eds.), *Sage Handbook of Gender and Education.* Thousand Oaks, CA: Sage.

Skjeie, Hege. 2007. "Religious exemptions to equality." *Critical Review of International Social and Political Philosophy* 10(4):471–90.

Small, Deborah A., Michele Gelfand, Linda Babcock, and Hilary Gettman. 2007. "Who goes to the bargaining table? The influence of gender and framing on the initiation of negotiation."

Journal of Personality and Social Psychology 93(4):600–13.

Smiler, Andrew P. 2006. "Living the image: A quantitative approach to delineating masculinities." *Sex Roles* 55:621–32.

Smiler, Andrew, and Susan Gelman. 2008. "Determinants of gender essentialism in college students." *Sex Roles* 58(11/12):864–74.

Smith, Andrea. 2006. "Appropriation of Native American religious traditions." In Rosemary Skinner Keller and Rosemary Radford Ruether (eds.), *Encyclopedia of Women and Religion in North America.* Bloomington, IN: Indiana University.

Smith, Barbara. 1995. "Myths to divert black women from freedom." In Sheila Ruth, *Issues in Feminism: An Introduction to Women's Studies.* Mountain View, CA: Mayfield.

Smith, Dorothy. 2003. "Women's perspectives as radical critique of sociology." In Sharlene Nagy Hesse-Biber and Michelle L. Yaiser (eds.), *Feminist Perspectives on Social Research.* New York: Oxford University.

Smith, Eric R.A.N. and Richard L. Fox. 2001. "The electoral fortunes of women candidates for Congress." *Political Science Quarterly* 54(1):205–21.

Smith, S.L. 2005. "From Dr. Dre to dismissed: Assessing violence, sex, and substance use on MTV." *Critical Studies in Mass Communication* 22:89–98.

Smith, Stacy L., and Aaron R. Boyston. 2002. "Violence in music videos: Examining the prevalence and context of physical aggression." *Journal of Communication* 52(1):61–83.

Smith, Yolanda L.S., L. Cohen, and Peggy T. Cohen-Kettenis. 2002. "Postoperative psychological functioning of adolescent transsexuals: A Rorschach study." *Archives of Sexual Behavior* 31(3):255–61.

Smith-Lovin, Lynn, and Charles Brody. 1989. "Interruptions in group discussions: The effects of gender and group composition." *American Sociological Review* 54:424–35.

Smyth, John. 2007. "Attrition from school." In Barbara J. Bank (ed.), *Gender and Education: Volume I.* (pp. 389–94). Westport, CT: Praeger.

Snow, Kate, and Michael Milberger. 2008, "New Hampshire Senate makes history: Becomes first state with more ladies than gentlemen." *ABC News* December 7. http://abcnews.go.com

So, Alvin Y. 2001. "Social relations between Pearl River Delta and Hong Kong." Presentation to the Pearl River Delta seminar, Asian Studies Development Program. Robert Black College, University of Hong Kong, May 29.

Sokal, Laura, Herb Katz et al. 2005. "Boys will be 'boys:' Variability of boys' experiences in literacy." *Alberta Journal of Educational Research* 51(3):216–30.

Solomon, Catherine Richards, Alan C. Acock, and Alexis J. Walker. 2004. "Gender ideology and investment in housework: Postretirement change." *Journal of Family Issues* 25(8):1050–71.

Sommers, Christa Hoff. 2000. *The War Against Boys: How Misguided Feminism is Harming our Young Men.* New York: Simon & Schuster.

Sorber, Ann Verbeck. 2001. "The role of peer socialization in the development of emotion display rules: Effects of age, gender, and emotion." *Dissertation Abstracts International Section B: Sciences and Engineering* 62(2-B):1119.

Sotirovic, Mira. 2008. "Gender differences in new media use and their political implications." *Media Report to Women* Summer. 36(3):14–20.

Speer, Susan A. 2005. *Gender Talk: Feminism, Discourse, and Conversational Analysis.* London: Routledge.

Spehr, Christiane. 2007. "Male-to-female sex reassignment surgery in transsexuals." *International Journal of Transgenderism* 10(1):25–37.

Spelke, Elizabeth S., and Ariel D. Grace. 2006. "Abilities. Motives, and personal styles." *American Psychologist* 61(7):725–26.

Spelke, Elizabeth S., and Ariel D. Grace. 2007. "Sex, math, and science." In Barbara J. Bank (ed.), *Gender and Education; Volume I.* (pp. 64–67). Westport, CT: Praeger.

Sperling, Valerie, Myra Marx Ferree, and Barbara Risman. 2001. "Constructing global feminism: Transnational advocacy networks and Russian women's activism." *Signs* 26(4):1155–86.

Sperling, Valerie. 1999. *Organizing Women in Contemporary Russia: Engendering Transition.* Cambridge, UK: Cambridge University.

Spongberg, Mary. 2002. *Writing Women's History Since the Renaissance.* New York: Palgrave Macmillan.

Sprecher, Susan, and Maura Toro-Morn. 2002. "A study of men and women from different sides of earth to determine if men are from Mars and women are from Venus in their beliefs about love and romantic relationships." *Sex Roles* 46(5/6):131–47.

Spriggs, Merle, and Julian Savulescu. 2006. "Ethnics of surgically assigning for intersex children." In David Benatar (ed.), *Cutting to the Core: Exploring the Ethics of Contested Surgeries.* Lanham, MD: Rowman and Littlefield.

St. John, Colin. 2006. "Coming out with dad." *Psychology Today* 39(3):43–44.

Stabile, Carol A. 2009. "Sweetheart, this ain't gender studies: Sexism and superheroes." *Communication and Critical/Cultural Studies* 6(1):86–92.

Staeger, Rob. 3003. *Native American Religion.* Philadelphia: Mason Crest.

Stahly, Geraldine B. 2004. "Battered women: Why don't they just leave?" In Joan C. Chrisler, Carla Golden and Patricia D. Rozee (eds.), *Lectures on the Psychology of Women.* (pp. 310–331). New York: McGraw-Hill.

Stamps, Leighton. 2002. "Maternal preference in child custody decisions." *Journal of Divorce and Remarriage* 37(1–2):1–11.

Stange, Mary Zeiss. 2002. "Female priests provide answer." *USA Today* April 4:13A.

Stankiewicz, Julie. 2008. "Women as sex objects and victims in print advertisements." *Sex Roles* 58(7/8):579–89.

Stanley, Alessandra. 2008. "Michelle Obama highlights her warmer side." *New York Times* June 19:A21.

———. 2009. "Plot lines for hard times." *New York Times* September 20:MT1.

Stanley, David. 2000. *Moon Handbooks: Tahiti.* Emeryville, CA: Avalon.

Stanley, Scott M., Galena H. Rhoades, and Howard J. Markman, (2006). "Sliding vs. deciding: Inertia and the premarital cohabitation effect." *Family Relations,* 55, 499–509.

Stansell, Christine. 2008. "All fired up: Women, feminism, and misogyny in the Democratic primaries." *Dissent* Fall:34–9.

Stark, Evan. 2009. *Coercive Control: How Men Entrap Women in Personal Life.* New York: Oxford University.

Stark, Rodney. 1996. *The Rise of Christianity: A Sociologist Reconsiders History.* Princeton, NJ: Princeton University.

Stark, Rodney. 2002. "Physiology and faith: Addressing the 'universal' gender differences in religious commitment." *Journal for the Scientific Study of Religion* 41(3):495–507.

Starrels, Marjorie, and Kristin E. Holm. 2000. "Adolescents' plans for family formation: Is parental socialization important." *Journal of Marriage and the Family* 62(2):416–29.

Stasio, Marilyn. 2001. "It's not just a 'women's issue' anymore." *Parade Magazine* January 21:14, 16.

Staudt, Kathleen. 1998. *Policy, Politics & Gender: Women Gaining Ground.* West Hartford, CT: Kumarian.

Steering Committee of the Physicians Health Study Research Group. 1989. "Final report of the aspirin component of the ongoing physician's health study." *New England Journal of Medicine* 321(3):129–35.

Steidel, Angel G. Lugo. 2006. "Attitudinal familism and psychological adjustment among Latinos: The moderating effect of structural familism." *Dissertation Abstracts International: Section B: The Sciences and Engineering* 66(10-B):5688.

Stein, Nan. 2007a. "Bullying, harassment, and violence among students." In Barbara J. Bank (ed.), *Gender and Education; Volume II.* (pp. 583–9). Westport, CT: Praeger.

———. 2007b. "Gender-based violence in schools." In Robert C. Davis, Arthur J. Lurigo, and Susan Herman (eds.), *Victims of Crime.* (pp. 201–10). Los Angeles: Sage.

Stein, Rob. 2008. "Premarital 'virginity pledges' ineffective, study finds." *The Honolulu Advertiser* December 29:A7.

Steinem, Gloria. 1995. "Sex, lies and advertising." In Jo Freeman (ed.), *Women: A Feminist Perspective.* Mountain View, CA: Mayfield.

Steiner, Elizabeth. 2007. "Why are divorced mothers economically disadvantaged? And what can be done about it? *Texas Journal of Women and the Law* 17(1):131–51.

Stengler, Mark. 2005. "Male menopause: Managing the midlife crisis." *Canadian Journal of Health and Nutrition* June:40, 42–43.

Stephens, Mary Ann Parris, Lynn M. Martire, and Jennifer Ann Druley. 2001. "Balancing parent care with other roles: Interrole conflict of adult daughter caregivers." *Journals of Gerontology: Series B: Psychological Sciences and Social Sciences* 56B(1):24–34.

Stephens, Walter. 2002. *Demon Lovers: Witchcraft, Sex, and the Crisis of Belief.* Chicago: University of Chicago.

Sternberg, Robert. 2008. "Triangulating love." In Thomas J. Oord (ed.), *The Altruism Reader: Selections from Writings on Love, Religion, and Science.* West Conshohoken, PA: Templeton Foundation.

Stets, Jan E., and Stacy A. Hammons. 2002. "Gender, control, and marital commitment." *Journal of Family Issues* 23(1):3–25.

Stevens, Daphne Perderson, Krista Lynn Minnotte, Susan E. Mannon, and Gary Kiger. 2007. "Examining the 'neglected side of the work-family interface': Antecedents of positive and negative family-to-work spillover." *Journal of Family Issues* 28(2):242–62.

Stevens, Evelyn P. 2000. "Marianismo: The other face of machismo in Latin America." In Anne Minas (ed.), *Gender Basics: Feminist Perspectives on Women and Men.* (pp. 456–63). Belmont, CA: Wadsworth.

Stikker, Allerd. 2002. *Closing the Gap: Exploring the History of Gender Relations.* Amsterdam: Amsterdam University.

Stockard, Jean. 2007. "Sex role socialization." In Barbara J. Bank (ed.), *Gender and Education: Volume I.* (pp. 79–85). Westport, CT: Praeger.

Stockley, Joshua. 2008. "Social forces and the primary vote: Examining race, gender, age, and class in the 2008 presidential primaries." *Race, Gender and Class* 15(3–4):32–50.

Stockwell, Peter. 2007. (ed.). *Sociolinguistics: A Resource Book for Students.* London: Routledge.

Stohs, Joanne Hoven. 2000. "Multicultural women's experience of household labor, conflicts, and equity." *Sex Roles* 42(5/6):339–61.

Stokar von Neuforn, Daniela. 2007. "Gender gap in the perception of communication in virtual learning environments." *Interactive Learning Environments* 15(3):209–15.

Stone, Kim. 2006. "Native American women and Christianity." In Rosemary Skinner Keller and Rosemary Radford Ruether (eds.), *Encyclopedia of Women and Religion in North America.* Bloomington, IN: Indiana University.

Stone, Merlin. 1990. *When God was a Woman.* New York: Dorset.

Stratton, Jo Anna L. 1981. *Pioneer Women: Voices from the Kansas frontier.* New York: Simon & Schuster.

Streitmatter, Janice L. 1999. *For Girls Only: Making a Case for Single-Sex Schooling.* Albany: State University of New York.

Strohschein, L., P. McDonough, G. Monette, and Q. Shao. 2005. "Marital transitions and mental illness: Are their gender differences in the short-term effects of marital status change?" *Social Science and Medicine* 61(11):2293–303.

Strough, JoNell, and Cynthia A. Berg. 2000. "Goals as a mediator of gender differences in high-affiliation dyadic conversations." *Developmental Psychology* 36(1):117–25.

Strow, Claudia W., and Chris Brasfield. 2006. "Divorce probability and the 'preference' for sons." *Journal of Applied Economics and Policy* 25(1):42–55.

Strum, Shirley C., and Linda M. Fedigan. 2000. "Changing views of primate society: A situated North American perspective." In Shirley C. Strum and Linda M. Fedigan (eds.), *Primate Encounters: Models of Science, Gender and Society.* (pp. 3–56). Chicago: University of Chicago.

Stuart, Jennifer. 2007. "Work and motherhood: Preliminary report of a psychoanalytic study." *The Psychoanalytic Quarterly* 76:439–86.

Sturt, Patrick. 2003. "The time-course of the application of binding constraints in reference resolution." *Journal of Memory and Language* 48(3):542–62.

Subramaniam, Mangala. 2006. *The Power of Women's Organizing: Gender, Caste, and Class In India.* Lanham, MD: Lexington.

Suitor, J. Jill, and Rebecca S. Carter. 1999. "Jocks, nerds, babes and thugs: Research notes on regional differences in adolescent gender norms." *Gender Issues* 17(3):87–101.

Sunderland, J. 2006. "Contradictions in gendered discourses: Feminist readings of sexist jokes?" *Gender and Language* 1(2):207–28.

Svirsky, Gila. 2003. "Local coalitions, global partners: The women's peace movement in Israel and beyond." *Signs: Journal of Women in Culture and Society* 29(2):543–50.

Swann, Joan. 2005. "Schooled language: Language and gender in educational settings." In Janet Holmes and Miriam Meyerhoff (eds.), *The Handbook of Language and Gender.* Malden, MA: Blackwell.

Sweeney, Megan M. 2002. "Remarriage and the nature of divorce: Does it matter which spouse chose to leave?" *Journal of Family Issues* 23(3):410–40.

Sweet, Elizabeth L. 2009. "Ethnographic understanding of gender and economic transition in Siberia: Implications for planners and policy makers." *European Planning Studies* 17(5):697–713.

Sweeting, Helen, and Patrick West. 2003. "Sex differences in health at ages 11, 13, and 15." *Social Science & Medicine* 56(1):31–39.

Swetkis, Doreen, Faith D. Gilroy, and Roberta Steinbacher. 2002. "Firstborn preference and attitudes toward using sex selection technology." *Journal of Genetic Psychology* 163(2):228–38.

Swidler, Leonard J. 2007. *Jesus Was a Feminist: What the Gospels Reveal about His Revolutionary Perspective.* Lanham, MD: Sheed and Ward.

Szymanski, Dawn M. and Erika R. Carr. 2008. "The roles of gender role conflict and internalized heterosexism in gay and bisexual men's psychological distress: Testing two mediation models." *Psychology of Men and Masculinity* 9(1):40–54.

Szymanski, Dawn M., Susan Kashubeck-West, and Jill Meyer. 2008. "Internalized heterosexism: Measurement, psychological correlates, and research directions." *Counseling Psychologist* 36(4):525–74.

Tager, David, Glenn E. Good, and Julie Bauer Morrison. 2006. "Our bodies, ourselves revisited: Male body image and psychological well-being." *International Journal of Men's Health* 5(3):228–37.

Taitz, Emily, Sondra Henry, and Cheryl Tallan. 2003. *JPS Guide to Jewish Women,* 600 B.C.E.–1900 C.E. Philadelphia: Jewish Publication Society.

Takacs, Sarolta A. 2008. *Vestal Virgins, Sibyls, and Matrons: Women in Roman Religion.* Austin, TX: University of Texas.

Takano, Deborah-Foreman. 2000. "Hit or myth: The perpetuation of popular Japanese stereotypes in Japan-published English textbooks" in M.J. Hardman and Anita Taylor (eds.), *Hearing Many Voices.* (pp. 119–32). Cresskill, NJ: Hampton.

Takano, Shoji. 2005. "Re-examining linguistic power : Strategic uses of directives by professional Japanese women in positions of authority and leadership." *Journal of Pragmatics* 37(5):633–66.

Takemaru, Naoko. 2005. "Japanese women's perceptions of sexism in language." *Women and Language* 28(1):39–48.

Tamborini, Christopher R. 2007. "The never-married in old age: Projections and concerns for the near future." *Social Security Bulletin* 67(2):25–40.

Tannen, Deborah. 2001a. *Talking from 9 to 5: Women and Men at Work.* New York: Quill.

———. 2001b. *You Just Don't Understand: Women and Men in Conversation.* New York: Quill.

Tasker, Fiona, and Charlotte J. Patterson. 2007. "Research on gay and lesbian parenting: Retrospect and prospect." *Journal of GLBT Studies* 3(2/3):9–34.

Tavernise, Sabrina. 2003. "Women redefine their roles in new Russia." *New York Times International* March 9:4.

Tavris, Carole. 2007. "Misdiagnosing the body: Premenstrual syndrome, postmenstrual syndrome." In Ira Silver (ed.), *Social Problems: Readings.* New York: W.W. Norton.

Ternikar, Farha. 2004. "Changing marriage trends in the South Asian American community." American Sociological Association, San Francisco.

Terborg-Penn, Rosalyn. 1991. "Discontented black feminists: Prelude and postscript to the passage of the Nineteenth Amendment." In Kathryn Kish Sklar and Thomas Dublin (eds.), *Women and Power in American History: A Reader, Volume II from 1870.* Englewood Cliffs, NJ: Prentice Hall.

Terkel, Amanda. 2009. "Operation rescue tries to distance itself from Roeders' activities on behalf of the group." *Think Progress* June 1. http://thinkprogress.org/2009/06/01/roeder-operation-rescue/

Tessier, Marie. 2002. "Bush appointees include fewer women." *Women's ENews* February 11. www.womensenews.org/org/article.cfm/dyn/aid/812

Tessina, Tina B. 2008. *The Commuter Marriage: Keeping Your Relationship Close while You're Far Apart.* Avon, MA: Adams Media.

Tharinger, Deborah J. 2008. "Maintaining the hegemonic masculinity through selective attachment, homophobia, and gay-baiting in schools: Challenges to intervention." *School Psychology Review* 37(2):221–27.

Thelwall, M. 2008. "Social networks, gender, and friendship: An analysis of MySpace member profiles." *Journal of the American Society for Information Science and Technology* 59(8):1321–30.

Theorell, Tores. 2001. "Stress and health from a work perspective." In Jack Dunham (ed.), *Stress in the Workplace: Past, Present, and Future.* (pp. 34–51). London: Whurr.

Theran, Sally A. 2004. "Ethnicity, attachment, and gender role socialization as predictors of level of voice in adolescent girls: The cumulative impact on relationships and psychological well-being." *Dissertation Abstracts International: Section B: The Sciences and Engineering* 65(4-B):2117.

Thomas, Jeannie Banks. 2003. *Naked Barbies, Warrior Joes, and Other Forms of Visible Gender.* Urbana, IL: University of Illinois.

Thompson, Edward H. 2006. "Images of old men's masculinity: Still a man?" *Sex Roles* 55:633–48.

Thompson, J. Kevin, and Guy Cafri (eds.). 2007. *The Muscular Ideal: Psychological, Social, and Medical Perspectives.* Washington, DC: American Psychological Association.

Thompson, Mark. 2009. "Why are army recruiters killing themselves." *Time* April 2.

Thompson, Nicola Diane (ed.). 1999. *Victorian Women Writers and the Woman Question.* Cambridge, UK: Cambridge University.

Thomson, Melissa. 2005. *Women of the Renaissance.* San Diego, CA: Lucent.

Thorne, Barrie. 1993. *Gender Play: Girls and Boys in School.* New Brunswick, NJ: Rutgers University.

———. 2002. "Do boys and girls have different cultures?" In Susan M. Bailey (ed.), *The Jossey-Bass Reader on Gender and Education.* (pp. 125–52). San Francisco: Jossey-Bass.

Thornton, Arland, William G. Axinn, and Yu Xie. 2007. *Marriage and Cohabitation.* Chicago: University of Chicago.

Thornton, J., and M. Lasswell. 1997. *Chore Wars: How Households Can Share the Work and Keep the Peace.* Berkeley, CA: Conari.

Tibbetts, Jane. 2008. "Women's monasteries and sacred space: The promotion of saints' cults and miracles." In Lisa M. Bitel and Felice Lifshitz (eds). *Gender and Christianity in Medieval Europe: New Perspectives.* Philadelphia: University of Pennsylvania.

Tichenor, Ronni. 2005. *Earning More and Getting Less.* New Brunswick, NJ: Rutgers University.

Tiessen, Rebecca. 2007. *Everywhere/Nowhere: Gender Mainstreaming in Development Agencies.* Bloomfield, CT: Kumarian.

Tin, Louis-Georges (ed.). 2008. *The Dictionary of Homophobia: A Global History of Gay and Lesbian Experience.* Vancouver: Arsenal Pulp.

Tirohl, Blu. 2003. "Fast talking dames." *Journal of Gender Studies* 12(2):145–6.

Tjaden, Patricia. 2007. "Stalking in America: Laws, research, and recommendations." In Robert C. Davis, Arthur J. Lurigio, and Susan Herman (eds.), *Victims of Crime.* (pp. 75–89). Thousand Oaks, CA: Sage.

Tokoro, Masabumi. 2005. "The shift towards American-style human resources management systems and the transformation of workers' attitudes at Japanese firms." *Journal of Asian Business and Management* 4(1):23–44.

Towner, Betsy. 2009. "50 and still a doll." *AARP Bulletin* March:35.

Townshend, Barbara K. 2007. "Community colleges." In Barbara J. Bank (ed.), *Gender and Education; Volume I.* (pp. 155–62). Westport, CT: Praeger.

Townshend, Tiffany G. 2008. "Protecting our daughters: Intersection of race, class and gender in African American mothers' socialization of their daughters' heterosexuality." *Sex Roles* 59:429–42.

Treas, Judith, and Esther de Ruijter. 2008."Earnings and Expenditures on household services in married and cohabiting unions." *Journal of Marriage and the Family* 70(3):796–805.

Tresaugue, Matthew. 2006. "College and universities find it difficult to enforce a line between a parent's involvement and interference: Family 101: No syllabus for letting go." *Houston Chronicle* August 21.

Trible, Phyllis. 1984. *The Texts of Terror.* Philadelphia: Fortress.

Trible, Phyllis. 2003. *Texts of Terror: Literary Feminist Readings of Biblical Narratives.* London :SCM Press.

Trost, Melanie A., and Jess K. Alberts. 2006. "How men and women communicate attraction: An evolutionary view." In Kathryn Dindia and Daniel J. Canary (eds.), *Sex Differences and Similarities in Communication.* (pp. 317–36). Mahwah, NJ: Lawrence Erlbaum.

Trudel, Gilles. 2002. "Sexuality and marital life: Results of a survey." *Journal of Sex & Marital Therapy* 28(3):229–49.

Tsui, Ming. 2007. "Gender and mathematics: Achievements in China and the United States." *Gender Issues* 24(3):1–11.

Tsuya, Noriko O., Larry L. Bumpass. Minja Kim Choe, and Ronald R. Rindfuss. 2005. "Is the gender division of labour changing in Japan?" *Asia Population Studies* 1(1):1744–730.

Tuch, Richard. 2000. *The Single Woman-Married Man Syndrome.* Northvale, NJ: Jason Aronson.

Tucker, Corinna Jenkins, Susan M. McHale, and Ann C. Crouter. 2003. "Dimensions of mothers' and fathers' differential treatment of siblings: Links with adolescents' sex-typed personal qualities." *Family Relations* 52(1):82–89.

U.S. Census Bureau. 2009. *Statistical Abstract of the United States.* Washington, DC: U.S. Department of Commerce.

U.S. Commission on Human Rights. 2000. "Indian tribes: A continuing quest for human survival." In Anne Minas (ed.), *Gender Basics: Feminist Perspectives on Women and Men.* (pp. 50–43). Belmont, CA: Wadsworth.

U.S. Department of Education. 2005. *Single-Sex Versus Coeducational Schooling: A Systematic Review.* Policy and Program Studies Service (PPSS). Washington, DC: Office of Planning, Evaluation and Policy Development.

Udeze, B., N. Abdelmawla, D. Khoosal, and T. Terry. 2008. "Psychological functions in male-to-female transsexual people before and after surgery." *Sexual and Relationship Therapy* 23(2):141–45.

Udry, J.R. 2000. "The biological limits of gender construction." *American Sociological Review* 65:443–57.

Ueno, Junko. 2006. "*Shojo* and adult women: A linguistic analysis of gender identity in manga (Japanese comics)." *Women and Language* 29(1):16–25.

Ulrich, Miriam, and Ann Weatherall. 2000. "Motherhood and infertility: Viewing motherhood through the lens of infertility." *Feminism & Psychology* (Special Issue: Reproduction) 10(3):323–36.

Umberson, Debra, Kristin Anderson, Jennifer Glick, and Adam Shapiro. 1998. "Domestic violence, personal control, and gender." *Journal of Marriage and the Family* 60(2):442–52.

Underwood, Marion K., and Lisa H. Rosen. 2009. Gender, peer relations, and challenges for girlfriends and boyfriends coming together in adolescence." *Psychology of Women Quarterly* 33(1):16–20.

UNDP. 2009. United Nations Development Programme. *Human Development Report, 2008.* New York: Palgrave Macmillan.

UNFPA. 2007. "Asian son preference will have severe social consequences, new studies warn." *UNFPA News* October 29. United Nations Population Fund. www.unfpa.org

———. 2008. *State of the World Population, 2008: Reaching Common Ground: Culture, Gender, and Human Rights.* United Nations Population Fund. New York: United Nations. www.unfpa.org/swp

———. 2009 United Nations Population Fund. *State of the World Population, 2008: Reaching Common Ground- Culture, Gender and Human Rights.* New York: United Nations. www.unfpa.org/swp

Unger, Donald N.S. 2008. "Judging fathers: The case for gender-neutral standards." In Shira Tarrant (ed.), *Men Speak Out: Views on Gender, Sex, and Power.* (pp. 212–19). New York: Routledge

UNHCR. 2008. United Nations High Commissioner for Refugees. *Statistical Yearbook, 2007: Trends in Displacement, Protection, and Solutions.* Oxford, UK: Oxford University.

UNICEF. 2008. *The State of the World's Children.* United Nations Children's Fund. London: Oxford University.

Uniform Crime Reports. 2009. *Crime in the United States.* Washington, DC: Federal Bureau of Investigation, U.S. Department of Justice.

Valenti, Jessica. 2008. "The sisterhood split." *The Nation* March 24. www.thenation.com/dod/20080324/valenti

Vargas, Virginia. 2002. "The struggle by Latin American feminists for rights and autonomy." In Nikke Craske and Maxine Molyneux (eds.), *Gender and the Politics of Rights and Democracy in Latin America.* (pp. 199–222). Houndmills, Hampshire, UK: Palgrave.

Vescio, Theresa, and Monica Biernat. 2003. "Family values and antipathy toward gay men." *Journal of Applied Social Psychology* 33(4):833–47.

Vindhya, U. 2000. "'Dowry deaths' in Andhra Pradesh, India." *Violence Against Women* 6(10):1085–108.

Vindhya, U. 2007. "Quality of women's lives in India: Some findings from two decades of psychological research on gender." *Feminism and Psychology* 17(3):337–56.

Von Drehle, Dave. 2003. *Triangle: The Fire that Changed America.* New York: Atlantic Monthly Press.

Voronina, Olga. 2009. "Has feminist philosophy a future in Russia? *Signs: Journal of Women in Culture and Society* 34(2):252–57.

Vuori, Jaana. 2009. "Guiding immigrants to the realm of gender equality." In Suvi Keskinen et al. (eds.), *Complying with Colonialism: Gender, Race and Ethnicity in the Nordic Region.* (pp. 207–24). Farnham, UK: Ashgate.

Wade, Terrence J., John Cairney, and David J. Pevalin. 2002. "Emergence of gender differences in depression during adolescence: National panel results from three countries." *Journal of the American Academy of Child and Adolescent Psychiatry* 41(2):190–98.

Wadud, Amina. 2005. "The Koran teaches that women have the same rights as men." In Margaret Speaker Yuan (ed.), *Women in Islam.* Detroit: Greenhaven/Thomson-Gale.

Wald, Kenneth D., and Calhoun-Brown. 2007. *Religion and Politics in the United States.* Lanham, MD: Rowman & Littlefield.

Walker, Martin. 2008. "The year of insurgents: The 2008 U.S. presidential campaign." *International Affairs* 84(6):1095–107.

Walker, Lenore E.A. 2009a. *The Battered Woman Syndrome.* New York: Springfield.

Walker, Tim. 2009b. "Assessing the threat: Are we doing enough to reduce the risk of violence against educators." *NEAToday* February. National Education Association. www.nea.org/neatoday

Walsh, Eileen. 2009. "Representations of race and gender in mainstream media coverage of the 2008 Democratic primary." *Journal of African American Studies* 13(2):121–30.

Walsh, Mary Williams. 2001. "So where are the corporate husbands?" *New York Times* June 24:3,13.

Walzer, Susan. 2008. "Redoing gender through divorce." *Journal of Social and Personal Relationships* 25(1):5–21.

Wang, Danyu. 2000. "Stepping on two boats: Urban strategies of Chinese peasants and their children." *International Review of Social History* 45(Suppl. 8):179–96.

Ward, Lo Monique, Edwina Hansbrough, and Eboni Walker. 2005. "Contributions of music exposure to black adolescents' gender and sexual schemas." *Journal of Adolescent Research* 20(2):143–66.

Waring, Marilyn. 1988. *If Women Counted: A New Feminist Economics.* San Francisco: Harper-SanFrancisco.

Warren, Anika K. 2009. "Cascading gender biases, compounding effects: An assessment of talent management systems." *Research Reports.* February Catalyst. www.catalyst.org/publications/292

Warren, Roland C. 2001. "Securing the home front: A father's role." *Our Children* 27(3):7.

Warwick, Ian, and Peter Aggleton. 2002. "Gay men's physical and emotional well-being: Re-orienting research and health promotion." In Adrian Coyle and Celia Kitzinger (eds.), *Lesbian and Gay Psychology: New Perspectives.* (pp. 135–53). Oxford, UK: BPS Blackwell.

Wasburn, Mara H. 2007. "Mentoring women faculty: An instrumental case study of strategic collaboration" *Mentoring and Tutoring* 15(1):57–72.

Watkins, Mirenda. 2006. "Divorce." *Georgetown Journal of Gender and the Law 2006 Annual Review* 7(3):1033–41.

Wax, Amy L. 2005. "What women want." *Wall Street Journal* August 25:A8.

Waxman, Sharon. 2002. "75 percent of roles are still male." *Washington Post* November 29.

Weathers, Charles. 2001. "Changing white-collar workplaces and female temporary workers in Japan." *Social Science Japan Journal* 4(2):201–18.

Weaver, Laura Adams. 2006. "Native American creation stories." In Rosemary Skinner Keller and Rosemary Radford Ruether (eds.), *Encyclopedia of Women and Religion in North America.* Bloomington: University of Indiana.

Weaver, Mary Jo. 1999. "American Catholics in the twentieth century." In Peter W. Williams (ed.), *Perspectives on American Religion and Culture.* (pp. 154–67). Malden, MA: Blackwell.

Weaver-Hightower, Robin. 2007. "The 'boy problem.' " In Barbara J. Bank (ed.), *Gender and Education, Volume II.* (pp. 717–22). Westport, CT: Praeger.

Weber, Max. 1946. *From Max Weber: Essays in Sociology.* H.H. Gerth and C.W. Mills, eds. (trans.). New York: Oxford University Press.

Webster, Alison R. 1995. *Found Wanting: Women, Christianity and Sexuality.* London: Cassell.

Weil, Elizabeth. 2008. "Teaching to the testosterone." Cover story: "Should boys and girls be taught separately? The gender wars go to school." *New York Times Magazine* March 2:37–45, 84–86, 87.

Weiler, Jeanne Drysdale. 2000. *Codes and Contradictions: Race, Gender Identity, and Schooling.* Albany: State University of New York.

Weinstein, Rhona S., Miriam H. Dimmler, and Nilofar Sami. 2007. "Expectations of teachers for boys and girls." In Barbara J. Bank (ed.), *Gender and Education, Volume II.* (pp. 541–47) Westport, CT: Praeger.

Weisgrau, Maxine K. 2000. "Vedic and Hindu traditions." In R. Scupin (ed.), *Religion and Culture: An Anthropological Focus.* (pp. 225–48). Upper Saddle River, NJ: Prentice Hall.

Wells, Barbara, and Maxine Baca Zinn. 2004. "The benefits of marriage reconsidered." *Journal of Sociology and Social Welfare* 31(4):59–80.

Welsch, Janice R. 2001. "On the road with Louise and Thelma." In Murray Pomerance (ed.), *Ladies and Gentlemen, Boys and Girls: Gender in Film at the End of the Twentieth Century.* (pp. 249–66). Albany: State University of New York.

Welsh, Patrick. 2001. "Unlearning machismo: Men changing men in post-revolutionary Nicaragua." In Bob Pease and Keith Pringle (eds.) *A Man's World? Changing Men's Practices in a Globalized World.* (pp. 177–90). London: Zed.

Welter, Barbara. 1996. "The cult of true womanhood, 1820–1860." In Mary Beth Norton and Ruth M. Alexander (eds.), *Major Problems in American Women's History.* Lexington, MA: D. C. Heath.

Werhane, Patricia et al. (eds.). 2008. *The Changing Face of Leadership.* Westport, CT: Praeger.

West, Michael O. 1999. "Like a river: The Million Man March and the black nationalist tradition in the United States." *Journal of Historical Sociology* 12(1):81–100.

Westley, Sidney, and Minja Kim Choe. 2007. "How does son preference affect population in Asia?" *AsiaPaciific Issues* (Analysis from the East-West Center No. 84) September.

Wexler, Barbara. 2003. *Violent Relationships: Battering and Abuse among Adults.* Detroit, MI: Gale.

Whisnant, Rebecca, and Christine Stark (eds.). 2005. *Not for Sale: Feminists Resisting Prostitution and Pornography.* Australia: Spinifex.

White, Linda. 2001. "Democracy in a Confucian-based society." In Lynn Walter (ed.), *Women's Rights: A Global View.* (pp. 141–54). Westport, CT: Greenwood.

White, Merry. 1991. *Challenging Tradition: Women in Japan.* New York: Japan Society.

Whitmire, Richard. 2008. *Boy Troubles.* New York: Doubleday.

Widestedt, Kristina. 2008. "Issues of gender equality and diversity in broadcast news policy." *Nordicom Review* 29(1):45–62.

Wiederman, Michael W. 2005. "The gendered nature of sexual scripts." *Family Journal* 13(4):496–502.

Wiener, Jon. 2007. "Feminist leaders oppose Hilary, endorse Obama." *Huffington Post* February 3. www.huffingtonpost.com/jon-wiener

Wiesner-Hanks, Merry E. 2008. *Women and Gender in Early Modern Europe*. Cambridge, UK: Cambridge University.

Wildfang, Robin Lorsch. 2006. *Rome's Vestal Virgins: A Study of Rome's Vestal Priestesses in the Late Republic and Early Empire*. London: Routledge.

Wiley, Juli Loesch. 2003. On the fatherhood of God. Is 'God the Mother' just as good?" In Philip E.Divine and Celia Wolf-Devine (eds.), *Sex and Gender: A Spectrum of Views*. (pp. 369–74). Belmont, CA: Wadsworth/Thomson.

Wilgus, Gay. 2005. "Gender, authority, and Montessori: Early childhood teachers' choices of interactional and disciplinary styles." In Janice Koch and Beverly J. Irby. (eds.), (pp. 1–28, 39–60). *Gender and Schooling in the Early Years*. Greenwich, CT: IAP.

Willemsen, Tineke M. 1998. "Widening the gender gap" Teenage magazines for girls and boys." *Sex Roles* 38(9/10):851–61.

Williams, Barbara Morrow. 2007. "Managing 'problem' boys and girls." In Barbara J. Bank (ed.), *Gender and Education, Volume II*. (pp. 555–61). Westport, CT: Praeger.

Williams, Christine. 2003a. "The glass escalator: Hidden advantages for men in the 'female' professions." In Michael S, Kimmel (ed.), *The Gendered Society Reader*. New York: Oxford University.

Williams, Jean Calterone. 2003b. *A Roof over My Head: Homeless Women and the Shelter Industry*. Boulder, CO: University Press of Colorado.

Williams, Kristi, and Alexandra Dunne-Bryant. 2006. "Divorce and adult psychological well-being: Clarifying the role of gender and child age." *Journal of Marriage and the Family* 68(5):1178–196.

Willmott, Ceri. 2002. "Constructing citizenship in the *Poblaciones* of Santiago, Chile: The Role of Reproductive and Sexual Rights." In Nikke Craske and Maxine Molyneux (eds.), *Gender and the Politics of Rights and Democracy in Latin America*. (pp. 124–48). Houndmills, Hampshire, UK: Palgrave.

Wilmerding, Ginny. 2006. *Smart Women and Small Business: How to Make the Leap from Corporate Careers to the Right Small Enterprises*. Hoboken, NJ: John Wiley.

Wilson, Calvin. 2002. "A Bond with 007." *St. Louis Post-Dispatch* November 22:F1–F4.

Wilson, Clint C., Felix Gutierrez, and Lena M. Chao. 2003. *Racism, Sexism, and the Media: The Rise of Class Communications in Multicultural America*. Thousand Oaks, CA: Sage.

Wilson, Edward O. 1975. *Sociobiology: The New Synthesis*. Princeton, NJ: Princeton University.

———. 1978. *On Human Nature*. Cambridge, MA: Harvard University.

Wilson, Robert A. 1966. *Feminine Forever*. New York: M. Evans.

Wilson, Steve R., and Eric S. Mankowski. 2000. "Beyond the drum: An exploratory study of group processes in a mythopoetic men's group." In Edward Read Barton (ed.). *Mythopoetic Perspectives of Men's Healing Work: An Anthology of Therapists and Others*. (pp. 21–45). Westport, CT: Bergin & Garvey.

Wingfield, Adia Harvey. 2009. "Men's experiences with women's work." *Gender & Society* 23(1):5–26.

Wiser, Paige. 2007. "Make no Ms.take: Ms. is here to stay." *Chicago Sun Times*. October 10.

Wolbrecht, Christina. 2000. *The Politics of Women's Rights: Parties, Positions and Change*. Princeton, NJ: Princeton University.

Wolensky, Kenneth C., Nicole H. Wolensky, and Robert P. Wolensky. 2002. *Fighting for the Union Label: The Women's Garment Industry and ILGWU in Pennsylvania*. University Park: Pennsylvania State University.

Wolf, Naomi. 2002. *The Beauty Myth: How Images of Beauty are Used Against Women*. New York: Perennial.

Wolf-Devine, Celia. 2002. "Proportional representation of women and minorities." In Stephan Cahn (ed.), *The Affirmative Action Debate*. (pp, 168–75). London: Routledge.

Wollstonecraft, Mary. 1792/1970. *The Vindication of the Rights of Woman*. Farnborough, UK: Gregg.

Women's Health Initiative. 2003. "WHI findings." www.whi.org/findings/default.asp

WomenDeliver. 2007. "The unfortunate facts of life in 2007." October. www.womendeliver.org/media/Fact_sheets

Wong, Eva. 2002. "Taoism." In Arvind Sharma and Katherine K. Young (eds.), *Her Voice, Her Faith: Women Speak on World Religions*. (pp. 119–44). Boulder, CO: Westview.

Woo, Stephanie M., and Carolyn Keatinge. 2008. *Diagnosis and Treatment of Mental Disorders Across the Lifespan*. Hoboken, NJ: John Wiley.

Woo, Terry. 2002. "Confucianism." In Arvind Sharma and Katherine K. Young (eds.), *Her Voice, Her Faith: Women Speak on World Religions*. (pp. 99–118). Boulder, CO: Westview.

Wood, Julia T. 2003a. *Gendered Lives: Communication, Gender and Culture*. Belmont, CA: Thomson/Wadsworth.

Wood, Peter. 2003b. "Diversity in America." *Society* 40, 4(264):60–67.

Worell, Judith, and Carol D. Goodheart (eds.). 2006. *Handbook of Girls' and Women's Psychological Health: Gender and Well-Being Across the Lifespan*. New York: Oxford University.

Worell, Judith. 1996. "Feminist identity in a gendered world." In Joan C. Chrisler, Carla Golden, and Patricia D. Rozee (eds.), *Lectures on the Psychology of Women*. New York: McGraw-Hill.

World Bank. 2008. "Girls' education: A World Bank priority." Topics: Education for All (EFA). http://web.worldbank.org

World Bank. 2009. *World Development Indicators (WDI), 2009*. Washington, DC: World Bank. http://web.worldbank.org

World Economic Forum. 2008. *The Global Gender Gap Report*. Geneva. www.weforum.org/en

World Health Organization. 2003. *World Health Report, 2003: Shaping the Future*. Geneva: WHO.

Woyshner, Christine. 2006. "Picturing women: Gender, images, and representations in social studies." *Social Education* 70(6):358–62.

Xiao, Hong. 2000. "Class, gender, and parental values in the 1990s." *Gender & Society* 14(6):785–803.

Xiaogan, Liu. 2001. "A Taoist perspective: Appreciating and applying the principle of femininity." In John C. Raines and Daniel C. Maguire (eds.), *What Men Owe to Women: Men's Voices from World Religions.* (pp. 239–58). Albany: State University of New York.

Xu, Feng. 2000. *Women Migrant Workers in China's Economic Reform.* Houndmills, Basingstoke, Hampshire, UK: Macmillan.

Yaish, Meir, and Vered Kraus. 2003. "The consequences of economic restructuring for the gender earning gap in Israel, 1972–1995." *Work, Employment and Society* 17(1):5–28.

Yamaguchi, Kazuo. 2000. "Married women's gender-role attitudes and social stratification: Communities and differences between Japan and the United States." *International Journal of Sociology* 30(2):52–89.

Yamokoski, Alexis, and Lisa A. Keister. 2006. "The wealth of single women: Marital status and parenthood in the asset accumulation of young baby boomers in the United States." *Feminist Economics* 12:167–79.

Yang, Anand A. 2008. "Whose sati? Widow burning in early nineteenth century India." In Sumit Sarkar and Tanika Sarkar (eds.), *Women and Social Reform in Modern India: A Reader.* Bloomington, IN: Indiana University.

Yardley, Jim. 2008. "China sticking with one-child policy." *New York Times* (International) March 11.

Yassin, Aksam A. 2006. "Brain-sex testosterone role in personality evolution: Females and males are different? *Journal of Sexual Medicine* 3(Suppl. 2):81–82.

Ybarra, M.L., D.L. Espelage, and K.J. Mitchell. 2007. "The co-occurrence of internet harassment and unwanted sexual solicitation and perpetration." *Journal of Adolescent Health.* 41(6 Suppl. 1):S31–41.

Yee, Nick, Jeremy N. Bailenson et al. 2007. "The unbearable likeness of being digital: The persistence of nonverbal social norms in online virtual environments." *CyberPsychology and Behavior* 10(1):115–21.

Yeung, W. Jean, John F. Sandberg, and Pamela E. Davis-Kean. 2001. "Children's time with fathers in intact families." *Journal of Marriage and the Family* 63(1):136–54.

Yoder, Janie D., Jessica Christopher, and Jeffrey D. Holmes. 2008. "Are television commercials still achievement scripts for women?" *Psychology of Women Quarterly* 32(3):303–11.

Young, Cathy. 2008. "Why feminists hate Sarah Palin." *Wall Street Journal* September 15:A21.

Young, Ellie L., and Betty Ashbaker. 2008. "Addressing sexual harassment." *Principle Leadership: Middle Level Edition* 9(3):10–14.

Young, Katherine K. 1987. "Introduction." In Arvind Sharma (ed.), *Women in World Religions.* Albany: State University of New York.

Younger, Paul. 2002. *Playing Host to Deity: Festival Religion in South Indian Tradition.* New York: Oxford University.

Yu, Wei-Hsin, and Kuo-Hsien Su. 2006. "Gender, sibship structure, and educational inequality in Taiwan: Son preference revisited." *Journal of Marriage and the Family* 68:1057–68.

Yu, Wei-hsin. 2002. Jobs for mothers: Married women's labor force reentry and part-time, temporary employment." *Sociological Forum* 17(3):493–52.

Zahl, Paul F.M. 2001. *Five Women of the English Reformation.* Grand Rapids, MI: William B. Eerdmans.

Zakaria, Rafia. 2009. "Muslim women between dual realities." In Anjana Narayan, and Bandana Purkayastha (eds.), *Living Our Religions; Hindu and Muslim South Asian American Women Narrate their Experiences.* Sterling, VA: Kumarian.

Zdravomyslova, Elena. 2002. "Overview of the feminist movement in contemporary Russia." *Diogenes* 49, 2(194):35–39.

Zhang, Shen, Toni Schmader, and Chad Forbes. 2009. "The effects of gender stereotypes on women's career choice: Opening the glass door." In Manuela Barreto, Michelle K. Ryan, and Michael T. Schmitt (eds.), *The Glass Ceiling in the 21st Century: Understanding Barriers to Gender Equity.* Washington DC: American Psychological Association.

Zhang, Yuanyuan, Laure E. Miller, and Kristen Harrison. 2008. "The relationship between exposure to sexual music videos and young adults' sexual attitudes." *Journal of Broadcasting and Electronic Media* 52(3):368–86.

Zhou, Xueguang, and Phyllis Moen. 2001. "Job-shift patterns of husbands and wives in urban China." In Hans-Peter Blossfeld and Sonja Drobnic (eds.), *Careers of Couples in Contemporary Societies: From Male Breadwinner to Dual Earner Families.* (pp. 332–37). New York: Oxford University.

Zia, Helen. 2009. "From nothing, a consciousness." In Estelle Disch (ed.), *Reconstructing Gender: A Multicultural Anthology.* (pp. 44–50). New York: McGraw-Hill.

Zick, Cathleen D., W. Keith Bryant, and Eva Oesterbacka. 2001. "Mothers' employment, parental involvement and the implications for intermediate child outcomes." *Social Science Research* 30(1):25–49.

Zimmer, Michael. 2001. "Explaining marital dissolution: The role of spouses' traits." *Social Science Quarterly* 82(3):464–77.

Zimmerman, Laura. 2003. "Where are the women? The strange case of the missing feminists: When was the last time you saw one on TV?" *Women's Review of Books.* October 21(1):5–6.

Zimmerman, T.S. (ed.). 2004. *Integrating Gender and Culture in Parenting.* Binghamton, NY: Hawthorne.

Zimmerman, Toni Schindler, Shelley A. Haddock, Lisa R. Current, and Scott Ziemba. 2003. "Intimate partnership: Foundation to the successful balance of family and work." *American Journal of Family Therapy* 31(2):107–24.

Znamensky, Vladimir, Keith T. Adams, Bruce S. McEwen, and Teresa A. Milner. 2003. "Estrogen levels regulate the subcellular distribution of phosphorylated akt in hippocampal CA1 dendrites." *Journal of Neuroscience* 23(March):2340–47.

Zunker, Vernon G. 2008. *Career, Work, and Mental Health: Integrating Career and Personal Counseling.* Los Angeles: Sage.

Glossary

agency   the power to adapt and sometimes to thrive in difficult situations

affirmative action   policies of preferential treatment for women and minorities underrepresented in certain job categories

agents of socialization   the people, groups, and social institutions that provide information for children to become functioning members of society

androcentrism   male-centered norms operating throughout all social institutions that become the standard to which all persons adhere

androgyny   the integration of traits considered to be feminine with those considered to be masculine

assortive mating   coupling based on similarity

battered women's syndrome   the powerless, dependence, and poor self-image of abused women associated with the belief that they are responsible for the violence against them

blended family   children from remarriages and parents' prior relationships who are brought together in a new family

bona fide occupational qualification (BFOQ)   legally allows for hiring an employee on the basis of one's sex under very specific circumstances

civil union   a legal classification entitling same-sex couples to the rights and responsibilities available to married partners

common law   those states where property belongs to the spouse in whose name it is held

community property   those states where all property acquired during the marriage is jointly owned by the spouses

companionate marriage   marriage based on romantic love and an emphasis on balancing individual needs with family needs

comparable worth   policies designed to upgrade the wages for jobs that employ large numbers of women

compensatory history   chronicles the lives of exceptional women

continuing socialization   learning that provides the basis for the varied roles an individual will fill throughout life

contribution history   chronicles women's contributions to specific social movements

countermodernization   a social movement that either resists modernization or promotes ways to neutralize its effects

culture   a society's total way of life that provides social heritage and guidelines for appropriate behavior

developing nations   countries and regions with poverty level incomes per capita; also referred to as the developing world

development   programs designed to upgrade the standard of living of the world's poor in ways that allow them to sustain themselves

doing gender   the notion that gender emerges not as an individual attribute but something that is accomplished through interaction with others

dominance model   argues that gendered language is a reflection of women's subordinate status

double standard   the idea that men are allowed to express themselves sexually and women are not

dramaturgical approach   viewing social interaction as if it were an enactment in a theatrical performance

dual-culture model   argues that the interactional styles of males and females are separate but equal

egalitarian marriage a marriage in which spouses share decision making and assign family roles based on talent and choice rather than on traditional beliefs about gender

empowerment the ability for women to control their own destinies

end-point fallacy the negotiation of social reality is an ongoing process where new definitions produce new behavior in a never-ending cycle

Equal Employment Opportunity Commission (EEOC) a federal agency created to ensure that Title VII of the 1964 Civil Rights Act is carried out

Equal Pay Act (EPA) a federal law requiring females and males to receive the same pay for the same job

Equal Rights Amendment (ERA) proposed constitutional amendment stating that equality of rights under the law shall not be denied on account of sex

essentialism the belief that males and females are inherently different because of their biology and genes

expressive role associated with the expectation that the wife–mother maintains the family through child rearing and nurturing

familism a Latino cultural value emphasizing the family and its collective needs over personal and individual needs

Family and Medical Leave Act (FMLA) federal policy allowing eligible employees to take 12 weeks of unpaid leave for the birth and care of child, spouse, or parent

family of orientation the family in which one grows up

family of procreation the family established when one marries or establishes a long-term partnership

female genital mutilation (FGM) a variety of genital operations designed to reduce or eliminate a girl's sexual pleasure and ensure her virginity; also referred to as female genital cutting

feminism an inclusive worldwide movement to end sexism and sexist oppression by empowering women

feminist theology draws on women's experience as a basic source of content previously shut out of theological reflection

feminization of aging the global pattern of women outliving men and the steady increase of women in the ranks of the elderly

feminization of poverty a global trend showing increase in the percentage of women in the poverty population

fictive kin networks among African Americans that absorb friends into kin structures

gender social, cultural, and psychological traits linked to males and females that define them as masculine or feminine

gender identity an awareness that there are two sexes who behave differently

gender gap in a political context, male–female differences in political choices, including vote choice, policy, and party preferences

gender roles the expected attitudes and behaviors a society associates with each sex

gender socialization the process by which individuals learn the cultural behavior of femininity or masculinity that is associated with the biological sex of female or male

gender-typing expectation for less pay and prestige when the majority of the occupation are those of one gender, usually female

glass ceiling describes women's failure to rise to senior-level positions because of invisible and artificial barriers constructed by male management

GLBT an inclusive term for gay, lesbian, bisexual and transgendered people who show a wide range of attitudes and behaviors related to sexual orientation and gender identity

globalization removal of barriers to increase the flow of capital between and within nations

gynocentrism an emphasis on female and feminine interests

hegemonic masculinity asserts that there are a number of competing masculinities that are enacted according to particular places and times

hermaphrodites infants born with both male and female sex organs or who have ambiguous genitals; also referred to as *intersexed*

heterosexism viewing the world only in heterosexual terms, thus denigrating other sexual orientations

hidden curriculum the informal and unwritten norms that serve to control students, including expectations about gender

homemaker the person responsible for "the making of a home," usually a full-time person, mostly women but increasingly men

homogamy becoming attracted to and marrying someone similar to yourself

homophobia the fear and intolerance of homosexuals (gay men and lesbians) and homosexuality

household a person or group of people occupying a housing unit

human capital model explains the gender wage gap as due to personal choices in matters of education, childbirth, child rearing, and occupation

informal sector the usually undocumented economic activities of people who work as subsistence farmers, landless agricultural laborers, street vendors, or day workers

instrumental role associated with the expectation that the husband–father maintains the family through earning income

intersexed infants born with both male and female sex organs or who have ambiguous genitals; also referred to as *hermaphrodites*

Islamization a religious fundamentalist movement seeking a return to an idealized version of Islam as a remedy against corrupt Western values

kibbutz an Israeli agricultural collective originally organized by gender egalitarian principles to allow all members to be full particpants in the community without regard to gender roles

Knights of Labor first major union opened for women and African Americans calling for equal pay for equal work

liberation theology calls for redistribution of wealth and economic equality grounded in biblical messages about God's concern for the poor and oppressed

life course the roles people play over a lifetime and the ages associated with those roles

machismo among Latinos, associating the male role with virility, sexual prowess, and the physical and ideological control of women

marianismo among Latinos, associating the female role with female over male spiritual and moral superiority, and glorification of motherhood

marriage gradient a pattern in which women tend to marry men of higher socioeconomic status

marriage squeeze an unbalanced ratio of marriage-age women to marriage-age men that limits the pool of potential marriage partners

Medicaid public health insurance program for those unable to pay medical expenses; women and children are majority of recipients

microcredit a system providing small loans to a group of very poor borrowers to start small businesses and open their first savings accounts; also called *microenterprise lending*

microenterprise programs provides for income-earning manufacturing or agricultural activities located in or around the households of very poor people

morbidity rate the amount of disease or illness in a population in a given time period

mortality rate the total number of deaths in a population in a given time period

motherhood mandate the belief that motherhood demands selfless devotion to children and a subordination of a mother's life to the needs of children and family

misogyny the disdain and hatred of women

National American Women's Suffrage Association   organization working for women's political rights formed in 1890 with the merger of two suffrage groups

National Organization for Women   organization formed in 1966 heralding the return of feminism in the United States

National Organization of Men Against Sexism   a male liberation group working to reduce the negative effects of power and unyielding masculinity

New Christian Right (NCR)   a fundamentalist political movement of conservative, Protestant groups that promotes morality based on the Bible and God's will as the ultimate source for political and social life

nongovernmental organizations (NGOs)   privately funded nonprofit groups concerned with relief and development and advocacy for the poor

nonverbal communication   using bodily and situational features in communication, such as posture, eye contact, touching, and personal space

norms   shared rules that guide people's behavior in specific situations

nuclear family   consists of wife, husband, and their dependent children who live apart from other relatives in their own residence

one-child policy   allowing only one child per couple in China, with severe penalties for violation; associated with negative consequences for girls

pater familias   the absolute power over all family members granted to the eldest man in the family in ancient Rome

patriarchy   male-dominated social structures leading to the oppression of women

pink-collar jobs   lower-level white-collar jobs held by women associated with low pay and few opportunities for advancement

primary socialization   begins in the family and allows the child to acquire necessary skills to fit into society, especially language learning and acceptable behavior to function effectively in a variety of social situations

queer theory   examines how sexuality and sexual identity in all its forms—from sexual orientation to sexual behavior—is socially constructed

register   sociolinguistic term for a variety of language defined by its use in social situations, such as female register and male register

Retirement Equity Act (REA)   requires employers to get spouse's approval before an employee waives spousal benefits offered through the employer, such as pensions or health insurance

Roe v. Wade   landmark 1973 Supreme Court case establishing the legal right to an abortion

role   the expected behavior associated with a status

rule of thumb   an English Common Law provision once allowing a husband to beat his wife with a stick no bigger than his thumb

sandwich generation   women caught between caring for the older and younger generations at the same time

sati   a Hindu widow who until the twentieth century was frequently expected to be buried alive or self-immolated with her dead husband on his funeral pyre

schemas   cognitive structures used to understand the world, interpret perception, and process new information

second shift   the shift of unpaid work in the home for women who are also employed full-time for pay

second wave feminism   phase of the women's movement (1960s–1980s) seeking to raise the consciousness of women about sexist oppression in the power structure and using political means to eradicate it

self   the unique and highly valued sense of identity that distinguishes each individual from all other individuals

Seneca Falls Convention 1848 convention held in Seneca Falls, New York, hailed as the birth of the women's movement in the United States

serial monogamy a pattern of marriage–divorce–remarriage

sex the biological characteristics distinguishing male and female

sexism the belief that the status of female is inferior to the status of male

sexual dimorphism the separation of the sexes into two distinct groups

sexual harassment legally includes physical or verbal conduct that is sexual in nature, is unwanted, and creates a hostile environment that interferes with school or work activities

sexual orientation a preference for sexual partners of one gender (sex) or the other

sex ratio at birth (SRB) the number of boys born for every hundred girls

sexual scripts shared beliefs concerning what society defines as acceptable sexual thoughts, feelings, and behaviors for each gender

social construction of reality the shaping of perception of reality by the subjective meanings brought to any experience or social interaction

social control measures a society uses to ensure that people generally conform to norms, including those related to gender

social institutions organizational structures that ensure the basic needs of society are met in established, predictable ways

social stratification the way a society divides people into ranked categories or statuses

socialization the lifelong process by which we learn culture, develop a sense of self, and become functioning members of society

sociobiology a field using evolutionary theory to examine the biological roots of social behavior

status a category or position a person occupies, such as gender, that is a significant determinant of how she or he will be defined and treated

status set statuses that are occupied simultaneously

stereotype oversimplified conception that people who occupy the same status share certain traits in common

subcultures segments of a culture that share characteristics distinguishing it from the broader culture

Texts of Terror parts of four books of the Torah that include the Old Testament of the Christian Bible documenting abuse and sexual violence against women often used as justifications for restricting women

theory an explanation that guides the research process and provides a means for interpreting the data

third wave feminism emerging in the 1990s—with attention to linking race, class, gender, and sexuality—it suggests there is no universal feminism and women define for themselves what it is and what it can become

third shift caregiving by employed women who simultaneously care for their children and frail parents, grandparents, or other friends and relatives

Title VII of the 1964 Civil Rights Act makes job discrimination and occupational segregation of women illegal

Title IX of the 1972 Educational Amendment Act prohibits sex (gender) discrimination in any school receiving federal assistance

transgender describes people who do not conform to culturally defined traditional gender roles associated with their sex

transsexuals genetic males or females who psychologically believe they are members of the other gender

True Womanhood the Victorian standard for women to subscribe to the virtues of piety, purity, submissiveness, and domesticity

work–family spillover attitudes and behaviors that carry over from roles in both these social institutions

Name Index

Subject Index